SIXTH EDITION

Leadership

THEORY, APPLICATION, & SKILL DEVELOPMENT

Robert N. Lussier, Ph.D.

Springfield College

Christopher F. Achua, D.B.A.

University of Virginia's College at Wise

CENGAGE
Learning·

Australia • Brazil • Mexico • Singapore • United Kingdom • United States

CENGAGE
Learning®

Leadership: Theory, Application, & Skill Development, 6e

Robert N. Lussier, Christopher F. Achua

Vice President, General Manager, Social Science & Qualitative Business: Erin Joyner

Product Director: Michael Schenk

Senior Product Manager: Scott Person

Senior Content Developer: Julia Chase

Product Assistant: Brian Pierce

Marketing Director: Kristen Hurd

Market Manager: Emily Horowitz

Marketing Coordinator: Christopher Walz

Art and Cover Direction, Production Management, and Composition: Lumina Datamatics, Inc.

Senior Media Developer: Sally Nieman

Manufacturing Planner: Ron Montgomery

Cover Image: © Ascent Xmedia/Taxi/Getty Images

Intellectual Property

　Analyst: Jennifer Nonenmacher

　Project Manager: Sarah Shainwald

> For product information and technology assistance, contact us at
> **Cengage Learning Customer & Sales Support, 1-800-354-9706**
>
> For permission to use material from this text or product,
> submit all requests online at **cengage.com/permissions**
> Further permissions questions can be emailed to
> **permissionrequest@cengage.com**

Library of Congress Control Number: 2014942594

Student Edition ISBN: 978-1-285-86635-2

Cengage Learning
20 Channel Center Street
Boston, MA 02210
USA

Cengage Learning is a leading provider of customized learning solutions with office locations around the globe, including Singapore, the United Kingdom, Australia, Mexico, Brazil, and Japan. Locate your local office at: **www.cengage.com/global**

Cengage Learning products are represented in Canada by Nelson Education, Ltd.

To learn more about Cengage Learning Solutions, visit **www.cengage.com**

Purchase any of our products at your local college store or at our preferred online store **www.cengagebrain.com**

Printed in the United States of America
Print Number: 01　　Print Year: 2014

Brief Contents

Contents

<table>
<tr><td>PART TWO</td><td>TEAM LEADERSHIP</td></tr>
</table>

CHAPTER 6
Communication, Coaching, and Conflict Skills   183

PART THREE   ORGANIZATIONAL LEADERSHIP

CHAPTER 12
Crisis Leadership and the Learning Organization   428

Preface

Target Market

This book is intended for leadership courses offered at the undergraduate and graduate levels in schools of business, public administration, health care, education, psychology, and sociology. No prior coursework in business or management is required. The textbook can also be used in management development courses that emphasize the leadership function, and can supplement management or organizational behavior courses that emphasize leadership, especially with an applications/skill development focus.

Goals and Overview of Competitive Advantages

In his book *Power Tools,* John Nirenberg asks, "Why are so many well-intended students learning so much and yet able to apply so little in their personal and professional lives?" Is it surprising that students cannot apply what they read and cannot develop skills, when most textbooks continue to focus on theoretical concepts? Textbooks need to take the next step and develop students' ability to apply what they read and to build skills using the concepts. I (Lussier) started writing management textbooks in 1988—prior to the call by the Association to Advance Collegiate Schools of Business (AACSB) for skill development and outcomes assessment—to help professors teach their students how to apply concepts and develop management skills. Pfeffer and Sutton concluded that the most important insight from their research is that knowledge that is actually implemented is much more likely to be acquired from learning by doing, than from learning by reading, listening, or thinking. We designed this book to give students the opportunity to learn by doing.

The overarching goal of this book is reflected in its subtitle: theory, application, skill development. We developed the total package to teach leadership theory and concepts, to improve ability to apply the theory through critical thinking, and to develop leadership skills. Following are our related goals in writing this book:

- To be the only traditional leadership textbook to incorporate the three-pronged approach. We make a clear distinction between coverage of theory concepts, their application, and the development of skills based on the concepts. The Test Bank includes questions under each of the three approaches.
- To make this the most "how-to" leadership book on the market. We offer behavior models with step-by-step guidelines for handling various leadership functions (such as how to set objectives, give praise and instructions, coach followers, resolve conflicts, and negotiate).
- To offer the best coverage of traditional leadership theories, by presenting the theories and research findings without getting bogged down in too much detail.
- To create a variety of high-quality application material, using the concepts to develop critical-thinking skills.
- To create a variety of high-quality skill-development exercises, which build leadership skills that can be used in students' personal and professional life.
- To offer behavior-modeling leadership skills training.
- To make available a DVD, including 7 Behavior Model Videos and 12 Video Cases.
- To suggest self-assessment materials that are well integrated and illustrate the important concepts discussed in the text. Students begin by determining their personality profile in Chapter 2, and then assess how their personality affects their leadership potential in the remaining chapters.

- To provide a flexible teaching package, so that professors can design the course to best meet the leadership needs of their students. The total package includes more material than can be covered in one course. Supplemental material is included, thus only one book is needed—making it a low-cost alternative for the student.

Flexibility Example

The textbook, with 12 chapters, allows time for other materials to be used in the leadership course. The textbook includes all the traditional topics in enough detail, however, to use only the textbook for the course. It offers so much application and skill-development material that it cannot all be covered in class during one semester. Instructors have the flexibility to select only the content and features that best meet their needs.

Specific Competitive Advantage— Pedagogical Features

Three-Pronged Approach

We created course materials that truly develop students into leaders. As the title of this book implies, we provide a balanced, three-pronged approach to the curriculum:

- A clear understanding of the traditional theories and concepts of leadership, as well as of the most recently developed leadership philosophies
- Application of leadership concepts through critical thinking
- Development of leadership skills

The three-pronged approach is clear in the textbook and is carried throughout the Instructor's Manual and Test Bank.

Theory

Leadership Theories, Research and References, and Writing Style: This book has been written to provide the best coverage of the traditional leadership theories, presenting the theories and research findings clearly without being bogged down in too much detail. The book is heavily referenced with classic and current citations. Unlike the textbooks of some competitors, this book does not use in-text citations, to avoid distracting the reader and adding unnecessary length to the text chapters. Readers can refer to the notes for complete citations of all sources. Thus, the book includes all the traditional leadership topics, yet we believe it is written in a livelier, more conversational manner than those of our competitors.

The following features are provided to support the first step in the three-pronged approach—theory.

Learning Outcomes: Each chapter begins with Learning Outcomes. At the end of the chapter, the Learning Outcomes are integrated into the chapter summary.

Key Terms: A list of key terms appears at the end of each chapter. Clear definitions are given in the text for approximately 15 of the most important concepts from the chapter (with the key term in bold and the definition in italic).

Chapter Summary: The summary lists the Learning Outcomes from the beginning of the chapter and gives the answers. For each chapter, the last Learning Outcome requires students to define the key terms of the chapter by writing the correct key term in the blank provided for each definition.

Review Questions: These questions require recall of information generally not covered in the Learning Outcomes.

Application

The second prong of our textbook is to have students apply the leadership theories and concepts so that they can develop critical-thinking skills. Students develop their application skills through the following features.

Opening Case Application: At the beginning of each chapter, information about an actual manager and organization is presented. The case is followed by four to eight questions to get students involved. Throughout the chapter, the answers to the questions are given to illustrate how the manager/organization actually uses the text concepts to create opportunities and solve problems through decision making. A distinctive head (Opening Case APPLICATION) appears when the opening case is applied in the text.

OPENING CASE Application

1. What Big Five and leadership personality traits does Ellen Kullman possess?

To a large extent, Ellen Kullman is a successful leader because of her strong personality in the Big Five.

She has a strong need for *surgency* that helped her climb the corporate ladder at DuPont, which is dominated by men. It took energy and determination to become the first woman CEO of DuPont. She is ranked #3 on the Fortune 50 Most Powerful Women list.

Kullman has *agreeableness*. She gets along well with people having strong interpersonal skills with EI. Kullman relies more on her personal relationships than her power as CEO to get the job done. She is also sociable and sensitive to others.

She is *conscientious* at getting the job done. Being very dependable by achieving great success was a cornerstone of her climbing the corporate ladder at DuPont. Plus she is viewed has having a high level of integrity.

Kullman is well *adjusted*. Competing in a company and industry dominated by men, she has self-control and self-confidence. She is calm, good under pressure, relaxed, secure, and positive. She praises the accomplishments of her employees at all levels.

She is *open* to new experience because of her innovating and bringing to market new products at a faster clip. Kullman is highly intelligent, has an internal locus of control as she takes charge to bring changes, and is flexible.

WORK
Application **2-1**

Based on your personality profile, identify which dimensions are stronger, moderate, and weaker.

Work Applications: Open-ended questions, called Work Applications, require students to explain how the text concepts apply to their own work experience; there are over 100 of these scattered throughout the text. Student experience can be present, past, summer, full-time, or part-time employment. The questions help the students bridge the gap between theory and the real world. The Work Applications are also included in the Test Bank, to assess students' ability to apply the concepts.

Concept Applications: Every chapter contains a series of two to six Concept Application boxes that require students to determine the leadership concept being illustrated in a specific, short example. All the recommended answers appear in the Instructor's Manual with a brief explanation. In addition, the Test Bank has similar questions, clearly labeled, to assess students' ability to apply the concepts.

CONCEPT APPLICATION 2-1

Big Five Personality Dimensions

Identify each of these seven traits/behaviors by its personality dimension. Write the appropriate letter in the blank before each item.

a. surgency
b. agreeableness
c. affiliation
d. conscientiousness
e. openness to experience

_____ 1. A leader is saying a warm, friendly hello to followers as they arrive at the meeting.

_____ 2. A leader is brainstorming ideas with followers on new products.

_____ 3. A follower is yelling about a problem, a leader calmly explains how to solve it.

_____ 4. A leader is not very talkative when meeting some unexpected customers.

_____ 5. A leader is letting a follower do the job his or her own way to avoid a conflict.

_____ 6. A leader is giving detailed instructions to a follower to do the job.

_____ 7. A purchasing agent submitted the monthly report on time as usual.

Critical-Thinking Questions: There are more than 80 critical-thinking questions (an average of seven per chapter) that can be used for class discussion and/or written assignments to develop communication and critical thinking skills.

Cases: Following the Review Questions and Critical Thinking Questions, students are presented with another actual manager and organization. The students learn how the manager/organization applies the leadership concepts from that chapter. Each Case is followed by questions for the student to answer. Chapters 2 through 11 also include cumulative case questions. Cumulative questions relate case material from prior chapters. Thus, students continually review and integrate concepts from previous chapters. Answers to the Case questions are included in the Instructor's Manual.

Video Cases: All chapters include one Video Case. Seeing actual leaders tackling real management problems and opportunities enhances student application of the concepts. The 12 Video Cases have supporting print material for both instructors and students, including a brief description and critical-thinking questions. Answers to the Video Case questions are included in the Instructor's Manual.

VIDEO ▶ CASE

"P.F." Chang's Serves Its Workers Well

P.F. Chang's has over 120 full-service, casual dining Asian bistros and contemporary Chinese diners across the country, and its employees have the authority to make decisions that benefit customers. Giving employees the freedom to make decisions has had a huge impact on their attitudes and performance. Managers at P.F. Chang's receive extensive training on how to create and nurture a positive attitude among their employees, and all workers receive an employee handbook, which clearly spells out exactly what is expected of them.

1. In what ways does P.F. Chang's create organizational commitment among its workers?

2. How might a manager at P.F. Chang's use the Big Five personality factors to assess whether a candidate for a position on the wait staff would be suitable?

Skill Development

The difference between learning about leadership and learning to be a leader is the acquisition of skills, our third prong. This text focuses on skill development so students can use the leadership theories and concepts they learn to improve their personal and professional life.

Self-Assessments: Scattered throughout the text are 37 Self-Assessments. Students complete these exercises to gain personal knowledge. All information for completing and scoring the assessments is contained within the text. Students determine their personality profile in Chapter 2, and then assess how their personality affects their leadership in the remaining chapters. Self-knowledge leads students to an understanding of how they can and will operate as leaders in the real world. Although Self-Assessments do not develop a specific skill, they serve as a foundation for skill development.

SELF-ASSESSMENT 9-3   **Personality and Charismatic and Transformational Leadership**

Charismatic leaders have charisma based on personality and other personal traits that cut across all of the Big Five personality types. Review the ten qualities of charismatic leaders in Exhibit 9.3 on page 333. Which traits do you have?

_____

_____

If you have a high surgency Big Five personality style and a high need for power, you need to focus on using socialized, rather than personalized, charismatic leadership.

Transformational leaders tend to be charismatic as well. In Self-Assessment 9-1 on page 329 you determined if you were more transformational or transactional. How does your personality affect your transformational and transactional leadership styles?

_____

_____

You Make the Ethical Call   The boxes present issues of ethics for class discussion, with many presenting actual situations faced by real companies. Each dilemma contains two to four questions for class discussion.

YOU
Make the
ETHICAL
Call

1.1   *Is Leadership Really Important?*

Scott Adams is the creator of the cartoon character Dilbert. Adams makes fun of managers, in part because he distrusts top-level managers, saying that leadership is really a crock. Leadership is about manipulating people to get them to do something they don't want to do, and there may not be anything in it for them. CEOs basically run the same scam as fortune-tellers, who make up a bunch of guesses, and when by chance one is correct, they hope you forget the other errors. First, CEOs blame their predecessors for anything that is bad, then they shuffle everything around, start a new strategic program, and wait. When things go well, despite the CEO, the CEO takes the credit and moves on to the next job. Adams says we may be hung up on leadership as part of our DNA. It seems we have always sought to put somebody above everybody else.

1. Do you agree with Scott Adams that leadership is a crock?

2. Do we really need to have someone in the leadership role?

Case Role-Play Exercise: Following each Case are instructions to prepare students to conduct an in-class role-play, based on a situation presented in the Case. Through role-playing, students develop their skills at handling leadership situations. For example, students are asked to conduct a motivational speech and to develop a vision and mission statement for an organization.

Step-by-Step Behavior Models: In addition to traditional theories of leadership, the text includes behavior models: how-to steps for handling day-to-day leadership functions, such as how to set objectives, give praise, coach, resolve conflicts, delegate, and negotiate.

Behavior Model Videos: There are seven Behavior Model Videos that reinforce the development of skills. The videos demonstrate leaders successfully handling common leadership functions, using the step-by-step behavior models discussed earlier in the Theory section. Students learn from watching the videos and/or using them in conjunction with the Skill-Development Exercises. Material in the text integrates the videos into the chapters. Ideas for using all videos are detailed in the Instructor's Manual.

Behavior Model Video   6.1

Situational Communications

Objectives

To better understand the four situational communication styles and which style to use in a given situation

Video (12 minutes) Overview

You will first listen to a lecture to understand how to use the situational communications model. Then, you will view two managers, Steve and Darius, meeting to discuss faulty parts. You are asked to identify the communication style Darius uses in four different scenes. Write the letters of the style on the scene line after each scene. This may be completed as part of Developing Your Leadership Skills Exercise 6-2.

Scene 1.   Autocratic (S1A)

Scene 2.   Consultative (S2C)

Scene 3.   Participative (S3P)

Scene 4.   Empowerment (S4E)

Developing Your Leadership Skills: There are between one and four Exercises at the end of each chapter. We use the term *developing your leadership skills* only in referring to an exercise that will develop a skill that can be used in the students' personal or professional life at work. Full support of 30 activities can be found in the Instructor's Manual, including detailed information, timing, answers, and so on. There are three primary types of exercises:

Individual Focus. Students make individual decisions about exercise questions before or during class. Students can share their answers in class discussions, or the instructor may elect to go over recommended answers.

Group/Team Focus. Students discuss the material presented and may select group answers and report to the class.

Role-Play Focus. Students are presented with a model and given the opportunity to use the model to apply their knowledge of leadership theories through role-playing exercises.

Behavior Model Skills Training: Six of the Developing Your Leadership Skills Exercises may be used as part of behavior modeling by using the step-by-step models in the text and the Behavior Model Videos. Meta-analysis research has concluded that behavior modeling skills training is effective at developing leadership skills. For example, students read the conflict resolution model in the text, watch the video in class, and then complete an Exercise (role-play) to resolve a conflict, using the model and feedback from others.

Behavior Model Skills Training   2

Session 2

In this behavior model skills training session, you will perform three activities:

1 Read "Improving Performance with the Coaching Model" (to review how to use the model).

2 Watch Behavior Model Video 6.2, "Coaching."

3 Complete Developing Your Leadership Skills Exercise 6-3 (to develop your coaching skills).

For further practice, use the coaching model in your personal and professional life.

Supplements Support

Instructor's Companion Site. Access important teaching resources on this companion Web site. For your convenience, you can download electronic versions of the instructor supplements from the password-protected section of the site, including the Instructor's Manual, Cognero Testing files, Word Test Bank files, PowerPoint® slides, and a DVD Guide.

- ***Instructor's Manual.*** The accompanying Instructor's Manual, prepared by Robert Lussier and Christopher Achua, contains the following for each chapter of the book: a detailed outline for lecture enhancement, Review Question answers, Concept Application answers, Case and Video Case question answers, instructions on use of videos, and Developing Your Leadership Skills Exercise ideas (including setup and timing). The Instructor's Manual also contains an introduction that discusses possible approaches to the course and provides an overview of possible uses for various features and how to test and grade them. It explains the use of permanent groups to develop team leadership skills and provides guidance in the development of a course outline/syllabus.
- ***Cengage Learning Testing Powered by Cognero.*** This is a flexible, online system that allows you to author, edit, and manage test bank content from multiple Cengage Learning solutions; create multiple test versions in an instant; and deliver tests from your LMS, your classroom, or wherever you want. Cengage Learning Testing Powered by Cognero works on any operating system or browser, no special installs or downloads needed. You can create tests from school, home, the coffee shop—anywhere with Internet access.
- ***Word Test Bank*** *files.* These files are converted from the Cognero testing system. All questions have been scrutinized for accuracy, the test bank for each chapter includes true/false, multiple-choice, and essay questions, all correlated to national business standards, learning objectives, level of difficulty, and page references.
- ***PowerPoint® Lecture Presentations.*** An asset to any instructor, the lectures provide outlines for every chapter, illustrations from the text, and emphasize key concepts providing instructors with a number of learning opportunities for students.
- ***DVD Guide.*** Designed to facilitate use of the accompanying DVD, this guide provides summaries of each Video Case, as well as the Behavior Model Video segments. Discussion starter question and suggested answers are included.

DVD. Chapter closing videos and Behavior Model videos compiled specifically to accompany *Leadership* allow students to engage with the textual materials by applying theories and concepts of real-world situations.

Summary of Key Innovations

Our goal is to make both students and instructors successful by providing learning features that not only teach about leadership but also help students become leaders. Here are the special ways in which this is done:

- Three-pronged approach (theory, application, skill development) in the textbook and corresponding assessment of the three areas in the Test Bank
- Unique skill-development materials that build leadership skills for use in students' personal and professional life
- Unique application material to develop critical-thinking skills in applying the leadership concepts and theories
- Unsurpassed video package, with 12 Video Cases and 7 Behavior Model Videos
- Flexibility—use any or all of the features that work for you!

Changes to the Sixth Edition

The sixth edition and accompanying supplements have been thoroughly revised.

Chapter 1

The chapter has been updated and 90 percent of the references are new to this edition. Learning outcomes 5 and 6 have been combined because they are related, and learning outcome 7 has been deleted, but the review and list of key terms remains in the Chapter Summary. There is a new Opening Case Application about Amazon. The opening section headings (level 1 and 2 heads) have been changed to better match the first learning outcome. The subsection (level 3 head) on the Importance of Leadership has been rewritten with all new current references. There is a new subsection, Why Study Leadership? to answer this question. There is a new sub-section, The Need for Self-Assessment in Leadership Development, so that students understand the value of the self-assessment exercises in each chapter. Also, it gets student self-assessment in the very first section of the chapter. Self-Assessment 1-1 has been expanded to include more questions, which makes some changes to the Five Elements of Leadership. Within the Five Elements of Leadership, The Leader–Follower subsection now has level 4 headings and the influencing, organizational objectives, change, and people subsections have been heavily revised and shortened with new references. The section "Can Leadership Skills be Taught and Skills Developed" has been rewritten and shortened with all new references. The introduction to the Management Leadership Skills and the discussion of the three management skills has been shortened with new references. The Interpersonal Roles now begins with the leader, and the discussion of all ten roles has been condensed. You Make the Ethical Call 1.2, Executive Compensation, has been shortened and updated with all new references. Each of the Leadership Theory Paradigms has been shortened by removing some of the details of the findings of each paradigm that is discussed in later chapters. AACSB standards have been updated using the 2013 AACSB Business Accreditation Standards, General Skills Areas. The listing of AACSB skills developed in each of the Skill Building Exercises throughout the book has also been updated. The case is essentially new as indicated in the new title "From Steve Jobs to Tim Cook—Apple." The information on Jobs has been decreased and the information on Cook has been increased, with several new references and current performance reported with Cook as CEO.

Chapter 2

The chapter has been updated and 92 percent of the references are new to this edition. The opening case is still DuPont, but it has been rewritten and updated with new references.

The first major section has been re-titled "Personality Traits and Leadership Trait Universality" and reorganized to better focus on Learning Outcome 1, "Explain the universality of traits of effective leaders." The number 2 head "Applying Trait Theory" has been replaced with "Leadership Trait Universality," and the discussion of "We Can Improve" and "Derailed Leadership Traits" level 3 heads has been moved to the "Personality Profile" section. The introduction to the Ethical Leadership section has been rewritten with all new references. The section "Does Ethical Behavior Pay?" has been rewritten with all new references. There is a new subsection, "Why Do Good People Do Bad Things?" The subsection "The Situation" has been expanded to include the "bad apple bad barrel" concept and include more situations in which unethical behavior may occur. In the "Guides to Ethical Behavior" section, subsection discussing codes of ethics and discernment and getting advice have been added. There is a new Work Application 2-4 to apply how people justify unethical behavior at work. The section "Being an Ethical Leader" has been deleted to shorten the chapter a bit. The end-of-chapter case is new—TOMS.

Chapter 3

The chapter has been updated and 86 percent of the references are new to this edition while listing the classical references to leadership and motivation theory. The opening case is still Trader Joe's, but it has been updated and shortened. The introduction to the chapter has been rewritten with all new references. The "University of Michigan and Ohio State University Studies" section has been shortened a bit. The section, Motivation and Leadership, has been rewritten with all new references. The section on Reinforcement Theory has been shortened some, and the subsection "The Folly of Rewarding A, While Hoping for B" with Exhibit 3.12 has been deleted. The end-of-chapter case is new, Facebook COO Sheryl Sandberg. There is also a new role-play exercise that goes with it.

Chapter 4

The chapter has been updated throughout. However, this chapter is based on older contingency leadership theories. Therefore, it includes more classical references than several of the other chapters. There are 46 references and 13 are from the fifth edition, so 33 or 72 percent of the references are new to this edition. The opening case is still Indra Nooyi at PepsiCo, but the case has been completely rewritten. The Contingency Leadership Theory and Models section introduction has been updated with all new references. The closing case name has been changed by dropping the name Terry Gou from the title. It has been updated and the information about Foxconn has been shortened a bit. There are changes to all of the applying the concept boxes. The skill building exercises include the new AACSB General Skills Areas.

Chapter 5

The chapter has been updated throughout. There are 80 references and 5 are from the fifth edition; so 75, or 94 percent, of the references are new to this edition. The opening case is Mark Cuban, but the case has been completely rewritten and shorter. The introduction to the Power section has been essentially rewritten with all new references. The amount of explanation of the Types of Power and Influencing Tactics, and Ways to Increase Your Power has been reduced. The subsection "Acquiring and Losing Power" has been deleted. The introduction to the Networking section has been rewritten with all new references. The second level heading Social Networking at Work has been dropped to a third level, rewritten and shortened. The key term definition of *negotiation* has been changed. The end-of-chapter case title and the people's names in the case have been changed.

Chapter 6

The chapter has been updated throughout. There are 87 references and 3 are from the fifth edition; so 84, or 97 percent, of the references are new to this edition. The entire Communications section has been shortened a bit throughout. The section "Communication and Leadership" has been completely rewritten with all new references. The second level heading 360-Degree Multirater Feedback is now a level 3 head. Learning Outcome 6 and the section "Common Approaches to "Getting Feedback on Messages, and Why They Don't Work" have been changed by dropping the four reasons why people don't ask questions. The introduction to the Coaching section has been rewritten with new references. The Managing Conflict section has been reorganized, moving the Conflict and Leadership section into the introduction and Psychological Contract sections. The end-of-chapter cases is still Netflix, but it has been updated and shortened a bit.

Chapter 7

More than 90 percent of the references are new to this edition. Learning Outcomes 1 through 4 and 8 are new. The opening case has been updated with new references. We changed the opening section title heading to read as follows: "From Vertical Dyadic Linkage Theory to Leader–Member Exchange Theory." We redirected the discussion away from Evolution of Dyadic Theory and focused only on VDL and LMX. The subsection on Team Member Exchange Theory is eliminated from Chapter 7 and moved to Chapter 8 that deals with Team Leadership. The subsection on factors that influence LMX relationships has been rewritten with two new level 3 headings: The Role of the Leader and The Role of the Follower in Influencing LMX relationships. We eliminated the subsection titled "Developing High-Quality LMX Relationships." The content in this section is now discussed under the newly created subsection titled "The Role of the Follower in Influencing LMX Relationships." The subsection on strengths and limitations of LMX theory has been eliminated. In its place is a new subsection titled "The Two Main Criticisms of LMX Theory." The subsection "Determinants of Follower Influence" has been renamed "Factors That Can Enhance Follower Influence." The subsection "Follower Evaluation and Feedback" has been renamed "Evaluating Followers: Guidelines for Success."

Chapter 8

This chapter has been broadly updated with a significant amount of references new to this edition. The opening case is still Southwest Airlines, but it has been rewritten and updated with new references. There is a new Concept Application 8-2 to test the student's understanding of organizational culture and team creativity. There has been a major revision of the opening heading "The Use of Teams in Organizations" with new references. The subsection "Groups versus Teams: What is the Difference" has been re-titled "Is It a Group or a Team?" This section has been completely revised and shortened. Exhibit 8-2, "The Team Leader's Role in Creating Effective," has been deleted. The listed activities in the exhibit have been summarized into a concise but easy to understand narrative. Exhibit 8.3, "Guidelines for Improving Cross-Functional Team Effectiveness," has been deleted due to its redundancy to the characteristics of effective teams presented in Exhibit 8-1. The end-of-chapter case has been revised with new references and updates.

Chapter 9

This chapter has been broadly updated with a significant amount of references new to this edition. The opening case still features Oprah Winfrey, but it has been completely rewritten from a different vantage point and updated with new references. The introduction to the chapter has been shortened. All Concept Application exercises have been updated and, in many cases, new questions added. The subsection on the *Effects of Transformational Leadership* has been rewritten and the content shortened. The subsection on the *Transformational versus Transactional Leadership* has been rewritten and the content shortened. The section on *Stewardship and Servant Leadership* has been restructured from three subheadings to just two subheadings. The new sub-headings are: *Stewardship and Attributes of the Effective Steward Leader* and *Servant Leadership and Attributes of the Effective Servant Leader.* The end-of-chapter case still features Ursula Burns and Xerox Corporation but with new information and updates.

Chapter 10

The chapter has been updated throughout. There are 117 references and 4 are from the fifth edition; so 113, or 97%, of the references are new to this edition. The opening case is Avon Corporation, but the case has been completely rewritten to focus on Avon's a new CEO—Sheri McCoy. All the Concept Application Exercises have been changed or modified. A new subsection on Culture Creation and Sustainability has been added. Two subheadings—Characteristics of Strong Cultures and Characteristics of Weak Cultures—have been dropped from level 2 to level 3 subheadings. These two subheadings have been significant shortened by not discussing each characteristic as a separate subheading. Instead, a summary narrative is given and the specific characteristics presented in the exhibits. The four subheadings on types of culture—Cooperative, Competitive, Adaptive, and Bureaucratic—have been dropped from level 2 to level 3 subheadings. Each of Hofstede's Five Value Dimensions for Understanding National Cultures has been dropped from a level 2 to a level 3 subheading. The four recommended practices for fostering an ethical work environment have been dropped from level 2 to level 3 subheadings. The subsection on the Characteristics of Authentic Leaders has been dropped. Its content is included in the subsection titled "What is Authentic Leadership?" The subheading formerly titled "Changing Demographics and Workforce Diversity" has been re-titled "The Changing Workplace." Also, *demographic diversity* has been deleted as a key term. The subsection titled "The Downside of Diversity" has been deleted. Each of the factors that support a pro-diversity organizational culture has been changed from level 2 to level 3 subheadings. The end-of-chapter case is new.

Chapter 11

The chapter has been updated throughout. There are 98 references and 12 are from the fifth edition; so 86, or 90 percent, of the references are new to this edition. The opening case has been updated. All the Concept Application Exercises have been modified. The subsection on strategic leadership failures has been dropped. The focus of the chapter is on strategic leadership; as such, we made it is the first major heading (level 1) and converted Globalization and Environmental Sustainability into a level 2 subheading under Strategic Leadership. The first part of the chapter on strategic leadership and the strategic management process has undergone significant restructuring and rewriting. A new subheading titled "Leading the Strategic Management Process" has been added under strategic leadership. Each of the five tasks of the strategic management process is discussed as level 2 subheadings with significant revisions and updates. Exhibit 11-1 (Strategic Management Framework) has been replaced with a new exhibit). It is now titled "The Strategic Management Process." We have eliminated the subsection (level 3 heading) titled "Recommendations for Minimizing Resistance to Change." The subsection titled "Strategic Management in Action" has been dropped. Exhibit 11-2 (Change Implementation Process) has been dropped. The end-of-chapter case has been updated.

Chapter 12

The chapter has been updated throughout. There are 121 references, and only 13 are from the fifth edition; so 108, or 89 percent, of the references are new to this edition. The opening chapter case is new. It focuses on Antonio Perez and Eastman Kodak. The subsection on crisis leadership training has been dropped. Content has been incorporated under Crisis Leadership. The section on formulating a crisis management plan has been reorganized with two new subsections added and one deleted. Also, in this section, crisis risk assessment has received expanded coverage and elevated to a level 2 subheading now titled "The Five-Step Risk Assessment Model." The subsection titled "Spotlight on the African Crisis" has been deleted. The end-of-chapter case is still on Ken Frazier and Merck but completely new in its content and focus.

Acknowledgments

I'm deeply honored that Judi Neal, CEO of Edgewalkers, **http://edgewalkers.org/** (wrote the Appendix, "Leadership and Spirituality in the Workplace"). I also want to thank my mentor and coauthor of many publications, Joel Corman, for his advice and encouragement during and after my graduate education at Suffolk University.

I hope everyone who uses this text enjoys teaching from these materials as I do.

Robert N. Lussier, *Springfield College*

As it has been with past editions of this book, working with Bob Lussier is always a learning and growth experience that I value very much. He is a good friend and a mentor. To my students, friends, and colleagues who have encouraged and supported me morally, I say thanks. And, finally, I give recognition and thanks to the leadership of my institution, the University of Virginia's College at Wise, for their support of scholarship of this kind.

Christopher F. Achua, *University of Virginia's College at Wise*

Finally, we both would like to acknowledge the superb assistance we received from our editorial team. The guidance, support, and professionalism of Scott Person, Julia Chase, Jennifer Ziegler, the team at Lumina Datamatics, Inc., and Sally Nieman were invaluable to the completion of this project. We would also like to thank Amy Richard for her preparation of support material. We sincerely acknowledge the reviewers and survey respondents of this and past editions who provided feedback that greatly improved the quality of this book in many areas.

Reviewers

Chris Adalikwu, *Concordia College—Selma, Alabama*
Josje Andmore, *Camosun College School of Business*
Kathy Bohley, *University of Indianapolis*
John Bonosoro, *Webster University*
Brenda D. Bradford, *Missouri Baptist University*
Brian W. Bridgeforth, *Herzing College*
Carl R. Broadhurst, *Campbell University*
Jon Burch, *Trevecca Nazarene University*
Debi Cartwright, *Truman State University*
Don Cassiday, *North Park University*
Ken Chapman, *Webster University*
Felipe Chia, *Harrisburg Area Community College*
Valerie Collins, *Sheridan College*
George W. Crawford, *Clayton College & State University*
Janice Cunningham, *Indiana Tech*

Sue Cunningham, *Rowan Cabarrus Community College*
Joseph Daly, *Appalachian State University*
Frederick T. Dehner, *Rivier College*
Melinda Drake, *Limestone College*
Rex Dumdum, *Marywood University*
Ray Eldridge, *Freed-Hardeman University*
Debi Carter-Ford, *Wilmington College*
Dave Foster, *Montana State University*
Gerald A. Garrity, *Anna Maria College*
Thomas Garsombke, *Northland College*
Ronald Gayhart, *Lakeshore Tech College*
Michele Geiger, *College of Mount St. Joseph*
James Gelatt, *University of Maryland University College*
Don R. Gibson, *Houston Baptist University*
Eunice M. Glover, *Clayton College & State University*
Garry Grau, *Northeast State Community College*
Wade Graves, *Grayson County College*
Ray Grubbs, *Millsaps College*
Frank Hamilton, *Eckerd College*
Deborah Hanson, *University of Great Falls*
Nathan Hanson, *Palm Beach Atlantic*
Mary Ann Hazen, *University of Detroit Mercy*
Linda Hefferin, *Elgin Community College*
Marilyn M. Helms, *Dalton State College*
Mary Hogue, *Kent State University, Stark Campus*
Carol Himelhoch, *Siena Heights University*
Donny Hurwitz, *Austin Community College*
Stewart Husted, *Virginia Military Institute*
Dr. Katherine Hyatt, *Reinhardt University*
Gale A. Jaeger, *Marywood University*
Lori Happel-Jarratt, *The College of St. Scholastica*
David Jones, *North Carolina State University*
Thomas O. Jones, Jr., *Greensboro College*
Louis Jourdan, *Clayton State University*
Paul N. Keaton, *University of Wisconsin–La Crosse*
Gary Kleemann, *Arizona State University East*
Susan Kowalewski, *D'Youville College*
Bill Leban, *DeVry University*
Chet Legenza, *DeVry University*
Sondra Lucht, *Mountain State University*
Cheryl Macon, *Butler Community College*
James Maddox, *Friends University*
Kathleen B. Magee, *Anna Maria College*

Charles Mambula, *Suffolk University*
Gary May, *Clayton College & State University*
David McCalman, *University of Central Arkansas*
Lee E. Meadows, *Walsh College*
Ken Miller, *Mountain State University*
Michael Monahan, *Frostburg State University*
Steve Morreale, *Worcester State College*
Lorrie Mowry, *McCook Community College*
Jamie Myrtle, *MidAmerica Nazarene University*
Rhonda S. Palladi, *Georgia State University*
Patricia Parker, *Maryville University*
Jeff Pepper, *Chippewa Valley Tech College*
Nicholas Peppes, *St. Louis Community College*
Melinda Phillabaum, *Indiana University*
Laura Poppo, *Virginia Tech*
William Price, *North County Community College*
Dr. Kanu Priya, *Arkansas State University*
Gordon Rands, *Western Illinois University*
Kira K. Reed, *Syracuse University*
Marlys Rizzi, *Simpson College*
Mary Sacavage, *Alvernia College Schuylkill Center*
Khaled Sartawi, *Fort Valley State University*
Christopher Sieverdes, *Clemson University*
H. D. Sinopoli, *Waynesburg College*
Thomas G. Smith, *Fort Valley State University*
Emeric Solymossy, *Western Illinois University—Quad Cities*
Martha C. Spears, *Winthrop University*
Shane Spiller, *Morehead State University*
Karen Stephens, *Camosun College*
Bill Tracey, *Central Connecticut State University*
Dr. Robert Trumpy, *Central Washington University*
Robin Turner, *Rowan-Cabarrus Community College*
John Waltman, *Eastern Michigan University*
Fred A. Ware, Jr., *Valdosta State University*
Kerr F. Watson, *Mount Olive College*
Kristopher Weatherly, *Campbellsville University*
Amy Wojciechowski, *West Shore Community College*
Mike Woodson, *Northeast Iowa Community College*
Jan Wyatt, *Hesser College*
Benjamin R. Wygal, *Southern Adventist University*
Kimberly S. Young, *St. Bonaventure University*
Kenneth J. Zula, *Keystone College*
Joseph E. Zuro, *Troy State University*

About the Authors

ROBERT N. LUSSIER is a professor of management at Springfield College and has taught management for more than 25 years. He has developed innovative and widely copied methods for applying concepts and developing skills that can be used in one's personal and professional life. He was the director of Israel Programs and taught there. Other international experiences include Namibia and South Africa.

Dr. Lussier is a prolific writer, with over 400 publications to his credit. His articles have been published in the *Academy of Entrepreneurship Journal, Business Horizons, Entrepreneurship Theory and Practice, Journal of Business Strategies, Journal of Management Education, Journal of Small Business Management, Journal of Small Business Strategy, SAM* *Advanced Management Journal,* and others. His other textbooks include *Management Fundamentals: Concepts, Applications, Skill Development 6e* (Sage); *Human Relations in Organizations: Applications and Skill Building 9e* (Irwin/McGraw-Hill); *Business, Society and Government Essentials: Strategy and Applied Ethics* (Routledge); and others.

When not writing, Dr. Lussier consults to a wide array of commercial and nonprofit organizations. In fact, some of the material in the book was developed for such clients as Baystate Medical Center, Coca-Cola, Friendly's Ice Cream, the Institute of Financial Education, Mead, Monsanto, Smith & Wesson, the Social Security Administration, the Visiting Nurses Associations of America, and the YMCA.

Dr. Lussier holds a bachelor of science in business administration from Salem State College, two master's degrees in business and education from Suffolk University, and a doctorate in management from the University of New Haven.

CHRISTOPHER F. ACHUA is a professor in the Department of Business and Economics at the University of Virginia's College at Wise. His teaching has centered on three disciplines: strategic management, marketing, and organizational leadership. Dr. Achua's interest in engaging students in real-life learning opportunities led him to create and direct programs such as the Center for Entrepreneurship, Leadership, and Service and the Small Business Institute at his university. These programs focused on developing students' leadership and entrepreneurial skills by applying theory to real-world situations.

Dr. Achua has presented scholarly papers at regional and national conferences. His papers have been published in many refereed proceedings, the *Small Business Institute Journal,* and the *Journal of Small Business Strategy.* When not involved in academic pursuits, he lends his expertise to community development programs and initiatives. He has served on several boards of organizations in the local community, and was chair of the Mountain Empire Regional Business Incubator's board of directors.

Dr. Achua received his undergraduate degree in business administration and accounting from the University of Sioux Falls, South Dakota; his MBA from the University of South Dakota; and his doctorate from the United States International University (now Alliant International University) in San Diego, California.

Who Is a Leader and What Skills Do Leaders Need?

Learning Outcomes

After studying this chapter, you should be able to:

1 Briefly describe the five key elements of leadership. p. 5

2 Identify and define the managerial leadership skills. p. 8

3 List the ten managerial roles based on their three categories. p. 11

4 Explain the interrelationships among the levels of leadership analysis. p. 15

5 Describe the major similarity and difference between the trait and behavioral leadership theories, and the interrelationships between them and contingency theories. p. 16

OPENING CASE Application

Jeff Bezos Amazon.com

We begin each chapter by introducing an exceptional leader and company, followed by some questions for you to answer, and we answer the questions throughout the chapter.

Back in July 1995, e-commerce pioneer Jeff Bezos launched Amazon.com as an online bookstore at age 30. Over the years he transformed Amazon into "the everything store" that rivals Walmart as a store, Apple as a device maker, and IBM as a data services provider. Amazon is a **Fortune** 500 company, ranked in the top 50, with sales expected to exceed $75 billion in 2013.

Bezos is a demanding boss who doesn't tolerate stupidity. If employees don't have the right answers or try to bluff or show uncertainty or frailty, he has been known to make harsh comments. But his criticism is almost always on target that leads to improvements. He is obsessed with improving company performance and customer service and has a public e-mail. When he gets a complaint that irks him, employees get a Bezos question mark e-mail, and they react to resolve the issue quickly, like a ticking bomb.

Bezos is incredibly intelligent, even about things he knows little about. He has won numerous awards for his leadership, including *Time* magazine Person of the Year and *Fortune* named Bezos as the best CEO in 2012. He has an estimated net worth of close to $30 billion.

OPENING CASE QUESTIONS:

1. **Why is Amazon so successful?**
2. **Does Amazon use our definition of leadership?**
3. **What managerial leadership skills does CEO Jeff Bezos use at Amazon?**
4. **What managerial leadership roles does CEO Jeff Bezos perform at Amazon?**

Can you answer any of these questions? You'll find answers to these questions about Amazon and its leadership throughout the chapter.

To learn more about Amazon, visit the company's Web site at **http://www. amazon.com.**

[1] Reference for open case and answers to the question within the chapter.

The focus of this chapter is on helping you understand what leadership is and what this book is all about. As you can see in the chapter outline, we begin by discussing why leadership is important and defining leadership. Then we explain the three managerial leadership skills and the ten roles that managerial leaders perform. Next we explain the three levels of leadership analysis, which provides the framework for the book. After explaining the four major leadership paradigms that have developed over the years, we end this chapter by stating the objectives of the book and presenting its organization.

Leadership Described

In this section, we discuss the leadership course and define leadership as having five key elements.

Leadership Development

Leadership is everyone's business, so let's begin with a discussion of the importance of leadership, then answer the question, "Why study leadership?" and also state the importance of self-awareness in leadership development.

Why Leadership Development Is Important

Here are just a few reasons why leadership is so important and the need for self-awareness in leadership.

Leadership is a key issue in management and has been for more than 100 years,[2] as thousands of leadership studies have been conducted,[3] and interest in leadership remains strong.[4] I did a Google search and got "about 434,000,000 results."[5]

Organizations spend a great deal of effort and resources to teach employees how to lead.[6] More specifically, corporations spend more than $2.2 trillion on education and training, with an estimated $10 billion being spent on leadership development alone.[7] Leadership development is often cited as an important priority because it is viewed as a competitive advantage[8] as there can be significant positive returns to the investment in leadership development.[9]

Although it is generally agreed that leadership is important, critics of leadership development programs state that new college graduates lack the skills necessary to effectively lead people.[10]

As the examples illustrate, leadership matters, and there is a great need for leaders to use best practices.[11] To this end, the focus of this book is to help you develop your leadership skills, so that you can become a successful leader in your personal and professional life.

Why Study Leadership?

It's natural at this point to be thinking, "What can I get from this book?" or "What's in it for me?" These common questions are seldom asked or answered directly. The short answer is that the better you can work with people—and this is what most of this book is about—the more successful you will be in both your personal and your professional lives.[12] If you are a manager, or want to be a manager someday, you need good leadership skills to be successful.[13] Even if you are not interested in being a manager, you still need leadership skills to succeed in today's workplace.[14] The old workplace, in which managers simply told employees what to do, is gone. Today, employees want to be involved in management,[15] and organizations expect employees to work in teams and share in decision making and other management tasks.[16]

The study of leadership also applies directly to your personal life. You communicate with, and interact with, people every day; you make personal plans and decisions, set goals, prioritize what you will do, and get others to do things for you. Are you ever in conflict with family and friends? This book can help you develop leadership skills that you can apply in all of those areas.

The Need for Self-Assessment in Leadership Development

Instructors often incorporate self-assessment.[17] "Know Thyself" or self-awareness has been called the leadership first commandment,[18] so the first step to leadership development is self-awareness of leadership competencies.[19] To provide you with leadership self-awareness, every chapter has self-assessment exercises. Let's start now to better understand your leadership potential by completing Self-Assessment 1-1.

SELF-ASSESSMENT 1-1 | **Leadership Potential**

As with all of the self-assessment exercises in this book, there are no right or wrong answers, so don't try to pick what you think is the right answer. Be honest in answering the questions, so that you can better understand yourself and your behavior as it relates to leadership.

For each pair of statements, distribute 5 points, based on how characteristic each statement is of you. If the first statement is totally like you and the second is not like you at all, give 5 points to the first and 0 to the second. If it is the opposite, use 0 and 5. If the statement is usually like you, then the distribution can be 4 and 1, or 1 and 4.

If both statements tend to be like you, the distribution should be 3 and 2, or 2 and 3. Again, the combined score for each pair of statements must equal 5.

SELF-ASSESSMENT 1-1   **Leadership Potential (*continued*)**

Here are the scoring distributions for each pair of statements:

0–5 or 5–0   One of the statements is totally like you, the other not like you at all.
1–4 or 4–1   One statement is usually like you, the other not.
2–3 or 3–2   Both statements are like you, although one is slightly more like you.

1. _____ I'm interested in and willing to take charge of a group of people.
   _____ I want someone else to be in charge of the group.
2. _____ When I'm not in charge, I'm willing to give input to the leader to improve performance.
   _____ When I'm not in charge, I do things the leader's way, rather than offer my suggestions.
3. _____ I'm interested in and willing to get people to listen to my suggestions and to implement them.
   _____ I'm not interested in influencing other people.
4. _____ I offer ideas and suggestions that are commonly implemented by others.
   _____ I don't offer many ideas and suggestions, and they are often ignored.
5. _____ When I'm in charge, I want to share the management responsibilities with group members.
   _____ When I'm in charge, I want to perform the management functions for the group.
6. _____ I want to have clear goals and to develop and implement plans to achieve them.
   _____ I like to have very general goals and take things as they come.
7. _____ I like to change the way my job is done and to learn and do new things.
   _____ I like stability, or to do my job the same way; I don't like learning and doing new things.

8. _____ I enjoy working with people and helping them succeed.
   _____ I don't really like working with people and helping them succeed.
9. _____ I get greater pleasure in team accomplishments.
   _____ I get greater pleasure in personal accomplishments.
10. _____ I seek harmony in teams and try to resolve conflicts.
   _____ I avoid conflict and let group members resolve their own conflicts.

To determine your leadership potential score, add up the numbers (0–5) for the first statement in each pair; don't bother adding the numbers for the second statement. The total should be between 0 and 50. Place your score on the continuum at the end of this assessment.

0 — 5 — 10 — 15 — 20 — 25 — 30 — 35 — 40 — 45 — 50
Lower leadership potential   *Higher leadership potential*

Generally, the higher your score, the greater your potential to be an effective leader. However, essentially no one gets a perfect score. The key to success is not simply potential but persistence and hard work. You can develop your leadership ability through this course by applying the principles and theories to your personal and professional lives.

If you want to be a leader, what areas do you need to work on to improve your leadership skills?

OPENING CASE Application

1. Why is Amazon so successful?

Founder and CEO Jeff Bezos is the key to Amazon's success. Bezos is obsessed with improving company performance and customer service by offering wider selection, lower prices, and fast, reliable delivery. Amazon's mission is to seek to be Earth's most customer-centric company for four primary customer sets: consumers, sellers, enterprises, and content creators. Under Bezos's leadership, Amazon has grown to become the everything store, with global operation in Brazil, Canada, China, France, Germany, India, Italy, Japan, Mexico, Spain, and the United Kingdom, selling more than 20 million products. It is known as one of the most successful companies in the world, and is ranked 3rd as the *Fortune* World's Most Admired Companies and ranked 1st as the most trusted U.S. brand.

1.1   *Is Leadership Really Important?*

Scott Adams is the creator of the cartoon character Dilbert. Adams makes fun of managers, in part because he distrusts top-level managers, saying that leadership is really a crock. He says leadership is about manipulating people to get them to do something they don't want to do, and when there may not be anything in it for them. According to Adams, CEOs basically run the same scam as fortune-tellers, who make up a bunch of guesses and when by chance one is correct, they hope you forget the other errors. First, CEOs blame their predecessors for anything that is bad, then they shuffle everything around, start a new strategic program, and wait. When things go well, despite the CEO, the CEO takes the credit and moves on to the next job. Adams says we may be hung up on leadership as part of our DNA. It seems we have always sought to put somebody above everybody else.[20]

1. Do you agree with Scott Adams that leadership is a crock?
2. Do we really need to have someone in the leadership role?

Learning Outcome **1** · *Briefly describe the five key elements of leadership.*

Defining Leadership with Five Key Elements

When people think about leadership, images come to mind of powerful dynamic individuals who command victorious armies, shape the events of nations, develop religions, or direct corporate empires. Why are certain leaders so successful? Why do certain leaders have dedicated followers while others do not? Why were Gandhi, Mother Theresa, Martin Luther King, and Nelson Mandela such influential leaders? In this book, you will learn the major leadership theories and research findings regarding leadership effectiveness.

There is no universal definition of leadership because leadership is complex, and because leadership is studied in different ways that require different definitions. As in leadership research studies, we will use a single definition that meets our purpose in writing this book. Here, we define leadership and discuss its five elements, which are included in Self-Assessment 1-1, as each of the ten questions relates to the elements of our leadership definition and to your leadership potential.

Leadership *is the influencing process between leaders and followers to achieve organizational objectives through change.* Let's discuss the five key elements of our definition; see Exhibit 1.1 for a list.

EXHIBIT 1.1

Leadership Definition Key

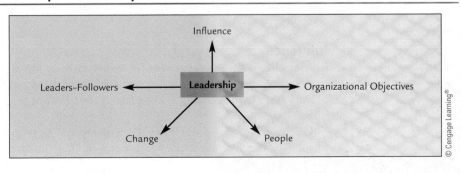

© Cengage Learning®

Leaders–Followers

Leadership is typically understood to take place where leaders and followers share a formal group membership,[21] and leadership is important as more organizations structure work around teamwork.[22] Question 1 of Self-Assessment 1-1 is meant to get you thinking about whether you want to be a leader or a follower. If you are not interested and not willing to be in charge, you are better suited to be a follower. However, leadership is shared.

Leadership is shared. One leader can't figure it all out.[23] Leadership is plural, not singular, as you can have many leaders.[24] Good followers also perform leadership roles when needed. And followers influence leaders. Thus, in our definition of leadership, the influencing process is *between* leaders and followers, not just a leader influencing followers; it's a two-way street.[25] Knowing how to lead and developing leadership skills will make you a better leader and follower.[26] So whether you want to be a leader or a follower, you will benefit from this book.

Organizations and managers or employees. Throughout this book, leadership is referred to in the context of formal organizational settings in business corporations (GE, IBM), government agencies (the Kent Police Department), and nonprofit organizations (Red Cross). Organizations have two major classifications of employees: managers, who have subordinates and formal authority to tell them what to do; and employees, who do not. All managers perform four major functions: planning, organizing, leading, and controlling. Leadership is thus a part of the manager's job. However, there are managers—you may know some—who are not effective leaders. There are also nonmanagers who have great influence on managers and peers.[27]

Manager or leader and followers? In this book, we do not use the terms *manager* and *leader* interchangeably. When we use the word *manager,* we mean a person who has a formal title and authority. When we use the term *leader,* we mean a person who may be either a manager or a nonmanager. A leader has the ability to influence others; a manager may not. Thus, a leader is not necessarily a person who holds some formal position such as manager.

A *follower* is a person who is being influenced by a leader. A follower can be a manager or a nonmanager—leadership is shared. Good followers are not "yes people" who simply follow the leader without giving input that influences the leader. The qualities needed for effective leadership are the same as those needed to be an effective follower. Throughout this book, we use the term *behavior* when referring to the activities of people or the things they do and say as they are influenced. You will learn more about followership in Chapter 7.

As implied in Question 2 of Self-Assessment 1-1, good followers give input and influence leaders. If you want to be an effective follower, you need to share your ideas. Also, as a leader you need to listen to others and implement their ideas to be effective. According to **GE** CEO Jeff Immelt, GE is not run like a big company; it is run like a big partnership, where every leader can make a contribution not just to their job, but to the entire company.[28]

Influence

Influencing *is the process of a leader communicating ideas, gaining acceptance of them, and motivating followers to support and implement the ideas through change.* The essence of leadership is influencing.[29] Let's face it; we all want to get our way, which is being influential.

Question 3 of Self-Assessment 1-1 asked if you were interested in, and willing to, influence others, as a leader or follower and Question 4 asked if you offer ideas and

WORK
Application **1-1**

Recall a present or past job. Were you both a leader and a follower? Explain.

WORK
Application **1-2**

Briefly explain the influencing relationship between the leader and followers where you work(ed).

WORK
Application **1-3**

State one or more objectives from an organization where you work(ed).

suggestions that are commonly implemented by others. When you have a management position, you have more power to influence others. But, effective followers also influence others. Your ability to influence others can be developed. Influencing includes power, politics, and negotiating; you will learn more about how to influence others in Chapter 5.

Question 5 asked if you want to share management responsibility as a leader. Influencing is also about the relationship between leaders and followers. Managers may coerce subordinates to influence their behavior, but leaders do not. Leaders gain the commitment and enthusiasm of followers who are willing to be influenced as they share leadership. Good leaders seek input from all team members.[30]

Organizational Objectives

Effective leaders influence followers, but to do what—to accomplish shared objectives.[31] Setting objectives clearly affects performance.[32] Members of the organization need to work together toward an outcome that the leader and followers both want, a desired future or shared purpose that motivates them toward this more preferable outcome. As implied in Question 6 of Self-Assessment 1, effective leaders set clear goals with their team. You will learn how to set objectives in Chapter 3.

WORK
Application **1-4**

Are the managers where you work(ed) effective at influencing their employees to bring about change? Explain.

Change

Influencing and setting objectives is about change, as leaders set objectives for behavioral change.[33] Leaders bring about change by asking followers for their input,[34] to change the status quo,[35] to continuously improve work processes, and to develop new innovative products and services.[36] As implied in Question 7 of Self-Assessment 1 and the information in this section, to be an effective leader and follower you must be open to change. To be successful, you need to change your systems and strategies.[37] When was the last time you did something new and different? You will learn more about leading change in Chapter 11.

WORK
Application **1-5**

Do managers where you work(ed) treat their employees as valuable assets? Explain.

People

Although the term *people* is not specifically mentioned in our definition of leadership, after reading about the other elements, you should realize that leadership is about leading people through relationships.[38] It's the people that accomplish the objectives.[39] As implied in Questions 8–10 of Self-Assessment 1-1, to be effective at almost every job today, you must be able to get along with people.[40] You will learn how to develop your people skills throughout this book.

OPENING CASE Application

2. Does Amazon use our definition of leadership?

Jeff Bezos is clearly the *leader* at Amazon, but he also gets ideas from his *followers*. Bezos is also very *influential*. He convinces investors to give him money to grow Amazon, gets other businesses to offer products and services through his Web site, and gets customers to buy those products. Bezos has a clear shared vision and *objectives* for the company. Amazon is fundamentally *changing* the way that people buy and read books with e-book readers and tablets. Amazon is about service to *people*.

> **Learning Outcome   2**   *Identify and define the managerial leadership skills.*

Leadership Skills

In this section, let's start by answering the age old question—are leaders born or made and can leadership be taught and skills developed—and then we will discuss the three skills managerial leaders need to succeed. But first complete Self-Assessment 1-2 to determine your managerial leadership skills.

Are Leaders Born or Made?

Are leaders born or made, or what determines leadership—nature or nurture? You may think this is a trick question, because most researchers say the answer is both. Effective leaders are not simply born or made. They are born with some leadership ability and develop it.[41] So both perspectives add to the debate on the origins of leadership skills.[42] Researchers estimate that 30 percent of leadership is heritable, whereas 70 percent is developed.[43] You will learn more about leadership traits (nature) in Chapter 2.

Some go so far as to say that leaders are definitely made, not born, and that everyone has equal potential to develop leadership skills (nurture). NFL Greenback Packers legendary football coach Vince Lombardi said, "Leaders are made, they are not born. They are made by hard effort."[44] Whatever your leadership ability is now, you can invest in developing your leadership skills, or you can allow them to remain as they are now. We'll talk more about this in the last section of this chapter.

SELF-ASSESSMENT 1-2   Managerial Leadership Skills

Rate each statement by how well the behavior describes you on a scale of 1–5.

I	2	3	4	5
Doesn't describe me			Describes me	

1. _____ I enjoy working with things.
2. _____ I enjoy working with people.
3. _____ I enjoy working with conceptual ideas.
4. _____ I like to work with technical things like computers and equipment.
5. _____ I like to figure out people's feeling, attitudes, and motives.
6. _____ I like to solve problems.
7. _____ Following directions and procedures comes easy for me.
8. _____ Getting along with a variety of people comes easy for me.
9. _____ Analytical and quantitative reasoning comes easy for me.
10. _____ I'm good at getting a task done by the deadline.

11. _____ I'm good at getting people to overcome conflict and work together.
12. _____ I'm good at figuring out ways of overcoming barriers to get things done.

To determine your score, add up the numbers (1–5) for each skill and place them on the following lines. Each skill score should be between 5 and 20.

_____ **Technical skill** (items 1, 4, 7, 10)
_____ **Interpersonal skill** (items 2, 5, 8, 11)
_____ **Decision-making skill** (items 3, 6, 9, 12)

Your score for each skill is essentially a measure of your preference. As the first three questions ask, do you prefer working with things, people, or conceptual ideas, or are they equal? In this section, you will learn about these three skills and throughout the book you will be given the opportunity to develop your managerial leadership skills.

Can Leadership Be Taught and Skills Developed?

Another question to answer is: Can leadership be taught and skills developed? Leadership is an individual capability.[45] Research supports that leadership is learnable,[46] that students can develop their leadership skills,[47] including their knowledge, skills, and abilities (KSA).[48] As already discussed, why would colleges and corporations spend a great deal of effort and resources (billions of dollars) on leadership training if leadership skills can't be developed?[49] Also, as stated, self-assessments aid in leadership development.[50] Leadership skills are developed through various forms of play, so it can be fun.[51] Because leadership skills are so important, the focus of this book is on developing our skills.

Managerial Leadership Skills

Now let's discuss the three management skills that you need to be successful,[52] as management skills have been identified as a core competency.[53] They are listed in Exhibit 1-2 and discussed here. We also point out the differences in the skills needed based on the level of management.

Management Skills

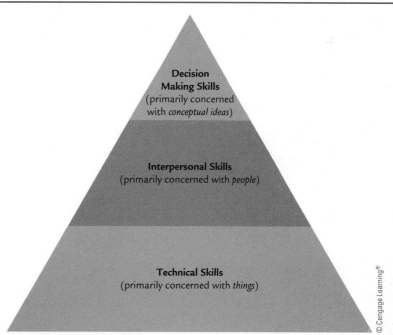

Decision
Making Skills
(primarily concerned
with *conceptual ideas*)

Interpersonal Skills
(primarily concerned with *people*)

Technical Skills
(primarily concerned with *things*)

© Cengage Learning®

Technical Skills

Technical skills *involve the ability to use methods and techniques to perform a task.* This includes knowledge about methods, processes, procedures, and techniques, and the ability to use tools and equipment to perform a task. Technical skills can also be called *business skills,* or can include them.[54] When managers are working on budgets, for example, they may need computer skills in order to use spreadsheet software such as **Microsoft®** Excel®. Most employees are promoted to their first management position primarily because of their technical skills. Technical skills vary widely from job to job, and they are the easiest of the three management skills to develop.[55] Therefore, we do not focus on developing technical skills.

Interpersonal Skills

Interpersonal skills *involve the ability to understand, communicate, and work well with individuals and groups through developing effective relationships.* Interpersonal skills are also called human, people, and soft skills. As we interact with others, we are using our interpersonal skills.[56] As discussed in our definition of leadership, relationships are critical to leadership success, and they are built on interpersonal skills.[57] Unfortunately, college grads have been found lacking it their interpersonal skills.[58]Interpersonal skills are based on several other skills, including communicating, teamwork, power, politics, negotiating, networking, motivating, conflict, diversity, and ethical skills. We will discuss these interpersonal skills throughout the book, and you will have the opportunity to develop your interpersonal skills through this course.

WORK
Application **1-7**

Select a manager, preferably one who is or was your boss, and state the specific management skills he or she uses(used) on the job.

_____

_____

_____

_____

Decision-Making Skills

Decision-making skills *are based on the ability to conceptualize situations and select alternatives to solve problems and take advantage of opportunities.* It's about how we reason and made decisions.[59] It involves critical thinking,[60] using a rational process,[61] analyzing alternatives,[62] and attempting to maximize positive outcomes for the organization.[63] Clearly the decisions you have made over the years affect who you are today and your success.

Decision-making skills are based on several other skills, including conceptual, diagnostic, analytical, critical-thinking, quantitative reasoning, and time management skills, as well as the ability to be creative, perceive trends, anticipate changes, and recognize problems and opportunities. We will discuss decision-making skills throughout the book, and you will have the opportunity to develop your decision-making skills through this course.

Skills Needed Based on Management Level

Although managers need all three skills, the need for each skill does vary based on the level of management. Top-level managers have a greater need for interpersonal and decision-making skills than technical skills. Middle-level managers have a balanced need for all three skills. First-level managers have a greater need for technical and interpersonal skills than decision-making skills. Complete Concept Application 1-1 to apply the management skills.

CONCEPT APPLICATION 1-1

Managerial Leadership Skills

Identify each activity as being one of the following types of management skills:

a. technical
b. interpersonal
c. decision-making

_____ 1. A manager is trying to figure out why a delivery hasn't been shipped out yet.

_____ 2. A manager is sending a text message from her smartphone.

_____ 3. A manager is making copies of a report he just finished at the copy machine downstairs.

_____ 4. A manager is praising an employee for a job well done.

_____ 5. A manager is determining the priority of orders to be filled next week.

OPENING CASE Application

3. What managerial leadership skills does CEO Jeff Bezos use at Amazon?

Jeff Bezos has technical skills as he developed the first online bookstore as a high-tech pioneer. He continues to challenge his employees' technical operations that expand the company performance and customer service. He also has interpersonal skills as he motivates employees to continually grow the business. Bezos clearly has decision-making skills as he is the one who has the conceptual ability to develop a successful business model and to continually change it to grow the company.

Learning Outcome 3

List the ten managerial roles based on their three categories.

Leadership Managerial Roles

In this section, we discuss what leaders do on the job—the management roles they play.[64] You will notice an overlap between the skills and roles because the leader needs the competencies (knowledge, skills, and ability—KSAs) to enact the managerial roles.[65] So we need to engage effectively in leadership roles.[66]

Henry Mintzberg identified ten managerial roles that leaders perform to accomplish organizational objectives.[67] He grouped these roles into three categories. *The **managerial role categories** are interpersonal, informational, and decisional.* Exhibit 1.3 shows the ten managerial roles, based on the three categories.

Managerial Roles

EXHIBIT 1.3

Interpersonal Roles	Informational Roles	Decisional Roles
Leader	Monitor	Entrepreneur Disturbance-
Figurehead	Disseminator	handler Resource-allocator
Liaison	Spokesperson	Negotiator

© Cengage Learning®

Interpersonal Roles

*The **interpersonal leadership roles** include figurehead, leader, and liaison.* Clearly, interpersonal skills are needed to successfully play interpersonal roles through managing interpersonal relationships.[68]

Leader Role

The *leader role* is that of performing the *management functions* (planning, organizing, leading, and controlling) to effectively operate the managers' unit to accomplish organizational objectives.[69] Therefore, the leader role influences how the leader performs the other roles. You will learn more about the leadership role throughout this book.

Figurehead Role

Leaders perform the *figurehead role* when they represent the organization or department in legal, social, ceremonial, and symbolic activities. Here are some of the figurehead activities: signing official documents; entertaining clients or customers as official

WORK
Application **1-8**

Give one job example of the specific behavior you or some other leader displayed when performing the figurehead, leader, and liaison roles. For each of the three roles, be sure to identify the leader as you or another, the role by its name, and the specific behavior.

representatives and receiving/escorting official visitors; informally talking to people and attending outside meetings as an organizational representative; presiding at meetings and ceremonial events.

Liaison Role

Leaders perform the *liaison role* when they interact with people outside their organizational unit. Liaison behavior includes networking to develop and maintain relationships, serving on committees with members from outside the organizational unit, and attending professional/trade association meetings.

Informational Roles

The **informational leadership roles** *include monitor, disseminator, and spokesperson.* Informational role success is also based on interpersonal skills.

Monitor Role

Leaders perform the *monitor role* when they gather information by talking to others, reading (memos, reports, professional/trade publications, newspapers, etc.), attending meetings, visiting competitor facilities, and so forth.

WORK
Application **1-9**

Give one job example of the specific behavior you or some other leader conducted when performing the monitor, disseminator, and spokesperson roles. For each of the three roles, be sure to identify the leader as you or another, the role by its name, and the specific behavior.

Disseminator Role

Leaders perform the *disseminator role* when they send information to others within the organizational unit. Using information translated into skills that advance the organization is now often being referred to as *knowledge management.*

Spokesperson Role

Leaders perform the *spokesperson role* when they provide information to people outside the organizational unit. People must report information to their boss and other departments, customers, suppliers, and so forth.

Decisional Roles

The **decisional leadership roles** *include entrepreneur, disturbance-handler, resource allocator, and negotiator.* Decision-making skills are important and they are needed to be successful in the decisional roles.[70]

Entrepreneur Role

Leaders perform the *entrepreneur role* when they innovate new or improved products and services and initiate improvements in business processes. Leaders often get ideas for improvements through the monitor role.

WORK
Application **1-10**

Give one job example of the specific behavior you or some other leader performed when fulfilling the entrepreneur, disturbance-handler, resource-allocator, and negotiator roles. For each of the four roles, be sure to identify the leader as you or another, the role by its name, and the specific behavior.

Disturbance-Handler Role

Leaders perform the *disturbance-handler role* when they take corrective action during crisis that interrupts business, such as a natural disaster, or emergencies like a breakdown of important machines/equipment or needed material not arriving as scheduled. Leaders typically give this role priority over all other roles during the disruption.

Resource-Allocator Role

Leaders perform the *resource-allocator role* when they schedule, request authorization, and perform budgeting activities. Deciding who gets the limited resources is important as people make decisions seeking self-interest that may not be in the best interest of the organization.[71]

Negotiator Role

Leaders perform the *negotiator role* when they represent their organizational unit during transactions that do not include set boundaries, such as only one price and term of a sale or purchase for a product/service, pay of an employee, or a raise for themselves. Leaders can try to negotiate a good deal to benefit the organization.

Although managers are responsible for all ten roles, which roles are most important—and which roles the manager performs and which are performed by other leaders—will vary based on the manager's job and the organizational environment.

After answering Work Applications 8 through 10, you should realize that we perform the leadership roles regardless of management title. Completing Concept Application 1-2, Questions 6-20, gives you practice at identifying the ten managerial roles.

OPENING CASE Application

4. What managerial leadership roles does CEO Jeff Bezos perform at Amazon?

Like all managers who are good leaders, Jeff Bezos plays all ten roles, and he delegates these roles to his followers. His interpersonal roles include signing documents; entertaining customers; running and attending meetings; leadership development and evaluation of followers; and serving on committees and boards.

His informational roles include extensive communications. Bezos is consistently analyzing information in the monitoring role, and sending information in his disseminator role, and is clearly the spokesperson for the company in the decisional role category. Bezos is an online entrepreneur. His other roles include developing new products to keep ahead of the competition and dealing with disturbances created by local and foreign government business laws and regulations.

CONCEPT APPLICATION 1-2

Leadership Managerial Roles

Identify each of the following 15 behaviors by its leadership role. Write the appropriate letter in the blank before each item.

Interpersonal roles	Informational roles	Decisional roles
a. leader	d. monitor	g. entrepreneur
b. figurehead	e. disseminator	h. disturbance-handler
c. liaison	f. spokesperson	i. resource-allocator
		j. negotiator

_____ 6. The supervisor is being promoted to middle management and is discussing her pay for the new job.

_____ 7. The supervisor is disciplining an employee for smoking on the job.

_____ 8. The leader is visiting a competitor's Web site to find out its prices.

_____ 9. The leader is getting maintenance to come fix a broken pipe and clean up a flood of water in the work area.

_____ 10. The manager has decided to stop having customers sign credit card receipts for less than $50 to speed up the checkout line.

_____ 11. The manager is breaking up a fight between two employees and getting the other employees to get back to work.

_____ 12. The manager is e-mailing the employees to inform them of their work hours for next week.

_____ 13. The manager in productions is talking to the manager in facilities about performing routine maintenance for the department equipment.

(continued)

CONCEPT APPLICATION 1-2

_____ 14. An employee quit and the manager is in the process of replacing the person.

_____ 15. The manager is signing a purchase order for new equipment.

_____ 16. The public relations leader is sending a press release to the local newspaper.

_____ 17. The manager has been given $1,000 to split and give to two of his 20 employees as bonuses.

_____ 18. The purchasing manager is discussing the price of an expensive new machine, and its installation and maintenance contract deal.

_____ 19. At the company annual employee meeting, the CEO is passing out awards for excellent performance.

_____ 20. The manager is reading the monthly trade journal.

Levels of Analysis of Leadership Theory

One useful way to classify leadership theory and research is by the levels of analysis.[72] *The three* **levels of analysis of leadership theory** *are individual, group, and organizational.* Most leadership theories are formulated in terms of processes at only one of these three levels.[73] You will briefly learn about each level in this section, and the details of each in Parts One through Three of this book.

Individual Level of Analysis

The individual level of analysis of leadership theory focuses on the individual leader and the relationship with individual followers.[74] The individual level can also be called the *dyadic process.* There is an implicit assumption that leadership effectiveness cannot be understood without examining how a leader and follower influence each other over time. You will also have multiple dyadic relationships at work. In Part One, "Individuals as Leaders" (Chapters 1 through 5), the focus is on the individual level of analysis.

Group Level of Analysis

The second level of analysis of leadership theory focuses on the relationship between the leader and the collective group of followers. This level is also called *group process.* Group process theories focus on how a leader contributes to group effectiveness. Extensive research on small groups has identified important determinants of group effectiveness, which you will learn about in Part Two, "Team Leadership" (Chapters 6 through 8). An important part of group process is meetings. In Chapter 8, you will learn how to conduct productive meetings.

Organizational Level of Analysis

The third level of analysis focuses on the organization, and is also called *organizational process.* Individuals and teams contribute to organizational success. Organizational performance in the long run depends on effectively adapting to the environment and acquiring the necessary resources to survive. You will learn more about determinants of organizational performance in Part Three, "Organizational Leadership" (Chapters 9 through 12).

1.2 *Executive Compensation*

Executive compensation is a complex and controversial subject. On one side of the debate, executive management skill has a direct impact on the success of the firm. Top executives should be paid multimillion-dollar compensation packages; after all, if it weren't for some effective CEOs, companies would not be making the millions of dollars of profits they make each year. They deserve a piece of the pie they helped create. In capitalist countries, talented CEOs, like in pro sports, are entitled to fetch their price.

On the other side, top executives have been criticized for being overpaid, especially as CEO pay rose while employees were getting laid off during the recession. Eight CEOs, led by J.C. Penny, made more than 1,000 times their average worker. The Oracle CEO made an estimated $189,000 per hour. Fortune 500 CEOs all make millions. Some say top executives are being overpaid.[75]

1. Do executives deserve to make around 300 times as much as the average worker?

2. Is it ethical for managers to take large pay increases while laying off employees and when giving them only small raises?

3. Are companies being socially responsible when paying executives premium compensation?

Learning Outcome 4 *Explain the interrelationships among the levels of leadership analysis.*

Interrelationships among the Levels of Analysis

Exhibit 1.4 illustrates the interrelationships among the levels of analysis of leadership theory. Note that the individual is placed at the bottom of the triangle because group and organizational performance are based on individual performance. It has been said that an organization is the sum of all of its individual transactions. Depending on the size of the group and organization you work for, your individual performance may influence the performance of the group and organization positively or negatively.[76]

EXHIBIT 1.4

Interrelationships among the Levels of Analysis of Leadership Theory

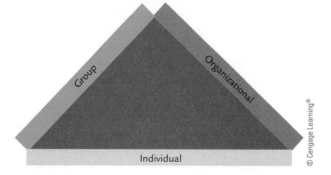

Group

Organizational

Individual

© Cengage Learning®

If individual performance is low throughout the organization, the triangle will fall because it will not have a firm foundation, or performance will be low. The group part of the triangle supports the organizational side. So if the groups are not effective, the triangle will fall or organizational performance will be low. At the same time, both group and organizational performance affect the performance of the individual. If groups are highly motivated and productive (or not productive), chances are the individual will be productive (or not) as well. Success tends to be contagious. Working for a winning organization like **Google** tends to motivate individuals to perform at their best to stay on top. However, an organization and its performance are more than the simple sum of its individuals and groups.

Leadership Theory Paradigms

The first thing we need to do is define the important concepts of this section. A **leadership theory** *is an explanation of some aspect of leadership; theories have practical value because they are used to better understand, predict, and control successful leadership.* So, the main purpose of a theory is to inform practice.[77] It has been said that there is nothing as practical as a good theory. There are four major classifications of leadership theory, also called research approaches, used to explain leadership. **Leadership theory classifications** *include trait, behavioral, contingency, and integrative theories.* In this section, we discuss each classification and indicate where it is covered in more detail later in this book.

A **leadership paradigm** *is a shared mindset that represents a fundamental way of thinking about, perceiving, studying, researching, and understanding leadership.* The leadership paradigm has changed in the 60 years during which it has been studied. The four major classifications of leadership theory all represent a change in leadership paradigm. You will also learn about the change in paradigm from management to leadership in this section.

Learning Outcome **5** *Describe the major similarity and difference between the trait and behavioral leadership theories, and the interrelationships between them and contingency theories.*

WORK
Application **1-11**

Give examples of traits and behaviors that helped make your past or present manager a successful leader.

The Trait Theory Paradigm

Early leadership studies were based on the assumption that leaders are born, not made. Researchers wanted to identify a set of characteristics or traits that distinguished leaders from followers, or effective leaders from ineffective leaders. **Leadership trait theories** *attempt to explain distinctive characteristics accounting for leadership effectiveness.* Researchers analyzed physical and psychological traits, or qualities, such as high energy level, appearance, aggressiveness, self-reliance, persuasiveness, and dominance, in an effort to identify a set of traits that all successful leaders possessed.

The list of traits was to be used as a prerequisite for promoting candidates to leadership positions. Only candidates possessing all the identified traits would be given leadership positions. You will learn more about trait theory in the next chapter.

The Behavioral Leadership Theory Paradigm

By the 1950s, most of the leadership research had changed its paradigm, going from trait theory to focusing on what the leader actually did on the job (behavior).[78] In the continuing quest to find the one best leadership style in all situations, researchers attempted to identify differences in the behavior of effective leaders versus ineffective leaders. Another subcategory of behavioral leadership focuses on the nature of management work. Thus, **behavioral leadership theories** *attempt to explain distinctive styles used by effective leaders, or to define the nature of their work.* Mintzberg's ten managerial roles are an example of behavioral leadership theory. Behavioral research focuses on finding ways to classify behavior that will facilitate our understanding of leadership. You will learn about some of the most popular behavioral leadership theories in Chapter 3.

The Contingency Leadership Theory Paradigm

Both the trait and behavioral leadership theories were attempts to find the one best leadership style in all situations; thus they are called *universal theories*. In the 1960s, it became apparent that there is no one best leadership style in all situations; the right answer often depends on the situation.[79] Thus, the leadership paradigm shifted to contingency theory. **Contingency leadership theories** *attempt to explain the appropriate leadership style based on the leader, followers, and situation.* In other words, which traits and/or behaviors will result in leadership success given the situational variables? You will learn about the major contingency leadership theories in Chapter 4.

The Integrative Leadership Theory Paradigm

In the mid-to-late 1970s, the paradigm began to shift to the integrative, to tie the theories together, or neo-charismatic theory. As the name implies, **integrative leadership theories** *attempt to combine the trait, behavioral, and contingency theories to explain successful, influencing leader–follower relationships.* Theories identify behaviors and traits that facilitate the leader's effectiveness, and explore why the same behavior by the leader may have a different effect on followers, depending on the situation. The integrative leadership theory paradigm is emphasized in our definition of leadership and thus influences this entire book, especially Chapters 6 through 12.

From the Management to the Leadership Theory Paradigm

WORK
Application **1-12**

Does your present or past manager focus more on management or leadership? Explain, using examples.

In the first section, we talked about some of the differences between a manager (formal position of authority) and a leader (has the ability to influence others), because the overarching paradigm has shifted from management to leadership. Successful managers tend to use a truly participative form of leadership as they share the responsibility of management with employees, or as leadership responsibilities are transitioned from managers to influential team members.

Some of the differences identified between managers and leaders are as follows. Managers focus on doing things right, and leaders focus on doing the right thing. Managers are concerned with stability and the best way to get the job done, and leaders place greater concern on innovation and change. The old command-and-control model of management just doesn't work in today's global economy.[80] The old-style autocratic managers are not climbing today's corporate ladder. Today, managers must be able to lead through motivating others and creating favorable conditions for success, as well as manage. So, going from the **management to the leadership theory paradigm** *is a shift from the older autocratic management style to the newer participative leadership style of management.*

Although we have made a comparison between managers and leaders, you should realize that successful leaders are also good at managing, and successful managers are good leaders. There is overlap between the two paradigms—a successful organization needs both managers and leaders. The focus is on how to integrate management and leadership, or on developing leadership skills of managers and employees, which we do in this book. To simplistically stereotype people as either managers or leaders does little to advance our understanding of leadership. Also, because the term *manager* is an occupational title, to foster an inaccurate, negative stereotype of managers is certainly not our intent.

CONCEPT APPLICATION 1-3

Leadership Theories

Identify each research approach by its leadership theory paradigm. Write the appropriate letter in the blank before each item.

a. trait
b. behavioral
c. contingency

d. integrative
e. management to leadership

_____ 21. A researcher is determining which leadership style is most appropriate.

_____ 22. A researcher is training managers to include employees in their decision making.

_____ 23. A researcher is observing managers' actions as they interact with employees.

_____ 24. A researcher is attempting to understand how managers influence employees to achieve high levels of performance.

_____ 25. A researcher is attempting to determine if the way managers dress influences their effectiveness.

Objectives of the Book

The overarching objectives of this book are reflected in its subtitle: *Theory, Application, and Skill Development.* We call it a three-pronged approach, with these objectives:

- To teach you the theory and concepts of leadership
- To develop your ability to apply leadership theory through critical thinking
- To develop your leadership skills in your personal and professional life

There has been a call to bridge the gap between research and practice (knowing and doing)[81] to teach students how to apply the concepts,[82] and for students to develop leadership skills.[83] To meet these calls, unlike most other books, ever since our first edition, we don't simply teach you leadership theory; we develop your ability to apply the theory and actually develop skills. This book offers some unique features relating to each of the three objectives (see Exhibit 1.5). We encourage you to turn back to the preface and read our goals in writing this book, and the descriptions of the features so that you can get the most from this book.

EXHIBIT 1.5

The Three-Pronged Approach: Features of the Book

Theory	Application	Skill Development
Research	Opening cases	Self-assessment exercises
References	Work applications	Case role-playing exercises
Learning	Concept applications	Step-by-step behavior models
Outcomes	Critical-thinking questions	Behavior model videos
Key terms	Cases	Developing your leadership
Summary	Video cases	skills exercises
Review questions	You make the ethical call	Behavior modeling training

© Cengage Learning®

Leadership Theory

Throughout this book, you will learn about several leadership theories and the concepts on which they are based. Conceptual knowledge is the foundation for its application and skill development.[84] As shown in Exhibit 1.5, this book offers six features to help you learn the leadership theory. The theories and concepts you will learn are based on research (EBM) and are considered important (AACSB), as discussed later in this chapter.

Evidence-Based Management

Research-based knowledge is relevant and useful to practice, and evidence-based management translates theory into workplace behavior.[85] **Evidence-based management (EBM)** *means that decisions and organizational practices are based on the best available scientific evidence.* The theories and concepts you will learn in this book are based on scientific research (not opinions, outdated research, or myths). If you look at the references at the end of this book, you will see that a majority of the journal articles are published by the premier professional association, the Academy of Management (AoM), and what it publishes is relevant to practicing leaders. However, unlike the AoM journals, we write about the theory and concepts at a level that is easy to read and understand.

Published research influences what people do in organizations; however, many organizations do not practice EBM.[86] Our objective is to move you away from making decisions based on personal preference and unsystematic experience toward EBM. If you go to the next level and apply EBM theory and concepts, you can develop your leadership skills.

AACSB 2013 Business Accreditation Standards

It is important to develop managerial leadership competencies. So how do we know what leadership competencies are important to your career success? For the answer, we turned to the Association to Advance Collegiate Schools of Business (AACSB), which gives accreditation to business schools, which states that "students engage in experiential and active learning designed to improve skills and the application of knowledge in practice is expected." Following is the list of "General Skills Areas" students are expected to develop taken from the 2013 AACSB Accreditation Standards, Standard 9.[87]

- **Written and oral communication** (able to communicate effectively orally and in writing). Chapter 6 covers communications.
- **Ethical understanding and reasoning** (able to identify ethical issues and address the issues in a socially responsible manner). Chapters 2 and 10 cover ethics, and each chapter includes "You Make the Ethical Call" situations
- **Analytical thinking** (able to analyze and frame problems). This general skill is developed throughout the book through multiple applications and skill-development exercises.
- **Information technology** (able to use current technologies in business and management contexts). This is not normally a topic of a leadership course.
- **Interpersonal relations and teamwork** (able to work effectively with others and in team environments). Chapter 8 focuses on team leadership.
- **Diverse and multicultural work environments** (able to work effectively in diverse environments). Chapter 10 covers these topics.
- **Reflective thinking** (able to understand oneself in the context of society). This general skill is developed throughout the book through multiple applications and skill-development exercises, especially the self-assessment exercises.
- **Application of knowledge** (able to translate knowledge of business and management into practice). This general skill is developed throughout the book through every application and skill-development exercise.

All of the Developing Your Leadership Skills exercises state which AACSB General Skills Area standards are developed through completing the exercise.

Application of Leadership Theory

Students need to learn to think critically,[88] but one of the most common criticisms of management education is the tendency to focus on teaching of theory but not on the application of theory to practice.[89] Thus, students lack the ability to apply knowledge.[90] Students need to be given the opportunity to practice applying what they learn.[91] To this end, this book offers you seven features (see Exhibit 1.5, the Application column) to practice applying the concepts and theory.

Leadership Skill Development

Many business programs do little to prepare leaders for their day-to-day realities.[92] There isn't enough effort given to developing leadership skills.[93] Thus, students need to be given the opportunity to practice their leadership skills.[94] To this end, this book offers you six features (see Exhibit 1.5, the Skill Development column) to help you develop your leadership skills. We also discuss a model versus an exhibit, behavior modeling, and the need to practice the skills next.

Models versus Exhibits

All of the behavioral "models" in this book provide specific, step-by-step instructions, and they are labeled as models. They are "prescriptive models." When we offer general advice without a specific instruction, we label the guidelines "exhibits." However, the purpose of both models and exhibits is to help you improve your performance.

Behavior Modeling Leadership Skills Training

Behavior modeling is the only multiple leadership skills training that has been empirically validated by rigorous procedures.[95] In some of the chapters, the features listed in Exhibit 1.5 are combined in behavior modeling skills training. For these exercises you may do a self-assessment. In any case, follow this procedure: (1) read the step-by-step models, (2) watch a behavior modeling video, and (3) practice the skill (which may include role-playing) through a skill-development exercise. The last step in this training is using the skill in your personal and/or professional life for further development of the leadership skill.

Practice

As with just about everything in life, you cannot become skilled by simply reading or trying something once. Vince Lombardi said that leaders are made by effort and hard work. If we want to develop our leadership skills, we need to learn the leadership concepts, apply the concepts, and do the preparation and skill-development exercises. But most important, to be successful, we need to be disciplined to practice using our leadership skills in our personal and professional lives. Think of leadership development like a sport. If you don't practice, you will not be good at it, and you will lose the skill you do have over time.

Flexibility

This book has so many features that they most likely cannot all be covered during a one-semester course. Your instructor will select the features to be covered that best meet the course objectives and the amount of class time available. You may do some or all of the features not covered in the course on your own, or do some exercises with the assistance of others outside of class.

Organization of the Book

This book is organized by level of leadership analysis and leadership theory paradigm. See Exhibit 1.6 for an illustration of the organization of this book.

Organization of the Book, Including Level of Analysis and Leadership Paradigm

PART ONE. INDIVIDUALS AS LEADERS (individual-level analysis of leadership theory——Trait, Behavioral, and Contingency Leadership Theories)

1. Who Is a Leader and What Skills Do Leaders Need?
2. Leadership Traits and Ethics
3. Leadership Behavior and Motivation
4. Contingency Leadership Theories
5. Influencing: Power, Politics, Networking, and Negotiation

PART TWO. TEAM LEADERSHIP (group-level analysis of leadership theory—— Integrative Leadership Theory Applications)

6. Communication, Coaching, and Conflict Skills
7. Leader–Member Exchange and Followership
8. Team Leadership and Self-Managed Teams

PART THREE. ORGANIZATIONAL LEADERSHIP (organizational-level analysis—— Integrative Leadership Theory Applications)

9. Charismatic and Transformational Leadership
10. Leadership of Culture, Ethics, and Diversity
11. Strategic Leadership and Change Management
12. Crises Leadership and the Learning Organization

© Cengage Learning®

"Take It To The Net". Access student resources at www.cengagebrain.com. Search for Lussier, Leadership 6e to find student study tools.

Chapter Summary

The chapter summary is organized to answer the six learning outcomes for Chapter 1.

1 **Briefly describe the five key elements of leadership.**

Leader–Follower—leaders influence the behavior of followers, and vice versa. *Influencing*—the relationship between leaders and followers, who change roles. *Organizational objectives*—outcomes that leaders and followers want to accomplish. *Change*—needed to achieve objectives. *People*—leadership is about leading people.

2 **Identify and define the managerial leadership skills.**

The three skills are technical, interpersonal, and decision making. *Technical skills* involve the ability to use methods and techniques to perform a task. *Interpersonal skills* involve the ability to understand, communicate, and work well with individuals and groups through developing effective relationships. *Decision-making skills* are based on the ability to conceptualize situations and select

alternatives to solve problems and take advantage of opportunities.

3 **List the ten managerial roles based on their three categories.**

Leaders perform the interpersonal role when they act as figurehead, leader, and liaison. Leaders perform the informational role when they act as monitor, disseminator, and spokesperson. Leaders perform the decisional role when they act as entrepreneur, disturbance-handler, resource-allocator, and negotiator.

4 **Explain the interrelationships among the levels of leadership analysis.**

The three levels of leadership analysis are individual, group, and organizational. The individual performance affects the group and organizational performance. The group performance affects the organizational performance. And both the group and organization affect the performance of the individual.

5 Describe the major similarity and difference between the trait and behavioral leadership theories, and the interrelationships between them and contingency theories.

The similarity between the trait and behavioral leadership theories is that they are both universal theories, or they are seeking one best leadership style for all situations. The difference is the approach to determining

leadership effectiveness. Trait theory attempts to explain personal characteristics of effective leaders, whereas behavioral theory attempts to explain what leaders actually do on the job.

The contingency theory is interrelated with the trait and behavioral leadership theories because it uses these two theories as the foundation for determining which leadership style is most appropriate—based on the leader, followers, and situation.

Key Terms

behavioral leadership theories, 16

contingency leadership theories, 17

decisional leadership roles, 12

decision-making skills, 10

evidence-based management (EBM), 19

influencing, 6

informational leadership roles, 12

integrative leadership theories, 17

interpersonal leadership roles, 11

interpersonal skills, 10

leadership, 5

leadership paradigm, 16

leadership theory, 16

leadership theory classifications, 16

leadership trait theories, 16

levels of analysis of leadership theory, 14

management to the leadership theory paradigm, 17

managerial role categories, 11

technical skills, 9

Review Questions

1 Why is leadership important?

2 What are the five key elements in our leadership definition? How do the elements interrelate to form this definition?

3 Are leaders born or made, and can leadership skills be developed?

4 List and define the interpersonal managerial leadership roles.

5 List and define the informational managerial leadership roles.

6 List and define the decisional managerial leadership roles.

7 List and define the levels of analysis of leadership theory.

8 List and define the leadership theory paradigms.

9 How can the shift in paradigm from management to leadership possibly help—and hurt—the management profession?

10 What are the three-pronged approach objectives to this book?

Critical-Thinking Questions

The following critical-thinking questions can be used for class discussion and/or as written assignments to develop communication skills. Be sure to give complete explanations for all questions.

1 Should leadership be the manager's job, or should leadership be a shared process?

2 Are you interested in sharing leadership, or do you prefer to be a follower?

3 Some people say the hard skills (e.g., finance, quantitative analysis) are more important for managers than soft skills

(e.g., interpersonal skills), and some say the opposite is true. What is your view?

4 Should leadership courses focus on teaching students about leadership or on teaching students to be leaders?

5 Can college students really develop their leadership skills through a college course? Why or why not?

6 Is leadership ability universal, or is a good leader in one environment also effective in another? For example, can a leader in one industry (e.g., a hospital) be successful in another industry (e.g., a bank)?

CASE

From Steve Jobs to Tim Cook—Apple

Steven Jobs cofounded Apple Computer with Steven Wozniak back in 1976 in Jobs's family garage. At age 21, Steven Jobs coproduced the first PC and Apple Computer; at 25 Jobs was running Apple with a net worth of $25 million, and at age 26 he made the cover of *Time* magazine. Over the years, Jobs was consistently ranked as one of the best CEO leaders of all times. In 2011, eight of the ten most read *Wall Street Journal* articles were about Steve Jobs and Apple products.[96]

Jobs also started two other companies. In 1985, Jobs started NeXT (a computer platform development). In 1986, he went to Hollywood starting what became Pixar Animated Studios. Jobs contracted with Disney to produce a number of computer-animated feature films, which Disney would cofinance and distribute. In 2006, Jobs sold Pixar to Disney and became its largest shareholder. In fact, Jobs's shares in Disney were worth more than five times the value of his Apple stock.

Most of us never have any real influence over any industry, but Jobs is ranked #1 for his leadership and power in influencing five industries: computers (coproducer of the PC—Mac), Hollywood (Pixar), music (iPod), retailing (iTunes and Apple stores), and wireless phones/telecom (iPhone and iPad). So far, no one has had more influence over a broader range of businesses than Jobs. Some say that his influence actually transformed these industries.[97]

On August 24, 2011, Jobs resigned as CEO, naming Tim Cook as his successor. Jobs died in October 2011. Many people questioned whether Apple could succeed without Jobs. Being seriously ill for a couple of years, without hype or fanfare, Jobs was quietly making sure Apple success would continue. In his resignation letter, Jobs wrote, "I believe Apple's brightest and most innovative days are ahead of it."[98] Apple insiders say that Cook was really the driving force for two years prior to Jobs's resignation.[99] To his own credit, in his first year as CEO, Tim Cook was ranked 8th on the *Fortune* 2011 Business Person of the Year.[100]

CEO Tim Cook's performance was assessed a year after the death of Steve Jobs. Tim Cook is not trying to be Jobs's clone and is making his own mark changing Apple.[101] He is a different type of leader than Jobs—being less emotional and more of a professional manager. Cook got the operations side working better than ever, coordinating suppliers to deliver on the unprecedented sale of the iPhone 5 in nearly 30 countries, and Apple is on track to launch it in 100 countries. Cook is quicker to admit product flaws and take corrective action than Jobs, such as the faulty Maps on the iPhone 5.[102] Cook has also given a stockholder dividend and is placing greater emphasis on corporate social responsibility, such as charitable contributions that Jobs was against.[103]

A year after Jobs's death, Apple stock was up 75 percent, making it the most valuable company in the world. In 2013, Apple was ranked 1st on the *Fortune* World's Most Admired Companies,[104] ranked 6th for revenues on the *Fortune* 500 U.S. largest corporations, 2nd by profits of $41,733,000,[105] and ranked 19th on the Global 500 largest corporations.[106] It is also ranked 4th as the most trusted U.S. brands.[107]

One thing Cook says he will not change is the Apple's focus on making the best products in the world—not just good ones, or lots of them—the absolute best. Cook really likes the fact that people really care so much about Apple and its products.[108] The final grade for Cook: No one is saying Apple is better off without Jobs, but to a surprising degree, Apple is doing fine without him.[109]

However, Cook is not without critics.[110] Even some who say he did a good job in his first year question, Can he keep it up?[111] One criticism is that there are no new product categories (such as no Apple TV set).[112] Only time will tell if Cook can keep Apple's momentum going.

Jobs found the secret to career fulfillment—he discovered something he was good at and loved to do. We can't all be another Steve Jobs, but we can find career fulfillment.

GO TO THE INTERNET: To learn more about Steve Jobs and Tim Cook and Apple, visit Apple's Web site **(http://www.apple.com).**

Support your answers to the following questions with specific information from the case and text or with information you get from the Web or another source.

1. Explain how each of the five elements of our definition of leadership applies to Tim Cook leading Apple.

2. Identify leadership skills Tim Cook has that led to his and Apple's success. Which skill is his strongest?

3. Identify managerial leadership roles played by Tim Cook as CEO of Apple. Which role was the most important?

4. Which level of analysis is the primary focus of this case?

5. Explain how each of the leadership theory classifications applies to this case, and which one is most relevant.

6. Can Tim Cook continue grow Apple, or will it be like so many other companies (like BlackBerry) that lose their competitive edge. Why or why not?

CASE EXERCISE AND ROLE-PLAY

Preparation: Assume that you were a powerful board member of Apple in the 1980s. You were involved in helping Jobs select the new CEO, John Sculley, and that you have worked with Jobs on the board for five years. The board has disagreed with Jobs's recommendation to replace Sculley as CEO, so Sculley stays in power and Jobs is out of power. You have to tell Jobs the bad news, which you know he will not want to hear.

Your instructor may elect to let you break into small groups to share ideas and develop a plan for your meeting with Jobs. If you develop a group plan, select one leader to present the meeting with Jobs.

Role-Play: One person (representing him- or herself or their group) conducts the meeting with Steve Jobs (to notify him that Sculley stays as CEO and he is removed from power) before the entire class. Or, multiple role-plays may take place in small groups of five to six; however, role-players can't conduct the meeting in front of the team that developed the meeting plan. They must present to a group that did not develop the plan for the meeting. The people role-playing Jobs should put themselves in his place. How would you feel about being thrown out of the company you cofounded and led? Don't forget that Jobs is rather hot tempered and very outspoken.

VIDEO CASE

Leadership at P. F. Chang's

Rick Federico is chairman and CEO of P.F. Chang's, which owns and operates a chain of Asian restaurants across the country. He has earned the respect of his managers, his workers, his customers, and even his competitors. He believes his greatest tasks as a leader involve remaining focused on his customers, his workers, and the food they serve. As P.F. Chang's grows, Federico wants to be sure that the quality of service, atmosphere, and food are always at their highest.

1. Describe some of Rick Federico's personal leadership traits.

2. Choose three of the leadership managerial roles and explain how Rick Federico might use them as head of P. F. Chang's.

Developing Your Leadership Skills   1-1

Getting to Know You by Name

Preparing for This Exercise
Complete Self-Assessment 1-2 on page 8, and read the accompanying information before class.

Objectives
1 To get acquainted with some of your classmates

2 To get to know your instructor

3 To develop your skill at remembering and calling people by their name

AACSB General Skills Area

The primary AACSB skill developed through this exercise is communication ability with application of knowledge.

In this chapter you learned about the importance of leader–follower relationships. An important part of leadership relations is making people feel important. Being able to call people by name will improve your leadership effectiveness.

Tips for Remembering People's Names

- The first thing you need to do is make a conscious effort to improve your skill at calling people by name. If you say you are no good at remembering names, you won't be. If you say, "I can be good at it," and work at it, you can.

- When you are introduced to a person, consciously greet them by name. For example, say, "Hi, Juan, glad to meet you." Then, during your conversation, say the name a few more times until it sticks with you. Use the person's name when you ask and answer questions.

- When you meet a person whom you will see again, without being introduced by someone else, introduce yourself by name—and get the other person to say their name. Then, as before, call them by name during your conversation. For example, if you get to class early and want to talk, introduce yourself to someone rather than just talking without learning the person's name. If someone you don't know just starts talking to you, introduce yourself.

- When you are in a small group being introduced to people, don't just say "hi" and ignore the names. Depending on the number of people, you can say "hello" and repeat each name as you look at the person. If you don't remember a name, ask. Just say, "I'm sorry, I didn't get your name." You may also want to mentally repeat the person's name several times. As you talk to the people in the group, use their names. If you forget a name, listen for others to say it as the discussion continues.

- If you have been introduced to a person and forget their name the next time you meet them, you have two choices. You can apologetically ask them their name. Or, before talking to the person, you can ask someone else for the person's name, and then greet them by name. Again, use the person's name during the conversation.

- Use association to help you remember. For example, if you meet John Higby, you could picture him hugging a bee. If the person's name is Ted, picture him with the body of a teddy bear. If you know the person likes something, say tennis, picture him or her with a tennis ball on his or her head. Think of other people you know who have the same name and make an association.

- Ask for a business card, or ask for the person's telephone number so you can write it down; this will help you remember the name.

- Write down the person's name and some information about them after you meet them. Sales representatives use this technique very effectively to recall personal information they may forget. If you are on a committee with people you don't know and don't see very often, use the membership list of names (or write them yourself).

Then write an association for each person, so that you can identify all members (this may be done during the meeting without drawing attention). Your notes might include personal characteristics (tall, thin, dark hair) or something about their work (marketing, engineer). Then, before the next meeting, review the list of names and characteristics so you can make the association and greet each person by name.

Doing This Exercise in Class

Procedure 1 *(5–8 minutes)* Break into groups of five or six, preferably with people you do not know. In the group, have each member give his or her name and two or three significant things about himself or herself. After all the members have finished, ask each other questions to get to know each other better.

Procedure 2 *(2–4 minutes)* Can anyone in the group call the others by name? If so, he or she should do so. If not, have each member repeat his or her name. Follow with each member calling all members by name. Be sure that each person has a turn to call everyone by name.

Procedure 3 *(5–8 minutes)* Select a person to play the spokesperson role for your group. Remember, this is a leadership course. The spokesperson writes down questions in the following two areas:

- *Course:* Is there anything more that you want to know about the course, such as any expectations or concerns that you have?

- *Instructor:* Make a list of questions for the instructor in order to get to know him or her better.

Procedure 4 *(10–20 minutes)* Each spokesperson asks the instructor one question at a time, until all questions are asked. If time permits, people who are not the spokesperson may ask questions.

Conclusion

The instructor may make concluding remarks.

Apply It *(2–4 minutes)* What did I learn from this experience? How will I use this knowledge in the future? Specifically state which tip for remembering names you will use in the future. Identify precisely when you will practice this skill: for example, on "*x*" day/date when I go to class—or to work, or to a party—I will introduce myself to someone I don't know.

Sharing

In the group, or to the entire class, volunteers may give their answers to the "Apply It" questions.

Developing Your Leadership Skills 1-2

Identifying Leadership Traits and Behaviors

Objective

To gain a better understanding of leadership traits and behavior

AACSB General Skills Area

The primary AACSB skill developed through this exercise is analytic skills and application of knowledge.

Preparing for This Exercise

Read and understand the trait and behavioral leadership theories. On the following lines, list specific traits and behaviors that you believe effective leaders have or should have. Your answers may or may not be based on your observation of successful leaders.

Traits: _____
_____
_____

Behaviors: _____
_____

Doing This Exercise in Class

Option 1 *(5–15 minutes)* Students give their answers to the instructor, who writes them on the board under the heading of Traits or Behaviors. During or after the answers are listed, the class may discuss them.

Option 2 *(10–20 minutes)* Break into groups of five or six, and select a leader to perform the spokesperson role (remember, this is a leadership class). The spokesperson records the answers of the group, and then writes them on the board (5–10 minutes). The instructor leads a class discussion (5–10 minutes).

Endnotes

1 Open case references: B. Stone, "The Secrets of Bezos: How Amazon Became the Everything Store," *Business-Week* (October 10, 2013): 58–76; "Scorecard," *Forbes* (October 28, 2013): 23; www.amazon.com, accessed October 24, 2013; "Largest U.S. Corporations—Fortune 500," *Fortune* (May 20, 2013): 1–20; G. Anders, "Jeff Bezos Gets It," *Forbes* (April 23, 2012): 77–86; P. Andruss, "Branding's Big Guns," *Entrepreneur* (April 2012): 50–55.

2 M. A. Hogg, D. Van Knippenberg, and D. E. Rast, "Intergroup Leadership in Organizations: Leading Across Group and Organizational Boundaries," *Academy of Management Review 37*(2) (2012): 232–255.

3 G. Yukl, "Effective Leadership Behavior: What We Know and What Questions Need More Attention," *Academy of Management Perspectives 26*(4) (2011): 66–85.

4 B. Schyns, T. Kiefer, R. Kerschreiter, and A. Tymon, "Teaching Implicit Leadership Theories to Develop Leaders and Leadership: How and Why It Can Make a Difference," *Academy of Management Learning & Education 10*(3) (2012): 397–408.

5 Google search (www.google.com), accessed October 3, 2013.

6. R. Kark, "Games Managers Play: Play as a Form of Leadership Development," *Academy of Management Learning & Education 10*(3) (2011): 507–527.

7. B. Benjamin and C. O'Reilly, "Becoming a Leader: Early Career Challenges Faced by MBA Graduates," *Academy of Management Learning & Education 10*(3) (2011): 452–472.

8. S. K. Johnson, L. L. Garrison, G. H. Bronnme, J. W. Fleenor, and J. L. Steed, "Go for the Goals: Relationship between Goal Setting and Transfer of Training Following Leadership Development," *Academy of Management Learning & Education 11*(4) (2012): 555–569.

9. B. Benjamin and C. O'Reilly, "Becoming a Leader: Early Career Challenges Faced by MBA Graduates," *Academy of Management Learning & Education 10*(3) (2011): 452–472.

10. B. Benjamin and C. O'Reilly, "Becoming a Leader: Early Career Challenges Faced by MBA Graduates," *Academy of Management Learning & Education 10*(3) (2011): 452–472.

11. "Call for Papers," *Academy of Management Learning & Education 12*(2) (2013): 324.

12. B. Benjamin and C. O'Reilly, "Becoming a Leader: Early Career Challenges Faced by MBA Graduates." *Academy of Management Learning & Education 10*(3) (2011), 452–472.

13. N. Breugst, H. Patzelt, D. A. Shepherd, and H. Aguinis, "Relationship Conflict Improves Team Performance Assessment Accuracy: Evidence from a Multilevel Study." *Academy of Management Learning & Education 11*(2) (2012): 187–206.

14. G. Yukl, "Effective Leadership Behavior: What We Know and What Questions Need More Attention." *Academy of Management Perspectives 26* (4) (2012): 66–85.

15. W. J. Henisz, "Leveraging the Financial Crisis to Fulfill the Promise of Progressive Management," *Academy of Management Learning & Education 10* (2) (2011): 298321.

16. R. E. Silverman, "Who's the Boss? There Isn't One." *The Wall Street Journal* (June 20, 2012): B1.

17. M. W. Ohland, "The Comprehensive Assessment of Team Member Effectiveness: Development of a Behaviorally Anchored Rating Scale for Self- and Peer Evaluation," *Academy of Management Learning & Education 11*(3) (2012): 609–630.

18. G. Petriglieri, J. D. Wood, and J. L. Petriglieri, "Up Close and Personal: Building Foundations for Leaders' Development through the Personalization of Management Learning," *Academy of Management Learning & Education 10*(3) (2011): 430–450.

19. M. Mayo, M. Kakarika, J. C. Pastor, and S. Brutus, "Aligning or Inflating Your Leadership Self-Image? A Longitudinal Study of Responses to Peer Feedback in MBA Teams," *Academy of Management Learning & Education 11*(4) (2012): 631–652.

20. G. Williams, "Comic Belief: Is Leadership Really a Crock?" *Entrepreneur* (April 2003): 28.

21. M. A. Hogg, D. Van Knippenberg, and D. E. Rast, "Intergroup Leadership in Organizations: Leading across Group and Organizational Boundaries," *Academy of Management Review 37*(2) (2012): 232–255.

22. S. B. Sitkin and J. R. Hackman, "Developing Team Leadership: An Interview with Coach Mike Krzyzewski," *Academy of Management Learning & Education 10*(3) (2011): 494–501.

23. B. P. Owens and D. R. Hekman, "Modeling How to Grow: An Inductive Examination of Humble Leader Behaviors, Contingencies, and Outcomes," *Academy of Management Journal 55*(4) (2012): 787–818.

24. S. B. Sitkin and J. R. Hackman, "Developing Team Leadership: An Interview with Coach Mike Krzyzewski," *Academy of Management Learning & Education 10*(3) (2011): 494–501.

25. B. P. Owens and D. R. Hekman, "Modeling How to Grow: An Inductive Examination of Humble Leader Behaviors, Contingencies, and Outcomes," *Academy of Management Journal 55*(4) (2012): 787–818.

26. D. S. DeRue and S. J. Ashford, "Who Will Lead and Who Will Follow? Social Process of Leadership Identity Construction in Organizations," *Academy of Management Review 35*(4) (2010): 627–647.

27. D. S. DeRue and S. J. Ashford, "Who Will Lead and Who Will Follow? Social Process of Leadership Identity Construction in Organizations," *Academy of Management Review 35*(4) (2010): 627–647.

28. J. Immelt, GE Annual Shareowners Meeting, April 26, 2006, http://www.ge.com/pdf/investors/events/068/ge_annualshar-eownersmeeting_042606_en.pdf.

29. G. Yukl, "Effective Leadership Behavior: What We Know and What Questions Need More Attention," *Academy of Management Perspectives 26*(4) (2011): 66–85.

30. B. Benjamin and C. O'Reilly, "Becoming a Leader: Early Career Challenges Faced by MBA Graduates," *Academy of Management Learning & Education 10*(3) (2011): 452–472.

31. G. Yukl, "Effective Leadership Behavior: What We Know and What Questions Need More Attention," *Academy of Management Perspectives 26*(4) (2011): 66–85.

32. S. K. Johnson, L. L. Garrison, G. H. Bronnme, J. W. Fleenor, and J. L. Steed, "Go for the Goals: Relationship between Goal Setting and Transfer of Training Following Leadership

Development," *Academy of Management Learning & Education 11*(4) (2012): 555–569.

33 S. K. Johnson, L. L. Garrison, G. H. Bronnme, J. W. Fleenor, and J. L. Steed, "Go for the Goals: Relationship between Goal Setting and Transfer of Training Following Leadership Development," *Academy of Management Learning & Education 11*(4) (2012): 555–569.

34 H. A. Richardson and S. G. Taylor, "Understanding Input Events: A Model of Employees' Responses to Requests for Their Input," *Academy of Management Review 37*(3) (2012): 471–491.

35 E. R. Burris, "The Risks and Rewards of Speaking Up: Managerial Responses to Employee Voice," *Academy of Management Journal 55*(4) (2012): 851–875.

36 J. Liang, C. I.C. Farh, and J. L. Farh, "Psychological Antecedents of Promotive and Prohibitive Voice: A Two-Wave Examination," *Academy of Management Journal 55*(1) (2012): 71–92.

37 S. B. Sitkin and J. R. Hackman, "Developing Team Leadership: An Interview with Coach Mike Krzyzewski," *Academy of Management Learning & Education 10* (3) (2011): 494–501.

38 B. Benjamin and C. O'Reilly, "Becoming a Leader: Early Career Challenges Faced by MBA Graduates," *Academy of Management Learning & Education 10*(3) (2011): 452–472.

39 A. J. Nyberg and R. E. Ployhart, "Context-Emergent Turnover (CET) Theory: A Theory of Collective Turnover," *Academy of Management Review 38*(1) (2013): 109–131.

40 M. A. Hogg, D. Van Knippenberg, and D. E. Rast, "Intergroup Leadership in Organizations: Leading across Group and Organizational Boundaries," *Academy of Management Review 37*(2) (2012): 232–255.

41 B. Benjamin and C. O'Reilly, "Becoming a Leader: Early Career Challenges Faced by MBA Graduates," *Academy of Management Learning & Education 10*(3) (2011): 452–472.

42 R. Kark, "Games Managers Play: Play as a Form of Leadership Development," *Academy of Management Learning & Education 10*(3) (2011): 507–527.

43 B. Benjamin and C. O'Reilly, "Becoming a Leader: Early Career Challenges Faced by MBA Graduates," *Academy of Management Learning & Education 10*(3) (2011): 452–472.

44 V. Lombardi, "Quote," *SBANC Newsletter* (May 19, 2009): 1.

45 B. Benjamin and C. O'Reilly, "Becoming a Leader: Early Career Challenges Faced by MBA Graduates," *Academy of Management Learning & Education 10*(3) (2011): 452–472.

46 J. Antonakis, M. Fenley, and S. Liechti, "Can Charisma Be Taught? Tests of Two Interventions," *Academy of Management Learning & Education 10*(3) (2011): 374–396.

47 R. Klimoski and B. Amos, "Practicing Evidence-Based Education in Leadership Development," *Academy of Management Learning & Education 11*(4) (2012): 685–702.

48 A. J. Nyberg and R. E. Ployhart, "Context-Emergent Turnover (CET) Theory: A Theory of Collective Turnover," *Academy of Management Review 38*(1) (2013): 109–131.

49 R. Kark, "Games Managers Play: Play as a Form of Leadership Development," *Academy of Management Learning & Education 10*(3) (2011): 507–527.

50 M. Feys, F. Anseel, and B. Wille, "Improving Feedback Reports: The Role of Procedural Information and Information Specificity," *Academy of Management Learning & Education 10*(4) (2011): 661–681.

51 R. Kark, "Games Managers Play: Play as a Form of Leadership Development," *Academy of Management Learning & Education 10*(3) (2011): 507–527.

52 G. Yukl, "Effective Leadership Behavior: What We Know and What Questions Need More Attention," *Academy of Management Perspectives 26*(4) (2011): 66–85.

53 B. Benjamin and C. O'Reilly, "Becoming a Leader: Early Career Challenges Faced by MBA Graduates," *Academy of Management Learning & Education 10*(3) (2011): 452–472.

54 R. B. Kaiser and R. B. Kaplan, "The Deeper Work of Executive Development: Outgrowing Sensitivities," *Academy of Management Learning & Education 5*(4) (2006): 463–483.

55 R. B. Kaiser and R. B. Kaplan, "The Deeper Work of Executive Development: Outgrowing Sensitivities," *Academy of Management Learning & Education 5*(4) (2006): 463–483.

56 E. R. Crawford and J. A. Lepine, "A Configural Theory of Team Process: Accounting for the Structure of Taskwork and Teamwork," *Academy of Management Review 38*(1) (2013): 32–48.

57 M. Crossan, D. Mazutis, G. Seijts, and J. Gandz, "Developing Leadership Character in Business Programs," *Academy of Management Learning & Education 12*(2) (2013): 285–305.

58 B. Benjamin and C. O'Reilly, "Becoming a Leader: Early Career Challenges Faced by MBA Graduates," *Academy of Management Learning & Education 10*(3) (2011): 452–472.

59 S. Mantere and M. Ketokivi, "Reasoning in Organization Science," *Academy of Management Review 38*(1) (2013): 70–89.

60 D. F. Baker and S. J. Baker, "To Catch the Sparkling Glow: A Canvas for Creativity in the Management Classroom," *Academy of Management Learning & Education 11*(4) (2012): 704–721.

61 H. R. Greve, "Microfoundations of Management: Behavioral Strategies and Levels of Rationality in Organizational Action," *Academy of Management Perspectives 27*(2) (2013): 103–119.

62 A. H. Van De Ven and A. Lifschitz, "Rational and Reasonable Microfoundations of Markets and Institutions," *Academy of Management Perspectives 27*(2) (2013): 156–172.

63 A. H. Jordan and P. G. Audia, "Self-Enhancement and Learning from Performance Feedback," *Academy of Management Review 37*(2) (2012): 211–231.

64 H. C. Vough, M. T. Cardador, J. S. Bendar, E. Dane, and M. G. Pratt, "What Clients Don't Get about My Profession: A Model of Perceived Role–Based Image Discrepancies," *Academy of Management Journal 56*(4) (2013): 1050–1080.

65 R. Grossman, E. Salas, D. Pavlas, and M. A. Rosen, "Using Instructional Features to Enhance Demonstration-Based Training in Management Education," *Academy of Management Learning & Education 12*(2) (2013): 219–243.

66 R. Kark, "Games Managers Play: Play as a Form of Leadership Development," *Academy of Management Learning & Education 10*(3) (2011): 507–527.

67 H. Mintzberg, *The Nature of Managerial Work* (New York: Harper & Row, 1973).

68 E. R. Crawford and J. A. Lepine, "A Configural Theory of Team Process: Accounting for the Structure of Taskwork and Teamwork," *Academy of Management Review 38*(1) (2013): 32–48.

69 G. Yukl, "Effective Leadership Behavior: What We Know and What Questions Need More Attention," *Academy of Management Perspectives 26*(4) (2011): 66–85.

70 S. Mantere and M. Ketokivi, "Reasoning in Organization Science," *Academy of Management Review 38*(1) (2013): 70–89.

71 A. H. Van De Ven and A. Lifschitz, "Rational and Reasonable Microfoundations of Markets and Institutions," *Academy of Management Perspectives 27*(2) (2013): 156–172.

72 H. R. Greve, "Microfoundations of Management: Behavioral Strategies and Levels of Rationality in Organizational Action," *Academy of Management Perspectives 27*(2) (2013): 103–119.

73 M. Crossan, D. Mazutis, G. Seijts, and J. Gandz, "Developing Leadership Character in Business Programs," *Academy of Management Learning & Education 12*(2) (2013): 285–305.

74 S. G. Winter, "Habit, Deliberation, and Action: Strengthening the Microfoundations of Routines and Capabilities," *Academy of Management Perspectives 27*(2) (2013): 120–137.

75 Information taken from the AFL-CIO's Web site at http://www.aflcio.org/corporatewatch/paywatch/pay/index.cfm, accessed October 21, 2013; R. Lowenstein, "Is Any CEO Worth $189,000 per hour?" *BusinessWeek* (February 20–26, 2012): 8–9; R. Fisman and T. Sullivan, "In Defense of the CEO," *The Wall Street Journal* (January 12–13, 2013): C1–C2; E. D. Smith and P. Kuntz, "Some CEOs Are More Equal Than Others," *BusinessWeek* (May 6–12, 2013): 70–73.e more equal than others. *BusinessWeek* (May 6 – 12, 2013), 70-73

76 S. G. Winter, "Habit, Deliberation, and Action: Strengthening the Microfoundations of Routines and Capabilities," *Academy of Management Perspectives 27*(2) (2013): 120–137.

77 B. Schyns, T. Kiefer, R. Kerschreiter, and A. Tymon, "Teaching Implicit Leadership Theories to Develop Leaders and Leadership: How and Why It Can Make a Difference," *Academy of Management Learning & Education 10*(3) (2012): 397–408.

78 A. H. Van De Ven and A. Lifschitz, "Rational and Reasonable Microfoundations of Markets and Institutions," *Academy of Management Perspectives 27*(2) (2013): 156–172.

79 H. R. Greve, "Microfoundations of Management: Behavioral Strategies and Levels of Rationality in Organizational Action," *Academy of Management Perspectives 27*(2) (2013): 103–119.

80 A. Murray, "The End of Management," *The Wall Street Journal* (August 21–22, 2010): W3.

81 R. Klimoski and B. Amos, "Practicing Evidence-Based Education in Leadership Development," *Academy of Management Learning & Education 11*(4) (2012): 685–702.

82 T. T. Baldwin, J. R. Pierce, R. C. Jones, and S. Farouk, "The Elusiveness of Applied Management Knowledge: A Critical Challenge for Management Education," *Academy of Management Learning & Education 10*(4) (2011): 583–605.

83 J. K. Nelson, L. W. Poms, and P. P. Wolf, "Developing Efficacy Beliefs for Ethics and Diversity Management," *Academy of Management Learning & Education 11*(1) (2012): 49–68.

84 T. T. Baldwin, J. R. Pierce, R. C. Jones, and S. Farouk, "The Elusiveness of Applied Management Knowledge: A Critical Challenge for Management Education," *Academy of Management Learning & Education 10*(4) (2011): 583–605.

85 R. Klimoski and B. Amos, "Practicing Evidence-Based Education in Leadership Development," *Academy of Management Learning & Education 11*(4) (2012): 685–702.

86 "Call for Papers," *Academy of Management Learning & Education 12*(2) (2013): 324.

87 AACSB Web site (http://www.aacsb.edu/accreditation /business/standards/2013/learning-and-teaching/standard9. asp), accessed October 24, 2013.

88 D. F. Baker and S. J. Baker, "To Catch the Sparkling Glow: A Canvas for Creativity in the Management Classroom," *Academy of Management Learning & Education 11*(4) (2012): 704–721.

89 S. Mantere and M. Ketokivi, "Reasoning in Organization Science," *Academy of Management Review 38*(1) (2013): 70–89.

90 T. T. Baldwin, J. R. Pierce, R. C. Jones, and S. Farouk, "The Elusiveness of Applied Management Knowledge: A Critical Challenge for Management Education," *Academy of Management Learning & Education 10*(4) (2011): 583–605.

91 R. Grossman, E. Salas, D. Pavlas, and M. A. Rosen, "Using Instructional Features to Enhance Demonstration-Based Training in Management Education," *Academy of Management Learning & Education 12*(2) (2013): 219–243.

92 B. Benjamin and C. O'Reilly, "Becoming a Leader: Early Career Challenges Faced by MBA Graduates," *Academy of Management Learning & Education 10*(3) (2011): 452-472.

93 R. Klimoski and B. Amos, "Practicing Evidence-Based Education in Leadership Development," *Academy of Management Learning & Education 11*(4) (2012): 685–702.

94 J. K. Nelson, L. W. Poms, and P. P. Wolf, "Developing Efficacy Beliefs for Ethics and Diversity Management," *Academy of Management Learning & Education 11*(1) (2012): 49–68.

95 M. Sorcher and A. P. Goldstein, "A Behavior Modeling Approach in Training," *Personnel Administration 35*(1972): 35–41.

96 J. E. Vascellaro, "Top Stories of 2011: All Apple All the Time," *The Wall Street Journal* (December 29, 2011): B4.

97 "America's Most Admired Companies," *Fortune* (March 17, 2008): 116–133; J. Hempel and B. Kowitt, "Smartest People in Tech," *Fortune* (June 26, 2010): 82–83.

98 M. Helft, "Steve Jobs' Real Legacy: Apple Inc," *Fortune* (September 26, 2011): 59–65.

99 P. Burrows and J. Tyrangiel, "Unfortunately, That Day Has Come," *BusinessWeek* (August 29–September 4, 2011): 33.

100 R. Murphy, "The 2011 Businessperson of the Year," *Fortune* (December 12, 2011): 87–91.

101 A. Lashinsky, "How Tim Cook Is Changing Apple," *Fortune* (July 11, 2012): 111–118.

102 B. Stone, A. Satariano, and P. Burrows, "Out of the Shadow," *BusinessWeek* (October 8–14, 2012): 6–8.

103 J. Tyrangiel, "Tim Cook's Freshman Year," *BusinessWeek* (December 6, 2012): 62–76.

104 Staff, "The World's Most Admired Companies," *Fortune* (March 18, 2013): 137–139.

105 Staff, "Largest U.S. Corporations," *Fortune* (May 20, 2013): 1–20.

106 Staff, "Global 500 World's Largest Corporations," *Fortune* (July 22, 2013): 134.

107 P. Andruss, "Brankding's Big Guns," *Entrepreneur* (April 2012): 50–56.

108 J. Tyrangiel, "Tim Cook's Freshman Year," *BusinessWeek* (December 6, 2012): 62–76.

109 B. Stone, A. Satariano, and P. Burrows, "Out of the Shadow," *BusinessWeek* (October 8–14, 2012): 6–8.

110 A. Lashinsky, "Game Over?," *Fortune* (July 22, 2013): 64–68.

111 B. Stone, A. Satariano, and P. Burrows, "Out of the Shadow," *BusinessWeek* (October 8–14, 2012): 6–8.

112 J. Tyrangiel, "Tim Cook's Freshman Year," *BusinessWeek* (December 6, 2012): 62–76.

Leadership Traits and Ethics

Learning Outcomes

After studying this chapter, you should be able to:

1. Explain the universality of traits of effective leaders. p. 35

2. Describe the Big Five personality dimensions. p. 35

3. Discuss why the trait of dominance is so important for managers to have. p. 36

4. State how the Achievement Motivation Theory and the Leader Motive Profile are related and different. p. 41

5. Identify similarities and differences among Theory X and Theory Y, the Pygmalion effect, and self-concept. p. 46

6. Describe how attitudes are used to develop four leadership styles. p. 49

7. Compare the three levels of moral development. p. 52

8. Explain the stakeholder approach to ethics. p. 56

OPENING CASE Application

Ellen Kullman DuPont

DuPont was founded over 200 years ago and continues to be a world leader in market-driven innovation and science. Its innovation includes thousands of new products and patent applications every year, serving markets as diverse as agriculture, nutrition, electronics and communications, safety and protection, home and construction, transportation and apparel.[1] Look closely at the things around your home and workplace, and chances are you'll find dozens of items made with DuPont materials.

Ellen Kullman received a BS in mechanical engineering from Tufts University, and later a master's degree in management from Northwestern University, and she began her career at GE. She started at DuPont in 1988 as a marketing manager. Kullman climbed the corporate ladder to the top in 2009, becoming chair of the board and CEO of DuPont.[2] Under Kullman's leadership DuPont's strategy shifted from selling commodity units into high-margin areas and the stock has more than doubled during her tenure.

DuPont operates in more than 90 countries, with revenues in excess of $39.5 billion. DuPont is ranked #72 on the Fortune 500 company list and 1st in the chemicals ranking,[3] ranked #267 on the Global 500,[4] and ranked #41 on the *Fortune* World's Most Admired Companies.[5]

OPENING CASE QUESTIONS:

1. **What Big Five personality traits does Ellen Kullman possess?**

2. **Does Ellen Kullman have the personality profile of an effective leader?**

3. **How did "attitude" help improve the performance of DuPont?**

4. **How did Ellen Kullman's self-concept affect her leadership?**

5. **What role does ethics play at DuPont?**

Can you answer any of these questions? You'll find answers to these questions and learn more about DuPont and its leadership throughout the chapter.

To learn more about Ellen Kullman and DuPont, visit its Web site at **http://www.dupont.com**.

Ellen Kullman is an effective leader. The focus of this chapter is on leadership traits, which includes ethics. We begin by learning about personality traits of leaders and the personality profile of effective leaders. Next we learn how attitudes affect leadership. We end with a discussion of ethics in leadership.

Personality Traits and Leadership Trait Universality

Recall that trait theory of leadership was the foundation for the field of leadership studies. Some authors believe that the most important thing about a leader is traits, rather than skills.[6] In this section, we discuss traits and personality, personality profiles, and leadership trait universality. But before you learn about personality traits, complete Self-Assessment 2-1 to determine your personality profile. Throughout this chapter, you will gain a better understanding of personality traits, which help explain why people do the things they do (behavior).

SELF-ASSESSMENT 2-1   Big Five Personality Profile

There are no right or wrong answers, so be honest and you will really increase your self-awareness. We suggest doing this exercise in pencil or making a copy before you write on it. We will explain why later.

Using the scale below, rate each of the 25 statements according to how accurately it describes you. Place a number from 1 to 7 on the line before each statement.

(continued)

Like me	Some what like me	Not like me
7 6	5 4 3	2 1

_____ 1. I step forward and take charge in leaderless situations.

_____ 2. I am concerned about getting along well with others.

_____ 3. I have good self-control; I don't get emotional, angry, or yell.

_____ 4. I'm dependable; when I say I will do something, it's done well and on time.

_____ 5. I try to do things differently to improve my performance.

_____ 6. I don't give up very easily, and push myself to achieve my objectives.

_____ 7. I enjoy having lots of friends.

_____ 8. I think positively about the outcomes of situations and perform well under pressure.

_____ 9. I work hard to be successful.

_____ 10. I'm flexible and go with the flow when things change.

_____ 11. I am outgoing and willing to be assertive when in conflict.

_____ 12. I try to see things from other people's points of view.

_____ 13. I have confidence in my judgments, decision making, ideas, and capabilities.

_____ 14. I am loyal to my boss, coworkers, and the organizations.

_____ 15. I'm good at problem solving and making decisions.

_____ 16. I want to climb the corporate ladder to as high a level of management as I can.

_____ 17. I want other people to like me and to view me as very friendly.

_____ 18. I give people lots of praise and encouragement; I don't put people down and criticize.

_____ 19. I follow the policies and rules of an organization.

_____ 20. I volunteer to be the first to learn and do new tasks at work.

_____ 21. I try to influence other people to get my way.

_____ 22. I enjoy working with others more than working alone.

_____ 23. I am relaxed and secure, rather than nervous and insecure.

_____ 24. I am considered to be trustworthy because I do a good job and support others.

_____ 25. I believe that my successful performance depends on me, not others or good luck

Surgency		Agreeableness		Adjustment		Conscientiousness		Openness to Experience	
	35		35		35		35		35
	30		30		30		30		30
____ 1.	25	____ 2.	25	____ 3.	25	____ 4.	25	____ 5.	25
____ 6.	20	____ 7.	20	____ 8.	20	____ 9.	20	____ 10.	20
____ 11.	15	____ 12.	15	____ 13.	15	____ 14.	15	____ 15.	15
____ 16.	10	____ 17.	10	____ 18.	10	____ 19.	10	____ 20.	10
____ 21.	5	____ 22.	5	____ 23.	5	____ 24.	5	____ 25.	5
____ Total	Scale	____ Total	Scale	____ Total	Scale	____ Total	Scale	____ Total	Scale

To determine your Big Five personality profile: (1) In the blanks, place the numbers from 1 to 7 that represents your score for each statement. (2) Add up each column; your total should be a number from 5 to 35. (3) On the number scale, circle the number that is closest to your total score. Each column in the chart represents a specific personality dimension.

The higher the total number, the stronger is the personality dimension that describes your personality. What is your strongest dimension? Your weakest dimension? Continue reading the chapter for specifics about your personality in each of the five dimensions.

You may visit **http://ipip.ori.org** for a more detailed 50- or 100-item Big Five Personality Assessment.

Personality and Traits

Why are some people outgoing and others shy, loud and quiet, warm and cold, aggressive and passive? This list of behaviors is made up of individual traits.

Personality and Traits Are Different but Related

Traits *are distinguishing personal characteristics.* The image we project is based largely on our character traits.[7] **Personality** *is a combination of traits that classifies an individual's behavior.* Researchers study personal characteristics[8] and personality[9] to understand and explain why people behave the way they do.[10]

Personality is developed based on genetics and environmental factors. The genes you received before you were born influence your personality traits today. Your family, friends, school, and work also influence your personality. So our personality is partly innate, partly learned, and we can change, but it takes time and effort.[11]

Why Understanding Personality Is Important

Understanding people's personalities is important because personality affects behavior as well as perceptions and attitudes.[12] Understanding personalities helps us explain and predict others' behavior and job performance.[13] For a simple example, if you know Kate is very shy, you can better understand why she is quiet when meeting new people. You can also predict that Kate will be quiet when going places and meeting new people. You can also better understand why Kate would not seek a job as a salesperson, and if she did, you could predict that she might not be highly successful.

Personality Profiles

> **WORK**
> Application **2-1**
>
> Based on your personality profile, identify which dimensions are stronger, moderate, and weaker.

Personality profiles *identify individual stronger and weaker traits.* Completing Self-Assessment 2-1 gives us our personality profile. Student profiles tend to have a range of scores for the five dimensions. Review your personality profile. Do you have higher scores (stronger traits) on some dimensions and lower scores (weaker traits) on others? There are many personality tests, such as the Myers-Briggs Type Indicator and the Minnesota Multiphasic Personality Inventory.

When we take personality tests, our self-awareness goes up as we figure out our stronger and weaker traits. But we have to make a realistic assessment and acceptance of our strengths and weaknesses and work to improve our behavior. We realize that we are different from other people, and, as stated above, we can change our behavior to improve our relationships and develop leadership skills.[14]

Job Performance

Many organizations (including the National Football League) give personality tests to ensure a proper match between the worker and the job. Personality profiles are also used to categorize people as a means of predicting job success, and high conscientiousness is a good predictor of job performance, whereas people who are unstable tend to have poor job performance. People who are high in openness to experience tend to lead innovation to improve organizational performance.[15]

The Big Five Correlates with Leadership

Researchers conducted a major meta-analysis combining 73 prior studies to correlate the Big Five personality dimensions with leadership. The highest correlation with leadership was surgency (.31), followed by conscientiousness (.28) and openness to experience (24). Agreeableness was weakly correlated (.08), and adjustment was negatively correlated with leadership (–.24).[16] In other words, people high in surgency are perceived as leaderlike—they work hard, and they bring about change. They are not too concerned about being well liked and trying to please everyone, and they are stable or not overly emotional.

Derailed Leadership Traits

Let's identify traits that led to leadership failure. A study was conducted that compared 21 derailed executives with 20 executives who had successfully climbed the corporate ladder to the top. The derailed executives had prior success and were expected to go far, but they were passed over for promotion again, were fired, or were forced to retire early. See Exhibit 2.1 for a list of the six major reasons for derailment.[17] Overall, the problem of derailed managers is poor human relations skills.

Why Executives Are Derailed

EXHIBIT 2.1

WORK
Application **2-2**

Select a present or past manager, and state whether he or she has any of the six traits of derailment. Give specific examples of weaknesses.

- They used a bullying style viewed as intimidating, insensitive, and abrasive.
- They were viewed as being cold, aloof, and arrogant.
- They betrayed personal trust.
- They were self-centered and viewed as overly ambitious and thinking of the next job.
- They had specific performance problems with the business.
- They overmanaged and were unable to delegate or build a team.

© Cengage Learning®

We Can Improve

As stated, we can change our behavior to be more effective. The key to success is to assess our personality strengths and weaknesses and to plan how to change our behavior to improve our relationships and leadership skills. Once we determine the behavior we want to improve, it takes deliberate practice to succeed. You are given the opportunity to apply what you learn throughout this book in your personal and professional lives.

Learning outcome 1 *Explain the universality of traits of effective leaders.*

Leadership Trait Universality

In applying trait theory, we need to remember that there are traits that many successful leaders have,[18] and we will discuss them in the next major section with the Big Five, but there is no agreed-upon list of traits that leaders need to be successful. So you don't need to have all of them to be a successful leader.

There are always exceptions to all the traits. For example, in Fortune 500 companies, 30 percent of the CEOs are 6 feet 2 inches or taller, compared to only 4 percent of the general U.S. population. However, there are lots of CEOs who are less than 6 feet.[19] Successful leaders are commonly extroverts, but 40 percent of CEOs describe themselves as introverts, including Microsoft's Bill Gates and investors Warren Buffet and Charles Schwab.[20] Also, certain personality traits have been shown to be important in some team settings, but not in others.

Learning outcome 2 *Describe the Big Five personality dimensions.*

The Big Five Including Traits of Effective Leaders

There are many personality classification methods.[21] However, the Big Five Model of Personality traits is the most widely accepted way to classify personalities because of its strong research support and its reliability across age, sex, race, and language groups.[22]

The purpose of the Big Five is to reliably categorize, into one of five dimensions, most if not all of the traits you would use to describe someone. Thus, each dimension includes multiple traits. *The* **Big Five Model of Personality** *categorizes traits into the dimensions of surgency, agreeableness, adjustment, conscientiousness, and openness to experience.* The dimensions are listed in Exhibit 2.2 and described in this section.

Note that some researchers have slightly different names for the five dimensions, and not all will agree under which dimension each leadership trait should be classified; there is some overlap. We include traits of effective leaders under each dimension based on their strong research support, and our definitions of each of the Big Five include the effective leadership traits in that category. However, again we should realize that there is no one list of traits accepted by all researchers, and that not all effective leaders have all these traits and, like all of us, are higher and lower in some than others.

Surgency

The **surgency personality dimension** *includes dominance, extraversion, and high energy with determination.* Review Self-Assessment 2-1 statements 1, 6, 11, 16, and 21 for examples of surgency traits. Let's discuss the three important dimensions of surgency here.

> **Learning Outcome 3** *Discuss why the trait of dominance is so important for managers to have.*

Dominance

Successful leaders assert themselves and want to be managers and to take charge.[23] If you do not want to be a leader, chances are you will not be an effective manager. Thus, the dominance trait affects all the other traits related to effective leaders. Do you want to be a leader?

EXHIBIT 2.2

The Big Five Including Traits of Effective Leaders

The Big Five Model of Personality	Leadership Traits within the Big Five
Surgency	a. Dominance
	b. Extroversion
	c. Energy/Determination
Agreeableness	d. Sociability/Sensitivity
	e. Emotional intelligence
Adjustment	f. Emotional Stability and Narcissism
	g. Self-confidence
Conscientiousness	h. Dependability
	i. Integrity
Openness	j. Flexibility
	k. Intelligence
	l. Locus of control

© Cengage Learning®

Extraversion

It is on a continuum between extravert and introvert. Extraverts are outgoing, like to meet new people, and are assertive and willing to confront others, whereas introverts are shy. Extraverts are frequently selected for leadership positions.[24] How outgoing are you?

High energy with determination

Leaders tend to have high energy with a positive drive to work hard to achieve goals, and they create energy in others.[25] Their positive attitude and optimism influence their high tolerance for frustration as they strive to overcome obstacles through being persistent; they don't give up easily. Do you have a high energy level with determination?

Agreeableness

The **agreeableness personality dimension** *includes traits of sociability and emotional intelligence.* Review Self-Assessment 2-1 statements 2, 7, 12, 17, and 22 for examples of agreeableness traits. Let's discuss the two important dimensions of agreeableness next.

Sociability/Sensitivity

Sociable people have an inclination to seek out enjoyable social relationships. Strong sociability personality types are friendly, courteous, easy to get along with, and diplomatic. How important is having good social relationships to you?

Sensitivity is part of being sociable. It refers to understanding group members as individuals. Recall that being insensitive is one of the reasons why executives are derailed. If you are concerned only about yourself and don't understand others, you probably will not be very successful. Are you sensitive to others?

Emotional Intelligence

An offshoot of IQ is EQ (emotional quotient—EQ or emotional intelligence—EI). EI is the ability to work well with people.[26] EQ is being used to identify future leaders.[27] There are four components of EQ:[28]

- *Self-awareness* relates to being conscious of your emotions and how they affect your personal and professional life. Self-awareness is the cornerstone of all insight. Use your self-awareness (the exercises in this book help) to accurately assess your strengths and limitations; this leads to higher self-confidence.
- *Social awareness* relates to the ability to understand others. Empathy is an ability to put yourself in other people's situations, sense their emotions, and understand things from their perspective.
- *Self-management* relates to the ability to control disruptive emotions, ours and others. Successful leaders are self-motivated and don't let negative emotions (worry, anxiety, fear, anger) interfere with getting things done.
- *Relationship management* relates to the ability to work well with others, which is dependent on the other three EI components. Most of this book focuses on developing relationship management skills. Do you have high EI skills in all four areas?

Adjustment

The **adjustment personality dimension** *includes traits of emotional stability and self-confidence.* Review Self-Assessment 2-1 statements 3, 8, 13, 18, and 23 for examples of adjustment traits. Let's discuss the two important dimensions of adjustment here.

WORK Application **2-3**

Select a present or past manager and assess his or her surgency traits of effective leaders. Give an example of the manager's strong or weak dominance, extroversion, and energy/determination in a typical specific situation.

WORK Application **2-4**

Using the same manager from Work Application 3, assess his or her agreeableness traits of effective leaders. Give an example of the manager's strong or weak sociability/sensitivity and emotional intelligence in a typical specific situation.

Emotional stability/self-control and narcissism

We all have emotions in leader–follower interactions. The question is how do we handle them? [29] Adjustment is on a continuum between being emotionally stable and unstable. *Stable* refers to self-control, being calm—good under pressure, relaxed, secure, and positive—praising others. *Unstable* is out of control—poor under pressure, nervous, insecure, negative, and hostile— criticizing others without helping them improve. How emotionally stable are you?

Narcissism is related to being unstable, and it is on the increase.[30] Narcissists are preoccupied with themselves, ignoring the needs of others, have an exaggerated sense of their own self-importance, and tend to make bad decisions.[31] Are you just looking out for yourself as #1 as a narcissist?

Self-confidence

It is on a continuum from strong to weak, indicating whether we are self-assured in our judgments, decision making, ideas, and capabilities. How can we succeed at anything if we don't believe we can? Our self-confidence builds with our success at setting and achieving our goals. Effective self-confidence is based on an accurate awareness of our strengths and weaknesses, with an orientation to self-improvement. Do you have effective self-confidence?

Conscientiousness

*The **conscientiousness personality dimension** includes traits of dependability and integrity.* Review Self-Assessment 2-1 statements 4, 9, 14, 19, and 24 for examples of conscientiousness. How strong is your desire to be successful?

Dependability

It is on a continuum between responsible/dependable to irresponsible/undependable. Highly dependable people get the job done and are characterized as loyal, committed to their coworkers and the organization. Are you dependable?

Integrity

It is on a continuum between being honest and ethical or not. Integrity is the foundation for trustworthiness.[32] We focus on honesty here and will discuss ethics in more detail in the last section of this chapter. Integrity is about being honest—no lying, cheating (manipulating), or stealing.[33] Clearly, to be effective, leaders need integrity.[34] Do you have integrity?

Openness

*The **openness-to-experience personality dimension** includes traits of flexibility, intelligence, and internal locus of control.* Review Self-Assessment 2-1 statements 5, 10, 15, 20, and 25 for examples of openness-to-experience traits.

Flexibility

It refers to the ability to adjust to different situations and change.[35] Without flexibility, you will not be successful. Flexible people are generally more creative and innovative—willing to try new things and change. How willing are you to change and try new things? Are you flexible?

Intelligence

It refers to cognitive ability to think critically, to solve problems, and to make decisions. It is also referred to as general mental ability intelligence quotient (IQ). Intelligence is the

WORK Application **2-5**

Using the same manager from Work Application 3, assess his or her emotional adjustment traits of effective leaders. Give an example of the manager's strong or weak emotional stability and narcissism and self-confidence in a typical specific situation.

WORK Application **2-6**

Using the same manager from Work Application 3, assess his or her conscientiousness traits of effective leaders. Give an example of the manager's strong or weak dependability and integrity in a typical specific situation.

YOU Make the ETHICAL Call

2.1 Downsizing and Part-Time Workers

As firms struggle to compete in the global economy, many have downsized. *Downsizing* is the process of cutting resources to increase productivity. The primary area of cutting is human resources, which has led to layoffs. Another method of keeping costs down is using part-time employees who do not receive benefits (e.g., health care) rather than full-time employees who receive benefits.

Walmart is known for having a heavy ratio of part- to full-time employees to keep costs down. Walmart is expanding its sales of grocery items, competing directly with supermarket chains. One of the reasons Walmart has lower prices is because it uses mostly part-time workers at or close to minimum wage and without benefits. Most supermarket chain employees are unionized and get higher wages and more benefits, and they want better pay and benefits. But supermarket chains state that they can't afford to pay more; they must compete with Walmart.

1. Do you view Walmart as a company with integrity?
2. Is downsizing ethical and socially responsible?
3. Is using part-time, rather than full-time, employees ethical and socially responsible?

WORK Application **2-7**

Using the same manager from Work Application 3, assess his or her openness to experience traits of effective leaders. Give an example of the manager's strong or weak flexibility, intelligence, and locus of control in a typical specific situation.

---

best predictor of job performance but not the only one as conscientiousness is also important. The founders of Microsoft (Bill Gates), Google (Sergey Brin and Larry Page), and Facebook (Mark Zuckerberg) all have 150+ IQs and math SAT skills at the 800 level, and they tend to have a bias for IQ when hiring.[36]

IQ, EQ, and I got a clue. It has been said that to be successful a high IQ is important[37] but not enough. We also need strong interpersonal skills, or a high EQ (leading). Plus, we have to have a clue of what we are trying to accomplish (objectives) and how we will get the job done (planning, organizing, and controlling). Can you think of any people who are intelligent but lack people skills or don't seem to have a clue about what to do or how to get things done?

Locus of control

It is on a continuum between external and internal belief in control over one's destiny/performance. *Externalizers* believe that they have no control over their fate and that their behavior has little to do with their performance. *Internalizers* believe that they control their fate and that their behavior directly affects their performance. Effective internalizer leaders take responsibility for who they are, for their behavior and performance, and for the performance of their organizational unit. Are you more of an internalizer or an externalizer?

OPENING CASE Application

1. What Big Five and leadership personality traits does Ellen Kullman possess?

To a large extent, Ellen Kullman is a successful leader because of her strong personality in the Big Five.

She has a strong need for *surgency* that helped her climb the corporate ladder at DuPont, which is dominated by men. It took energy and determination to become the first woman CEO of DuPont. She is ranked #3 on the Fortune 50 Most Powerful Women list.[38]

Kullman has *agreeableness*. She gets along well with people having strong interpersonal skills with El. Kullman relies more on her personal relationships than her power as CEO to get the job done. She is also sociable and sensitive to others.

She is *conscientious* at getting the job done. Being very dependable by achieving great success was a cornerstone of her climbing the corporate ladder at DuPont. Plus she is viewed has having a high level of integrity.

Kullman is well *adjusted*. Competing in a company and industry dominated by men, she has self-control and self-confidence. She is calm, good under pressure, relaxed, secure, and positive. She praises the accomplishments of her employees at all levels.

She is *open* to new experience because of her innovating and bringing to market new products at a faster clip. Kullman is highly intelligent, has an internal locus of control as she takes charge to bring changes, and is flexible.

CONCEPT APPLICATION 2-1

Big Five Personality Dimensions

Identify each of these seven traits/behaviors by its personality dimension. Write the appropriate letter in the blank before each item.

a. surgency   d. conscientiousness
b. agreeableness   e. openness to experience
c. affiliation

_____ 1. A leader is saying a warm, friendly hello to followers as they arrive at the meeting.

_____ 2. A leader is brainstorming ideas with followers on new products.

_____ 3. A follower is yelling about a problem, a leader calmly explains how to solve it.

_____ 4. A leader is not very talkative when meeting some unexpected customers.

_____ 5. A leader is letting a follower do the job his or her own way to avoid a conflict.

_____ 6. A leader is giving detailed instructions to a follower to do the job.

_____ 7. A purchasing agent submitted the monthly report on time as usual.

CONCEPT APPLICATION 2-2

Personality Traits of Effective Leaders

Identify each of the following eight behaviors by its trait. The leader may be behaving effectively, or the behavior may be the opposite of the effective trait behavior. Refer to Exhibit 2.2 and use the "leadership traits within the Big Five." Write the appropriate letter a–l in the blank before each item.

_____ 8. A leader telling his boss that he is right on schedule to finish the job, planning to catch up before the boss finds out.

_____ 9. A leader assigned a task to one follower, giving very specific instructions, and another task telling that follower to complete the task any way they want to.

_____ 10. A leader is fixing a broken machine.

_____ 11. A leader is acting very nervous while giving the follower a new task.

_____ 12. A leader tells a follower that he can have lunch at noon. But 15 minutes later, the leader tells the follower to have lunch at 1:00.

_____ 13. A leader listens to the follower complain and then paraphrases the complaint back to the follower.

_____ 14. A leader in situation 10 above is/has been working to fix the machine for three hours now.

_____ 15. A leader is giving excuses as to why performance is low and that nothing can be done to improve.

The Personality Profile of Effective Leaders

Effective leaders have a common personality profile. David McClelland's trait theories of Achievement Motivation Theory and Leader Motive Profile Theory have strong research support and a great deal of relevance to the practice of leadership. Achievement Motivation Theory identifies three major traits, which McClelland calls *needs*. Leader Motive Profile Theory identifies the personality profile of effective leaders.[39] You will learn about both of these theories in this section.

Learning Outcome 4	State how the Achievement Motivation Theory and the Leader Motive Profile are related and different

Achievement Motivation Theory

WORK Application **2-8**

How can you improve your leadership skills by understanding your manager's (and other people's) personality profile?

Achievement Motivation Theory *attempts to explain and predict behavior and performance based on a person's need for achievement, power, and affiliation.* Through an unconscious process, our behavior is motivated by our desire to satisfy our needs. McClelland stated that needs are based on personality and are developed as we interact with the environment. All people possess these three needs but to varying degrees.

The Need for Achievement (n Ach)

The *need for achievement* is the concern for excellence in accomplishments through individual efforts. High n Ach is categorized as the Big Five dimension of *conscientiousness* with dependability, but the person is not necessarily being high in integrity. People with high n Ach tend to be characterized as wanting to take personal responsibility for solving problems. They are goal oriented and set moderate, realistic, and attainable goals. They seek challenge, excellence, and individuality; take calculated, moderate risk; desire concrete feedback on their performance; and work hard. McClelland's research showed that only about 10 percent of the U.S. population has a very "strong" dominant need for achievement. There is evidence of a correlation between high achievement need and high performance in the general population.

The Need for Power (n Pow)

The *need for power* is the concern for influencing others and seeking positions of authority. High n Pow is categorized as the Big Five dimension of *surgency*. People with a high need for power tend to be characterized as wanting to control the situation, wanting influence or control over others, enjoying competition in which they can win (they don't like to lose), being willing to confront others, and seeking positions of authority and status. They tend to be ambitious and have a lower need for affiliation and agreeableness. They are attuned to power and politics as essential for successful leadership, and they tend to seek management positions.

WORK Application **2-9**

Explain how your need for achievement, power, and/or affiliation has affected your behavior and performance, or that of someone you work with or have worked with. Give an example of the behavior and performance, and list your predicted motive need.

The Need for Affiliation (n Aff)

The *need for affiliation* is the concern for developing, maintaining, and restoring close personal relationships. High n Aff is categorized as the Big Five dimension of *agreeableness*. People with strong n Aff have the trait of sociability/sensitivity and often high EI. People with high n Aff tend to be characterized as seeking close relationships with others, wanting to be liked by others, enjoying lots of social activities, and seeking to belong; so they join groups and organizations. People with high n Aff are more concerned about what others think of them than about getting their own way (influencing others). N Aff is negatively related to leadership. Those with a high n Aff tend to have a low n Pow; they tend to avoid management because they like to be one of the group rather than its leader.

CONCEPT APPLICATION 2-3

Achievement Motivation Theory

Identify each of the five behaviors below by its need, writing the appropriate letter in the blank before each item. The person may be behaving based on a strong need, or the behavior may be the opposite, indicating a weak need. Also state how the behavior meets the need and predict the performance.

a. achievement   b. power   c. affiliation

_____ 16. A person is refusing to be the chairman of the committee.

_____ 17. A person is going to talk to a coworker to resolve a conflict they have.

_____ 18. The other coworker above will not be the first one to make a move to resolve the conflict; but when the other party comes to him, he will be receptive.

_____ 19. A finance major has offered to calculate the financial analysis for the group's simulation game and to make the presentation to the class.

_____ 20. A management major is studying hard for many hours to maintain his A average.

Your Motive Profile

Note that McClelland does not have a classification for the *adjustment* and *openness-to-experience* Big Five personality dimensions; they are not needs. A person can have a high or low need for achievement, power, and affiliation and be either well adjusted or not, and either open or closed to new experiences. So these two dimensions of personality are ignored in determining the Achievement Motivation Theory personality profile. Complete Self-Assessment 2 to determine your motive profile now.

SELF-ASSESSMENT 2-2   Motive Profile

Return to Self-Assessment 2-1 on page 32 and place the scores from your Big Five personality profile in the following blanks, next to their corresponding needs. On the number scale, circle your total score for each need.

Need for Achievement (conscientiousness)	**Need for Power** (surgency)	**Need for Affiliation** (agreeableness)
35	35	35
30	30	30
25	25	25
20	20	20
15	15	15
10	10	10
5	5	5
Total Score _____	Total Score_____	Total Score_____

There is no right or wrong score for this profile. To interpret your score, check to see if there is much difference between the three need scores. If all three are about the same, one need is not stronger than the others are. If scores vary, one need is higher than the others and is called the stronger or dominant need, and the lower score is the weaker need. You can also have other combinations, such as two stronger and one weaker, or vice versa. Do you have stronger and weaker needs?

Knowing a motive profile is useful, because it can explain and predict behavior and performance. Read on to determine if you have the motive profile of an effective leader.

Leader Motive Profile Theory

Leader Motive Profile Theory *attempts to explain and predict leadership success based on a person's need for achievement, power, and affiliation.* McClelland found that effective leaders consistently have the same motive profile and that Leader Motive Profile has been found to be a reliable predictor of leader effectiveness.[40] Let's first define the profile of effective leaders and then discuss why it results in success. *The* **Leader Motive Profile (LMP)** *includes a high need for power, which is socialized, that is greater than the need for affiliation and with a moderate need for achievement.* The achievement score is usually somewhere between the power and affiliation score, and the reason is described below.

Power

Power is essential to leaders because it is a means of influencing followers. Without power, there is no leadership. To be successful, leaders need to want to be in charge and enjoy dominance in the leadership role,[41] with high energy and determination to succeed. We will need power to influence our followers, peers, and higher-level managers. We will discuss how to gain power and be successful in organizational politics in Chapter 5.

Socialized Power

McClelland further identified power as neither good nor bad. It can be used for personal gain at the expense of others (personalized power), or it can be used to help oneself and others (socialized power).[42] Social power is discussed again later, with ethics. Effective leaders use socialized power, which includes the traits of sensitivity to others and stability with good EI relationships,[43] and is the Big Five *adjustment* dimension. Thus, a person with a low need for affiliation can have a high sensitivity to others. McClelland's research supports the reasons for executive derailment, because these negative traits are personalized power. Socialized power is not included in the motive profile, so complete Self-Assessment 3 to determine your motive profile with socialized power.

Achievement

To be effective, leaders generally need to have a moderate need for achievement. They have high energy, self-confidence, and openness-to-experience traits, and they are dependable—*conscientious* (Big Five dimension). The reason for a moderate, rather than a high, need for achievement, which would include a lower need for power, is the danger of personalized power. People with a high need for achievement tend to seek individual achievement, and when they are not interested in being a leader, there is the chance for personalized power and derailment.

Affiliation

Effective leaders have a lower need for affiliation than power, so that relationships don't get in the way of influencing followers. If the achievement score is lower than that for affiliation, the probability of the following problems occurring may be increased. Leaders with high n Aff tend to have a lower need for power and are thus reluctant to play the bad-guy role, such as disciplining and influencing followers to do things they would rather not do—like change. However, recall that effective leaders do have concern for followers—socialized power.

WORK
Application **2-10**

Make an intelligent guess about your present or past manager's motive profile. Is it an LMP? Explain.

Motive Profile with Socialized Power

Return to Self-Assessment 2-1 on page 32 and place the scores from Self-Assessment 2 (your motive profile) in the following blanks. On the number scale, circle your total score.

Need for Achievement (conscientiousness)	**Need for Power** (surgency)	**Socialized Power** (adjustment)	**Need for Affiliation** (agreeableness)
35	35	35	35
30	30	30	30
25	25	25	25
20	20	20	20
15	15	15	15
10	10	10	10
5	5	5	5
Total Score _____	Total Score _____	Total Score _____	Total Score _____

Again, there is no right or wrong score. The adjustment score will give you an idea if your power is more social or personal. Also realize that the questions in Self-Assessment 2-1 (3, 8, 13, 18, and 23) are not totally focused on social power. Thus, if you believe you have higher sensitivity to others, your score on McClelland's LMP socialized power could be higher.

The Leader Motive Profile is included in the definition of leadership. Our definition of leadership includes the five key elements of leadership (see Exhibit 1.1 on page 5) in the LMP. Our definition of leadership includes *influencing* and *leaders–followers* (power) and getting along with *people* (social power with EI). It also includes *organizational objectives* (which achievers set and accomplish well) and *change* (which achievers are open to).

OPENING CASE Application

2. Does Ellen Kullman have the personality profile of an effective leader?

Ellen Kullman has an LMP. Her need for power is illustrated through climbing the corporate ladder in a male-dominated industry and company. She has a socialized need for power since she relies more on relationships than simply her power as CEO, and she uses participative management and does allow others to make decisions in local issues. Kullman has a need for achievement that leads to continued success. She also has a lower need for affiliation as she sets objectives and standards for improving performance and uses her power when needed.

Do you have an LMP? Complete Self-Assessment 4 now to find out.

Leadership Interest

Select the option that best describes your interest in leadership now.

_____ 1. I am, or want to become, a manager and leader.

_____ 2. I am, or want to become, a leader without being a manager.

_____ 3. I am not interested in being a leader; I want to be a follower.

If you want to be a leader, recall that research has shown that you can develop your leadership skills.

If you selected option 1, do you have an LMP? If you answered yes, it does not guarantee that you will climb the corporate ladder. However, having an LMP does increase your chances, because it is a predictor of leadership success. On the other hand, an LMP is not enough; you need leadership skills to be successful. If your Self-Assessment 3 score doesn't indicate that you have an LMP, go back to Self-Assessment 2-1 on page 33 and review questions 1, 6, 11, 16, and 21. Did you score them accurately? The most important question is 16. If you believe you have an LMP, be aware that your profile could be different using McClelland's LMP questionnaire. Also recall that not all successful leaders have an LMP; you can still be successful. Developing your leadership skills, through effort, will increase your chances of leadership success.

If you selected option 2, don't be concerned about your LMP. Focus on developing your leadership skills. However, your personality profile can help you better understand your strengths and weaknesses to identify areas to improve upon. This also holds true for people who selected option 1.

If you selected option 3, that's fine. Most people in the general population probably would select this option. Many professionals who have great jobs and incomes are followers, and they have no interest in becoming managers. However, recall that research has shown that leaders and followers need the same skills, that organizations are looking for employees with leadership skills, and that organizations conduct skills training with employees at all levels. To increase your chances of having a successful and satisfying career, you may want to develop your leadership skills. You may someday change your mind about becoming a leader and manager.

Your need for power and LMP can change over time, along with your interest in leadership and management and your skill level, regardless of which option you selected.

EXHIBIT 2.3

Combing the Big Five with Traits and Needs

The Big Five Model of Personality	Leadership Traits within the Big Five	Achievement Motivation Theory and Leader Motive Profile (LMP)
Surgency	a. Dominance b. Extroversion c. Energy/Determination	Need for power
Agreeableness	d. Sociability/Sensitivity e. Emotional intelligence	Need for affiliation
Adjustment	f. Emotional Stability and Narcissism g. Self-confidence	Socialized power (LMP)
Conscientiousness	h. Dependability i. Integrity	Need for achievement
Openness	j. Flexibility k. Intelligence l. Locus of control	No separate need; it is included in the other needs

© Cengage Learning®

Before we go on to discuss leadership attitudes, let's review what we've covered so far in Exhibit 2.3 by putting together the Big Five Model of Personality, the nine traits of effective leaders, and Achievement Motivation Theory and LMP.

Leadership Attitudes

Attitudes *are positive or negative feelings about people, things, and issues.* We all have favorable or positive attitudes, and unfavorable or negative attitudes about life, work, school, leadership, and everything else.[44] J.W. Marriott, Jr., president of Marriott Corporation, stated that the company's success depends more upon employee attitudes than any other single factor. Legendary football coach Lou Holtz says that attitude is the most important thing in this world and that we each choose the attitude we have. So, being a positive or negative person is your choice. Successful leaders have positive, optimistic attitudes. Do you?

In this section, we discuss the important question, "how does leadership affect the behavior of followers?"[45] We start with how attitudes relate to Theory X and Theory Y, and how the Pygmalion effect influences followers' behavior and performance. Then we discuss self-concept and how it affects the leader's behavior and performance. Lastly, we consider how the leader's attitudes about followers, and about his or her self-concept, affect the leadership style of the leader.

Learning Outcome **5**   *Identify similarities and differences among Theory X and Theory Y, the Pygmalion effect, and self-concept.*

Theory X and Theory Y

Today, **Theory X and Theory Y** *attempt to explain and predict leadership behavior and performance based on the leader's attitude about followers.* Before you read about Theory X and Y, complete Self-Assessment 2-5.

SELF-ASSESSMENT 2-5   Theory X and Theory Y Attitudes

For each pair of statements distribute 5 points, based on how characteristic each statement is of your belief system. The combined score for each pair of the ten statements must equal 5.

Here are the scoring distributions for each pair of statements:

0–5 or 5–0	I believe one statement and not the other.
1–4 or 4–1	I believe one statement much more than the other.
2–3 or 3–2	I believe both statements, although one more than the other.

---

1. _____ People enjoy working.
   _____ People do not like to work.
2. _____ Employees don't have to be closely supervised to do their job well.
   _____ Employees will not do a good job unless you closely supervise them.
3. _____ If the manager is not around, the employees will work just as hard.
   _____ If the manager is not around, the employees will take it easier than they will when being watched.
4. _____ Employees will do a task well for you if you ask them to.
   _____ If you want something done right, you need to do it yourself.
5. _____ Interesting, challenging work is the best motivator of employee.
   _____ Money is the best motivator of employees.

6. _____ Employees want to be involved in making decisions.
   _____ Employees want the managers to make the decisions.
7. _____ Employees will do their best work if you allow them to do the job their own way.
   _____ Employees will do their best work if they are taught how to do it the one best way.
8. _____ Managers should share the management responsibilities with group members.
   _____ Managers should perform the management functions for the group.
9. _____ Managers should let employees have full access to information that is not confidential.
   _____ Managers should give employees only the information they need to know to do their job.

(continued)

10. _____ The participative management style is the best leadership style.

_____ The autocratic management style is the best leadership style.

To determine your attitude about people at work, add up the numbers (0–5) for the first statement in each pair; don't bother adding the numbers for the second statements. The total should be between 0 and 50. Place your score on the continuum below.

0 — 5 — 10 — 15 — 20 — 25 — 30 — 35 — 40 — 45 — 50
Theory X   *Theory Y*

Generally, the higher your score, the greater are your Theory Y beliefs, and the lower the score, the greater your Theory X attitudes.

Douglas McGregor classified attitudes or belief systems, which he called *assumptions*, as *Theory X* and *Theory Y*.[46] People with Theory X attitudes hold that employees dislike work and must be closely supervised in order to do their work. Theory Y attitudes hold that employees like to work and do not need to be closely supervised in order to do their work. In each of the ten pairs of statements in Self-Assessment 2-5, the first lines are Theory Y attitudes and the second lines are Theory X attitudes.

Managers with Theory X attitudes tend to have a negative, pessimistic view of employees and display more coercive, autocratic leadership styles using external means of controls, such as threats and punishment. Managers with Theory Y attitudes tend to have a positive, optimistic view of employees and display more participative leadership styles using internal motivation and rewards.

It is widely accepted that managers with Theory Y attitudes are generally more productive than Theory X attitudes.[47] The six derailed executive traits reflect Theory X behaviors. If you scored higher in Theory X for Self-Assessment 2-5, it does not mean that you cannot be an effective leader. There are some situations, such as large-scale production and unskilled workers where a more autocratic style works well. As with personality traits, we can change our attitudes, with effort. We don't have to be autocratic leaders.

The Pygmalion Effect

The **Pygmalion effect** *proposes that leaders' attitudes toward and expectations of followers, and their treatment of them, explain and predict followers' behavior and performance.* We have already talked about attitudes, so let's add expectations and treatment. In business, expectations are stated as objectives and standards. Lou Holtz advises setting a higher standard; the worst disservice you can do as a coach, teacher, parent, or leader is to expect little and lower standards. Just treating employees well and getting them in a good mood as they start their day can have a huge impact on performance.[48]

WORK Application **2-11**

Give an example of when a person (parent, friend, teacher, coach, manager) really expected you either to perform well or to fail, and treated you like you would, which resulted in your success or failure

----

OPENING CASE Application

3. How did "attitude" help improve the performance of DuPont?

A major factor in Ellen Kullman's improving the performance of DuPont is in her positive attitude with a Theory Y attitude toward her employees. She has a positive optimistic view of employees and uses a participative leadership style. Kullman has faith in her employees and expects them to succeed, and they do.

Self-Concept

So far, we have discussed the leaders' attitudes about followers. Now we will examine leaders' attitudes about themselves. **Self-concept** *refers to the positive or negative attitudes people have about themselves.* If you have a positive view of yourself as being a capable person, you will tend to have the positive self-confidence trait. *Self-efficacy* is the belief in your own capability to perform in a specific situation, which is based on your self-concept and self-confidence.

What we think determines what happens to us. As Henry Ford put it, "If you think you can, you can; if you think you can't, you can't." Recall times when you had positive self-efficacy and were successful, or negative self-efficacy and failed. If you don't believe you can be a successful leader, you probably won't be.

OPENING CASE Application

4. How did Ellen Kullman's self-concept affect her leadership?

Ellen Kullman rarely doubted that she could do whatever she applied herself to accomplish. Back when she went to Tufts to major in engineering, there were not many women entering the male-dominated field, but she knew she would graduate and go on to a successful career. Without a positive self-attitude, she would not have had the confidence, especially being in a male-dominated company, that she could climb the corporate ladder at DuPont all the way to the top. Kullman has self-efficacy as CEO, as she knew she could improve the performance at DuPont, and she is doing that.

Developing a More Positive Attitude and Self-Concept

Our behavior and performance will be consistent with the way we see ourselves. Think and act like a winner, and you may become one. Self-awareness and self-development help.[49] Following are some ideas to help you change your attitudes and develop a more positive self-concept:

1. *Realize that there are few, if any, benefits to negative, pessimistic attitudes about others and yourself.* Do holding a grudge, worrying, and being afraid of failure help you to succeed?
2. *Consciously try to have and maintain a positive, optimistic attitude.* If you don't have a positive attitude, it may be caused by your unconscious thoughts and behavior. Only with conscious effort can you improve your self-concept.
3. *Cultivate optimistic thoughts.* Scientific evidence suggests that your thoughts affect every cell in your body. Every time you think positive thoughts, your body, mind, and spirit respond. Use positive self-talk—I will do a good job; it will be done on time; and so on. Also use mental imagery—picture yourself achieving your goal.
4. *If you catch yourself complaining or being negative in any way, stop and change to a positive attitude.* With time, you will catch yourself less often as you become more positive about yourself.
5. *Avoid negative people, especially those who make you feel negative about yourself.* Associate with people who have a positive self-concept, and use their positive behavior.
6. *Set and achieve goals.* Set short-term goals (daily, weekly, monthly) that you can achieve. Achieving specific goals will improve your self-concept.
7. *Focus on your success; don't dwell on failure.* We are all going to make mistakes and experience failure, but we need to bounce back. If you achieve five of six goals, dwell on the five and forget the one you missed. Lou Holtz says happiness is nothing more than a poor memory for the bad things that happen to you.

WORK
Application **2-12**

Recall a present or past manager. Using Exhibit 2.4, which combinations of attitudes best describe your manager's leadership style? Give examples of the manager's behavior that illustrate his or her attitudes.

8. *Don't belittle accomplishments or compare yourself to others.* If you meet a goal and say it was easy anyway, you are being negative. If you compare yourself to someone else and say they are better, you are being negative. No matter how good you are, there is almost always someone better. So focus on being the best that you can be, rather than putting yourself down for not being the best.

9. *Accept compliments.* When someone compliments you, say thank you; it builds self-concept. Don't say things like it was nothing, or anyone could have done it, because you lose the opportunity for a buildup.

10. *Be a positive role model.* If the leader has a positive attitude, the followers usually do too. We can choose to be optimistic or pessimistic—and we usually find what we are looking for. If you look for the positive, you are likely to be happier and get more out of life; why look for the negative and be unhappy?

11. *When things go wrong and you're feeling down, do something to help someone who is worse off than you.* You will realize that you don't have it so bad, and you will realize that the more you give, the more you get. Volunteering at a hospital, soup kitchen, or becoming a Big Brother or Sister can help change your attitude. This is also a great cure for loneliness.

Learning Outcome **6** *Describe how attitudes are used to develop four leadership styles.*

How Attitudes Develop Leadership Styles

We now put together the leader's attitudes toward others, using Theory X and Theory Y, and the leader's attitude toward self, using self-concept, to illustrate how these two sets of attitudes develop into four leadership styles. Combining attitudes with the Leader Motive Profile (LMP), an effective leader tends to have Theory Y attitudes with a positive self-concept. See Exhibit 2.4 to understand how attitudes toward self and others affect leadership styles.

EXHIBIT 2.4

Leadership Styles Based on Attitudes

	Theory Y Attitudes	Theory X Attitudes
Positive self-concept	The leader typically gives and accepts positive feedback, expects others to succeed, and uses a participative leadership style.	The leader typically is bossy, pushy, and impatient; does much criticizing with little praising; and uses an autocratic leadership style.
Negative self-concept	The leader typically is afraid to make decisions, is unassertive, and is self-blaming when things go wrong.	The leader typically blames others when things go wrong, is pessimistic about resolving personal or organizational problems, and promotes feeling of hopelessness among followers.

© Cengage Learning®

Ethical Leadership

Before we discuss ethical behavior, complete Self-Assessment 2-6 to find out how ethical your behavior is.

SELF-ASSESSMENT 2-6 **How Ethical Is Your Behavior?**

For this exercise, you will be using the same set of statements twice. The first time you answer them, focus on your own behavior and the frequency with which you use it for each question. On the line before the question number, place the numbers 1–4 that represent how often you "did do" the behavior in the past, if you "do the behavior now," or if you "would do" the behavior if you had the chance.

These numbers will allow you to determine your level of ethics. You can be honest without fear of having to tell others your score in class. Sharing ethics scores is not part of the exercise.

Frequently			Never
1	2	3	4

The second time you use the same statements, focus on other people in an organization that you work/worked for. Place an "O" on the line after the number if you observed someone doing this behavior. Also place an "R" on the line if you reported (whistle-blowing) this behavior within the organization or externally.

O—observed   R—reported
1–4   **O–R**

College

_____ 1. _____ Cheating on homework assignments.

_____ 2. _____ Cheating on exams.

_____ 3. _____ Passing in papers that were completed by someone else, as your own work.

Workplace

_____ 4. _____ Lying to others to get what you want or stay out of trouble.

_____ 5. _____ Coming to work late, leaving work early, taking long breaks/lunches and getting paid for it.

_____ 6. _____ Socializing, goofing off, or doing personal work rather than doing the work that should be done and getting paid for it.

_____ 7. _____ Calling in sick to get a day off, when not sick.

_____ 8. _____ Using the organization's phone, computer, Internet, copier, mail, car, and so on for personal use.

_____ 9. _____ Taking home company tools/equipment for personal use without permission and then returning them/it.

_____ 10. _____ Taking home organizational supplies or merchandise and keeping it.

_____ 11. _____ Giving company supplies or merchandise to friends or allowing them to take them without saying anything.

_____ 12. _____ Putting in for reimbursement for meals and travel or other expenses that weren't actually eaten or taken.

_____ 13. _____ Taking spouse/friends out to eat or on business trips and charging it to the organizational expense account.

_____ 14. _____ Accepting gifts from customers/suppliers in exchange for giving them business.

_____ 15. _____ Cheating on your taxes.

_____ 16. _____ Misleading customers to make a sale, such as short delivery dates.

_____ 17. _____ Misleading competitors to get information to use to compete against them, such as saying/pretending to be a customer/supplier.

_____ 18. _____ Manipulating data to make you look good, or others bad.

_____ 19. _____ Selling more of the product than the customer needs, to get the commission.

_____ 20. _____ Spreading false rumors about coworkers or competitors to make yourself look better for advancement or to make more sales.

_____ 21. _____ Lying for your boss when asked/told to do so.

_____22. _____ Deleting information that makes you look bad or changing information to look better than actual results—false information.

_____23. _____ Being pressured, or pressuring others, to sign off on documents with false information.

_____24. _____ Being pressured, or pressuring others, to sign off on documents you haven't read, knowing they may contain information or decisions that might be considered inappropriate.

_____25. _____ If you were to give this assessment to a person you work with and with whom you do not get along very well, would she agree with your answers? Use a scale of yes 4–1 on the line before the number 25 and skip O or R.

Other Unethical Behavior:

Add other unethical behaviors you observed. Identify if you reported the behavior by using R.

26. _____
27. _____
28. _____

Note: This self-assessment is not meant to be a precise measure of your ethical behavior. It is designed to get you thinking about ethics and your behavior and that of others from an ethical perspective. There is no right or wrong score; however, each of these actions is considered unethical behavior in most organizations. Another ethical issue of this exercise is your honesty when rating the frequencies of your behavior. How honest were you?

Scoring: To determine your ethics score, add the numbers 1–4. Your total will be between 25 and 100. Place the number here and on the continuum below that represents your score. The higher your score, the more ethical is your behavior, and vice versa for lower scores.

25—30—40—50—60—70—80—90—100
Unethical   Ethical

Members of organizations face moral issues,[50] and leaders set the ethical climate and are responsible for employee ethical or unethical behavior.[51] Unfortunately, scandals have become too commonplace,[52] often based on the greedy win at all cost philosophy.[53] Corporate scandals globally have led to a distrust of leaders,[54] to the point where only around 30 percent of developed countries trust organizational leaders.[55] **Ethics** _are the standards of right and wrong that influence behavior._ Right behavior is considered ethical, and wrong behavior is considered unethical.

Government laws and regulations are designed to help keep business honest. To this end, Congress passed the Sarbanes-Oxley Act of 2002 to help ensure that complaints about financial irregularities would surface and be swiftly acted upon, without retaliation against the person who exposed the unethical behavior ("whistle-blower"). However, the government can't make people be ethical. But recall that AACSB (Chapter 1) lists ethical understanding as an important competency.[56] Thus, business schools are focusing on ethics,[57] as it is generally agreed that ethics can be taught.[58]

In this section, we discuss that ethical behavior does pay; how personality traits and attitudes, moral development, and the situation affect ethical behavior; how people justify unethical behavior; some simple guides to ethical behavior; and being an ethical leader.

Does Ethical Behavior Pay?

Generally, the answer is yes. Research has found a direct link to bottom-line performance.[59] Unethical decisions have led to dramatic costs in fines, reputational damage, and imprisonment.[60] Society also suffers, such as the financial crisis that plunged world economies into recession.[61] Most highly successful people are ethical.[62] Being ethical may be difficult, but it has its rewards.[63] It actually makes you feel better.[64] Honest people have fewer mental health and physical complaints, like anxiety and back pain, and better social interactions.[65]

Ethics is so important that large organizations have ethics officers who are responsible for developing and implementing ethics codes (standards of what is ethical and what is not) to help guide employees to ethical behavior.[66]

Leadership success is based on personal traits, including integrity—having character of being honest (no lying, steeling, or cheating).[67] Trust among employees is vital, and trust is based on integrity.[68] If you are not honest with people and take advantage of them, they will not trust you and you will not have the ability to influence them. So there is a direct link between being ethical and being an effective leader.[69]

Learning Outcome 7   *Compare the three levels of moral development.*

Factors Influencing Ethical Behavior

In this subsection, we discuss why good people do bad things, and three related concepts: how personality traits and attitudes, moral development, and the situation affect ethical behavior.

Why Do Good People Do Bad Things?

Most people understand right and wrong behavior and have a conscience. So why do good people do bad things? Most often, when people behave unethically, it is not because they have some type of character flaw or were born bad. It can be incredibly tempting to be unethical.[70] Most people aren't simply good or bad. Just about everyone has the capacity to be dishonest.[71] One percent of people will always be honest, one percent will always be dishonest, and 98 percent will be unethical at times but just a little.[72] We respond to "incentives" and can usually be manipulated to behave ethically or unethically, if you find the right incentives.[73] The incentive is usually looking out for our own self-interest,[74] and can be personal gain or to avoid getting into trouble.[75]

Most people don't go into business thinking, "I'm going to be unethical." It often starts with the temptation to do something unethical for personal gain. Without getting caught and punished, people tend to get worse over time as they become desensitized to their unethical behavior. In most cases, the person is eventually caught and punished. This is illustrated in the film *The Wolf of Wall Street*. Leonardo DiCaprio plays the role of Jordan Belfort, whose unethical behavior starts small and leads to his imprisonment.[76] So once you start down the road of unethical behavior, it is difficult to pull a u-turn.

Personality Traits and Attitudes

Our ethical behavior is related to our individual needs and personality traits of character with integrity.[77] But personality alone is not a good predictor of unethical behavior. Leaders with surgency (dominance) personality traits have two choices: to use power for personal benefit or to use socialized power. To gain power and to be conscientious with high achievement, some people will use unethical behavior.

An agreeableness personality sensitive to others can lead to following the crowd in either ethical or unethical behavior. Emotionally unstable people and those with external locus of control are more likely to use unethical behavior. People with positive attitudes about ethics tend to be more ethical than those with negative or weak attitudes about ethics.[78]

Moral Development

A second factor affecting ethical behavior is *moral development*, which refers to understanding right from wrong and choosing to do the right thing with a moral identity.[79]

Our ability to make ethical choices is related to our level of moral development and judgments.[80] There are three levels of personal moral development, as discussed in Exhibit 2.5, and we can improve our character development.[81]

Levels of Moral Development

EXHIBIT 2.5

3. Postconventional

Behavior is motivated by universal principles of right and wrong, regardless of the expectations of the leader or group. One seeks to balance the concerns for self with those of others and the common good. He or she will follow ethical principles even if they violate the law at the risk of social rejection, economic loss, and physical punishment (Martin Luther King, Jr., broke what he considered unjust laws and spent time in jail seeking universal dignity and justice).

"I don't lie to customers because it is wrong."

The common leadership style is visionary and committed to serving others and a higher cause while empowering followers to reach this level.

2. Conventional

Living up to expectations of acceptable behavior defined by others motivates behavior to fulfill duties and obligations. It is common for followers to copy the behavior of the leaders and group. If the group (can be society/organization/department) accepts lying, cheating, stealing, and so on, when dealing with customers/suppliers/government/competitors, so will the individual. On the other hand, if these behaviors are not accepted, the individual will not do them either. Peer pressure is used to enforce group norms.

"I lie to customers because the other sales reps do it too."

It is common for lower-level managers to use a similar leadership style of the higher-level managers.

1. Preconventional

Self-interest motivates behavior to meet one's own needs to gain rewards while following rules and being obedient to authority to avoid punishment.

"I lie to customers to sell more products and get higher commission checks."

The common leadership style is autocratic toward others while using one's position for personal advantage.

Source: Adapted from Lawrence Kohlberg, "Moral Stages and Moralization: The Cognitive-Development Approach." In Thomas Likona (ed.),

Moral Development and Behavior: Theory, Research, and Social Issues (Austin, TX: Holt, Rinehart and Winston, 1976), 31–53.

At the first level, preconventional, we choose right and wrong behavior based on our self-interest and the consequences (reward and punishment). With ethical reasoning at the second level, conventional, we seek to maintain expected standards and live up to the expectations of others. One does what the others do. At the third level, postconventional, we make an effort to define moral principles regardless of leader or group ethics. Although most of us have the ability to reach the third level of moral development, postconventional, only about 20 percent of people reach this level.

Source: Adapted from Lawrence Kohlberg, "Moral Stages and Moralization: The Cognitive-Development Approach." In Thomas Likona (ed.), Moral Development and Behavior: Theory, Research, and Social Issues (Austin, TX: Holt, Rinehart and Winston, 1976), 31–53.

WORK
Application **2-13**

Give an organizational example of behavior at each of the three levels of moral development.

Most people behave at the second level, conventional, while some have not advanced beyond the first level, preconventional. How do you handle peer pressure to be unethical? What level of moral development are you on? What can you do to further develop your ethical behavior? We will discuss how to be an ethical leader.

The Situation

Our third factor affecting ethical behavior is the situation. People consider the situational forces in determining ethical behavior.[82] We are susceptible to social influence.[83] Unethical organizational behavior has been attributed to the effects of individual unethical "bad apples."[84] The bad is stronger than the good effect as a bad apple can spoil the whole barrel (organization).[85]

Highly competitive and unsupervised situations increase the odds of unethical behavior. Unethical behavior occurs more often when there is no formal ethics policy or code of ethics, and when unethical behavior is not punished, and it is especially prevalent when it is rewarded. In other words, people are more unethical when they believe they will not get caught and punished.[86] Unethical behavior is also more likely when performance falls below aspiration levels. People also tend to be more ethical in the morning.[87] People are also less likely to report unethical behavior (blow the whistle) when they perceive the violation as not being serious and when the offenders are their friends.

Integration

To tie the three factors affecting ethical behavior together, we need to realize that personality traits and attitudes and moral development interact with the situation to determine if a person will use ethical or unethical behavior. In this chapter we use the individual level of analysis: Am I ethical, and how can I improve my ethical behavior? At the organizational level, many firms offer training programs and develop codes of ethics to help employees behave ethically. The organizational level of analysis is examined in Part Three of this book; therefore, ethics and whistle-blowing will be further discussed in Chapter 10.

OPENING CASE Application

5. What role does ethics play at DuPont?

It always has been, and continues to be, the intent of DuPont that its employees maintain the highest ethical standards in their conduct of company affairs. Here are some of its ethical principles. In living up to its ethical philosophy, DuPont will be fair and honest in all dealings on behalf of the company, do what is right rather than what is expedient, and conduct all dealings with suppliers, customers, and others in a manner that excludes consideration of personal advantage.[88]

How People Justify Unethical Behavior

As we seek our own self-interest,[89] most of us give in to temptation and do the wrong thing sometimes.[90] Few people see themselves as unethical. We all want to view ourselves in a positive manner. If we only cheat a little, we can still feel good about our sense of integrity.[91] Therefore, when we do use unethical behavior, we often justify the behavior to protect our self-concept so that we don't have to feel bad.[92] **Moral justification** *is the thinking process of rationalizing why unethical behavior is used.* We *rationalize* with statements like "this is a widespread business practice," "everybody does it," and "I deserve it." Let's discuss several thinking processes used to justify unethical behavior.

- **Higher purpose** is rationalizing immoral behavior in terms of a higher purpose. "It's for a greater good."[93] People lie, cheat, and steal, claiming it is for the good of the organization, department, or employees.
- **Displacement of responsibility** is the process of blaming one's unethical behavior on others. "I was only following orders; my boss told me to inflate the figures."[94]
- **Diffusion of responsibility** is the process of the group using the unethical behavior with no one person being held responsible. "It isn't my decision."[95] Everyone does it.[96] "We all take bribes/kickbacks; it's the way we do business," or "We all take merchandise home (steal)." If you hear others are doing something, you will tend to be tempted to be unethical to.[97]
- **Advantageous comparison** is the process of comparing oneself to others who are worse. "I call in sick when I'm not sick only a few times a year; Tom and Ellen do it all the time." "We pollute less than our competitors do." I'm only fudging a little."[98]
- **Disregard or distortion of consequences** is the process of minimizing the harm caused by the unethical behavior. [99] "If I inflate the figures, no one will be hurt and I will not get caught. And if I do, I'll just get a slap on the wrist anyway." Was this the case at Enron?
- **Attribution of blame** is the process of claiming the unethical behavior was caused by someone else's behavior. "It's my coworker's fault that I hit him. He called me/did xxx, so I had to hit him."
- **Euphemistic labeling** is the process of using "cosmetic" words to make the behavior sound acceptable. *Terrorist group* sounds bad but *freedom fighter* sounds justifiable. *Misleading* or *covering up* sounds better than *lying to others.*

> **WORK**
> Application **2-14**
>
> Give at least two organizational examples of unethical behavior and the process of justification.
>
> _____
>
> _____
>
> _____

It is important to understand the subtlety of how unethical behavior can take hold of you. Simply doing what "works for you," what "makes you feel good," or "doing whatever it takes," often leads to unethical behavior. Unethical behavior that you justify might give you some type of short-term gain, but in the long run, you've sabotaged yourself.[100] Which justification processes have you used? How can you improve your ethical behavior by not using justification?

CONCEPT APPLICATION 2-4

Justifying Unethical Behavior

Identify each thinking process used to justify the unethical behavior below.

a. moral justification
b. displacement of responsibility
c. diffusion of responsibility
d. advantageous comparison
e. disregard or distortion of consequences
f. attribution of blame
g. euphemistic labeling

_____ 21. Yes. We have to take the other team's play book so that we can win the game.

_____ 22. I only take candy once in a while. Jean takes one every day.

_____ 23. We all do it, so don't worry about it. Everyone takes candy without paying for it.

_____ 24. It's not my fault. Kevin started breaking it, so I just joined in.

_____ 25. Yes. I'm keeping it. I found it and the company will never miss it anyway.

_____ 26. I lied to the customer because my boss told me too.

_____ 27. Yes. Our boss is married, but that is no stopping her from having an affair with the president.

YOU Make the **ETHICAL** Call

2.2 *Sex and Violence*

Over the years, various social activist groups, including the Parents Television Council, the National Viewers and Listeners Association, and the National Coalition against Censorship, have taken a stance for and against censorship of sex and violence on TV and in the movies. People call for more censorship to protect children from seeing sex and violence, while others don't want censorship, stating it violates free speech laws.

Advocates of regulation state the fact than many cable stations show reruns of major network shows in the daytime and early evening when children are watching. For example, *Sex and the City* and *Jersey Shore* are aired in different areas at all hours of the day and night.

1. Does the media (TV, movies, and music) influence societal values?

2. Does the media, with sex and violence, reflect current religious and societal values?

3. The Federal Communications Commission (FCC) has the power to regulate television. Should the FCC regulate the media, and, if yes, how far should it go? Should it require toning down the sex and violence, airing the shows only later at night, or should it take shows like *Sex and the City* and *Jersey Shore* off the air?

4. Is it ethical and socially responsible to show sex and violence against women, and to portray women as sex objects?

5. Which of the seven justifications of unethical behavior do the media use to defend sex and violence?

Guides to Ethical Behavior

Every day in our personal and professional life, we face situations in which we can make ethical or unethical choices. As discussed, you make these choices based on your personality traits and attitudes, level of moral development, and the situation. Research shows that making a decision without using an ethical guide leads to less ethical choices.[101] So ethical guidelines can have a positive influence on our making ethical decisions.[102] Following are some guides that can help us make ethical decisions.

Golden Rule

The golden rule is, "Do unto others as you want them to do unto you." Or, put other ways, "Don't do anything to other people that you would not want them to do to you." "Lead others as you want to be led." Sammy Hagar says, "You have to treat people the way you want to be treated."[103] Do you like it when people lie to you, cheat you, or steal from you?

Four-Way Test

Rotary International developed the four-way test of the things we think and do to guide business transactions. The four questions are (1) Is it the truth? (2) Is it fair to all concerned? (3) Will it build goodwill and better friendship? (4) Will it be beneficial to all concerned? When making your decision, if you can answer yes to these four questions, it is probably ethical. Anne Beiler, founder of **Auntie Anne's**, advice is to tell the truth, even if it hurts.[104]

Learning Outcome **8**   *Explain the stakeholder approach to ethics.*

Codes of Ethics

Also called *codes of conduct*, state the importance of conducting business in an ethical manner and provide guidelines or standards for ethical behavior.[105] Most large businesses have written codes of ethics you should follow.

Stakeholder Approach to Ethics

Under the **stakeholder approach to ethics**, *one creates a win–win situation for relevant parties affected by the decision.* A win–win situation meets the needs of the organization and employees as well as those of other stakeholders, so that everyone benefits from the decision. Stakeholders include everyone affected by the decision.[106] You can ask yourself one simple question to help you determine if your decision is ethical from a stakeholder approach:

> *"Am I proud to tell relevant stakeholders my decision?"*

If you are proud to tell relevant stakeholders your decision, it is probably ethical. If you are not proud to tell others your decision, or you keep justifying it, the decision may not be ethical. Justifying is usually a cop-out. You can't always create a win for everyone, but you can try.

Discernment and Advice

Making an immediate decision leads to increased odds of unethical behavior, whereas taking time to contemplate the decision and talking to others for advice lead to increased odds of ethical behavior.[107] If you are unsure whether a decision is ethical, talk to your boss, higher-level managers, and other people with high ethical standards. If you are reluctant to ask others for advice because you may not like their answers, and you keep justifying it, the decision may not be ethical. Seeking advice is especially important in the global economy because what is considered unethical in one country may be considered ethical in another country.[108]

"Take It To The Net". Access student resources at www.cengagebrain.com. Search for Lussier, Leadership 6e to find student study tools.

Chapter Summary

The chapter summary is organized to answer the ten learning outcomes for this chapter.

1 Explain the universality of traits of effective leaders.

Traits are universal in the sense that there are certain traits that most effective leaders have. However, traits are not universal in the sense that there is no one list of traits that is clearly accepted by all researchers, and not all effective leaders have all the traits.

2 Describe the Big Five personality dimensions.

The surgency personality dimension includes leadership and extraversion traits. The agreeableness personality dimension includes traits related to getting along with people. The adjustment personality dimension includes traits related to emotional stability. The conscientiousness personality dimension includes traits related to achievement. The openness-to-experience personality dimension includes traits related to being willing to change and try new things.

3 Discuss why the trait of dominance is so important for managers to have.

Because the dominance trait is based on the desire to be a leader, this trait affects the other traits in a positive or negative way based on that desire.

4 **State how the Achievement Motivation Theory and the Leader Motive Profile are related and different.**

Achievement Motivation and Leader Motive Profile theories are related because both are based on the need for achievement, power, and affiliation. They are different because the Achievement Motivation Theory is a general motive profile for explaining and predicting behavior and performance, while the LMP is the one profile that specifically explains and predicts leadership success.

5 **Identify similarities and differences among Theory X and Theory Y, the Pygmalion effect, and self-concept.**

The concept of Theory X and Theory Y is similar to the Pygmalion effect, because both theories focus on the leader's attitude about the followers. The Pygmalion effect extends Theory X and Theory Y attitudes by including the leader's expectations and how he or she treats the followers, using this information to explain and predict followers' behavior and performance. In contrast, Theory X and Theory Y focus on the leader's behavior and performance. Both approaches are different from self-concept because they examine the leader's attitudes about others, whereas self-concept relates to the leader's attitude about him- or herself. Self-concept is also different because it focuses on how the leader's attitude about him- or herself affects his or her behavior and performance.

6 **Describe how attitudes are used to develop four leadership styles.**

The leader's attitude about others includes Theory Y (positive) and Theory X (negative) attitudes. The leader's attitude about him- or herself includes a positive self-concept or a negative self-concept. Combinations of these variables are used to identify four leadership styles: Theory Y positive self-concept, Theory Y negative self-concept, Theory X positive self-concept, and Theory X negative self-concept.

7 **Compare the three levels of moral development.**

At the lowest level of moral development, preconventional, behavior is motivated by self-interest, seeking rewards, and avoiding punishment. At the second level, conventional, behavior is motivated by meeting the group's expectations to fit in by copying others' behavior. At the highest level, postconventional, behavior is motivated to do the right thing, at the risk of alienating the group. The higher the level of moral development, the more ethical is the behavior.

8 **Explain the stakeholder approach to ethics.**

Under the stakeholder approach to ethics, the leader (or follower) creates a win–win situation for relevant parties affected by the decision. If you are proud to tell relevant stakeholders your decision, it is probably ethical. If you are not proud to tell others your decision, or you keep justifying it, the decision may not be ethical.

Key Terms

Achievement Motivation Theory, 41

adjustment personality dimension, 37

agreeableness personality dimension, 37

attitudes, 45

Big Five Model of Personality, 36

conscientiousness personality dimension, 38

ethics, 51

Leader Motive Profile (LMP), 43

Leader Motive Profile Theory, 43

moral justification, 54

openness-to-experience personality dimension, 38

personality, 34

personality profiles, 34

Pygmalion effect, 47

self-concept, 48

stakeholder approach to ethics, 57

surgency personality dimension, 36

Theory X and Theory Y, 46

traits, 34

Review Questions

1 What are the Big Five dimensions of traits?

2 What is the primary use of personality profiles?

3 What are some of the traits that describe the high-energy trait?

4 Is locus of control important to leaders? Why?

5 What does intelligence have to do with leadership?

6 Does sensitivity to others mean that the leader does what the followers want to do?

7 Does McClelland believe that power is good or bad? Why?

8 Should a leader have a dominant need for achievement to be successful? Why or why not?

9 How do attitudes develop leadership styles?

10 Which personality traits are more closely related to ethical and unethical behavior?

11 Do people change their level of moral development based on the situation?

12 Why do people justify their unethical behavior?

Critical-Thinking Questions

The following critical-thinking questions can be used for class discussion and/or as written assignments to develop communication skills. Be sure to give complete explanations for all questions.

1 Would you predict that a person with a strong agreeableness personality dimension would be a successful computer programmer? Why or why not?

2 McGregor published Theory X and Theory Y over 30 years ago. Do we still have Theory X managers? Why?

3 In text examples related to the Pygmalion effect, Lou Holtz calls for setting a higher standard. Have the standards in school, society, and work increased or decreased over the last five years?

4 Do you believe that if you use ethical behavior it will pay off in the long run?

5 Can ethics be taught and learned?

6 Which justification do you think is used most often?

7 As related to the simple guide to ethical behavior, how do you want to be led?

CASE

Blake Mycoskie and TOMS

By age 29, Blake Mycoskie had already started four businesses. He got the idea to start his fifth business on a trip to Argentina. Blake observed that many people were wearing alpargatas—soft casual canvas shoes—and he thought they would sell in America. But he also realized that there were also many poor people without any shoes who had blisters, sores, and infections. So he decided to help.

Back home in America, Blake got involved in a volunteer shoe drive to ship shoes overseas. But he realized that there was a need for a constant flow of shoes and that even a nonprofit organization couldn't be very sustainable through simply donations. He was also an entrepreneur and wanted to make money. So Blake came up with the idea of being a social entrepreneur by combining business and charity to help others and make the world a better place.[109]

Blake Mycoskie founded TOMS, which stands for TOMmorrowS shoes, in 2006. He developed the One for One business model—for every pair of shoes TOMS sells, it gives away a free pair to a child in need. But as with entrepreneurial new ventures, it wasn't easy. In fact, Blake was told that he didn't understand the shoe industry and that his business wouldn't be successful. But that didn't stop Blake. To date, TOMS has given away more than 10 million pairs of shoes.[110]

Blake realized that he couldn't just buy the alpargate shoes. They needed to be more stylish, comfortable, and durable to sell in the United States. So with no knowledge of the shoe industry and not speaking Spanish, he returned to Argentina to find a local partner, and teamed up with shoemaker Alejo for help. Together they developed a prototype and Blake brought 250 pairs home to Los Angeles.

Blake ran a focus group by inviting a bunch of friends, mostly women, to his place. He told them his story and One for One, and they discussed the potential market and price for the shoes and where they could be sold. They loved the story, bought a pair of shoes, and spread the word.

Blake went to retail stores and told his story and tried to get them to sell TOMS, but he got lots of rejections. Blake would tell his story to anyone who would listen. He would wear two different shoes just to get people to talk to him so he could tell his story. Blake's first two big breaks came when American Rag agreed to sell TOMS and the *LA Times* ran his story in the newspaper. Orders started pouring in. So Blake started the business on a shoestring budget by using his apartment and three interns he found through Craigslist.

Blake went back to Argentina to give away free shoes and develop a supply chain of TOMS shoes. Blake believes that success is more than status and money and that it's about contributing to the world and living and working on your own terms. He has personal, professional, and philanthropic success. Today, TOMS gives free shoes to 60 countries.

Blake has expanded his social entrepreneurship mission to include writing a book, *Start Something That Matters*, to inspire others to contribute to the world.[111] He also expanded his unique One for One business model to include TOMS Eyewear, helping save and restore sight for those in need. TOMS Web site **(www.toms.com)** includes the Marketplace where people can shop for a variety of other products and contribute to funding education. TOMS has Giving Partners to increase its charity, and it has given millions to nonprofit organizations. To encourage social entrepreneurship, TOMS develops ways to use its platform to support their ventures. In addition, the Start Something That Matters Foundation has begun to help innovators bring their ideas to life.[112]

GO TO THE INTERNET: To learn more about Blake Mycoskie and TOMS, visit the Web site **(http://www.toms.com).**

Support your answers to the following questions with specific information from the case and text or with other information you get from the Web or other sources.

1. What do you think Blake Mycoskie's personality traits are for each of the Big Five dimensions?

2. Which of the traits of effective leaders would you say has had the greatest impact on Blake Mycoskie success at TOMS?

3. Which motivation would McClelland say was the major need driving Blake Mycoskie to continue to work so hard despite being worth millions of dollars?

4. Does Blake Mycoskie have an LMP?

5. What type of self-concept does Blake Mycoskie have, and how does it affect his success?

6. Is Blake Mycoskie ethical in business? Which level of moral development is he on?

CUMULATIVE CASE QUESTION

7. Which leadership managerial role(s) played by Blake Mycoskie have an important part in the success of TOMS (Chapter 1)?

CASE EXERCISE AND ROLE-PLAY

Preparation: Think of a business that you would like to start some day and answer these questions, which will help you develop your plan. (1) What would be your company's name? (2) What would be its mission (purpose or reason for being)? (3) What would your major products and/or services be? (4) Who would be your major competitors? (5) What would be your competitive advantage? (What makes you different from your competitors? Why would anyone buy your product or service rather than the competition's?) (6) As Blake would say, what is your story?

Your instructor may elect to let you break into groups to develop a group business idea. If you do a group business, select one leader with a thick skin who can handle a "Blake" meeting to present the proposal to the entire class. An alternative is to have a student(s) who has an actual business idea/project/proposal of any type present it for feedback.

Role-Play "Blake" Meeting: One person (representing oneself or a group) may give the business proposal idea to the entire class; or break into groups of five or six and, one at a time, deliver proposals. The members of the class that listen play the role of Blake at the "Blake" meeting, or they challenge presenters and offer suggestions for improvement.

VIDEO CASE

"P.F." Chang's Serves Its Workers Well

P.F. Chang's has over 120 full-service, casual dining Asian bistros and contemporary Chinese diners across the country, and its employees have the authority to make decisions that benefit customers. Giving employees the freedom to make decisions has had a huge impact on their attitudes and performance. Managers at P.F. Chang's receive extensive training on how to create and nurture a positive attitude among their employees, and all workers receive an employee handbook, which clearly spells out exactly what is expected of them.

1. In what ways does P.F. Chang's create organizational commitment among its workers?
2. How might a manager at P.F. Chang's use the Big Five personality factors to assess whether a candidate for a position on the wait staff would be suitable?

Developing Your Leadership Skills 2-1

Improving Attitudes and Personality Traits

Preparing for This Exercise

You should have read and now understand attitudes and personality traits. Effective leaders know themselves and work to maximize their strengths and minimize their weaknesses. As the name of this exercise implies, you can improve your attitudes and personality traits through this exercise by following these steps.

1 Identify strengths and weaknesses. Review the six self-assessment exercises in this chapter. List your three major strengths and areas that can be improved:

We don't always see ourselves as others do. Research has shown that many people are not accurate in describing their own personalities, and that others can describe them more objectively. Before going on with this exercise, you may want to ask someone you know well to complete your personality profile (see Self-Assessment 2-1 on page 32), rate your attitude as positive or negative, and list your strengths and areas for improvement.

2 Develop a plan for improving. Start with your Number One area to improve on. Write down specific things that you can do to improve. List specific times, dates, and places that you will implement your plans. You may want to review the 11 tips for developing a more positive attitude and self-concept for ideas.

3 Work on other areas for improvement. After you see improvement in your first area, develop a new plan for your second area, and proceed through the steps again.

Optional Way to Improve: If you have a negative attitude toward yourself or others—or you would like to improve your behavior with others (family, coworkers), things, or issues (disliking school or work)—try following the internationally known motivational speaker and trainer Zig Ziglar's system.[113] Thousands of people have used this system successfully. This system can also be used for changing personality traits as well.

Here are the steps to follow, with an example plan for a person who has a negative self-concept and also wants to be more sensitive to others. Use this example as a guide for developing your own plan.

1 *Self-concept.* Write down everything you like about yourself. List all your strengths. Then go on and list all your weaknesses. Get a good friend to help you.

2 Make a clean new list, and using positive affirmations, write all your strengths. Example: "I am sensitive to others' needs."

3 *On another sheet of paper, again using positive affirmations, list all your weaknesses.* For example, don't write "I need to lose weight." Write "I am a slim (whatever you realistically can weigh in 30 days) pounds." Don't write "I have to stop criticizing myself." Write "I positively praise myself often, every day." Write "I have good communications skills," not "I am a weak communicator." The following list gives example affirmations for improving sensitivity to others. Note the repetition; you can use a thesaurus to help.

I am sensitive to others.

My behavior with others conveys my warmth for them. I convey my concern for others.

My behavior conveys kindness toward others.

My behavior helps others build their self-esteem. People find me easy to talk to.

I give others my full attention. I patiently listen to others talk.

I answer others slowly and in a polite manner.

I answer questions and make comments with useful information.

My comments to others help them feel good about themselves.

I compliment others regularly.

4 *Practice.* Every morning and night for at least the next 30 days, look at yourself in the mirror and read your list of positive affirmations. Be sure to look at yourself between each affirmation as you read. Or, record the list on a tape recorder and listen to it while looking at yourself in the mirror. If you are really motivated, you can repeat this step at other times of the day. Start with your areas for improvement. If it takes five minutes or more, don't bother with the list of your strengths. Or stop at five minutes; this exercise is effective in short sessions. Although miracles won't happen overnight, you may become more aware of your behavior in the first week. In the second or third week, you may become aware of yourself using new behavior successfully. You may still see some negatives, but the number will decrease in time as the positive increases.

Psychological research has shown that if a person hears something believable repeated for 30 days, he or she will tend to believe it. Ziglar says that you cannot consistently perform in a manner that is inconsistent with the way you see yourself. So, as you listen to your positive affirmations, you will believe them, and you will behave in a manner that is consistent with your belief. Put simply, your behavior will change with your thoughts without a lot of hard work. For example, if you listen to the affirmation, "I am an honest person" (not, "I have to stop lying"), in time— without having to work at it—you will tell the truth. At first you may feel uncomfortable reading or listening to positive affirmations that you don't really believe you have. But keep looking at yourself in the mirror and reading or listening, and with time you will feel comfortable and believe it and live it.

Are you thinking you don't need to improve, or that this method will not work? Yes, this system often does work. Zig Ziglar has trained thousands of satisfied people. One of this book's authors tried the system himself, and within two or three weeks, he could see improvement in his behavior. The question isn't will the system work for you, but rather will you work the system to improve?

5 *When you slip, and we all do, don't get down on yourself.* In the sensitivity-to-others example, if you are rude to someone and catch yourself, apologize and change to a positive tone. Effective leaders admit when they are wrong and apologize. If you have a hard time admitting you are wrong and saying you are sorry, at least be obviously nice so that the other person realizes you are saying you are sorry indirectly. Then forget about it and keep trying. Focus on your successes, not your slips. Don't let ten good discussions be ruined by one insensitive comment. If you were an MLB player and got nine out of ten hits, you'd be the best in the world.

6 *Set another goal.* After 30 days, select a new topic, such as developing a positive attitude toward work, school, or trying a specific leadership style that you want to develop. You can also include more than one area to work on.

Doing This Exercise in Class

Objective

To develop your skill at improving your attitudes and personality traits. As a leader, you can also use this skill to help your followers improve.

AACSB General Skills Area

The primary AACSB skills developed through this exercise are analytic and reflective thinking skills and application of knowledge.

Preparation You should have identified at least one area for improvement and developed a plan to improve.

Procedure 1 *(1–2 minutes)* Break into groups of two or preferably three; be sure the others in your group are people you feel comfortable sharing with.

Procedure 2 *(4–6 minutes)* Have one of the group members volunteer to go first. The first volunteer states the attitude or personality trait they want to work on and describes the plan. The other group members give feedback on how to improve the plan. Try to give other plan ideas that can be helpful and/or provide some specific help. You can also make an agreement to ask each other how you are progressing at set class intervals. Don't change roles until you're asked to do so.

Procedure 3 *(4–6 minutes)* A second group member volunteers to go next. Follow the same procedure as above.

Procedure 4 *(4–6 minutes)* The third group member goes last. Follow the same procedure as above.

Conclusion

The instructor may lead a class discussion and/or make concluding remarks.

Apply It *(2–4 minutes)* What did I learn from this exercise? Will I really try to improve my attitude and personality by implementing my plan?

Sharing

In the group, or to the entire class, volunteers may give their answers to the "Apply It" questions.

Developing Your Leadership Skills (2-2)

Personality Perceptions

Preparing for This Exercise

Read the section on "Personality Traits and Leadership," and complete Self-Assessment 2-1 on page 32. From that exercise, rank yourself below from the highest score (1) to lowest (5) for each of the Big Five traits. Do not tell anyone your ranking until asked to do so.

– surgency   – adjustment
– openness to experience   – agreeableness
– conscientiousness

Doing This Exercise in Class

Objective

To develop your skill at perceiving personality traits of other people. With this skill, you can better understand and predict people's behavior, which is helpful to leaders in influencing followers.

AACSB General Skills Area

The primary AACSB skills developed through this exercise are analytic and reflective thinking skills and application of knowledge.

Procedure 1 (2–4 minutes) Break into groups of three. This group should be with people you know the best in the class. You may need some groups of two. If you don't know people in the class, and you did Skill-Development Exercise 1 in Chapter 1, "Getting to Know You by Name," get in a group with those people.

Procedure 2 (4–6 minutes) Each person in the group writes down their perception of each of the other two group members. Simply rank which trait you believe to be the highest and lowest (put the Big Five dimension name on the line) for each person. Write a short reason for your perception, including some behavior you observed that leads you to your perception.

Name _____ Highest personality score
_____ Lowest score _____

Reason for ranking _____

_____

Name _____ Highest personality score
_____ Lowest score _____
Reason for ranking _____

Procedure 3 (4–6 minutes) One of the group members volunteers to go first to hear the other group members' perceptions.

1 One person tells the volunteer which Big Five dimension he or she selected as the person's highest and lowest score, and why these dimensions were selected. Do not discuss this information yet.

2 The other person also tells the volunteer the same information.

3 The volunteer gives the two others his or her actual highest and lowest scores. The three group members discuss the accuracy of the perceptions.

Procedure 4 (4–6 minutes) A second group member volunteers to go next to receive perceptions. Follow the same procedure as above.

Procedure 5 (4–6 minutes) The third group member goes last. Follow the same procedure as above.

Conclusion The instructor may lead a class discussion and/or make concluding remarks.

Apply It (2–4 minutes) What did I learn from this exercise? How will I use this knowledge in the future?

Sharing

In the group, or to the entire class, volunteers may give their answers to the "Apply It" questions.

Developing Your Leadership Skills (2-3)

Ethics and Whistle-blowing

Preparing for This Exercise

Now that you have completed Self-Assessment 2-6 on pages 50–51 regarding ethical behavior, answer the discussion questions based on that assessment.

Discussion Questions

1 For the "College" section, items 1–3, who is harmed and who benefits from these unethical behaviors?

2 For the "Workplace" section, items 4–24, select the three items (circle their numbers) you consider the most seriously unethical behavior. Who is harmed and who benefits by these unethical behaviors?

3 If you observed unethical behavior but didn't report it, why didn't you report the behavior? If you did blow the whistle, why did you report the unethical behavior? What was the result?

4 As a manager, it is your responsibility to uphold ethical behavior. If you know employees are using any of these unethical behaviors, will you take action to enforce compliance with ethical standards?

Doing This Exercise in Class

Objective

To better understand ethics and whistle-blowing, and decide what you will do about unethical behavior.

AACSB General Skills Area

The primary AACSB skills developed through this exercise are ethical understanding, analytic and reflective thinking skills, and application of knowledge.

Preparation

You should have completed the preparation for this exercise.

Experience

You will share your answers to the preparation questions but are not requested to share your ethics score.

Procedure 1 *(5–10 minutes)* The instructor writes the numbers 1–24 on the board. For each statement, students first raise their hands if they have observed this behavior, then if they have

reported the behavior. The instructor writes the numbers on the board. (Note: Procedure 1 and Procedure 2A can be combined.)

Procedure 2 *(10–20 minutes)* Option A: As the instructor takes a count of the students who have observed and reported unethical behavior, he or she leads a discussion on the statements.

Option B: Break into groups of four to six, and share your answers to the four discussion questions at the end of the preparation part of this exercise. The groups may be asked to report the general consensus of the group to the entire class. If so, select a spokesperson before the discussion begins.

Option C: The instructor leads a class discussion on the four discussion questions at the end of the preparation part of this exercise.

Conclusion

The instructor may make concluding remarks.

Apply It *(2–4 minutes)* What did I learn from this exercise? How will I use this knowledge in the future to be ethical? When will I use a simple guide to ethics?

Sharing

Volunteers may give their answers to the "Apply It" questions.

Endnotes

1. DuPont Web site (www.dupont.com), accessed November 7, 2013.
2. DuPont Web site (www.dupont.com), accessed November 7, 2013.
3. "Largest U.S. Corporations—Fortune 500," *Fortune* (May 20, 2013): 1–20.
4. "Global 500," *Fortune* (July 22, 2013): F1–F7.
5. "The World's Most Admired Companies," *Fortune* (March 18, 2013): 137–147.
6. G. Colvin, "Ignore These Leadership Lessons at Your Peril," *Fortune* (October 28, 2013): 85.
7. H. C. Vough, M.T. Cardador, J.S. Bendar, E. Dane, and M.G. Pratt, "What Clients Don't Get about My Profession: A Model of Perceived Role-Based Image Discrepancies," *Academy of Management Journal* 56(4) (2013): 1050–1080.
8. B. Schyns, T. Kiefer, R. Kerschreiter, and A. Tymon, "Teaching Implicit Leadership Theories to Develop Leaders and Leadership: How and Why It Can Make a Difference," *Academy of Management Learning & Education* 10(3) (2012): 397–408.
9. J. Antonakis, M. Fenley, and S. Liechti, "Can Charisma Be Taught? Tests of Two Interventions," *Academy of Management Learning & Education* 10(3) (2011): 374–396.
10. M.R. Barrick, M.K. Mount, and N. Li, "The Theory of Purposeful Work Behavior: The Role of Personality, Higher-Order Goals, and Job Characteristics," *Academy of Management Review* 38(1) (2013): 132–153.
11. J. Antonakis, M. Fenley, and S. Liechti, "Can Charisma Be Taught? Tests of Two Interventions," *Academy of Management Learning & Education* 10(3) (2011): 374–396.
12. G. Yukl, "Effective Leadership Behavior: What We Know and What Questions Need More Attention," *Academy of Management Perspectives* 26(4) (2011): 66–85.
13. J. Antonakis, M. Fenley, and S. Liechti, "Can Charisma Be Taught? Tests of Two Interventions," *Academy of Management Learning & Education* 10(3) (2011): 374–396.
14. J. Antonakis, M. Fenley, and S. Liechti, "Can Charisma Be Taught? Tests of Two Interventions," *Academy of Management Learning & Education* 10(3) (2011): 374–396.
15. C. Bendersky and N.P. Shah, "The Downfall of Extraverts and Rise of Neurotics: The Dynamic Process of Status Allocation in Task Groups," *Academy of Management Journal* 56(2) (2013): 387–406.
16. T. A. Judge, R. Ilies, J.E. Bono, and M.W. Gerhardt, "Personality and Leadership: A Qualitative and Quantitative Review," *Journal of Applied Psychology* 87(4) (2002): 765–768.

17. M. W. Morgan and M.M. Lombardo, *Off the Track: Why and How Successful Executives Get Derailed* (Greensboro, NC: Center for Creative Leadership, January 1988), Technical Report Nos. 21 & 34.

18. Staff, "Follow My Lead," *Entrepreneur* (September 2013): 8.

19. M. Rosenwald, "The Origin of C-Suites," *BusinessWeek* (January 24–30, 2011): 116–117.

20. J. B. Kahnweiler, "Why Introverts Can Make the Best Leaders," *Forbes* (December 28, 2009): 8.

21. B. L. Blume, T.T. Baldwin, and K.C. Ryan, "Communication Apprehension: A Barrier to Students' Leadership, Adaptability, and Multicultural Appreciation," *Academy of Management Learning & Education* 12(2) (2013): 158–172.

22. M. R. Barrick, M.K. Mount, and N. Li, "The Theory of Purposeful Work Behavior: The Role of Personality, Higher-Order Goals, and Job Characteristics," *Academy of Management Review* 38(1) (2013): 132–153.

23. C. Bendersky and N.P. Shah, "The Downfall of Extraverts and Rise of Neurotics: The Dynamic Process of Status Allocation in Task Groups," *Academy of Management Journal* 56(2) (2013): 387–406.

24. C. Bendersky and N.P. Shah, "The Downfall of Extraverts and Rise of Neurotics: The Dynamic Process of Status Allocation in Task Groups," *Academy of Management Journal* 56(2) (2013): 387–406.

25. G. Colvin, "Ignore These Leadership Lessons at Your Peril," *Fortune* (October 28, 2013): 85.

26. T.T. Baldwin, J.R. Pierce, R.C. Jones, and S. Farouk, "The Elusiveness of Applied Management Knowledge: A Critical Challenge for Management Education," *Academy of Management Learning & Education* 10(4) (2011): 583–605.

27. M. Korn, "Business Schools Know How You Think, but How Do You Feel?" *Wall Street Journal* (May 2, 2013): B1.

28. R. E. Boytzis and D. Goleman, *The Emotional Competence Inventory* (Boston: Hay Group, 2001).

29. G. Toegel, M. Kilduff, and N. Anand, "Emotion Helping by Managers: An Emergent Understanding of Discrepant Role Expectations and Outcomes," *Academy of Management Journal* 56(2) (2013): 334–357.

30. C. Bendersky and N.P. Shah, "The Downfall of Extraverts and Rise of Neurotics: The Dynamic Process of Status Allocation in Task Groups," *Academy of Management Journal* 56(2) (2013): 387–406.

31. B. P. Owens and D.R. Hekman, "Modeling How to Grow: An Inductive Examination of Humble Leader Behaviors, Contingencies, and Outcomes," *Academy of Management Journal* 55(4) (2012): 787–818.

32. G. Yukl, "Effective Leadership Behavior: What We Know and What Questions Need More Attention," *Academy of Management Perspectives* 26(4) (2011): 66–85.

33. R. Hurley, "Trust Me," *Wall Street Journal* (October 24, 2011): R4.

34. G. Colvin, "Ignore These Leadership Lessons at Your Peril," *Fortune* (October 28, 2013): 85.

35. G. Yukl, "Effective Leadership Behavior: What We Know and What Questions Need More Attention," *Academy of Management Perspectives* 26(4) (2011): 66–85.

36. R. Karlgaard, "Scary Smart: The Next Trillion-Dollar Industry," *Forbes* (October 25, 2010): 26.

37. T. T. Baldwin, J.R. Pierce, R.C. Jones, and S. Farouk, "The Elusiveness of Applied Management Knowledge: A Critical Challenge for Management Education," *Academy of Management Learning & Education* 10(4) (2011): 583–605.

38. C. Dunn, B. Kowitt, C. Leahey, and A. Vandermey, "The 50 Most Powerful Women," *Fortune* (October 2013): 133–140.

39. D. McClelland, *The Achieving Society* (New York: Van Nostrand Reinhold, 1961); and D. McClelland and D. H. Burnham, "Power Is the Great Motivator," *Harvard Business Review* (March/April 1978): 103.

40. D. C. McClelland and R. E. Boyatzis, "Leadership Motive Pattern and Long-Term Success in Management," *Journal of Applied Psychology* 6(1982): 737–743.

41. C. Bendersky and N.P. Shah, "The Downfall of Extraverts and Rise of Neurotics: The Dynamic Process of Status Allocation in Task Groups," *Academy of Management Journal* 56(2) (2013): 387–406.

42. D. C. McClelland, *Human Motivation* (Glenview, IL: Scott Foresman, 1985).

43. G. Toegel, M. Kilduff, and N. Anand, "Emotion Helping by Managers: An Emergent Understanding of Discrepant Role Expectations and Outcomes," *Academy of Management Journal* 56(2) (2013): 334–357.

44. S. S. Wiltermuth and F.J. Flynn, "Power, Moral Clarity, and Punishment in the Workplace," *Academy of Management Journal* 56(4) (2013): 1002–1023.

45. D. M. Mayer, K. Aquino, R.L. Greenbaum, and M. Kuenzi, "Who Displays Ethical Leadership, and Why an Examination of Antecedents and Consequences of Ethical Leadership," *Academy of Management Journal* 55(1) (2012): 151–171.

46. D. McGregor, *Leadership and Motivation* (Cambridge, MA: MIT Press, 1966).

47. Mind Tools Web site "Comparing Theory X and Theory Y" (www.mindtools.com), accessed November 27, 2013.

48. N. Rothbard, "Put on a Happy Face, Seriously," *Wall Street Journal* (October 24, 2011): R2.

49 S. Waddock and J.M. Lozano, "Developing More Holistic Management Education: Lessons Learned from Two Programs," *Academy of Management Education & Learning* 12(2) (2013): 265–284.

50 M. Pitesa and S. Thau, "Compliant Sinners, Obstinate Saints: How Power and Self-Focus Determine the Effectiveness of Social Influences in Ethical Decisions Making," *Academy of Management Journal* 56(3) (2013): 635–658.

51 A. Simha and J.B. Cullen, "Ethical Climates and Their Effects on Organizational Outcomes: Implications from the Past and Prophecies for the Future," *Academy of Management Perspectives* 26(4) (2012): 20–34.

52 A. W. Martin, S.H. Lopez, V.J. Roscigno, and R. Hodson, "Against the Rules: Synthesizing Types and Processes of Bureaucratic Rule-Breaking," *Academy of Management Review* 38(4) (2013): 550–574.

53 R.A. Giacalone and M.D. Promislo, "Broken When Entering: The Stigmatization of Goodness and Business Ethics Education," *Academy of Management Learning & Education* 12(1) (2012): 86–101.

54 M. Crossan, D. Mazutis, G. Seijts, and J. Gandz, "Developing Leadership Character in Business Programs," *Academy of Management Learning & Education* 12(2) (2013): 285–305.

55 N. M. Pless, T. Moak, and D.A. Waldman, "Different Approaches toward Doing the Right Thing: Mapping the Responsibility Orientations of Leaders," *Academy of Management Perspectives* 26(4) (2012): 51–65.

56 AACSB Web site (http://www.aacsb.edu/accreditation/business/standards/2013/learning-and-teaching/standard9.asp), accessed October 24, 2013.

57 J. K. Nelson, L.W. Poms, and P.P. Wolf, "Developing Efficacy Beliefs for Ethics and Diversity Management," *Academy of Management Learning & Education* 11(1) (2012): 49–68.

58 M. Crossan, D. Mazutis, G. Seijts, and J. Gandz, "Developing Leadership Character in Business Programs," *Academy of Management Learning & Education* 12(2) (2013): 285–305.

59 D. M. Mayer, K. Aquino, R.L. Greenbaum, and M. Kuenzi, "Who Displays Ethical Leadership, and Why an Examination of Antecedents and Consequences of Ethical Leadership," *Academy of Management Journal* 55(1) (2012): 151–171.

60 B. C. Gunia, L. Wang, L. Huang, J. Wang, and J.K. Murnighan, "Contemplation and Conversation: Subtle Influences on Moral Decision Making," *Academy of Management Journal* 55(1) (2012): 13–33.

61 K. Leavitt, S.J. Reynolds, C.M. Barnes, P. Schilpzand, and S.T. Hannah, "Different Hats, Different Obligations: Plural Occupational Identities and Situated Moral Judgments," *Academy of Management Journal* 55(6) (2012): 1316–1333.

62 R. Murphree, "Visionary Leader: Gospel Is Key to Unlimited Success," *AFA Journal* (March 2013): 11.

63 C. Bonanos, "The Lies We Tell at Work," *BusinessWeek* (February 4–10, 2013): 71–73.

64 P. Zak, *The Moral Molecule* (New York: Penguin, 2012).

65 C. Downs, "Liar, Liar—Back's on Fire," *AARP Magazine* (October/November 2012): 22.

66 S.S. Wiltermuth and F.J. Flynn, "Power, Moral Clarity, and Punishment in the Workplace," *Academy of Management Journal* 56(4) (2013): 1002–1023.

67 F. Farley, "What's a Hero?" *Entrepreneur* (December 2013): 64.

68 J. A. Colquitt, J.A. Lepine, C.P. Zapata, and R.E. Wild, "Trust in Typical and High-Reliability Contexts: Building and Reacting to Trust among Firefighters," *Academy of Management Journal* 54(5) (2011): 999–1015.

69 G. Yukl, "Effective Leadership Behavior: What We Know and What Questions Need More Attention," *Academy of Management Perspectives* 26(4) (2011): 66–85.

70 B. C. Gunia, L. Wang, L. Huang, J. Wang, and J.K. Murnighan, "Contemplation and Conversation: Subtle Influences on Moral Decision Making," *Academy of Management Journal* 55(1) (2012): 13–33.

71 D. Ariely, "Why We Lie," *Wall Street Journal* (May 26–27, 2012): C1–C2.

72 D. Ariely, "Why We Lie," *Wall Street Journal* (May 26–27, 2012): C1–C2.

73 S. D. Levitt and S.J. Dubner, Super Freakonomics: Global cooling, patriotic prostitutes, and why suicide bombers should buy life insurance. *Academy of Management Perspectives* 25(2) (2011): 86–87.

74 M. Pitesa and S. Thau, "Compliant Sinners, Obstinate Saints: How Power and Self-Focus Determine the Effectiveness of Social Influences in Ethical Decisions Making," *Academy of Management Journal* 56(3) (2013): 635–658.

75 D. Ariely, "Why We Lie," *Wall Street Journal* (May 26–27, 2012): C1–C2.

76 S. Kolhathar, "The Man, the Myth, the Wolf," *BusinessWeek* (November 11–17, 2013): 72–76.

77 M. Crossan, D. Mazutis, G. Seijts, and J. Gandz, "Developing Leadership Character in Business Programs," *Academy of Management Learning & Education* 12(2) (2013): 285–305.

78 S. S. Wiltermuth and F.J. Flynn, "Power, Moral Clarity, and Punishment in the Workplace," *Academy of Management Journal* 56(4) (2013): 1002–1023.

79 D. M. Mayer, K. Aquino, R.L. Greenbaum, and M. Kuenzi, "Who Displays Ethical Leadership, and Why an Examination of Antecedents and Consequences of Ethical Leadership," *Academy of Management Journal* 55(1) (2012): 151–171.

80 K. Leavitt, S.J. Reynolds, C.M. Barnes, P. Schilpzand, and S.T. Hannah, "Different Hats, Different Obligations: Plural Occupational Identities and Situated Moral Judgments," *Academy of Management Journal* 55(6) (2012): 1316–1333.

81 R. L. Dufresne and E.H. Offstein, "Holistic and Intentional Student Character Development Process: Learning from West Point," *Academy of Management Learning & Education* 11(4) (2012): 570–590.

82 M. Pitesa and S. Thau, "Compliant Sinners, Obstinate Saints: How Power and Self-Focus Determine the Effectiveness of Social Influences in Ethical Decisions Making," *Academy of Management Journal* 56(3) (2013): 635–658.

83 M. Pitesa and S. Thau, "Compliant Sinners, Obstinate Saints: How Power and Self-Focus Determine the Effectiveness of Social Influences in Ethical Decisions Making," *Academy of Management Journal* 56(3) (2013): 635–658.

84 J. M. Schaubroeck, "Embedding Ethical Leadership within and across Organizational Levels," *Academy of Management Journal* 55(5) (2012): 1053–1078.

85 R. Sutton, "How a Few Bad Apples Ruin Everything," *Wall Street Journal* (October 24, 2011): R5.

86 D. Ariely, "Why We Lie," *Wall Street Journal* (May 26–27, 2012): C1–C2.

87 D. Akst, "Ethics' Afternoon Swoon," *Wall Street Journal* (November 9–10, 2013): C4.

88 Information taken from the DuPont Web site November 21, 2013.

89 M. Pitesa and S. Thau, "Compliant Sinners, Obstinate Saints: How Power and Self-Focus Determine the Effectiveness of Social Influences in Ethical Decisions Making," *Academy of Management Journal* 56(3) (2013): 635–658.

90 B.C. Gunia, L. Wang, L. Huang, J. Wang, and J.K. Murnighan, "Contemplation and Conversation: Subtle Influences on Moral Decision Making," *Academy of Management Journal* 55(1) (2012): 13–33.

91 D. Ariely, "Why We Lie," *Wall Street Journal* (May 26–27, 2012): C1–C2.

92 K. Leavitt, S.J. Reynolds, C.M. Barnes, P. Schilpzand, and S.T. Hannah, "Different Hats, Different Obligations: Plural Occupational Identities and Situated Moral Judgments," *Academy of Management Journal* 55(6) (2012): 1316–1333.

93 D. Ariely, "Why We Lie," *Wall Street Journal* (May 26–27, 2012): C1–C2.

94 C. Bonanos, "The Lies We Tell at Work," *BusinessWeek* (February 4–10, 2013): 71–73.

95 C. Bonanos, "The Lies We Tell at Work," *BusinessWeek* (February 4–10, 2013): 71–73.

96 D. Ariely, "Why We Lie," *Wall Street Journal* (May 26–27, 2012): C1–C2.

97 C. Bonanos, "The Lies We Tell at Work," *BusinessWeek* (February 4–10, 2013): 71–73.

98 D. Ariely, "Why We Lie," *Wall Street Journal* (May 26–27, 2012): C1–C2.

99 C. Bonanos, "The Lies We Tell at Work," *BusinessWeek* (February 4–10, 2013): 71–73.

100 C. Bonanos, "The Lies We Tell at Work," *BusinessWeek* (February 4–10, 2013): 71–73.

101 B. C. Gunia, L. Wang, L. Huang, J. Wang, and J.K. Murnighan, "Contemplation and Conversation: Subtle Influences on Moral Decision Making," *Academy of Management Journal* 55(1) (2012): 13–33.

102 B. C. Gunia, L. Wang, L. Huang, J. Wang, and J.K. Murnighan, "Contemplation and Conversation: Subtle Influences on Moral Decision Making," *Academy of Management Journal* 55(1) (2012): 13–33.

103 S. Hagar, "The Sammy Hagar School of Business," *Inc.* (November 2013): 102.

104 A. Beiler, "My Advice," *Fortune* (July 22, 2013): 24.

105 S. S. Wiltermuth and F.J. Flynn, "Power, Moral Clarity, and Punishment in the Workplace," *Academy of Management Journal* 56(4) (2013): 1002–1023.

106 K. Leavitt, S.J. Reynolds, C.M. Barnes, P. Schilpzand, and S.T. Hannah, "Different Hats, Different Obligations: Plural Occupational Identities and Situated Moral Judgments," *Academy of Management Journal* 55(6) (2012): 1316–1333.

107 B. C. Gunia, L. Wang, L. Huang, J. Wang, and J.K. Murnighan, "Contemplation and Conversation: Subtle Influences on Moral Decision Making," *Academy of Management Journal* 55(1) (2012): 13–33.

108 J. M. Schaubroeck, "Embedding Ethical Leadership within and across Organizational Levels," *Academy of Management Journal* 55(5) (2012): 1053–1078.

109 B. Mycoskie, *Start Something That Matters* (New York: Spiegel & Grau, 2012).

110 TOMS Web site (www.TOMS.com), accessed December 5, 2013.

111 B. Mycoskie, *Start Something That Matters* (New York: Spiegel & Grau, 2012).

112 TOMS Web site (www.TOMS.com), accessed December 5, 2013.

113 For more information on Zig Ziglar training, go to his Web site (www.ziglar.com).

CHAPTER

3

Leadership Behavior and Motivation

Learning Outcomes

After studying this chapter, you should be able to:

1 List the University of Iowa leadership styles. p. 70

2 Describe similarities and differences between the University of Michigan and Ohio State University leadership models. p. 72

3 Discuss similarities and differences between the Ohio State University Leadership Model and the Leadership Grid. p. 75

4 Discuss similarities and differences among the three content motivation theories. p. 80

5 Discuss the major similarities and differences among the three process motivation theories. p. 87

6 Explain the four types of reinforcement. p. 93

7 State the major differences among content, process, and reinforcement theories. p. 98

OPENING CASE *Application*

Trader Joe's

Trader Joe's mission is to bring you the best-quality products at the best prices. It's not complicated; it just focuses on what matters—great food + great prices = Value. Joe Coulombe named the store Trader Joe's to evoke images of the South Seas. As part of its unique culture, employees wear Hawaiian shirts because they're traders on the culinary seas, searching the world over for cool items to bring home to its customers. They sail those seven seas, so customers can have some fun with its finds at their neighborhood Trader Joe's.

Joe Coulombe opened the first Trader Joe's over 40 years ago in Pasadena, California, with a quirky in-store culture with a different business model to make shopping at Trader Joe's different from what people were used to in a supermarket—it's an adventure. It's an offbeat, fun discovery zone that elevates food shopping from being a chore to a cultural experience. Trader Joe's stocks its shelves with a winning combination of low-cost, yuppie-friendly staples and exotic affordable luxuries.

Although Joe moved on, Joe's fingerprints are still all over the company that bears his name, from the business model, robust selection of products, and culture to the Hawaiian-print shirts that employees wear. Trader Joe's is family-owned, not having any publicly owned stock. The current CEO Dan Bane runs the company with around 20,000 employees in 400 stores. [1]

OPENING CASE QUESTIONS:

1. **Which Ohio State University, University of Michigan, and Leadership Grid leadership style is emphasized at Trader Joe's?**

2. **What does Trader Joe's do to motivate its employees, and how does it affect performance?**

3. **(a–c). How does Trader Joe's meet its employees' content motivation needs?**

4. **(a–c). How does Trader Joe's meet its employees' process motivation needs?**

5. **How does Trader Joe's use reinforcement theory to motivate its employees?**

Can you answer any of these questions? You'll find answers to these questions and learn more about Trader Joe's and its leadership throughout the chapter.

To learn more about Trader Joe's, visit the company's Web site at **http://www.traderjoes.com**.

In this chapter, we discuss two related topics: leadership behavior and motivation. The goal of behavioral scientists is to explain why people do what they do at work.[2] Much of the leadership research has focused on behavior.[3] Research findings include that behavior of leaders affects follower performance,[4] and that leaders need to use behaviors that promote, develop, and maintain team performance.[5] The fundamental task for leaders is to motivate followers.[6] Thus, leader behavior is used to motivate followers.[7] In this chapter, we discuss four behavioral leadership models and seven motivation theories.

Leadership Behavior and Styles

In this section, we discuss leadership behavior and the University of Iowa leadership styles.

Leadership Behavior

By the late 1940s, most of the leadership research had shifted from the trait theory paradigm (Chapters 2 and 3) to the behavioral theory paradigm, which focuses on what the leader says and does. In the continuing quest to find the one best leadership style in all situations, researchers attempted to identify the differences in the behavior of effective leaders versus ineffective leaders. Although the behavioral leadership theory made major contributions to leadership research, it never achieved its goal of finding one best style. However, today research continues to seek a better understanding of behavior in the workplace.[8]

Leadership Behavior Is Based on Traits

Although the behavioral theorists focus on behavior, it's important to realize that leaders' behavior is based on their traits and skills. The manager's leadership personality traits and attitudes directly affect his or her behavior and relationship with employees.[9] Recall that the Pygmalion effect is based on traits, attitude expectations, and the manager's behavioral treatment of employees, which in turn determines the followers' behavior and performance.

Leading by example is important to managers, and it takes place as followers observe the leader's behavior and copy it. And the leader's behavior is based on his or her traits. However, behavior is easier to learn and change than traits. We need to select relevant behaviors to influence follower behavior and performance.[10]

> **Learning Outcome** (1)
>
> *List the University of Iowa leadership styles.*

Leadership Styles and the University of Iowa Research

Leadership style *is the combination of traits, skills, and behaviors leaders use as they interact with followers.* Although a leadership style is based on traits and skills, the important component is the behavior, because it is a relatively consistent pattern of behavior that characterizes a leader.

University of Iowa Leadership Styles

WORK
Application **3-1**

Recall a present or past manager. Which of the University of Iowa leadership styles does or did your manager use most often? Describe the behavior of your manager.

In the 1930s, before behavioral theory became popular, Kurt Lewin and associates conducted studies at the University of Iowa that concentrated on the leadership style of the manager.[11] Their studies identified two basic leadership styles:

- *Autocratic leadership style.* The autocratic leader makes the decisions, tells employees what to do, and closely supervises workers.
- *Democratic leadership style.* The democratic leader encourages participation in decisions, works with employees to determine what to do, and does not closely supervise employees.

The autocratic and democratic leadership styles are often placed at opposite ends of a continuum, as shown in Exhibit 3.1; thus a leader's style usually falls somewhere between the two styles. The Iowa studies contributed to the behavioral movement and led to an era of behavioral, rather than trait, research. It started a taxonomy, or classification, of leadership behavior still used today.[12]

EXHIBIT 3.1

University of Iowa Leadership Styles

Autocratic-------------------------------Democratic

Source: Adapted from K. Lewin, R. Lippett, and R. K. White. 1939. "Patterns of Aggressive Behavior in Experimentally Created Social Climates." Journal of Social Psychology 10:271–301.

University of Michigan and Ohio State University Studies

Leadership research was conducted at Ohio State and the University of Michigan at about the same time during the mid-1940s to mid-1950s. These studies were not based on prior autocratic and democratic leadership styles but rather sought to determine the behavior of effective leaders. In this section, we discuss leadership styles identified by these two universities. Before reading about these studies, complete Self-Assessment 3-1 to determine your behavioral leadership style.

SELF-ASSESSMENT 3-1   Your Behavioral Leadership Style

For each of the following statements, select one of the following:

1– "I **would not** tend to do this."
0– "I **would** tend to do this."

as a manager of a work unit. There are no right or wrong answers, so don't try to select correctly.

1. _____ I (would or would not) let my employees know that they should not be doing things during work hours that are not directly related to getting their jobs done.

2. _____ I (would or would not) spend time talking to my employees to get to know them personally during work hours.

3. _____ I (would or would not) have a clearly written agenda of things to accomplish during department meetings.

4. _____ I (would or would not) allow employees to come in late or leave early to take care of personal issues.

5. _____ I (would or would not) set clear goals so employees know what needs to be done.

6. _____ I (would or would not) get involved with employee conflicts to help resolve them.

7. _____ I (would or would not) spend much of my time directing employees to ensure that they meet department goals.

8. _____ I (would or would not) encourage employees to solve problems related to their work without having to get my permission to do so.

9. _____ I (would or would not) make sure that employees do their work according to the standard method to be sure it is done correctly.

10. _____ I (would or would not) seek the advice of my employees when making decisions.

11. _____ I (would or would not) keep good, frequent records of my department's productivity and let employees know how they are doing.

12. _____ I (would or would not) work to develop trust between my employees and me, and among the department members.

13. _____ I (would or would not) be quick to take corrective action with employees who are not meeting the standards or goals.

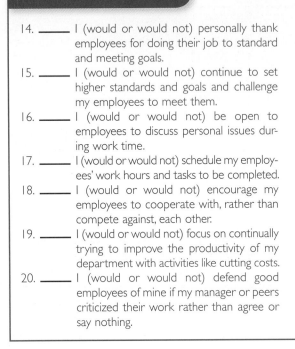

Learning Outcome 2   *Describe similarities and differences between the University of Michigan and Ohio State University leadership models.*

University of Michigan: Job-Centered and Employee-Centered Behavior

The University of Michigan's Survey Research Center, under the principal direction of Rensis Likert, conducted studies to determine how leaders functioned in small groups. Researchers created a questionnaire called the *Survey of Organizations* and conducted interviews to gather data on leadership styles. They gave the survey, similar to the one in Self-Assessment 3-1, to employees to complete based on their managers behavior. You can give Self-Assessment 3-1 to others to determine if they perceive your leadership style the same as you assessed it.

The researchers' goals were to (1) classify the leaders as effective and ineffective by comparing the behavior of leaders from high-producing units and low-producing units and (2) determine reasons for effective leadership.[13] The researchers identified two styles of leadership behavior, which they called *job-centered* and *employee-centered*. The University of Michigan model stated that a leader is either more job-centered or more employee-centered. *The* **University of Michigan Leadership Model** *thus identifies two leadership styles: job-centered and employee-centered.* See Exhibit 3.2 for the University of Michigan Leadership Model: It is a one-dimensional continuum between two leadership styles.

EXHIBIT 3.2

The University of Michigan Leadership Model: Two

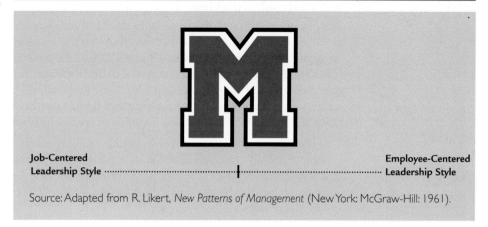

Job-Centered
Leadership Style ⋯⋯⋯⋯⋯⋯⋯⋯⋯⋯⋯⋯⋯⋯⋯⋯⋯⋯ Employee-Centered
Leadership Style

Source: Adapted from R. Likert, *New Patterns of Management* (New York: McGraw-Hill: 1961).

- *Job-Centered Leadership Style.* The job-centered style has scales measuring two job-oriented behaviors of goal emphasis and work facilitation. Job-centered behavior refers to the extent to which the leader takes charge to get the job done. The leader closely directs subordinates with clear roles and goals, whereas the manager tells them what to do and how to do. Review the odd-numbered items in Self-Assessment 3-1 for examples of job-(task-)oriented leadership behavior.
- *Employee-Centered Leadership Style.* The employee-centered style has scales measuring two employee-oriented behaviors of supportive leadership and interaction facilitation. Employee-centered behavior refers to the extent to which the leader focuses on meeting the human needs of employees while developing relationships. The leader is sensitive to subordinates and communicates to develop trust, support, and respect while looking out for their welfare. Review the even-numbered items in Self-Assessment 3-1 for examples of employee-(people-)oriented leadership behavior.

Based on Self-Assessment 3-1, is your leadership style more job-(task-) or employee (people-)centered?

CONCEPT APPLICATION 3-1

University of Michigan Leadership Styles

Identify each of these five behaviors by its leadership style. Write the appropriate letter in the blank before each item.

a. job-centered   b. employee-centered

_____   1. A manager is motivating employees to meet a difficult deadline.

_____   2. A manager is giving detailed instructions to the follower to ensure the job is done right.

_____   3. A manager is quietly observing employees as they do their jobs.

_____   4. A manager is praising an employee for a job well done.

_____   5. A manager is in the office developing the employee work schedule for next week.

Ohio State University: Initiating Structure and Consideration Behavior

The Personnel Research Board of Ohio State University, under the principal direction of Ralph Stogdill, began a study to determine effective leadership styles. These researchers developed an instrument known as the *Leader Behavior Description Questionnaire (LBDQ)*. The LBDQ had 150 examples of definitive leader behaviors, which were narrowed down from 1,800 leadership functions. Respondents to the questionnaire perceived their manager's behavior toward them on two distinct dimensions or leadership types, which they eventually called *initiating structure* and *consideration:*[14]

- *Initiating structure behavior.* The initiating structure leadership style is essentially the same as the job-centered leadership style; it focuses on getting the task done.
- *Consideration behavior.* The consideration leadership style is essentially the same as the employee-centered leadership style; it focuses on meeting people's needs and developing relationships.

WORK
Application **3-2**

Recall a present or past manager. Which of the four Ohio State leadership styles does or did your manager use most often? Describe the behavior of your manager.

Because a leader can be high or low on initiating structure and/or consideration, four leadership styles are developed. *The* **Ohio State University Leadership Model** *identifies four leadership styles: low structure and high consideration, high structure and high consideration, low structure and low consideration, and high structure and low consideration.* Exhibit 3.3 illustrates the four leadership styles and their two dimensions.

Leaders with high structure and low consideration behavior use one-way communications, and decisions are made by the managers, whereas leaders with high consideration and low structure use two-way communications and tend to share decision making. To determine your two-dimensional leadership style from Self-Assessment 3-1, put your two separate ("task" and "people") scores together and determine which of the four styles in Exhibit 3.3 is the closest match.

The Ohio State University Leadership Model: Four Leadership Styles, Two Dimensions

EXHIBIT 3.3

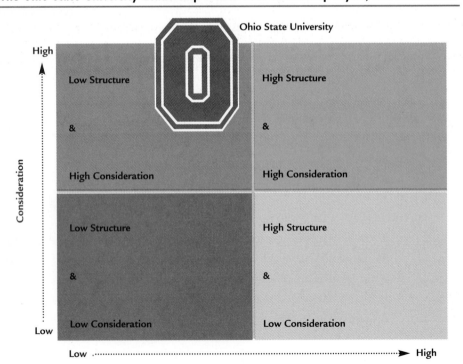

Source: Adapted from R. Likert, *New Patterns of Management.* (New York: McGraw-Hill: 1961).

Differences, Contributions, and Applications of Leadership Models

Differences between the Models

The Ohio State and University of Michigan leadership models are different in that the University of Michigan places the two leadership behaviors at opposite ends of the same continuum, making it one-dimensional. The Ohio State University model considers the two behaviors independent of one another, making it two-dimensional; thus this model has four leadership styles.

Contributions of the Models

There is no one best leadership style in all situations; this is the first contribution to leadership theory, because it has helped lead researchers to the next paradigm—that of contingency leadership theory (the topic of Chapter 4). Thus, the contribution of the behavioral leadership paradigm was to identify two generic dimensions of leadership behavior that continue to have importance in accounting for leader effectiveness today.

Prior to the two university leadership studies, many organizations had focused on getting the job done with little, if any, concern for meeting employee needs. So there was a shift to place more emphasis on the human side of the organization to increase productivity; this is a second contribution. The saying that a happy worker is a productive worker comes from this period of research, and still has research support today.[15]

Another important research finding was that most leadership functions can be carried out by someone besides the designated leader of a group. Thus, more organizations began training managers to use participative leadership styles. Thus, as a third contribution of these leadership models, Likert has been credited as being the first to identify the participative leadership style that is commonly used today.

Applications of the Models

The two models don't tell the leader how to behave, but they do provide a classification system reminding us that our behavior affects others through the "task" we perform as well as the "relationships" we develop. Many leadership development programs are structured along the behavioral styles approach, and almost all give managers a questionnaire that in some way assesses their task and relationship behavior toward followers. Managers use the assessment to improve their overall leadership style.

The behavioral styles approach is easily applied to leadership by assessing our behavioral style. Through our ongoing self-assessment, we can determine how we are coming across to others and how we could change our behavior to be more effective in performing our task and in developing our relations.

The Leadership Grid

In this section, we discuss the Leadership Grid theory, including research and contributions of the high-concern-for-people and high-concern-for-production (team leader) leadership styles.

Learning Outcome 3 *Discuss similarities and differences between the Ohio State University Leadership Model and the Leadership Grid.*

Leadership Grid Theory

Robert Blake and Jane Mouton, from the University of Texas, developed the Managerial Grid® and published it in 1964, updated it in 1978 and 1985, and in 1991 it became the Leadership Grid® with Anne Adams McCanse replacing Mouton, who died in 1987. Blake and Mouton published numerous articles and around 40 books describing their theories.[16]

The Leadership Grid builds on the Ohio State and Michigan studies; it is based on the same two leadership dimensions, which Blake and Mouton called *concern for production* and *concern for people*. The concern for both people and production is measured through a questionnaire on a scale from 1 to 9. Therefore, the grid has 81 possible combinations of concern for production and people. However, *the* **Leadership Grid** *identifies five leadership styles: 1,1 impoverished; 9,1 authority compliance; 1,9 country club; 5,5 middle of the road; and 9,9 team leader.* See Exhibit 3.4 for an adaptation of the Leadership Grid.

Following are descriptions of leadership styles in the Leadership Grid:

- The *impoverished leader* (1,1) has low concern for both production and people. The leader does the minimum required to remain employed in the position.
- The *authority-compliance leader* (9,1) has a high concern for production and a low concern for people. The leader focuses on getting the job done while people are treated like machines.
- The *country-club leader* (1,9) has a high concern for people and a low concern for production. The leader strives to maintain a friendly atmosphere without regard for production.
- The *middle-of-the-road leader* (5,5) has balanced, medium concern for both production and people. The leader strives to maintain satisfactory performance and morale.
- The *team leader* (9,9) has a high concern for both production and people. This leader strives for maximum performance and employee satisfaction. According to Blake, Mouton, and McCanse, the team leadership style is generally the most appropriate for use in all situations.

To estimate your Leadership Grid leadership style, using Self-Assessment 3-1, use your task score as your concern for production and your people score, and

WORK
Application **3-3**

Recall a present or past manager. Which of the five Leadership Grid styles does or did your manager use most often? Describe the behavior of your manager.

<EXHIBIT   3.4

Blake, Mouton, and McCanse Leadership Grid

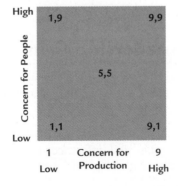

Source: Adapted from Robert R. Blake and Jane S. Mouton, The Managerial Grid III (Houston: Gulf, 1985); and Robert R. Blake and Anna Adams McCanse, Leadership Dilemmas-Grid Solutions (Houston: Gulf, 1991), 29.

OPENING CASE Application

1. Which Ohio State University and Leadership Grid leadership style is emphasized at Trader Joe's?

Trader Joe's emphasizes the Ohio State University high structure and high consideration style, which is called the Leadership Grid team leader's high concern for people and high concern for production (9,9) leadership style. Trader Joe's treats its employees well but at the same time stresses high levels of performance. We will provide more detail with the answers to the other case application answers.

CONCEPT APPLICATION 3-2

The Leadership Grid

Identify the five statements by their leader's style. Write the appropriate letter in the blank before each item.

a. 1,1 (impoverished)   c. 9,1 (authority compliance)   e. 9,9 (team)
b. 1,9 (country club)   d. 5,5 (middle of the road)

_____ 6. A group has an average productivity level compared to the other departments in the company.

_____ 7. A group dislikes its leader and has one of the lowest levels of morale in the company, but it is a top performer.

_____ 8. A group has a leader that doesn't seem to care about the employees or how much work gets done.

_____ 9. A group has a leader that is very supportive of the employees, while also exceeding expectations as a top performer.

_____ 10. A group has very high morale but the department is one of the lowest performers in the company.

plot them on the Leadership Grid in Exhibit 3.4. Then select the closest of the five leadership styles.

Leadership Grid and High-High Leader Research

The *high-high leader* has concern for both production and people; this is the *team* leadership style. Blake and Mouton did conduct an extensive empirical research study that measured profitability before and after a ten-year period. In the study, one company subsidiary used an extensive Grid Organizational Development program designed to teach managers how to be 9,9 team leaders (experimental group), whereas another subsidiary did not use the program (control group). The subsidiary using the team leadership style increased its profits four times more than the control subsidiary. Thus, the researchers claimed that team leadership usually results in improved performance, low absenteeism and turnover, and high employee satisfaction.

However, another researcher disagreed with these findings, calling high-high leadership a myth. A more objective meta-analysis (a study combining the results of many prior studies) found that although task and relationship behavior tends to correlate positively with subordinate performance, the correlation is usually weak.[17] In conclusion, although there is some support for the universal theory, the high-high leadership style is not accepted as the one best style in all situations.

Behavioral Theory Contributions and Applications

Critics of behavioral theories suggested that different leadership styles are more effective in different situations. Thus, a contribution of behavioral research is that it led to the shift in paradigm to contingency leadership theory. As you will learn in Chapter 4, contingency leadership theory is based on the behavioral theory of production and people leadership styles. Situational leadership models don't agree with using the same leadership style in all situations but rather prescribe using the existing behavioral leadership style that best meets the situation.

A second contribution of behavioral leadership theory was the recognition that organizations need both production and people leadership. A generic set of production-oriented and people-oriented leadership functions must be performed to ensure effective organizational performance.

A third related contribution of behavioral leadership theory supports coleadership. The manager does not have to perform both production and people functions. Thus, strong production-oriented leaders can be successful if they have coleaders to provide the people-oriented functions for them, and vice versa. So, if you tend to be more production- or people-oriented, seek coleaders to complement your weaker area.

Before we go on to motivation, let's tie personality traits from Chapter 2 together with what we've covered so far. Complete Self-Assessment 3-2 now.

SELF-ASSESSMENT 3-2   **Your Personality Traits and Leadership Styles**

We stated in the first section that *traits affect leadership behavior*. How does this relate to you? For the University of Michigan Leadership Model, generally, if you had a high personality score for the Big Five surgency dimension in Self-Assessment 2-1 in Chapter 2 (dominance trait, high need for power), you most likely have a high score for the task (job-centered) leadership style. If you had a high score for agreeableness (sensitivity to others trait, high need for affiliation), you most likely have a high score for the people (employee-centered) leadership style. My U of M leadership style is primarily _____

For the Leadership Grid, you need to score your personality for surgency and agreeableness on a scale of 1 to 9. Then you combine them on the grid, and these personality scores should generally provide about the same score as Self-Assessment 3-1. My Leadership Grid style is primarily _____

For the Ohio State University Leadership Model, you need to score your personality for surgency and agreeableness as high or low. Then you combine them, and these personality scores should generally provide the same two-dimensional behaviors corresponding to one of the four leadership styles. My OSU leadership style is primarily _____

If you scored a Leader Motive Profile, your score for tasks should generally be higher than your score for people, because you have a greater need for power than affiliation. However, your leadership style on the Ohio State model could be high structure and high consideration, because this implies socialized power. You could also have a 9,9 team leader score on the Leadership Grid. My LMP is primarily _____

Leadership and Major Motivation Theories

In this section, we discuss motivation and leadership, the motivation process (which explains how motivation affects behavior), and three classifications of motivation theories (content, process, and reinforcement).

Motivation and Leadership

Leadership success requires motivating followers,[18] and leadership behavior is used to motivate followers.[19] **Motivation** *is anything that affects behavior in pursuing a certain outcome.* Outcomes in business are usually organizational goals or objectives, and it takes motivation to reach our goals.[20] So you have to know how to motivate yourself,[21] and you have to be able to motivate others.[22] To be truly successful, you have to get people to do more than the minimum required.[23]

So what motivates us?[24] We tend to seek job satisfaction as we satisfy our self-interest.[25] So, if we want to motivate others, we should answer their often-unasked question, "What's in it for me?"[26] If we give people what they want, they will in turn tend to give us what we want. But the truly great leaders get followers to go beyond their own self-interest for the good of the team or organization.[27] Unfortunately, it's easier said than done, but you will learn how in the rest of this chapter.

The Motivation Process

The motivation process results from the joint effects of personality traits and task or social job characteristics that explain work behavior.[28] *Through the* **motivation process**, *people go from need to motive to behavior to consequence to satisfaction or dissatisfaction.* For example, you are thirsty (need) and have a drive (motive) to get a drink. You get a drink (behavior) that quenches (consequence and satisfaction) your thirst. However, if you could not get a drink, or a drink of what you really wanted, you would be dissatisfied. Satisfaction is usually short-lived. Getting that drink satisfied you, but sooner or later you will need another drink. For this reason, the motivation process has a feedback loop. See Exhibit 3.5 for an illustration of the motivation process.

The Motivation Process

EXHIBIT 3.5

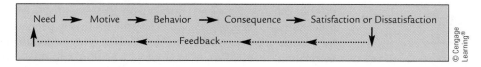

Some need or want motivates all behavior. However, needs and motives are complex: We don't always know what our needs are, or why we do the things we do. Have you ever done something and not known why you did it? Understanding needs will help you better understand motivation and behavior, or you will gain a better understanding of why people do the things they do for their rational self-interest.[29]

Like traits, motives cannot be observed, but you can observe behavior and infer what the person's motive is (*attribution theory*). However, it is not easy to know why people behave the way they do, because people do the same things for different reasons. Also, people often attempt to satisfy several needs at once. Thus, a one-size-fits-all assumption about what motives people doesn't work.[30]

OPENING CASE Application

2. What does Trader Joe's do to motivate its employees, and how does it affect performance?
Trader Joe's primary motivator is creating an innovative fun environment to work in with good pay and benefits. Providing good compensation with above industry average salaries and great benefits to full-time crew members and store management (mates, commanders, captains) allows Trader Joe's to hire highly self-motivated crew members.

Employees are motivated and provide a high-quality customer experience. The results are more than $8 billion in sales with around 400 stores in 30 states. Sales are estimated at $1,750 in merchandise per square foot, more than double Whole Foods. Trader Joe's has no debt and funds all growth from its own profits.[31]

An Overview of Three Major Classifications of Motivation Theories

There is no single, universally accepted theory of how to motivate people, or how to classify the theories. We will discuss motivation theories and how we can use them to motivate ourselves and others. In the following sections, you will learn about content motivation theories, process motivation theories, and reinforcement theory. See Exhibit 3.6 for this classification, which is commonly used, with a listing of major motivation theories you will learn.

After studying all of the theories separately, we can put them back together using the unifying motivation process to see the relationship between the theories. You can select one theory to use, or take from several to make your own theory, or apply the theory that best fits the specific situation.

 Learning Outcome 4 *Discuss similarities and differences among the three content motivation theories.*

Content Motivation Theories

Before we present the content motivation theories, let's discuss content motivation theories in general. **Content motivation theories** *focus on explaining and predicting behavior based on people's needs.* The primary reason people do what they do is to meet their needs or wants—to be satisfied. Thus, it is important to understand needs (content motivation) theory. People want job satisfaction, and they will leave one organization for another to meet this need.[32] The key to successful leadership is to meet the needs of employees while achieving organizational objectives.

Hierarchy of Needs Theory

In the 1940s, Abraham Maslow developed his hierarchy of needs theory, which is based on four major assumptions. (1) Only unmet needs motivate. (2) People's needs are arranged in order of importance (hierarchy) going from basic to complex needs. (3) People will not be motivated to satisfy a higher-level need unless the lower-level need(s) has been at least minimally satisfied. (4) Maslow assumed that people have five classifications of needs, which are presented here in hierarchical order from low to high level of need.[33]

EXHIBIT **3.6**

Major Motivation Theories

CLASSIFICATION OF MOTIVATION THEORIES	SPECIFIC MOTIVATION THEORY
1. Content motivation theories focus on explaining and predicting behavior based on employee need motivation.	A. *Hierarchy of needs theory proposes that employees are motivated through five levels of need—physiological, safety, social, esteem, and self-actualization.* B. *Two-factor theory proposes that employees are motivated by motivators (higher-level needs) rather than maintenance (lower-level needs) factors.* C. *Acquired needs theory proposes that employees are motivated by their need for achievement, power, and affiliation.*
2. Process motivation theories focus on understanding how employees choose behaviors to fulfill their needs.	A. *Equity theory proposes that employees will be motivated when their perceived inputs equal outputs.* B. *Expectancy theory proposes that employees are motivated when they believe they can accomplish the task, they will be rewarded, and the rewards for doing so are worth the effort.* C. *Goal-setting theory proposes that achievable but difficult goals motivate employees.*
3. Reinforcement theory proposes that behavior can be explained, predicted, and controlled through the consequences for behavior.	Types of Reinforcement • Positive • Avoidance • Extinction • Punishment

© Cengage Learning®

Hierarchy of Needs

The **hierarchy of needs theory** *proposes that people are motivated through five levels of needs—physiological, safety, belongingness, esteem, and self-actualization:*

1. *Physiological needs:* These are people's primary or basic needs: air, food, shelter, sex, and relief from or avoidance of pain.
2. *Safety needs:* **Once the physiological needs are met, the individual is concerned with safety and security.**
3. *Belongingness needs:* **After establishing safety, people look for love, friendship, acceptance, and affection. Belongingness is also called** *social needs.*
4. *Esteem needs:* **After the social needs are met, the individual focuses on ego, status, self-respect, recognition for accomplishments, and a feeling of self-confidence and prestige.**
5. *Self-actualization needs:* The highest level of need is to develop one's full potential. To do so, one seeks growth, achievement, and advancement.

Maslow's hierarchy of needs is commonly taught in psychology and business courses, because it offers a very rich theory of human motivation and its determinants at the individual level. However, Maslow's work was criticized because it did not take into consideration that people can be at different levels of needs based on different aspects of their lives. Nor did he mention that people can revert back to lower-level needs. Today, Maslow's followers and others realize that needs are not on a simple five-step hierarchy. Maslow's assumptions have recently been updated to reflect this insight, and many organizations today are using some of the management methods he proposed 30 years ago. Maslow has also been credited with influencing many management authors, including Douglas McGregor, Rensis Likert, and Peter Drucker.

Motivating Employees with Hierarchy of Needs Theory

An important contribution of this theory is that we realize that people have a need for more than just pay. Second, even if we don't have much money to give raises, we can have inexpensive socials, like barbecues, and there is no cost to giving compliments.[34] Also, employees are more motivated when they perceive the organization supports them, which again does not have to be costly.

People want to fulfill higher-level needs,[35] including self-esteem and recognition from peers,[36] so a major recommendation to leaders is to meet employees' lower-level needs so that they will not dominate the employees' motivational process. You should get to know and understand people's needs and meet them as a means of increasing performance. See Exhibit 3.7 for a list of ways in which managers attempt to meet all five needs.

OPENING CASE Application

3-a. How does Trader Joe's meet its employees' content motivation needs?

Trader Joe's allows people to climb the *hierarchy of needs*. As stated in opening case answer to question 2, it pays well with great working conditions (*physiological*), with great benefits (*safety*). There is continual employee and customer contact (*social*). The job itself is interesting and challenging, with participation in decision making and employee development with opportunity for advancement through the Career Adventure path (*esteem and self-actualization*).

Two-Factor Theory

In the 1960s, Frederick Herzberg published his two-factor theory.[37] Herzberg combined lower-level needs into one classification he called *hygiene* or *maintenance*; and higher-level needs into one classification he called *motivators*. The **two-factor theory** *proposes that people are motivated by motivators rather than maintenance factors*. Before you learn about two-factor theory, complete Self-Assessment 3-3.

Maintenance—Extrinsic Factors

Maintenance factors are also called *extrinsic motivators* because motivation comes from outside the person and the job itself.[38] Extrinsic motivators include pay, job security, working conditions, fringe benefits, and relationships. These factors are related to meeting lower-level needs. Review Self-Assessment 3-3, the even-numbered questions, for a list of extrinsic job factors.

Motivators—Intrinsic Factors

Motivators are called *intrinsic motivators* because motivation comes from within the person through the work itself.[39] Intrinsic motivators include achievement, recognition,

© Cengage Learning®

EXHIBIT 3.7

How Organizations Motivate With Hierarchy of Needs Theory

Self-Actualization Needs

Organizations meet these needs by the development of employees' skills, the chance to be creative, achievement and promotions, and the ability to have complete control over their jobs.

Esteem Needs

Organizations meet these needs through titles, the satisfaction of completing the job itself, merit pay raises, recognition, challenging tasks, participation in decision making, and change for advancement.

Social Needs

Organizations meet these needs through the opportunity to interact with others, to be accepted, to have friends. Activities include parties, picnics, trips, and sports teams.

Safety Needs

Organizations meet these needs through safe working conditions, salary increases to meet inflation, job security, and fringe benefits (medical insurance/sick pay/pensions) that protect the physiological needs.

Physiological Needs

Organizations meet these needs through adequate salary, breaks, and working conditions.

SELF-ASSESSMENT 3-3 Job Motivators and Maintenance Factors

Here are 12 job factors that contribute to job satisfaction. Rate each according to how important it is to you by placing a number from 1 to 5 on the line before each factor.

Very important		Somewhat important		Not important
5	4	3	2	1

1. _____ An interesting job I enjoy doing
2. _____ A boss who treats everyone the same regardless of the circumstances
3. _____ Getting praise and other recognition and appreciation for the work that I do
4. _____ A job that is routine without much change from day to day

(continued)

SELF-ASSESSMENT 3-3   **Job Motivators and Maintenance Factors (continued)**

5. _____ The opportunity for advancement
6. _____ A nice title regardless of pay
7. _____ Job responsibility that gives me freedom to
do things my way
8. _____ Good working conditions (safe environment, cafeteria, etc.)
9. _____ The opportunity to learn new things
10. _____ An emphasis on following the rules, regulations, procedures, and policies
11. _____ A job I can do well and succeed at
12. _____ Job security; a career with one company

For each factor, write the numbers from 1 to 5 that
represent your answer. Total each column (should be
between 6 and 30 points).

Motivating factors	Maintenance factors
1. _____	2. _____
3. _____	4. _____
5. _____	6. _____
7. _____	8. _____
9. _____	10. _____
11. _____	12. _____

Totals

Did you select motivators or maintenance factors as
being more important to you? The closer to 30 (6) each
score is, the more (less) important it is to you. Continue
reading to understand the difference between motivators
and maintenance factors.

challenge, and advancement. These factors are related to meeting higher-level needs, and
are better at motivating than extrinsic factors.[40] Review Self-Assessment 3-3, the odd-
numbered questions, for a list of intrinsic job factors.

Herzberg's Two-Factor Motivation Model

Based on research, Herzberg and associates disagreed with the traditional view that satisfaction and dissatisfaction were at opposite ends of one continuum (a one-dimensional
model). There are two continuums: not dissatisfied with the environment (maintenance)
to dissatisfied, and satisfied with the job itself (motivators) to not satisfied (a two-
dimensional model). See Exhibit 3.8 for Herzberg's motivation model.

EXHIBIT 3.8

Two-Factor Motivation Theory

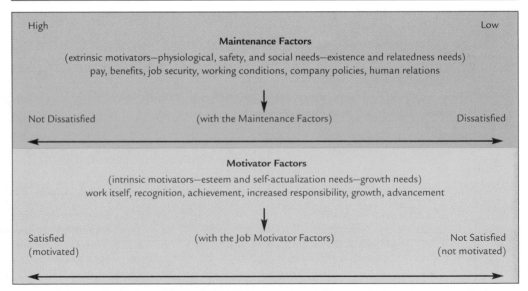

Source: Adapted from F. Herzberg. "The Motivation-Hygiene Concept and Problems of Manpower." Personnel
Administrator: 3–7 (1964); and F. Herzberg. "One More Time: How Do You Motivate Employees?" Harvard
Business Review (January–February 1967):53.

Employees are on a continuum from dissatisfied to not dissatisfied with their environment. Herzberg contends that providing maintenance factors will keep employees from being dissatisfied, but it will not make them satisfied or motivate them. For example,

Herzberg believes that if employees are dissatisfied with their pay and they get a raise, they will no longer be dissatisfied. However, before long people get accustomed to the new standard of living and will become dissatisfied again. Employees will need another raise to not be dissatisfied again. The vicious cycle goes on. So, Herzberg says you have to focus on motivators.

Money as a Motivator

The current view of money as a motivator is that money matters more too some people than others, and that it may motivate some employees but not others. Money, however, does not necessarily motivate employees to work harder. Have you ever gotten a raise? Were you more motivated and more productive? Money also is limited in its ability to motivate. For example, many commissioned workers get to a comfortable point and don't push to make extra money; and some employees get to the point where they don't want overtime work, even though they are paid two or three times their normal wage for overtime.

Motivating Employees with Two-Factor Theory

Under the old management paradigm, money (and other extrinsic motivators) was considered the best motivator. Under the new leadership paradigm, pay is important, but it is not the best motivator; intrinsic motivators are.[41] Herzberg's theory has been criticized for having limited research support. However, current research does support that making work more meaningful increases motivation and performance.[42]

Herzberg fits the new paradigm: He said that managers must first ensure that the employees' level of pay and other maintenance factors are adequate. Once employees are not dissatisfied with their pay (and other maintenance factors), they can be

WORK
Application **3-5**

Recall a present or past job; are you or were you dissatisfied or not dissatisfied with the maintenance factors? Are or were you satisfied or not satisfied with the motivators? Be sure to identify and explain your satisfaction with the specific maintenance and motivator factors.

_____

_____

_____

_____

OPENING CASE Application

3-b. How does Trader Joe's meet its employees' content motivation needs?

Related to *two-factor theory*, although Trader Joe's offers great pay and benefits (*maintenance*), its focus is really more on *motivators* so employees can grow and meet their high-level needs of esteem and self-actualization. Its motto is "Where fun, food and opportunity align." The Trader Joe's Career Adventure (career path) has three levels.

1. *Store Crew* members do a little of everything—run registers, stock shelves, merchandise products, and chat up terrific customers. They have the opportunity to advance.

2. *Store Leadership*. Leaders are out on the store floor with their customers and crew creating a WOW! experience. Store leadership begins at the Novitiate level (entry-level supervisor). They participate in all aspects of managing a Trader Joe's.

3. Store *Management* includes working up to becoming a 2nd and 1st Mate (assistant store managers) to Commander and Captain (store managers). There is also a Regional Mobile Thriver (RMT) Training Program for fast-tracking *experienced* and *relocatable* retail store managers through its promote-from-within structure.

motivated through their jobs. Herzberg also developed *job enrichment,* the process of building motivators into the job itself by making it more interesting and challenging. Job enrichment methods are commonly used today.[43] Job enrichment has been used successfully to motivate employees to higher levels of performance at many organizations,[44] including **AT&T, GM, IBM, Maytag, Monsanto, Motorola, Polaroid**, and the **Traveler**'s.

Acquired Needs Theory

Acquired needs theory *proposes that people are motivated by their need for achievement, power, and affiliation.* This is essentially the same definition given for achievement motivation theory in Chapter 2. It is now called *acquired needs theory* because David McClelland was not the first to study these needs. Because other management writers call McClelland's theory *acquired needs theory*, a general needs theory was developed by Henry Murray, then adapted by John Atkinson, and David McClelland.[45] You have already learned about McClelland's work, so we will be brief here.

Acquired needs theory says that all people have the need for achievement, power, and affiliation but to varying degrees. McClelland's affiliation need is essentially the same as Maslow's belongingness need; and power and achievement are related to esteem, self-actualization, and growth. McClelland's motivation theory does not include lower-level needs for safety and physiological needs. Here are some ideas for motivating employees based on their dominant needs:

WORK
Application **3-6**

Explain how your need for achievement, power, and/or affiliation has affected your behavior, or that of someone you work with or have worked with. What were the consequences of the behavior, and was the need satisfied?

_____

_____

_____

_____

- *Motivating employees with a high n Ach.* Give them nonroutine, challenging tasks with clear, attainable objectives. Give them fast and frequent feedback on their performance. Continually give them increased responsibility for doing new things. Keep out of their way.
- *Motivating employees with a high n Pow.* Let them plan and control their jobs as much as possible. Try to include them in decision making, especially when they are affected by the decision. They tend to perform best alone rather than as team members. Try to assign them to a whole task rather than just part of a task.
- *Motivating employees with a high n Aff.* Be sure to let them work as part of a team. They derive satisfaction from the people they work with rather than the task itself. Give them lots of praise and recognition. Delegate responsibility for orienting and training new employees to them. They make great buddies and mentors.

OPENING CASE Application

3-c. How does Trader Joe's meet its employees' content motivation needs?

Trader Joe's does help employees meet all three *acquired needs.* It provides support they can do a good job, and it has a career path so that employees can *achieve* their goal of advancing. They have the *power* to be in control at the crew, leader, and manager positions. Employees are also encouraged to develop an *affiliation* with employees and customers.

Before we discuss the need to balance professional and personal needs, see Exhibit 3.9 for a comparison of the three content theories of motivation.

EXHIBIT 3.9

A Comparison of Content Motivation Theories

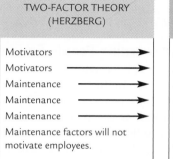

HIERARCHY OF NEEDS THEORY (MASLOW)	TWO-FACTOR THEORY (HERZBERG)	ACQUIRED NEEDS THEORY (MCCLELLAND)
Self-Actualization ⟶	Motivators ⟶	Achievement and Power
Esteem ⟶	Motivators ⟶	Achievement and Power
Belongingness ⟶	Maintenance ⟶	Affiliation
Safety ⟶	Maintenance ⟶	Not classified
Physiological ⟶	Maintenance ⟶	Not classified
Needs must be met in a hierarchical order.	Maintenance factors will not motivate employees.	Employees must be motivated differently based on their acquired needs.

© Cengage Learning®

Balancing Work–Life Needs

Work–life balance is also called work–home and work–family balance. As discussed, we all have personal life needs and we have work needs, and both needs overlap and influence each other. We need a healthy balance between our life and our work. However, with organizations working around the clock competing in a global marketplace, with a focus on getting more done with fewer people, and with technology making it easy to check our cell phones and work all hours of the day and night from anywhere, life and work are blurring together for many people. Negative consequences of imbalance (often called work–life conflict) include stress, burnout, absenteeism, turnover, and dissatisfaction with job, family, and life. Balance is a much sought-after, but rarely claimed, state of being.

Two major things organizations are doing to help employees meet their personal needs are providing on-site day care centers—or giving employees information to help them find good day and elder care—and offering flextime.[46] Some leaders are also telling employees to go home and "get a life" before it is too late.

Learning Outcome 5 *Discuss the major similarities and differences among the three process motivation theories.*

Process Motivation Theories

Process motivation theories *focus on understanding how people choose behavior to fulfill their needs.* Process motivation theories are more complex than content motivation theories. Content motivation theories simply focus on identifying and understanding people's needs. Process motivation theories go a step further by attempting to understand the following: why people have different needs, why their needs change, how and why people choose to try to satisfy needs in different ways, the mental processes people go through as they understand situations, and how they evaluate their need satisfaction.

In this section you learn about three process motivation theories: equity theory, expectancy theory, and goal-setting theory.

Equity Theory

Do you want to be treated fairly? If we perceive organizational decisions and managerial actions, such as pay, to be unfair or unjust, we are likely to experience feelings of anger, outrage, and resentment.[47] Conversely, if we believe we are being treated fairly, we are more willing to accept managerial authority.[48] Equity theory is primarily J. Stacy Adams's motivation theory, in which people are said to be motivated to seek social equity in the rewards they receive (output) for their performance (input).[49] **Equity theory** *proposes that people are motivated when their perceived inputs equal outputs.*

Rewarding People Equitably

Through the equity theory process, people compare their inputs (effort, experience, loyalty, commitment, seniority, etc.) and outputs (financial compensation and intangibles of praise, recognition, etc.) to that of relevant others.[50] A relevant other could be a co-worker or group of employees from the same or different organizations, or even from a hypothetical situation. Notice that our definition says *perceived* and not *actual* inputs to outputs. Others may perceive that equity actually exists and that the person complaining about inequity is wrong.

Equitable distribution of pay is crucial to organizations.[51] Unfortunately, many employees tend to inflate their own efforts or performance when comparing themselves to others. Employees also tend to overestimate what others earn. A comparison with relevant others leads to one of three conclusions: The employee is under-rewarded, over-rewarded, or equitably rewarded. When inequity is perceived, employees attempt to correct the balance by reducing input (e.g., put forth less effort) or increasing output (e.g., get a raise).

Motivating with Equity Theory

People who believe they are over-rewarded usually don't change their behavior. Instead, they often rationalize that they deserve the outputs. One view of equity is that it is like Herzberg's maintenance factors. When employees are not dissatisfied, they are not actively motivated, but maintenance factors do demotivate when employees are dissatisfied. According to equity theory, when employees believe they are equitably rewarded, they are not actively motivated. However, when employees believe they are under-rewarded, or not being treated fairly, they are demotivated.[52] Unethical leaders tend to be viewed as unfair.[53] Using equity theory in practice can be difficult, because you don't always know who the employee's reference group is, or his or her view of inputs and outcomes. However, this theory does offer some useful general recommendations: Be aware that equity is based on perception, do reward equitably, and be sure to reward high performers so they don't decrease their performance.

> **WORK**
> Application **3-7**
>
> Give an example of how equity theory has affected your motivation, or that of someone else you work with or have worked with. Be sure to specify if you were under-rewarded, over-rewarded, or equitably rewarded.

OPENING CASE Application

4-a. How does Trader Joe's meet its employees' process motivation needs?

Trader Joe's treats all employees with *equity.* The management style is participative so everyone shares in the management at each store. Employees who put in the effort (*inputs*) to climb the corporate ladder have potential rewards (*outputs*). However, not everyone is expected to move to leadership and store management. But even the part-time crew get good pay and benefits—yes, health insurance for all.

Expectancy Theory

Expectancy theory is based on Victor Vroom's formula: motivation = expectancy × instrumentality × valence.[54] **Expectancy theory** *proposes that people are motivated when they believe they can accomplish the task, they will get the reward, and the rewards for doing the task are worth the effort.* The theory is based on the following assumptions:

Both internal (needs) and external (environment) factors affect behavior; behavior is the individual's decision; people have different needs, desires, and goals; and people make behavior decisions based on their perception of the outcome.

Three Variables

All three variable conditions must be met in Vroom's formula for motivation to take place:

- *Expectancy* refers to the person's perception of his or her ability (probability) to accomplish an objective—self-efficacy.[55] Generally, the higher one's expectancy, the better the chance for motivation. When we do not believe that we can accomplish objectives, we will not be motivated to try.[56]
- *Instrumentality* refers to belief that the performance will result in getting the reward. If employees are certain to get the reward, they probably will be motivated. When not sure, employees may not be motivated.
- *Valence* refers to the value a person places on the outcome or reward. Generally, the higher the value (importance) of the outcome or reward, the better the chance of motivation.

Motivating with Expectancy Theory

The following conditions should be implemented to make expectancy theory result in motivation:

1. Clearly define objectives and the performance necessary to achieve them.[57]
2. Tie performance to rewards. High performance should be rewarded. When one employee works harder to produce more than other employees and is not rewarded, he or she may slow down productivity.
3. Be sure rewards are of value to the employee. Managers should get to know employees as individuals. Develop good human relations as a people developer.
4. Make sure our employees believe we will do what we say we will do. For example, employees must believe we will give them a merit raise if they do work hard.
5. Founder of Walmart Sam Walton said, "High expectations are the key to everything." So use the Pygmalion effect (Chapter 2) to increase expectations. Your high expectations can result in follower self-fulfilling prophecy. As the level of expectation increases, so will performance.

> **WORK**
> Application **3-8**
>
> Give an example of how expectancy theory has affected your motivation, or that of someone else you work with or have worked with. Be sure to specify the expectancy and valence.
>
> ---------------
> ---------------
> ---------------
> ---------------

OPENING CASE Application

4-b. How does Trader Joe's meet its employees' process motivation needs?

Trader Joe's focuses on attracting people who have the *expectancy* that they can be successful at the level of their choice, and it provides the training to help them succeed as store crew, leader, and manager. Employees know that if they do a good job they will get rewarded (*instrumentality*). The *valence* of employees does vary, but as discussed, Trader Joe's offers good pay and benefits.

Goal-Setting Theory

Based on his extensive research, goal-setting theory is primarily attributed to Edwin Locke. **Goal-setting theory** *proposes that specific, difficult goals motivate people*. Goal setting increases commitment, motivation, energy, and persistence toward goals.[58]

Writing Objectives

To help you to write effective objectives that meet the criteria you will learn next, use the model. The parts of the **writing objectives model** *are (1) To + (2) action verb + (3) singular, specific, and measurable result to be achieved + (4) target date.* This is shown in Model 3.1, with and objective, that is adapted from Max E. Douglas's model.

MODEL 3.1

Writing Effective Objectives Model

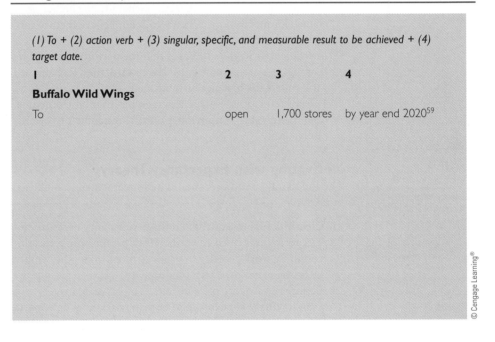

(1) To + (2) action verb + (3) singular, specific, and measurable result to be achieved + (4) target date.

1	2	3	4
Buffalo Wild Wings			
To	open	1,700 stores	by year end 2020[59]

© Cengage Learning®

WORK
Application **3-9**

1. Using the writing objectives model, write one or more objectives for an organization you work for or have worked for that meet the criteria for objectives.

2. Give an example of how a goal(s) affected your motivation and performance, or those of someone else you work with or have worked with.

Criteria for Objectives

For an objective to be effective, it should include the four criteria listed in steps 3 and 4 of the writing objectives model:

1. *Singular result.* To avoid confusion, each objective should contain only one end result. When multiple objectives are listed together, one may be met but the other(s) may not.
2. *Specific.* The objective should not be vague, such as to learn a lot in this leadership course. It should state the exact level of performance expected, such as to get an A.
3. *Measurable.* The saying "what gets measured gets done" is true. If people are to achieve objectives, they must be able to observe and measure their progress regularly to monitor progress and to determine if the objective has been met.
4. *Target date.* A specific date should be set for accomplishing the objective. When people have a deadline, they usually try harder to get the task done on time.[60] If people are simply told to do it when they can, they don't tend to "get around to it" until they have to. It is also more effective to set a specific date, such as October 29, 2015, rather than a set time, such as in two weeks, because you can forget when the time began and should end. However, some objectives are ongoing and do not require a stated date. The target date is indefinite until it is changed, such as the Domino's objective to deliver pizza within 30 minutes.

In addition to the four criteria from the model, there are three other criteria that do not always fit within the model:

1. *Difficult but achievable.* Research shows that individuals perform better with challenging objectives rather than (1) easy objectives, (2) objectives that are too difficult, or (3) simply told "do your best."[61]
2. *Participatively set.* People that participate in setting their objectives generally outperform those that are assigned objectives, because it helps gain commitment.[62]
3. *Commitment.* For objectives to be met, employees must accept them. If employees are not committed to striving for the objective, even if they meet the other criteria, they may not meet the objective.[63]

Microsoft

Microsoft has a long tradition of having individuals set goals as part of its high performance–based culture. All employees are trained to set "SMART" (Specific, Measurable, Achievable, Results-based, and Time-specific) written goals. Managers are trained to assist in the goal-setting process, including how to provide relevant performance feedback during the review process.

YOU
Make the
ETHICAL
Call

3.1   *Academic Standards*

Lou Holtz, former successful Notre Dame football coach, said that the power of goal setting is an incredible motivator for high performance; to be successful we need to set a higher goal. Have colleges followed his advice? Have academic standards dropped, maintained, or increased over the years?

The academic credit-hour system was set many years ago to establish some formal standardization across colleges throughout the country so that academics and employers had the same expectations of the workload that a college student carried to earn a degree. This also allowed students to transfer credit from one university to another, assuming the same standards were met.

The credit-hour system was set at students doing two hours of preparation for each hour of in-class time. So, a student taking five classes should spend 15 hours in class and 30 hours preparing for class, or a total of 40+ hours per week—which is a full-time schedule.

1. How many hours outside of class, on average, do you and other students use to prepare for class each week?
2. Are college professors throughout the country assigning students two hours of preparation for every hour in class today? If not, why have they dropped the standard?
3. Are students who are putting in part-time hours (20–30 hours) during college being well prepared for a career after graduation (40–60 hours)?
4. Is it ethical and socially responsible for professors to drop standards and for colleges to award degrees for doing less work today than 5, 10, or 20 years ago?

Using Goal Setting to Motivate Employees

Need we say anything more about setting objectives besides to follow the guidelines above? Yes. Setting a goal is just the first step; the next step is just as important as we need to plan how we will accomplish it.[64] Relying on willpower is a horrible strategy; it's doomed to fail, and this is why so few people keep their New Year's resolutions. We will provide details on tying goals and plans in the subsection "Changing Behavior."

CONCEPT APPLICATION 3-3

Objectives

For each objective, state which "must" criteria is not met.

a. singular result   c. measurable
b. specific   d. target date

_____ 11. To sell 12 percent more cars and 3 percent more services in 2015

_____ 12. To increase sales in 2016

_____ 13. To be perceived as the best bar in the Houston area by the end of 2017

_____ 14. To write personal objectives within two weeks

_____ 15. To double iPad production in China

OPENING CASE Application

4-c. How does Trader Joe's meet its employees' process motivation needs?

Trader Joe's does use *goal-setting* theory. One of its ongoing goals is to introduce 10–15 new products a week. Some of the new products are sold nationally, and some are selected by the store to take advantage of local products, such as farm fresh produce.

Reinforcement Theory

B. F. Skinner, reinforcement motivation theorist, contended that to motivate employees it is really not necessary to identify and understand needs (content motivation theories), or to understand how employees choose behaviors to fulfill them (process motivation theories). All the manager needs to do is understand the relationship between behaviors and their consequences, and then arrange contingencies that reinforce desirable behaviors and discourage undesirable behaviors.[65] **Reinforcement theory** *proposes that through the consequences for behavior, people will be motivated to behave in predetermined ways.*

Let's face it; all organizations develop systems to control employee behavior,[66] and that is what reinforcement theory is all about. Reinforcement theory uses behavior modification (apply reinforcement theory to get employees to do what you want them to do) and operant conditioning (types and schedules of reinforcement). Skinner stated that behavior is learned through experiences of positive and negative consequences. Employees learn what is, and is not, desired behavior as a result of the consequences for specific behavior. The three components of Skinner's framework are shown with an example in Exhibit 3.10.

In this section, we have five subsections, as we discuss the two important concepts used to modify behavior (1 the types of reinforcement and 2 the schedules of reinforcement): 3 that you get what you reinforce, 4 how to motivate using reinforcement, and 5 how to give praise.

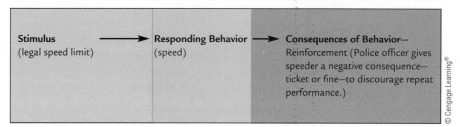

Components of Reinforcement Theory

| Stimulus (legal speed limit) | → | Responding Behavior (speed) | → | Consequences of Behavior— Reinforcement (Police officer gives speeder a negative consequence—ticket or fine—to discourage repeat performance.) |

© Cengage Learning®

Learning Outcome **6**

Explain the four types of reinforcement.

Types of Reinforcement

The four types of reinforcement are positive, avoidance, punishment, and extinction. Exhibit 3.11 illustrates the four types of reinforcement.

Positive Reinforcement

A method of encouraging continued behavior is to offer attractive consequences (rewards) for desirable performance. Positive reinforcements are pay, promotions, time off, increased status, and so forth. Giving praise is a positive reinforcement, and you will learn how to give praise at the end of this section.

Motivating with rewards. There has been an ongoing debate about using the carrot (reward) or the stick (punishment), and the general consensus is to use rewards (be positive not negative) when possible. Ever heard of the *Angry Birds*? A big part of its success is that the game gives lots of positive reinforcement, and doesn't punish players. So when possible, use rewards to motivate yourself and others.

Avoidance Reinforcement

Avoidance is also called *negative reinforcement*. *Rules* with punishment for violations are designed to get employees to avoid certain behavior. Employees don't necessarily want to follow the rules, but they usually do to avoid the negative consequence of punishment.

Motivating with avoidance. Organizational leaders do need to develop rules, but rules in and of themselves are not a punishment. Punishment is given only if the rule is broken, which we hope will not happen. So note that with avoidance there is no actual punishment; it's the "threat" of the punishment that controls behavior. So when needed, set rules that will contribute to performance.

Punishment

Punishment is used to provide an undesirable consequence for undesirable behavior. Methods of punishment include harassing, taking away privileges, probation, fining, demoting, firing, and so forth.

Motivating with punishment. Punishment is the most controversial and the least effective method in motivating employees to do a good job. Punishment may reduce the undesirable behavior; but its overuse may cause other undesirable behaviors, such as poor morale, lower productivity, and acts of theft or sabotage. However, leaders need to enforce the rules, so there are times when only punishment will do. So punish when rules are broken.

Extinction

Rather than encourage desirable behavior, extinction (and punishment) attempts to reduce or eliminate undesirable. Extinction also includes ignoring the behavior to get the employee to stop it. From another perspective, managers who do not reward good performance can cause its extinction. In other words, if you ignore good employee performance, good performance may stop because employees think, "Why should I do a good job if I'm not rewarded in some way?"

Motivating with extinction.   When employees don't earn rewards, withhold them. For example, the manager may withhold a reward of value, such as a pay raise, until the employee performs to set standards. Also, don't ignore good performance.

3.2   *Airlines*

An airline often charges higher fares for one-way tickets than round-trip tickets, and for direct flight tickets to its hub than for flight connections from its hub to another destination. So some travelers buy round-trip tickets and only go one way, and some end their travel at the hub instead of taking the connection (a "hidden city" itinerary), to save money. The airlines call this breach of contract: They have *punished* travel agencies for tickets that aren't properly used, they sometimes demand higher fares from travelers caught, and they have seized some travelers' frequent-flier miles, saying they were fraudulently obtained.

1. Not using the full travel of a ticket breaks airline rules but not the law, so it's not illegal, unless travelers lie about what they are doing. But is it ethical and socially responsible behavior of travelers?
2. Is it ethical and socially responsible for airlines to charge more for less travel?
3. Is it ethical and socially responsible to punish people who break the ticket rules?
4. Is reinforcement theory effective (does it motivate you and others) in today's global economy?
5. Is reinforcement theory ethical and socially responsible, or is it manipulative?

Schedules of Reinforcement

The second reinforcement consideration in controlling behavior is determining when to reinforce performance. The two major schedule classifications are *continuous* and *intermittent*.

Continuous Reinforcement

With a continuous method, each and every desired behavior is reinforced. Examples of this method would be a machine with an automatic counter that lets the employee know (at any given moment) exactly how many units have been produced, and a sales rep who gets a commission on every sale.

Motivating with a continuous schedule.   Continuous reinforcement is generally better at sustaining desired behavior. It works well as an incentive to produce. For example, a piece rate reward of $1 for each unit produced or a 10 percent commission on every sale.

Intermittent Reinforcement

The reward is given based on the passage of time or output. When the reward is based on the passage of time, it is called an *interval* schedule. When it is based on output, it is

Types of Reinforcement

EXHIBIT 3.11

As a manager, you have an assistant who makes many errors when completing correspondence. Your objective, which you discussed with the assistant, is to decrease the error rate by 50 percent by Friday, June 3, 2016. Based on the assistant's performance at that time, you have four types of reinforcement that you can use with her when you next review her work.

EMPLOYEE BEHAVIOR	TYPE OF REINFORCEMENT	MANAGER ACTION (CONSEQUENCE)	EMPLOYEE BEHAVIOR MODIFICATION (FUTURE)
Improved performance	Positive	Praise improvements	Repeat quality work*
Improved performance	Avoidance	Do not give any reprimand	Repeat quality work
Performance not improved	Extinction	Withhold praise/raise	Do not repeat poor work
Performance not improved	Punishment	Discipline action, such as a written warning	Do not repeat poor work

*Assuming the employee improved performance, positive reinforcement is the best motivator.

© Cengage Learning®

called a *ratio* schedule. When electing to use intermittent reinforcement, you have four alternatives:

1. *Fixed interval schedule.* Giving a salary paycheck every week, or breaks and meals at the same time every day
2. *Variable interval schedule.* Giving praise only now and then, a surprise inspection, or a pop quiz
3. *Fixed ratio schedule.* Giving a piece rate or bonus after producing a standard rate
4. *Variable ratio schedule.* Giving praise for excellent work, or a lottery for employees who have not been absent for a set amount of time

Motivating with an intermittent schedule. Continuous reinforcement is not always possible or practical, such as with giving praise. To be more effective, praise is generally only given for exceptional, not routine, performance. Otherwise, it becomes routine and tends to lose its effect. Ratios are generally better motivators than intervals. The variable ratio tends to be the most powerful schedule for sustaining behavior.

You Get What You Reinforce

One of the important things you should learn in this course is that people will do what they are reinforced for doing. People seek information concerning what activities are reinforced, and then seek to do (or at least pretend to do) those things, often to the exclusion of activities not reinforced. The extent to which this occurs, of course, depends on the attractiveness of the rewards offered and the punishment for the behavior.

For example, if the professor says, "A, B, and C from this chapter are important and I'll test you on them, but X, Y, and Z will not be on the test," will students spend equal time studying both groups of material? In the business setting, if the manager repeatedly says quality is important, but there is no reward for taking the time and effort to do a quality job, or punishment for poor quality, many employees will not really care about quality.

Motivating with Reinforcement
General Guides

Here are some general guidelines for using reinforcement:

1. Make sure employees know exactly what is expected of them. Set clear objectives—goal-setting theory.
2. Select the appropriate type of reinforcement. A reward may work better for some, and avoidance, punishment, or extinction for others. Know your employees' needs.
3. Select the appropriate reinforcement schedule—continuous in some situations and intermittence in others.
4. Do not reward mediocre or poor performance (use extinction), and punish rule violators.
5. Look for the positive and give praise, rather than focus on the negative and criticize. Listen to people and make them feel good about themselves (Pygmalion effect).
6. Never go a day without giving sincere praise.
7. Do things for your employees, instead of to them, and you will see productivity increase.

Changing Behavior

If we are going to change our behavior, we need to retrain our brain to form new habits by conditioning ourselves to new behavior. Here are some tips on using reinforcement to change our behavior. The tips include a personal example, which is the same process as for professional behavior changes.

1. Begin by setting an objective using goal-setting theory. For example, to get into shape by working out three days a week for 30 minutes starting (list a specific date).
2. Specify the who, what, when, where, and how of your plan. I will go to the gym (or walk from my home) every Monday, Wednesday, and Friday at 6:00 a.m. before going to school/work.
3. Next, further develop the plan by implementing the following ideas within your overall plan.
   - Reduce other life stress, if possible, so you can focus on your new behavior without distractions. I'm going to stop my relationship with Chris.
   - Think in advance about what might cause you to slip and plan how you can avoid those things. Why would you skip a workout?
   - Expect setbacks and slips and how you will bounce back as part of your plan. The next tip can help.
   - Plan your reinforcement. Have punishments for undesirable behavior. If I skip a workout, I will not watch TV that day, or I will make it up on another day. Have rewards for desired behavior. After working out for the three days of the week, I will treat myself to an ice cream.

Giving Praise

Pay is not the only, nor necessarily the best, reinforcer for performance. Employees want to know that their organization values their contributions and cares about their well-being. Giving praise sends this message as it develops a positive self-concept in employees and leads to better performance—the Pygmalion effect and self-fulfilling prophecy. Praise is a motivator (not maintenance) because it meets employees' needs for esteem and self-actualization, growth, and achievement. Giving praise creates a win–win situation, only takes a minute, and doesn't cost anything. It is probably the most powerful, simplest, least costly, and yet most underused motivational technique there is.

Ken Blanchard and Spencer Johnson popularized giving praise back in the 1980s through their best-selling book, *The One-Minute Manager.* They developed a technique that involves giving one-minute feedback of praise. Model 3.2, Giving Praise, is an adaptation. *The steps in the* **giving praise model** *are (1) Tell the employee exactly what was done correctly. (2) Tell the employee why the behavior is important. (3) Stop for a moment of silence. (4) Encourage repeat performance.* Blanchard calls it one-minute praise because it should not take more than one minute to give the praise. It is not necessary for the employee to say anything. The four steps are described below and illustrated in Model 3.2.

Giving Praise

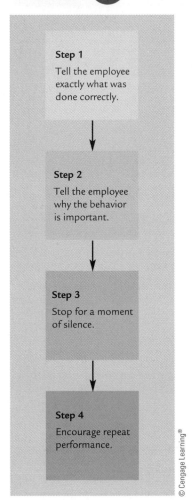

Model 3.2

Step 1
Tell the employee exactly what was done correctly.

Step 2
Tell the employee why the behavior is important.

Step 3
Stop for a moment of silence.

Step 4
Encourage repeat performance.

© Cengage Learning®

Step 1.　Tell the employee exactly what was done correctly. When giving praise, look the person in the eye. Eye contact shows sincerity and concern. It is important to be very specific and descriptive. General statements, like "you're a good worker," are not as effective.

Step 2.　Tell the employee why the behavior is important. Briefly state how the organization and/or person benefits from the action. It is also helpful to tell the employee how you feel about the behavior. Be specific and descriptive.

Step 3.　Stop for a moment of silence. Being silent is tough for many managers. The rationale for the silence is to give the employee the chance to "feel" the impact of the praise. It's like "the pause that refreshes." When you are thirsty and take the first sip or gulp of a refreshing drink, it's not until you stop, and maybe say, "Ah," that you feel your thirst quenched.

Step 4.　Encourage repeat performance. This is the reinforcement that motivates the employee to continue the desired behavior.

As you can see, giving praise is easy, and it doesn't cost a penny. One supermarket manager stated that an employee was taking his time stacking cans on a display. He gave the employee praise for stacking the cans so straight, rather than punishment for working slow. The employee was so pleased with the praise that the display went up with about a 100 percent increase in productivity. Being positive and giving praise first thing in the work day can get employees in a good mood, and it can increase performance.[67]

In this global environment, it is not always possible to give praise in person, so when you don't see people face to face, use written communication, including e-mail, instead. The personal handwritten note is considered to be special. Disney CEO Bob Iger writes personal, handwritten notes on Disney stationery to praise employees, even those he has never met. He says that writing a simple note goes a long way with people.

OPENING CASE Application

5. How does Trader Joe's use reinforcement theory to motivate its employees?

Trader Joe's uses *positive reinforcement* with good pay and benefits and its career path opportunities. Sales are on a *continuous reinforcement schedule* as managers know the sales volume throughout the day. Paychecks are given on a *fixed interval schedule.* Praise and other recognition for accomplishments are given on a *variable interval and ratio schedule.*

CONCEPT APPLICATION 3-4

Motivation Theories

Identify each supervisor's statement of how to motivate employees by the theory behind the statement. Write the appropriate letter in the blank before each item.

a. hierarchy of needs   d. equity   f. expectancy
b. two-factor   e. goal setting   g. reinforcement
c. acquired needs

_____ 16. A manager treats everyone fairly to motivate them.

_____ 17. A manager knows Jose likes people, so she gives him jobs working with others.

_____ 18. Edie would often make a sound because he knew it bothered the manager. So the manager decided to ignore it.

_____ 19. A manager knows employees values so she can offer rewards that will motivate them when they achieve attainable task performance.

_____ 20. Shaw retail store offers good working conditions, salaries, and benefits, so Shaw is working at meeting socialization needs by having monthly barbecues.

_____ 21. A manager thanks employees using a four-step model for doing a good job everyday.

_____ 22. A manager used to focus on improving working conditions, but stopped and now focuses on making the job more interesting and challenging.

_____ 23. A manager tells employees what he want them to do, with a tough deadline that is achievable.

_____ 24. A manager now realizes that she tends to be autocratic because it helps fill her needs. But now she is giving employees more autonomy on how they do their jobs.

_____ 25. A manager motivates employees by giving them more responsibility so they can grow and develop new skills.

Learning Outcome **7**   *State the major differences among content, process, and reinforcement theories.*

The Motivation Process with the Motivation Theories

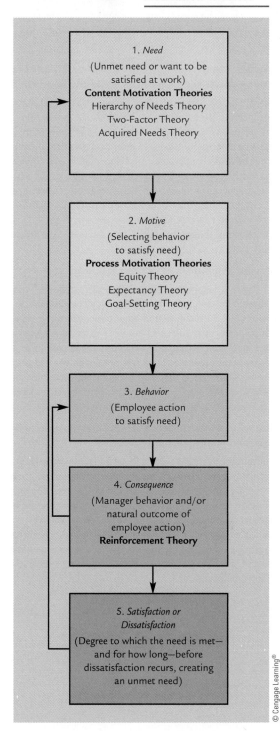

Putting the Motivation Theories Together within the Motivation Process

Motivation is important because it helps explain why employees behave the way they do. At this point you may be wondering: How do these theories fit together? Is one the best? Should I try to pick the correct theory for a given situation? Actually, the groups of theories are complementary; each group of theories refers to a different stage in the motivation process. Each group of theories answers a different question. Content motivation theories answer the question: What needs do employees have that should be met on the job? Process motivation theories answer the question: How do employees choose behavior to fulfill their needs? Reinforcement theory answers the question: What can managers do to get employees to behave in ways that meet the organizational objectives?

In this chapter you learned that the motivation process went from need to motive to behavior to consequence to satisfaction or dissatisfaction. Now let's make the motivation process a little more complex by incorporating the motivation theories, or answers to the preceding questions, into the process. See Exhibit 3.12 for an illustration.

Note that step 4 loops back to step 3 because, according to reinforcement theory, behavior is learned through consequences. Step 4 does not loop back to steps 1 or 2 because reinforcement theory is not concerned about needs, motives, or satisfaction; it focuses on getting employees to behave in predetermined ways, through consequences provided by managers. Also note that step 5 loops back to step 1 because meeting needs is ongoing; meeting our needs is a never-ending process. Finally, be aware that according to two-factor theory, step 5 (satisfaction or dissatisfaction) is not on one continuum but on two separate continuums (satisfied to not satisfied, or dissatisfied to not dissatisfied), based on the level of need being met (motivator or maintenance).

"Take It To The Net". Access student resources at www.cengagebrain.com. Search for Lussier, Leadership 6e to find student study tools.

Chapter Summary

The chapter summary is organized to answer the eight learning outcomes for this chapter.

1 **List the University of Iowa leadership styles.**

The University of Iowa leadership styles are autocratic and democratic.

2 **Describe similarities and differences between the University of Michigan and Ohio State University leadership models.**

The University of Michigan and Ohio State University leadership models are similar because they are both based on the same two distinct leadership behaviors, although the models use different names for the two behaviors. The models are different because the University of Michigan model identifies two leadership styles based on either job- or employee-centered behavior. The Ohio State University model states that a leader uses high or low structure and consideration, resulting in four leadership style combinations of these two behaviors.

3 **Discuss similarities and differences between the Ohio State University Leadership Model and the Leadership Grid.**

Both theories are based on the same two leadership behaviors, but they use different names for the two dimensions. The theories are different because the Leadership Grid identifies five leadership styles, with one being middle of the road, whereas the Ohio State model identifies four leadership styles. The Leadership Grid also gives each combination of the two-dimensional behaviors one leadership style name.

4 **Discuss similarities and differences among the three content motivation theories.**

Similarities among the content motivation theories include their focus on identifying and understanding employee needs. The theories identify similar needs but are different in the way they classify the needs. Hierarchy of needs theory includes physiological, safety, belongingness, esteem, and self-actualization needs. Two-factor theory includes motivators and maintenance factors. Acquired needs theory includes achievement, power, and affiliation needs, and includes no lower-level needs, as the other two theories do.

5 **Discuss the major similarities and differences among the three process motivation theories.**

The similarity among the three process motivation theories includes their focus on understanding how employees choose behaviors to fulfill their needs. However, they are very different in their perceptions of how employees are motivated. Equity theory proposes that employees are motivated when their perceived inputs equal outputs. Expectancy theory proposes that employees are motivated when they believe they can accomplish the task and the rewards for doing so are worth the effort. Goal-setting theory proposes that achievable, difficult goals motivate employees.

6 **Explain the four types of reinforcement.**

(1) Positive reinforcement provides the employee with a reward consequence for performing the desired behavior. (2) Avoidance reinforcement encourages employees to perform the desired behavior to avoid a negative consequence. (3) Extinction reinforcement withholds a positive consequence to get the employee to stop performing undesirable behavior. (4) Punishment reinforcement gives the employee a negative consequence to get the employee to stop performing undesirable behavior.

7 **State the major differences among content, process, and reinforcement theories.**

Content motivation theories focus on identifying and understanding employees' needs. Process motivation goes a step farther to understand how employees choose behavior to fulfill their needs. Reinforcement theory is not as concerned about employee needs; it focuses on getting employees to do what managers want them to do through the consequences provided by managers for their behavior. The use of rewards is the means of motivating employees.

Key Terms

Review Questions

1 Why was there a shift from the trait to the behavioral theory paradigm?

2 How is leadership behavior based on traits?

3 What are the University of Iowa leadership styles?

4 What are the University of Michigan leadership styles?

5 What are the Ohio State University leadership styles?

6 What are three important contributions of the University of Michigan and Ohio State University studies?

7 What are the Leadership Grid leadership styles?

8 What are the three important contributions of the Leadership Grid and high-high research?

9 What is motivation, and why is it important to know how to motivate employees?

10 What are the content motivation theories?

11 What are the process motivation theories?

12 What are the types and schedules of reinforcement theory?

Critical-Thinking Questions

The following critical-thinking questions can be used for class discussion and/or as written assignments to develop communication skills. Be sure to give complete explanations for all questions.

1 Which leadership model do you prefer?

2 Do you agree with the University of Michigan model (with two leadership styles) or with the Ohio State model (with four leadership styles)?

3 Do you agree with the Leadership Grid's claim that the one best leadership style is the team leader (9,9)?

4 Which of the three content motivation theories do you prefer? Why?

5 Which of the three process motivation theories do you prefer? Why?

6 What is your motivation theory? What major methods, techniques, and so on do you plan to use on the job as a manager to increase motivation and performance?

7 Reinforcement theory is unethical because it is used to manipulate employees. Do you agree with this statement? Explain your answer.

8 Which type and schedule of reinforcement do you plan to use most often as a leader?

9 Do you really get what you reinforce? Explain.

Facebook COO Sheryl Sandberg

Sheryl Sandberg is the chief operating officer (COO) at Facebook. Sandberg is second in command and is said to actually manage Facebook as an equal partner with CEO Mark Zuckerberg so that he can focus on what he likes to do: product development and engineering. There has never been an executive like her. Sheryl is the world's most famous COO and a billionaire best-selling author, and is ranked fifth on the Fortune Most Powerful Women list.[68] She tends to use a participative leadership style as she spends much of her time e-mailing and in meetings, with an emphasis on influencing and motivating others to achieve the Facebook mission: to make the world more open and connected.[69]

Sheryl Sandberg published a thought-provoking book on the role of women in the office and at their home. The book is Sheryl's attempt to help other women be successful in business. It was an instant best seller and has already generated meaningful discussion about the roles of men and women at work.

What is so controversial? Sheryl titled her book *Lean In: Women, Work and the Will to Lead*. The book is being sold around the world under the following different titles to reflect the meaning of "Lean In" in each country. In France it is *En Avant Toutes* ("Forward All"), in Italy it is *Facciamoci avanti* ("Step Forward"), in Spanish it is *Vayamos Adelante* ("Let's Go"), and in Brazil it is *Faça Acontecer* ("Make It Happen").[70]

What does "Lean In" mean? Sandberg is calling on other women, as she puts it, to "lean in" and embrace success. Sandberg feels that "if more women lean in, we can change the power structure of our world and expand opportunities for all. More female leadership will lead to fairer treatment for *all* women."[71] She also feels the half of the companies around the world should be run by women and half of the houses run by men—which is far from the reality of the situation.[72]

Sandberg also states that her success was not just because she worked hard—but that she removed internal barriers that often hold women back. These barriers that women create are a lack of self-confidence, not raising their hands, and by pulling back when they should be leaning in. If women expect to crack the glass ceiling and access more powerful positions at work, they are going to have to Lean In.[73]

When the book was released, many newspapers and television disputed the merits of her theory. The first reply was that it is easy for a woman that is wealthy and voted the fifth most powerful woman in the world to say that a woman can be a leader at work and at home.

Is a woman successful if she opts to Lean Out and just become a stay-at-home mom? Or, is she less successful if she just has a good middle-level job at work without the high levels of stress often associated with executive-level positions and decisions?

One of the goals of *Lean In* was to bring women together to discuss the issue. Facebook, and many other social media sites, already have a large number of groups formed that are meeting online and in person. You can join the lean in community at **www.facebook.com/leaninorg** or **www.leanin.org.**

GO TO THE INTERNET: To learn more about Sheryl Sandberg and Facebook, visit their Web sites **www.facebook.com.**

Support your answers to the following questions with specific information from the case and text or with other information you get from the Web or other sources.

1. How would Sheryl Sandberg's leadership style be described based on the four behavioral leadership styles?

2. How does Sandberg's book *Lean In* emphasize the three content motivation theories?

3. How does Sandberg's book *Lean In* emphasize the three process motivation theories?

4. Which type and schedule of reinforcement will help women advance in business?

CUMULATIVE CASE QUESTIONS

5. How do the five dimensions of our leadership definition (Chapter 1) apply to Sandberg as COO of Facebook?

6. What managerial leadership skills does Sandberg need as COO of Facebook (Chapter 1)?

7. How would you describe Sandberg's Big Five Personality, and do you believe she has the personality profile of an effective leader (Chapter 2)?

CASE EXERCISE AND ROLE-PLAY

Preparation: Think about reasons why women should and shouldn't be given more opportunities to advance in organizations.

In-Class Groups: Break into groups of four to six members and develop a list of reasons for and against giving women more opportunities for advancement in organizations.

Role-Play: One person (representing him- or herself or a group) gives the reasons for giving women more opportunities to advance, and another to give the reasons against it.

VIDEO ▶ CASE

Motivation at Washburn Guitars

Founded in the late 1800s in Chicago, Washburn Guitars boasts a rich tradition of fine instrument making. Washburn Guitars produces a variety of acoustic and electric guitars. Washburn craftsmen also enjoy making custom guitars. In recent years, custom shop production has grown dramatically. Having a motivated workforce is essential because guitar making is labor intensive and requires attention to detail.

1. What motivates most employees at Washburn Guitars?

2. What kinds of guitars do employees most like to produce?

3. What is the connection between quality guitars and workforce motivation?

Developing Your Leadership Skills (3-1)

Writing Objectives

Preparing for This Exercise

For this exercise, you will first work at improving objectives that do not meet the criteria for objectives. Then you will write nine objectives for yourself.

Part 1. For each objective below, identify the missing criteria and rewrite the objective so that it meets all essential criteria. When writing objectives, use the model:

To + action verb + singular, specific, and measurable result + target date

1 To improve our company image by year-end 2018.

Criteria missing: ———————————————

Improved objective: ———————————————

2 To increase the number of customers by 10 percent.

Criteria missing: ———————————————

Improved objective: ———————————————

3 To increase profits during 2016.

Criteria missing: ———————————————

Improved objective: ———————————————

4 To sell 5 percent more hot dogs and 8 percent more soda at the baseball game on Sunday, June 12, 2016.

Criteria missing: ———————————————

Improved objective: ———————————————

Part 2. Write three *educational*, *personal*, and *career* objectives you want to accomplish. Your objectives can be as short term as something you want to accomplish today, or as long term as 20

years from now. Be sure your objectives meet the criteria for effective objectives.

Doing This Exercise in Class

Objective

To develop your skill at writing objectives.

AACSB General Skills Area

The primary AACSB learning skills developed through this exercise are written communications, analytic thinking, and application of knowledge.

Preparation

You should have corrected the objectives in Part 1 and have written objectives in Part 2 during the preparation for this exercise.

Experience

You will get feedback on how well you corrected the four objectives and share your written objectives with others.

Options (8–20 minutes)

A. The instructor goes over suggested corrections for the four objectives in Part 1 of the preparation, and then calls on class members to share their written objectives with the class in Part 2.

B. The instructor goes over suggested corrections for the four objectives in Part 1 of the preparation, and then the class breaks into groups of four to six to share their written objectives.

C. Break into groups of four to six and go over the corrections for the four objectives in Part 1. Tell the instructor when your group is done, but go on to Part 2, sharing your written objectives, until all groups are finished with the four corrections. The instructor goes over the corrections and may allow more time for sharing objectives. Give each other feedback for improving your written objectives during Part 2.

Behavior Model Skills Training (3-1)

Giving Praise

This training for leadership behavior modeling skills has four parts, as follows:

1. First, read how to use the model.

2. Then, view the behavior model video that illustrates how to give praise, following the four steps in the model.

3. Develop the skill in class by doing Developing Your Leadership Skills Exercise 1.

4. Further develop this skill by using the model in your personal and professional life.

Conclusion

The instructor may lead a class discussion and/or make concluding remarks.

Apply It *(2–4 minutes)* What did I learn from this experience? How will I use the knowledge in the future?

Giving Praise Model

Review Model 3.2, "Giving Praise," in the text.

Behavior Model Video (3-1)

Giving Praise

Objective

To assist you in giving praise that motivates others to high levels of performance.

Video (4½ minutes) Overview

You will watch a bank branch manager give praise to an employee for two different jobs well done.

Developing Your Leadership Skills (3-2)

Giving Praise

Preparing for This Exercise

Think of a job situation in which you did something well deserving of praise and recognition. For example, you may have saved the company some money, you may have turned a dissatisfied customer into a happy one, and so forth. If you have never worked, interview someone who has. Put yourself in a management position and write out the praise you would give to an employee for doing what you did. Be sure to write your praise using the Giving Praise Model 3-2.

Doing This Exercise in Class

Objective

To develop your skill at giving praise.

AACSB General Skills Area

The primary AACSB learning skills developed through this exercise are communication, and application of knowledge.

Preparation

You will need your prepared praise.

Experience

You will give and receive praise.

Procedure *(10–15 minutes)* Break into groups of four to six. One at a time, give the praise you prepared.

1. Explain the situation.

2. Select a group member to receive the praise.

3. Give the praise. (Talk; don't read it off the paper.) Try to select the position you would use if you were actually giving the praise on the job (both standing, both sitting, etc.).

4. Integration. The group gives the praise-giver feedback on how he or she did:

Step 1.   Was the praise very specific and descriptive? Did the giver look the employee in the eye?

Step 2.   Was the importance of the behavior clearly stated?

Step 3.   Did the giver stop for a moment of silence?

Step 4. Did the giver encourage repeat performance?

Did the giver of praise touch the receiver (optional)?

Step 5. Did the praise take less than one minute? Was the praise sincere?

Conclusion

The instructor may lead a class discussion and/or make concluding remarks.

Apply It *(2–4 minutes)* What did I learn from this experience? How will I use this knowledge in the future? When will I practice?

Endnotes

1. Trader Joe's Web site (www.traderjoes.com), retrieved January 2, 2013.

2. M.R. Barrick, M.K. Mount, and N. Li, "The Theory of Purposeful Work Behavior: The Role of Personality, Higher-Order Goals, and Job Characteristics," *Academy of Management Review* 38(1) (2013): 132–153.

3. B. Schyns, T. Kiefer, R. Kerschreiter, and A. Tymon, "Teaching Implicit Leadership Theories to Develop Leaders and Leadership: How and Why It Can Make a Difference," *Academy of Management Learning & Education* 10(3) (2012): 397–408.

4. S.L. Martin and H. Liao, "Directive versus Empowering Leadership: A Field Experiment Comparing Impacts on Task Proficiency and Proactivity," *Academy of Management Journal* 56(5) (2013): 1372–1395.

5. N.M. Lorinkova, M.J. Pearsall, and H.P. Sims, "Examining the Differential Longitudinal Performance of Directive versus Empowering Leadership in Teams," *Academy of Management Journal* 56(2) (2013): 573–596.

6. A.M. Grant, "Leading with Meaning: Beneficiary Contact, Prosocial Impact, and the Performance Effects of Transformational Leadership," *Academy of Management Journal* 55(2) (2012): 458–476.

7. G. Yukl, "Effective Leadership Behavior: What We Know and What Questions Need More Attention," *Academy of Management Perspectives* 26(4) (2012): 66–85.

8. R. Klimoski and B. Amos, "Practicing Evidence-Based Education in Leadership Development," *Academy of Management Learning & Education* 11(4) (2012): 685–702.

9. G. Yukl, "Effective Leadership Behavior: What We Know and What Questions Need More Attention," *Academy of Management Perspectives* 26(4) (2012): 66–85.

10. G. Yukl, "Effective Leadership Behavior: What We Know and What Questions Need More Attention," *Academy of Management Perspectives* 26(4) (2012): 66–85.

11. K. Lewin, R. Lippitt, and R.K. White, "Patterns of Aggressive Behavior in Experimentally Created Social Climates," *Journal of Social Psychology* 10(1939): 271–301.

12. G. Yukl, "Effective Leadership Behavior: What We Know and What Questions Need More Attention," *Academy of Management Perspectives* 26(4) (2012): 66–85.

13. R. Likert, *New Patterns of Management* (New York: McGraw-Hill, 1961).

14. R. M. Stogdill and A.E. Coons (Eds.), *Leader Behavior: Its Description and Measurement* (Columbus: Ohio State University Bureau of Business Research, 1957).

15. A. Edmans, "The Link between Job Satisfaction and Firm Value, with Implications for Corporate Social Responsibility," *Academy of Management Perspectives* 26(4) (2012): 1–19.

16. R. Blake and J. Mouton, *The Managerial Grid* (Houston, TX: Gulf Publishing, 1964); R. Blake and J. Mouton, *The New Managerial Grid* (Houston, TX: Gulf Publishing, 1978); R. Blake and J. Mouton, *The Managerial Grid III: The Key to Leadership Excellence* (Houston, TX: Gulf Publishing, 1985); and R. Blake and A. A. McCanse, *Leadership Dilemmas— Grid Solutions* (Houston, TX: Gulf Publishing, 1991). "R. Blake and J. Mouton: The Managerial Grid," *Thinkers* (March 2002).

17. B. M. Fisher and J. E. Edwards, "Consideration and Initiating Structure and Their Relationship with Leader Effectiveness: A Meta-Analysis," *Proceeding of the Academy of Management* (August 1988): 201–205.

18. M.A. Hogg, D. Van Knippenberg, and D.E. Rast, "Intergroup Leadership in Organizations: Leading across Group and Organizational Boundaries," *Academy of Management Review* 37(2) (2012): 232–255.

19. G. Yukl, "Effective Leadership Behavior: What We Know and What Questions Need More Attention," *Academy of Management Perspectives* 26(4) (2012): 66–85.

20. R.L. Dufresne and E.H. Offstein, "Holistic and Intentional Student Character Development Process: Learning from West Point," *Academy of Management Learning & Education* 11(4) (2012): 570–590.

21. M. Cuban, "Motivate Yourself," *BusinessWeek* (April 11, 2013): online.

22 G.K. Stahl and M.Y. Brannen, "Building Cross-Cultural Leadership Competence: An Interview with Carlos Chosn," *Academy of Management Learning & Education* 12(3) (2013): 494–502.

23 K. H. Dekas, T.N. Bauer, B. Welle, J. Kurkoski, and S. Sullivan, "Organizational Citizenship Behavior, Version 2.0: A Review and Qualitative Investigation of OCBs for Knowledge Workers at Google and Beyond," *Academy of Management Perspectives* 27(3) (2013): 219–237.

24 S. Boivie, S.D. Graffin, and T.G. Pollock, "Time for Me to Fly: Predicting Director Exit at Large Firms," *Academy of Management Journal* 55(6) (2012): 1334–1359.

25 L.M. Leslie, C.F. Manchester, T.Y. Park, and S. A. Mehng, "Flexible Work Practices: A Source of Career Premiums or Penalties?" *Academy of Management Journal* 55(6) (2012): 1407–1428.

26 L. Colan, "4 Questions to Help Build a Purpose-Driven Team," *Inc.* (December 2013/January 2014): 12.

27 A.M. Grant and S.V. Patil, "Challenging the Norm of Self-Interest: Minority Influence and Transitions to Helping Norms in Work Units," *Academy of Management Review* 37(4) (2012): 547–568.

28 M.R. Barrick, M.K. Mount, and N. Li, "The Theory of Purposeful Work Behavior: The Role of Personality, Higher-Order Goals, and Job Characteristics," *Academy of Management Review* 38(1) (2013): 132–153.

29 A.H. Van De Ven and A. Lifschitz, "Rational and Reasonable Microfoundations of Markets and Institutions," *Academy of Management Perspectives* 27(2) (2013): 156–172.

30 J. Eisenberg, C. E. J. Härtel, and G. K. Stahl, "From the Guest Editors: Cross-Cultural Management Learning and Education—Exploring Multiple Aims, Approaches, and Impacts," *Academy of Management Learning & Education* 12(3) (2013): 323–329; A.H. Van De Ven and A. Lifschitz, "Rational and Reasonable Microfoundations of Markets and Institutions," *Academy of Management Learning & Education* 27(2) (2013): 156–172.

31 B. Kowitt, "Inside Trader Joe's," *Fortune* (September 6, 2010): 86–96.

32 D. Liu, T.R. Mitchell, T.W. Lee, B.R. Holtom, and T.R. Hinkin, "When Employees Are Out of Step with Coworkers: How Job Satisfaction Trajectory and Dispersion influence Individual- and Unit-Level Voluntary Turnover," *Academy of Management Journal* 55(6) (2012): 1360–1380.

33 A. Maslow, "A Theory of Human Motivation," *Psychological Review* 50(1943): 370–396.

34 "Using the Malsow Hierarchy of Needs Theory," Mind Tools Web site (www.mindtools.com), accessed January 17, 2014.

35 H.A. Richardson and S.G. Taylor, "Understanding Input Events: A Model of Employees' Responses to Requests for Their Input," *Academy of Management Review* 37(3) (2012): 471–491.

36 D. Ariely, "For Quick Decisions, Depend on Deadlines," *Wall Street Journal* (August 3–4, 2013): C12.

37 F. Herzberg, "The Motivation-Hygiene Concept and Problems of Manpower," *Personnel Administrator* (1964): 3–7; and F. Herzberg, "One More Time: How Do You Motivate Employees?" *Harvard Business Review* (January–February 1968): 53–62.

38 M. Kownatzki, J. Walter, S.W. Floyd, and C. Lechner, "Corporate Control and the Speed of Strategic Business Unit Decision Making," *Academy of Management Journal* 56(5) (2013): 1295–1324.

39 M. Kownatzki, J. Walter, S.W. Floyd, and C. Lechner, "Corporate Control and the Speed of Strategic Business Unit Decision Making," *Academy of Management Journal* 56(5) (2013): 1295–1324.

40 S. Boivie, S.D. Graffin, and T.G. Pollock, "Time for Me to Fly: Predicting Director Exit at Large Firms," *Academy of Management Journal* 55(6) (2012): 1334–1359.

41 S. Boivie, S.D. Graffin, and T.G. Pollock, "Time for Me to Fly: Predicting Director Exit at Large Firms," *Academy of Management Journal* 55(6) (2012): 1334–1359.

42 A.M. Grant, "Leading with Meaning: Beneficiary Contact, Prosocial Impact, and the Performance Effects of Transformational Leadership," *Academy of Management Journal* 55(2) (2012): 458–476.

43 S.K. Parker, A. Johnson, C. Collins, and H. Nguyen, "Making the Most of Structural Support: Moderating Influence of Employees' Clarity and Negative Affect," *Academy of Management Journal* 56(3) (2013): 867–892.

44 M.R. Barrick, M.K. Mount, and N. Li, "The Theory of Purposeful Work Behavior: The Role of Personality, Higher-Order Goals, and Job Characteristics," *Academy of Management Review* 38(1) (2013): 132–153.

45 H. Murray, *Explorations in Personality* (New York: Oxford University Press, 1938); J. Atkinson, *An Introduction to Motivation* (New York: Van Nostrand Reinhold, 1964); D. McClelland, *The Achieving Society* (New York: Van Nostrand Reinhold, 1961); and D. McClelland and D. H. Burnham, "Power Is the Great Motivator," *Harvard Business Review* (March/April 1978): 103.

46 L.M. Leslie, C.F. Manchester, T.Y. Park, and S.A. Mehng, "Flexible Work Practices: A Source of Career Premiums or Penalties?" *Academy of Management Journal 55*(6) (2012): 1407–1428.

47 A. Edmans, "The Link between Job Satisfaction and Firm Value, with Implications for Corporate Social Responsibility," *Academy of Management Perspectives 26*(4) (2012): 1–19.

48 C.R. Long, C. Bendersky, and C. Morrill, "Fairness Monitoring: Linking Managerial Controls and Fairness Judgments in Organizations," *Academy of Management Journal 54*(5) (2011): 1045–1056.

49 J. S. Adams, "Toward an Understanding of Inequity," *Journal of Abnormal and Social Psychology 67* (1963): 422–436.

50 M.K. Duffy, K. L. Scott, J.D. Shaw, B.J. Tepper, and K Aquino, "A Social Context Model of Envy and Social Undermining," *Academy of Management Journal 55*(2) (2012): 643–666.

51 C.O. Trevor, G. Reilly, and B. Gerhart, "Reconsidering Pay Dispersion's Effect on the Performance of Interdependent Work: Reconciling Sorting and Pay Inequality," *Academy of Management Journal 55*(3) (2012): 585–610.

52 A.H. Van De Ven and A. Lifschitz, "Rational and Reasonable Microfoundations of Markets and Institutions," *Academy of Management Perspectives 27*(2) (2013): 156–172.

53 D.M. Mayer, K. Aquino, R.L. Greenbaum, and M. Kuenzi, "Who Displays Ethical Leadership, and Why an Examination of Antecedents and Consequences of Ethical Leadership," *Academy of Management Journal 55*(1) (2012): 151–171.

54 V. Vroom, *Work and Motivation* (New York: John Wiley & Sons, 1964).

55 J.K. Nelson, L.W. Poms, and P.P. Wolf, "Developing Efficacy Beliefs for Ethics and Diversity Management," *Academy of Management Learning & Education 11*(1) (2012): 49–68.

56 H.J. Klein, J.C. Molloy, and C.T. Brinsfield, "Reconceptualizing Workplace Commitment to Redress a Stretched Construct: Revisiting Assumptions and Removing Confounds," *Academy of Management Review 37*(1) (2012): 130–151.

57 A.H. Van De Ven and A. Lifschitz, "Rational and Reasonable Microfoundations of Markets and Institutions," *Academy of Management Perspectives 27*(2) (2013): 156–172.

58 R.L. Dufresne and E.H. Offstein, "Holistic and Intentional Student Character Development Process: Learning from West Point," *Academy of Management Learning & Education 11*(4) (2012): 570–590.

59 B. Southward, "The Crowd Goes Wild," *Fortune* (July 22, 2013): 18.

60 D. Ariely, "For Quick Decisions, Depend on Deadlines," *Wall Street Journal* (August 3–4, 2013): C12.

61 S.K. Johnson, L.L. Garrison, G.H. Bronnme, J.W. Fleenor, and J.L. Steed, "Go for the Goals: Relationship between Goal Setting and Transfer of Training Following Leadership Development," *Academy of Management Learning & Education 11*(4) (2012): 555–569.

62 L.M. Leslie, C.F. Manchester, T.Y. Park, and S. A. Mehng, "Flexible Work Practices: A Source of Career Premiums or Penalties?" *Academy of Management Journal 55*(6) (2012): 1407–1428.

63 H.J. Klein, J.C. Molloy, and C.T. Brinsfield, "Reconceptualizing Workplace Commitment to Redress a Stretched Construct: Revisiting Assumptions and Removing Confounds," *Academy of Management Review 37*(1) (2012): 130–151.

64 D. Ariely, "For Quick Decisions, Depend on Deadlines," *Wall Street Journal* (August 3–4, 2013): C12.

65 B. F. Skinner, *Beyond Freedom and Dignity* (New York: Alfred A. Knopf, 1971).

66 M. Kownatzki, J. Walter, S.W. Floyd, and C. Lechner, "Corporate Control and the Speed of Strategic Business Unit Decision Making," *Academy of Management Journal 56*(5) (2013): 1295–1324.

67 N. Rothbard, "Put on a Happy Face, Seriously," *Wall Street Journal* (October 24, 2011): R2.

68 M. Helft, "Sheryl Sandberg: The Real Story," *Fortune* (October 28, 2013): 122–130.

69 C. Rose, "Charlie Rose Talks to Mark Zuckerberg and Sheryl Sandberg," *BusinessWeek* (November 14–20, 2011): 50.

70 C. Suddath, "Sheryl-Sandberg's 'Lean In' Brand Goes Global," *Businessweek.com*, March 22, 2013.

71 S. Sandberg, *Lean In* (New York: Alfred A. Knopf, 2013), p. 171.

72 S. Sandberg, *Lean In* (New York: Alfred A. Knopf, 2013), p. 7.

73 S. Sandberg, *Lean In* (New York: Alfred A. Knopf, 2013), p. 8.

CHAPTER

4

Contingency Leadership Theories

Learning Outcomes

After studying this chapter, you should be able to:

1. State the major difference between behavioral and contingency leadership theories, and explain the behavioral contribution to contingency theories. p. 109

2. Describe the contingency leadership theory variables. p. 110

3. Identify the contingency leadership model styles and variables. p. 112

4. State the leadership continuum model major styles and variables. p. 116

5. Identify the path–goal leadership model styles and variables. p. 119

6. State the normative leadership model styles and the number of variables. p. 123

7. Discuss the major similarities and differences between the behavioral and contingency leadership theories. p. 128

8. Compare and contrast four major differences among the four contingency leadership models. p. 128

9. List which leadership models are prescriptive and descriptive, and explain why they are classified as such. p. 129

10. Explain substitutes and neutralizers of leadership. p. 131

OPENING CASE Application

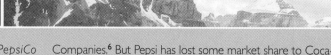

PepsiCo has four major global business units: *PepsiCo Americas Beverages (PAB)* spans carbonated soft drinks (Pepsi, Mountain Dew), juices and juice drinks (Tropicana, Naked Juice), ready-to-drink teas and coffees (Lipton, Starbucks, Tazo), sports drinks (Gatorade), and bottled waters (Aquafina, Propel, IZZE). *PepsiCo Americas Foods* is the provider of many of the most popular food and snacks throughout North and Latin America. Its portfolio of businesses includes Frito-Lay North America (snack foods), Quaker Foods (cereal, granola bars) North America, and Latin American food and snack businesses, including Sabritas and Gamesa brands. *PepsiCo Europe* includes all beverage, food, and snack businesses in Europe and South Africa. *PepsiCo Asia, Middle East and Africa (AMEA)* includes all beverage, food, and snack businesses in these areas.[1]

Indra K. Nooyi is chairman and CEO of PepsiCo, and she is consistently ranked at or near the top of the Fortune 50 Most Powerful Women list.[2] Nooyi is a different kind of CEO, not just because she is an Indian woman. She says her approach boils down to "Performance with Purpose," the goal of providing sustained financial performance through human sustainability, environmental sustainability, and talent sustainability. She was one of the first executives to realize that the health and green movements were not just fads, and she demanded true innovation.[3]

By the numbers, PepsiCo has done well under CEO Nooyi.[4] Its stock price hit an all-time high in 2013. PepsiCo is ranked in the top 50 (43rd and Coca-Cola is 57th) on the Fortune 500 Largest U.S. Corporations list, with more than $6 billion in profits,[5] and it is ranked in the top 40 (37th and Coca-Cola is 4th) of the Fortune World's Most Admired

Companies.[6] But Pepsi has lost some market share to Coca-Cola. Critics say Nooyi put too much focus on healthy foods. In response, Pepsi is fighting back in the cola war with its first new ad campaign in three years.[7] Can PepsiCo every win the cola war and outsell Coke? Some investors would like PepsiCo to split into two companies, separating food and beverages.[8] Can Nooyi keep PepsiCo together?

OPENING CASE QUESTIONS:

1. What does climbing the corporate ladder to CEO of PepsiCo have to do with contingency leadership? What life, educational, and job experiences qualified Indra Nooyi for her job as CEO?

2. What do colleagues say about Indra Nooyi's leadership—is it task or relationship, does she have a life outside of PepsiCo, and does she have any future career plans?

3. Which continuum leadership style does Indra Nooyi tend to use in making acquisitions at PepsiCo?

4. Which path–goal leadership styles does Indra Nooyi tend to use at PepsiCo?

5. Which normative leadership styles does Indra Nooyi tend to use at PepsiCo?

Can you answer any of these questions? You'll find answers to these questions about PepsiCo and Indra Nooyi throughout the chapter.

To learn more about Indra Nooyi and PepsiCo, visit the company's Web site at www.pepsico.com.

Learning Outcome **1**

State the major difference between behavioral and contingency leadership theories, and explain the behavioral contribution to contingency theories.

Contingency Leadership Theories and Models

Both the trait and behavioral leadership theories were attempts to find the one best leadership style in all situations. By the late 1960s, it became apparent that there is no one best leadership style in all situations. Thus, contingency leadership theory became the third major leadership paradigm (Chapter 1), and the leadership styles used in its models are based on the behavioral leadership theories.

Leadership is typically understood as taking place in a situation,[9] so leaders need to change their behavior to meet the situational characteristics,[10] which is called contingency or situational leadership.[11] Duke's basketball Coach K says you have to adjust your leadership to the composition of your team.[12] In this section, we discuss theories versus models, the contingency theory factors, and the need for global contingency leadership.

Leadership Theories versus Leadership Models

As defined in Chapter 1, a *leadership theory* is an explanation of some aspect of leadership; theories have practical value because they are used to better understand, predict, and control successful leadership. A **leadership model** *is an example for emulation or use in a given situation.* Models are used to represent the world of managers,[13] and there are many academic models of leadership.[14] In this chapter, we discuss using models in a given situation to improve performance of leaders, followers, or both.

All of the contingency leadership theories in this chapter have leadership models. The leadership theory is the longer text that explains the variables and leadership styles to be used in a given contingency situation. The leadership model is the short (one-page) summary of the theory to be used when selecting the appropriate leadership style for a given situation.[15] Models have been compared to baseball in this way. A model can't teach you to get a hit every time at bat, but if you use the model, it will improve your batting average.

Learning Outcome **2**   *Describe the contingency leadership theory variables.*

Contingency Theory and Model Variables

Contingency means "it depends." One thing depends on other things, and for a leader to be effective, there must be an appropriate fit between the leader's behavior and style and the followers and the situation.[16] Recall from Chapter 1 that *contingency leadership theories* attempt to explain the appropriate leadership style based on the leader, followers, and situation. Much of today's contingency research focuses on team leadership,[17] as leaders find themselves reacting to situational contingencies.[18]

See Exhibit 4.1 for a list of general contingency leadership variables that can be used as a framework in which to place all the contingency leadership model variables for analyzing leadership. Throughout this chapter, each contingency leadership model's variables are described in terms of this framework. For each model, the *leader* variable also includes the leadership styles of each model.

EXHIBIT 4.1

Framework for Contingency Leadership Variables

FOLLOWERS	LEADER	SITUATION
Capability	Personality traits	Task
Motivation	Behavior	Structure
	Experience	Environment

© Cengage Learning®

4.1   Leadership Gender

Should gender be a contingency variable in leadership? Are there differences in the leadership of men and women? Some researchers say that women tend to be more participative, relationship-oriented leaders and men are more assertive and task oriented. However, others say that men and women leaders are more alike than different because they do the same things. Thus, there currently is no consensus in the literature that men and women lead differently or the same as men.[19]

1. Do you think that men and women lead the same or differently?
2. Are men or women more ethical and socially responsible leaders?
3. Would you prefer to have a man or woman for a boss?
4. Is it ethical and socially responsible to say that one gender makes better leaders?
5. Should global companies appoint women as managers in countries that believe in equal rights for women, but not allow women to be managers in countries that don't have these beliefs?

Global Contingency Leadership

Before we get into all the theories, let's take a minute to quickly realize how important contingency leadership is in the global economy of today.[20] Leadership is critical especially with the importance of the globalization of business,[21] and because executives have stated that new business school graduates have a weak global perspective.[22] Multinational companies have long abandoned the parochial "one-size-fits-all" assumptions in management practices.[23] Global companies like McDonald's, with restaurants all over the world, realize that successful leadership styles can vary greatly from place to place. In Europe and other parts of the world, managers have more cultural than technical variables to deal with as they encounter diverse value systems and religious backgrounds among employees. Employees in some countries prefer domineering, self-centered, and autocratic leaders, whereas other countries prefer a more democratic and participative leadership style. The focus of Chapter 10 is on organizational culture, ethics, and diversity. With respect to the discussion on diversity, we emphasize that the growing cultural diversity of the workforce and the increasing globalization of the marketplace create the need for leaders with multicultural backgrounds and experiences. This reinforces the message of global contingency leadership.

Companies, including IBM, are training their managers to work with a variety of foreigners to become successful global players. In countries that are more like the United States (such as Australia, Canada, and England), Americans have fewer adjustments to make, whereas countries with cultures that are quite different from that of the United States (such as China, India, and Japan) require greater adjustment.

GLOBE stands for *Global Leadership and Organizational Behavior Effectiveness*, which is an ongoing cross-cultural investigation of leadership and national culture. The GLOBE research team used data from 825 organizations, with 18,000 managers, in 62 countries to identify nine dimensions in which national cultures are diverse.[24] See Chapter 10 for an expanded discussion of national culture identities using Hofstede's Model of five dimensions that he used to distinguish a nation's culture from other nations.

OPENING CASE Application

I. What does climbing the corporate ladder to CEO of PepsiCo have to do with contingency leadership? What life, educational, and job experiences qualified Indra Nooyi for her job as CEO?

Contingency theory is about using the right style in the right situation to succeed, which Indra Nooyi continues to do. Having grown up in India, Nooyi was the right person to continue to take PepsiCo global. On special occasions, Nooyi wears a traditional Indian sari. Her South Asian heritage gives her a wide-angle view on the world. She grew up in Chennai (formerly Madras), on the southeast coast of India, the daughter of a stay-at-home mom and an accountant father. Although her family is Hindu, Nooyi attended a Catholic school, was an avid debater, played cricket and the guitar, and formed an all-girl rock band. She earned a BS degree from Madras Christian College, an MBA from the Indian Institute of Management in Kolkata (formerly Calcutta), and a master of public and private management from Yale University. Before coming to PepsiCo, Nooyi was Senior VP and Director of Corporate Strategy and Planning at Motorola from 1986 to 1990 and Senior VP of Strategy and Strategic Marketing at Asea Brown Boveri from 1990 to 1994. She spent 12 years climbing the corporate ladder at PepsiCo. Nooyi started as Senior VP of Strategic Planning in 1994, was promoted to Senior VP of Corporate Strategy and Development in 1996, was promoted to President and CFO in 2001, and was promoted to CEO in 2006.

Learning Outcome **3**

Identify the contingency leadership model styles and variables.

Contingency Leadership Theory and Model

In 1951, Fred E. Fiedler began to develop the first situational leadership theory. It was the first theory to specify how situational variables interact with leader personality and behavior. He called the theory "Contingency Theory of Leader Effectiveness."[25] Contingency suggests that a leader's effectiveness depends on how well the leader's style fits the context of the job. So he was the first to develop a model to match the leadership style to the job. Although it is dated, researchers continue to conduct studies based on contingency theory.[26]

Fiedler believed that leadership style is a reflection of personality (trait theory–oriented) and behavior (behavioral theory–oriented), and that leadership styles are basically constant. Leaders should not change styles; they should change the context of their job. Because his was the first, today his term "contingency theory" is used in other contexts that have nothing to do with Fiedler's theory and model. You may have noticed that the title of this chapter is "Contingency Leadership Theories." The objective of all four contingency theories we present is to choose the leadership style that matches the situation to maximize performance.[27]

The **contingency leadership model** *is used to determine if a person's leadership style is task- or relationship-oriented, and if the situation (leader–member relationship, task structure, and position power) matches the leader's style to maximize performance.* In this section, we discuss Fiedler's leadership styles, situational favorableness, determining the appropriate leadership style for the situation, and research by Fiedler and others. See Exhibit 4.2 to see how Fiedler's model fits into the framework of contingency leadership variables.

EXHIBIT 4.2

Contingency Leadership Model Variables within the Contingency Leadership Framework

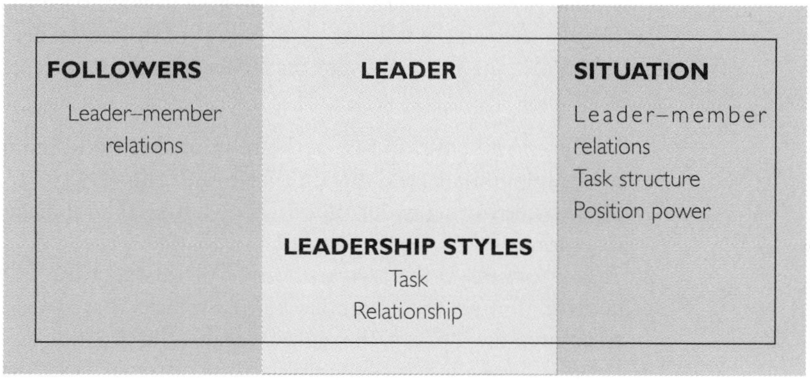

FOLLOWERS	LEADER	SITUATION
Leader–member relations		Leader–member relations Task structure Position power
	LEADERSHIP STYLES Task Relationship	

© Cengage Learning®

Leadership Style and the LPC

Although we may be able to change your behavior with different followers (although Fiedler didn't think we can), we also have a dominant leadership style. The first major factor in using Fiedler's model is to determine whether your dominant leadership style is task-motivated or relationship-motivated. People primarily gain satisfaction either from task accomplishment or from forming and maintaining relationships with followers.[28] To determine leadership style, using Fiedler's model, you must complete the *least-preferred coworker (LPC)* scales. The LPC essentially answers the question, "Are you more task-oriented or relationship-oriented?" The two leadership styles are (1) *task* and (2) *relationship*. To determine your Fiedler leadership style, complete Self-Assessment 4-1.

SELF-ASSESSMENT 4-1 **Leadership Style Your**

Fiedler LPC

1. Return to Chapter 3, Self-Assessment 1 on page 71, and place your score for tasks on the following Task line and your score for people on the Relationship line.

   10 — 9 — 8 — 7 — 6 — 5 — 4 — 3 — 2 — 1
   High Task Leadership Style

   10 — 9 — 8 — 7 — 6 — 5 — 4 — 3 — 2 — 1
   High Relationship Leadership Style

   According to Fiedler, you are primarily either a task- or relationship-oriented leader. Your highest score is your primary leadership style. Neither leadership style is the one best style. The one appropriate leadership style to use is based on the situation—our next topic.

Situational Favorableness

After determining your leadership style, determine the situational favorableness. *Situational favorableness* refers to the degree to which a situation enables the leader to exert influence over the followers. The more control the leader has over the followers, the more favorable the situation is for the leader. The three variables, in order of importance, are as follows.

1. *Leader–member relations.* Is the relationship good (cooperative and friendly) or poor (antagonistic and difficult)? Do the followers trust, respect, accept, and have confidence in the leader (good)? The better the relations, the more favorable the situation.
2. *Task structure.* Is the task structured or unstructured? Do employees perform repetitive, routine, unambiguous, standard tasks that are easily understood? The more structured the jobs are, the more favorable the situation.
3. *Position power.* Is position power strong or weak? Does the leader have the power to assign work, reward and punish, hire and fire, give raises and promotions? The more power, the more favorable the situation.

The relative weights of these three factors together create a continuum of situational favorableness of the leader. Fiedler developed eight levels of favorableness, going from 1 (highly favorable) to 8 (very unfavorable). See Exhibit 4.3 for an adapted model.

Determining the Appropriate Leadership Style

To determine whether task or relationship leadership is appropriate, you answer the three questions pertaining to situational favorableness, using the Fiedler contingency theory model (Exhibit 4.3). Start with question 1 and follow the decision tree to Good or Poor depending on the relations. Next, answer question 2 and follow the decision tree to Repetitive or Non repetitive. When answering question 3, you end up in one of eight possible situations. If the LPC leadership style matches, you do nothing, since you may be successful in that situation because your leadership style matches the situation.

Changing the Situation

However, if the leadership style does not match the situation, the leader may be ineffective. One option is to change to a job that matches the leadership style. Fiedler recommends (and trained people to) change the situation, rather than their leadership styles. Here are a few general examples of how to change the situation variables to make a more favorable match for the leader's style:

- If relations are poor, the leader can work to improve them by showing interest in followers, listening to them, and spending more time getting to know them personally.
- The *task* can be more or less structured by stating more or less specific standards and procedures for completing the task, and giving or not giving clear deadlines.
- Leaders with strong *position power* do not have to use it; they can empower employees.[29] Leaders with weak power can try to get more power from their manager and play up the power by being more autocratic.

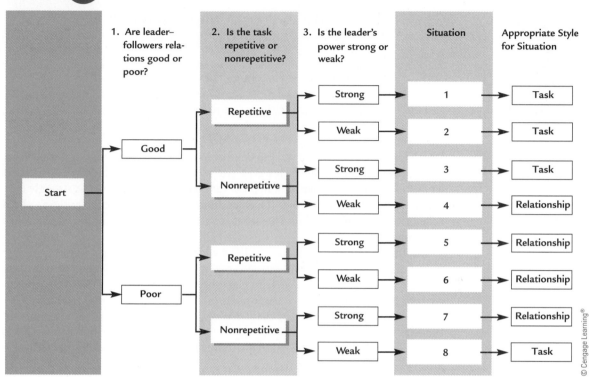

EXHIBIT 4.3

Fiedler Contingency Leadership Model

	1. Are leader–followers relations good or poor?	2. Is the task repetitive or nonrepetitive?	3. Is the leader's power strong or weak?	Situation	Appropriate Style for Situation
		Repetitive	Strong	1	Task
	Good		Weak	2	Task
		Nonrepetitive	Strong	3	Task
Start			Weak	4	Relationship
		Repetitive	Strong	5	Relationship
	Poor		Weak	6	Relationship
		Nonrepetitive	Strong	7	Relationship
			Weak	8	Task

© Cengage Learning®

CONCEPT APPLICATION 4-1

Contingency Leadership Theory

Using the contingency model in Exhibit 4.3, answer the three questions at the top of the model to get to the situation (numbered 1–8). Follow the situation to the appropriate style in the last column of the model to determine the situation number with its corresponding appropriate leadership style (task or relationship). Select two answers below based on the answers you get from the model, writing the appropriate two letters in the blanks before each item.

Situation number   a. 1   b. 2   c. 3   d. 4   e. 5   f. 6   g. 7   h. 8
Leadership style   A. task-oriented   B. relationship-oriented

_____ 1. Shawn, the manager, is from the human resources department. He helps the other departments write job descriptions. Shawn is viewed as not understanding the various departments. Employees tend to be rude in their dealings with Shawn.

_____ 2. Juan, the manager, oversees the processing of canceled checks for the bank. He is well liked by the employees. Juan's manager enjoys hiring and evaluating his employees' performance.

_____ 3. Sally, the principal of a school, assigns teachers to classes and has various other duties. The school atmosphere is tense. She hires and decides on tenure appointments.

WORK
Application **4-1**

Select a present or past manager. Which LPC leadership style is, or was, dominant for that manager? Using the Fiedler model (see Exhibit 4.3 on page 115), which situation number is the manager in? What is the appropriate leadership style for the manager in this situation? Does it match his or her style? How successful a leader is your manager? Do you think there is a relationship between the manager's leadership style and the situation?

If you are a manager, you may want to repeat this work application, using yourself as the manager.

CONCEPT APPLICATION **4-1**(*continued*)

_____ 4. Carlos, the chairperson of the HR committee, is highly regarded by its volunteer members from a variety of departments. The committee members are charged with recommending ways to increase minority hiring and promotions.

_____ 5. Tania, the manager, oversees the assembly of mass-produced pens. She has the power to reward and punish, and is viewed as a highly demanding manager.

Research, Criticism, and Applications

Despite its groundbreaking start to contingency theories, Fiedler's work was criticized for weak statistical results.[30] However, two meta-analyses concluded that the research tends to support the model, although not for every situation and not as strongly for field studies as for laboratory studies.[31] Fiedler disagreed with some of the criticism and published two rejoinders.[32] Thus, the debate continues over the validity and usefulness of the model.

Another major criticism is of Fiedler's view that we leaders should not change our style, but rather the context of our job should be changed. It is generally agreed that it is much easier to change our style to meet the context of the job than to change the job context. Fiedler's model also doesn't really teach us how to change our job context. The other situational writers in this chapter suggest changing leadership styles, not our job context.

Despite the critics, Fiedler has helped contribute to the other contingency theories. It has application as it can be used to answer questions about the leadership of individuals in different types of organizations. It can help explain why a hard-working manager is not effective in a specific job—no match of style to context.

OPENING CASE Application

2. **What do colleagues say about Indra Nooyi's leadership—is it task or relationship, does she have a life outside of PepsiCo, and does she have any future career plans?**

Indra Nooyi's colleagues say she is intense, decisive, an excellent negotiator, very open and very direct, demanding, and she challenges you. Nooyi is charismatic. She can rouse an audience and rally them around any project. Although she is task oriented, Nooyi also has strong relationships with her colleagues. She insists that everybody's birthday be celebrated with a cake. She has a supportive husband (Raj) and two daughters (Preetha and Tara), and she enjoys being a soccer mom. Nooyi is a karaoke fan, and her karaoke machine is the ubiquitous party game at every PepsiCo gathering. Being CEO of PepsiCo will not be Nooyi's last job. She says that she eventually wants to give back by going to Washington to work for the government.

Learning Outcome **4**   *State the leadership continuum model major styles and variables.*

Leadership Continuum Theory and Model

Robert Tannenbaum and Warren Schmidt also developed a contingency theory in the 1950s.[33] They stated that leadership behavior is on a continuum from boss-centered to subordinate-centered leadership. Their model focuses on who makes the decisions. They noted that a leader's choice of a leadership pattern should be based on forces in the boss, forces in the subordinates, and forces in the situation. Look at Exhibit 4.4 to see how Tannenbaum and Schmidt's variables fit within the framework of contingency leadership variables.

EXHIBIT 4.4

Leadership Continuum Model Variables within the Contingency Leadership Framework

FOLLOWERS	LEADER	SITUATION
Subordinates	Boss	Situation (time)
	LEADERSHIP STYLES	
	Boss-centered to subordinate-centered leadership with seven leadership styles along the continuum in Exhibit 4.5	

© Cengage Learning®

Tannenbaum and Schmidt identify seven major styles the leader can choose from. Exhibit 4.5 is an adaptation of their model, which lists the seven styles. *The* **leadership continuum model** *is used to determine which one of seven styles to select, based on the use of boss-centered versus subordinate-centered leadership, to meet the situation (boss, subordinates, situation/time) to maximize performance.*

Before selecting one of the seven leadership styles, the leader must consider the following three forces or variables:

- *Boss.* The leader's personality and behavioral preferred style—based on experience, expectation, values, and confidence in the subordinates—are considered in selecting a leadership style. Based on personality and behavior, some leaders tend to be more autocratic and others more participative.[34]
- *Subordinates.* The followers' preferred style for the leader is based on personality and behavior, as with the leader. Generally, the more willing and able the followers are to participate, the more freedom of participation should be used, and vice versa.
- *Situation (time).* The environmental considerations, such as the organization's size, structure, climate, goals, and technology, are considered in selecting a leadership style.

The *time* available is another consideration. It takes more time to make participative decisions. Thus, when there is no time to include followers in decision making, the leader uses an autocratic leadership style.

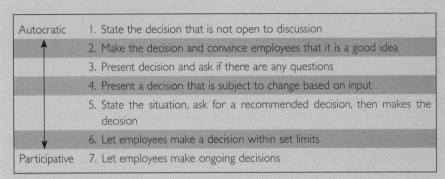

EXHIBIT 4.5

Tannenbaum and Schmidt's Leadership Continuum Model

Autocratic   1. State the decision that is not open to discussion

2. Make the decision and convince employees that it is a good idea

3. Present decision and ask if there are any questions

4. Present a decision that is subject to change based on input

5. State the situation, ask for a recommended decision, then makes the decision

6. Let employees make a decision within set limits

Participative   7. Let employees make ongoing decisions

Source: Adapted from *How to Choose a Leadership Pattern* by Robert Tannenbaum and Warren H. Schmidt, May–June 1973.

CONCEPT APPLICATION **4-2**

Leadership Continuum

Using the continuum model in Exhibit 4.5, *identify these five statements by their leadership style (numbered 1–7 in the model). Select each answer, writing the appropriate letters in the blank before each item.*

    a. 1   b. 2   c. 3   d. 4   e. 5   f. 6   g. 7

____ 6. "This is the way I think we should do the job. Does anyone have any other ideas for how to do it?"

____ 7. "Here is list of holidays you can get paid for. Tania, you get seven paid, so you can pick the ones you want."

____ 8. "I'd like your ideas on how to solve the problem. But I have the final say on the solution we implement."

____ 9. "Tony, I selected you to take on the new assignment. Do you have any questions about this assignment?"

____ 10. "Helen, I like your report. Send it to the VP right away."

WORK
Application **4-2**

Using the leadership continuum model (Exhibit 4.5), identify your manager's most commonly used leadership style by number and description. Would you say this is the most appropriate leadership style based on the leader, the followers, and the situation? Explain.

Although the leadership continuum model was very popular, it did not undergo research testing like the contingency leadership model. One major criticism of this model is that the three factors to consider when selecting a leadership style are very subjective. In other words, determining which style to use, and when, is not clear in the model. The Situational Leadership® Model and Normative Leadership Model (to be discussed later in this chapter) thus took over in popularity, most likely because they clearly identified which leadership style to use in a given, clearly defined situation.

You will determine your major leadership continuum style later in Self-Assessment 4-4 on page 143, which puts together three of the contingency leadership styles (continuum, path–goal, and normative).

OPENING CASE Application

3. Which continuum leadership style does Indra Nooyi tend to use in making acquisitions at PepsiCo?

Nooyi tends to use #5—the leader presents the problem, gets suggested solutions, and makes the decision. She has others look into possible acquisition targets and gets recommendations from them, but Nooyi has the final say on which companies will be acquired.

Learning Outcome **5** *Identify the path–goal leadership model styles and variables.*

Path–Goal Leadership Theory and Model

The path–goal leadership theory was developed by Robert House, based on an early version of the theory by M. G. Evans, and published in 1971 and other articles over years.[35] His theory specified a number of situational moderators of relationships between task- and person-oriented leadership and their effects. House attempted to explain how the behavior of a leader influences the performance and satisfaction of the followers (subordinates). Look at Exhibit 4.6 to see how House's model fits into the framework of contingency leadership variables. Note that unlike the earlier contingency leadership models, House's model does not have a leader trait and behavior variable. The leader is supposed to use the appropriate leadership style (one of four), regardless of preferred traits and behavior to motivate employees to enhance their performance.

The **path–goal leadership model** *is used to select the leadership style (directive, supportive, participative, or achievement-oriented) appropriate to the situation (subordinate and environment) to maximize both performance and job satisfaction.* Note that path–goal leadership theory is based on motivation theories of goal-setting and expectancy theory. The leader is responsible for increasing followers' motivation to attain personal and organizational goals. Motivation is increased by (1) clarifying the follower's path to the rewards that are available or (2) increasing the rewards that the follower values and desires. *Path clarification* means that the leader works with followers to help them identify and learn the behaviors that will lead to successful task accomplishment and organizational rewards.

EXHIBIT 4.6 **Path–Goal Leadership Model Variables within the Contingency Leadership Framework**

FOLLOWERS	LEADER	SITUATION
Subordinates (authoritarianism, locus of control, ability)	None	Environment (task structure, formal authority, and work group)
	LEADERSHIP STYLES Directive Supportive Participative Achievement-oriented	

© Cengage Learning®

The path–goal model is used to determine employee objectives and to clarify how to achieve them using one of four leadership styles. It focuses on how leaders influence employees' perceptions of their goals and the paths they follow toward goal attainment. As shown in Exhibit 4.7 (an adaptation of the model), the situational factors are used to determine the leadership style that affects goal achievement through performance and satisfaction.

EXHIBIT 4.7

House Path–Goal Leadership Model

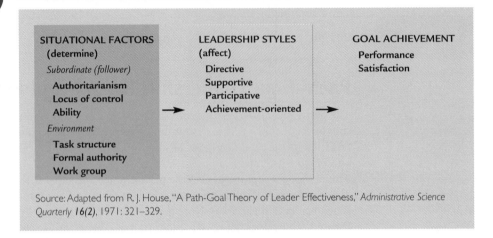

SITUATIONAL FACTORS
(determine)
Subordinate (follower)
Authoritarianism
Locus of control
Ability
Environment
Task structure
Formal authority
Work group

LEADERSHIP STYLES
(affect)
Directive
Supportive
Participative
Achievement-oriented

GOAL ACHIEVEMENT
Performance
Satisfaction

Source: Adapted from R. J. House, "A Path-Goal Theory of Leader Effectiveness," *Administrative Science Quarterly 16(2)*, 1971: 321–329.

Situational Factors

Subordinate

Subordinate situational characteristics are:

1. *Authoritarianism* is the degree to which employees defer to others, and want to be told what to do and how to do the job.
2. *Locus of control* (Chapter 2) is the extent to which employees believe they control goal achievement (internal) or if goal achievement is controlled by others (external).
3. *Ability* is the extent of the employees' ability to perform tasks to achieve goals.

Environment

Environment situational factors are:

1. *Task structure* is the extent of repetitiveness of the job.
2. *Formal authority* is the extent of the leader's position power. Note that task structure and formal authority are essentially the same as Fiedler's.
3. *Work group* is the extent to which coworkers contribute to job satisfaction or the relationship between followers. Note that House identifies work group as a situational variable. However, under the contingency framework, it would be considered a follower variable.

YOU Make the **ETHICAL** Call

4.2 *Drug Research*

Several drug companies, including GlaxoSmithKline and Merck, have been accused of situationally favorable research reporting. When results support the use of the drug, they are reported; when they don't, results are not reported. Although all medications have side effects, some drug users have died because of medication. As a result, the Food and Drug Administration (FDA) has been criticized for its process of approving drugs and monitoring their safety.

1. Is it ethical and socially responsible to report only the results that help gain FDA approval of drugs?

2. If you worked for a drug company and knew that the results of a study showed negative effects but were not included in a report, what would you do?

3. If you worked for a drug company and your boss asked you to change negative results into positive results, or to make results even better, what would you do?

4. What would you do if you gave your boss a negative report on a drug and found out the results were changed to positive results?

5. Is the FDA doing a good job of monitoring the safety of drugs? If not, what else should it do?

Leadership Styles

Based on the situational factors in the path–goal model, the leader can select the most appropriate leadership style by using the following general guidelines for each style.

Directive

The leader provides high structure. Directive leadership is appropriate when the followers want authority leadership and have external locus of control, and when the follower ability is low. Directive leadership is also appropriate when the environmental task is complex or ambiguous, formal authority is strong, and the work group provides job satisfaction.

Supportive

The leader provides high consideration. Supportive leadership is appropriate when the followers do not want autocratic leadership and have internal locus of control, and when follower ability is high. Supportive leadership is also appropriate when the environmental tasks are simple, formal authority is weak, and the work group does not provide job satisfaction.

Participative

The leader includes employee input into decision making. Participative leadership is appropriate when followers want to be involved and have internal locus of control, and when follower ability is high; when the environmental task is complex, authority is either strong or weak, and job satisfaction from coworkers is either high or low.

Achievement-Oriented

The leader sets difficult but achievable goals, expects followers to perform at their highest level, and rewards them for doing so. In essence, the leader provides both high directive (structure) and high supportive (consideration) behavior. The leader tries to make the job challenging.[36] Achievement-oriented leadership is appropriate when followers are open to autocratic leadership and have external locus of control, and when follower ability is high; when the environmental task is simple, authority is strong, and job satisfaction from coworkers is either high or low.

CONCEPT APPLICATION 4-3

Path–Goal Leadership

2. Using Exhibit 4.7 on page 120 and text descriptions, identify the appropriate leadership style for the five situations. Write the appropriate letter in the blank before each item.

a. directive   c. participative

b. supportive   d. achievement-oriented

_____ 11. A manager is assembling a new task force that will have an ambiguous task to complete. The members don't know each other.

_____ 12. A manager has decided to give a new task to an employee who tends to be insecure and may feel threatened by taking on a new task.

_____ 13. The quarter just ended and the sales team easily met the quota. The manager has strong position power and has decided to increase the quota to make the job more challenging.

_____ 14. A manager has an employee who has been coming in late for work. The manager has decided to get the employee to get to work on time.

_____ 15. A manager has a new task, and he is not sure how it should be done. Employees are experienced and like to be involved.

Research, Criticism, and Applications

A meta-analysis based on 120 studies examined directive and supportive behavior and showed that support for path–goal theory was significantly greater than chance, but results were quite mixed. An extensive review of the research on moderator variables in leaders also had inconclusive findings.[37]

Although path–goal theory is more complex and specific than leadership continuum, it is also criticized by managers because it is difficult to know which style to use when. As you can see, there are many situations in which not all six situational factors are exactly as presented in the guidelines for when to use the style. Judgment calls are required to select the appropriate style as necessary. Plus, House suggests adding your own variables to the model.

Despite its limitations, the path–goal model has already made an important contribution to the study of leadership by providing a conceptual framework to guide researchers in identifying potentially relevant situational variables. Path–goal leadership theory led to the development of the theory of *charismatic leadership* in 1976.

Path–goal theory was considerably broadened in scope, and in 1996, House referred to it as *value-based leadership theory*. You will learn about charismatic and values-based leadership in Chapter 9. Path–goal theory also provides a useful way for leaders to think about motivating followers. You will determine your path–goal leadership style in Self-Assessment 4-4 on page 143, which puts together the contingency leadership styles.

WORK
Application **4-3**

Identify your manager's most commonly used path–goal leadership style. Would you say this is the most appropriate leadership style based on the situational factors? Explain.

_____

_____

_____

_____

OPENING CASE Application

4. Which path–goal leadership styles does Indra Nooyi tend to use at PepsiCo?

Nooyi tends to use the achievement-oriented and participative styles. She sets high standards and expects everyone around her to measure up. She has red, green, and purple pens and uses them liberally to mark up everything that crosses her desk. Her scribbles are legendary, and include the following: "I have never seen such gross incompetence," and "This is unacceptable," with "unacceptable" underlined three times. Nooyi believes in people; you give them an objective and get them all to buy into it, and they can move mountains. She uses input from others, including her second-in-command, whom she treats like a partner, and her "Team Pepsi" members.

Learning Outcome 6   *State the normative leadership model styles and the number of variables.*

Normative Leadership Theory and Models

An important leadership question today is, "When should the manager take charge and when should the manager let the group make the decision?" In 1973, Victor Vroom (yes, the same guy who developed expectancy theory) and Philip Yetton published a decision-making model to answer this question while improving decision-making effectiveness. Vroom and Arthur Jago refined the model and expanded it to four models in 1988. In 2000, Victor Vroom published a revised version titled "Leadership and the Decision-Making Process." We present the latest.[38]

The **normative leadership model** *has a time-driven and development-driven decision tree that enables the user to select one of five leadership styles (decide, consult individually, consult group, facilitate, and delegate) appropriate for the situation (seven questions/ variables) to maximize decisions.* See Exhibit 4.8 to see how the normative leadership model fits into the contingency leadership framework variables. It is called a *normative model* because it provides a sequential set of questions that are rules (norms) to follow to determine the best leadership style for the given situation.

EXHIBIT 4.8   **Normative Leadership Model Variables within the Contingency Leadership Framework**

FOLLOWERS	LEADER	SITUATION
Development-Driven Decision Model	3. Leader expertise	*Time-Driven Decision Model*
2. Importance of commitment	**LEADERSHIP STYLES**	1. Decision significance
4. Likelihood of commitment	Decide	
5. Group support for objectives	Consult individually	
6. Group expertise	Consult group	
7. Team competence	Facilitate	
	Delegate	

© Cengage Learning®

To use the normative model, you must have a specific decision to make, have the authority to make the decision, and have specific potential followers to participate in the decision.

Leadership Participation Styles

Vroom identified five leadership styles based on the level of participation in the decision by the followers. Vroom's five leadership styles follow.

Decide

The leader makes the decision alone and announces it, or sells it, to the followers.

Consult Individually

The leader tells followers individually about the problem, gets information and suggestions, and then makes the decision.

Consult Group

The leader holds a group meeting and tells followers the problem, gets information and suggestions, and then makes the decision.

Facilitate

The leader holds a group meeting and acts as a facilitator to define the problem and the limits within which a decision must be made. Leaders seek participation and concurrence on the decision without pushing their ideas.

Delegate

The leader lets the group diagnose the problem and make the decision within stated limits. The role of the leader is to answer questions and provide encouragement and resources.

Model Questions to Determine the Appropriate Leadership Style

To determine which of the five leadership styles is the most appropriate for a given situation, you answer a series of diagnostic questions based on seven variables. The seven variables presented in Exhibit 4.8 are repeated in Exhibit 4.9 and in Exhibit 4.10.

We now explain how to answer the questions, based on the variables, when using the two models.

1. *Decision Significance.* How important is the decision to the success of the project or organization? Is the decision of high (H) importance or low (L) importance to the success? When making highly important decisions, leaders need to be involved.

2. *Importance of Commitment.* How important is follower commitment to implement the decision? If acceptance of the decision is critical to effective implementation, importance is high (H). If commitment is not important, it's low (L). When making highly important commitment decisions that followers may not like and may not implement, followers generally need to be involved in making the decision.

3. *Leader Expertise.* How much knowledge and expertise does the leader have with this specific decision? Is expertise high (H) or low (L)? The more expertise the leader has, the less need there is for follower participation.

4. *Likelihood of Commitment.* If the leader were to make the decision alone, is the certainty that the followers would be committed to the decision high (H) or low (L)? When making decisions that followers will like and want to implement, there is less need to involve them in the decision.

5. *Group Support for Objectives.* Do followers have high (H) or low (L) support for the team or organizational goals to be attained in solving the problem? Higher levels of participation are acceptable with high levels of support.

Normative Leadership Time-Driven Model

EXHIBIT 4.9

Instructions: The model is a decision tree that works like a funnel. Define the problem statement and then answer the questions from left to right as high (H) or low (L), skipping questions when not appropriate to the situation and avoiding crossing any horizontal lines. The last column you come to contains the appropriate leadership participation decision-making style for the situation.

	1. Decision Significance?	2. Importance of Commitment?	3. Leader Expertise?	4. Likelihood of Commitment?	5. Group Support?	6. Group Expertise?	7. Team Competence?	Leadership Style
P R O B L E M S T A T E M E N T	H	H	H	H	–	–	–	Decide
				L	H	H	H	Delegate
							L	Consult (Group)
						L	–	Consult (Group)
					L	–	–	
			L	H	H	H	H	Facilitate
							L	Consult (Individually)
						L	–	Consult (Individually)
					L	–	–	
				L	H	H	H	Facilitate
							L	Consult (Group)
						L	–	Consult (Group)
					L	–	–	
		L	H	–	–	–	–	Decide
			L	–	H	H	H	Facilitate
							L	Consult (Individually)
					L	–	Consult (Individually)
				L	–	–	
	L	H	–	H	–	–	Decide
			L	–	–	H	Delegate
						L	Facilitate
	L	–	–	–	–	Decide

Source: Adapted from *Organizational Dynamics 28*, Victor H. Vroom, "Leadership and the Decision-Making Process," p. 87.

6. *Group Expertise.* How much knowledge and expertise do the individual followers have with this specific decision? Is expertise high (H) or low (L)? The more expertise the followers have, the greater the individual or group participation can be.

Normative Leadership Development-Driven Model

Instructions: *The model is a decision tree that works like a funnel. Define the problem statement, then answer the questions from left to right as high (H) or low (L), skipping questions when not appropriate to the situation and avoiding crossing any horizontal lines. The last column you come to contains the appropriate leadership participation decision-making style for the situation.*

The far-left column is labeled **PROBLEM STATEMENT** (spanning all rows).

1. Decision Significance?	2. Importance of Commitment?	3. Leader Expertise?	4. Likelihood of Commitment?	5. Group Support?	6. Group Expertise?	7. Team Competence?	Leadership Style
H	H	–	H	H	H	H	Delegate
H	H	–	H	H	H	L	Facilitate
H	H	–	H	H	L	–	Consult (Group)
H	H	–	H	L	–	–	Consult (Group)
H	H	–	L	H	H	H	Delegate
H	H	–	L	H	H	L	Facilitate
H	H	–	L	H	L	–	Facilitate
H	H	–	L	L	–	–	Consult (Group)
H	L	–	–	H	H	H	Delegate
H	L	–	–	H	H	L	Facilitate
H	L	–	–	H	L	–	Consult (Group)
H	L	–	–	L	–	–	Consult (Group)
L	H	–	H	–	–	–	Decide
L	H	–	L	–	–	–	Delegate
L	L	–	–	–	–	–	Decide

Source: Adapted from *Organizational Dynamics 28,* Victor H. Vroom, "Leadership and the Decision-Making Process," p. 88.

7. *Team Competence.* Is the ability of the individuals to work together as a team to solve the problem high (H) or low (L)? With high team competence, more participation can be used.

Not all seven variables/questions are relevant to all decisions. All seven or as few as two questions are needed to select the most appropriate leadership style in a given situation. The great thing about the models is that they tie the relevant variables together for us as we answer the questions to determine the most appropriate leadership style for the given situation.

Selecting the Time-Driven or Development-Driven Model for the Situation

The first step is actually to select one of the two models, based on whether the situation is driven by the importance of time or development of followers. The characteristics of the decision are focus, value, and orientation.

The Time-Driven Model

See Exhibit 4.9 for the three characteristics:

1. *Focus.* The model is concerned with making effective decisions with minimum cost. Time is costly, as it takes longer for groups to make decisions than the leader alone.
2. *Value.* Value is placed on time, and no value is placed on follower development.
3. *Orientation.* The model has a short-term horizon.

The Development-Driven Model

See Exhibit 4.10 for these three characteristics:

1. *Focus.* The model is concerned with making effective decisions with maximum development of followers. Follower development is worth the cost.
2. *Value.* Value is placed on follower development, and no value is placed on time.
3. *Orientation.* The model has a long-term horizon, as development takes time.

Computerized Normative Model

Vroom has developed a computerized CD-ROM model that is more complex and more precise, yet easier to use. It combines the time-driven and development-driven models into one model, includes 11 variables/questions (rather than seven), and has five variable measures (rather than H or L). It guides users through the process of analyzing the situation with definitions, examples, and other forms of help as they progress through the use of the model. The computerized model is beyond the scope of this course, but you will learn how to use the time-driven and development-driven models presented here in Exhibits 4.9 and 4.10 and used with Developing Your Leadership Skills Exercise 4-2.

Determining the Appropriate Leadership Style

To determine the appropriate style for a specific situation, use the best model (time-driven or development-driven) for the situation and answer the questions, some of which may be skipped based on the model used and answers to prior questions. The questions are sequential and are presented in a decision-tree format similar to the Fiedler model, in which you end up with the appropriate style to use. If we use both models for the same situations, for some decisions the appropriate style will be the same, and different for others.

Research, Criticism, and Applications

The current normative model is based on the research of Vroom and colleagues at Yale University on leadership and decision-making processes, with more than 100,000 managers making decisions.[39] Numerous studies conducted by others have tested the normative leadership model. In general, the results found in the empirical research have supported the model.[40] In a summary of prior research, managers—contrary to Fiedler—do change

WORK
Application **4-4**

Recall a specific decision you or your boss has or had to make. Is or was the decision time-driven or development-driven? Using Exhibit 4.9 on page 125 or 4.10 on page 126, select the appropriate participation style for the situation. Be sure to state the questions you answered and how (H or L) you answered each.

WORK
Application **4-5**

1. Identify the one contingency leadership model you prefer to use on the job, and state why.

2. Describe the type of leader that you want to be on the job. Identify specific behavior you plan to use as a leader. You may also want to identify behavior you will not use.

their style to meet the situation. Managers using the decision style recommended by the normative model were almost twice as likely to be successful as were managers using decisions not recommended by the model. Higher-level managers use more participation in decision making. Women managers tend to use more participation than men. Almost all managers view themselves as using a higher level of participation than do their followers. Over the 25 years of research, there has been a move toward higher levels of participation, greater empowerment, and use of teams.[41]

The model is not without its critics. Vroom treats decisions as a single, discrete episode that occurs at one point in time, but most important decisions are not made that way. Important decisions often involve multiple meetings with various people. Thus, the leader may have to use a sequence of different decision procedures with different people at different times before the final decision is made. Also, the leader is assumed to have the skills needed to use each of the five leadership styles, and the leader's skills are not included in the model.

The Vroom and Vroom Yetton/Jago model tends to be popular in the academic community because it is based on research and it is complex. It is not very popular with managers because they find it cumbersome to select models and to pull out the model and follow a seven-question decision tree every time they have to make a decision.

You will determine your major normative leadership style in Self-Assessment 4-3 on pages 138, and you will learn how to use the models in Developing Your Leadership Skills Exercise 4-1 and 4-2.

OPENING CASE Application

5. Which normative leadership styles does Indra Nooyi tend to use at PepsiCo?

Based on the decision to be made, Nooyi consults and facilitates others. As chairman and CEO, she has the final say in major decisions affecting PepsiCo. However, she also delegates some decisions down the chain of command that involve specific products in American and international markets.

Learning Outcome **7,8**

Discuss the major similarities and differences between the behavioral and contingency leadership theories.

Compare and contrast four major differences among the four contingency leadership models.

Putting the Behavioral and Contingency Leadership Theories Together

Exhibit 4.11 is a review of different words that are used to describe the same two leadership behavior concepts. It includes the number of leadership styles based on the two behavior concepts and the different names given to the leadership styles. We should realize that all the leadership styles are based on the same two behavior concepts. We developed Exhibits 4.11 and 4.12 to put all these contingency leadership theories together with behavioral leadership styles. These exhibits should help you better understand the similarities and differences between these theories.

Learning Outcome **9**	*List which leadership models are prescriptive and descriptive, and explain why they are classified as such.*

Prescriptive and Descriptive Models

One last difference between models, not shown in any exhibits, is the difference between prescriptive and descriptive models. The contingency leadership model and the normative leadership model are **prescriptive leadership models**: *They tell the user exactly which style to use in a given situation.* However, the continuum and path–goal leadership models are **descriptive leadership models**: *They identify contingency variables and leadership styles without specifying which style to use in a given situation.* In other words, users of the descriptive model select the appropriate style based more on their own judgment. Look at all the leadership models and you will see what we mean.

‹EXHIBIT 4.11   **Names Given to the Same Two Leadership Behavior Concepts**

	LEADERSHIP & BEHAVIOR/STYLE		NUMBER OF LEADERSHIP STYLES BASED ON BEHAVIOR CONCEPTS
Behavioral Theories			
University of Iowa	Autocratic	Democratic	2
University of Michigan	Job-centered	Employee-centered	2
Ohio State University	Structure	Consideration	4
Leadership Grid®	Concern for production	Concern for people	5
Contingency Theories			
Contingency model	Task	Relationship	2
Leadership continuum	Boss-centered	Subordinate-centered	7
Path-goal model	Directive	Supportive	4
Normative model	Autocratic	Group	5

© Cengage Learning®

EXHIBIT 4.12   Putting the Behavioral and Contingency Leadership Theories Together

BEHAVIORAL THEORIES	LEADERSHIP STYLES				CONTINGENCY VARIABLES	CONTINGENCY CHANGE	DESIRED OUTCOME
U. of Michigan	Job-Centered		Employee-Centered				
Ohio State U.	High Structure/ Low Consideration	High Structure/ High Consideration	Low Structure/ High Consideration	Low Structure/ Low Consideration			
CONTINGENCY THEORIES							
Contingency Leadership Model	Task		Relationship		Leader/Follower Relations Task Structure Position Power	Situation	Performance
Leadership Continuum Model Path–Goal Model	1 Directive	2&3 Achievement	4&5 Supportive	6&7 Participative	Manager Subordinates Situation/time Subordinate (authoritarianism, locus of control, ability) Environment (task structure, formal authority, work group)	Leadership Style Leadership Style	Performance Performance Job Satisfaction
Normative Leadership Model	Decide	Consult Individual or Group	Facilitate	Delegate	Development-Driven or Time-Driven Models: (1) Decision significance (2) Importance of commitment (3) Leader expertise (4) Likelihood of commitment (5) Group support for objectives (6) Group expertise (7) Team competence	Leadership Style	Decisions

Many managers prefer prescriptive models; this is a reason why they are more commonly used in organizational leadership training programs than the descriptive leadership models. On the other hand, many academic researchers scoff at prescriptive models, especially simple ones, and prefer the more complex descriptive models based on solid theoretical foundations.

Learning Outcome 10   *Explain substitutes and neutralizers of leadership.*

Leadership Substitutes Theory

The four leadership theories presented assume that some leadership style will be effective in each situation. However, in keeping with contingency theory, there are factors outside the leader's control that have a larger impact on outcomes than do leadership actions. Contingency factors provide guidance and incentives to perform, making the leader's role unnecessary in some situations. Steven Kerr and John Jermier argued that certain situational variables prevent leaders from affecting subordinates' (followers') attitudes and behaviors.[42] **Substitutes for leadership** *include characteristics of the subordinate, task, and organization that replace the need for a leader or neutralize the leader's behavior.* This is the motivation for some organizations adopting self-managed teams. Self-managed teams are discussed in Chapter 8.

Substitutes and Neutralizers

Thus, *substitutes* for leadership make a leadership style unnecessary or redundant. Highly skilled workers do not need a leader's task behavior to tell them how to do their job. *Neutralizers* reduce or limit the effectiveness of a leader's behavior. For example, managers who are not near an employee cannot readily give task-directive behavior. See Exhibit 4.13 to see how the substitutes for leadership fit into the framework of contingency leadership variables. Then, read a description of each substitute.

EXHIBIT 4.13 **Substitutes for Leadership Variables within the Contingency Leadership Framework**

FOLLOWERS	LEADER	SITUATION
Subordinates	None	Task Organization

© Cengage Learning®

The following variables may substitute or neutralize leadership by providing task-oriented direction and/or people-oriented support rather than a leader.

1. *Characteristics of followers.* Ability, knowledge, experience, training. Need for independence. Professional orientation. Indifference toward organizational rewards.
2. *Characteristics of the task.* Clarity and routine. Invariant methodology. Provision of own feedback concerning accomplishment. Intrinsic satisfaction for completing the task.
3. *Characteristics of the organization.* Formalization (explicit plans, goals, and areas of responsibility). Inflexibility (rigid, unbending rules and procedures). Highly specified and active advisory and staff functions. Closely knit, cohesive work groups. Organizational rewards not within the leader's control. Spatial distance between leader and followers.

Leadership Style

Leaders can analyze their situation and better understand how these three characteristics substitute or neutralize their leadership style and thus can provide the leadership and followership most appropriate for the situation. The leader role is to provide the direction and support not already being provided by the task, group, or organization. The leader fills the gaps in leadership.

Changing the Situation

WORK
Application **4-6**

Identify your present or past manager. Can the characteristics of followers, task, and/ or the organization substitute for this leader? In other words, is his or her leadership necessary?

Like Fiedler suggested, leaders can change the situation rather than their leadership style. Thus, substitutes for leadership can be designed in organizations in ways to complement existing leadership, to act in leadership absence, and to otherwise provide more comprehensive leadership alternatives. After all, organizations have cut middle-management numbers, and something has to provide the leadership in their absence. One approach is to make the situation more favorable for the leader by removing neutralizers. Another way is to make leadership less important by increasing substitutes such as job enrichment, self-managing teams, and automation.

Research, Criticism, and Applications

A meta-analysis was conducted to estimate bivariate relationships among leadership behaviors, substitutes for leadership, followers' attitudes, and role perceptions and performance, and to examine the relative strengths of the relationships among these variables. It was based on 435 relationships obtained from 22 studies containing 36 independent samples. Overall, the theory was supported.[43]

However, the theory does have its critics. As with the other theories, results are mixed. Research has found support for some aspects of the theory, but other aspects have not been tested or supported. Critics point out that for many of the substitutes, the behavior of the formal leader is merely replaced by similar leadership behavior carried out by peers or other informal leaders—so leadership still exists anyway.

Applications of leadership substitute theory include its strong evidence that situational variables can directly affect job satisfaction and motivation. As already discussed, changing the situation is a major application of substitute theory.

To close this chapter, complete Self-Assessment 4-2 to determine how your personality influences your use of contingency leadership theory.

SELF-ASSESSMENT 4-2   **Your Personality and Contingency Leadership Theories**

In Self-Assessment 4-1 on page 113 were you more task or relationship oriented? Your being more task- or relationship-oriented is based very much on your personality.

Based on surgency, if you have a high need for power, you may tend to be more task oriented. Based on agreeableness, if you are a real "people" person with a high need for affiliation, you may tend to be more relationship oriented. Based on conscientiousness, if you have a high need for achievement, you may tend to be more task oriented to make sure the job gets done, and done your way.

Based on your personality profile, does it match Fiedler's contingency leadership theory, as presented in Self-Assessment 1? If you have a higher need for power, do you tend to use the autocratic (1–3) leadership continuum styles, the directive and achievement path–goal leadership styles, and then decide and consult normative leadership styles?

If you have a higher need for affiliation, do you tend to use more participative leadership continuum styles, the supportive and participative path–goal styles, and the facilitate and delegate normative leadership styles?

You will better be able to understand which leadership style you do tend to use when you complete Self-Assessment 4-3 on page 138, "Determining Your Preferred Normative Leadership Style." The leadership continuum and path–goal styles are explored in Self-Assessment 4-4 on page 143. It is important to realize that your personality does affect your leadership style. However, you can use the leadership style that is most appropriate for the situation. You will learn how in Developing Your Leadership Skills Exercises 4-1 and 4-2.

"Take It To The Net". Access student resources at www.cengagebrain.com. Search for Lussier, Leadership 6e to find student study tools.

Chapter Summary

The chapter summary is organized to answer the 11 learning outcomes for this chapter.

1 **State the major difference between behavioral and contingency leadership theories, and explain the behavioral contribution to contingency theories.**

Behavioral theories attempt to determine the one best leadership style for all situations. Contingency leadership theories contend that there is no one best leadership style for all situations. Behavioral theories contributed to contingency theories because their basic leadership styles are used in contingency leadership models.

2 **Describe the contingency leadership theory variables.**

The contingency leadership variables used to explain the appropriate leadership style are the leader, followers, and situation. The leader factor is based on personality traits, behavior, and experience. The followers factor is based on capability and motivation. The situational factor is based on task, structure, and environment.

3 **Identify the contingency leadership model styles and variables.**

The contingency leadership model styles are task and relationship. The variables include (1) the leader–follower relationship, (2) the leadership styles—task or relationship, and (3) the situation—task structure and position power.

4 **State the leadership continuum model major styles and variables.**

The two major continuum leadership model styles are boss centered and subordinate centered. The variables include (1) the boss, (2) the subordinates, and (3) the situation (time).

5 **Identify the path–goal leadership model styles and variables.**

The path–goal leadership model styles include directive, supportive, participative, and achievement-oriented.

Variables used to determine the leadership style are the subordinate and the environment.

6 **State the normative leadership model styles and the number of variables.**

The five normative leadership model styles are decide, consult individually, consult group, facilitate, and delegate. The model has seven variables.

7 **Discuss the major similarities and differences between the behavioral and contingency leadership theories.**

The primary similarity between these theories is that their leadership styles are all based on the same two leadership concepts, although they have different names. The major difference is that the contingency leadership models identify contingency variables on which to select the most appropriate behavioral leadership style for a given situation.

8 **Compare and contrast four major differences among the four contingency leadership models.**

Using Exhibit 4.12 on page 130, note that the first difference is in the number of leadership styles used in the four models, which ranges from 2 (contingency) to 7 (continuum). The second difference is in the number of contingency variables used to select the appropriate leadership style, which ranges from 2 (path–goal) to 7 (normative). The third difference is what is changed when using the model. When using the contingency as example for emulation or use in a given model, the leader changes the situation; with the other three models, the leader changes behavior (leadership style). The last difference is the desired outcome. Contingency and continuum leadership models focus on performance, and the path–goal model adds job satisfaction. The normative model focuses on decisions.

9 **List which leadership models are prescriptive and descriptive, and explain why they are classified as such.**

The contingency and normative leadership models are prescriptive models, because they specify exactly which leadership style to use in a given situation. The continuum and path–goal leadership models are descriptive models, because users select the appropriate leadership style for a given situation based on their own judgment.

10 **Explain substitutes and neutralizers of leadership.**

Substitutes for leadership include characteristics of the subordinate, task, and organization that make leadership behavior unnecessary or redundant; neutralizers reduce or limit the effectiveness of a leader's behavior.

Key Terms

Review Questions

1 What is the difference between a theory and a model?

2 What contingency leadership variables are common to all of the theories?

3 How does the global economy relate to contingency leadership?

4 What are the two contingency leadership theory leadership styles?

5 Do the three situational favorableness factors of the contingency leadership model (see Exhibit 4.3 on page 115) fit in only one of the three variables (follower, leader, situation) or all contingency leadership variables (see Exhibit 4.1 on page 110)? Explain.

6 What is the difference in the outcomes of the contingency leadership and the continuum leadership models and that of the path–goal model?

7 What are the three subordinate and environment situational factors of the path–goal model?

8 What are the path–goal theory leadership styles?

9 What are the normative leadership theory leadership styles?

10 What is the primary difference between the contingency leadership model and the other leadership models (leadership continuum, path–goal, and normative leadership)?

11 What are the three substitutes for leadership?

Critical-Thinking Questions

The following critical-thinking questions can be used for class discussion and/or as written assignments to develop communication skills. Be sure to give complete explanations for all questions.

1 Do you agree with Fiedler's belief that people have one dominant leadership style and cannot change styles? Explain.

2 Do you believe that managers today are using more boss- or more subordinate-centered leadership styles?

3 Do you agree that time is an important situational factor to consider in selecting a leadership style for the situation? Explain.

4 The normative leadership model is the most complex. Do more variables improve the model?

5 One group of authors believes that Fiedler's contingency leadership model is the model best supported by research. However, a different author believes that it is the normative leadership model. Which model do you believe is best supported by research? Why?

6 Which contingency leadership theory do you think is the best?

7 Which contingency leadership theory do you actually plan to use, and how? If you don't plan to use any, give a detailed reason for not wanting to use any of the models.

CASE

Foxconn Technology Group

Have you ever heard of Foxconn Technology Group and its founder and CEO Terry Gou? It is the largest exporter out of China. Gou started Hon Hai Precision Industry Company, the anchor company of Foxconn Technology Group, in 1974 at age 23 with a $7,500 loan from his mother to provide the lowest "total cost" solution to increase the affordability of electronics products for everyone. Foxconn has been the most trusted name in contract manufacturing services.[44] Some of the major companies Foxconn makes contracted products for include IBM, Cisco, Microsoft, Nokia, Sony, Dell, Hewlett-Packard, and Apple. If you have a PlayStation, computer, or smart phone, there is a good chance that all or part of it was made by Foxconn.

Terry Gou has been characterized as always thinking about a way to shave another nickel off the cost of a product, as a charming salesman, as a daring strategist, as a ruthless taskmaster, and as a reincarnated Henry Ford. Gou is a billionaire, but he says, "I think for me, I am not interested in knowing how much I have. I don't care. I am working not for the money at this moment, I am working for society, I am working for my employees."[45]

Although Terry Gou's story is interesting, in this case we focus on lower-level manager Li Chang. (Please note: Foxconn is an existing company. However, Chang and Jackie Lee are not the names of actual managers at Foxconn; they are used to illustrate contingency leadership.)

Li Chang worked her way up to become the manager in a department making parts for the iPad. Chang's job was to supervise the production of one part that is used as a component in other products. Running the machines to make the standard parts is not complicated, and her employees generally find the job to be boring with low pay. Chang closely supervised the employees to make sure they kept production on schedule. She believed that if she did not watch the employees closely and keep them informed of their output, they would slack off and miss production goals. Chang's employees viewed her as an okay boss to work for, as she did take a personal interest in them, and employees were productive. Chang did discipline employees who did not meet standard productivity, and she ended up firing some workers.

Jackie Lee, the manager of a larger department that made instruments to customer specifications, retired, and Chang was given a promotion to manage this department because she did

a good job running her old department. Chang never did any design work, nor supervised it. The designers are all engineers who are paid well and who were doing a good job according to their prior supervisor Lee. As Chang observed workers in her usual manner, she realized that all of the designers did their work differently. So she closely observed their work and looked for good ideas that all her employees could follow. It wasn't long before Chang was telling employees how to do a better job of designing the custom specifications. Things were not going too well, however, as employees told Chang that she did not know what she was talking about. Chang tried to rely on her authority, which worked while she was watching employees. However, once she left one employee to observe another, the workers went back to doing things their own way. Chang's employees were complaining about her being a poor manager behind her back.

The complaints about Chang being a poor manager got to Terry Gou. Gou also realized that performance in the design department had gone down since Chang took over as manager. Gou decided to call Chang into his office to discuss how things are going.

GO TO THE INTERNET: To learn more about Terry Gou and Foxconn, visit its Web site **(http://www.foxconn.com).**

Support your answers to the following questions with specific information from the case and text or with other information you get from the Web or other sources.

1. Which leadership style would Fiedler say Li Chang uses?

2. Using Exhibit 4.3 on page 115, Fiedler's contingency leadership model, what situation and leadership style are appropriate for the production department and for the custom design department?

3. Why isn't Chang doing an effective job in the design department?

4. What would Fiedler and Kerr and Jermier recommend that Chang do to improve performance?

5. Which of the two basic continuum leadership styles would Tannenbaum and Schmidt recommend for Chang and other managers of the design department?

6. Which path–goal leadership style would House recommend for Chang and other managers of the design department?

CUMULATIVE CASE QUESTIONS

7. Describe Chang's personality based on the Big Five model of personality (Chapter 2). How does Chang's personality influence her leadership style?

8. How is Chang's leadership style and behavior affecting employee needs and motivation (Chapter 3)?

CASE EXERCISE AND ROLE-PLAY

Preparation: Put yourself in the role of Terry Gou. (1) Which normative leadership style would you use with Chang during the meeting? (2) How would you handle the meeting with Chang? (3) What will you say to her?

In-Class Meeting: Break into groups of four to six members, and discuss the three preparation questions.

Role-Play: One person (representing themselves or a group) meets with Chang to role-play the meeting for the class

to observe. The person does not identify which normative leadership style they are using. You can discuss the role-play, as discussed next. More than one role-play may also take place.

Observer Role: As the rest of the class members watch the role-play, they should: (1) Identify the leadership style used by the person playing the role of Gou. (2) State if it is the appropriate leadership style for this situation. (3) Look for things that Gou does well, and does not do so well. For your suggested improvements, be sure to have alternative behaviors that are coaching.

Discussion: After the first role-play, the class (1) votes for the leadership style used by the person role-playing Gou, (2) determines the appropriate leadership style, and (3) discusses good behavior and better behavior that could be used. If additional role-plays are used, skip step 2.

VIDEO ▶ CASE

Leadership at McDonald's

McDonald's has achieved the status of one of the most recognizable franchises across the globe through a mixture of successful marketing, consistent service and products, and strong leadership. Ray Kroc was a visionary leader who inspired others through his charisma. He saw the potential for standardizing an efficient, systematized restaurant model and replicating it across the country. Kroc is quoted as saying, "If you've got time to lean, you've got time to clean,"

which highlights his goal-oriented and task-focused leadership style that still exists in the corporation today.

1. What kind of normative leadership style do you think Ray Kroc, as a leader in the first years of McDonald's, likely used? Explain your answer.

2. What are the benefits of a corporate leadership strategy?

SELF-ASSESSMENT 4-3 | Determining Your Preferred Normative Leadership Style

Following are 12 situations. Select the one alternative that most closely describes what you would do in each situation. Don't be concerned with trying to pick the right answer; select the alternative you would really use. Circle a, b, c, or d. Ignore the S part, which will be explained later in Developing Your Leadership Skills Exercise 1.

1. Your rookie crew seems to be developing well. Their need for direction and close supervision is diminishing. What do you do?

a. Stop directing and overseeing performance unless there is a problem. S _____

b. Spend time getting to know them personally, but make sure they maintain performance levels. S _____

c. Make sure things keep going well; continue to direct and oversee closely. S _____

d. Begin to discuss new tasks of interest to them. S _____

2. You assigned Jill a task, specifying exactly how you wanted it done. Jill deliberately ignored your directions and did it her way. The job will not meet the customer's standards. This is not the first problem you've had with Jill. What do you decide to do?

a. Listen to Jill's side, but be sure the job gets done right. S _____

b. Tell Jill to do it again the right way, and closely supervise the job. S _____

c. Tell her the customer will not accept the job, and let Jill handle it her way. S _____

d. Discuss the problem and possible solutions to it. S _____

3. Your employees work well together; the department is a real team. It's the top performer in the organization. Because of traffic problems, the president okayed staggered hours for departments. As a result, you can change your department's hours. Several of your workers have suggested changing. You take what action?

a. Allow the group to decide its hours. S _____

b. Decide on new hours, explain why you chose them, and invite questions. S _____

c. Conduct a meeting to get the group members' ideas. Select new hours together, with your approval. S _____

d. Send around a memo stating the hours you want. S _____

4. You hired Bill, a new employee. He is not performing at the level expected after one month's training. Bill is trying, but he seems to be a slow learner. What do you decide to do?

a. Clearly explain what needs to be done and oversee his work. Discuss why the procedures are important; support and encourage him. S _____

b. Tell Bill that his training is over and it's time to pull his own weight. S _____

c. Review task procedures and supervise Bill's work closely. S

d. Inform Bill that his training is over, and tell him to feel free to come to you if he has any problems. S

5. Helen has had an excellent performance record for the last five years. Recently you have noticed a drop in the quality and quantity of her work. She has a family problem. What do you do?

a. Tell Helen to get back on track and closely supervise her. S _____

b. Discuss the problem with Helen. Help her realize that her personal problem is affecting her

work. Discuss ways to improve the situation. Be supportive and encourage her. S _____

c. Tell Helen you're aware of her productivity slip, and that you're sure she'll work it out soon. S _____

d. Discuss the problem and solution with Helen, and supervise her closely. S _____

6. Your organization does not allow smoking in certain areas. You just walked by a restricted area and saw Joan smoking. She has been with the organization for 10 years and is a very productive worker. Joan has never been caught smoking before. What action do you take?

a. Ask her to put it out, and then leave. S _____

b. Discuss why she is smoking, and ask what she intends to do about it. S _____

c. Give her a lecture about not smoking, and check up on her in the future. S _____

d. Tell her to put it out, watch her do it, and tell her you will check on her in the future. S _____

7. Your department usually works well together with little direction. Recently a conflict between Sue and Tom has caused problems. As a result, you take what action?

a. Call Sue and Tom together and make them realize how this conflict is affecting the department. Discuss how to resolve it and how you will check to make sure the problem is solved. S _____

b. Let the group resolve the conflict. S _____

c. Have Sue and Tom sit down and discuss their conflict and how to resolve it. Support their efforts to implement a solution. S _____

d. Tell Sue and Tom how to resolve their conflict and closely supervise them. S _____

8. Jim usually does his share of the work with some encouragement and direction. However, he has migraine headaches occasionally and doesn't pull his weight when this happens. The others resent doing Jim's work. What do you decide to do?

a. Discuss his problem and help him come up with ideas for maintaining his work; be supportive. S _____

b. Tell Jim to do his share of the work and closely watch his output. S _____

c. Inform Jim that he is creating a hardship for the others and should resolve the problem by himself. S _____

d. Be supportive, but set minimum performance levels and ensure compliance. S _____

9. Barbara, your most experienced and productive worker, came to you with a detailed idea that could increase your department's productivity at a very low cost. She can do her present job and this new assignment. You think it's an excellent idea; what do you do?

    a. Set some goals together. Encourage and support her efforts. S _____

    b. Set up goals for Barbara. Be sure she agrees with them and sees you as being supportive of her efforts. S _____

    c. Tell Barbara to keep you informed and to come to you if she needs any help. S _____

    d. Have Barbara check in with you frequently, so that you can direct and supervise her activities. S _____

10. Your boss asked you for a special report. Frank, a very capable worker who usually needs no direction or support, has all the necessary skills to do the job. However, Frank is reluctant because he has never done a report. What do you do?

    a. Tell Frank he has to do it. Give him direction and supervise him closely. S _____

    b. Describe the project to Frank and let him do it his own way. S _____

    c. Describe the benefits to Frank. Get his ideas on how to do it and check his progress. S _____

    d. Discuss possible ways of doing the job. Be supportive; encourage Frank. S _____

11. Jean is the top producer in your department. However, her monthly reports are constantly late and contain errors. You are puzzled because she does everything else with no direction or support. What do you decide to do?

    a. Go over past reports with Jean, explaining exactly what is expected of her. Schedule a meeting so that you can review the next report with her. S _____

    b. Discuss the problem with Jean, and ask her what can be done about it; be supportive. S _____

    c. Explain the importance of the report. Ask her what the problem is. Tell her that you expect the next report to be on time and error free. S _____

    d. Remind Jean to get the next report in on time without errors. S _____

12. Your workers are very effective and like to participate in decision making. A consultant was hired to develop a new method for your department using the latest technology in the field. What do you do?

    a. Explain the consultant's method and let the group decide how to implement it. S _____

    b. Teach them the new method and closely supervise them. S _____

    c. Explain the new method and the reasons that it is important. Teach them the method and make sure the procedure is followed. Answer questions. S _____

    d. Explain the new method and get the group's input on ways to improve and implement it. S _____

To determine your preferred normative leadership style, follow these steps:

1. In this chart, circle the letter you selected for each situation.

    The column headings (S1 through S4) represent the style you selected.

    S1 = Decide, S2 = Consult (Individually or Group), S3 = Facilitate, S4 = Delegate

	S1D	S2C	S3F	S4DL
1	c	a	d	a
2	b	a	d	c
3	d	b	c	a
4	c	a	d	b
5	a	d	b	c
6	d	c	b	a
7	d	a	c	b
8	b	d	a	c
9	d	b	a	c
10	a	c	d	b
11	a	c	b	d
12	b	c	d	a
Totals	_____	_____	_____	_____

2. Add up the number of circled items per column. The column with the highest total is your preferred leadership style. There is no correct or best normative leadership style. Below is an explanation about each style.

S1 Decide Leadership Style. The decide style includes making the decision alone. As a decider, you autocratically tell people how to implement your decision and follow up to make sure performance is maintained, or you tell people what to do and make sure they continue to do it.

S2 Consult (Individually or Group) Leadership Style. As they are both consult styles, we combine individual and group styles for this exercise. The consult style includes talking to individuals or groups for input in a supportive way before you make the decision. As a consulter, after making the decision, you also tell people how to implement your decision and follow up to make sure performance is maintained, while you support and encourage them as they implement your decision.

S3 Facilitate Leadership Style. The facilitate style includes having a group meeting to get input from members as you attempt to support the group to agree on a decision within boundaries set by you; in other words, you still have the final say on the decision. As a facilitator, you are supportive and encouraging to the group members to both make the decision and implement the decision.

S4 Delegate Leadership Style. The delegate style includes letting the group make the decision within limits. As a delegator, you don't tell the group what to do or facilitate the group during the decision making and its implementation.

To determine your flexibility to change styles, do the following. Look at your total score for each column leadership style. The more evenly distributed the totals (for example 4, 4, 4, 4), the more flexible you appear to be at changing your leadership style. Having high numbers in some columns and low in others indicates a strong preference to use or avoid using one or more leadership styles.

Note: There is no right, correct, or best normative leadership style. What this self-assessment exercise does is allow you to know your preferred leadership style and your flexibility at changing styles. In Developing Your Leadership Skills Exercise 1, you will develop your skill to identify the normative leadership styles. In Skill-Development Exercise 2, you will learn to use the normative leadership models to select the most appropriate leadership style for a given situation.

Developing Your Leadership Skills 4-1

Identifying Normative Leadership Styles

Preparing for This Exercise

Return to the 12 situations in Self-Assessment 3. This time, instead of selecting one of the four options, a–d, identify the normative leadership style used in each option, with the aid of the leadership style definitions in Self-Assessment 3 above. Let's do the following example.

Example

Your rookie crew seems to be developing well. Their need for direction and close supervision is diminishing. What do you do?

1. Stop directing and overseeing performance unless there is a problem. S_DL_

2. Spend time getting to know them personally, but make sure they maintain performance levels. S_C_

4. Make sure things keep going well; continue to direct and oversee closely. S_D_

4. Begin to discuss new tasks of interest to them. S_F_

Answers

5. As indicated on the S_DL_line, this is the delegate leadership style. As in the definition of delegate, you are leaving the group alone—unless there is a problem (limits)—to make and implement its own decisions about work.

6. As indicated on the S_C_ line, this is the consult leadership style. As in the definition of consult, you are being

supportive by getting to know them, yet you are still following up to make sure they get the job done.

7. As indicated on the S_D_ line, this is the decide leadership style. As in the definition of decide, you are following up to make sure performance is maintained.

8. As indicated on the S_F_ line, this is the facilitate leadership style. As in the definition of facilitate, you are facilitating a group decision on possible new tasks for the group to perform.

Now, complete situation numbers 2–12 by determining the leadership style and placing the letters D, C, F, and DL on each of the a–d S_ lines as illustrated above. All four alternative behaviors do represent a different normative leadership style.

Doing This Exercise in Class

Objective

To develop the skill of identifying normative leadership styles.

AACSB General Skills Area

The primary AACSB competencies developed through this exercise are communication, analytic skills, and application of knowledge.

Procedure (5–30 minutes) Select an option:

9. The instructor goes over the answers.

10. The instructor calls on students and goes over the answers.

Developing Your Leadership Skills **4-2**

Using the Normative Leadership Models

Preparing for This Exercise

You should have studied the normative leadership model text material. Using Exhibits 4.9 and 4.10 on pages 125 and 126, determine the appropriate leadership style for the given problem statements below. Follow these steps:

1 Determine which normative leadership model to use for the given situation.

2 Answer the variable questions (between 2 and 7) for the problem.

3 Select the appropriate leadership style from the model.

1. Production department manager. You are the manager of a mass-produced manufactured product. You have two major machines in your department with 10 people working on each. You have an important order that needs to be shipped first thing tomorrow morning. Your boss has made it very clear that you must meet this deadline. It's 2:00 and you are right on schedule to meet the order deadline. At 2:15 an employee comes to tell you that one of the machines is smoking a little and making a noise. If you keep running the machine, it may make it until the end of the day and you will deliver the important shipment on time. If you shut down the machine, the manufacturer will not be able to check the machine until tomorrow and you will miss the deadline. You call your boss and there is no answer, and you don't know how else to contact the boss or how long it will be before the boss gets back to you if you leave a message. There are no higher-level managers than you or anyone with more knowledge of the machine than you. Which leadership style should you use?

Step 1   Which model should you use? (_____ time-driven _____ development-driven)

Step 2   Which questions on the normative model Exhibit 4.9 or 4.10 did you answer and how? (H = high, L = low, NA = not answered/skipped)

1. H L or NA   3. H L or NA   5. H L or NA   7. H L or NA
2. H L or NA   4. H L or NA   6. H L or NA

Step 3   Which leadership style is the most appropriate? _____ decide _____ consult individually _____ consult _____ group _____ facilitate delegate

2. Religious leader. You are the top religious leader of your church with 125 families and 200 members. You have a doctor of religious studies degree with just two years' experience as the head of a church, and no business courses. The church has one paid secretary, three part-time program directors for religious instruction, music, and social activities, plus many volunteers. Your paid staff serves on your advisory board with 10 other church members who are primarily top-level business leaders in the community. You make a yearly budget with the board's approval. The church source of income is weekly member donations. The board doesn't want to operate in the red, and the church has very modest surplus funds. Your volunteer accountant (CPA), who is a board member, asked to meet with you. During the meeting, she informed you that weekly collections are 20 percent below budget and the cost of utilities has increased 25 percent over the yearly budget figure. You are running a large deficit, and at this rate your surplus will be gone in two months. Which leadership style will you use in this crisis?

Step 1   Which model should you use? (_____ time-driven _____ development-driven)

Step 2   Which questions did you answer and how? (H = high, L = low, NA = not answered/skipped)

1. H L or NA   3. H L or NA   5. H L or NA   7. H L or NA
2. H L or NA   4. H L or NA   6. H L or NA

Step 3   Which leadership style is the most appropriate? ___ decide ___consult individually ___ consult group___ facilitate ___ delegate

3. School of business dean. You are the new dean of the school of business at a small private university. Your faculty includes around 20 professors, only two of whom are nontenured, and the average length of employment at the school is 12 years. Upon taking the job, you expect to leave for a larger school in three years. Your primary goal is to start a business school faculty advisory board to improve community relations and school alumni relations, and to raise money for financial aid scholarships. You have already done this in your last job as dean. However, you are new to the area and have no business contacts. You need help to develop a network of alumni and other community leaders fairly quickly if you are to show achieved results on your resume in two-and-a-half years. Your faculty gets along well and is talkative, but when you approach small groups of them they tend to become quiet and disperse. Which primary leadership style would you use to achieve your objective?

Step 1   Which model should you use? (___ time-driven ___ development-driven)

Step 2   Which questions did you answer and how? (H = high, L = low, NA = not answered/skipped)

1. H L or NA   3. H L or NA   5. H L or NA   7. H L or NA
2. H L or NA   4. H L or NA   6. H L or NA

Step 3 Which leadership style is the most appropriate?

1. H L or NA 3. H L or NA 5. H L or NA 7. H L or NA
2. H L or NA 4. H L or NA 6. H L or NA

Step 3 Which leadership style is the most appropriate?
___ decide ___ consult individually ___ consult group ___ facilitate ___ delegate group ___ facilitate ___ delegate

4. Dot.com president. You are the president of a dot.com company that has been having financial problems for a few years. As a result, your top two managers left for other jobs. One left four months ago and the other two months ago. With your networking contacts you replaced both managers within a month; thus, they don't have a lot of time on the job and haven't worked together for very long. Plus, they currently do their own thing to get their jobs done. However, they are both very bright, hardworking, and dedicated to your vision of what the company can be. You know how to turn the company around and so do your two key managers. To turn the company around, you and your two managers will have to work together, with the help of all your employees. Virtually all the employees are high-tech specialists who want to be included in decision making. Your business partners have no more money to invest. If you cannot turn a profit in four to five months, you will most likely go bankrupt. Which primary leadership style would you use to achieve your objective?

Step 1 Which model should you use? (___ time-driven ___ development-driven)

Step 2 Which questions did you answer and how? (H = high, L = low, NA = not answered/skipped)

1. H L or NA 3. H L or NA 5. H L or NA 7. H L or NA
2. H L or NA 4. H L or NA 6. H L or NA

Step 3 Which leadership style is the most appropriate?
____ decide ____ consult individually ____ consult group ____ facilitate ____ delegate

Doing This Exercise in Class

Objective

To develop your skill at determining the appropriate leadership style to use in a given situation using the normative leadership models, Exhibits 4.9 and 4.10.

AACSB General Skills Area

The primary AACSB competencies developed through this exercise are communications, analytic skills, and application of knowledge.

Experience

You will use the normative leadership models in four given problem situations.

Procedure 1 *(5–8 minutes)* The instructor goes over the normative leadership models and uses the models to illustrate how to select the appropriate leadership style for problem situation 1.

Procedure 2 *(10–20 minutes)* Break into groups of two or three and use the models to determine the appropriate leadership style for situations 2–4 in the preparation above. This is followed by the instructor going over or just stating the answers to situations 2–4.

Conclusion

The instructor may lead a class discussion and/or make concluding remarks.

Apply It *(2–4 minutes)* What did I learn from this experience? How will I apply normative leadership in the future?

_____

_____

_____

Sharing

In the group, or to the entire class, volunteers may give their answers to the "Apply It" questions.

SELF-ASSESSMENT 4-4 | **Your Leadership Continuum and Path–Goal Leadership Styles**

You have already determined your preferred LPC contingency leadership style (Self-Assessment 4-1 on page 113) and your preferred normative leadership style (Self-Assessment 4-3 on pages 138–141). Using Self-Assessment 4-4, you can determine your other preferred styles by checking your preferred normative leadership style in the first column. In the same row, the columns to the right show your continuum and path–goal preferred leadership styles. Does your preferred leadership style match your personality for Self-Assessment 4-2 on page 132?

NORMATIVE LEADERSHIP STYLE	LEADERSHIP CONTINUUM STYLE	PATH–GOAL LEADERSHIP STYLE
Decide	1 Boss-centered	Directive
Consult (individually or group)	2 or 3	Achievement-oriented
Facilitate	4 or 5	Supportive
Delegate	6 or 7 Subordinate-centered	Participative

Endnotes

1. PepsiCo Web site (www.pepsico.com), accessed January 28, 2014.

2. "The 50 Most Powerful Women," *Fortune* (October 28, 2013): 133–138.

3. PepsiCo Web site (www.pepsico.com), accessed January 28, 2014.

4. G. Colvin, "Indra Nooyi's Challenge," *Fortune* (June 11, 2012): 149–156.

5. "Largest U.S. corporations—Fortune 500," *Fortune* (May 20, 2013): 1–20.

6. "The World's Most Admired Companies," *Fortune* (March 18, 2013): 137–148.

7. M. Esterl and V. Baurlein, "PepsiCo Wakes Up and Smells the Cola," *Wall Street Journal* (June 28, 2011): B1, B2.

8. M. Esterl, "PepsiCo Board Stands by Nooyi," *Wall Street Journal* (January 13, 2012): B1.

9. M.A. Hogg, D. Van Knippenberg, and D.E. Rast, "Intergroup Leadership in Organizations: Leading across Group and Organizational Boundaries," *Academy of Management Review 37*(2) (2012): 232–255.

10. H.R. Greve, "Microfoundations of Management: Behavioral Strategies and Levels of Rationality in Organizational Action," *Academy of Management Perspectives 27*(2) (2013): 103–119.

11. A.M. Grant and S.V. Patil, "Challenging the Norm of Self-Interest: Minority Influence and Transitions to Helping Norms in Work Units," *Academy of Management Review 37*(4) (2012): 547–568.

12. S.B. Sitkin and J.R. Hackman, "Developing Team Leadership: An Interview with Coach Mike Krzyzewski," *Academy of Management Learning & Education 10*(3) (2011): 494–501.

13. J.D. Harris and S.G. Sounder, "Model-Theoretic Knowledge Accumulation: The Case of Agency Theory and Incentive Alignment," *Academy of Management Review 38*(3) (2013): 442–454.

14. B. Benjamin and C. O'Reilly, "Becoming a Leader: Early Career Challenges Faced by MBA Graduates," *Academy of Management Learning & Education 10*(3) (2011): 452–472.

15. B.P. Owens and D.R. Hekman, "Modeling How to Grow: An Inductive Examination of Humble Leader Behaviors, Contingencies, and Outcomes," *Academy of Management Journal 55*(4) (2012): 787–818.

16. G. Yukl, "Effective Leadership Behavior: What We Know and What Questions Need More Attention," *Academy of Management Perspectives 26*(4) (2011): 66–85.

17. N.M. Lorinkova, M.J. Pearsall, and H.P. Sims, "Examining the Differential Longitudinal Performance of Directive versus Empowering Leadership in Teams," *Academy of Management Journal 56*(2) (2013): 573–596.

18. G. Toegel, M. Kilduff, and N. Anand, "Emotion Helping by Managers: An Emergent Understanding of Discrepant Role Expectations and Outcomes," *Academy of Management Journal 56*(2) (2013): 334–357.

19. M.C. Sonfield and R.N. Lussier, "Gender in Family Business Ownership and Management: A Six Country Analysis," *International Journal of Gender and Entrepreneurship 1*(2) (2009): 96–117.

20. J. Eisenberg, C.E.J. Härtel, and G.K. Stahl, "From the Guest Editors: Cross-Cultural Management Learning and Education—Exploring Multiple Aims, Approaches, and Impacts," *Academy of Management Learning & Education 12*(3) (2013): 323–329; A.H. Van De Ven and A. Lifschitz, "Rational and Reasonable Microfoundations of Markets and Institutions," *Academy of Management Learning & Education 27*(2) (2013): 156–172.

21. Y. Zhu and F.B. Chiappini, "Balancing Emic and Etic: Situated Learning and Ethnography of Communication in Cross-Cultural Management Education," *Academy of Management Learning & Education 12*(3) (2013): 380–395.

22. M.E. Mendenhall, A.A. Arnardottir, G.R. Oddou, and L.A. Burke, "Developing Cross-Cultural Competencies in Management Education via Cognitive-Behavior Therapy," *Academy of Management Learning & Education 12*(3) (2013): 436–451.

23. J. Eisenberg, C.E.J. Härtel, and G.K. Stahl, "From the Guest Editors: Cross-Cultural Management Learning and Education—Exploring Multiple Aims, Approaches, and Impacts," *Academy of Management Learning & Education 12*(3) (2013): 323–329; A.H. Van De Ven and A. Lifschitz, "Rational and Reasonable Microfoundations of Markets and Institutions," *Academy of Management Learning & Education 27*(2) (2013): 156–172.

24. R.J. House; et al., eds. *Culture, Leadership, and Organizations: The GLOBE Study of 62 Societies* (Thousand Oaks, CA: Sage, 2004).

25. F.E. Fiedler, *A Theory of Leadership Effectiveness* (New York: McGraw-Hill, 1967); F.E. Fiedler and M.M. Chemers, *Improving Leadership Effectiveness: The Leader Match Concept*, 2nd ed. (New York: Wiley, 1982).

26. P. Puranam, M. Raveendran, and T. Knudsen, "Organization Design: The Epistemic Interdependence Perspective," *Academy of Management Review 37*(3) (2012): 419–440.

27. G. Yukl, "Effective Leadership Behavior: What We Know and What Questions Need More Attention," *Academy of Management Perspectives* 26(4) (2011): 66–85.

28. G. Toegel, M. Kilduff, and N. Anand, "Emotion Helping by Managers: An Emergent Understanding of Discrepant Role Expectations and Outcomes," *Academy of Management Journal* 56(2) (2013): 334–357.

29. N.M. Lorinkova, M.J. Pearsall, and H.P. Sims, "Examining the Differential Longitudinal Performance of Directive versus Empowering Leadership in Teams," *Academy of Management Journal* 56(2) (2013): 573–596.

30. G. Yukl, "Effective Leadership Behavior: What We Know and What Questions Need More Attention," *Academy of Management Perspectives* 26(4) (2011): 66–85.

31. M.J. Strube and J.E. Garcia, "A Meta-Analytical Investigation of Fiedler's Contingency Model of Leadership Effectiveness," *Psychology Bulletin 90* (1981): 307–321; and L.H. Peters, D.D. Hartke, and J.T. Pohlmann, "Fiedler's Contingency Theory of Leadership: An Application of the Meta-Analysis Procedure of Schmidt and Hunter," *Psychological Bulletin 97* (1985): 274–285.

32. F.E. Fiedler, "A Rejoinder to Schriesheim and Kerr's Premature Obituary of the Contingency Model," in J.G. Hunt and L.L. Larson, eds., *Leadership: The Cutting Edge* (Carbondale, IL: Southern Illinois University Press, 1977): 45–50; and F.E. Fiedler, "The Contingency Model: A Reply to Ashour," *Organizational Performance and Human Behavior 9* (1973): 356–368.

33. R. Tannenbaum and W.H. Schmidt, "How to Choose a Leadership Pattern," *Harvard Business Review* (March–April 1958): 95–101; R. Tannenbaum and W.H. Schmidt, "How to Choose a Leadership Pattern," *Harvard Business Review* (May–June 1973): 166. R. Tannenbaum and W.H. Schmidt, excerpts from "How to Choose a Leadership Pattern," *Harvard Business Review* (July–August 1986): 129.

34. B.P. Owens and D.R. Hekman, "Modeling How to Grow: An Inductive Examination of Humble Leader Behaviors, Contingencies, and Outcomes," *Academy of Management Journal* 55(4) (2012): 787–818.

35. R.J. House, "A Path-Goal Theory of Leader Effectiveness," *Administrative Science Quarterly 16*(2) (1971): 321–329; M.G. Evans, "The Effects of Supervisory Behavior on the Path-Goal Relationship," *Organizational Behavior and Human Performance 5* (1970): 277–298; and R.N. House and R.J. Aditya, "The Social Scientific Study of Leadership: Quo Vadis?" *Journal of Management 23* (May–June 1997): 409–474.

36. M.R. Barrick, M.K. Mount, and N. Li, "The Theory of Purposeful Work Behavior: The Role of Personality, Higher-Order Goals, and Job Characteristics," *Academy of Management Review* 38(1) (2013): 132–153.

37. J.C. Wofford and L.Z. Liska, "Path-Goal Theories of Leadership: A Meta-Analysis," *Journal of Management 19* (1993): 858–876; and P.M. Podsakoff, S.B. MacKenzie, M. Ahearne, and W.H. Bommer, "Searching for a Needle in a Haystack: Trying to Identify the Illusive Moderators of Leadership Behavior," *Journal of Management 21* (1995): 423–470.

38. V.H. Vroom and P.W. Yetton, *Leadership and Decision Making* (Pittsburgh: University of Pittsburgh Press, 1973); V.H. Vroom and A.G. Jago, *The New Leadership: Managing Participation in Organizations* (Englewood Cliffs, NJ: Prentice Hall, 1988); and V.H. Vroom, "Leadership and the Decision-Making Process," *Organizational Dynamics 28* (Spring 2000): 82–94.

39. V.H. Vroom, "Leadership and the Decision-Making Process," *Organizational Dynamics 28* (Spring 2000): 82–94.

40. J.B. Miner, "The Uncertain Future of the Leadership Concept: An Overview," in J.G. Hunt and L.L. Larson, eds., *Leadership Frontiers* (Kent, OH: Kent State University, 1975); R.H.G. Field, "A Critique of the Vroom-Yetton Contingency Model of Leadership Behavior," *Academy of Management Review 4* (1979): 249–257; R.H.G. Field, "A Test of the Vroom-Yetton Normative Model of Leadership," *Journal of Applied Psychology* (October 1982): 523–532; and R.H.G. Field, P.C. Read, and J.J. Louviere, "The Effect of Situation Attributes on Decision Method Choice in the Vroom-Jago Model of Participation in Decision Making," *Leadership Quarterly 1* (1990): 165–176.

41. N.M. Lorinkova, M.J. Pearsall, and H.P. Sims, "Examining the Differential Longitudinal Performance of Directive versus Empowering Leadership in Teams," *Academy of Management Journal* 56(2) (2013): 573–596.

42. S. Kerr and J. Jermier, "Substitutes for Leadership: Their Meaning and Measurement," *Organizational Behavior and Human Performance 22* (1978): 375–403.

43. P.M. Podsakoff, S.B. MacKenzie, and W.H. Bommer, "Meta-Analysis of the Relationships between Kerr and Jermier's Substitutes for Leadership and Employee Job Attitudes, Role Perceptions, and Performance," *Journal of Applied Psychology 81* (August 1996): 380–400.

44. Foxconn Web site (www.foxconn.com), accessed February 4, 2014.

45. F. Balfour and T. Culpan, "Chairman Gou," *BusinessWeek* (September 13–19, 2010): 58–69.

Influencing: Power, Politics, Networking, and Negotiation

Learning Outcomes

After studying this chapter, you should be able to:

1 Explain the differences between position power and personal power. p. 145

2 Discuss the differences among legitimate, reward, coercive, and referent power. p. 146

3 Discuss how power and politics are related. p. 154

4 Describe how money and politics have a similar use. p. 154

5 List and explain the steps in the networking process. p. 160

6 List the steps in the negotiation process. p. 166

7 Explain the relationships among negotiation and conflict, influencing tactics, power, and politics. p. 166

OPENING CASE Application

Serial entrepreneur Mark Cuban has ventured into many diverse businesses. Cuban's first step into the business world occurred at age 12, when he sold garbage bags door to door. Soon after, he was selling stamps, coins, and baseball cards, which paid for his business degree at Indiana University (IU). While attending IU, Cuban bought a Bloomington bar and named it Motley's, raising the money by selling shares to his friends. Cuban and Martin Woodall founded MicroSolutions, and they sold the company for $6 million. With Woodall, he also invested in the Landmark Theatres, Magnolia Pictures, AXS TV (formerly HDNet), and audio and video portal Broadcast.com; he was also a day trader. Cuban also took acting lessons and was on the TV show *Shark Tank*. But Cuban is most famous, however, for his 90 percent ownership and controversial, zealous management of the NBA team Dallas Mavericks. Cuban is listed on the Forbes 400 Richest People in America, with a net worth of $2.5 billion.[1]

OPENING CASE QUESTIONS:

1. **What sources and types of power does Mark Cuban have, and why has he had problems with power?**

2. **Why are organizational politics important to Mark Cuban's enterprises?**

3. **How has Mark Cuban used networking?**

4. **What types of negotiations does Mark Cuban engage in?**

5. **Is Mark Cuban ethical in influencing others?**

Can you answer any of these questions? You'll find answers to these questions and learn more about Mark Cuban's businesses and leadership style throughout the chapter.

To learn more about Mark Cuban, do an Internet search.

Besides excellent work, what does it take to get ahead in an organization? To climb the corporate ladder, you will have to influence people[2]—to gain power, play organizational politics, network, and negotiate to get what you want. These related concepts are the topics of this chapter. Recall from our definition of leadership (Chapter 1) that leadership is the "*influencing*" process of leaders and followers to achieve organizational objectives through change. Leaders and followers influence each other. This chapter focuses on leadership behavior by explaining how leaders influence others at the individual level of analysis. Let's begin with power because if you want to make a difference, you need to have power.[3]

Power

Power is the fundamental concept in social science,[4] and power skills can be taught and developed.[5] If we want to understand why organizations do the things they do, we must consider the power of managers and how power differences affect team and organizational performance.[6] Power is about achieving influence over others. However, **power** *is the leader's potential influence over followers.* Because power is the *potential* to influence, you do not actually have to use power to influence others. Often, it is the perception of power, rather than the actual use of power, that influences others. In this section, we discuss sources of power, types of power, influencing tactics, and ways to increase your power.

Learning Outcome 1 *Explain the differences between position power and personal power.*

Sources of Power

There are different sources of power,[7] and here we discuss position power and personal power.

Position Power

Position power is derived from top management, and it is delegated down the chain of command. Position status can give you power.[8] Thus, a person who is in a management position has more potential power to influence than an employee who is not a manager.[9] Some people view power as the ability to make people do what they want them to do or the ability to do something to people or for people. These definitions may be true, but they tend to give power a manipulative, negative connotation, as does the old saying by Lord Acton, "Power corrupts. Absolute power corrupts absolutely." Power can also make people more self-focused.[10]

Within an organization, power should be viewed in a positive sense. Without power, managers could not achieve organizational objectives, so leadership and power go hand in hand. Managers rely on position power to get the job done.[11] Dr. Martin Luther King Jr. said, "Power properly understood is nothing but the ability to achieve purpose. It is the strength to bring about change."

Personal Power

Personal power is derived from the followers based on the leader's behavior. Charismatic leaders have personal power. Again, followers do have some power over leaders. So you don't have to be a manager to have power.

A manager can have only position power or both position and personal power, but a nonmanager can have only personal power. Today's successful leaders share power (*empowerment*) by pushing power and decision making down the organization.[12] As former NBA coach Phil Jackson puts it, you need to empower your players.[13]

> **Learning Outcome 2** *Discuss the differences among legitimate, reward, coercive, and referent power.*

Types of Power and Influencing Tactics, and Ways to Increase Your Power

Seven types of power are illustrated, along with their source and influencing tactics, in Exhibit 5.1. In the late 1950s, French and Raven distinguished five types of power (reward, coercive, legitimate, expert, and referent).[14] Connection (politics) and information power have been added to update the important types of power. We will discuss these seven types of power and explore ways to increase each type with *influencing tactics, or actions*.[15] You can acquire power, without taking it away from others. Generally, power is given to those who get results and have good human relations skills that are useful to those in power.[16]

Legitimate Power

Legitimate power *is based on the user's position power, given by the organization*. It is also called the *legitimization influencing tactic*. Managers assign work, coaches decide who plays, and teachers award grades. These three positions have formal authority from the organization. Without this legitimate authority, they could not influence followers in the same way.[17] Employees tend to have a felt obligation and feel that they ought to do what their manager says within the scope of the job.[18]

Appropriate Use of Legitimate Power. Employees agree to comply with management authority in return for the benefits of membership. The use of legitimate power is appropriate when asking people to do something that is within the scope of their job. Most day-to-day manager–employee interactions are based on legitimate power.

When using legitimate power, it is also helpful to use the *consultation influencing tactic.* With consultation, you seek others' input about achieving an objective and are open to developing a plan together to achieve the objective. This process is also known as *participative management* and *empowering employees.* We will talk more about participative management throughout the book.

Legitimate Use of Rational Persuasion. When we as managers are meeting objectives through our employees or dealing with higher-level managers and people over whom we have no authority, it is often helpful to use the *rational persuasion influencing tactic.* Rational persuasion includes logical arguments with factual evidence to persuade others to implement your recommended action.

When we use rational persuasion, we need to develop a persuasive case based on the other party's needs, not ours. What seems logical and reasonable to you may not be to others. With multiple parties, a different logical argument may be made to meet individual needs. Logical arguments generally work well with people whose behavior is more influenced by thinking than by emotions. It works well when the leader and follower have the same shared interest and objectives.

When trying to persuade others to do something for us, it is helpful to use the *ingratiation influencing tactic.* Be friendly and praising others before you ask them for what you want—complements cost you nothing[19] (use the giving praise model in Chapter 3).

Sources and Types of Power with Influencing Tactics

EXHIBIT 5.1

Source	Position Power ⟶			⟵ Personal Power			
Types	Legitimate	Reward	Coercive	Connection	Information	Expert	Referent
Tactics	Legitimization Consultation Rational persuasion Ingratiation	Exchange	Pressure	Coalitions	Rational persuasion Inspirational appeal	Rational persuasion	Personal appeal Inspirational appeal

© Cengage Learning®

Using Rational Persuasion. When you develop a rational persuasion, follow these guidelines:

- Explain the reason why the objective needs to be met.
- Explain how the other party will benefit by meeting the objective. Try to think of the other party's often-unasked question: what's in it for me?
- Provide evidence that the objective can be met.
- Explain how potential problems and concerns will be handled. Know the potential problems and concerns and deal with them in the rational persuasion.

Increasing Legitimate Power. To increase legitimate power, follow these guidelines:

- To have legitimate power, we need management experience, which could also be a part of the job—for example, being in charge of a team project with peers.
- Exercise authority regularly. Follow up to make sure that objectives are achieved.

- Follow the guidelines for using rational persuasion, especially when authority is questioned.
- Back up your authority with *rewards and punishment,*[20] our next two types of power, which are primarily based on having legitimate power.

Reward Power

Reward power *is based on the user's ability to influence others with something of value to them.* In a management position, use positive reinforcements to influence behavior, with incentives such as praise, recognition (with pins, badges, hats, or jackets), special assignments or desirable activities, pay raises, bonuses, and promotions. Many organizations, including Kentucky Fried Chicken (KFC), have employee-of-the-month awards. Tupperware holds rallies for its salespeople, and almost everyone gets something—ranging from pins to lucrative prizes for top performers. A leader's power is strong or weak based on ability to punish and reward followers. An important part of reward power is having control over getting and allocating resources.[21]

Appropriate Use of Reward Power.   When employees do a good job, they should be rewarded, as discussed with reinforcement motivation theory (Chapter 3). When dealing with higher-level managers and people over whom we have no authority, we can use the *exchange influencing tactic* by offering some type of reward for helping meet our objective. The incentive for exchange can be anything of value, such as scarce resources, information, advice or assistance on another task, or career and political support. Exchange is common in reciprocity[22] (you do something for me and I'll do something for you—or you owe me one, for a later reward), which we will discuss in a later section on organizational politics.

Increasing Reward Power.   To increase reward power, follow these guidelines:

- Gain and maintain control over evaluating employees' performance and determining their raises, promotions, and other rewards.
- Find out what others value, and try to reward people in that way.
- Let people know you control rewards, and state our criteria for giving rewards.

Coercive Power

The use of **coercive power** *involves punishment and withholding of rewards to influence compliance.* It is also called the *pressure influencing tactic.* From fear of reprimands, probation, suspension, or dismissal, employees often do as their manager requests. Other examples of coercive power include verbal abuse, humiliation, and ostracism. Group members also use coercive power (peer pressure) to enforce group norms.

Appropriate Use of Coercive Power.   Coercive power is appropriate to use in maintaining discipline and enforcing rules. When employees are not willing to do as requested, coercive power may be the only way to gain compliance. Employees tend to resent managers' use of coercive power. So keep the use of coercive power to a minimum by using it only as a last resort.

Increasing Coercive Power.   To increase coercive power, follow these guidelines.

- Gain authority to use punishment and withhold rewards.
- Don't make rash threats; do not use coercion to manipulate others or to gain personal benefits.
- Be persistent. If we request that followers do something, we need to follow up to make sure it is done.

WORK
Application **5-1**

Select a present or past manager who has or had coercive power. Give a specific example of how he or she uses or used reward and punishment to achieve an objective. Overall, how effective is (or was) this manager at using rewards and punishment?

5.1 *Following Orders*

The armed forces are hierarchical by rank, based on power. Officers tend to give orders to troops by using legitimate power. When orders are followed, reward power is common. When orders are not followed, coercive power is commonly used to get the troops to implement the order. The conditioning of the military is to respect the power of authority and to follow orders, usually without questioning authority.

1. Is it ethical and socially responsible to teach people to follow orders without questioning authority in the military or any other organization?

2. What would you do if your boss asked you to follow orders that you thought might be unethical? (Some options include the following: just do it; don't say anything but don't do it; question the motives; look closely at what you are asked to do; go to your boss's boss to make sure it's okay to do it; tell the boss you will not do it; ask the boss to do it him- or herself; blow the whistle to an outside source like the government or media; etc.)

3. Is following orders a good justification for unethical practices?

Referent Power

Referent power *is based on the user's personal relationships with others.* It is also called the *personal appeals influencing tactic* based on loyalty and friendship. Power stems primarily from relationships with the person using power. Charismatic leaders tend to use referent power.

Leaders can also use the *inspirational appeals influencing tactic.* You appeal to the follower's values, ideals, and aspirations, or increase self-confidence by displaying your feelings to appeal to the follower's emotions and enthusiasm. So rational persuasion uses logic, whereas inspirational persuasion appeals to emotions and enthusiasm. Thus, inspirational appeals generally work well with people whose behavior is more influenced by emotions than logical thinking.

To be inspirational, we need to understand the values, hopes, fears, and goals of followers. We need to be positive and optimistic and create a vision of how things will be when the objective is achieved. You can also include the ingratiation influencing tactic within your inspirational appeal.

Appropriate Use of Referent Power.   The use of referent power is particularly appropriate for people with weak, or no, position power, such as with peers. Referent power is needed in self-managed teams because leadership should be shared.

Increasing Referent Power.   To increase referent power, follow these guidelines:

• Develop people skills, which are covered in all chapters. Remember that we don't have to be a manager to have referent power.
• Work at relationships with managers and peers.

Expert Power

Expert power *is based on the user's skill and knowledge.* Being an expert makes other people dependent on you. People often respect an expert, and the fewer people who possess an expertise and knowledge, the more power the expert individual has.[23]

The more people come to us for advice, the greater is our expert power. Experts commonly use the *rational persuasion influencing tactic* because people believe they know what they are saying and that it is correct.

Appropriate Use of Expert Power. Managers, particularly at lower levels, are often—but not always—experts within their departments. New managers frequently depend on employees who have expertise in how the organization runs and know how to get things done politically. Thus, followers can have considerable influence over the leader. Expert power is essential to employees who are working with people from other departments and organizations.

Increasing Expert Power. To increase expert power, follow these guidelines:

- To become an expert, take all the training and educational programs the organization provides.
- Attend meetings of your trade or professional associations, and read their publications (magazines and journals) to keep up with current trends in your field. Write articles to be published. Become an officer in the organization.
- Keep up with the latest technology. Volunteer to be the first to learn something new.
- Project a positive self-concept (Chapter 2),[24] and let people know about your expertise by developing a reputation for having expertise.

Information Power

Information power *is based on the user's data desired by others.* Information power involves access to vital information and knowledge and control over its distribution to others.[25] Managers often have access to information that is not available to subordinates, giving them power. Managers also rely on employees for information, giving them some power. Some administrative assistants have more information and are more helpful in answering questions than the managers they work for.

Appropriate Use of Information Power. An important part of the manager's job is to convey information. Employees often come to managers for information on what to do and how to do it. Leaders use information power when making *rational persuasion* and often with *inspirational appeals.*

Increasing Information Power. To increase information power, follow these guidelines:

- Have information flow through you.
- Know what is going on in the organization. Serve on committees because it gives both information and a chance to increase connection power.
- Develop a network of information sources, and gather information from them.[26] You will learn how to network later in this chapter.

Connection Power

Connection power *is based on the user's relationships with influential people.* Connection power is also a form of politics, the topic of our next major section. The right connections can give power or at least the perception of having power. If people know you are friendly with people in power, they are more apt to do as you request.

Sometimes it is difficult to influence others all alone. With a *coalition influencing tactic* you use influential people to help persuade others to meet your objective. The more people you can get on your side, the more influence you can have on others. Coalitions are also a political strategy—a tactic that will be discussed again later in this chapter.

Appropriate Use of Connection Power. When you are looking for a job or promotions, connections can help. There is a lot of truth in the statement "It's not what you know; it's who you know." Connection power can also help you get resources you need.[27]

WORK
Application **5-2**

Select a past or present job. Who did (or do) you usually go to for expertise and information? Give examples of when you went to someone for expertise and when you went to someone for information.

WORK
Application **5-3**

1. Think of a present or past manager. Which type of power does (or did) the manager use most often? Explain.

2. Which one or two suggestions for increasing your power base are the most relevant to you? Explain.

WORK
Application **5-4**

Give three different influencing tactics you or someone else used to achieve an objective in an organization you have worked for.

Increasing Connection Power.   To increase connection power, follow these guidelines:

- Expand your network of contacts with important managers who have power.
- Join the "in-crowd" and the "right" associations and clubs. Participating in sports like golf may help you meet influential people.
- Follow the guidelines for using the coalition influencing tactic. When you want something, identify the people who can help you attain it, make coalitions, and win them over to your side.
- Get people to know your name. Get all the publicity you can. Have your accomplishments known by the people in power; send them notices without sounding like a bragger.

Now that you have read about nine influencing tactics within seven types of power, see Exhibit 5.1 for a review, and test your ability to apply them in Concept Applications 5-1 and 5-2. Then, complete Self-Assessment 5-1 to better understand how your personality traits relate to how you use power and influencing tactics to get what you want.

CONCEPT APPLICATION 5-1

Influencing Tactics

For each situation, select the most appropriate individual tactic that will enhance your chances of getting a desired outcome. Write the appropriate letter in the blank before each item.

a. rational persuasion   d. ingratiation   g. coalition
b. inspirational appeals   e. personal appeals   h. legitimization
c. consultation   f. exchange   i. pressure

_____ 1. Sonia is resisting helping a coworker thinking, "What's in it for me?"

_____ 2. You have an employee Hank with a big ego and who is very moody at times. You want Hank to complete an assignment ahead of schedule.

_____ 3. You believe you have accomplished things deserving a pay raise. So you decide to ask your manager for it.

_____ 4. Next week the committee you serve on will elect officers. Nominations and elections will be done at the same time. You are interested in being the president. But you don't want to nominate yourself and you don't want to run and lose.

_____ 5. Your employee Nikki regularly passes in assignments late. The assignment you are giving her now is very important and must be done on time.

_____ 6. You have an idea about how to increase performance of your department. But you are not too sure if it will work or if the employees will like the idea.

_____ 7. You are a production manager and heard rumors that the company will be purchasing some new high-tech manufacturing equipment. You would like to know if it is true, and, if so, are you getting it. You know a person in the purchasing department, so you decide to contact that person to try to find out.

_____ 8. The purchasing person from situation 7 gave you the information you were looking for. She is calling to ask you for some information.

_____ 9. Some of your workers did not come in to work today. You have a large order that a sales rep said would go out today. It will be tough for the small crew to meet the deadline.

_____ 10. Although the crew members in situation 9 have agreed to push to meet the deadline, you would like to give them some help besides your own. You have an administrative assistant who doesn't work on processing orders. You decide to talk to this nonunion employee about working with the crew today.

CONCEPT APPLICATION 5-2

Using Power

Identify the relevant type of power to use in each situation to get the best results. Write the appropriate letter in the blank before each item.

a. coercive
b. connection
c. reward or legitimate

d. referent
e. information or expert

_____ 11. One of your best workers, Carl, who needs little direction from you, is not performing to standard. You believe that a personal problem is affecting his work.

_____ 12. A committee, which is very political, allocates money for resources. You want a new larger truck to help your crew be more productive.

_____ 13. One of your best workers, Latoya, wants to be a manager. Latoya is asking you to help prepare her for a promotion.

_____ 14. Shawn is not doing much work today. As occasionally happens, he claims that he does not feel well but cannot afford to take time off without pay. There is work that needs to be done today.

_____ 15. You gave Helen an assignment specifying exactly how it had to be done. She ignored your directives and the assignment doesn't meet the customer's request. This is not the first time this has happened.

SELF-ASSESSMENT 5-1   Influencing Tactics, Power, and Personality Traits

Review the nine influencing tactics. Which ones do you tend to use most often to help you get what you want? Also review your personality profile self-assessment exercises in Chapter 2.

Surgency/High Need for Power

If you have a high need for power (n Pow), you are apt to try to influence others, and you enjoy it. You tend to hate to lose, and when you don't get what you want, it bothers you. Thus, you are more likely to use harder methods of influence and power, such as pressure, exchange, coalitions, and legitimization, than other personality types. You probably also like to use rational persuasion and don't understand why people don't think or see things the way you do. Be careful; use socialized, rather than personalized, power to influence others.

Agreeableness/High Need for Affiliation

If you have a high need for affiliation (n Aff), you are apt to be less concerned about influencing others and gaining power than about getting along with them. Thus, you are more likely to use softer methods of influence, such as personal and inspirational appeals and ingratiation, as well as rational appeals. You may tend not to seek power, and even avoid it.

Conscientiousness/High Need for Achievement

If you have a high need for achievement (n Ach), you tend to be between the other two approaches to influencing others. You tend to have clear goals and work hard to get what you want, which often requires influencing others to help you. So, you don't want power for its own sake, only to get what you want. But you like to play by the rules and may tend to use rational persuasion frequently.

Based on the preceding information, briefly describe how your personality affects the ways you attempt to influence others.

_____

_____

_____

OPENING CASE Application

1. What sources and types of power does Mark Cuban have, and why has he had problems with power?

Mark Cuban is used to getting his own way, and he wants to be famous and influential as he attempts to reorder the landscape of professional sports and entertainment. He has position power as an owner of multiple businesses. As a business owner, Cuban has legitimate power, and he rewards his employees for doing a good job. He has used coercive power (he fired the Mavericks coach), he has some referent power, and he is viewed as an expert in business. He also has information power and has connections with some influential people.

On the dark side, Cuban's behavior has cost him money and respect. Cuban is not your typical pro sports team owner who watches the games from the owner's box. He sits next to the Mavericks team bench and yells at the players. He has gone out on the court during games and listens in on team huddles. Cuban has stormed into the locker room and cursed out the players when they lost. He has berated the referees, which has led to fines and problems with the NBA.

Organizational Politics

Just as the nine influencing tactics (see Exhibit 5.1) are used within the seven types of power, these tactics are also used in organizational politics. In this section, we discuss the nature of organizational politics, political behavior, and guidelines for developing political skills. But first, determine your own use of political behavior by completing Self-Assessment 5-2.

SELF-ASSESSMENT 5-2 | Use of Political Behavior

Select the response that best describes your actual or planned use of the following behavior on the job. Place a number from 1 to 5 on the line before each statement.

1 — 2 — 3 — 4 — 5
Rarely   Occasionally   Usually

_____ 1. I use my personal contacts to get a job and promotions.

_____ 2. I try to find out what is going on in all the organizational departments.

_____ 3. I dress the same way as the people in power and take on the same interests (watch or play sports, join the same clubs, etc.).

_____ 4. I purposely seek contacts and network with higher-level managers.

_____ 5. If upper management offered me a raise and promotion requiring me to move to a new location, I'd say yes even if I did not want to move.

_____ 6. I get along with everyone, even those considered to be difficult to get along with.

_____ 7. I try to make people feel important by complimenting them.

_____ 8. I do favors for others and use their favors in return, and I thank people and send them thank-you notes.

_____ 9. I work at developing a good working relationship with my manager.

_____ 10. I ask my manager and other people for their advice.

_____ 11. When a person opposes me, I still work to maintain a positive working relationship with that person.

_____ 12. I'm courteous, pleasant, and positive with others.

_____ 13. When my manager makes a mistake, I never publicly point out the error.

_____ 14. I am more cooperative (I compromise) than competitive (I seek to get my own way).

_____ 15. I tell the truth.

SELF-ASSESSMENT 5-2   **Use of Political Behavior (Continued)**

_____ 16. I avoid saying negative things about my manager and others behind their backs.

_____ 17. I work at getting people to know me by name and face by continually introducing myself.

_____ 18. I ask some satisfied customers and people who know my work to let my manager know how good a job I'm doing.

_____ 19. I try to win contests and get prizes, pins, and other awards.

_____ 20. I send notices of my accomplishments to higher-level managers and company newsletters.

To determine your overall political behavior, add the 20 numbers you selected as your answers. The number will range from 20 to 100. The higher your score, the more political behavior you use. Place your score here and on the continuum below.

20 — 30 — 40 — 50 — 60 — 70 — 80 — 90 — 100
Nonpolitical   _Political_

To determine your use of political behavior in four areas, add the numbers for the following questions and divide by the number of questions to get the average score in each area.

A. _Learning the organizational culture and power players_

Questions 1–5 total: ____ divided by 5 = ____

B. _Developing good working relationships, especially with your boss_

Questions 6–12 total: ____ divided by 7 = ____

C. _Being a loyal, honest team player_

Questions 13–16 total: ____ divided by 4 = ____

D. _Gaining recognition_

Questions 17–20 total: ____ divided by 4 = ____

The higher the average score of items A–D, the more you use this type of political behavior. Do you tend to use them all equally, or do you use some more than others?

Learning Outcome (3) _Discuss how power and politics are related._

The Nature of Organizational Politics

Organizations are political,[28] as they are a social process,[29] and power and politics are related.[30] **Politics** _is the process of gaining and using power._ Some managers believe that playing the political game is not necessary and that they will advance based just on job performance. But they couldn't be more wrong because research findings support that political skills are needed to climb the corporate ladder, or at least avoid getting thrown off it as many promising managers' careers were derailed because of poor political skills.[31] The amount and importance of politics vary from organization to organization. However, larger organizations tend to be more political, and the higher the level of management, the more important politics becomes.

Learning Outcome (4) _Describe how money and politics have a similar use._

Politics Is a Medium of Exchange

Like power, politics often has a negative connotation because of people who abuse political power. A positive way to view politics is to realize that it is simply a social medium of exchange. _Social exchange theory_ regards exchanges between people as "social," as opposed to economic, in nature.

Like money, politics in and of itself is inherently neither good nor bad. Politics is simply a system of getting things done, or getting what we want. In our economy, money is the medium of exchange (tangible currency); in an organization, social politics is the medium of exchange (political behavior). Favors are the currency by which productivity is purchased and goodwill is gained. Political behavior creates energy and commitment, a valuable currency.[32]

Politically effective leaders marshal resources to accomplish personal and professional goals through the power and influence of their relationships. So political skill is not about taking advantage of others or backstabbing to enhance self-interest at the expense of others, it's about building relationships to help you meet your objectives.[33]

Political Behavior

How well you play politics directly affects your success.[34] Networking, reciprocity, and coalitions are common organizational political behaviors.

Networking

Networking is a critical facet of political skills.[35] **Networking** *is the process of developing relationships for the purpose of socializing and politicking.* Successful managers spend more time networking than average managers, so reach out to establish an ongoing network of contacts to help you bring about change to meet your objectives.[36] Because networking is so important to career success, we are going to discuss it as our next major section, after we finish our other political skills discussions.

Reciprocity

Using **reciprocity** *involves creating obligations and developing alliances, and using them to accomplish objectives.* Notice that the exchange influencing tactic is used with reciprocity. When people do something for you, you incur an obligation that they may expect to be repaid. When you do something for people, you create a debt that you may be able to collect at a later date when you need a favor. Isn't part of relationships doing things (favors) for each other?[37] Thus, ongoing reciprocal relationships build community needed to meet your objectives,[38] and reciprocity builds trust in social exchange relationships.[39]

Here is a tip to increase your chances of getting help from others. When asking for help, use the word *favor,* because the mere mention of that word can persuade people to help you. People have a modal, rote response to a favor request, which is, "Yeah, sure, what is it?" So start with the phrase "Will you please do me a favor?"

WORK
Application **5-5**

Give a job example of how networking, reciprocity, or a coalition was used to achieve an organizational objective

Coalitions

Using coalitions as an influencing tactic is political behavior. Each party helps the others get what they want. Reciprocity and networking are commonly used to achieve ongoing objectives, whereas coalitions are developed for achieving a specific objective. A political tactic when developing coalitions is to use co-optation. *Co-optation is the process of getting a person whose support you need to join your coalition rather than compete.*

The reality of organizational life is that most important decisions are made by coalitions outside of the formal meeting in which the decision is made. For example, let's say you are on a team and the captain is selected by a nomination and vote of the team members. If you want to be captain, you can politic by asking close teammates who they will vote for to try to get their votes, and if they are supportive, you can ask them to promote you for captain to others. If the majority of the team says they will vote for you, you have basically won the election before the coach even starts the meeting, nominating, and voting by building a coalition. If you don't get any support from your close teammates and others, you can drop the effort to build a coalition, knowing that you will lose. This same coalition-building process is used to influence all types of decisions.

The upcoming guidelines can be used with any of the three political behaviors. Before considering how to develop political skills, review Exhibit 5.2 for a list of political behaviors and guidelines.

OPENING CASE Application

2. Why are organizational politics important to Mark Cuban's enterprises?

Mark Cuban has clearly used politics to gain and use power in creating his business empire. For the owner of multiple businesses, organizational politics is not as important as using political skills outside the organization. The NBA is an organization of multiple team owners, so politics is important for making changes in the league. Because of Cuban's behavior, the NBA owners voted to pass rules of conduct that were really meant for Cuban. The NBA commissioner said that the more stringent rules were called for to prevent individual owners from overshadowing the games. Cuban was so upset that he walked out of the meeting before the vote. So Cuban can improve on his organizational politics skills.

◀ **EXHIBIT   5.2**

Political Behavior and Guidelines for Developing Political Skills

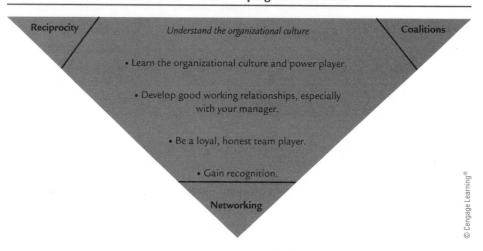

Reciprocity / *Understand the organizational culture* / Coalitions

• Learn the organizational culture and power player.

• Develop good working relationships, especially with your manager.

• Be a loyal, honest team player.

• Gain recognition.

Networking

© Cengage Learning®

Guidelines for Developing Political Skills

Researchers have found that women and minorities tend to have weak political skills and will have many more opportunities for advancement if they expand and exercise their political skills.[40] Carly Fiorina stated that she lost her job as CEO of HP because of politics. Successfully implementing the behavior guidelines presented here can result in increased political skills. However, if you don't agree with a particular political behavior, don't use it. You do not have to use all of the political behaviors to be successful. Learn what it takes in the organization where you work as you follow the guidelines.

Understand the Organizational Culture and Power Players

Develop your connection power through politicking. It is natural, especially for young people, to take a purely rational approach to a job without considering politics. But many business decisions are not very rational; they are based on power and politics. Learn the cultural (Chapter 10) shared values and beliefs and how business and politics operate where you work. Learn to read between the lines.

In all organizations, there are some powerful key players. Your manager is a key player to you.[41] Don't just find out who the managers are; gain an understanding of what makes each of them tick. By understanding them, you can tailor the presentation of your ideas and style to fit each person's needs.[42] For example, some managers want to see detailed financial numbers and statistics, while others don't. Some managers expect you to continually follow up with them, while others will think you are bugging them.

Review Self-Assessment 2, questions 1 through 5.   You can use these tactics to increase your political skills. Network with power players. Try to do favors for power players to help them.[43] When developing coalitions, get key players on your side. When selecting a mentor, try to get one who is good at organizational politics to teach you. Also try to observe people who are good at politics, and copy their behavior.

Develop Good Working Relationships, Especially with Your Manager

The ability to work well with others is critical to your career success, and it's an important foundation of politics.[44] The more people like and respect you, the more power you will gain. Managers often promote informal leaders to supervise their peers. Let's focus on the relationship with our boss because it is a major indicator of job satisfaction today.

Advancement.   If we want to get ahead, we need to have a good supportive working relationship with our manager—your manager says you're a top performer. Your boss usually gives you formal performance appraisals, which are the primary bases for raises and promotions. Fair or not, many evaluations are influenced by the manager's relationship with the employee. If your manager likes and supports you, you have a better chance of getting a good review, raises, and promotions. If you lose your bosses support, you will most likely lose your advancement with the organization.[45] It helps to phrase your own ideas as if they were your managers, and to complement your boss.[46]

Do more than what is required.   Supervisors also give higher ratings to employees who share their goals (goal congruence) and priorities than they give to those who don't.[47] Thus, get to know what your manager expects from you (key performance indicators and objectives), and do it.[48] Beat or at least meet deadlines, and don't miss them. Impress your boss by doing more than you are asked to do.

Share bad news.   It's common to put off telling the manager bad news. But if you are having a problem on the job, don't put off letting your manager know about it. Most managers, and peers, like to be asked for advice. If you are behind schedule to meet an important deadline and your manager finds out about it from others, it is embarrassing, especially if your manager finds out from his or her manager. Also avoid showing up your manager in public, such as during a meeting.

Don't go to your boss's manager.   If you cannot get along with your manager and are in conflict, avoid going to his or her manager to resolve the conflict. There are two dangers in going over the manager's head. First, chances are your manager has a good working relationship with his or her manager, who will side with your manager. Even if the higher-level manager agrees with you, you will most likely hurt your relationship with your manager. He or she may consciously or unconsciously take some form of retaliation, such as giving you a lower performance review, which can hurt you in the long run.

Review Self-Assessment 2, questions 6 through 12. You can use these tactics to increase your political skills. Include your manager in your network, try to do favors for your manager, and include your manager in your coalitions. Use the ingratiation tactic with everyone. When was the last time you gave anyone, including your manager, a compliment? When was the last time you sent a thank-you or congratulations note?

Be a Loyal, Honest Team Player

Many managers reward loyalty.[49] Ethical behavior is important in organizational power and politics.[50] Some backstabbing gossips may get short-term benefits from such behavior, but in the long run they are generally unsuccessful because others gun them down in return. In any organization, you must earn others' respect, confidence, and trust.[51] There are very few, if any, jobs in which objectives can be achieved without the support of a group or team. The trend is toward teamwork,[52] so if you're not a team player, work at it.

Review Self-Assessment 2, questions 13 through 16. You can use these tactics to increase your political skills. Be a loyal, honest team player in your network, in your reciprocity, and with your coalition members.

Gain Recognition

Doing a great job does not help you get ahead in an organization if no one knows about it or doesn't know who you are. Author Ken Blanchard says, "It's not who you know that counts; it's who knows you and what they think of you."[53] Recognition and knowing the power players go hand in hand. You want people higher in the organization to know your expertise and the contributions you are making to them and the organization.[54]

Review Self-Assessment 2, questions 17 through 20. You can use these tactics to increase your political skills. Let people in your network and coalitions, and people you reciprocate with, know of your accomplishments. You can also serve on committees and try to become an officer, which gives you name recognition.

WORK
Application **5-6**

Which one or two suggestions for developing political skills are the most relevant to you? Explain.

CONCEPT APPLICATION 5-3

Political Behavior

Identify the behavior in each situation as effective or ineffective political behavior. Write the appropriate letter in the blank before each item.

a. effective   b. ineffective

_____ 16. The manager, Breonna, has to drop off a daily report by noon. She delivers the report at around 11:00 a.m. on Friday, so that she can run into some executives who meet at that time. On the other days, Breonna drops the report off at around noon on her way to lunch.

_____ 17. Jamal is taking golf lessons so he can join the company golf group, which includes some executives.

_____ 18. A manager made a poor decision, and Chris told his manager's boss about it.

_____ 19. Sonia really wants to do an excellent job, so she avoids socializing at work.

_____ 20. Juan sent a very positive performance report to three executives who did not request copies.

Networking

Recall that networking is part of politics, and through networking you can develop your power and influence to get others to help you reach your objectives.[55] Through networking you develop relationships,[56] and the relationships build a community support system to help you in your career.[57] There are many benefits to networking.[58] For example, more people find jobs through networking than all the other methods combined. Companies have been recruiting talented workers through social media site LinkedIn for years,[59] and more companies are now also using Facebook to recruit as well as to increase sales.[60] Assess your networking skills now in Self-Assessment 5-3 before reading on.

SELF-ASSESSMENT 5-3   **Networking**

Identify each of the 16 statements according to how accurately it describes your behavior. Place a number from 1 to 5 on the line before each statement.

5 — 4 — 3 — 2 — 1

Describes me   *Does not describe me*

_____ 1. When I start something (a new project, a career move, a major purchase), I seek help from people I know and seek new contacts for help.

_____ 2. I view networking as a way to create win–win situations.

_____ 3. I like to meet new people; I can easily strike up a conversation with people I don't know.

_____ 4. I can quickly state two or three of my most important accomplishments.

_____ 5. When I contact business people who can help me (such as with career information), I have goals for the communication.

_____ 6. When I contact business people who can help me, I have a planned short opening statement.

_____ 7. When I contact business people who can help me, I praise their accomplishments.

_____ 8. When I contact people who can help me, I have a set of questions to ask.

_____ 9. I know contact information for at least 100 people who can potentially help me.

_____ 10. I have a file/database with contact information of people who can help me in my career, and I keep it updated and continue to add new names.

_____ 11. During communications with people who can help me, I ask them for names of others I can contact for more information.

_____ 12. When seeking help from others, I ask them how I might help them.

_____ 13. When people help me, I thank them at the time and for big favors with a follow-up thanks.

_____ 14. I keep in touch with people who have helped or can potentially help me in my career at least once a year, and I update them on my career progress.

_____ 15. I have regular communications with people in my industry who work for different organizations, such as members of trade professional organizations.

_____ 16. I attend trade/professional/career types of meetings to maintain relationships and to make new contacts.

Add up your score and place it here _____ and on the continuum below.

80 — 70 — 60 — 50 — 40 — 30 — 16
Effective Networking   *Ineffective Networking*

If you are a full-time student, you may not score high on networking effectiveness, but that's okay as you can develop networking skills by following the steps and guidelines in this chapter.

Networking is not about asking everyone you know for a job (or whatever you need assistance with). How would you react if someone directly said "Can you give me a job?" Although the same networking process applies to broad career development, we focus more on the job search. Whenever you start something—a new project, a career move, a car or house purchase—use your networks.

You may have a social networking account, like Facebook, to communicate with your friends, but "career" networking is more than this. This section provides a how-to network process that can enhance career development.[61] The process is summarized in Exhibit 5.3.

EXHIBIT 5.3

The Networking Process

1. Perform a self-assessment and set goals.
2. Create your one-minute self-sell.
3. Develop your network.
4. Conduct networking interviews.
5. Maintain your network.

© Cengage Learning®

Learning Outcome 5 *List and explain the steps in the networking process.*

Perform a Self-Assessment and Set Goals

The self-assessment includes writing down your skills, competencies, and knowledge. Self-assessment gives you insight into your transferable skills and the criteria that are important to you in a new job. Listing the major criteria that are most important to you in the new job and prioritizing these can help to clarify your ideal next position.

Factors to consider are industry, company size and growth, location, travel and commuting requirements, compensation package/benefits, job requirements, and promotion potential. Other factors to assess are the style of management, culture, and work style of the organization. Critical to career satisfaction is the ability to use your talents, grow in your field, and do what you do best in your job. Although many tools exist to assess skills and preferences, a simple list with priorities can suffice to clarify your talents and the characteristics of an ideal new career or job.

Accomplishments

After completing a self-assessment, you are ready to translate your talents into accomplishments. The results you achieved in your jobs and/or college are the best evidence of your skills. Your future employer knows that your past behavior helps predicts your future behavior and that if you achieved results in the past, you will likely produce similar results again. Accomplishments are what set you apart and provide evidence of your skills and abilities. We must articulate what we have accomplished in a way that is clear, concise, and compelling. Write down your accomplishments (at least two or three) and include them in your résumé. Whether you are looking for a job or not, you should always have an updated résumé handy.

Tie Your Accomplishments to the Job Interview

You want to be sure to state your accomplishments that are based on your skill during the job interview. Many interviews begin with a broad question such as "Tell me about yourself." Oftentimes candidates do not reveal anything compelling. Sell yourself by elaborating on a problem that was solved or an opportunity taken and how you achieved it using your skills.

Set Networking Goals

For example: to get a mentor; to determine the expertise, skills, and requirements needed for XYZ position; to get feedback on my résumé and job and/or career preparation for a career move into XYZ; or to attain a job as XYZ. Be sure to write objectives using the setting objectives Model 3.1 from Chapter 3.

WORK Application **5-7**

Write a networking goal.

Create Your One-Minute Self-Sell

Our next step is to create a one-minute sell to help accomplish your goal. *The* **one-minute self-sell** *is an opening statement used in networking that quickly summarizes your history and career plan and asks a question.* It is also referred to as an elevator pitch. To take 60 seconds or less, your message must be concise, but it also needs to be clear and compelling. It gives the listener a sense of your background, identifies your career field and a key result you've achieved, plus provides the direction of your next job. It tells the listener what you plan to do next and why. It also stimulates conversation by asking your network for help in the area of support, coaching, contacts, or knowledge of the industry.

Part 1. History: Start with a career summary, the highlights of your career to date. Include your most recent career or school history and a description of the type of work/internship or courses you have taken. Also include the industry and type of organization.

Part 2. Plans: Next, state the target career you are seeking, the industry you prefer, and a specific function or role. You can also mention names of organizations you are targeting as well as let the acquaintance know why you are looking for work.

Part 3. Question: Last, ask a question to encourage two-way communication. The question will vary depending on the person and your goal or the reason you are using the one-minute self-sell, for example:

- In what areas might there be opportunities for a person with my experience?
- In what other fields can I use these skills or this degree?
- In what other positions in your organization could my skills be used?
- How does my targeted future career sound to you? Is it a match with my education and skills?
- Do you know of any job openings in my field?

Write and Practice Your One-Minute Self-Sell

WORK Application **5-8**

Write a one-minute self-sell to achieve your networking goal from Work Application 7.

Write out your one-minute self-sell. Be sure to clearly separate your history, plans, and question, and customize your question based on the contact with whom you are talking. For example, *Hello, my name is Will Smith. I am a senior at Springfield College majoring in marketing, and I have completed an internship in the marketing department at the Big Y supermarket. I am seeking a job in sales in the food industry. Can you give me some ideas on the types of sales positions available in the food industry?* Practice delivering it with family and friends and get feedback to improve it. The more opportunities you find to use this brief introduction, the easier it becomes.

Develop Your Network

Begin with who you know. Everyone can create a written network list of about 200 people consisting of professional and personal contacts. You may already have a network on an online social networking site, such as Facebook or LinkedIn, and you most likely have phone and an e-mail account with an address book. Address books and rolodexes are written network lists, but you need to continually develop and expand them. An e-mail or Facebook/LinkedIn account is a good place to store your network list and information on each person because you can easily contact one or more people.

One word of caution regarding social networking and other Web sites: Be careful with what is online. If a potentially helpful person or employer looks you up online and finds unflattering pictures of you (under the influence of drugs or alcohol, not fully dressed, doing embarrassing things, etc.), it may cost you a contact or potential job. You may want to do a search on yourself to make sure that others don't have unflattering pictures or other things of you posted.

Professional contacts include colleagues (past and present), professional organizations, alumni associations, vendors, suppliers, managers, mentors, and many other professional acquaintances. On a personal level, your network includes family, neighbors, friends, religious groups, and other personal service providers (doctor, dentist, insurance agent, stock broker, accountant, hairstylist, politician). Compose a list of your network using the above categories, and continually update and add to your list with referrals from others. You will discover that your network grows exponentially and can get you closer to the decision makers in a hiring position. In today's job market, it is critical to engage in a "passive job hunt" using your network and having your résumé ready.

Now expand your list to people you don't know. Who do you want to build a tie to? Where should you go to develop your network? Anywhere people gather. Talk to everyone because you never know who's connected to whom. To be more specific, get more involved with professional associations. Many have special student memberships, and some even have college chapters. If you really want to develop your career reputation, become a leader in your associations and not just a member. Volunteer to be on committees and boards, to give presentations, and so on. Other opportunities to network with people you don't know include the chamber of commerce, college alumni clubs/reunions, civic organizations (Rotary, Lions, Kiwanis, Elks, Moose, Knights of Columbus, etc.), courses of any type, trade shows and career fairs, community groups, charities and religious groups (Goodwill, American Cancer Society, your local church), and social clubs (exercise, boating, golf, tennis, etc.).

Another important point is to work at developing your ability to remember people by name. If you want to impress people you have never met or hardly know, call them by their name. Ask others who they are, then go up and call them by name and introduce yourself with your one-minute self-sell. When you are introduced to people, call them by name during the conversation two or three times. If you think the person can help you, don't stop with casual conversation; make an appointment at a later time for a phone conversation, personal meeting, coffee, or lunch. Get their business cards to add to your network list, and give your business card and/or résumé when appropriate.

Conduct Networking Interviews

Even though the trend is toward more online communications, networking in person is important. Based on your goal, use your network list of people to set up a networking interview to meet your goal. It may take many interviews to meet a goal, such as to get a job. An informational interview is a phone call or preferably a meeting that you initiate to meet a goal, such as to gain information from a contact with hands-on experience in your field of interest.

You are the interviewer (in contrast to a job interview) and need to be prepared with specific questions to ask the contact regarding your targeted career or industry based on your self-assessment and goal. Keep your agenda short; focus on what is most important. Ask for a 15- to 20-minute meeting, and, as a result, many people will talk to you.

These meetings can be most helpful when you have accessed someone who is in an organization you'd like to join or has a contact in an industry you are targeting. A face-to-face meeting of 20 minutes can have many benefits. Your contact will remember you after a personal meeting, and the likelihood of getting a job lead increases. Keeping the person posted on your job search progress as well as a thank-you note after the meeting also solidifies the relationship. The interviewing steps are the following:

Step 1.   **Establish Rapport:** Provide a brief introduction and thank the contact for his or her time. Clearly state the purpose of the meeting; be clear that you are not asking for a job. Don't start selling yourself; project an interest in the other person. Do some research and impress the person by stating an accomplishment, such as "I enjoyed your presentation at the Rotary meeting on…."

Step 2.   **Deliver Your One-Minute Self-Sell:** Even if the person has already heard it, say it again. This enables you to quickly summarize your background and career direction.

Step 3.   **Ask Prepared Questions:** As stated above, do your homework before the meeting and compose a series of questions to ask during the interview. Your questions should vary depending on your goal, the contact, and how he or she may help you with your job search. Sample questions include the following:

- What do you think of my qualifications for this field?
- With your knowledge of the industry, what career opportunities do you see in the future?
- What advice do you have for me as I begin/advance in my career?
- If you were exploring this field, who else would you talk with?

During the interview, if the interviewee mentions anything that could hinder your search, ask how such obstacles could be overcome. Take notes during the interview.

Step 4.   **Get Additional Contacts for Your Network:** As mentioned previously, always ask who else you should speak with—a referral.[62] Most people can give you three names, so if you are only offered one, ask for others—seek more referrals.[63] Add the new contacts to your network list; be sure to write them down. When contacting new people, be sure to use your network person's name. Be sure not to linger beyond the time you have been offered, unless invited to stay. Leave a business card and/or résumé so the person can contact you in case something comes up.

Step 5.   **Ask Your Contacts How You Might Help Them:** Offer a copy of a recent journal article or any additional information that came up in your conversation. Remember, it's all about building relationships, and making yourself a resource for other people.

Step 6. **Follow Up with a Thank-You Note and Status Report:** By sending a thank-you note, along with another business card/résumé, and following up with your progress, you are continuing the networking relationship and maintaining a contact for the future.

Be sure to assess the effectiveness of your networking meetings using the six steps as your criteria. Did you implement all of the steps successfully? How can you improve next time? It is always helpful to create a log of calls, meetings, and contacts to maintain your network as it expands.

Maintain Your Network

After you build your network, you should maintain it.[64] If an individual was helpful in finding your new job, be sure to let him or her know the outcome. Saying thank you to those who helped in your transition will encourage the business relationship; providing this information will increase the likelihood of getting help in the future.

It is also a good idea to notify everyone in your network that you are in a new position and provide contact information. Go to trade shows and conventions, make business friends, and continue to update, correct, and add to your network list. Always thank others for their time.

Networking is also about helping others, especially your mentor.[65] As you have been helped, you should help others. You will be amazed at how helping others comes back to you. Jack Gherty, former CEO of Land O'Lakes, said that he got ahead by helping other people win.

Try to contact everyone on your network list at least once a year (calls, e-mail, and cards are good). Send congratulations on recent achievements. By contacting everyone, we don't mean sending a note to your 500 friends at the same time. You need to maintain regular personal contact, which is generally limited to around 150 people.

Social Networking at Work

Once you land that new position, should you network on or off the job—or both? With increasing technology advances, people are blurring the differences between their personal and professional lives, including the use of social networking media, including LinkedIn, Facebook, and Twitter.[66] Although many companies are encouraging employees to use social networking media on the job, it brings new challenges. Is it business or personal? Will employees get the company into legal problems? To deal with potential problems, many companies are developing social media policies and rules. So on the new job, be sure to know the policy on social media and follow the rules, and be careful what you say about your boss and company.

OPENING CASE Application

3. How has Mark Cuban used networking?

Mark Cuban first started networking by selling garbage bags door to door and then by selling stamps and baseball cards before the Internet was available. As the owner of Motley's, between bartending and spinning records, he schmoozed customers. In fact, people came to see him, and when he wasn't there, business wasn't as good. When Cuban was selling computers, he was constantly socializing and trading business cards. To be successful in the entertainment business, you have to network with the right people.

Negotiation

We negotiate to secure a more favorable outcome,[67] so negotiating is an essential career skill,[68] because good negotiators get more favorable outcomes, such as more pay.[69] Let's face it, whether you realize it or not, and whether you like it or not, we are all negotiators because we attempt to get what we want everyday. **Negotiating** *is a process in which two or more parties have something the other wants and attempt to come to an agreement.*

Influence tactics, power, and politics are commonly used during the negotiation process. Walmart keeps its everyday low prices because it is such a good negotiator. In this section, we focus on getting what we want by influencing others through negotiation. Before we get into the details of negotiating, complete Self-Assessment 5-4.

SELF-ASSESSMENT 5-4   Negotiating

Identify each of the 16 statements according to how accurately it describes your behavior. Place a number from 1 to 5 on the line before each statement.

5 — 4 — 3 — 2 — 1

Describes me   *Does not describe me*

_____ 1. Before I negotiate, if possible, I find out about the person I will negotiate with to determine what they want and will be willing to give up.

_____ 2. Before I negotiate, I set objectives.

_____ 3. When planning my negotiating presentation, I focus on how the other party will benefit.

_____ 4. Before I negotiate, I have a target price I want to pay, a lowest price I will pay, and an opening offer.

_____ 5. Before I negotiate, I think through options and trade-offs in case I don't get my target price.

_____ 6. Before I negotiate, I think of the questions and objections the other party might have, and I prepare answers.

_____ 7. At the beginning of negotiations, I develop rapport and read the person.

_____ 8. I let the other party make the first offer.

_____ 9. I listen to what the other parties are saying and focus on helping them get what they want, rather than focusing on what I want.

_____ 10. I don't give in too quickly to others' offers.

_____ 11. When I compromise and give up something, I ask for something in return.

_____ 12. If the other party tries to postpone the negotiation, I try to create urgency and tell them what they might lose.

_____ 13. If I want to postpone negotiation, I don't let the other party pressure me into making a decision.

_____ 14. When I make a deal, I don't second-guess, wonder whether I got the best price, and check prices.

_____ 15. If I can't make an agreement, I ask for advice to help me with future negotiations.

_____ 16. During the entire business negotiating process, I'm trying to develop a relationship, not just a onetime deal.

Add up your score and place it here _____ and on the continuum below.

80 — 70 — 60 — 50 — 40 — 30 — 16
Effective Networking   *Ineffective Networking*

If you did not score high on negotiating effectiveness, that's okay, as you can develop negotiating skills by following the steps and guidelines in this chapter.

Negotiating

At certain times, negotiations are appropriate, such as when conducting management–union collective bargaining, buying and selling goods and services, accepting a new job and compensation offer, and getting a raise—all situations without a fixed price or deal. If there's a set, take-it-or-leave-it deal, there is no negotiation.

All Parties Should Believe They Got a Good Deal

Negotiation is often a *zero-sum game* in which one party's gain is the other party's loss. For example, every dollar less that you pay for a car is your gain and the seller's loss. But it doesn't have to be an "I win and you lose" negotiation. Like power and politics, negotiating is not about taking advantage of others, it's about building relationships and helping each other get what we want.

To get what we want, we have to sell our ideas and convince the other party to give us what we want. However, negotiation should be viewed by all parties as an opportunity for everyone to win. When possible, make the pie larger rather than fight over how to split it. If union employees believe they lost and management won, employees may experience job dissatisfaction, resulting in lower performance in the long run. If customers believe they got a bad deal, they may not give repeat business.

Negotiation Skills Can Be Developed

Not everyone is born a great negotiator. Taking the time to learn how to negotiate before entering a deal is the best way to arrive at a successful settlement.[70] Following the steps in the negotiation process can help develop negotiation skills.

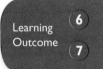

Learning Outcome 6

List the steps in the negotiation process.

Learning Outcome 7

Explain the relationships among negotiation and conflict, influencing tactics, power, and politics.

The Negotiation Process

The negotiation process has three, and possibly four, steps: plan, negotiations, possibly a postponement, and an agreement or no agreement. These steps are summarized in Model 5.1 and discussed in this section. Like the other models in this book, Model 5.1 is meant to give us step-by-step guidelines. However, in making it apply to varying types of negotiation, you may have to make slight adjustments.

Plan

The key to any negotiation is preparation, so develop a plan. Know what's negotiable and what's not. Be clear about what it is you are negotiating over. Is it price, options, delivery time, sales quantity, or all four? Ask yourself "What exactly do I want?" Planning has four steps.

Step 1. **Research the other party(ies).** Put yourself in the other party's shoes. Try to find out what the other parties want, and what they will and will not be willing to give up, before you negotiate. Find out their personality traits and negotiation style by networking with people who have negotiated with the other party before. If possible, establish a personal relationship before the negotiation. If you have experience working with the other party (e.g., your manager or a potential customer), what worked and did not work in the past?

Step 2.   **Set objectives.** Based on your research, what can you expect from the nego-tiation—what is your objective? Set a lower limit, a target objective, and an opening objective. The objective may be price, but it could be working condi-tions, longer vacation, job security, and so on. Follow steps a, b, and c: (a) Set a specific lower limit and be willing to walk away; do not come to an agree-ment unless you get it. You need to be willing to walk away from a bad deal. (b) Set a target objective of what you believe is a fair deal. (c) Set an opening objective offer that is higher than you expect; you might get it.[71] Remember that the other party is probably also setting three objectives. So don't view their opening offer as final. The key to successful negotiations is for all parties to get between their minimum and target objective. This creates a win–win; everyone got a good deal situation.

The Negotiation Process

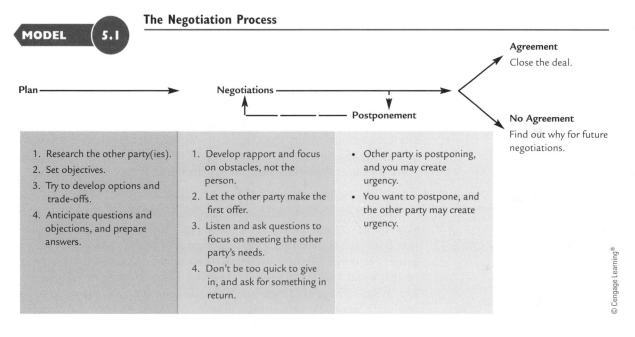

MODEL 5.1

Plan →

Negotiations —

Postponement

Agreement
Close the deal.

No Agreement
Find out why for future negotiations.

1. Research the other party(ies).
2. Set objectives.
3. Try to develop options and trade-offs.
4. Anticipate questions and objections, and prepare answers.

1. Develop rapport and focus on obstacles, not the person.
2. Let the other party make the first offer.
3. Listen and ask questions to focus on meeting the other party's needs.
4. Don't be too quick to give in, and ask for something in return.

- Other party is postponing, and you may create urgency.
- You want to postpone, and the other party may create urgency.

© Cengage Learning®

Step 3.   **Try to develop options and trade-offs.** In purchasing something as well as in looking for a job, if you have multiple sellers and job offers, you are in a stron-ger power position to get your target price. It is common practice to quote other offers and to ask if the other party can beat them.

   If you have to give up something, or cannot get exactly what you want, be prepared to ask for something else in return. If you cannot get the higher raise you want, maybe you can get more days off, more in your retirement account, a nicer office, an assistant, and so on. Based on your research, what trade-offs do you expect from the other party?

Step 4.   **Anticipate questions and objections, and prepare answers.** The other party may want to know why you are selling something, looking for a job, how the product or service works, or what are the features and benefits. You need to be prepared to answer the unasked question "What's in it for me?" Don't focus on what you want but on how your deal will benefit the other party.

   There is a good chance that you will face some objection—reasons why the negotiations will not result in agreement or sale. Be prepared to overcome the no's you are bound to encounter. Unfortunately, not everyone comes out to state their real objections. So we need to listen and ask open-ended questions to get them talking so we can find out what is preventing the agreement.

Negotiations

After we have planned, we are now ready to negotiate the deal. Face-to-face negotiations are generally preferred because you can see the other person's nonverbal behavior and better understand objections. However, telephone and written negotiations (e-mail) work too. Again, know the other party's preference. Handling negotiations also has four steps.

Step 1.   **Develop rapport and focus on obstacles, not the person.** The first thing we sell in any negotiation is ourselves. The other party needs to trust us. Smile and call the other party by name as you greet them. Open with some small talk, like the weather, to get to know them. Deciding on how much time to wait until you get down to business depends on the other party's style. Some people like to get right down to business; others want to get to know you first. However, you usually want the other party to make the first offer, so don't wait too long or you may lose your chance.

    "Focus on the obstacle, not the person" means never to attack the other's personality or put others down with negative statements like "You are being unfair to ask for such a price cut." If we do so, the other party will become defensive, we may end up arguing, and it will be harder to reach an agreement. So even if the other person starts it, refuse to fight on a name-calling level. Make statements like "You think my price is too high" to calm them down.

Step 2.   **Let the other party make the first offer.** This usually gives you the advantage, because if the other party offers you more than your target objective, you can close the agreement. For example, if you are expecting to be paid $35,000 a year (your target objective) and the other party offers you $40,000, are you going to reject it? On the other hand, if you are offered $30,000 you can realize that it may be low and work at increasing the compensation. Ask questions like "What is the salary range?" or "What do you expect to pay for such a fine product?" Some say there are exceptions to the rule, such as salary negotiations for experienced professionals because if you state your requested salary first, the first number influences the rest of the negotiation.[72]

    Try to avoid negotiating simply on price. When others pressure you to make the first offer with a common question like "Give us your best price, and we'll tell you whether we'll take it," try asking them a question such as "What do you expect to pay?" or "What is a reasonable price?" When this does not work, say something like "Our usual (or list) price is xxx. However, if you make me a proposal, I'll see what I can do for you."

    If things go well during steps 1 and 2, you may skip to closing the agreement. If you are not ready to agree, proceed to the next step or two.

Step 3.   **Listen and ask questions to focus on meeting the other party's needs.** Create an opportunity for the other party to disclose reservations and objections. When you speak, you give out information, but when you ask questions and listen, you receive information that will help you overcome the other party's objections.

    If you go on and on about the features you have to offer, without finding out what features the other party is really interested in, you may be killing the deal. Ask questions such as "Is the price out of the ballpark?" or "Is it fast enough for you?" or "Is any feature you wanted missing?" If the objection is a "want" criteria, such as two years of work experience and you have only one, play up the features you know they want and that you do have, and you may reach an agreement.

If the objection is something you cannot meet, at least you found out and don't waste time chasing a deal that will not happen. However, be sure the objection is really a "must" criterion: What if the employer gets no applicants with two years' experience and you apply? You may get the job offer.

Step 4. **Don't be too quick to give in, and ask for something in return.** Those who ask for more get more. Be persistent, don't just give up.[73] If our competitive advantage is service, and during negotiation we quickly give in for a lower price, we lose all the value in a minute. We want to satisfy the other party without giving up too much during the negotiation. Remember not to go below your minimum objective. If it is realistic, be prepared to walk away.

When we are not getting what we want, having other planned options can help give us bargaining power. If we do walk away, we may be called back, and, if not, we may be able to come back for the same low price—but not always. If other parties know we are desperate or just weak and will accept a low agreement, they will likely take advantage of us. Have you ever seen a sign on a product saying "must sell—need cash"? What type of price do you think that seller gets? You also need to avoid being intimidated by comments such as this said in a loud voice: "Are you kidding me, that's too much." Many people will quickly drop the price, but you don't have to be intimidated.

However, when you are dealing with a complex deal, such as a management–union contract negotiation with trade-offs, be willing to be the first to make a concession. The other party tends to feel obligated, and then we can come back with a counter trade-off that is larger than the one we gave up.

Avoid giving unilateral concessions. Recall your planned trade-offs. If the other party asks for a lower price, ask for a trade-off such as a large-volume sale to get it, or a longer delivery time, a less popular color, and so on. We need to send the message that we don't just give things away.

Postponement

Take your time. When there doesn't seem to be any progress, it may be wise to postpone the negotiations.

The Other Party Is Postponing, and You May Create Urgency. The other party says, "I'll get back to you." When we are not getting what we want, we may try to create urgency. For example, "This product is on sale, and the sale ends today." However, honesty is the best policy. The primary reason people will negotiate with you is that they trust and respect you. If we do have other options, we can use them to create urgency, such as saying "I have another job offer pending; when will you let me know if you want to offer me the job?"

But what if urgency does not apply—or does not work—and the other party says, "I'll think about it?" You might say, "That's a good idea." Then at least review the major features the other party liked about our proposed deal and ask if it meets their needs. The other party may decide to come to an agreement or sale. If not, and they don't tell you when they will get back to you, ask, for example, "When can I expect to hear if I got the job?" Try to pin the other party down for a specific time; tell the person that if you don't hear from them by then, you will call them. If you are really interested, follow up with a letter (mail/e-mail) of thanks for their time and again highlight the features you think they liked. If you forgot to include any specific points during the negotiation, add them in the letter.

One thing to remember when the other party becomes resistant to making the agreement is that the hard sell will not work. Take the pressure off. Ask something like "Where do you want to go from here?" If we press for an answer, it may be no agreement; however, if we wait, we may have a better chance. To your manager, you might say, "Why don't we think about it and discuss it some more later?" (Then pick an advantageous time to meet with your manager.)

We also need to learn to read between the lines, especially when working with people from different cultures. Some people will not come right out and tell us there is no deal. We should be persistent in trying to come to an agreement, but we also don't want to waste our time chasing a deal that will not happen.

You Want to Postpone, and the Other Party May Create Urgency.   Don't be hurried by others, and don't hurry yourself. If we are not satisfied with the deal, or want to shop around, tell the other party you want to think about it. You may also need to check with your manager or someone else, which simply may be for advice, before you can finalize the deal. If the other party is creating urgency, be sure it really is urgent. In many cases, we can get the same deal at a later date; don't be pressured into making a deal you are not satisfied with or may regret later. If we do want to postpone, give the other party a specific time that we will get back to them, and do so with more prepared negotiations or simply to tell them we cannot make an agreement.

Agreement

Once the agreement has been made, restate it and/or put it in writing when appropriate. It is common to follow up an agreement with a letter of thanks, restating the agreement to ensure the other parties have not changed their mind about what they agreed to. Also, after the deal is made, stop selling it. Change the subject to a personal one and/or leave, depending on the other person's preferred negotiations. If they want a personal relationship, stick around; if not, leave.

No Agreement

Our goal is to come to an agreement, but rejection, refusal, and failure happen to us all, even the superstars. The difference between the also-rans and the superstars lies in how they respond to the failure. The successful people keep trying, learn from their mistakes, and continue to work hard; failures usually don't persevere. When there is no agreement, analyze the situation and try to determine what went wrong to improve in the future. We may also ask the other party for advice, such as "I realize I did not get the job; thanks for your time. Can you offer me any suggestions for improving my résumé and interview skills, or other ideas to help me to get a job in this field?"

WORK
Application **5-9**

8. How would you rate your negotiation skills? How can you improve?

4.   What types of negotiations does Mark Cuban engage in?

A large part of Mark Cuban's job is negotiating. He had to negotiate to buy the Dallas Mavericks and to get HDNet and HDNet Movies on DirecTV. Cuban still needs to negotiate to distribute his 2929 Productions and Magnolia Pictures through big studios. The Mavericks won the championship in 2011 and many of the fans like Mark Cuban.

Ethics and Influencing

Recall that leadership is the *influencing* process of leaders and followers to achieve organizational objectives through change (Chapter 1). We usually influence others to get what we want. Power, politics, networking, and negotiating are all forms of influencing that can be used by leaders and followers. When influencing, recall that it pays to be ethical[74] (Chapter 2). The number 1 reason people will help you is because you have integrity—you are honest and they can trust you.[75] With deception comes loss of trust and influence.[76]

People respond to incentives and can usually be motivated for good or bad if we find the right levers.[77] So influence is neither good nor bad; it's what we do with it. *Power* is ethical when it is used to help meet organizational objectives and those of its members, as well as to get what we want (socialized power, Chapters 2 and 9). Power is unethical when used to promote self-interest and manipulate others at their expense (personalized power).[78]

YOU Make the **ETHICAL** Call

5.2   *Facebook Hired Firm to Target Google*

The social networking company secretly hired the public-relations firm Burson-Marsteller to push stories critical of Google's privacy practices to shift the online privacy spotlight away from itself and onto rival Google. But the controversial strategy backfired when bloggers and journalists disclosed Facebook's behind-the-scenes role, forcing the company to explain its tactic.

Facebook said that it didn't authorize or intend to run a "smear campaign" but wanted to highlight that Facebook didn't approve of Google's data collection from its social-network accounts.

The nonprofit Public Relations Society of America said that Burson-Marsteller's lack of disclosure of Facebook is "deceptive" and violated its ethical standards.

Burson-Marsteller said that Facebook requested that its name be withheld because it was merely asking to bring publicly available information to light. But withholding Facebook's name was against its policy and the assignment on those terms should have been declined.

Google did not respond to a request for a comment on the newspaper story.[79]

1. Was Facebook's hiring of Burson-Marsteller to shift the online privacy spotlight away from itself and onto rival Google ethical and socially responsible? Do you believe that Facebook was or was not really trying to run a "smear campaign" to get itself out of the headline and Google into the news for lack of privacy? If your boss asked you to be the one to hire Burson-Marsteller, what would you have done?

2. Do you agree with the Public Relations Society of America's statement that Burson-Marsteller's lack of disclosure of Facebook is "deceptive" and is an unethical business tactic?

3. Was Burson-Marsteller ethical and socially responsible in taking the job from Facebook? Do you believe that the company simply made a mistake in taking the job or that it took the job knowing it was against company policy? If your boss asked you to be the one to smear Facebook against company policy, what would you have done?

4. Was it ethical and socially responsible of Google not to respond on this story when asked to do so? If you were the CEO of Google, what would your comment be about the behavior or your rival Facebook and Burson-Marsteller?

When playing *organizational politics* (and to a lesser extent *networking*), it can be tempting to be unethical, but don't do it. Even if others are using unethical behavior, don't stoop to their level. We should confront others if we believe they are being unethical and try to resolve the issues. You will learn how to resolve conflict in Chapter 6.

An ethical challenge in *negotiation* is telling the truth or not lying to the other party or being lied to. There is a difference between not giving extra information that is not asked for and lying to the other party. The person who caught us lying may tell others, and we can lose even more friends and business.

So when influencing others, try to use the stakeholders' approach to ethics by creating a win–win situation for relevant parties.

OPENING CASE Application

5. Is Mark Cuban ethical in influencing others?

As discussed, Mark Cuban's behavior has not always been appropriate and thus has gotten him into some trouble in sports and entertainment. Cuban is aware of this shortcoming, and only time will tell if he will earn the respect he believes he deserves as he strives to be famous and influential.

"Take It To The Net". Access student resources at www.cengagebrain.com. Search for Lussier, Leadership 6e to find student study tools.

Chapter Summary

The chapter summary is organized to answer the eight learning outcomes for this chapter.

1 Explain the differences between position power and personal power.

Position power is derived from top management and is delegated down the chain of command. Thus, people at the top of the organization have more power than those at the bottom of the organization. Personal power is derived from the followers based on the leader's behavior. All managers have position power, but they may or may not have personal power. Nonmanagers do not have position power, but they may have personal power.

2 Discuss the differences among legitimate, reward, coercive, and referent power.

Legitimate, reward, and coercive power are all related. A leader with position power usually has the power to reward and punish (coercive). However, a person with referent power may or may not have position power to reward and punish, and the leader influences followers based on relationships.

3 Discuss how power and politics are related.

Power is the ability to influence others' behavior. Politics is the process of gaining and using power. Therefore, political skills are a part of power.

4 Describe how money and politics have a similar use.

Money and politics have a similar use, because they are mediums of exchange. In our economy, money is the medium of exchange. In an organization, politics is the medium of exchange.

5 List and explain the steps in the networking process.

The first step in the networking process is to perform a self-assessment to determine accomplishments and to set goals. Second, create a one-minute self-sell that quickly summarizes history and career plans and asks a question. Third, develop a written network list. Fourth, conduct networking interviews to meet your goals. Finally, maintain your network for meeting future goals.

6 **List the steps in the negotiation process.**

The first step in the negotiation process is to plan for the negotiation. The second step is to conduct the actual negotiation, which can be postponed and results in an agreement or no agreement.

7 **Explain the relationships among negotiation and conflict, influencing tactics, power, and politics.**

Negotiations take place when there is a conflict, and influencing tactics, power, and politics can be used during the negotiation process.

Key Terms

coercive power, 148

connection power, 150

expert power, 149

information power, 150

legitimate power, 146

negotiating, 165

networking, 155

one-minute self-sell, 161

politics, 154

power, 145

reciprocity, 155

referent power, 149

reward power, 148

Review Questions

1 What are the seven types of power?

2 What are the nine influencing tactics?

3 What is ingratiation influencing?

4 What is the difference between inspirational appeal and personal appeal influencing?

5 What are the three political behaviors and four guidelines for developing political skills?

6 How many interview questions should you bring to a networking interview?

7 Which step of "conduct networking interviews" involves getting additional contacts for your network?

8 What type of situation (win/lose) is the goal of negotiation?

9 What are the steps in negotiations?

10 What are the steps in planning a negotiation?

Critical-Thinking Questions

The following critical-thinking questions can be used for class discussion and/or as written assignments to develop communication skills. Be sure to give complete explanations for all questions.

1 Is power good or bad for organizations?

2 Which influencing tactics do you tend to use most and least? How will you change and develop the ability to influence using influencing tactics?

3 How would you rate your political skills, and which political behavior do you use most often? How will you change and develop your political skills?

4 How would you rate your relationship with your current or past boss? What will you do differently in the future to improve your relationship with your boss?

5 Can management stop the use of power and politics in their organizations?

6 Should people be judged based on their social skills?

7 How would you rate your networking skills? What will you do differently in the future to improve your networking skills?

8 Do people really need a written networking list?

9 How would you rate your negotiation skills? What will you do differently in the future to improve your negotiation skills?

10 Do you believe that most managers use influencing (power, politics, networking, and negotiating) for the good of the organization or for their own personal benefit? What can be done to help managers be more ethical in influencing others?

CASE

Organizational Power and Politics

Jose Gonzalez, a Hispanic man, was highly sought after receiving his PhD in accounting. Today, he is a tenured professor at a small teaching college in the Midwest.[80] The Department of Accounting (DA) has nine faculty members; it is one of five departments in the School of Business (SB). The accounting department chair is Helen Canton, who is in her first year as chair. Six faculty members, including Jose, have been in the department longer than Helen. Helen likes to have policies in place so that faculty members have guides for their behavior. On the college-wide level, however, there is no policy about the job of graduate assistant. Helen asked the dean of the SB about the policy. After a discussion with the vice president for academic affairs, the dean told Helen that there is no policy. The vice president and dean suggested letting the individual departments develop their own policy regarding what graduate assistants can and cannot do in their position. So, Helen made developing a policy for graduate assistants an agenda item for the department meeting.

During the DA meeting, Helen asked for members' views on what graduate assistants should and should not be allowed to do. She was hoping that the department could come to a consensus on a policy. It turns out that Jose was the only faculty member using graduate assistants to grade exams. Two other faculty members speak out against having graduate assistants grade exams. They believe it is the professor's job to grade exams. Jose makes a few statements in hopes of not having to correct his own exams. Because his exams are objective, requiring a correct answer, Jose believes it's not necessary for him to personally grade the exams. He also points out that across the campus, and across the country, other faculty members are using graduate assistants to teach entire courses and to correct subjective papers and exams. Jose states that he does not think it fair that he can no longer use graduate assistants to grade objective exams when others are doing so. He also states that the department does not need to have a policy and requests that the department not set a policy. However, Helen states that she wants a policy. Jose is the only one to speak in favor of allowing graduate assistants to grade exams, although three others made no comments either way. But, after the meeting, one other member, Joel Corman, who said nothing during the meeting, tells Jose he agrees that it is not fair to deny him this use of a graduate assistant.

There was no department consensus, as Helen hoped there would be. She said that she would draft a department policy, which will be discussed at a future DA meeting. The next day, Jose sent a memo to department members asking if it is ethical and legal to deny him the same resources as others are using across the campus. Jose also states that if the department sets a policy stating that he can no longer use graduate assistants to correct objective exams, he will appeal the policy decision to the dean, vice president, and president.

Support your answers to the following questions with specific information from the case and text, or with other information you get from the Web or other sources.

1. (a) What source of power does Helen have, and (b) what type of power is she using? (c) Which influencing tactic is Helen using during the meeting? (d) Is negotiation and/or the (e) exchange tactic appropriate in this situation?

2. (a) What source of power does Jose have, and (b) what type of power is he using during the meeting? (c) Which two influencing tactics is Jose primarily using during the meeting? (d) Which influencing tactic is Jose using with the memo? (e) Is the memo a wise political move for Jose? What might he gain and lose by sending it?

3. What would you do if you were Helen? (a) Would you talk to the dean, letting her know that Jose said he would appeal the policy decision? (b) Which influencing tactic would this discussion involve? (c) Which political behavior would the discussion represent? (d) Would you draft a policy directly stating that graduate assistants cannot be used to grade objective exams? (e) Would your answer to (d) be influenced by your answer to (a)?

4. (a) If you were Jose, knowing you had no verbal supporters during the meeting, would you have continued to defend your position or agreed to stop using a graduate assistant? (b) What do you think of Jose sending the memo? (c) As a tenured full professor, Jose is secure in his job. Would your answer change if you (as Jose) had not received tenure or promotion to the top rank?

5. (a) If you were Jose, and Helen drafted a policy and department members agreed with it, what would you do? Would you appeal the decision to the dean? (b) Again, would your answer change if you had not received tenure or promotion to the top rank?

6. If you were the dean of the School of Business (SB), knowing that the vice president does not want to set a college-wide policy, and Jose appealed to you, what would you do? Would you develop a school-wide policy for SB?

7. At what level (college-wide, by schools, or by departments within each school) should a graduate assistant policy be set?

8. (a) Should Joel Corman have spoken up in defense of Jose during the meeting? (b) If you were Joel, would you have taken Jose's side against the other seven members? (c) Would your answer change if you were or were not friends with Jose, and if you were or were not a tenured full professor?

CUMULATIVE CASE QUESTIONS

9. Which level(s) of analysis of leadership theory is (are) presented in this case (Chapter 1)?

10. Is it ethical for graduate students to correct undergraduate exams (Chapter 2)?

11. Which of the four Ohio State University leadership styles did Helen use during the department meeting (Chapter 3)?

CASE EXERCISE AND ROLE-PLAY

Preparation: Read the case and think about whether you agree or disagree with using graduate assistants to correct objective exams. If you do this exercise, we recommend that you complete it before discussing the questions and answers to the case.

In-Class DA Meeting: A person who strongly agrees with Jose's position volunteers to play this role (can be female) during a DA meeting. A second person who also agrees with the use of graduate assistants correcting exams plays the role of Joel (can be a male). However, recall that Joel cannot say anything during the meeting to support Jose. One person who strongly disagrees with Jose—who doesn't want graduate assistants to correct exams and who also feels strongly that there should be a policy stating what graduate assistants can and cannot do—volunteers to play the role of the department chair (Helen) who runs the DA meeting. Six others who are neutral or disagree with graduate assistants grading exams play the roles of other department members.

The ten role-players sit in a circle in the center of the room, with the other class members sitting around the outside of the circle. Observers just quietly watch and listen to the meeting discussion.

Role-Play: *(about 15 minutes)* Helen opens the meeting by simply stating that the agenda item is to set a graduate assistants policy stating what they can and cannot do and that he or she hopes the department can come to a consensus on a policy. Helen states his or her position on why graduate students should not be allowed to correct exams and then asks for other views. Jose and the others, except Joel, jump in anytime with their opinions.

Discussion: After the role-play is over, or when time runs out, the person playing the role of Jose expresses to the class how it felt to have everyone against him or her. Other department members state how they felt about the discussion, followed by observers' statements as time permits. A discussion of the case questions and answers may follow.

VIDEO ▶ CASE

Employee Networks at Whirlpool Corporation

Since 1911, Whirlpool Corporation has grown from a small company to a global corporation, with manufacturing locations on every major continent worldwide. Like many organizations, one of Whirlpool's strategies for creating a culture of pluralism is encouraging the formation of employee network groups. These are voluntary groups formed around primary dimensions such as gender and ethnicity, which meet regularly to focus on business issues. The groups are also a resource to the employees by providing a supportive community, decreasing social isolation, and promoting career development. Further, they help retain employees by providing them a forum for expressing ideas. These discussions often spark new ideas that benefit the company as a whole.

1. Using the Whirlpool Corporation Web site (http://www.whirlpoolcorp.com), identify the employee network groups at Whirlpool and the mission of each.

2. Do you think Whirlpool's encouragement of employee networks works for or against creating a culture of diversity? Explain your answer.

Developing Your Leadership Skills   5-1

Influencing Tactics

Preparing for This Exercise

Following are three situations. For each situation, select the most appropriate influencing tactic(s) to use. Write the tactic(s) on the lines following the situation. At this time, don't write out how you would behave (what you would say and do).

1 You are doing a college internship, which is going well.

You would like to become a full-time employee in a few weeks, after you graduate.

Which influencing tactic(s) would you use? _____

Who would you try to influence? _____

How would you do so (behavior)? _____

2 You have been working at your job for six months, and you are approaching the elevator. You see a powerful person who could potentially help you advance in your career waiting for the elevator. You have never met her, but you do know that her committee has recently completed a new five-year strategic plan for the company and that she plays tennis and is active at the same religious organization (church, synagogue, mosque) as you. Although you only have a couple of minutes, you decide to try to develop a connection.

Which influencing tactic(s) would you use? _____

How would you strike up a conversation? What topic(s) do you raise? _____

3 You are the manager of the production department. Some of the sales staff has been scheduling deliveries for your product that your department can't meet. Customers are blaming you for late delivery. This is not good for the company, so you decide to talk to the sales staff manager about it over lunch.

Which influencing tactic(s) would you use? _____

How would you handle the situation (behavior)? _____

Now select one of the three situations that seems real to you—you can imagine yourself in the situation. Or briefly write in a real-life situation that you can quickly explain to a small group. Now, briefly write out the behavior (what you would do and say) that you would use in the situation to influence the person to do what you want.

Situation # _____ Or, my situation: _____

Influencing tactic(s) to use: _____

Behavior: _____

Doing This Exercise in Class

Objective

To develop your persuasion skills by using influencing tactics

AACSB General Skills Area

The primary AACSB skills developed through this exercise are analytic skills and application of knowledge—students learn to achieve their goals by influencing others.

Experience

You will discuss which influencing tactics are most appropriate for the preparation situations. You may also be given the opportunity to role-play how you would handle the one situation you selected; you will also play the role of the person to be influenced and observer.

Procedure 1 *(10–20 minutes)*

Break up into groups of three, with one or two groups of two if needed. Try not to have two members in a group who selected the same situation; use people who selected their own situation. First, try to quickly agree on which influencing tactics are most appropriate in each situation. Select a spokesperson to give group answers to the class. In preparation to role-play, have each person state the behavior selected to handle the situation. The others give feedback for improvement: suggestions to delete, change, and/or add to the behavior (e.g., I would not say … , I'd say it this way … , I'd add … to what you have now).

Procedure 2 *(5–10 minutes)*

One situation at a time, each group spokesperson tells the class which influencing styles it would use, followed by brief remarks from the professor. The professor may also ask people who selected their own situation to tell the class the situation.

Conclusion

The instructor may lead a class discussion and/or make concluding remarks.

Apply It *(2–4 minutes)*

What did I learn from this exercise? How will I use this knowledge in the future?

Sharing

In the group, or to the entire class, volunteers may give their answers to the "Apply It" questions.

Developing Your Leadership Skills   5-2

Influencing, Power, and Politics

Preparing for This Exercise

Your instructor will tell you to select one, two, or all three of the following topics (influencing, power, and/or politics) for this preparation.

To get what you want, you need to develop your ability to influence others and gain power through politics. It is helpful to read about these topics and how to improve your skills, but unless you apply the concepts in your personal and professional life, you will not develop these skills.

This preparation covers three skills, each with two activities. The first activity is to develop a general guide to daily actions you can take to increase your influence, power, and/or understanding of politics. The second is to think of a specific situation in the future, and develop a plan to get what you want. Use additional paper if you need more space to write your plan.

Influencing

- Write down the influencing tactic that you are the strongest at using:_____. The weakest: _____. The one you would like to improve on: _____ (it does not have to be your weakest). Review the ideas for using this tactic, and write down a few ways in which you will work at developing your skill.

- Think of a specific situation in the near future in which you can use this type of power to help you get what you want. Briefly describe the situation, and explain how you will use this tactic—what you will say and do, and so on.

Power

- Write down the one type of your power you would like to improve on:_____. Review the ideas for increasing this type of power, and write down a few ways in which you will work at developing your power.

- Think of a specific situation in the near future in which you can use this tactic to help you get what you want. Briefly describe the situation, and explain how you will use this tactic—what you will say and do, and so on.

Politics

- Write down the one area of politics you would like to improve on:_____. Review the ideas for using this type of politics, and write down a few ways in which you will work at developing your skill.

- Think of a specific situation in the near future in which you can use this type of politicking to help you get what you want. Briefly describe the situation, and explain how you will use this tactic—what you will say and do, and so on.

Doing This Exercise in Class

Objective

To develop your ability to influence others and gain power through politics

AACSB General Skills Area

The primary AACSB skills developed through this exercise are analytic skills and application of knowledge—students learn to achieve their goals by influencing others.

Experience

You will develop a general guide to daily actions you can take to increase your influence, power, and/or understanding of politics. You'll also develop a plan to get what you want.

Preparation

You should have completed the preparation for this exercise, unless told not to do so by your instructor.

Procedure 1 *(10–20 minutes)* Break into groups of three, with some groups of two if necessary. If group members developed plans for more than one skill area, select only one to start with. One group member volunteers to share first and states his or her preparation for influencing, power, or politics. The other members give input into how effective they think the plan is and offer ideas on how to improve the plan. After the first member shares, the other two have their turn, changing roles with each round. If there is time remaining after all have shared, go on to another skill area until the time is up.

Procedure 2 *(2–3 minutes)* Each member commits to implementing his or her plan by a set time, and to telling the others how well the influence, power, or politics went by a specific date—before or after the class ends.

Name _____

Date of implementation _____

Date to report results _____

Name _____

Date of implementation _____

Date to report results _____

Name _____

Date of implementation _____

Date to report results _____

Conclusion

The instructor may make concluding remarks.

Apply It *(2–4 minutes)* What did I learn from this experience? How will I use this knowledge in the future?

Sharing

In the group, or to the entire class, volunteers may give their answers to the "Apply It" questions.

Developing Your Leadership Skills   5-3

Networking Skills*

Preparing for This Exercise

Based on the section "Networking" and the subsection on the networking process, complete the following steps.

1 Perform a self-assessment and set goals. List two or three of your accomplishments and set a goal. The goal can be to learn more about career opportunities in your major; to get an internship, part-time, summer, or full-time job; and so on.

2 Create your one-minute self-sell. Write it out. See page 161 for a written example.

History: _____

Plan: _____

Question: _____

3 Develop your network. List at least five people to be included in your network, preferably people who can help you achieve your goal.

4 Conduct networking interviews. To help meet your goal, select one person for a personal 20-minute interview or to interview by phone if it is difficult to meet in person. List the person and write questions to ask during the interview. This person can be a person in your college career center or a professor in your major.

*Source: This exercise was developed by Andra Gumbus, professor of management, College of Business, Sacred Heart University. © Andra Gumbus, 2002. It is used with Dr. Gumbus's permission.

Doing This Exercise in Class

Objective

To develop networking skills by implementing the steps in the networking process

AACSB General Skills Area

The primary AACSB skills developed through this exercise are analytic skills and application of knowledge—students learn to achieve their goals by networking.

Experience

You will deliver your one-minute self-sell from the preparation and get feedback for improvement. You will also share your network list and interview questions and get feedback for improvement.

Procedure 1 (7–10 minutes) A. Break into groups of two. Show each other your written

one-minute self-sell. Is the history, plan, and question clear (do you understand it), concise (60 seconds or less to say), and compelling (does it promote interest to help)? Offer suggestions for improvement.

B. After perfected, each person states (no reading) the one-minute self-sell. Was it stated clearly, concisely, and with confidence? Offer improvements. State it a second and third time, or until told to go on to the next procedure.

Procedure 2 (7–10 minutes) Break into groups of three with people you did not work with during procedure 1. Follow procedures A and B above in your triad. Repeating your self-sell should improve your delivery and confidence.

Procedure 3 (10–20 minutes) Break into groups of four with people you did not work with during procedures 1 and 2, if possible. Share your answers from steps 3 (your network list) and 4 (your interview questions). Offer each other improvements to the questions and new questions. You should also get ideas for writing new questions for your own interview.

Applications (done outside of class)

Expand your written network list to at least 25 names. Conduct the networking interview using the questions developed through this exercise.

Conclusion

The instructor may make concluding remarks, including requiring the network lists and/or networking interview in the "Applications" section. Written network lists and/or interview questions and answers (following the name, title, and organization of interviewee; date, time, and type of interview—phone or in person) may be passed in.

Apply It (2–4 minutes) What did I learn from this experience? How will I use this knowledge in the future?

Sharing

In groups, or to the entire class, volunteers may give their answers to the "Apply It" questions.

*Source: This exercise was developed by Andra Gumbus, professor of management, College of Business, Sacred Heart University. © Andra Gumbus, 2002. It is used with Dr. Gumbus's permission.

Developing Your Leadership Skills 5-4

Car Dealer Negotiation*

Preparing for This Exercise

You should have read and should understand the negotiation process.

Doing This Exercise in Class

Objective

To develop your negotiation skills

AACSB General Skills Area

The primary AACSB skills developed through this exercise are analytic skills and application of knowledge—students learn to achieve their goals through negotiating.

Experience

You will be the buyer or seller of a used car.

Procedure 1 *(1–2 minutes)* Break up into groups of two and sit facing each other, so that you cannot read each other's confidential sheet. Each group should be as far away from other groups as possible, to avoid overhearing each other's conversations. If there is an odd number of students in the class, one student will be an observer or work with the instructor. Select who will be the buyer and who will be the seller of the used car.

Procedure 2 *(1–2 minutes)* The instructor goes to each group and gives each buyer and seller their confidential sheet.

Procedure 3 *(5–6 minutes)* Buyers and sellers read their confidential sheets and write down some plans (what will be your basic approach, what will you say) for the lunch meeting.

Procedure 4 *(3–7 minutes)* Negotiate the sale of the car. Try not to overhear your classmates' conversations. You do not have to buy or sell the car. After you make the sale, or agree not to sell, read the confidential sheet of your partner in this exercise and discuss the experience.

Integration *(3–7 minutes)*

Answer the following questions:

1. Which of the nine influencing tactics (see Exhibit 5.1) did you use during the negotiations?

2. Which of the seven types of power (Exhibit 5.1) did you use during the negotiations? Did both parties believe that they got a good deal?

3. During your planning, did you (1) research the other party, (2) set an objective (price to pay or accept), (3) develop

options and trade-offs, and (4) anticipate questions and objections and prepare answers?

4. During the negotiations, did you (1) develop a rapport and focus on obstacles, not the person; (2) let the other party make the first offer; (3) listen and ask questions to focus on meeting the other party's needs; and (4) did you refuse to give in too quickly, and did you remember to ask for something in return?

5. Did you reach an agreement to sell/buy the car? If yes, did you get exactly, more than, or less than your target price?

6. When negotiating, is it a good practice to ask for more than you expect to receive, or to offer less than you expect to pay?

7. When negotiating, is it better to be the one to give or receive the initial offer?

8. When negotiating, is it better to appear to be dealing with strong or weak power? In other words, should you try to portray that you have other options and don't really need to make a deal with this person? Or, should you appear to be in need of the deal?

9. Can having the power to intimidate others be helpful in negotiations?

Conclusion

The instructor leads a class discussion, or simply gives the answers to the "Integration" questions, and makes concluding remarks.

Apply It *(2–4 minutes)*

What did I learn from this experience? How will I use this knowledge in the future? What will I do differently?

Sharing

In the group, or to the entire class, volunteers may give their answers to the "Apply It" questions.

Source: The car dealer negotiation confidential information is from Arch G. Woodside, Tulane University. The Car Dealer Game is part of a paper, "Bargaining Behavior in Personal Selling and Buying Exchanges," that was presented at the 1980 *Eighth Annual Conference of the Association for Business Simulation and Experiential Learning (ABSEL)*. It is used with Dr. Woodside's permission.

Endnotes

1 *Forbes* Web site (www.forbes.com/profile/mark-cuban), retrieved February 4, 2014.

2 J. Pfeffer, "Don't Dismiss Office Politics—Teach It," *Wall Street Journal* (October 24, 2011): R6.

3 J. Pfeffer, "Don't Dismiss Office Politics—Teach It," *Wall Street Journal* (October 24, 2011): R6.

4 D. Ma, Mo. Rhee, and D. Yang, "Power Source Mismatch and the Effectiveness of Interorganizational Relations: The Case of Venture Capital Syndication," *Academy of Management Journal* 56(3) (2013): 711–734.

5 J. Pfeffer, "Don't Dismiss Office Politics—Teach It," *Wall Street Journal* (October 24, 2011): R6.

6 L.P. Tost, F. Gino, and R.P. Larrick, "When Power Makes Others Speechless: The Negative Impact of Leader Power on Team Performance," *Academy of Management Journal* 56(5) (2013): 1465–1486.

7 D. Ma, Mo. Rhee, and D. Yang, "Power Source Mismatch and the Effectiveness of Interorganizational Relations: The Case of Venture Capital Syndication," *Academy of Management Journal* 56(3) (2013): 711–734.

8 A.G. Acharya and T.G. Pollock, "Shoot for the Starts' Predicting the Recruitment of Prestigious Directors at Newly Public Firms," *Academy of Management Journal* 56(3) (2013): 711–734.

9 N.M. Lorinkova, M.J. Pearsall, and H.P. Sims, "Examining the Differential Longitudinal Performance of Directive versus Empowering Leadership in Teams," *Academy of Management Journal* 56(2) (2013): 573–596.

10 M. Pitesa and S. Thau, "Compliant Sinners, Obstinate Saints: How Power and Self-Focus Determine the Effectiveness of Social Influences in Ethical Decisions Making," *Academy of Management Journal* 56(3) (2013): 635–658.

11 N.M. Lorinkova, M.J. Pearsall, and H.P. Sims, "Examining the Differential Longitudinal Performance of Directive versus Empowering Leadership in Teams," *Academy of Management Journal* 56(2) (2013): 573–596.

12 N.M. Lorinkova, M.J. Pearsall, and H.P. Sims, "Examining the Differential Longitudinal Performance of Directive versus Empowering Leadership in Teams," *Academy of Management Journal* 56(2) (2013): 573–596.

13 J. Saraceno, "Phil Jackson," *AARP Bulletin* (January–February 2014): 10.

14 J. R. P. French and B. H. Raven, "The Bases of Social Power," in D. Cartwright, Ed., *Studies of Social Power* (Ann Arbor, MI: Institute for Social Research, 1959): 150–167.

15 S.S. Wiltermuth and F.J. Flynn, "Power, Moral Clarity, and Punishment in the Workplace," *Academy of Management Journal* 56(4) (2013): 1002–1023.

16 J. Pfeffer, "Don't Dismiss Office Politics—Teach It," *Wall Street Journal* (October 24, 2011): R6.

17 S.S. Wiltermuth and F.J. Flynn, "Power, Moral Clarity, and Punishment in the Workplace," *Academy of Management Journal* 56(4) (2013): 1002–1023.

18 J. Liang, C.I.C. Farh, and J.L. Farh, "Psychological Antecedents of Promotive and Prohibitive Voice: A Two-Wave Examination," *Academy of Management Journal* 55(1) (2012): 71–92.

19 M. Selman, "Manipulate Creative People," *BusinessWeek* (April 11, 2013): 92.

20 S.S. Wiltermuth and F.J. Flynn, "Power, Moral Clarity, and Punishment in the Workplace," *Academy of Management Journal* 56(4) (2013): 1002–1023.

21 G. Ertug and F. Castellucci, "Getting What You Need: How Reputation and Status Affect Team Performance, Hiring, and Salaries in the NBA," *Academy of Management Journal* 56(2) (2013): 407–431.

22 Staff, "Success with Help," *Entrepreneur* (December 2013): 64.

23 R. Nag and D. Gioia, "From Common to Uncommon Knowledge: Foundations of Firm-Specific Use of Knowledge as a Resource," *Academy of Management Journal* 55(2) (2012): 421–457.

24 S. Shellenbarger, "Strike a Powerful Pose," *Wall Street Journal* (August 21, 2013): D1, D2.

25 G. Ertug and F. Castellucci, "Getting What You Need: How Reputation and Status Affect Team Performance, Hiring, and Salaries in the NBA," *Academy of Management Journal* 56(2) (2013): 407–431.

26 C. Galunic, G. Ertug, and M. Gargiulo, "The Positive Externalities of Social Capital: Benefiting from Senior Brokers," *Academy of Management Journal* 55(5) (2012): 1213–1231.

27 G. Ertug and F. Castellucci, "Getting What You Need: How Reputation and Status Affect Team Performance, Hiring, and Salaries in the NBA," *Academy of Management Journal* 56(2) (2013): 407–431.

28 J. Battilana and T. Casciaro, "Change Agents, Networks, and Institutions: A Contingency Theory of Organizational Change," *Academy of Management Journal* 55(2) (2012): 381–398.

29 B. Schyns, T. Kiefer, R. Kerschreiter, and A. Tymon, "Teaching Implicit Leadership Theories to Develop Leaders and Leadership: How and Why It Can Make a Difference," *Academy of Management Learning & Education* 10(3) (2012): 397–408.

30 L.P. Tost, F. Gino, and R.P. Larrick, "When Power Makes Others Speechless: The Negative Impact of Leader Power on Team Performance," *Academy of Management Journal* 56(5) (2013): 1465–1486.

31 J. Pfeffer, "Don't Dismiss Office Politics—Teach It," *Wall Street Journal* (October 24, 2011): R6.

32 G. Colvin, "Ignore These Leadership Lessons at Your Peril," *Fortune* (October 28, 2013): 85.

33 J. Pfeffer, "Don't Dismiss Office Politics—Teach It," *Wall Street Journal* (October 24, 2011): R6.

34 J. Pfeffer, "Don't Dismiss Office Politics—Teach It," *Wall Street Journal* (October 24, 2011): R6.

35 M. Reinholt, T. Pedersen, and N.J. Foss, "Why a Central Network Position Isn't Enough: The Role of Motivation and Ability for Knowledge Sharing in Employee Networks," *Academy of Management Journal* 54(6) (2011): 1277–1297.

36 J. Battilana and T. Casciaro, "Change Agents, Networks, and Institutions: A Contingency Theory of Organizational Change," *Academy of Management Journal* 55(2) (2012): 381–398.

37 J. Liang, C.I.C. Farh, and J.L. Farh, "Psychological Antecedents of Promotive and Prohibitive Voice: A Two-Wave Examination," *Academy of Management Journal* 55(1) (2012): 71–92.

38 P. Andruss, "How the Great Ones Got Great," *Entrepreneur* (December 2013): 64.

39 G. Toegel, M. Kilduff, and N. Anand, "Emotion Helping by Managers: An Emergent Understanding of Discrepant Role Expectations and Outcomes," *Academy of Management Journal* 56(2) (2013): 334–357.

40 P.J. Frederickson, "Political Skill at Work," *Academy of Management Perspectives* 20(2) (2006): 95–96.

41 B. Benjamin and C. O'Reilly, "Becoming a Leader: Early Career Challenges Faced by MBA Graduates," *Academy of Management Learning & Education* 10(3) (2011): 452–472.

42 J. Pfeffer, "Don't Dismiss Office Politics—Teach It," *Wall Street Journal* (October 24, 2011): R6.

43 Staff, "Success with Help," *Entrepreneur* (December 2013): 64.

44 B. Benjamin and C. O'Reilly, "Becoming a Leader: Early Career Challenges Faced by MBA Graduates," *Academy of Management Learning & Education* 10(3) (2011): 452–472.

45 J. Pfeffer, "Don't Dismiss Office Politics—Teach It," *Wall Street Journal* (October 24, 2011): R6.

46 M. Selman, "Manipulate Creative People," *BusinessWeek* (April 11, 2013): 92.

47 B. Benjamin and C. O'Reilly, "Becoming a Leader: Early Career Challenges Faced by MBA Graduates," *Academy of Management Learning & Education* 10(3) (2011): 452–472.

48 J. Pfeffer, "Don't Dismiss Office Politics—Teach It," *Wall Street Journal* (October 24, 2011): R6.

49 E.R. Burris, "The Risks and Rewards of Speaking Up: Managerial Responses to Employee Voice," *Academy of Management Journal* 55(4) (2012): 851–875.

50 S.S. Wiltermuth and F.J. Flynn, "Power, Moral Clarity, and Punishment in the Workplace," *Academy of Management Journal* 56(4) (2013): 1002–1023.

51 G. Colvin, "Ignore These Leadership Lessons at Your Peril," *Fortune* (October 28, 2013): 85.

52 N.M. Lorinkova, M.J. Pearsall, and H.P. Sims, "Examining the Differential Longitudinal Performance of Directive versus Empowering Leadership in Teams," *Academy of Management Journal* 56(2) (2013): 573–596.

53 K. Blanchard, D. Hutson, and E. Wills, *The One Minute Entrepreneur* (New York: Currency/Doubleday, 2008).

54 J. Pfeffer, "Don't Dismiss Office Politics—Teach It," *Wall Street Journal* (October 24, 2011): R6.

55 J. Battilana and T. Casciaro, "Change Agents, Networks, and Institutions: A Contingency Theory of Organizational Change," *Academy of Management Journal* 55(2) (2012): 381–398.

56 M. Baer, "Putting Creativity to Work: The Implementation of Creative Ideas in Organizations," *Academy of Management Journal* 55(5) (2012): 1102–1119.

57 P. Andruss, "How the Great Ones Got Great," *Entrepreneur* (December 2013): 64.

58 C. Galunic, G. Ertug, and M. Gargiulo, "The Positive Externalities of Social Capital: Benefiting from Senior Brokers," *Academy of Management Journal* 55(5) (2012): 1213–1231.

59 E. Glazer, "Problem—and—Solutions," *Wall Street Journal* (October 24, 2011): R2.

60 S. Raice, "Friends—and Possible Employee," *Wall Street Journal* (October 24, 2011): R4.

61 This section is adapted from A. Gumbus and R.N. Lussier, "Career Development: Enhancing Your Networking Skill," *Clinical Leadership & Management Review* 17(1) (January–February 2003).

62 V. Harnish, "Five Ways to Boost Revenue," *Fortune* (September 16, 2013): 45.

63 E. Glazer, "Problem—and—Solutions," *Wall Street Journal* (October 24, 2011): R2.

64 C. Galunic, G. Ertug, and M. Gargiulo, "The Positive Externalities of Social Capital: Benefiting from Senior Brokers," *Academy of Management Journal* 55(5) (2012): 1213–1231.

65 P. Andruss, "How the Great Ones Got Great," *Entrepreneur* (December 2013): 64.

66 S. Raice, "Friends—and Possible Employee," *Wall Street Journal* (October 24, 2011): R4.

67 M. Pitesa and S. Thau, "Compliant Sinners, Obstinate Saints: How Power and Self-Focus Determine the Effectiveness of Social Influences in Ethical Decisions Making," *Academy of Management Journal* 56(3) (2013): 635–658.

68 W.M. Murphy, "From E-Mentoring to Blended Mentoring: Increasing Students' Developmental Initiation and Mentors' Satisfaction," *Academy of Management Learning & Education* 10(4) (2011): 606–622.

69 C. Suddath, "The Art of Haggling," *BusinessWeek* (November 26–December 2, 2012): 98.

70 W.S. Helms, C. Oliver, and K. Webb, "Antecedents of Settlement on a New Institutional Practice: Negotiation of the ISO 26000 Standard on Social Responsibility," *Academy of Management Journal* 55(5) (2012): 1120–1145.

71 C. Suddath, "The Art of Haggling," *BusinessWeek* (November 26–December 2, 2012): 98.

72 C. Suddath, "The Art of Haggling," *BusinessWeek* (November 26–December 2, 2012): 98.

73 C. Suddath, "The Art of Haggling," *BusinessWeek* (November 26–December 2, 2012): 98.

74 M. Pitesa and S. Thau, "Compliant Sinners, Obstinate Saints: How Power and Self-Focus Determine the Effectiveness of Social Influences in Ethical Decisions Making," *Academy of Management Journal* 56(3) (2013): 635–658.

75 G. Colvin, "Ignore These Leadership Lessons at Your Peril," *Fortune* (October 28, 2013): 85.

76 Staff, "What's a Hero?" *Entrepreneur* (December 2013): 64.

77 R. Pinheiro, "Super Freakonomics," *Academy of Management Perspectives* 25(2) (2011): 86–87.

78 S.S. Wiltermuth and F.J. Flynn, "Power, Moral Clarity, and Punishment in the Workplace," *Academy of Management Journal* 56(4) (2013): 1002–1023.

79 G. A. Fowler and A. Efati, "Facebook Hired Firm to Target Google," *Wall Street Journal* (May 13, 2011): B1, B-2.

80 This is an actual case, but the names have been changed to protect identities.

Communication, Coaching, and Conflict Skills

Learning Outcomes

After studying this chapter, you should be able to:

1 List the steps in the oral message-sending process. p. 186

2 List and explain the three parts of the message-receiving process. p. 189

3 Describe paraphrasing and state why it is used. p. 191

4 Identify two common approaches to getting feedback, and explain why they don't work. p.192

5 Describe the difference between criticism and coaching feedback. p. 197

6 Discuss the relationship between the performance formula and the coaching model. p. 198

7 Define the five conflict management styles. p. 201

8 List the steps in the initiating conflict resolution model. p. 206

OPENING CASE Application

The Ranch Golf Club (The Ranch), where every player is a special guest for the day, opened in 2001 in Southwick, Massachusetts. The Ranch's competitive advantage is its upscale public course with links, woods, and a variety of elevations with unsurpassed service in New England. From the start, The Ranch strived to be the best golf club in New England. In less than a year, The Ranch earned a 4-star course rating, one of only four in New England. It has gone on to win numerous other awards.

So how did The Ranch get started? Prior to being a golf club, it was a dairy farm owned by the Hall family. The Hall family wanted to turn the farm into a golf club with the help of Rowland Bates as project coordinator. The Halls were to provide the land, and investors would provide the capital.

Peter and Korby Clark were part owners of nearly 50 Jiffy Lubes, selling most to Pennzoil in 1991. Bates offered Peter Clark the opportunity to create and help manage a new golf club. Although Clark played golf, it was not so much the golf but the challenge of creating a new course and also playing an ongoing part in its management that interested him. Bates found two more investors, Bernard Chiu and Ronald Izen, to provide the additional funding, creating a one-third ownership by the Halls, Clarks, and Chiu and Izen.

The Clarks were happy to have the professional golf management team of Willowbend run day-to-day operations because they had no experience managing a golf club and they would not have to work full time at

The Ranch. However, in 2005 Willowbend stopped managing golf courses and sold its business. By then the Clarks had gained enough experience running The Ranch and no longer needed professional management. Peter Clark stopped his part-time coaching of football and baseball and increased his management role to become the managing partner, overseeing day-to-day operations, and Korby works full time too.[1]

OPENING CASE QUESTIONS:

1. **Why is communication important to the management of The Ranch?**

2. **How does management use feedback at The Ranch?**

3. **Is there a difference in managing an oil change business, a golf course, and a sports team, and how does Peter Clark use coaching at The Ranch?**

4. **Which conflict management style does Peter Clark tend to use at The Ranch?**

5. **What types of conflict resolutions do the Clarks deal with at The Ranch?**

Can you answer any of these questions? You'll find answers to these questions and learn more about The Ranch and its leadership throughout the chapter.

To learn more about The Ranch, or take a virtual tour of the course, visit its Web site at **http:// www .theranchgolfclub.com**.

Leadership success is based on interpersonal skills,[2] and the focus of this chapter is on three important interrelated parts of interpersonal skills. They are communication, coaching, and conflict skills. We begin with sending and receiving *communications,* because it is the foundation for coaching and managing conflict. We also discuss feedback as it relates to both communication and coaching. Based on this foundation, you will learn how to *coach followers,* and then how to *manage conflicts.*

Communication

In this section, we discuss the importance of communication in leadership and examine the communication process of sending and receiving messages. **Communication** *is the process of conveying information and meaning.* True communication takes place only when all parties understand the message (information) from the same perspective (meaning).

Communication and Leadership

Leaders use communications to influencing others,[3] so leaders need to have good communication skills.[4] Formal authority affects communication and, ultimately, performance.[5] Managers use communications to monitor and reinforce performance standards;[6] they share information.[7] Information processing is so important that organizations are designed as a means to meet the information processing requirements generated by interdependent activities.[8] Unfortunately, some managers distort information.[9] Thus, managers are not trusted today, as only 17 percent of U.S. respondents stated the information provided by top leaders is credible, and this level does not exceed 30 percent in most developed countries.[10]

With changing technology, how we communicate has changed over the years as mobile technologies provide a constant pattern of communication,[11] which blurs our work and nonwork lives.[12] Communicating is a social process,[13] and the trend is to use networking[14] and social media.[15] Facebook tends to be more personal and LinkedIn more professional networking,[16] and people are using Twitter to get quick answers to questions.[17] But no matter which technology we use to communicate, two important parts of communication remain: sending and receiving messages.

Sending Messages and Giving Instructions

Leaders send a variety of messages orally, in writing, and nonverbally. An important part of a manager's job is to give instructions, which is sending a message. As managers, how well we give instructions directly affects performance.[18] Have you ever heard a manager say "This isn't what I asked for"? This tends to happen when managers do a poor job of giving instructions. Let's discuss how to avoid this problem.

Planning the Message

Before sending a message, we should plan it, remembering that brevity rules. Answer these questions while planning. *What* is the goal of my message? *Who* should receive my message? *When* will my message be transmitted? *Where* will my message be transmitted? *How* will I send the message?

With the receivers in mind, plan how you will convey the message so that it will be understood. Select the appropriate method for the audience and situation[19] (see Concept Application 6-1 for a list).

CONCEPT APPLICATION 6-1

Methods of Sending Messages

For each of these ten communication situations, select the most appropriate channel for transmitting the message. Write the most appropriate letter in the blank before each item.

Oral communication

a. face-to-face
b. meeting
c. presentation
d. telephone

Written communication (includes e-mail/texting and traditional methods)

e. memo
f. letter
g. report

h. bulletin board
i. poster
j. newsletter

(continued)

CONCEPT APPLICATION 6-1

____ 1. You want one of your employees to stop being disruptive during meetings.

____ 2. You have beaten the deadline on a major project and you want your boss to know about it so that it can have a positive influence on your next performance review.

____ 3. Your child asked you to sell candy at work for a fund-raiser. However, you don't want to ask anyone in person.

____ 4. You have been asked for some financial information relating to your job.

____ 5. You have been asked to speak at your union meeting.

____ 6. You write well and want to be formally involved in sharing information throughout the organization.

____ 7. You have been given a letter of complaint from a supplier and asked to respond.

____ 8. You are waiting for an important letter to arrive, and you want to know if it is in the mail room yet.

____ 9. You want workers to save electricity by shutting off the lights in the break room when no one is in it.

____ 10. You have four employees from other departments who will be working on a new project. You need to explain the project to them.

Learning Outcome 1 — *List the steps in the oral message-sending process.*

The Oral Message-Sending Process

Oral face-to-face communication is the richest channel because it allows for a maximum amount of information to be transmitted through dialogue between the parties.[20] The big advantage over the other channels is that it allows us to read the person's nonverbal communication. When using electronics, we lose the personal touch.

It is helpful to follow these steps in the **oral message-sending process**: (1) *develop rapport*; (2) *state your communication objective*; (3) *transmit your message*; (4) *check the receiver's understanding*; and (5) *get a commitment and follow up.* Model 6.1 lists these steps.

Step 1.   Develop rapport. Put the receiver at ease. It is usually appropriate to begin communications with small talk correlated to the message. It helps prepare the person to receive the message.

MODEL 6.1

The Oral Message-Sending Process

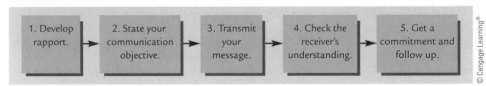

1. Develop rapport. → 2. State your communication objective. → 3. Transmit your message. → 4. Check the receiver's understanding. → 5. Get a commitment and follow up.

© Cengage Learning®

Step 2.   State your communication objective. It is helpful for the receiver to know the desired end result of the communication before covering all the details.

Step 3.   Transmit your message. Tell the people what you want them to do—give instructions. Be sure to set deadlines for completing tasks. Take it a step at a time so you don't have information overload.[21] We will discuss how to delegate task in Chapter 7.

Step 4. **Check the receiver's understanding.** When communicating, we should ask direct questions and/or use paraphrasing. To simply ask "Do you have any questions?" does not check understanding. In the next section of this chapter, you will learn how to check understanding by using feedback.

Step 5. **Get a commitment and follow up**. When giving instructions, it is important to get a commitment to the action. We need to make sure that followers can do the task and have it done by the deadline.

Written Communication and Writing Tips

Because the use of mobile technology will continue to increase, your written communication skills are more important than ever.[22] Even if people aren't telling you that you're using incorrect grammar, they are evaluating you and may conclude you're not intelligent. So we have included some simple but important tips that can help you to improve your writing.

- Lack of organization is a major writing problem. Before you begin writing, set an objective for your communication. Keep the audience in mind. What do you want them to do? Make an outline, using letters and/or numbers, of the major points you want to get across. Now put the outline into written form. The first paragraph states the purpose of the communication. The middle paragraphs support the purpose of the communication: facts, figures, and so forth. The last paragraph summarizes the major points and clearly states the action, if any, to be taken by you and other people.
- Write to communicate, not to impress. Keep the message short and simple. Follow the 1-5-15 rule. Limit each paragraph to a single topic and an average of five sentences. Sentences should average 15 words. Vary paragraph and sentence length. Write in the active voice (I recommend …) rather than the passive voice (it is recommended …).
- Edit your work and rewrite where necessary. To improve sentences and paragraphs, add to them to convey full meaning, cut out unnecessary words and phrases, and/or rearrange the words. Check your work with the computer spelling and grammar checkers. Have others edit your important work as well.

YOU Make the ETHICAL Call

6.1 *Advertising*

Companies use oral, nonverbal, and written communications to advertise their products to increase sales. Selecting the best words to sell a product or service is important. However, some of the terms used in ads are misleading and even deceptive, although in some cases the words are legal.

For example, some companies use the word "natural" on foods that are highly processed, such as products including white sugar. So, some question the use of the term "natural." Bags of chips are advertised as being "all natural," which leads people to think they are healthy, when in fact others classify them as junk food. Because obesity has become such a major health problem, the Food and Drug Administration's (FDA) obesity task force is trying to crack down on misleading labels and ads, and is calling for warnings and fines for violators.

1. Is it ethical and socially responsible for food companies to use terms (like "natural") that can be misleading to increase sales and profits?

2. Should companies use terms that are considered misleading by some but are not illegal?

3. How would you define "natural"?

4. How should the FDA define "natural" so that it is not used to mislead people to buy food thinking that it is healthy, when in fact it is not?

Receiving Messages

The second communication process that leaders are involved in is receiving messages, which includes listening[23] and responding to messages.[24] Responding effectively improves communications.[25] Let's begin by completing the Self-Assessment 6-1 to determine the level and quality of your listening skills, and be honest.

SELF-ASSESSMENT 6-1	Listening Skills

Select the response that best describes the frequency of your actual behavior. Write the letters A, U, F, O, or S on the line before each of the 15 statements.

A—almost always   U—usually   F—frequently   O—occasionally   S—seldom

---

_____ 1. I like to listen to people talk. I encourage others to talk by showing interest, smiling, nodding, and so forth.

_____ 2. I pay closer attention to people who are more similar to me than I do to people who are different from me.

_____ 3. I evaluate people's words and their non-verbal communication ability as they talk.

_____ 4. I avoid distractions; if it's noisy, I suggest moving to a quiet spot.

_____ 5. When people come to me and interrupt me when I'm doing something, I put what I was doing out of my mind and give them my complete attention.

_____ 6. When people are talking, I allow them time to finish. I do not interrupt, anticipate what they are going to say, or jump to conclusions.

_____ 7. I tune people out who do not agree with my views.

_____ 8. While the other person is talking, or professors are lecturing, my mind wanders to personal topics.

_____ 9. While the other person is talking, I pay close attention to the nonverbal communication to help me fully understand what they are trying to communicate.

_____ 10. I tune out and pretend I understand when the topic is difficult for me to understand.

_____ 11. When the other person is talking, I think about and prepare what I am going to say in reply.

_____ 12. When I think there is something missing or contradictory, I ask direct questions to get the person to explain the idea more fully.

_____ 13. When I don't understand something, I let the other person know I don't understand.

_____ 14. When listening to other people, I try to put myself in their position and to see things from their perspective.

_____ 15. During conversations I repeat back to the other person what has been said in my own words to be sure I correctly understand what has been said.

If people you talk to regularly were to answer these questions about you, would they have the same responses that you selected? To find out, have friends fill out the questions with you in mind rather than themselves. Then compare answers.

To determine your score, give yourself 5 points for each A, 4 for each U, 3 for each F, 2 for each O, and 1 for each S for statements 1, 4, 5, 6, 9, 12, 13, 14, and 15. Place the numbers on the line next to your response letter. For items 2, 3, 7, 8, 10, and 11, the score reverses: 5 points for each S, 4 for each O, 3 for each F, 2 for each U, and 1 for each A. Place these score numbers on the lines next to the response letters. Now add your total number of points. Your score should be between 15 and 75. Place your score on the continuum below. Generally, the higher your score, the better your listening skills.

15–20–25–30–35–40–45–50–55–60–65–70–75
Poor listener   *Good listener*

If someone asks us "Are you a good listener," most likely we would say yes. What was your score on the self-assessment? Unfortunately, a recent survey found that the number 1 thing lacking in new college grads is listening skills.[26] Constant multitasking (including checking screens) is deteriorating our ability to pay attention for long and listen. For how long can you pay attention and listen effectively at school and work? Next time you begin reading a textbook, time how long you can go before you "have" to stop and multitask. By using the message-receiving process below, we can become better listeners.

Learning Outcome **2**	*List and explain the three parts of the message-receiving process.*

The Message-Receiving Process

The **message-receiving process** *includes listening, analyzing, and checking under standing.* To improve your listening skills, spend one week focusing your attention on listening by concentrating on what other people say and the nonverbal communications they send when they speak. Notice if their verbal and nonverbal communication are consistent. Talk only when necessary, so that you can listen and "see" what others are saying. If you apply the following tips, you will improve your listening skills. The tips are presented in the depiction of the message-receiving process (Exhibit 6.1): We should listen, analyze, and then check understanding.

EXHIBIT 6.1

The Message-Receiving Process

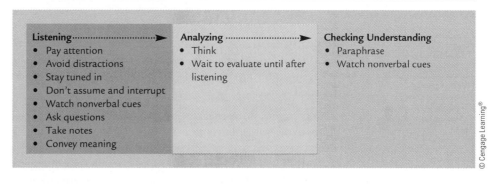

Listening ··········>
- Pay attention
- Avoid distractions
- Stay tuned in
- Don't assume and interrupt
- Watch nonverbal cues
- Ask questions
- Take notes
- Convey meaning

Analyzing ····················>
- Think
- Wait to evaluate until after listening

Checking Understanding
- Paraphrase
- Watch nonverbal cues

© Cengage Learning®

Listening

Listening is the process of giving the speaker your undivided attention. As the speaker sends the message, you should listen by:

- *Paying attention.* When people interrupt, stop what you are doing and give them your complete attention before you begin the conversation.
- *Avoiding distractions.* Keep your eye on the speaker. Avoid distractions; let your phone "take a message." If you are in a noisy or distracting place, suggest moving to a quiet spot.
- *Staying tuned in.* Do not let your mind wander. If it does, gently bring it back or repeat in your mind what the person is saying to force yourself to pay attention. Do not think about what you are going to say in reply; just listen.
- *Not assuming and interrupting.* Do not assume you know what the speaker is going to say, or listen to the beginning and jump to conclusions. Listen to the entire message without interrupting the speaker.

- *Watching nonverbal cues*. People sometimes say one thing and mean something else. So watch as you listen to be sure that the speaker's eyes, body, and face are sending the same message as the verbal message. If something seems out of sync, get it cleared up by asking questions.
- *Asking questions*. When you feel there is something missing, contradictory, or you just do not understand, ask direct questions to get the person to explain the idea more fully.
- *Taking notes*. Part of listening is writing important things down so you can remember them later and document them when necessary. This is especially true when you're listening to instructions.
- *Conveying meaning*. The way to let the speaker know you are listening to the message is to use verbal clues, such as "you feel…," "uh huh," "I see," and "I understand." Use nonverbal communication such as eye contact, appropriate facial expressions, nodding of the head, or leaning slightly forward in your chair to indicate interest and listening.

Analyzing

Analyzing is the process of thinking about, decoding, and evaluating the message. As the speaker sends the message, we should analyze by the following:

- *Thinking*. Listen actively by organizing, summarizing, reviewing, interpreting, and critiquing often. These activities will help do an effective job of decoding the message.
- *Waiting to evaluate until after listening*. When we try to listen and evaluate what is said at the same time, we tend to miss part or the entire message. Just listen to the entire message, and then come to a conclusion.[27]

Checking Understanding

Checking understanding is the process of giving feedback. After we have listened to the message—or during the message, if it's a long one—check understanding of the message by the following:

- *Paraphrasing*. Begin speaking by giving feedback, using paraphrasing to repeat the message to the sender in your own words. When you can paraphrase the message correctly, you convey that you have listened and understood the other person.
- *Watching nonverbal cues*. As you speak, watch the other person's nonverbal cues. If the person does not seem to understand what you are talking about, clarify the message before finishing the conversation.

Work to change your behavior to become a better listener. Review the 15 statements in Self-Assessment 6-1. To improve your listening skills, practice doing items 1, 4, 5, 6, 9, 12, 13, 14, and 15; and avoid doing items 2, 3, 7, 8, 10, and 11.

WORK
Application **6-3**

Refer to Self-Assessment 6-1 and the listening tips. What is your weakest listening skill area on the job? How will you improve your listening ability?

OPENING CASE Application

I. Why is communication important to the management of The Ranch?

The key to success at The Ranch is clear, open communications of expectations. Peter Clark has to continually communicate with his partners and department heads, and nothing takes the place of sitting down face-to-face during regular weekly meetings and listening to each other to continually improve operations. Meetings of department managers with employees continually focus on the importance of communicating the philosophy of unsurpassed professional service. To communicate professionalism, all employees wear The Ranch uniforms and name tags, and they are trained with instructions on how to perform high-quality service. Even the words used are chosen to communicate professionalism. For example, The Ranch has player assistants (PAs), not rangers; golf cars, not golf carts; and it has a golf shop, not a pro shop.

Learning Outcome **3**	*Describe paraphrasing and state why it is used.*

Feedback

In this section, we discuss the importance of feedback, the common approaches to getting feedback (and why they don't work), and how to get feedback. In the next section, we discuss how to give feedback as part of coaching.

The Importance of Feedback

Communications influence behavior,[28] as feedback motivates employees to achieve high levels of performance.[29] **Feedback** *is the process of verifying messages and determining if objectives are being met.* In Chapter 7, we discuss leader–follower performance feedback. Effective leader–follower feedback focuses on the leader's assessment of a follower's job performance on assigned tasks and responsibilities.

The Role of Feedback in Verifying Messages

Recall that checking receiver understanding is the fourth step in the oral message sending process. The best way to make sure communication has taken place is to get feedback from the receiver of the message through questioning and paraphrasing. **Paraphrasing** *is the process of having the receiver restate the message in his or her own words.* If the receiver of the message can answer the questions or paraphrase the message, communication has taken place.

The Role of Feedback in Meeting Objectives

Leaders set objective for the desired level of performance.[30] Thus, leaders should set specific measurable objectives (Chapter 3) and monitor the process through ongoing feedback to increase motivation toward goal accomplishment.[31] Feedback is also used in recognition of good work.[32] See Guidelines for Effective Leader Feedback in Chapter 7.

The Need to Be Open to Feedback—Criticism

To improve our performance and get ahead in an organization, we have to be open to feedback commonly called *criticism*.[33] We should actually solicit feedback. However, if we're asking for personal feedback, remember that we are asking to hear things that may surprise, upset, or insult us, and even hurt our feelings. If we become defensive and emotional—and it is tough not to when we feel attacked—feedback will stop.

We do not really enjoy being criticized by our manager, peers, or others, even when it is constructive, because it tends to be painful. But keep the phrase "no pain, no gain" in mind when it comes to criticism. When criticized, whether you asked for it or not, stay calm[34] (even when the other person is emotional), don't get defensive, and don't blame others. View it as an opportunity to improve. If the feedback is vague, ask what specific behavior they want that will improve performance. Although it is difficult to change our behavior, it is the only way we will improve.

WORK
Application **6-4**

Are you really open to feedback or criticism from others at work? How can you improve on accepting criticism?

YOU
Make the
ETHICAL
Call

6.2   *Academic Grades*

Grades are a form of feedback and are often criticized. (Recall Ethical Call "Academic Standards" in Chapter 3.) Successful managers set and maintain high expectations for all their employees, and as Lou Holtz said, we need to set a higher standard. While students are doing less work than in prior years, grades continue to increase, which is called grade inflation. At one time, most colleges had a set grade point average (GPA) to determine honors. But today, most colleges use a ranking system of GPA, because of grade inflation, to limit the number of students graduating with honors.

1. How do you react when you get a grade that is lower than you wanted or expected?
2. Do you use the feedback of correcting and grades to help you improve? Why or why not, and, if yes, how?
3. Why are professors giving higher grades today than were given 5, 10, or 20 years ago?
4. Are students who are putting in less time and getting higher grades being well prepared for a career with high standards after graduation?
5. Is it ethical and socially responsible for professors to drop standards and for colleges to award degrees with higher grades today than 5, 10, or 20 years ago?

Learning Outcome 4   *Identify two common approaches to getting feedback, and explain why they don't work.*

Common Approaches to Getting Feedback on Messages—and Why They Don't Work

The first common approach is to send the entire message and then assume that the message has been conveyed with mutual understanding without getting any feedback. The second approach is to give the entire message and then ask "Do you have any questions?" Feedback usually does not follow, because people have a tendency "not" to ask questions. Asking questions, especially if no one else does, is often considered an admission of not paying attention or not being bright enough to understand, or the receiver doesn't know what to ask.

After managers send a message and ask if there are questions, they then proceed to make another common error: Managers assume that no questions means communication is complete and that there is mutual understanding of the message. In reality, the message is often misunderstood. When "this isn't what I asked for" happens, the task often has to be done all over again. The end result is often wasted time, materials, and effort.

The most common cause of messages not resulting in communication is the lack of getting feedback that ensures mutual understanding. The proper use of questioning and paraphrasing can help you ensure that your messages are communicated.

How to Get Feedback on Messages

Here are four guidelines we can use to ensure getting feedback on messages:

- *Be open to feedback.* There are no dumb questions. When someone asks a question, we need to be responsive, patiently answer questions, and explain things clearly. If people sense that we get upset if they ask questions, they will not ask questions.

- *Be aware of nonverbal communication.* Be sure nonverbal communications encourage feedback. For example, if you say, "I encourage questions," but when people ask questions you look at them as though they are stupid, or you act impatient, people will learn not to ask questions. You must also be aware of, and read, people's nonverbal communications. For example, if you are explaining a task to Larry and he has a puzzled look on his face, he is probably confused but may not be willing to say so. In such a case, you should stop and clarify things before going on.
- *Ask questions.* When sending messages, it is better to know whether the messages are understood before action is taken, so that the action will not have to be changed or repeated. Ask questions to check understanding, rather than simply asking "Do you have any questions?" Direct questions dealing with the *specific information* you have given will indicate if the receiver has been listening, and whether he or she understands enough to give a direct reply. If the response is not accurate, try repeating, giving more examples, or elaborating further on the message.
- *Use paraphrasing.* The most accurate indicator of understanding is paraphrasing. How we ask the receiver to paraphrase will affect attitudes. For example, if we say "Joan, tell me what I just said so that I can be sure you will not make a mistake as usual," this will probably result in defensive behavior on Joan's part. Joan will probably make a mistake. Here are two examples of proper requests for paraphrasing:

"Now tell me what you are going to do, so we will be sure that we are in agreement."

"Would you tell me what you are going to do, so that I can be sure that I explained myself clearly?"

Notice that the second statement takes the pressure off the employee. The sender is asking for a check on *his or her* ability, not that of the employee. These types of requests for paraphrasing should result in a positive attitude toward the message and the sender. They show concern for the employee and for communicating effectively.

<aside>
WORK
Application **6-5**

Recall a past or present manager. Did or does your manager use the common approach to getting feedback on messages regularly? Was or is he or she open to feedback and aware of nonverbal communication on a regular basis? Did the manager regularly ask questions and ask you to paraphrase?
</aside>

360-Degree Multi-Rater Feedback

The use of feedback from multiple sources, especially peers,[35] is popular as a means of improving performance[36] So far, we have discussed the informal methods of getting feedback. We now turn to a formal evaluation process using 360-degree multi-rater feedback. As the name implies, **360-degree feedback** *is based on receiving performance evaluations from many people.* Usually a 360-degree evaluation form is completed by the person being evaluated, his or her manager, peers, and subordinates when applicable. Customers, suppliers, and other outside people are also asked for an evaluation when applicable. See Exhibit 6.2 for an illustration of the 360-degree feedback process.

> **EXHIBIT 6.2**

360-Degree Feedback Sources

may be customers

Manager

Peers   360-degree multirater   Self
             feedback form results

Employees

may be suppliers

© Cengage Learning®

If you are serious about getting ahead, it is critical to focus on feedback from your manager and any other evaluators and do what it takes to receive a good formal performance evaluation. You should work together with your manager to develop and implement a plan for improvement during the next evaluation period.

OPENING CASE Application

2. How does management use feedback at The Ranch?

Feedback is critical to success at The Ranch, because it is how the Clarks and the managers know if the players are getting quality service and learn how to improve service. The Clarks, managers, and employees are open to player criticism because they realize that the only way to improve is to listen and make changes to improve performance. In fact, Peter and Korby Clark spend much of their time at The Ranch talking to players about their experience, with the focus on listening for ways to make improvements. The Clarks and managers set clear objectives and have regular meetings with employees to get and give feedback on how The Ranch is progressing toward meeting its objectives.

Although it is a small business, during the summer 80 people work at The Ranch, and it has a sophisticated information system for its three departments—golf (greens and practice, tournaments/outings, golf shop), maintenance (the course and other facilities), and food and beverage (The Ranch Grille, bar, and functions)—that include many performance measures that are monitored for continuous improvements.

Coaching

Coaching is based on feedback and communications,[37] and it improves performance.[38] **Coaching** *is the process of giving motivational feedback to maintain and improve performance.* In this section, we discuss how to give coaching feedback, and what criticism is— and why that doesn't work. We then present a coaching model you can use on the job, and we end by briefly discussing mentoring, which may be considered a form of coaching.

How to Give Coaching Feedback

When people hear the word *coaching*, they often think of athletes, but managers should also be looking for steady performance and continual improvement. Here we discuss some guidelines that will help us to be effective coaches; the guidelines are also shown in Exhibit 6.3. The guidelines are designed primarily for use with employees who are doing a good job.

Coaching Guidelines

EXHIBIT 6.3

1. Develop a supportive working relationship.
2. Give praise and recognition.
3. Avoid blame and embarrassment.
4. Focus on the behavior, not the person.
5. Have employees assess their own performance.
6. Give specific and descriptive feedback.
7. Give coaching feedback.
8. Provide modeling and training.
9. Make feedback timely, but flexible.
10. Don't criticize.

© Cengage Learning®

WORK
Application **6-6**

Recall the best and worst manager you ever had. With which manager did you have the best working relationship? Which one gave you the most encouragement, praise, and recognition for a job well done? Which one gave you the most negative criticism? Was your performance at a higher level for your best or worst manager?

Develop a Supportive Working Relationship

Manager and employee do not have to be personal friends and socialize together—it's about having a good working relationship. Our relationship with followers needs to convey concern for them as individuals and our commitment to coach them to success. We should periodically ask employees if there is anything we can do to help them do a better job. Take the time to listen to them. Our job as a manager is to run interference and to remove the stumbling blocks for the employees to improve their performance and that of the business unit.

Give Praise and Recognition

In Chapter 3, you learned the importance of giving praise, and how to use the giving praise model. We cannot overemphasize the importance of giving praise and recognition. Recognition includes praise, awards, and recognition ceremonies. Awards include certificates of achievement, a letter of commendation, a pin/plaque/trophy/medal, clothing, cash, trips, employee of the month, and so on.

Avoid Blame and Embarrassment

The objective of coaching is to develop employees.[39] Thus, any behavior that focuses on placing blame and making the person feel bad does not help.[40] For example, if an employee makes a mistake and realizes it, verbalizing it is not needed; doing so only makes them feel bad. Statements like "I'm surprised that you did XYZ" or "I'm disappointed in you" should be avoided. Besides, effective leaders treat mistakes as learning experiences.

Focus on the Behavior, Not the Person

Let's use examples to illustrate the difference between coaching by focusing on changing behavior and coaching by focusing on the person. Notice that the statements focusing on the person place blame and embarrassment—or belittle the person:

- *Situation 1.* The employee is dominating the discussion at a meeting. Focus on person—You talk too much; give others a chance. Focus on behavior—I'd like to hear what some of the other group members have to say.
- *Situation 2.* The employee is late for a meeting again. Focus on person—You are always late for meetings; why can't you be on time like the rest of us?

 Focus on behavior—This is the second time in a row that you arrived late for our meeting. The group needs your input right from the start of the meeting.

Have Employees Assess Their Own Performance

Here are some examples of criticism and of self-evaluation coaching feedback to help explain the difference:

- *Situation 3.* The employee has been making more errors lately. Criticism—You haven't been working up to par lately; get on the ball. Self-evaluation—How would you assess the number of errors you have been making this week?
- *Situation 4.* The employee is working on a few reports, and one is due in two days. The manager believes the employee may not meet the deadline. Criticism—Are you going to meet the deadline for the report? Self-evaluation—How are you progressing on the cost-cutting report that's due this Thursday? Is there something I can do to help?

Give Specific and Descriptive Feedback

Specific feedback is needed to avoid confusion over which particular behavior needs to be improved.[41] Compare the preceding criticism statements, which are not specific, to the self-evaluation statements, which are specific.

Descriptive feedback can be based on *facts* or *inferences*. Facts can be observed and proven; inferences cannot. In situation 3, the manager can observe and prove that the employee made more errors this week than in prior weeks. However, the manager cannot observe or prove why. The manager may infer many reasons for the changed behavior, such as laziness, illness, a personal problem, and so on.

In situation 4, the manager cannot prove that the report will be late; the manager is inferring that it will be and attempting to coach the employee to make sure it is completed on time. Give factual, rather than inferential, feedback, because factual feedback tends to be specific and more positive, while inferential feedback tends to be more negative criticism.

Give Coaching Feedback

Self-assessment can work well.[42] However, it is not always appropriate; if overused, it can have limited success. Here are some examples of how to coach versus criticize:

- *Situation 5.* The manager just saw an employee, who knows how it should be done, incorrectly pick up a fairly heavy box.
- Criticism—You just picked up the box wrong. Don't let me catch you again. Coaching feedback—If you don't want to injure your back, use your legs—not your back.
- *Situation 6.* A student sees a fellow student going to the Yahoo! Web site by typing in the entire address, http://www.yahoo.com.
  Criticism—You just wasted time typing in the entire Yahoo! Web site address.
  Coaching feedback—Would you like me to show you a faster way to get to the Yahoo! home page?

Provide Modeling and Training

A good manager leads by example. If employees see the manager doing things in an effective manner, they will tend to copy the manager. As illustrated in situations 4 and 5, coaching often requires some training.[43] The job instructional training method is widely used (see Model 6.2). *The* **job instructional training (JIT)** *steps include* (1) *trainee receives preparation;* (2) *trainer presents the task;* (3) *trainee performs the task; and* (4) *trainer follows up.* Remember that tasks we know well seem very simple, but they are usually difficult for the new trainee.

Step 1. **Trainee receives preparation.** Put the trainee at ease as you create interest in the job and encourage questions. Explain the quantity and quality requirements and why they are important.

Job Instructional Training Steps

MODEL 6.2

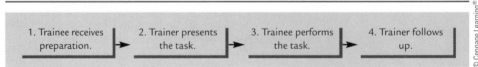

1. Trainee receives preparation. → 2. Trainer presents the task. → 3. Trainee performs the task. → 4. Trainer follows up.

© Cengage Learning®

Step 2. **Trainer presents the task.** Perform the task yourself at a slow pace, explaining each step several times. Once the trainee seems to have the steps memorized, have the trainee explain each step as you slowly perform the task again. For complex tasks with multiple steps, it is helpful to write them out and to give a copy to the trainee.

Step 3. **Trainee performs the task.** Have the trainee perform the task at a slow pace, while explaining each step to you. Correct any errors and be patiently willing to help the trainee perform any difficult steps. Continue until the trainee is proficient at performing the task.

Step 4. **Trainer follows up.** Tell the trainee whom to ask for help with any questions or problems. Observe the trainee performing the task, and be sure to correct any errors or faulty work procedures before they become a habit. As you follow up, be sure to be patient and encouraging.

WORK
Application **6-7**

Recall a present or past manager. Which of the ten guidelines does or did the manager use most frequently and least frequently?

Make Feedback Timely, but Flexible

Feedback should be given *as soon as possible* after the behavior has been observed. For example, in situation 5 you will want to give the coaching feedback as soon as you see the employee lift the box incorrectly. To tell the employee about it a few days later will have less impact on changing the behavior, and the employee could be injured by then. The *flexibility* part comes into play in two ways: (1) When you don't have the time to do the full coaching job, make an appointment to do so; (2) when emotions are high, wait until everyone calms down to discuss the issue.

Remember that you can be a good coach by following the simple guidelines presented here. These general guidelines apply to any leadership situation. So start coaching—today.

What Is Criticism—and Why Doesn't It Work?

Placing blame and embarrassment and focusing on the person are types of criticism. Criticism is rarely effective. Criticism involves a judgment, which is that either the person is right or wrong. Criticism is also the process of pointing out mistakes, which places blame and is embarrassing.

Once we tell people they are wrong or made a mistake, directly or indirectly, four things usually happen. (1) They become defensive and justify their behavior, or they blame it on someone or something. (2) They don't really listen to so-called constructive feedback. (3) They are embarrassed and feel bad about themselves, or they view themselves as losers. (4) They begin to dislike the task or job, as well as the critic. Plus, yelling at people makes things worse, and we tend to regret yelling.[44] Conversely, when people feel good about the feedback they receive; they will be more open to changing their behavior, which increases performance.[45]

Demotivating

Employees with overly critical managers tend to develop a negative attitude: "My manager doesn't care about me or appreciate my work, so why should I work hard to do a good job?" They play it safe by doing the minimum, taking no risks, focusing on not making errors, and covering up any errors so they aren't criticized. They avoid contact with the manager and they feel stress just seeing the manager approach them. They think, "What did I do this time?"

Learning
Outcome **5**   *Describe the difference between criticism and coaching feedback.*

The Difference between Criticism and Coaching Feedback

Coaching feedback *is based on a good, supportive relationship; it is specific and descriptive; and it is not judgmental criticism.* And coaching is often based on the employee doing a self-assessment of performance. Criticism makes employees feel like losers; praise and coaching feedback makes them feel like winners. And nothing breeds success like good coaches.

CONCEPT APPLICATION 6-2

Criticism or Coaching Feedback

Identify each of these five statements as criticism or coaching feedback. For each criticism only, write a coaching feedback statement to replace it.

a. criticism   b. coaching feedback

_____ 11. *In a loud, angry voice:* What are you doing?

_____ 12. Would you like to know a faster way to get it done?

_____ 13. This is still dirty. Clean it again.

_____ 14. Would you like me to tell you how you can minimize this problem in the future?

_____ 15. Make sure you don't forget to use the spell check this time before you pass it in.

Learning Outcome **6**   *Discuss the relationship between the performance formula and the coaching model.*

The Coaching Model for Employees Who Are Performing Below Standard

Coaching is needed when performance falls below expected levels.[46] When giving feedback to employees who are performing below standard, all nine of the coaching guidelines are important. They need your one-on-one coaching at its best. Be patient but persistent; don't give up on them. Before getting into the coaching model, let's discuss attribution theory and the performance formula because they affect the coaching model.

Attribution Theory

Attribution theory *is used to explain the process managers go through in determining the reasons for effective or ineffective performance and deciding what to do about it.* The reaction of a manager to poor performance has two stages. First, we try to determine the cause of the poor performance, and then to select an appropriate corrective action. To help determine the cause of poor performance, we provide the performance formula; and to take corrective action, the coaching model.

Determining the Cause of Poor Performance and Corrective Coaching Action

The **performance formula** *explains performance as a function of ability, motivation, and resources.* Model 6.3 is a simple model that can help us determine the cause of poor performance and the corrective action to take based on the cause. When ability, motivation, or resources are low, performance will be lower.

When the employee's *ability* is the reason for keeping performance from being optimal, the corrective coaching action is training.[47] When *motivation* is lacking, coach the employee.[48] Motivational techniques (discussed in Chapter 3) such as giving praise might help. When *resources* (tools, material, equipment, etc.) are the problem, look at getting the needed resources. When obstacles are getting in the way of performance, we need to overcome them.

The Performance Formula

MODEL 6.3	Performance (f)* Ability, Motivation, and Resources *(f) = is a function of

© Cengage Learning®

Improving Performance with the Coaching Model

The steps in the coaching model are below.

Step 1. **Describe current performance.** In detail, using specific examples, describe the current behavior that needs to be changed.

For example, for an ability or motivation problem, say something like, "There is a way to lift boxes without straining our back that will decrease chances of getting injured."

Step 2. **Describe desired performance.** Tell the employee exactly what the desired performance is, in detail. If *ability* is the reason for poor performance, modeling and training the employee with JIT are very appropriate. If the employee knows the proper way, the reason for poor performance is *motivational*. Demonstration is not needed; just describe desired performance as you ask the employee to state why the performance is important.

For example: *Ability*—"If you squat down and pick up the box using your legs instead of your back, it is easier and there is less chance of injuring yourself. Let me demonstrate for you." *Motivation*—"Why should you squat and use your legs rather than your back to pick up boxes?"

Step 3. **Get a commitment to the change.** When dealing with an *ability* performance issue, it is not necessary to get employees to verbally commit to the change if they seem willing to make it. However, if employees defend their way, and you're sure it's not as effective, explain why your proposed way is better. If you cannot get the employee to understand and agree based on rational persuasion, get a verbal commitment through coercive power, such as a threat of discipline. For *motivation* performance issues, this is important because, if employees are not willing to commit to the change, they will most likely not make the change.

For example: *Ability*—the employee will most likely be willing to do it correctly, so skip the step. *Motivation*—"Will you squat rather than use your back from now on?"

Step 4. **Follow up.** Remember, some employees do what managers inspect, not what they expect. We should follow up to ensure that the employee is behaving as desired.

When we are dealing with an *ability* performance issue, the person is receptive, and we skip step 3, say nothing. But watch to be sure the task is done correctly in the future. Coach again, if necessary. For a *motivation* problem, make a statement that you will follow up, and describe possible consequences for repeated poor performance.

For example: *Ability*—say nothing, but observe. *Motivation*—"You know that picking up boxes with your back is dangerous; if I catch you doing it again, I will take disciplinary action."

See Model 6.4 for a review of the steps in the coaching model.

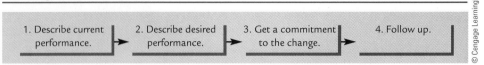

MODEL   6.4

Coaching Model

| 1. Describe current performance. | → | 2. Describe desired performance. | → | 3. Get a commitment to the change. | → | 4. Follow up. |

© Cengage Learning®

Mentoring

Mentoring *is a form of coaching in which a more experienced manager helps a less experienced protégé.* Thus, the ten tips for coaching apply to mentoring. However, mentoring includes more than coaching, and it is more involved and personal than coaching. The formal mentor is usually at a higher level of management and is not the protégé's immediate manager. Family, friends, and peers can also be mentors.

WORK
Application **6-8**

Recall a person who is or was a mentor to you. Briefly describe the relationship and type of advice you got from your mentor.

The primary responsibility is to coach the protégé by providing good, sound career advice and to help develop leadership skills necessary for a successful career.[49] Mentors can nurture your inner greatness.[50] Mentoring is especially important in progressing from middle management to upper level management, especially for women and minorities because they are very underrepresented in Fortune 500 companies. We all need mentors, so don't wait for someone to ask you. Seek out a good mentor.[51] If your organization has a formal mentoring program, try to sign up for it. If it is informal, ask around about getting a mentor, and remember that a mentor can be from another organization and in today's global economy, e-mentoring is becoming more popular.[52] Whenever you have job- or career-related questions and would like advice, contact your mentor.

OPENING CASE Application

3. Is there a difference in managing an oil change business, a golf course, and a sports team; and how does Peter Clark use coaching at The Ranch?

Peter Clark says there are more similarities than differences in running a Jiffy Lube business and a golf club and coaching sports. The focus is the same—high-quality service. You have to treat the customer or player right. Clark uses the same 3 I's coaching philosophy for all three: You need Intensity to be prepared to do the job right, Integrity to do the right thing when no one is watching, and Intimacy to be a team player. If one person does not do the job right, everyone is negatively affected. In business and sports, you need to strive to be the best. You need to set and meet challenging goals.

Clark strongly believes in being positive and in the need to develop a supportive working relationship, which includes sitting down to talk and really listening to the other person. He also strongly believes in the need for good training. Employees at The Ranch give high-quality service because they are thoroughly trained to do so, and they are continually coached to maintain and improve performance. Although The Ranch does not have a formal mentoring program, Clark clearly sees mentoring as an important role he plays at The Ranch.

Managing Conflict

Poor communications, feedback, and coaching can lead to conflict. A **conflict** *exists whenever people are in disagreement and opposition.* Conflict is part of everyday life in organizations;[53] it affects everyone involved[54] and how we manage conflict affects performance.[55] With the trend toward teamwork, conflict skills are increasingly important;[56] as managers spend about 25 percent of their time resolving conflicts.[57] Thus, ability to resolve conflicts will have a direct effect on your leadership success.[58] In this section, we discuss the psychological contract and the five conflict management styles we can use to resolve conflicts.

The Psychological Contract

All human relations rely on the psychological contract. The *psychological contract* is the unwritten implicit expectations of each party in a relationship. At work, you have a set of expectations of what you will contribute to the organization (effort, time, skills) and what it will provide to you (compensation, job satisfaction, etc.). We are often not aware of our expectations until they have not been met (for example, how we are treated by a manager).

Conflict Arises by Breaking the Psychological Contract

The psychological contract is broken for two primary reasons: (1) We fail to make explicit our own expectations and fail to inquire into the expectations of the other parties; and/ or (2) we further assume that the other party(ies) has the same expectations that we hold. To help form the psychological contract, organizations have values, norms, and rules to guide fair and legitimate behavior.[59]

So as long as people meet our expectations, everything is fine; when they don't meet our expectations, we are in conflict. Thus, it is important to share information and negotiate expectations assertively. After all, how can you expect others to meet your expectations when they don't know what they are? However, we can't confront people for every little thing that bothers us, but we should resolve conflicts that impede our work.[60] It is especially important to resolve conflicts with our boss.[61]

> **Learning Outcome 7**   *Define the five conflict management styles.*

Conflict Can Be Dysfunctional or Functional

People often think of conflict as fighting and view it as disruptive, which it can be.[62] When conflict is not resolved effectively, negative consequences occur.[63] When conflict prevents the achievement of organizational objectives, it is negative or *dysfunctional conflict*. However, some say conflict is not only inevitable, it can be good.[64] *Functional conflict* exists when disagreement and opposition supports change and the achievement of organizational objectives.[65] The real question today is not whether conflict is dysfunctional or functional but how to manage conflict to benefit the organization.[66]

Conflict Management Styles

When we are in conflict, we have five conflict management styles to choose from. The five styles are based on two dimensions of concern: concern for others' needs and concern for our own needs. These concerns result in three types of behavior:

- A low concern for your own needs and a high concern for others' needs results in passive behavior.
- A high concern for your own needs and a low concern for others' needs results in aggressive behavior—only looking out for one's own self-interest.[67]
- A moderate or high concern for your own needs and others' needs results in assertive behavior.

Each conflict style of behavior results in a different combination of win–lose situations. The five styles, along with concern for needs and win–lose combinations, are presented in Exhibit 6.4 and discussed here in order of passive, aggressive, and assertive behavior. The conflict style that we tend to use the most is based on our personality and leadership style. There is no one best conflict management style for all situations. In this section, we present the advantages and disadvantages and the appropriate use of each of the five conflict management styles.

Conflict Management Styles

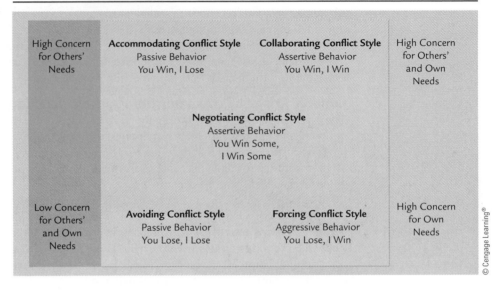

© Cengage Learning®

Avoiding Conflict Style

The *avoiding conflict style* user attempts to passively ignore the conflict rather than resolve it. When we avoid a conflict, we are being unassertive and uncooperative. People avoid conflict by refusing to take a stance, or escape conflict by mentally withdrawing and physically leaving. A lose–lose situation is created because the conflict is not resolved.

Advantages and Disadvantages of the Avoiding Conflict Style. The advantage of the avoiding style is that it may maintain relationships that would be hurt through conflict resolution. The disadvantage of this style is that conflicts do not get resolved, so avoiding is often not the best option. People tend to walk all over the consistent avoider. Avoiding problems usually does not make them go away; the problems usually get worse.[68] And the longer you wait to confront others, the more difficult the confrontation usually is.

Appropriate Use of the Avoiding Conflict Style. The avoiding style is appropriate to use when (1) the conflict is trivial, (2) our stake in the issue is not high, (3) confrontation will damage an important relationship, (4) we don't have time to resolve the conflict, or (5) emotions are high. When we don't have time to resolve the conflict or people are emotional, we should confront the person(s) later. However, it is inappropriate to repeatedly avoid confrontation until you get so upset that you end up yelling at the other person(s). This passive–aggressive behavior tends to make the situation worse by hurting human relations.[69] Often people do not realize they are doing something that bothers us (that we are in conflict), and when approached properly, they are willing to change.

Accommodating Conflict Style

The *accommodating conflict style* user attempts to resolve the conflict by passively giving in to the other party. When we use the accommodating style, we are being unassertive but cooperative. We attempt to satisfy the other party, neglecting our own needs by letting others get their own way. A win–lose situation is created, as we try to please everyone.

Differences between the Avoiding Accommodating Style.   A common difference between the avoiding and accommodating styles is based on behavior. With the avoiding style, we don't have to do anything we really do not want to do; with the accommodating style, we do. For example, if you are talking to someone who makes a statement that you disagree with, to avoid a conflict you can say nothing, change the subject, or stop the conversation. However, suppose you have to put up a display with someone who says "Let's put up the display this way." If you don't want to do it the other person's way, but say nothing and put it up the other person's way, you have done something you really did not want to do—accommodation.

Advantages and Disadvantages of the Accommodating Conflict Style.   The advantage of the accommodating style is that relationships are maintained by doing things the other person's way. The disadvantage is that giving in may be counterproductive. You may have a better solution, such as a better way to put up a display. An overuse of this style tends to lead to people taking advantage of the accommodator, and the type of relationship the accommodator tries to maintain is usually lost.

Appropriate Use of the Accommodating Conflict Style.   The accommodating style is appropriate when (1) the person enjoys being a follower, (2) maintaining the relationship outweighs all other considerations, (3) the changes agreed to are not important to the accommodator but are to the other party, or (4) the time to resolve the conflict is limited. This is often the only style that can be used with an autocratic manager who uses the forcing style.

Forcing Conflict Style

The *forcing conflict style* user attempts to resolve the conflict by using aggressive behavior to get his or her own way. When we use the forcing style, we are uncooperative and *aggressive*, doing whatever it takes to satisfy our own needs—at the expense of others, if necessary. Forcers use authority, threaten, intimidate, and call for majority rule when they know they will win. Forcers commonly enjoy dealing with avoiders and accommodators. If you try to get others to change without being willing to change yourself, regardless of the means, then you use the forcing style. A win–lose situation is created.

Advantages and Disadvantages of the Forcing Style.   The advantage of the forcing style is that better organizational decisions will be made, when the forcer is correct, rather than less-effective compromised decisions. The disadvantage is that overuse of this style leads to hostility and resentment toward its user. Forcers tend to have poor human relations.

Appropriate Use of the Forcing Style.   Some managers commonly use their position power to force others to do what they want them to do.[70] The forcing style is appropriate to use when (1) unpopular action must be taken on important issues; (2) commitment by others to proposed action is not crucial to its implementation—in other words, people will not resist doing what we want them to do; (3) maintaining relationships is not critical; or (4) the conflict resolution is urgent.

Negotiating Conflict Style

The *negotiating conflict style* user attempts to resolve the conflict through assertive, give-and-take concessions. This is also called the *compromising style*. When you use the compromising approach, you are moderate in assertiveness and cooperation. An "I win some, you win some" situation is created through compromise. As discussed in Chapter 5, negotiation skills are important in both your personal and your professional life.[71]

Advantages and Disadvantages of the Negotiating Conflict Style. The advantage of the negotiating style is that the conflict is resolved relatively quickly and working relationships are maintained. The disadvantage is that the compromise may lead to counterproductive results, such as suboptimum decisions. An overuse of this style leads to people playing games such as asking for twice as much as they need to get what they want. It is commonly used during management and labor collective bargaining.

Appropriate Use of the Negotiating Conflict Style. The negotiating style is appropriate to use when (1) the issues are complex and critical, and there is no simple and clear solution; (2) parties have about equal power and are interested in different solutions; (3) a solution will be only temporary; or (4) time is short. Note that we are being assertive, not aggressive, to get what we want without being taken advantage of.

Collaborating Conflict Style

The *collaborating conflict style* user assertively attempts to jointly resolve the conflict with the best solution agreeable to all parties. It is also called the *problem-solving style*. When we use the collaborating approach, we are being assertive and cooperative. Although avoiders and accommodators are concerned about others' needs, and forcers are concerned about their own needs, the collaborator is concerned about finding the best solution to the problem that is satisfactory to all parties. Unlike the forcer, the collaborator is willing to change if a better solution is presented. While negotiating is often based on secret information, collaboration is based on open and honest communication. This is the only style that creates a true win–win situation.

Differences between the Negotiation and Collaborating Style. A common difference between negotiating and collaborating is the solution. Let's continue with the example of putting up a display. With negotiation, the two people may trade off by putting up one display one person's way and the next display the other person's way. This way they each win and lose. With collaboration, the two people work together to develop one display method that they both like. It may be a combination of both, or simply one person's idea if, after an explanation, the other person really agrees that the method is better. The key to collaboration is agreeing that the solution is the best possible one.

Advantages and Disadvantages of the Collaborating Style. The advantage of the collaborating style is that it tends to lead to the best solution to the conflict, using assertive behavior. Again, assertiveness, not aggression, is often a good option. The disadvantage is that the skill, effort, and time it takes to resolve the conflict are usually greater and longer than the other styles. There are situations, mentioned under "Negotiating Conflict Style," when collaboration is difficult, and when a forcer prevents its use. The collaborating style offers the most benefit to the individual, group, and organization.

CONCEPT APPLICATION 6-3

Selecting Conflict Management Styles

For each of these five conflict situations, identify the most appropriate conflict management style. Write the appropriate letter in the blank before each item.

a. avoiding   c. forcing   e. collaborating

b. accommodating   d. negotiating

CONCEPT APPLICATION 6-3

____ 16. You have joined a task force to meet people. Your interest in what the committee does is low. While serving on the task force, you make a recommendation that is opposed by another member. You realize that you have the better idea. The other party is using a forcing style.

____ 17. You are on a task force that has to select a new company smart phone. The alternatives will all do the job. It's the brand, price, and service that members disagree on.

____ 18. You are a sales manager. Jose, one of your competent salespeople, is trying to close a big sale. The two of you are discussing the next sales call he will make. You disagree on the strategy to use to close the sale.

____ 19. You're late and on your way to an important meeting. As you leave, at the other end of the work area you see one of your employees goofing off instead of working.

____ 20. There aren't many customers in the store, so you ask Tony, a part-time employee, to leave work early. Tony tells you he want to stay because he needs the money.

WORK
Application **6-9**

Select a present or past manager. Which conflict management style did that manager use most often? Explain by giving a typical example. Which one of the five conflict management styles do you tend to use most often? Explain your answer

---

Appropriate Use of the Collaborating Conflict Style. The collaborating style is appropriate when (1) you are dealing with an important issue that requires an optimal solution, and compromise would result in suboptimizing; (2) people are willing to place the group goal before self-interest, and members will truly collaborate; (3) maintaining relationships is important; (4) time is available; and (5) it is a peer conflict.

Of the five styles, the relatively easiest to use are the avoiding and accommodating styles. We generally want to avoid using the forcing style. The most difficult to implement successfully, due to the complexity and level of skill needed, is the collaborative style. It is most likely to be underutilized when it would have been appropriate. Therefore, to develop your conflict skills, the collaborative style is the only one that we cover in detail in the next section. Recall that you learned how to negotiate in Chapter 5.

OPENING CASE Application

4. Which conflict management style does Peter Clark tend to use at The Ranch?

At The Ranch, with partners and managers, conflict is inevitable. Peter Clark prefers to use the collaborating conflict style, which goes back to the importance he places on open communications and a good supportive working relationship. He prefers to sit down and work through problem issues together and agree on solutions. He believes that when you have a conflict problem, ignoring it using the avoiding conflict style usually does not solve the problem. When Clark is in conflict with a manager, he does not like to simply accommodate when he does not agree with what the manager wants to do, but he has accommodated.

Clark does not like to use the forcing conflict style, but there are times when he says no to managers. Clark's guiding question is: Will spending the money clearly improve player satisfaction enough to pay for itself? Clark also has to negotiate with outside organizations.

Collaborating Conflict Management Style Models

We can develop our skill to assertively confront (or be confronted by) people we are in conflict with, and in a manner that resolves the conflict without damaging relationships. In this last section, we provide a model with the steps we can follow when initiating, responding to, and mediating a conflict resolution in or out of work.

Learning Outcome **8** List the steps in the initiating conflict resolution model.

Initiating Conflict Resolution

We are the initiators when we confront the other person(s) to resolve the conflict. If we did or said something that was wrong and hurt the other person or when we make a mistake, placing us in conflict, we should apologize. Telling others we are sorry is very beneficial for building and maintaining relationship. Apologizing to our boss, rather than trying to defend our action when we were wrong or made a mistake, can help our performance reviews.[72]

When initiating a conflict resolution using the collaborating style, there is a model to use. *The* **initiating conflict resolution model** *steps are (1) plan a BCF statement that maintains ownership of the problem; (2) present your BCF statement and agree on the conflict; (3) ask for, and/or give, alternative conflict resolutions; and (4) make an agreement for change.*

Step 1. **Plan a Behavior, Consequence, and Feeling (BCF) statement that maintains ownership of the problem.** Planning is the starting point. Let's begin by stating what *maintains ownership of the problem* means. Assume you don't smoke, and someone visits you while smoking. Is it you or the smoker who has a problem? The smoke bothers you, not the smoker. It's your problem. So we should open the confrontation with a request for the respondent to help us solve our problem. This approach reduces defensiveness and establishes an atmosphere of problem solving that will maintain the relationship.

There are three things we *should NOT do in the BCF statement*:

(1) Don't make judgments that evaluate others' behavior ("You are wrong"). Avoid judging and trying to determine who is to blame for something or who is right and wrong. Fixing blame or correctness only makes people defensive and argue about who is right as opposed to resolving the conflict.[73]

(2) Don't make threats ("I'm going to tell the boss on you"). This can hurt your relationship. Using threats should be our last, not first option.

(3) Don't give solutions. This is done step 3, so don't start with a solution.

Don't make statements like "You are inconsiderate of others," "You shouldn't smoke" (judgmental evaluation), "You are going to get cancer, I'm going to tell on you and you will get in trouble" (threats), and "Just quit smoking" (solution).

The **BCF model** *describes a conflict in terms of behavior, consequences, and feelings.* When you do B (behavior), C (consequences) happens, and I feel F (feelings). The longer the statement, the longer it will take to resolve the conflict, so keep the opening BCF statement short. For example, when you smoke in my room (behavior), I have trouble breathing and become nauseous (consequence), and I feel uncomfortable and irritated (feeling). You can vary the BCF sequence. For example, I fear (feeling) that the advertisement is not going to work (behavior), and that we will lose money (consequences).

Try to put yourself in the other person's position. If you were the other person, would you like the BCF presented? Would it make you defensive? If so, change it. After planning our BCF statement, we should practice saying it before confronting the other party. In addition, think of some possible alternatives we can offer to resolve the conflict.

WORK
Application **6-10**

Use the BCF model to describe a conflict you face or have faced on the job.

Step 2. **Present your BCF statement and agree on the conflict.** After making the short, planned BCF statement, let the other party respond. If the other party does not understand or avoids acknowledgment of the problem, repeat the planned statement by explaining it in different terms until getting an acknowledgment or realizing it's hopeless. But don't give up too easily; be assertive. If you cannot agree on a conflict, you may have to change our approach and use one of the other four conflict management styles.

Step 3. **Ask for, and/or give, alternative conflict resolutions.** Begin by asking the other party what can be done to resolve the conflict. If both agree, great; if not, offer your resolution. However, remember that you are collaborating, not simply trying to change others. When the other party acknowledges the problem, but is not responsive to resolving it, appeal to common goals. Make others realize the benefits to them in resolving the conflict.

Step 4. **Make an agreement for change.** Our goal is not to win but to agree on a plan of action so that the same error, mistake, or problem doesn't occur again. Try to come to an agreement on specific action you will both take to resolve the conflict. Clearly state—or, better yet for complex change, write down—the specific behavior changes necessary by all parties to resolve the conflict. Again, remember that you are collaborating, not forcing. The steps are also listed in Model 6.5.

Responding to Conflict Resolution

As the responder, an initiator has confronted you.[74] Here's how to handle the role of the responder to a conflict. Most initiators do not follow the model. Therefore, we must take responsibility for successful conflict resolution by following the conflict resolution model steps, which are also listed in Model 6.5:

1. Listen to and paraphrase the conflict using the BCF model. You need to state the conflict in your own words to make sure you get it and agree to the conflict.
2. Agree with some aspect of the complaint. Rarely is only one party the problem. So even if you don't think you are wrong, at least agree with something (I agree that I upset you) so the conflict can be resolved.
3. Ask for, and/or give, alternative conflict resolutions. This is the same as step 3 of initiating conflict discussed above.
4. Make an agreement for change. This is the same as step 4 of initiating conflict.

Mediating Conflict Resolution

Frequently, conflicting parties cannot resolve their dispute alone. In these cases, a mediator should be used. A **mediator** *is a neutral third party who helps resolve a conflict.* Some organizations have trained and designated employees as mediators. In unionized organizations, the mediator is usually a professional from outside the organization. However, a conflict resolution should be sought internally first.

Before bringing the conflicting parties together, we should decide whether to start with a joint meeting or conduct individual meetings. If one employee comes to complain but has not confronted the other party, or if there is a serious discrepancy in employee perceptions, meet one-on-one with each party before bringing them together. On the other hand, when both parties have a similar awareness of the problem and motivation to solve it, you can begin with a joint meeting when all parties are calm. The leader should be a mediator, not a judge. Get the employees to resolve the conflict, if possible. Remain impartial, unless one party is violating company policies. Do a good job of coaching. Avoid blame and embarrassment. Don't make comments such as "I'm disappointed in you two" or "you're acting like babies."

The Collaborating Conflict Style

MODEL 6.5

Initiating Conflict Resolution	Responding to Conflict Resolution	Mediating Conflict Resolution
Step 1. Plan a BCF statement that maintains ownership of the problem.	Step 1. Listen to and paraphrase the conflict using the BCF model.	Step 1. Have each party state his or her complaint using the BCF model.
Step 2. Present your BCF statement and agree on the conflict.	Step 2. Agree with some aspect of the complaint.	Step 2. Agree on the conflict problem(s).
Step 3. Ask for, and/or give, alternative conflict resolutions.	Step 3. Ask for, and/or give, alternative conflict resolutions.	Step 3. Develop alternative conflict resolutions.
Step 4. Make an agreement for change.	Step 4. Make an agreement for change.	Step 4. Make an agreement for change.
		Step 5. Follow up to make sure the conflict is resolved.

© Cengage Learning®

When bringing conflicting parties together, follow the mediating conflict model steps listed in Model 6.5.

If either party blames the other, make a statement such as "We are here to resolve the conflict; placing blame is not productive." Focus on how the conflict is affecting their work. Discuss the issues by addressing *specific behavior*, not personalities. If a person says "We cannot work together because of a personality conflict," ask the parties to state the specific behavior that is bothering them. The discussion should make the parties aware of their behavior and the consequences of their behavior. The mediator may ask questions or make statements to clarify what is being said. The mediator should develop one problem statement that is agreeable to all parties, if possible.

If the conflict has not been resolved, an arbitrator may be used. *An* **arbitrator** *is a neutral third party who makes a binding decision to resolve a conflict.* The arbitrator is like a judge; the decision must be followed. However, the use of arbitration should be kept to a minimum because it is not a collaborative conflict style. Arbitrators commonly use a negotiating style in which each party wins some and loses some.

OPENING CASE Application

5. What types of conflict resolutions do the Clarks deal with at The Ranch?

At The Ranch, Peter Clark more often responds to conflict than initiating conflict resolutions since, when problems arise, he is asked for solutions or to approve actions. Clark also has to occasionally mediate a conflict between partners or between managers and employees.

As we end this chapter, you should understand how important communication, feedback, coaching, and conflict resolution are to leadership effectiveness in all organizations. Self-Assessment 6-2 will help you understand how your personality traits affect your communication, feedback, coaching, and conflict management style.

| **SELF-ASSESSMENT 6-2** | **Your Personality Traits and Communication, Feedback, Coaching, and Conflict Management Style** |

Let's tie personality traits from Chapter 2 together with what we've covered in this chapter. We are going to present some general statements about how your personality may affect your communication, feedback, coaching, and conflict management styles. For each area, determine how the information relates to you. This will help you better understand your behavior strengths and weaknesses, and identify areas you may want to improve.

Communication

If you have a high *surgency* personality, you most likely are an extrovert and have no difficulty initiating and communicating with others. However, you may be dominating during communication and may not listen well and be open to others' ideas. Be careful not to use communications simply as a means of getting what you want; be concerned about others and what they want. If you are low in surgency, you may be quiet and reserved in your communications. You may want to be more vocal.

If you are high in *agreeableness* personality trait, you are most likely a good listener and communicator. Your *adjustment* level affects the emotional tone of your communications. If you tend to get emotional during communications, you may want to work to keep your emotions under control. We cannot control our feelings, but we can control our behavior. If you are high in *conscientiousness,* you tend to have reliable communications. If you are not conscientious, you may want to work at returning messages quickly. People who are *open to new experience* often initiate communication, because communicating is often part of the new experience.

Feedback and Coaching

If you have a high *surgency* personality, you have a need to be in control. Watch the tendency to give feedback, but not listen to it. You may need to work at *not* criticizing. If you have low surgency, you may want to give more feedback and do more coaching. If you have a high *agreeableness* personality, you are a people person and probably enjoy coaching others. However, as a manager, you must also discipline when needed, which may be difficult for you.

If you are high on the *adjustment* personality trait, you may tend to give positive coaching; people with low *adjustment* need to watch the negative criticism. If you have a high *conscientiousness* with a high need for achievement, you may tend to be more concerned about your own success. This is also true of people with a high *surgency* personality. Remember that an important part of leadership is coaching others. If you have a low *conscientiousness,* you may need to put forth effort to be a good coach. Your *openness to experience* personality affects whether you are willing to listen to others' feedback and make changes.

Conflict Styles

Generally, the best conflict style is collaboration. If you have a high *surgency* personality, you most likely have no problem confronting others when in conflict. However, be careful not to use the forcing style with others; remember to use social, not personal power. If you have a high *agreeableness* personality, you tend to get along well with others. However, be careful not to use the avoiding and accommodating styles to get out of confronting others; you need to satisfy your needs too.

Adjustment will affect how to handle a conflict situation. Try not to be low in adjustment and get too emotional. If you are *conscientious,* you may be good at conflict resolution; but again, be careful to meet others' needs too. *Openness to experience* affects conflicts, because their resolution often requires change; be open to new things.

Action Plan

Based on your personality, what specific things will you do to improve your communication, feedback, coaching, and conflict management style?

_____

_____

_____

"Take It To The Net". Access student resources at www.cengagebrain.com. Search for Lussier, Leadership 6e to find student study tools.

Chapter Summary

This chapter summary is organized to answer the nine learning outcomes for Chapter 6.

1 **List the steps in the oral message-sending process.**

The five steps in the oral message-sending process are (1) develop rapport; (2) state your communication objective; (3) transmit your message; (4) check the receiver's understanding; (5) get a commitment and follow up.

2 **List and explain the three parts of the message-receiving process.**

The three parts of the message-receiving process are listening, analyzing, and checking understanding. Listening is the process of giving the speaker your undivided attention. Analyzing is the process of thinking about, decoding, and evaluating the message. Checking understanding is the process of giving feedback.

3 **Describe paraphrasing and state why it is used.**

Paraphrasing is the process of having the receiver restate the message in his or her own words. Paraphrasing is used to check understanding of the transmitted message. If the receiver can paraphrase the message accurately, communication has taken place. If not, communication is not complete.

4 **Identify two common approaches to getting feedback, and explain why they don't work.**

The first common approach is to send the entire message and to assume that the message has been conveyed with mutual understanding without getting any feedback. The second approach is to give the entire message followed by asking "Do you have any questions?" Feedback usually does not follow because people have a tendency not to ask questions. Asking questions, especially if no one else does, is often considered an admission of not paying attention or not being bright enough to understand, or the receiver doesn't know what to ask.

5 **Describe the difference between criticism and coaching feedback.**

Criticism is feedback that makes a judgment about behavior being wrong. Coaching feedback is based on a supportive relationship and offers specific and descriptive ways to improve performance. Criticism focuses on pointing out mistakes, while coaching feedback focuses on the benefits of positive behavior.

6 **Discuss the relationship between the performance formula and the coaching model.**

The performance formula is used to determine the reason for poor performance and the corrective action needed. The coaching model is then used to improve performance.

7 **Define the five conflict management styles.**

(1) The *avoiding conflict style* user attempts to passively ignore the conflict rather than resolve it. (2) The accommodating conflict style user attempts to resolve the conflict by passively giving in to the other party. (3) The forcing conflict style user attempts to resolve the conflict by using aggressive behavior to get his or her own way. (4) The negotiating conflict style user attempts to resolve the conflict through assertive, give-and-take concessions. (5) The collaborating conflict style user assertively attempts to jointly resolve the conflict with the best solution agreeable to all parties.

8 **List the steps in the initiating conflict resolution model.**

The initiating conflict resolution model steps are (1) plan a BCF statement that maintains ownership of the problem; (2) present your BCF statement and agree on the conflict; (3) ask for, and/or give, alternative conflict resolutions; and (4) make an agreement for change.

Key Terms

Review Questions

1 What should be included in your plan to send a message?

2 What are the three parts of a written outline?

3 As an average, how many words should a sentence have, and how many sentences should there be in a paragraph?

4 Which personality traits are associated with being closed to feedback?

5 What are the four guidelines to getting feedback on messages?

6 What is 360-degree feedback, and are many organizations using it?

7 Should a supportive working relationship be a true friendship?

8 Why doesn't criticism work?

9 Are all managers mentors?

10 How do you know when you are in conflict?

11 What is the difference between functional and dysfunctional conflict, and how does each affect performance?

12 What is meant by *maintaining ownership of the problem*?

13 How is the BCF model used?

14 What is the difference between a mediator and an arbitrator?

Critical-Thinking Questions

The following critical-thinking questions can be used for class discussion and/or as written assignments to develop communication skills. Be sure to give complete explanations for all questions.

1 How would you assess communications in organizations? Give examples of good and poor communications in organizations.

2 How did you score on Self-Assessment 6-1, "Listening Skills"? State your plan for improving your listening skills.

3 How would you assess managers at giving feedback? Specifically, what should managers do to improve?

4 Is 360-degree multi-rater feedback really better than a boss-based assessment? As a manager, would you elect to use 360?

5 Do you agree with the statement "Don't criticize"? Do managers tend to give criticism or coaching feedback? How can managers improve?

6 Women and minorities are less likely to have mentors, so should they get mentors? Will you seek out career mentors?

7 What are your psychological contract expectations of your boss and coworkers? Give examples of conflicts you have had at work, listing the expectation that was not met.

8 What percentage of the time do you think a manager can actually use the collaborating conflict management style? Give detailed examples of when managers have used collaboration at work.

CASE

Reed Hastings—Netflix

In January 2005, Wedbush Securities stock analysts Michael Pachter called Netflix a "worthless piece of crap." He put a price target of $3 on the stock that was trading at around $11. Doubters thought Blockbuster, Walmart, or Amazon.com, with their economies of scale and established customer bases, would simply destroy Netflix. Founder and CEO Reed Hastings

wasn't supposed to be *Fortune*'s Businessperson of the Year in 2010, five years after his demise was predicted. Not only did Hasting earn the No. 1 spot; he and Netflix also killed it. Netflix was the stock of the year, up more than 200 percent in 2010, while the S&P 500 was up only 7 percent. Netflix shares ran laps around even Apple's.[75] Between 2010 and 2013

(continued)

Netflix subscribers doubled to over 40 million and its stock price quadrupled to $375, making it again the best-performing stock on the S&P 500.[76] Don't you wish you bought it back in 2005 when it was selling for $11? In Fortune's List of 2013's Top People in Business, Reed Hastings was ranked #5, ahead of Amazon's Jeff Bezos, Google's Larry Page, Facebook's Mark Zuckerberg, and Apple's Tim Cook.[77]

So how did Hastings do it? A lot of his success is based on how he built his company on a hard-driving and risk-taking culture, and Hastings never stops looking over his shoulder to stay one step ahead of the competition. Unlike Blockbuster, which went into bankruptcy, Netflix wasn't afraid to change its business model by abandoning the past to build its future.[78] How, by cannibalizing its own mail order DVD customers to focus on streaming existing program and even to launching original series, including the highly successful House of Cards that won three Emmy awards, with more to come.[79] Although the change in focus from mailing DVDs to streaming with a pricing revamping was clumsily handled, resulting in angry and lost mail customers, it clearly was a good strategic move.[80] With streaming, Netflix is now stealing customers from cable and pay movie channels HBO, Showtime, and Starz, as it is the world's largest video subscription company.[81] Growth is also coming from Netflix global expansion from Canada (2010), to Latin America (2011) and most recently to Europe (2012), where streaming is new in many countries.[82]

Let's talk about Hastings's leadership style that led to success. It has changed over the years between the two companies he created. As a young founding CEO of Pure Software, Hastings was considered as hard headed as they come and couldn't take criticism. He used the autocratic style to push for his ways of doing things, and he sometimes embarrassed employees with nonverbal eye rolling and critical comments about dumb ideas. So much so that Hastings earned the nickname "Animal." Hastings sold Pure for $750 million, and it made him realize he had helped build a company he didn't want to be part of.[83]

So when he used the money to start Netflix, as CEO Hastings was determined to create a culture in which people enjoyed coming to every day. He wanted the company to be run differently, so he changed his style to be participative. He is more honest and direct with employees but not confrontational, but he still has a Steve Jobs–like perfectionist streak. Instead of simply telling others what to do, he actively seeks out ideas and advice from his employees. Now when he hears ideas that seem silly, he doesn't roll his eyes and humiliate employees by making critical comments about the idea or person being dumb. Hastings digs deeper by responding with comments like "I don't understand how your idea will work, so help me to understand how it will solve the problem."[84]

Hastings was ahead of the technology curve. Even back in 1997 when Hastings cofounded Netflix, he anticipated that consumers would eventually prefer to get movies instantly delivered via the Internet. This is actually amazing foresight because back then less than 7 percent of U.S. homes even had broadband. Hastings actually had a team working on the technology to bring movies to the home via the Internet back in 2000. They even developed a Netflix-branded box with a hard drive that connected to your movie queue, but it took six hours to download a movie back in the early 2000s. Once Hastings saw YouTube videos, he killed the hard-drive device and put this team to work on a streaming machine, a sort of YouTube-in-a-box. This again was meant to be a branded piece of hardware produced and sold by Netflix. However, even though they built the technology, once again Hasting killed the idea in favor of software that could be embedded in all kinds of devices— the software today is known as apps. [85]

No. This wasn't wasted time. Netflix built on this base to be able to come out streaming a year and a half, in 2007, after YouTube showed the world instant viewing over the Internet. Also, it spun off the hardware technology into an existing company called Roku, which today makes a digital device that plays content via software from Netflix, as well as Hulu, Amazon, and others.

Does this mean that Netflix doesn't face any present and future threats? As Hastings admits, there are plenty of challenges ahead. Analysts like Pachter now are warning that Netflix could be crushed or acquired by the likes of Amazon.com, Google, or Apple. Anyone can come after Netflix by streaming bits via contracts with data-delivery companies like Level 3, Limelight, and Akamai. Who knows what Facebook will come up with? Also, Netflix has to pay the studios for contents. Content acquisition could be denied or costs could go through the roof, and new expensive original series may not have the success of House or Cards. In February 2014, Netflix agreed to pay Comcast extra to speed up its streaming service to its customers, which could lead to having to pay other cable providers extra.[86] The European media companies across the continent are girding for battle to stop Netflix from taking market share.[87] But Hastings is confident, as he enjoys solving subtle, yet tough, problems alongside the smartest people he can find. He said, "For me the thrill is making a contribution by solving hard problems." Only time will tell if he can stay ahead of the competition and technology curve.

GO TO THE INTERNET: To learn more about Reed Hastings and Netflix, visit their Web site **(http://www.netflix.com)**.

Support your answers to the following questions with specific information from the case and text or with other information you get from the Web or other sources.

1. How did Hastings change his use of communications in sending and receiving messages from Pure Software to Netflix?

2. How did Hastings change his use of feedback from Pure Software to Netflix?

3. How did Hastings change his use of coaching guidelines (Exhibit 6.3) from Pure Software to Netflix?

4. Which conflict management style did Hastings tend to use at Pure and Netflix?

5. In making a deal with content suppliers, which conflict management style was most likely used by Netflix?

6. How would you improve Netflix's product offerings (i.e., what things can't you watch that you would like to watch) or processes (i.e., how can it improve its delivery or service)?

CUMULATIVE CASE QUESTIONS

7. Which level or levels of analysis and leadership paradigm are presented in this case, and did Hastings use the management or leadership paradigm (Chapter 1)?

8. How did Hastings's Big Five model of personality leadership traits change from Pure Software to Netflix (Chapter 2)?

9. Which University of Iowa leadership styles did Hastings use at Pure Software and Netflix (Chapter 3)?

10. Explain how power, organizational politics, networking, and negotiation are, or are not, discussed in the case (Chapter 5)?

CASE EXERCISE AND ROLE-PLAY

Preparation: An important part of success is to continually improve products and processes. So we are going to use answers to case question 6.

In-Class Groups: Break into groups of four to six members, and develop a list of improvements for Netflix. Select a spokesperson to record the ideas and then present them to Hastings in front of the class.

Role-Play: One person from each group at a time presents the group's suggested improvements to Hastings (played by the professor or one or more students as a committee). During and/or after the presentation, Hastings and/or committee members ask questions and make comments on the ideas. Are the ideas practical? Would you consider implementing the ideas? What research would you need to make a decision?

VIDEO ▶ CASE

Communication at Navistar International

The decision to dedicate the resources needed to fund and support the Department of Communications within Navistar International sends a signal that corporate communication is seen as vital to the health of this $12 billion truck and engine manufacturing and financial services corporation. The Department of Communications functions as a business partner with the company's three major business units. Each plant has a communications manager who reports to both the plant manager and the corporate director of the Department of Communications. The role of the communications manager is to drive the message to the target audience. The manager uses different approaches depending on the audience and the direction of the message, whether it's heading up or down the corporate ladder or across business units.

1. Explain why the communication skills and techniques used within a business unit (department) are not always effective in communicating across business units or up and down the corporate ladder.

2. Explain why conflict resolution communication skills are not always present in everyday workplace situations and how a skilled communications professional would add value to that workplace.

Developing Your Leadership Skills 6-1

Giving Instructions

Doing This Exercise in Class

Objective

To develop your ability to give and receive messages (communication skills)

AACSB General Skills Area

The primary AACSB skill developed through this exercise is communication.

Preparation

No preparation is necessary except reading and understanding the chapter. The instructor will provide the original drawings that must be drawn.

Experience

You will plan, give, and receive instructions for completing a drawing of three objects.

Procedure 1 *(3–7 minutes)* Read all of procedure 1 twice. The task is for the manager to give an employee instructions for completing a drawing of four objects. The objects must be drawn to scale and look like photocopies of the originals. You will have up to 15 minutes to complete the task.

The exercise has four separate parts or steps:

1. The manager plans.

2. The manager gives the instructions.

3. The employee does the drawing.

4. Evaluation of the results takes place.

Rules: The rules are numbered to correlate with the four parts of the exercise.

1. *Planning.* While planning, the manager may write out instructions for the employee, but may not do any drawing of any kind.

2. *Instructions.* While giving instructions, the manager may not show the original drawing to the employee. (The instructor will give it to you.) The instructions may be given orally, and/or in writing, but no nonverbal hand gestures are allowed. The employee may take notes while the instructions are being given, but cannot do any drawing with or without a pen. The manager must give the instructions for all four objects before drawing begins.

3. *Drawing.* Once the employee begins the drawing, the manager should watch but no longer communicate in any way.

4. *Evaluation.* When the employee is finished or the time is up, the manager shows the employee the original drawing.

Discuss how you did. Turn to the "Integration" section of this exercise, and answer the questions. The manager, not the employee, writes the answers. The employee will write when playing the manager role.

Procedure 2 *(2–5 minutes)* Half of the class members will act as the manager first and give instructions. Managers move their seats to one of the four walls (spread out). They should be facing the center of the room with their backs close to the wall.

Employees sit in the middle of the room until called on by a manager. When called on, bring a seat to the manager. Sit facing the manager so that you cannot see any managers' drawing.

Procedure 3 *(Up to 15 minutes for drawing and integration)* The instructor gives each manager a copy of the drawing, being careful not to let any employees see it. The manager plans the instructions. When a manager is ready, she or he calls an employee and gives the instructions. It is helpful to use the message-sending process. Be sure to follow the rules. The employee should do the drawing on an 8½ by 11 sheet of paper, not in this book. If you use written instructions, they may be on the reverse side of the page that the employee draws on or on a different sheet of paper. You have up to 15 minutes to complete the drawing and about 5 minutes for integration (evaluation). When you finish the drawing, turn to the evaluation questions in the "Integration" section.

Procedure 4 *(Up to 15 minutes)* The employees are now the managers, and they sit in the seats facing the center of the room. New employees go to the center of the room until called for.

Follow procedure 3, with the instructor giving a different drawing. Do not work with the same person; change partners.

Integration

Evaluating Questions: You may select more than one answer. The manager and employee discuss each question; and the manager, not the employee, writes the answers to the questions.

1. The goal of communication was to:

   a. influence   b. inform
   c. express feelings

2. The manager transmitted the message through _____ communication channel(s).

   a. oral   b. written
   c. nonverbal   d. combined

3. The manager spent _____ time planning.

   a. too much   b. too little
   c. the right amount of

Questions 4 through 8 relate to the steps in the message-sending process.

4. The manager developed rapport. (Step 1)

   a. true   b. false

5. The manager stated the communication objective. (Step 2)

   a. true   b. false

6. The manager transmitted the message _____. (Step 3)

   a. effectively   b ineffectively

7. The manager checked understanding by using _____. (Step 4)

   a. direct questions   b. paraphrasing
   c. both   d. neither

8. The amount of checking was _____.

   a. too frequent   b. too infrequent
   c. about right

9. The manager got a commitment and followed up. (Step 5)

   a. true   b. false

10. The employee did an _____ job of listening, an job of analyzing, and an _____ job of checking understanding through the receiving message process.

    a. effective   b ineffective

11. When going over this integration, the manager was _____ and the employee was _____ to criticism that can help improve communication skills.

    a. open   b. closed

12. Were the objects drawn to approximate scale (same size)? If not, why not?

13. Did you follow the rules? If not, why not?

14. If you could do this exercise again, what would you do differently to improve communications?

Conclusion

The instructor leads a class discussion and/or makes concluding remarks.

Apply It *(2–4 minutes)* What did I learn from this experience? How will I use this knowledge in the future? When will I practice?

Behavior Model Skills Training (6-1)

Session 1

In this behavior model skills training session, you will perform four activities:

1 Complete Self-Assessment 6-3 (to determine your preferred communication style).

2 Read "The Situational Communications Model."

3 Watch Behavior Model Video 6.1, "Situational Communications."

4 Complete Developing Your Leadership Skills Exercise 6-2 (to apply the model to various situations).

For practice, use the situational communications model in your personal and professional communication.

SELF-ASSESSMENT 6-3   Determining Your Preferred Communication Style

To determine your preferred communication style, select the one alternative that most closely describes what you would do in each of the 12 situations described. Do not be concerned with trying to pick the correct answer; select the alternative that best describes what you would actually do. Circle the letter a, b, c, or d.

For now, ignore these three types of lines:

1. (before each number)
   _____ time _____ information
   _____ acceptance _____ capability
   _____ communication style
• S _____ (following each letter)

They are explained later, and will be used during the n-class part of Developing Your Leadership Skills Exercise 6-2.

1. Wendy, a knowledgeable person from another department, comes to you, the engineering supervisor, and requests that you design a special product to her specifications. You would:
   _____ time _____ information
   _____ acceptance _____ capability
   _____ communication style

   a. Control the conversation and tell Wendy what you will do for her. S _____

   b. Ask Wendy to describe the product. Once you understand it, you would present your ideas. Let

   (continued)

her realize that you are concerned and want to help by offering your ideas. S _____

c. Respond to Wendy's request by conveying under-standing and support. Help clarify what is to be done by you. Offer ideas, but do it her way. S _____

d. Find out what you need to know. Let Wendy know you will do it her way. S _____

2. Your department has designed a product that is to be fabricated by Saul's department. Saul has been with the company longer than you have; he knows his department. Saul comes to you to change the product design. You decide to:
_____ time _____ information
_____ acceptance _____ capability
_____ communication style

a. Listen to the change and why it would be beneficial. If you believe Saul's way is better, change it; if not, explain why the original design is superior. If neces-sary, insist that it be done your way. S _____

b. Tell Saul to fabricate it any way he wants to. S _____

c. You are busy; tell Saul to do it your way. You don't have time to listen and argue with him. S _____

d. Be supportive; make changes together as a team. S _____

3. Upper management has a decision to make. They call you to a meeting and tell you they need some infor-mation to solve a problem they describe to you. You:
_____ time _____ information
_____ acceptance _____ capability
_____ communication style

a. Respond in a manner that conveys personal support and offer alternative ways to solve the problem. S _____

b. Just answer their questions. S _____

c. Explain how to solve the problem. S _____

d. Show your concern by explaining how to solve the problem and why it is an effective solution. S _____

4. You have a routine work order. The work order is to be placed verbally and completed in three days. Sue, the receiver, is very experienced and willing to be of service to you. You decide to:
_____ time _____ information
_____ acceptance _____ capability
_____ communication style

a. Explain your needs, but let Sue make the order decision. S _____

b. Tell Sue what you want and why you need it. S _____

c. Decide together what to order. S _____

d. Simply give Sue the order. S _____

5. Work orders from the staff department normally take three days; however, you have an emergency and need the job today. Your colleague Jim, the department su-pervisor, is knowledgeable and somewhat cooperative. You decide to:
_____ time _____ information
_____ acceptance _____ capability
_____ communication style

a. Tell Jim that you need it by three o'clock and will return at that time to pick it up. S _____

b. Explain the situation and how the organization will benefit by expediting the order. Volunteer to help in any way you can. S _____

c. Explain the situation and ask Jim when the order will be ready. S _____

d. Explain the situation and together come to a solution to your problem. S _____

6. Danielle, a peer with a record of high performance, has recently had a drop in productivity. Her problem is affecting your performance. You know Danielle has a family problem. You:
_____ time _____ information
_____ acceptance _____ capability
_____ communication style

a. Discuss the problem; help Danielle realize the problem is affecting her work and yours. Support-ively discuss ways to improve the situation. S _____

b. Tell the manager about it and let him decide what to do about it. S _____

c. Tell Danielle to get back on the job. S _____

d. Discuss the problem and tell Danielle how to solve the work situation; be supportive. S _____

7. You are a knowledgeable supervisor. You buy sup-plies from Peter regularly. He is an excellent salesperson and very knowledgeable about your situation. You are placing your weekly order. You decide to:
_____ time _____ information
_____ acceptance _____ capability
_____ communication style

a. Explain what you want and why. Develop a supportive relationship. S _____

b. Explain what you want, and ask Peter to recommend products. S _____

c. Give Peter the order. S _____

d. Explain your situation and allow Peter to make the order. S _____

8. Jean, a knowledgeable person from another department, has asked you to perform a routine staff function to her specifications. You decide to:

   _____ time _____ information
   _____ acceptance _____ capability
   _____ communication style

   a. Perform the task to her specifications without questioning her. S _____
   b. Tell her that you will do it the usual way. S _____
   c. Explain what you will do and why. S _____
   d. Show your willingness to help; offer alternative ways to do it. S _____

9. Tom, a salesperson, has requested an order for your department's services with a short delivery date. As usual, Tom claims it is a take-it-or-leave-it offer. He wants your decision now, or within a few minutes, because he is in the customer's office. Your action is to:

   _____ time _____ information
   _____ acceptance _____ capability
   _____ communication style

   a. Convince Tom to work together to come up with a later date. S _____
   b. Give Tom a yes or no answer. S _____
   c. Explain your situation, and let Tom decide if you should take the order. S _____
   d. Offer an alternative delivery date. Work on your relationship; show your support. S _____

10. As a time-and-motion expert, you have been called regarding a complaint about the standard time it takes to perform a job. As you analyze the entire job, you realize that one element of the job should take longer, but other elements should take less time. The end result is a shorter total standard time for the job. You decide to:

    _____ time _____ information
    _____ acceptance _____ capability
    _____ communication style

    a. Tell the operator and foreman that the total time must be decreased and why. S _____
    b. Agree with the operator and increase the standard time. S _____
    c. Explain your findings. Deal with the operator and/or foreman's concerns, but ensure compliance with your new standard. S _____
    d. Together with the operator, develop a standard time. S _____

11. You approve budget allocations for projects. Marie, who is very competent in developing budgets, has come to you. You:

    _____ time _____ information
    _____ acceptance _____ capability
    _____ communication style

    a. Review the budget, make revisions, and explain them in a supportive way. Deal with concerns, but insist on your changes. S _____
    b. Review the proposal and suggest areas where changes may be needed. Make changes together, if needed. S _____
    c. Review the proposed budget, make revisions, and explain them. S _____
    d. Answer any questions or concerns Marie has and approve the budget as is. S _____

12. You are a sales manager. A customer has offered you a contract for your product, but the contract has a short delivery date—only two days. The contract would be profitable for you and the organization. The cooperation of the production department is essential to meet the deadline. Tim, the production manager, and you do not get along very well because of your repeated request for quick delivery. Your action is to:

    _____ time _____ information
    _____ acceptance _____ capability
    _____ communication style

    a. Contact Tim and try to work together to complete the contract. S _____
    b. Accept the contract and convince Tim in a supportive way to meet the obligation. S _____
    c. Contact Tim and explain the situation. Ask him if he and you should accept the contract, but let him decide. S _____
    d. Accept the contract. Contact Tim and tell him to meet the obligation. If he resists, tell him you will go to his manager. S _____

To determine your preferred communication style, do the following. (1) Circle the letter you selected as the alternative you chose in situations 1 through 12. The column headings indicate the style you selected. (2) Add up the number of circled items per column. The total for all the columns should not be more than 12. The column with the highest number represents your preferred communication style. There is no one best style in all situations. The more evenly distributed the numbers are between the four styles, the more flexible are your communications. A total of 0 or 1 in any column may indicate a reluctance to use the style(s). You could have problems in situations calling for the use of this style.

Communication has the following five dimensions, which are each on a continuum:

	Autocratic (S1A)	Consultative (S2C)	Participative (S3P)	Empowerment (S4E)
1.	a	b	c	d
2.	c	a	d	b
3.	c	d	a	b
4.	d	b	c	a
5.	a	b	d	c
6.	c	d	a	b
7.	c	a	b	d
8.	b	c	d	a
9.	b	d	a	c
10.	a	c	d	b
11.	c	a	b	d
12.	d	b	a	c
	Totals			

The Situational Communications Model

The Interactive Process System

Initiation ———————————————— **Response**

- *Initiation.* The sender starts, or initiates, the communication. The sender may or may not expect a response to the initiated message.
- *Response.* The receiver's reply or action taken to the sender's message. In responding, the receiver can become an initiator. As two-way communication takes place, the role of initiator (sender) and responder (receiver) may change.

Presentation ———————————————— **Elicitation**

- *Presentation.* The sender's message is structured, directive, or informative. A response may not be needed, although action may be called for. ("We are meeting to develop next year's budget." "Please open the door.")
- *Elicitation.* The sender invites a response to the message. Action may or may not be needed. ("How large a budget do we need?" "Do you think we should leave the door open?")

Closed ———————————————— **Open**

- *Closed.* The sender expects the receiver to follow the message. ("This is a new form to fill out and return with each order.")
- *Open.* The sender is eliciting a response as a means of considering the receiver's input. ("Should we use this new form with each order?")

Rejection ———————————————— **Acceptance**

- *Rejection.* The receiver does not accept the sender's message. ("I will not fill out this new form for each order!")
- *Acceptance.* The receiver agrees with the sender's message. ("I will fill out the new form for each order!")

Strong ———————————————— **Mild**

- *Strong.* The sender will use force or power to have the message acted upon as directed. ("Fill in the form or you're fired.")
- *Mild.* The sender will not use force or power to have the message acted upon as directed. ("Please fill in the form when you can.")

Situational Communication Styles

Following is the interactive process. Acceptance or rejection can come from any of the styles because, to a large extent, it is out of the sender's control.

The Autocratic Communication Style (S1A). This style demonstrates high task/low relationship behavior (HT-LR), initiating a closed presentation. The other party has little, if any, information and is low in capability.

- *Initiation/Response.* You initiate and control the communication with minimal, if any, response.
- *Presentation/Elicitation.* You make a presentation letting the other parties know they are expected to comply with your message; there is little, if any, elicitation.
- *Closed/Open.* You use a closed presentation; you will not consider the receiver's input.

The Consultative Communication Style (S2C). This style demonstrates high task/high relationship behavior (HT-HR), using a closed presentation for the task with an open elicitation for the relationship. The other party has moderate information and capability.

- *Initiation/Response.* You initiate the communication by letting the other party know that you want him or her to buy into your influence. You desire some response.
- *Presentation/Elicitation.* Both are used. You use elicitation to determine the goal of the communication. For example, you may ask questions to determine the situation and follow up with a presentation. When the communication goal is known, little task elicitation is needed. Relationship communication is elicited to determine the interest of the other party and acceptance of the message. The open elicitation should show your concern for the other party's point of view and motivate him or her to follow your influence.
- *Closed/Open.* You are closed to having the message accepted (task), but open to the person's feelings (relationship). Be empathetic.

The Participative Communication Style (S3P). This style demonstrates low task/high relationship behavior (LT-HR), responding with open elicitation, some initiation, and little presentation. The other party is high in information and capability.

- *Initiation/Response.* You respond with some initiation. You want to help the other party solve a problem or get him or her to help you solve one. You are helpful and convey personal support.
- *Presentation/Elicitation.* Elicitation can occur with little presentation. Your role is to elicit the other party's ideas on how to reach objectives.
- *Closed/Open.* Open communication is used. If you participate well, the other party will come to a solution you can accept. If not, you may have to reject the other party's message.

The Empowerment Communication Style (S4E). This style demonstrates low task/low relationship behavior (LT-LR), responding with the necessary open presentation. The other party is outstanding in information and capability.

- *Initiation/Response.* You respond to the other party with little, if any, initiation.
- *Presentation/Elicitation.* You present the other party with information, structure, and so forth, which the sender wants.
- *Closed/Open.* Open, you convey that the other party is in charge; you will accept the message.

Situational Variables

When selecting the appropriate communication style, you should consider four variables: time, information, acceptance, and capability. Answering the questions related to each of these variables can help you select the appropriate style for the situation.

Time. Do I have enough time to use two-way communication—yes or no? When there is no time, the other three variables are not considered; the autocratic style is appropriate. When time is available, any of the other styles may be appropriate, depending on the other variables. Time is a relative term; in one situation, a few minutes may be considered a short time —in another situation, a month may be a short time.

Information. Do I have the necessary information to communicate my message, make a decision, or take action? When you have all the information you need, the autocratic style may be appropriate. When you have some of the information, the consultative style may be appropriate. When you have little information, the participative or empowerment style may be appropriate.

Acceptance. Will the other party accept my message without any input? If the receiver will accept the message, the autocratic style may be appropriate. If the receiver will be reluctant to accept it, the consultative style may be appropriate. If the receiver will reject the message, the participative or empowerment style may be appropriate to gain acceptance. There are situations in which acceptance is critical to success, such as in the area of implementing changes.

Capability. Capability has two parts. *Ability:* Does the other party have the experience or knowledge to participate in two way communications? Will the receiver put the organization's goals ahead of personal needs or goals? *Motivation:* Does the other party want to participate? When the other party is low in capability, the autocratic style may be appropriate; moderate in capability, the consultative style may be appropriate; high in capability, the participative style may be appropriate; outstanding in capability, the empowerment style may be appropriate. In addition, capability levels can change from one task to another. For example, a professor may have outstanding capability in classroom teaching but be low in capability for advising students.

Selecting Communication Styles

Successful managers rely on different communication styles according to the situation. There are three steps to follow when selecting the appropriate communication style in a given situation. After reading these steps and looking at Model 6.6, you will get to practice this selection process in the section "Determining the Appropriate Communications Style for Situation 1."

Step 1. **Diagnose the situation.** Answer the questions for each of the four situational variables (time, information, acceptance, and capability). In Self-Assessment 6-3 at the beginning of this training session, you were asked to select an alternative to 12 situations. You were told to ignore certain lines. When completing the in-class part of Developing Your Leadership Skills Exercise 6-2, you will place the style letters (S1A, S2C, S3P, S4E) on the lines provided for each of the 12 situations.

Step 2. **Select the appropriate communication style for the situation.** After analyzing the four variables, you select the appropriate communication style for the situation. In some situations, variables may have conflicting styles; you should select the style of the most important variable

for the situation. For example, capability may be outstanding (S4E) but you have all the information needed (S1A). If the information is more important, use the autocratic style even though the capability is outstanding. When doing the in-class part of Developing Your Leadership Skills Exercise 6-2, place the letters (S1A, S2C, S3P, S4E) for the appropriate communication styles on the style lines (S _____).

Step 3. **Use the appropriate communication style for the situation.** During the in-class part of Developing Your Leadership Skills Exercise 6-2, you will identify one of the four communication styles for each alternative action; place the S1A, S2C, S3P, or S4E on the S _____ lines. Select the alternative (a, b, c, or d) that represents the appropriate communication style for each of the 12 situations, and place it on the line before the number of the situation.

Model 6.6 summarizes the material in this preparation for the exercise. Use it to determine the appropriate communication style in situation 1 and during the in-class part of Developing Your Leadership Skills Exercise 6-2.

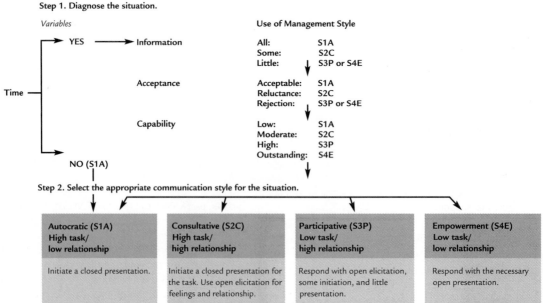

Situational Communication

MODEL 6.6

Determining the Appropriate Communication Style for Situation 1

Step 1. **Diagnose the situation.** Answer the four variable questions from the model, and place the letters on the four variable lines for situation 1.

_____ 1. Wendy, a knowledgeable person from another department, comes to you, the engineering supervisor, and requests that you design a special product to her specifications. You would:

_____ time _____ information

_____ acceptance _____ capability

_____ communication style

    a. Control the conversation and tell Wendy what you will do for her. S _____

    b. Ask Wendy to describe the product.

    Once you understand it, you would present your ideas. Let her realize that you are concerned and want to help by offering your ideas. S _____

    c. Respond to Wendy's request by conveying understanding and support. Help clarify what is to be done by you. Offer ideas, but do it her way. S _____

    d. Find out what you need to know. Let Wendy know you will do it her way. S _____

Step 2. **Select the appropriate communication style for the situation.** Review the four variables. If they are all consistent, select one style. If they are conflicting, select the most important variable as the style to use. Place its letters (S1A, S2C, S3P, or S4E) on the style line.

Step 3. **Use the appropriate communication style for the situation.** Review the four alternative actions. Identify the communication style for each,

placing its letters on the S _____ line, then place the appropriate match (a, b, c, d) on the line before the number.

Let's See How You Did

1 _Time:_ Time is available (or yes, you have time); it can be any style. _Information:_ You have little information, so you need to use a participative or empowerment style to find out what Wendy wants done (S3P or S4E). _Acceptance:_ If you try to do it your way rather than Wendy's way, she will most likely reject it. You need to use a participative or empowerment style (S3P or S4E). _Capability:_ Wendy is knowledgeable and has a high level of capability (S3P).

2 Reviewing the four variables, you see that there is a mixture of S3P and S4E. Because you are an engineer, it is appropriate to participate with Wendy to give her what she needs. Therefore, the choice is S3P.

3 Alternative (a) is S1A; this is the autocratic style, high task/ low relationship. Alternative (b) is S2C; this is the consultative style, high task/high relationship. Alternative (c) is S3P; this is the participative style, low task/high relationship. Alternative (d) is S4E; this is empowerment style, low task/low relationship behavior. If you selected (c) as your action, you chose the most appropriate action for the situation. This was a three-point answer. If you selected (d) as your answer, this is also a good alternative; it scores two points. If you selected (b), you get one point for overdirecting. If you selected (a), you get zero points; this is too much directing and will most likely hurt communications.

The better you match your communication style to the situation, the more effective you will be at communicating. In the in-class part of Developing Your Leadership Skills Exercise 6-3, you will apply the model to the other 11 situations in Self-Assessment 6-3 to develop your ability to communicate as a situational communicator.

Behavior Model Video   6-1

Situational Communications

Objectives

To better understand the four situational communication styles and which style to use in a given situation

Video (12 minutes) Overview

You will first listen to a lecture to understand how to use the situational communications model. Then, you will view two managers, Steve and Darius, meeting to discuss faulty parts. You are asked to identify the communication style Darius uses in four

different scenes. Write the letters of the style on the scene line after each scene. This may be completed as part of Developing Your Leadership Skills Exercise 6-2.

Scene 1.   Autocratic (S1A)

Scene 2.   Consultative (S2C)

Scene 3.   Participative (S3P)

Scene 4.   Empowerment (S4E)

Developing Your Leadership Skills

Situational Communications

Doing This Exercise in Class

Objectives

To develop your ability to communicate using the appropriate style for the situation

AACSB General Skills Area

The primary AACSB skills developed through this exercise are communication, using analytical thinking to select which style to use in a given situation—application of knowledge.

Preparation

You should have competed Self-Assessment 6-3, and finished the reading about situational communications. You may also want to view Behavior Model Video 6.1.

Experience

You will select the appropriate style for the 12 situations in Self-Assessment 6-3. On the *time* line, place Y (yes); on the *information*, *acceptance*, and *capability* lines, place the letters S1A, S2C, S3P, or S4E that are appropriate for the situation. Based on your diagnoses, select the one style you would use by placing its letters (S1A, S2C, S3P, or S4E) on the *communication style* line. On the four S lines, write the letters S1A, S2C, S3P, or S4E to identify each style being used. Place the letters a, b, c, or d on the line before the exercise number that represents the most appropriate communication style for the situation.

Procedure 1 *(10–20 minutes)* The instructor shows the video and then reviews the situational communications model, explaining how to apply it to determine the appropriate style for situation 2.

Procedure 2 *(4–8 minutes)* Students, working alone, complete situation 3 of Self-Assessment 6-3 using the model. The instructor then goes over the recommended answers.

Procedure 3 *(20–50 minutes)*

A. Break into groups of two or three. As a team, apply the model to situations 4 through 8. The instructor will go over the appropriate answers when all teams are finished, or the time is up.

B. Break into new groups of two or three and do situations 9 through 12. The instructor will go over the appropriate answers.

Conclusion

The instructor leads a class discussion and/or makes concluding remarks.

Apply It *(2–4 minutes)* What did I learn from this experience? How will I use this knowledge in the future? When will I practice using the model?

_____

_____

_____

Behavior Model Skills Training

Session 2

In this behavior model skills training session, you will perform three activities:

1 Read "Improving Performance with the Coaching Model" (to review how to use the model).

2 Watch Behavior Model Video 6.2, "Coaching."

3 Complete Developing Your Leadership Skills Exercise 6-3 (to develop your coaching skills).

For further practice, use the coaching model in your personal and professional life.

The Coaching Model

In the text, read about the coaching model and review Model 6.4.

Behavior Model Video

Coaching

Objective

To assist you in coaching to improve performance of employees who are not performing to standard

Video (3½ minutes) Overview

You will watch a Web development manager coach an employee who has missed deadlines for completing Web sites.

Developing Your Leadership Skills

Coaching

Preparing for This Exercise

You should have read and understood the text material on coaching. You may also view Behavior Model Video 6.2.

Doing This Exercise in Class

Objective

To develop your skill at improving performance through coaching

AACSB General Skills Area

The primary AACSB skills developed through this exercise are communication, using analytical thinking to effectively coach an employee to improve performance—application of knowledge.

Experience

You will coach, be coached, and be observed coaching using Model 6.4 from the text.

Procedure 1 *(2–4 minutes)* Break into groups of three. Make some groups of two, if necessary. Each member selects one of the following three situations in which to be the manager, and a different one in which to be the employee. In each situation, the employee knows the standing plans but is not motivated to follow them. You will take turns coaching and being coached.

Three Employee-Coaching Situations

1 *Employee 1 is a clerical worker.* The person uses paper medical files, as do the other three employees in the department. The employees all know that they are supposed to return the files when they are finished so that others can find the files when they need them. Employees should have only one file out at a time. The supervisor notices that employee 1 has five files on the desk, and another employee is looking for one of them. The supervisor thinks that employee 1 will complain about the heavy

workload as an excuse for having more than one file out at a time.

2 *Employee 2 is a server in an ice cream shop.* The person knows that the tables should be cleaned up quickly after customers leave so that new customers do not have to sit at dirty tables. It's a busy night. The supervisor finds dirty dishes on two of this employee's occupied tables. Employee 2 is socializing with some friends at one of the tables. Employees are supposed to be friendly; employee 2 will probably use this as an excuse for the dirty tables.

3 *Employee 3 is an auto technician.* All employees at the garage where this person works know that they are supposed to put a paper mat on the floor of each car so that the carpets don't get dirty. When the service supervisor got into a car repaired by employee 3, the car did not have a mat and there was grease on the carpet. Employee 3 does excellent work and will probably mention this fact when coached.

Procedure 2 *(3–7 minutes)* Prepare for coaching to improve performance. On the following lines, each group member writes an outline of what he or she will say when coaching employee 1, 2, or 3, following the coaching steps listed:

1 Describe current performance. _____

_____

_____

2 Describe the desired behavior. _____

_____

_____

3 Get a commitment to the change. _____

_____

_____

④ Follow up. _____
_____
_____

Procedure 3 *(5–8 minutes)*

- Role-playing. The manager of employee 1, the clerical worker, coaches him or her as planned. (Use the actual name of the group member playing employee 1. Talk— do not read your written plan.) Employee 1, put yourself in the worker's position. You work hard; there is a lot of pressure to work fast. It's easier when you have more than one file. Refer to the workload while being coached. Both the manager and the employee will have to improvise their roles.

The person not playing a role is the observer. He or she takes notes using the observer form. Try to make positive coaching feedback comments for improvement. Give the manager alternative suggestions for what he or she could have said to improve the coaching session.

Observer Form

① How well did the manager describe current behavior?
_____
_____
_____

② How well did the manager describe desired behavior?
_____
_____
_____

③ How successful was the manager at getting a commitment to the change? Do you think the employee would change?
_____
_____
_____

④ How well did the manager describe how he or she was going to follow up to ensure that the employee performed the desired behavior?
_____
_____
_____

- Feedback. The observer leads a discussion on how well the manager coached the employee. (This should be a coaching discussion, not a lecture.) Focus on what the manager did well, and on how the manager could improve. The employee should also give feedback on how he or she felt, and what might have been more effective in getting him or her to change.

Do not go on to the next interview until you are told to do so. If you finish early, wait for the others to finish.

Procedure 4 *(5–8 minutes)* Same as procedure 3, but change roles so that employee 2, the server, is coached. Employee 2 should make a comment about the importance of talking to customers to make them feel welcome. The job is not much fun if you can't talk to your friends.

Procedure 5 *(5–8 minutes)* Same as procedure 3, but change roles so that employee 3, the auto technician, is coached. Employee 3 should comment on the excellent work he or she does.

Conclusion

The instructor leads a class discussion and makes concluding remarks.

Apply It *(2–4 minutes)* What did I learn from this experience? How will I use this knowledge in the future? When will I practice?
_____
_____
_____

Developing Your Leadership Skills **6-4**

Session 3

In this behavior model skills training session, you will perform three activities:

① Read "Initiating Conflict Resolution" to review how to use the model.

② Watch Behavior Model Video 6.3, "Initiating Conflict Resolution."

③ Complete Developing Your Leadership Skills Exercise 6-4 (to develop your conflict resolution skills).

For further practice, use the conflict resolution model in your personal and professional life.

The Initiating Conflict Resolution Model **6-5**

In the text, read the initiating conflict resolution model and review Model 6.5.

Behavior Model Video **6-3**

Initiating Conflict Resolution

Objective

To assist you in resolving conflicts

Video (4½ minutes) Overview

You will watch an advertising agency's employees. Alex initiates a conflict resolution with Catherine to resolve a conflict over a client.

Developing Your Leadership Skills **6-5**

Initiating Conflict Resolution

Preparing for This Exercise

During class you will be given the opportunity to role-play a conflict you face, or have faced, to develop your conflict skills. Students and workers have reported that this exercise helped prepare them for a successful initiation of a conflict resolution with roommates and coworkers. Fill in the following information.

Other party(ies). (You may use fictitious names.)

_____

Describe the conflict situation:

_____

List pertinent information about the other party (i.e., relationship with you, knowledge of the situation, age, background, etc.).

_____

_____

_____

Identify the other party's possible reaction to your confrontation. (How receptive will they be to collaborating? What might they say or do during the discussion to resist change?)

_____

_____

How will you overcome this resistance to change?

_____

_____

_____

Following the initiating conflict resolution model steps, write out your planned opening BCF statement that maintains ownership of the problem.

_____

_____

_____

Doing This Exercise in Class

Objective

To experience and develop skills in resolving a conflict.

AACSB General Skills Area

The primary AACSB skills developed through this exercise are communication, using analytical thinking to select which style to resolve a conflict—application of knowledge.

Preparation

You should have completed the questionnaire in Developing Your Leadership Skills Exercise 6-4.

Experience

You will initiate, respond to, and observe a conflict role-play, and then evaluate the effectiveness of its resolution.

Procedure 1 *(2–3 minutes)* Break into as many groups of three as possible. If there are any people not in a triad, make one or two groups of two. Each member selects the number 1, 2, or 3. Number 1 will be the first to initiate a conflict role-play, then 2, followed by 3.

Procedure 2 *(8–15 minutes)*

1 Initiator number 1 gives his or her information from the preparation to number 2 (the responder) to read. Once number 2 understands, proceed with role-play (see item B). Number 3 is the observer.

2 Role-play the conflict resolution. Number 3, the observer, writes his or her observations on the feedback form at the end of this exercise.

3 Integration. When the role-play is over, the observer leads a discussion on the effectiveness of the conflict resolution. All three should discuss the effectiveness. Number 3 is not a lecturer. Do not go on until told to do so.

Procedure 3 *(8–15 minutes)* Same as procedure 2, only number 2 is now the initiator, number 3 is the responder, and number 1 is the observer.

Procedure 4 *(8–15 minutes)* Same as procedure 2, only number 3 is the initiator, number 1 is the responder, and number 2 is the observer.

Conclusion

The instructor leads a class discussion and/or makes concluding remarks.

Apply It *(2–4 minutes)* What did I learn from this experience? How will I use this knowledge in the future? When will I practice?

_____

_____

_____

Feedback Form

Try to have positive coaching improvement feedback comments for each step in initiating conflict resolution. Remember to be *specific* and *descriptive*, and for all improvements have an alternative positive behavior (APB). (For example: "If you would have said/done…, it would have improved the conflict resolution by …")

Initiating Conflict Resolution Model Steps

Step 1. **Plan a BCF statement that maintains ownership of the problem.** (Did the initiator have a well-planned, effective BCF statement?)

_____

_____

_____

_____

Step 2. **Present your BCF statement and agree on the conflict.** (Did the initiator present the BCF statement effectively? Did the two agree on the conflict?)

_____

_____

_____

_____

Step 3. **Ask for, and/or give, alternative conflict resolutions.** (Who suggested alternative solutions? Was it done effectively?)

_____

_____

_____

_____

Step 4. **Make an agreement for change.** (Was there an agreement for change?)

_____

_____

_____

_____

Behavior Model Video   **6-4**

Mediating Conflict Resolution

Objective

To view the process of mediating a conflict resolution between employees.

Video *(6½ minutes)* Overview

This is a follow-up to the advertising agency conflict (Video 6.3). The two employees end up in conflict again. Their manager, Peter,

brings them together to resolve the conflict by following the steps in "Mediating Conflict Resolution" (Model 6.5).

Note: There is no skill-development exercise.

Endnotes

1. Information taken from personal interviews with the Clarks and The Ranch Web site: http://www.theranchgolfclub.com, accessed February 18, 2014.

2. B.L. Blume, T.T. Baldwin, & K.C. Ryan, "Communication Apprehension: A Barrier to Students' Leadership, Adaptability, and Multicultural Appreciation," *Academy of Management Learning & Education* 12(2) (2013): 158–172.

3. A. Simha & J.B. Cullen, "Ethical Climates and Their Effects on Organizational Outcomes: Implications from the Past and Prophecies for the Future," *Academy of Management Perspectives* 26(4) (2012): 20–34.

4. S.B. Sitkin & J.R. Hackman, "Developing Team Leadership: An Interview with Coach Mike Krzyzewski," *Academy of Management Learning & Education* 10(3) (2011): 494–501.

5. L.P. Tost, F. Gino, & R.P. Larrick, "When Power Makes Others Speechless: The Negative Impact of Leader Power on Team Performance," *Academy of Management Journal* 56(5) (2013): 1465–1486.

6. C.R. Long, C. Bendersky, & C. Morrill, "Fairness Monitoring: Linking Managerial Controls and Fairness Judgments in Organizations," *Academy of Management Journal* 54(5) (2011): 1045–1056.

7. A. Edmans, "The Link between Job Satisfaction and Firm Value, with Implications for Corporate Social Responsibility," *Academy of Management Perspectives* 26(4) (2012): 1–19.

8. P. Puranam, M. Raveendran, & T. Knudsen, "Organization Design: The Epistemic Interdependence Perspective," *Academy of Management Review* 37(3) (2012): 419–440.

9. M. Orlitzky, "Corporate Social Responsibility, Noise, and Stock Market Volatility," *Academy of Management Perspectives* 27(3) (2013): 238–254.

10. N.M. Pless, T. Moak, & D.A. Waldman, "Different Approaches toward Doing the Right Thing: Mapping the Responsibility Orientations of Leaders," *Academy of Management Perspectives* 26(4) (2012): 51–65.

11. M. Mazmania, "Avoiding the Trap of Constant Connectivity: When Congruent Frames Allow for Heterogeneous Practices," *Academy of Management Journal* 56(5) (2013): 1225–1250.

12. L. Ramarajan & E. Reid, "Shattering the Myth of Separate Worlds: Negotiating Nonwork Identities at Work," *Academy of Management Review* 38(4) (2013): 621–644.

13. B. Schyns, T. Kiefer, R. Kerschreiter, and A. Tymon, "Teaching Implicit Leadership Theories to Develop Leaders and Leadership: How and Why It Can Make a Difference," *Academy of Management Learning & Education* 10(3) (2012): 397–408.

14. P. Andruss, "How the Great Ones Got Great," *Entrepreneur* (December 2013): 64.

15. E. Glazer, "Problem—and—Solutions," *Wall Street Journal* (October 24, 2011): R2.

16. W.M. Murphy, "From E-Mentoring to Blended Mentoring: Increasing Students' Developmental Initiation and Mentors' Satisfaction," *Academy of Management Learning & Education* 10(4) (2011): 606–622.

17. A.O. Malaterre, N.P. Rothbard, & J.M. Berg, "When Worlds Collide in Cyberspace: How Boundary Work in Online Social Networks Impacts Professional Relationships," *Academy of Management Review* 38(4) (2013): 645–669.

18. S.B. Sitkin & J.R. Hackman, "Developing Team Leadership: An Interview with Coach Mike Krzyzewski," *Academy of Management Learning & Education* 10(3) (2011): 494–501.

19. B.L. Blume, T.T. Baldwin, & K.C. Ryan, "Communication Apprehension: A Barrier to Students' Leadership, Adaptability, and Multicultural Appreciation," *Academy of Management Learning & Education* 12(2) (2013): 158–172.

20. B.L. Blume, T.T. Baldwin, & K.C. Ryan, "Communication Apprehension: A Barrier to Students' Leadership, Adaptability, and Multicultural Appreciation," *Academy of Management Learning & Education* 12(2) (2013): 158–172.

21. J.B. Oldroyd & S.S. Morris, "Catching Falling Stars: A Human Resource Response to Social Capital's Detrimental Effect of Information Overload on Start Employees," *Academy of Management Review* 37(3) (2012): 396–418.

22. M. Mazmania, "Avoiding the Trap of Constant Connectivity: When Congruent Frames Allow for Heterogeneous Practices," *Academy of Management Journal* 56(5) (2013): 1225–1250.

23. C.R. Long, C. Bendersky, & C. Morrill, "Fairness Monitoring: Linking Managerial Controls and Fairness Judgments in Organizations," *Academy of Management Journal* 54(5) (2011): 1045–1068.

24. H.A. Richardson & S.G. Taylor, "Understanding Input Events: A Model of Employees' Responses to Requests for Their Input," *Academy of Management Review* 37(3) (2012): 471–491.

25. L.T. Madden, D. Duchon, T.M. Madden, & D.A. Plowman, "Emergent Organizational Capacity for Compassion," *Academy of Management Review* 37(4) (2012): 689–708.

26 Public Radio, News Broadcast, WFCR 88.5, aired May 28, 2010.

27 B. Benjamin & C. O'Reilly, "Becoming a Leader: Early Career Challenges Faced by MBA Graduates," *Academy of Management Learning & Education 10*(3) (2011): 452–472.

28 S.B. Sitkin & J.R. Hackman, "Developing Team Leadership: An Interview with Coach Mike Krzyzewski," *Academy of Management Learning & Education 10*(3) (2011), 494–501.

29 M. Feys, F. Anseel, & B. Wille, "Improving Feedback Reports: The Role of Procedural Information and Information Specificity," *Academy of Management Learning & Education 10*(4) (2011): 661–681.

30 A.H. Jordan & P.G. Audia, "Self-Enhancement and Learning from Performance Feedback," *Academy of Management Review 37*(2) (2012): 211–231.

31 R.L. Dufresne & E.H. Offstein, "Holistic and Intentional Student Character Development Process: Learning from West Point," *Academy of Management Learning & Education 11*(4) (2012): 570–590.

32 A. Edmans, "The Link between Job Satisfaction and Firm Value, with Implications for Corporate Social Responsibility," *Academy of Management Perspectives 26*(4) (2012): 1–19.

33 A.H. Jordan & P.G. Audia, "Self-Enhancement and Learning from Performance Feedback," *Academy of Management Review 37*(2) (2012): 211–231.

34 S. Shellenbarger, "Shouting Is Less Tolerated in the Workplace, but Nasty Emails and Other Ways of Venting Take a Toll," *Wall Street Journal* (August 15, 2012): D1, D2.

35 M. Mayo, M. Kakarika, J.C. Pastor, & S. Brutus, "Aligning or Inflating Your Leadership Self-Image? A Longitudinal Study of Responses to Peer Feedback in MBA Teams," *Academy of Management Learning & Education 11*(4) (2012): 631–652.

36 R.L. Dufresne & E.H. Offstein, "Holistic and Intentional Student Character Development Process: Learning from West Point," *Academy of Management Learning & Education 11*(4) (2012): 570–590.

37 T.T. Baldwin, J.R. Pierce, R.C. Jones, & S. Farouk, "The Elusiveness of Applied Management Knowledge: A Critical Challenge for Management Education," *Academy of Management Learning & Education 10*(4) (2011): 583–605.

38 "Need Coaching?" *HR Magazine* (February 2013): 66.

39 J. Pfeffer, "Don't Dismiss Office Politics—Teach It," *Wall Street Journal* (October 24, 2011): R6.

40 T. Lenski, "Talk It Out," *BusinessWeek* (December 10–16, 2012): 85.

41 R.L. Dufresne & E.H. Offstein, "Holistic and Intentional Student Character Development Process: Learning from West Point," *Academy of Management Learning & Education 11*(4) (2012): 570–590.

42 J. Pfeffer, "Don't Dismiss Office Politics—Teach It," *Wall Street Journal* (October 24, 2011): R6.

43 T.T. Baldwin, J.R. Pierce, R.C. Jones, & S. Farouk, "The Elusiveness of Applied Management Knowledge: A Critical Challenge for Management Education," *Academy of Management Learning & Education 10*(4) (2011): 583–605.

44 S. Shellenbarger, "Shouting Is Less Tolerated in the Workplace, but Nasty Emails and Other Ways of Venting Take a Toll," *Wall Street Journal* (August 15, 2012): D1, D2.

45 M. Feys, F. Anseel, & B. Wille, "Improving Feedback Reports: The Role of Procedural Information and Information Specificity," *Academy of Management Learning & Education 10*(4) (2011): 661–681.

46 A.H. Jordan & P.G. Audia, "Self-Enhancement and Learning from Performance Feedback," *Academy of Management Review 37*(2) (2012): 211–231.

47 R.L. Dufresne & E.H. Offstein, "Holistic and Intentional Student Character Development Process: Learning from West Point," *Academy of Management Learning & Education 11*(4) (2012): 570–590.

48 A.H. Jordan & P.G. Audia, "Self-Enhancement and Learning from Performance Feedback," *Academy of Management Review 37*(2) (2012): 211–231.

49 P.B. Lester, S.T. Hannah, P.D. Harms, G.R. Vogelgesang, & B.J. Avolio, "Mentoring Impact on Leader Efficacy Development: A Field Experiment," *Academy of Management Learning & Education 10*(3) (2012): 409–429.

50 Staff, "Success with Help," *Entrepreneur* (December 2013): 64.

51 Staff, "Success with Help," *Entrepreneur* (December 2013): 64.

52 W.M. Murphy, "From E-Mentoring to Blended Mentoring: Increasing Students' Developmental Initiation and Mentors' Satisfaction," *Academy of Management Learning & Education 10*(4) (2011): 606–622.

53 R. Fehr & M.J. Gelfand, "The Forgiving Organization: A Multilevel Model of Forgiveness at Work," *Academy of Management Review 37*(4) (2012): 664–688.

54 B. Benjamin & C. O'Reilly, "Becoming a Leader: Early Career Challenges Faced by MBA Graduates," *Academy of Management Learning & Education 10*(3) (2011): 452–472.

55 T.T. Baldwin, J.R. Pierce, R.C. Jones, & S. Farouk, "The Elusiveness of Applied Management Knowledge: A Critical Challenge for Management Education," *Academy of Management Learning & Education* 10(4) (2011): 583–605.

56 R. Fehr & M.J. Gelfand, "The Forgiving Organization: A Multilevel Model of Forgiveness at Work," *Academy of Management Review* 37(4) (2012): 664–688.

57 S. Shellenbarger, "Shouting Is Less Tolerated in the Workplace, but Nasty Emails and Other Ways of Venting Take a Toll," *Wall Street Journal* (August 15, 2012): D1, D2.

58 M.A. Hogg, D. Van Knippenberg, & D.E. Rast, "Intergroup Leadership in Organizations: Leading across Group and Organizational Boundaries," *Academy of Management Review* 37(2) (2012): 232–255.

59 A.H. Van De Ven & A. Fifschitz, "Rational and Reasonable Microfoundations of Markets and Institutions," *Academy of Management Perspectives* 27(2) (2013): 156–172.

60 T. Lenski, "Talk It Out," *BusinessWeek* (December 10–16, 2012): 85.

61 B. Benjamin & C. O'Reilly, "Becoming a Leader: Early Career Challenges Faced by MBA Graduates," *Academy of Management Learning & Education* 10(3) (2011): 452–472.

62 M.A. Hogg, D. Van Knippenberg, & D.E. Rast, "Intergroup Leadership in Organizations: Leading across Group and Organizational Boundaries," *Academy of Management Review* 37(2) (2012): 232–255.

63 R. Fehr & M.J. Gelfand, "The Forgiving Organization: A Multilevel Model of Forgiveness at Work," *Academy of Management Review* 37(4) (2012): 664–688.

64 T. Lenski, "Talk It Out," *BusinessWeek* (December 10–16, 2012): 85.

65 A.M. Grant & S.V. Patil, "Challenging the Norm of Self-Interest: Minority Influence and Transitions to Helping Norms in Work Units," *Academy of Management Review* 37(4) (2012): 547–568.

66 R. Fehr & M.J. Gelfand, "The Forgiving Organization: A Multilevel Model of Forgiveness at Work," *Academy of Management Review* 37(4) (2012): 664–688.

67 A.H. Van De Ven & A. Fifschitz, "Rational and Reasonable Microfoundations of Markets and Institutions," *Academy of Management Perspectives* 27(2) (2013): 156–172.

68 S. Shellenbarger, "Shouting Is Less Tolerated in the Workplace, but Nasty Emails and Other Ways of Venting Take a Toll," *Wall Street Journal* (August 15, 2012): D1, D2.

69 S. Shellenbarger, "Shouting Is Less Tolerated in the Workplace, but Nasty Emails and Other Ways of Venting Take a Toll," *Wall Street Journal* (August 15, 2012): D1, D2.

70 L. P. Tost, F. Gino, & R.P. Larrick, "When Power Makes Others Speechless: The Negative Impact of Leader Power on Team Performance," *Academy of Management Journal* 56(5) (2013): 1465–1486.

71 C. Suddath, "The Art of Haggling," *BusinessWeek* (November 26–December 2, 2012): 98.

72 One of the authors uses this technique at work.

73 T. Lenski, "Talk It Out," *BusinessWeek* (December 10–16, 2012): 85.

74 R. Fehr & M.J. Gelfand, "The Forgiving Organization: A Multilevel Model of Forgiveness at Work," *Academy of Management Review* 37(4) (2012): 664–688.

75 M.V. Copeland, "Reed Hastings: Leader of the Pack," *Fortune* (December 6, 2010): 212–130.

76 Staff, "Being Reed Hastings," *Forbes* (January 20, 2014): 16.

77 M. Adamo & C. Leahey, "The List: 2013's Top People in Business," *Fortune* (December 9, 2013): 90–96.

78 R. Grover, D. Edwards, & A. Fixmer, "Can Netflix Find Its Future by Abandoning the Past?" *BusinessWeek* (September 26–October 2, 2011): 29–30.

79 Staff, "Being Reed Hastings," *Forbes* (January 20, 2014): 16.

80 R. Ebert, "Don't Bash My Netflix," *BusinessWeek* (October 3–9, 2011): 113.

81 C. Edwards, A. Pringle, & N. Summers, "The Battle over Netflix," *BusinessWeek* (November 11–17, 2013): 49–50.

82 S. Schechner & A. Sharma, "Europe's Media Giants Prep for Netflix Landing," *Wall Street Journal* (January 29, 2014): A1.

83 M. Jarzemsky, "Netflix to Enter Latin America," *Wall Street Journal* (July 6, 2011): B5.

84 M. Jarzemsky, "Netflix to Enter Latin America," *Wall Street Journal* (July 6, 2011): B5.

85 M. Jarzemsky, "Netflix to Enter Latin America," *Wall Street Journal* (July 6, 2011): B5.

86 S. Ramachandran, "Netflix Will Pay Comcast for Speed," *Wall Street Journal* (February 24, 2014): A1.

87 S. Schechner & A. Sharma, "Europe's Media Giants Prep for Netflix Landing," *Wall Street Journal* (January 29, 2014): A1.

Leader–Member Exchange and Followership

Learning Outcomes

After studying this chapter, you should be able to:

1 Describe the two subgroups that can form under Vertical Dyadic Linkage Theory. p. 232

2 Define the two kinds of relationships that can occur between a leader and followers under Leader–Member Exchange Theory. p. 234

3 Describe the role of the leader and follower in influencing LMX relationships. p. 235

4 Discuss the main Criticisms of LMX Theory. p. 238

5 Describe the two behaviors identified in the Kelley Model and the resulting five follower types. p. 240

6 Briefly describe the three factors than can enhance a follower's influence. p. 246

7 List five things a leader should delegate. p. 250

8 An effective evaluation should accomplish at least three things. Name them. p. 253

OPENING CASE Application

Mark Zuckerberg—Facebook Founder and CEO

In 2010, Zuckerberg was named *Time* magazine's Person of the Year. Since then, much has changed in terms of his leadership performance. The company's stock hit an all-time high (above $50) in October 2013 after falling to just $18 a year ago. This has been due to strong 2013 quarterly earnings reports in which the company has steadily beaten analysts' estimates.

According to its latest survey, career site Glassdoor, named Mark Zuckerberg No. 1 on its list of Top 50 CEOs in 2013. Facebook employees gave Mark Zuckerberg a 99 percent approval rating for his role as CEO of the company. Zuckerberg replace Apple's Tim Cook, who came in first in 2012. Zuckerberg's ratings rose from 85 percent last year, while Cook's dropped to 93 percent from 97 percent. According to Glassdoor, CEO approval ratings are calculated similar to Presidential approval ratings; employees are asked: "Do you approve or disapprove of the way your CEO is leading the company?" Current and former employees described Facebook as an "intense and fun," "awesome," "amazing," and "fantastic" place to work—this in keeping with the way Zuckerberg relates with his staff. He does not have one of those plush executive suites typical of corporate CEOs. His desk is near the middle of the office, within arm's length of his most senior employees. He is said to be a hands-on-type leader. His best friends are his staff; there are no separate offices. Zuckerberg, it is said, loves being around people—a far cry from the shy recluse that he has been portrayed to be.

Facebook has been able to recruit and hire some of the best minds in the industry. According to one analyst, everyone at Facebook was a star in their previous employment. "You don't get a lot of shy, retiring types at Facebook," said one writer. These are intelligent, experienced, productive and highly sought-after talents, "power nerds" for sure. Debate is the hallmark of staff meetings at Facebook and employees describe what an intense listener Zuckerberg is during these debates. It is said that he is often one of the last persons to leave the office.[1]

OPENING CASE QUESTIONS:

1. Describe the quality of the LMX relationship between Mark Zuckerberg and his followers?

2. What leadership qualities does Mark Zuckerberg possess, and how have these qualities influenced the quality of LMX relationships at Facebook?

3. According to the followership model of follower types, what types of followers has Facebook generally attracted?

4. The text discusses factors that can determine follower influence; when applied to Facebook employees, which factor(s) in your opinion stands out?

Can you answer any of these questions? You'll find answers to these questions and learn more about Mark Zuckerberg and his leadership approach throughout the chapter.

To learn more about Mark Zuckerberg and Facebook, visit the company's Web site at http://www.facebook.com.

There is ample research support for the proposition that effective leadership is a function of the interactions between leaders and followers.[2] Leadership and followership represent active and dynamic roles in every level of organizational functions.[3] In this chapter, you will explore the intricate nature of the relationship between a leader and a follower. The relationship that develops between a follower and the leader does influence the follower's job satisfaction, commitment, and performance.[4] Often one of the reasons given for why employees quit their jobs is the lack of a good working relationship with the leader.[5] In fact, for a new employee, leader–member exchange (LMX) acts as an important mediator in explaining his/her attachment to the job and organization.[6] There is evidence from the literature showing that a high LMX relationship does indeed enhance follower organizational commitment and decreases their likelihood of quitting the job.[7,8,9,10]

We will discuss leader–member exchange (LMX) theory and followership. The chapter concludes with a discussion of delegation, including a model that can help you develop your delegation skills.

From Vertical Dyadic Linkage Theory to Leader–Member Exchange Theory

For decades, the nature of the exchange relationship between a leader and a follower has been a topic of much interest for scholars and practitioners alike.[11] [12] Some have suggested that it is one of the most important relationships for followers, arguing that the quality of the social exchange between a leader and a follower is be more predictive of follower outcomes than traits or behaviors of leaders.[13] [14] [15]

Vertical dyadic linkage (VDL) theory focuses on the notion that the state of the relationship (or linkage) between a leader and a follower can affect the leadership process. It focuses attention on follower participation and influence in the decision-making process.[16] In the 1980s, this theory was renamed leader–member exchange (LMX) theory.[17] We take a closer look at VDL theory and its evolution to leader–member exchange theory.

 Learning Outcome **1**   *Describe the two subgroups that can form under the vertical dyadic linkage theory.*

Vertical Dyadic Linkage Theory

Leader–follower interactions have come to be viewed as a function of dyadic characteristics.[18] Supporters of VDL theory believe that leadership is better understood by examining dyads (pairs of relations) made up of a leader and a follower (a vertical hierarchy) rather than a focus on Average Leadership Style (ALS), which in effect held that all subordinates are treated equally.[19] A **dyad** is defined as *the individualized relationship between a leader and each follower in a work unit.* Dyadic relationships and work roles are developed and negotiated over time through a series of exchanges between leader and member. For instance, many aspects of organizational life such as the employment interview, mentoring, negotiation, coaching, conflict management, and performance evaluation inherently involve dyadic relationships and interactions between a leader and a follower.[20] As such, it is important to understand the nature of these relationships.

Dyadic theory *approaches leadership as an exchange relationship that develops between a leader and a follower over time during role-making activities.* VDL theory focuses on the heterogeneity of dyadic relationships, arguing that a single leader will form different relationships with different followers. Such differential treatment by a leader creates situations in which the leader treats the various members of his/her work unit or team differently. The leader treats followers differently on social or task-related aspects of employment and distributes resources and rewards differently.[21] With a select subset of followers known as the *in-group,* the leader perceives them as competent, trustworthy, and motivated to work hard and accept responsibility. With others known as the *out-group,* the leader does not see them as possessing these traits.[22] It is the "similarity-attraction" phenomenon.

The **in-group** *includes followers with strong social ties to their leader in a supportive relationship characterized by high mutual trust, respect, loyalty, and influence.* The leader is inclined to assign responsibility for important tasks to members of the in-group. The knowledge that in-group members are those willing to go out of their

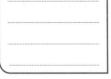

WORK
Application **7-1**

Recall a work unit or organization you worked at that had both in-groups and out-groups. Describe some of the ways in which the manager's behavior and actions toward in-group and out-group members varied.

----

way to help the leader makes him/her feel grateful and thus the desire by the leader to reciprocate.[23] The leader is more likely to offer strong support, positive feedback, and high consideration to in-group followers. The governing principle for in-group members is expanded to include a social contract. Leaders primarily use expert, referent, and reward power to influence members of the in-group.

The **out-group** *includes followers with few or no social ties to their leader, in a strictly task-centered relationship characterized by low exchange and top-down influence.* The leader is less inclined to involve out-group members in major decisions or give them significant responsibilities. Leaders mostly use position power to influence out-group members. Out-group members are more likely to be managed according to the requirements of the employment contract and the leader's formal authority. As long as such compliance is forthcoming, the out-group follower receives the standard benefits for the job (such as a salary) and no more.[24] Before we begin, determine the dyadic relationship with your manager by completing Self-Assessment 7-1.

OPENING CASE Application

I. Describe the quality of the LMX relationship between Mark Zuckerberg and his followers?

As mentioned in the case, his best friends are his staff. It is said that he loves being around people. His desk is near the middle of the office, within arm's length of his most senior employees. He is said to be a hands-on-type leader. Debate is the hallmark of staff meetings at Facebook, and employees describe what an intense listener Zuckerberg is during these debates. From this description, it's a good bet that Mr. Zuckerberg has a high quality LMX relationship with his followers.

SELF-ASSESSMENT 7-1   Dyadic Relationship with Your Manager

Select a present or past manager and answer each question describing your relationship using the following scale:

1	—	2	—	3	—	4	—	5
Is descriptive of our relationship						*Is not descriptive of our relationship*		

_____ 1. I have quick, easy access to talk with my manager anytime I want to.

_____ 2. I get along well with my manager.

_____ 3. I can influence my manager to get things done my way—to get what I want.

_____ 4. When I interact with my manager, our conversation is often relationship-oriented (we talk on a personal level), rather than just task-oriented (we talk only about the job).

_____ 5. We have a loyal, trusting relationship. We look out for each other's interest.

_____ 6. My manager understands my job and the problems that I face; he or she appreciates the work I do.

_____ 7. My manager recognizes my potential and gives me opportunities to grow on the job.

_____ 8. My manager listens carefully to what I have to say and seeks my advice.

_____ 9. My manager gives me good performance evaluations.

_____ 10. My manager gives me rewards (raises and other perks) in excess of the minimum. Add up the numbers on lines 1 through 10 and place your score here and on the continuum below.

10	—	20	—	30	—	40	—	50
In-group								*Out-group*

The lower your score, the more characteristic your relationship is of the in-group.

CONCEPT APPLICATION 7-1

In-Groups versus Out-Groups

From each of the following statements from a subordinate, identify the group to which he or she belongs. Write the appropriate letter in the blank before each item.

a. in-group   b. out-group

____   1. My boss helps me fulfill some of my social or personal goals.

____   2. I am highly committed to and energized by my work and organization and therefore, I am reciprocating with my best ideas and performance.

____   3. I seldom have any direct contact with my boss unless something is wrong with the way I have done my job.

____   4. For fear of being criticized, I do not take the initiative to seek out and successfully complete assignments that go above and beyond your job.

____   5. I do help out my boss, making him look good, even when I don't get any credit.

Learning Outcome 2   *Define the two kinds of relationships that can occur between a leader and followers under leader–member exchange theory.*

Leader–Member Exchange (LMX) Theory

LMX focuses on the *quality of the exchange relationship* that develops between leaders and followers. Therefore, we define **leader–member exchange (LMX)** *as the quality of the exchange relationship between a leader and a follower.*[25] The underlying assumption of LMX theory is that leaders or superiors have limited amounts of social, personal, and organizational resources (such as energy, time, attention, and discretion) and as a result tend to distribute them among followers selectively. Leaders do not always have positive relationships with all followers, which ultimately results in the formation of LMX exchanges that vary in quality. Leaders form *high-quality social exchanges* (based on trust and liking) with some members and *low-quality economic exchanges* with others.[26][27] The low-quality LMX relationship does not extend beyond the formal employment contract.[28] Such differentiated leadership does affect individual and organizational effectiveness.

The theory predicts that followers in high-quality relationships with the leader will experience positive outcomes such as higher job satisfaction, better performance, lower turnover, greater commitment, creativity, innovation and organizational citizenship behavior.[29]

YOU Make the ETHICAL Call

7.1 LMX at Work

Leader–member exchange theory states that in each work group some employees belong to the in-group and others belong to the out-group. Think about your present or past employment. Can you identify members of the in-group and the out-group? Which group were you in?

1. Is it ethical to exclude employees from the in-group?

2. Do you think people in the in-group tend to think exclusion is ethical and those in the out-group tend to think it is unethical?

3. Is your answer to question I based on whether you were a member of the in-group or the out-group?

4. Is it possible for all employees to be in the in-group?

5. Should managers work to overcome LMX theory by including all employees in the in-group?

OPENING CASE Application

2. What leadership qualities does Mark Zuckerberg possess, and how have these qualities influenced the quality of LMX relationship at Facebook?

Zuckerberg is close to all his employees. He is sociable and considerate. He has created a work environment that does not reflect rankings in the organizational hierarchy. He does not have one of those plush executive suites typical of corporate CEO offices. He maintains an office location that keeps him physically close to his most senior employees. This symbolic gesture conveys a sense of camaraderie and teamwork to his associates. He has earned the trust and respect of his coworkers, so much so that they they're adamant in their avowals of affection for him. He is seen as a leader with high integrity, intelligence, and self-confidence. It seems the quality of the exchange relationship between Zuckerberg and his followers is quite high.

CONCEPT APPLICATION 7-2

From VDL to LMX

Which concept is described by the following statements? Write the appropriate letter in the blank before each item.

a. vertical dyadic linkage theory   b. leader–member exchange theory

____ 6. The notion that leaders do not interact with all followers equally but rather focus on the formation of relationships that varies in quality.

____ 7. A theory in which leadership is better understood by examining pairs of relations made up of a leader and a follower.

____ 8. A hierarchical relationship in which leader–follower dyads (or pairs) develops.

____ 9. A relationship in which leader–follower interactions do lead to the creation of in-groups and out-groups.

Learning Outcome **3**   *Describe the role of the leader and follower in influencing LMX relationships.*

Factors That Influence LMX Relationships

LMX relationships are based on social exchanges, meaning that there is reciprocity.[30] Each party must contribute something that is valued by the other party. According to LMX theory, a leader varies his or her behavior according to the quality of the interpersonal relationship with each individual. Within the same work unit, there may exist a

WORK
Application **7-2**

Recall a work
situation in which
you were required
to do something
that was beyond
your employment
contract. How did
you respond to your
manager's request, and
what consequences
did it have on your
relationship with
him or her?

wide variation in the quality of each dyadic relationship.[31] It takes at least two parties to form a relationship, and for our purpose the two parties will be the leader and the follower. Each plays a role in influencing the relationship that ensues between them. Therefore, we will examine the role of the leader and the follower in influencing the exchange relationship.

The Role of the Leader

The leader's ability or willingness to develop a working relationship with a follower that goes beyond an economic-based exchange (which is strictly contractual in nature) to a socially based exchange relationship (characterized by friendship, mutual trust, loyalty, and respect between the leader and the follower) is critical in influencing the LMX relationship. Followers associated with the latter are more likely to exhibit greater organizational citizenship behavior (OCB).[32] **Organizational citizenship behavior** is defined as *individual behavior that is discretionary, not directly or explicitly recognized by the formal reward system, and that in the aggregate promotes the effective functioning of the organization.*[33] It is behavior that goes above and beyond the expected duties of an employee. Followers perceived by the leader to be hard working and willing to go the extra mile tend to have a higher-quality exchange relationship with the leader than those who are perceived to be lazy or unwilling to go the extra mile for the leader.

A leader's resource strength is a major factor in influencing the quality of the exchange relationship with followers. An underlying assumption of LMX is that due to limited time and social resources, a leader cannot form close positive LMX relationships with all followers. Therefore, a leader has to ration these scarce resources. With some followers, the leader will develop high-quality LMX relationships (the in-group) and with others, low-quality LMX relationships (the out-group).[34] Take, for example, a leader's span of control. A leader's *span of control* is the number of direct followers to a particular leader. The wider the span of control, the more difficult it is for the leader to form strong positive relationships with every follower and thus the disparity in the quality of exchange relationship. The same is true for time as a resource.

A leader's ability to create a work environment that fosters positive exchange relationships between members of the work group is critical. A work climate of trust, respect, and openness may provide a setting for positive LMX relationships to develop not just between the leader and followers but between followers. This is the type of work environment that allows members to align their social identities with the group's identity.[35] **Social identity** is the degree to which members form close social ties with the group and how it subsequently influences interactions within and between group members.[36] Within the work group, members who show a positive social identity to the organization are more likely to exhibit OCB and develop high-quality LMX relationships than members with a negative social identity or a lack of it.[37] [38]

The Role of the Follower

The difference between traditional leadership theories and LMX is that while the former focused on the leader primarily, the latter was one of the first attempts in leadership studies to formally recognize the role of the follower in the leadership process. A follower's behavior and attributes influence how the leader and other members perceive such a follower. For example, a follower's feedback-seeking behavior and self-promoting personality can have a positive or negative effect on the LMX relationship. A proactive follower who takes the time to actively seek information and feedback about his or her role expectations and how to successfully perform them sets the right tone for forming not just a working relationship, but a high-quality relationship with the leader. Such followers show initiative even in areas outside their immediate responsibility, possess a strong sense of commitment to work unit goals, and show a greater sense of responsibility for unit success. In short, they have the right attitude.[39] As the saying goes, "attitude affects altitude."

Proactive followers who want to form positive relationships with their leaders can employ any number of tactics. Here we discuss three such tactics: impressions management, ingratiation, and self-promotion. Effective followers can use these tactics to influence the relationship with their leaders

Impressions management *is a follower's effort to project a favorable image to gain an immediate benefit or improve a long-term relationship with the leader.* Employees seeking to form a positive relationship with the leader will often be the ones seeking feedback on how to improve their work performance. Researchers have identified two kinds of motives associated with follower feedback-seeking behavior: performance-driven motive and impressions-driven motive. The *performance-driven motive* is the follower's genuine attempt to seek information from the leader that will help improve work performance, while the *impressions-driven motive* refers to the desire to control how one appears to the leader.[40 41]

Ingratiation *is the effort to appear supportive, appreciative, and respectful.* Ingratiatory influence tactics include favor rendering and behavioral conformity. In this instance, followers go beyond the call of duty to render services to the leader and to conform their behavior to the expectations of the leader. Studies have found a positive correlation between ingratiation by a follower and affection (or liking) by the leader for the follower. Affection, in turn, is positively related to the quality of the exchange relationship and the leader's assessment of the follower's competence, loyalty, commitment, and work ethic. These tactics are valuable tools that can enhance the visibility of the follower's strengths and performance.

Self-promotion *is the effort to appear competent and dependable.*[42] A positive relationship is more likely when the follower is perceived to be competent and dependable, and when the follower's values and ideals are similar to those of the leader. This in turn influences the leader to show support, delegate more, allow greater discretion, and engage in open communication with the follower. This reciprocation strengthens the LMX relationship. In other words, high-quality LMX not only increases job satisfaction, but that job satisfaction can also enhance high-quality supervisor–employee relationships.[43] What this reveals is that follower traits and personality do influence the relationship between the leader and follower. However, there is the risk that these tactics can have a negative effect on the LMX relationship if deemed to be self-serving.[44]

WORK
Application **7-3**

Recall an occasion when you had the opportunity to make a positive first impression on your manager. Describe what tactics you employed and their effects on your manager.

The Benefits of High-Quality LMX Relationships

LMX takes a relationship-based approach to leadership, focusing on social dimensions of trust, loyalty, honesty, support, and respect that help define the nature of the dyadic relationship between a leader and a follower.[45] As discussed earlier, there are high-quality and low-quality LMX relationships. Followers in high-quality relationships with their leader show greater motivation and job performance, experience lower staff turnover, and report higher levels of satisfaction with their leaders. High-quality LMX employees exhibit greater OCB.[46] In return, these followers routinely receive higher performance ratings on their job evaluations compared to followers in low-quality LMX relationships.[47]

A leader's control over outcomes that are desirable to followers increases the leader's reward power. For example, the leader can influence follower behavior with rewards such as helping with a follower's career by recommending promotion, giving pay raises, offering special favors (bigger office, better work schedule), and allowing greater participation

WORK
Application **7-4**

Think of a leader you've had or now have a very positive high-quality relationship with. Describe some of the work-related benefits you received that can be directly or indirectly tied to your relationship with this leader/supervisor.

_____

_____

_____

_____

in decision making.[48] In return for these benefits, members in high-quality LMX relationships have certain obligations and expectations beyond those required of members in low-quality LMX relationships. In high-quality LMX relationships, members are expected to be loyal to the leader, to be more committed to task objectives, to work harder, and to share some of the leader's administrative duties.

It is evident that high-quality LMX relationships create a reciprocal exchange.[49] Unless this cycle of reciprocal reinforcement is interrupted, the relationship is likely to develop to a point where there is a high degree of mutual dependence, support, and loyalty. The greater the perceived value of the tangible and intangible benefits exchanged between the leader and followers, the higher the quality of LMX.

We should also note that the special relationship that exists between a leader and a follower in a high-quality LMX relationship does create certain obligations and constraints for the leader.[50] The leader cannot resort to coercion or heavy-handed influencing approaches without endangering the quality of the relationship. It is under such situations that followers are said to have earned **social capital**, defined as *the set of resources that inheres in the structure of relations between members of the group, which helps them get ahead.*[51]

Now that you understand LMX, complete Self-Assessment 7-2.

SELF-ASSESSMENT 7-2   **In-Group and Out-Group**

Based on Self-Assessment 7-1 on page 233 and your reading of VDL and LMX theory, think of a current work environment or one that you once were a part of and separate the workers into two groups—those who in your opinion had a high-quality LMX relationship with the leader and those who had a low-quality LMX relationship. Be sure to include yourself. Explain your thinking.

High-Quality LMX Members	Low-Quality LMX Members
_____	_____
_____	_____
_____	_____

 Learning Outcome **4**   *Discuss the main criticisms of LMX theory.*

Criticisms of LMX Theory

Deficiencies in measurement of LMX quality have been raised.[52] The quality of the exchange relationship between a leader and a follower is measured through a survey called the LMX-7 questionnaire. The LMX-7 scale features such structured questions as the following:

• How well does your leader understand your job problems and needs? (Not a bit, a little, a fair amount, quite a bit, and a great deal)
• How well does your leader recognize your potential? (Not at all, a little, moderately, mostly, and fully)
• How would you characterize your working relationship with your leader? (Extremely ineffective, worse than average, average, better than average, and extremely effective)

A criticism of LMX-7 is that it determines the quality of the exchange relationship solely from the follower's perspective. Leader variables have been found to explain the most variance in LMX quality.[53] However, LMX-7 measures the quality of the exchange relationship only from the perspective of the follower.

Another criticism of LMX is attribution bias in favor of some group members. A leader who appreciates in-group members for making his life easier may reciprocate by giving favorable performance evaluations and feedback to such members. Positive job performance ratings often then become part of an individual's employment record. An employee's employment record is ultimately used as a resource to justify future selection, development, and promotion decisions. In many instances, those who get promoted are also those who consistently achieve higher scores in performance evaluations. Therefore, the development and career advancement of other group members who (regardless of their performance) are not similar to, familiar to, or well liked by their leader may be jeopardized. The out-group members may be paying a price for not having the same social standing or personal relationship with their leader as in-group members. This inherent bias in the system raises questions of fairness and equality in the treatment of all employees.

Finally, there have been criticisms of the predictive power of LMX theory. For example, the research evidence on staff turnover is mixed at best and reservations about the performance measures used.

Complete Self-Assessment 7-3 to determine your LMX relationship with your manager.

SELF-ASSESSMENT 7-3   Your LMX Relationship with Your Manager

Self-Assessment 7-1 determined your status in terms of your relationship with your manager—whether you were part of the in-group or out-group. Your score in Self-Assessment 7-1 also indicates the quality of the relationship that you have with your manager. Place your score from Self-Assessment 7-1 here _____ and on the following continuum. Note that some of the questions in Self-Assessment 7-1 are similar to the LMX-7 questions.

10 — 20 — 30 — 40 — 50
High-quality LMX relationship   *Low-quality LMX relationship*

The lower your score, generally, the better is your relationship with your manager. We say generally, because you could have a manager who does not have a good relationship with any employee. Thus, a good LMX can be a relative measure.

Followership

While leader-centric studies have dominated the scholarship sphere on this topic, there is increasing evidence that follower-centric studies are showing significant promise in helping us understand the dynamics of the leader–follower relationship.[54] [55] Most scholars would agree that there is increasing use of the words *follower* and *followership* in discussions of organizational leadership.[56] Past leadership research has focused on leaders and ignored the role of followers in explaining organizational successes or failures.[57] This has led to criticism of existing leadership theories for being too "leader-centric."[58] The focus of these theories has been almost exclusively on the impact of leader traits and behaviors on follower outcomes. However, like leadership, good followership is increasingly being recognized as an important component for strong organizational performance.[59] Good followership is about 'upward influencing.'[60] Leaders have to put aside their egos and recognize that there are times when they have to listen to and take their followers' counsel on how to proceed. This is a cultural change that needs top management support, else nothing happens.[61] Robert Kelley, a pioneer and early proponent of followership, states that "without followers, leadership is meaningless and leaders don't exist."[62] To adequately understand the cognitions, attributes, behaviors, and contexts of followership, researchers have focused on such questions as the following: Why do some people choose to follow? Are there different types of followers? How does one become an effective follower? Can the leadership–followership relationship be nurtured? In this section, we address these questions and more. But first, we start with a definition of followership.

Defining Followership

Followership is not merely the actions of a subordinate who blindly follows the dictates of formal authority figures in an organization. As such, followership is not the same as following. Following is reacting (consciously or unconsciously) to a leader's orders. In contrast, followership is a self-conscious choice of the follower in the context of his or her relationship to the nominal leader. Issues of rank and authority play little or no role in such a choice. Followers are in control of the situation by the choices made.[63] Therefore, **followership** refers to *the behavior of followers that result from the leader–follower mutual influencing relationship.* It is an interactive concept. To a large extent, societal views about followers have contributed to our limited understanding of followership. From an early age we are taught that organizations succeed because of the leader, with very little or no mention of the role of followers. The follower is seen as someone whose sole duty is to carry out the instructions of the leader. From this perspective, the **follower** is defined as *someone who is under the direct influence and authority of a leader.*

Leaders are just one part of a duality, because there can be no leaders without followers. Effective leadership requires effective followership. Kelley and Chaleff are two early pioneers who brought focus to the role of followers in the leadership process. No work unit or organized effort can succeed and be sustained without followers; this, according to Kelley, is the power of followership.[64] Chaleff discussed the fact that effective followers are also courageous followers who tend to demonstrate certain behaviors. He identifies the five behaviors as *courage* to accept responsibility, *courage* to serve, *courage* to question, *courage* to be part of necessary change, and *courage* to take a moral stand when necessary.[65][66]

Effective followers do more than fulfill the vision laid out by their leader; they are partners in creating the vision.[67] They take responsibility for their actions, they take initiative in fixing problems, and they question leaders when they think they are wrong. According to Kelley, "Effective followers have the vision to see both the forest and the trees, the social capacity to work well with others, the strength of character to flourish without heroic status, the moral and psychological balance to pursue personal and corporate goals at no cost to either, and above all, the desire to participate in a team effort for the accomplishment of some greater purpose."[68]

Learning Outcome **5**   *Describe the two behaviors identified in the Kelley Model and the resulting five follower types.*

Types of Followers

There are contextual influences that may affect both followership constructions and behavior in the follower role. For example, personal qualities such as obedience, expressing opinions, and taking initiative have been found to be most disparate across different types of followers.[69] In her book titled *Followership: How Followers Are Creating Change and Changing Leaders,* Barbara Kellerman classifies followers into five categories based on their level of engagement: *isolates, bystanders, participants, activists,* or *diehards.*[70] Another typology of follower types is that of Robert Kelley.[71] Based on their intellectual capacity to think critically and their level of involvement in organizational affairs—Kelley groups followers into five categories that we will elaborate on next.

Exhibit 7.1 depicts these two behavioral dimensions—level of independent critical thinking and the level of involvement. The high independent critical thinker refers to the follower who is able to examine, analyze, and evaluate matters of significance in the organization's life. Conversely, the opposite of this person is someone who is low in ability to think critically. The second behavior dimension—level of involvement—refers to the follower who takes a visible and active role in organizational affairs. The opposite of this person is someone who prefers to be in the background and take a passive role in organizational affairs.

According to Kelley, combining these dimensions results in five basic follower types, identified as the following: alienated, passive, conformist, pragmatic, and effective follower (see Exhibit 7.1):

Follower Types

EXHIBIT 7.1

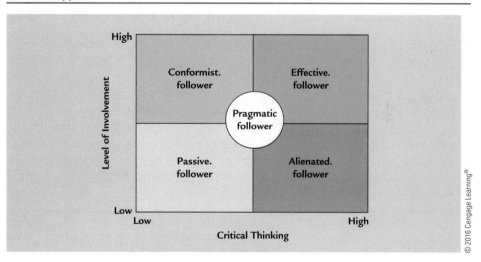

© 2016 Cengage Learning®

- The lower-left quadrant identifies the Passive Follower. *The* **passive follower** *is someone who is* *low on critical thinking and low on involvement.* The passive follower looks to the leader or others to do all the thinking and does not get involved. Lacking in initiative and commitment to the team, this invisible follower requires constant supervision and never goes beyond the job description. They are often described by their leaders as lazy, unmotivated, and incompetent.
- The upper-left quadrant identifies the Conformist Follower. *The* **conformist follower** *is someone who is high on involvement but low on critical thinking.* In other words, conformists are the "yes people" of the organization. They carry out all orders without

considering the consequences of such orders. A conformist would do anything to avoid conflict. Authoritarian leaders prefer conformist followers.

- The upper-right quadrant identifies the Effective Follower. *The* **effective follower** *is someone who is high on critical thinking and involvement.* Effective followers are not risk-averse, nor do they shy from conflict. They have the courage to initiate change and put themselves at risk or in conflict with others, even their leaders, to serve the best interest of the organization. As such, they are often described as proactive. Effective followers tend to function very well in self-managed teams. They are a manager's best asset in that they complement the leader and can be relied upon to relieve the leader of many tasks.

- The lower-right quadrant identifies the Alienated Follower. *The* **alienated follower** *is someone who is low on involvement, yet is high on critical thinking.* The alienated follower is someone who feels cheated, or unappreciated, by his or her organization for exemplary work. Often cynical in their behavior, alienated followers are capable but unwilling to participate in developing solutions to problems. They are just happy to dwell on the negatives and ignore the positives as far as organizational life goes.

- *The* **pragmatic follower** *exhibits a little of all four styles—depending on which style fits the prevailing situation.* Pragmatic followers are "stuck in the middle" most of the time. Because it is difficult to discern just where they stand on issues, they present an ambiguous image, with positive and negative sides. On the positive side, when an organization is going through desperate times, the pragmatic follower knows how to "work the system to get things done." On the negative side, this same behavior can be interpreted as "playing political games," or adjusting to maximize self-interest.

OPENING CASE Application

5. According to the followership model of follower types, what types of followers has Facebook generally attracted?

Facebook has been able to recruit and hire some of the best minds in the industry. According to one analyst, everyone at Facebook was a star in their previous employment. Sheryl Sandberg, a veteran of Google, was the chief of staff for former treasury secretary Lawrence Summers. She joined Facebook as the company's chief operating officer (COO). Chris Cox, Facebook's vice president of product, was doing a master's in artificial intelligence at Stanford when Zuckerberg personally convinced him to join Facebook. "You don't get a lot of shy, retiring types at Facebook," said one writer. These are intelligent, experienced, productive, and highly sought-after talents, "power nerds" to say the least. Remember, the effective follower is someone who is high on critical thinking and involvement. It is a safe bet that Zuckerberg and Facebook have mostly attracted effective followers.

Becoming an Effective Follower

How individuals see their role as followers informs how they function. While some scholars construct follower definitions around passivity, deference, and obedience, others emphasize the importance of constructively questioning and challenging their leaders.[72] To be effective as a follower, it is important to acquire the skills necessary to combine two opposing follower roles—namely, to execute decisions made by a leader, and yet be able to raise issues about those decisions when they are deemed misguided or unethical. This is often referred to as "speaking truth to power."[73] Although this is not always easy to do, followers must be willing to risk the leader's displeasure with such feedback. Moral integrity and a willingness to take stands based on principle are distinguishing characteristics of the effective follower.[74] It could be argued that the effective follower has the greatest potential to become an effective leader. Developing a high level of mutual trust and respect between the leader and follower can mitigate the risk of falling out of favor with the leader. In such a relationship, a leader is likely to view criticism and dissenting views as an honest effort to facilitate achievement of shared objectives, rather than as an intentional expression of personal disagreement or disloyalty.[75]

The effective follower has a high self-efficacy compared to the ineffective follower. **Self-efficacy** is defined *as a person's beliefs in his or her capabilities to produce at a certain level of performance.*[76] Self-efficacy determines how people feel, think, and see themselves, which in turn influences their work ethic.

How followers perceive a leader plays a critical role in their ability to help the leader grow and succeed.[77] Just as leaders make attributions about follower competence, followers make attributions about leader competence and intentions. Followers assess whether the leader's primary motivation is more for his or her personal benefit or career advancement than for their own welfare and the organization's well-being. Credibility is increased and follower commitment is enhanced when the leader makes self-sacrifices to gain support for his or her ideas, rather than imposing on followers. Leaders who appear insincere or motivated only by personal gain create an atmosphere in which integrating the two opposing follower roles is impossible. Here, followers would play the passive role of conforming to the leader's expectations without offering any constructive criticism, even when it is called for in a leader's decisions and actions. Complete Self-Assessment 7-4 to learn how effective you are as a follower.

SELF-ASSESSMENT 7-4   Effective Followers

Select a present or past boss and answer each question describing your behavior using the following scale.

5 — 4 — 3 — 2 — 1
I do this regularly   *I do not do this*

_____ 1. I offer my support and encouragement to my boss when things are not going well.

_____ 2. I take initiative to do more than my normal job without having to be asked to do things.

_____ 3. I counsel and coach my boss when it is appropriate, such as with a new, inexperienced boss, and in a unique situation in which the boss needs help.

_____ 4. When the boss has a bad idea, I raise concerns and try to improve the plans, rather than simply implement a poor decision.

_____ 5. I seek and encourage the boss to give me honest feedback, rather than avoid it and act defensively when it is offered.

_____ 6. I try to clarify my role in tasks by making sure I understand my boss's expectations of me and my performance standards.

_____ 7. I show my appreciation to my boss, such as saying thanks when the boss does something in my interest.

_____ 8. I keep the boss informed; I don't withhold bad news.

_____ 9. I would resist inappropriate influence by the boss; if asked, I would not do anything illegal or unethical.

Add up the numbers on lines 1 through 9 and place your score here _____ and on the continuum below.

9 — 15 — 25 — 35 — 45
Ineffective Follower   *Effective Follower*

The higher your score, generally, the more effective you are as a follower. However, your boss also has an effect on your followership. A poor boss can affect your followership behavior; nevertheless, make sure you do try to be a good follower. Read on to better understand how to be an effective follower.

Guidelines to Becoming an Effective Follower

Research focused on followership has identified certain behaviors that are associated with effective followers.[78][79] These behaviors distinguish followers on top-performing teams from their counterparts on marginally performing teams. Exhibit 7.2 presents nine guidelines for effective followership; note that the nine questions in Self-Assessment 7-4 are based on these guidelines.

EXHIBIT 7.2

Guidelines to Becoming an Effective Follower

a. Offer support to leader.

b. Take initiative.

c. Play counseling and coaching roles to leader when appropriate.

d. Raise issues and/or concerns when necessary.

e. Seek and encourage honest feedback from the leader.

f. Clarify your role and expectations.

g. Show appreciation.

h. Keep the leader informed.

i. Resist inappropriate influence of leader.

© Cengage Learning®

Offer Support to Leader

A good follower looks for ways to express support and encouragement to a leader who is encountering resistance in trying to introduce needed change in his or her organization. Successful organizations are characterized by followers whose work ethic and philosophy are in congruence with those of the organization and the leader.

Take Initiative

Effective followers take the initiative to do what is necessary without being told, including working beyond their normally assigned duties. They look for opportunities to make a positive impact on the organization's objectives. When serious problems arise that impede the organization's ability to accomplish its objectives, effective followers take the risk to initiate corrective action by pointing out the problem to the leader, suggesting alternative solutions, or, if necessary, resolving the problem outright. While taking the initiative often involves risks, if done carefully and properly, it can make the follower a valuable part of the team and a member of the leader's trusted circle.

Counsel and Coach the Leader When Appropriate

Contrary to the myth that leaders have all the answers, most people now recognize that followers also have opportunities to coach and counsel leaders, especially when a leader is new and inexperienced.[80] A mutually trusting relationship with a leader facilitates upward coaching and counseling. An effective follower must be alert for opportunities to provide helpful advice, and ask questions, or simply be a good listener when the leader needs someone to confide in. Because some leaders may be reluctant to ask for help, it is the follower's responsibility to recognize such situations and step in when appropriate. For example, a leader whose interpersonal relationship with another follower may be having a different effect than the leader intended could be counseled to see the ineffectiveness of his approach or style by another follower: "I am sure you intended for Bob to see the value of being on time when you said…, but that is not how he took it." When coaching and counseling a leader is done with respect, it is most effective. Respect creates symmetry, empathy, and connection in all kinds of relationships, including that between a leader and a follower.[81]

Raise Issues and/or Concerns When Necessary

When there are potential problems or drawbacks with a leader's plans and proposals, a follower's ability to bring these issues or concerns to light is critical. How the follower raises these issues is crucial, because leaders often get defensive in responding to negative feedback. Followers can minimize such defensiveness by acknowledging the leader's superior status and communicating a sincere desire to be of help in accomplishing the organization's goals, rather than personal interest. When challenging a leader's flawed plans and proposals, it is important for the follower to pinpoint specifics rather than vague generalities, and to avoid personalizing the critique. This guideline is consistent with the prevailing view of the courageous follower as a person who is highly involved and very much an independent thinker with initiative and a well-developed sense of responsibility.

Seek and Encourage Honest Feedback from the Leader

Followers can play a constructive role in how their leaders evaluate them. Some leaders are uncomfortable with expressing negative concerns about a follower's performance, so they tend to focus only on the follower's strengths. One way to overcome this tendency is for the follower to show willingness to accept both positive and negative feedback without being defensive. Encourage the leader to point out the strongest and weakest aspects of your work.

Clarify Your Role and Expectations

Where there is evidence of role ambiguity or uncertainty about job expectations, this must be clarified with the leader. As will be revealed in Chapter 8 on leading effective teams, it is the leader's responsibility to clearly communicate role expectations for followers. Nevertheless, some leaders fail to communicate clear job expectations, scope of authority and responsibility, performance targets, and deadlines. Followers must insist on clarification in these areas by their leaders. In some cases the problem is that of role conflict. The leader directs a follower to perform mutually exclusive tasks and expects results on all of them at the same time. Followers should be assertive but diplomatic about resolving role ambiguity and role conflict.

Show Appreciation

Everyone, including leaders, loves to be appreciated when they perform a good deed that benefits others. When a leader makes a special effort to help a follower, such as helping to protect the follower's interest, or nurturing and promoting the follower's career, it is appropriate for the follower to show appreciation. Even if the leader's actions don't directly benefit a particular follower but represent a significant accomplishment for the organization, it is still an appropriate gesture for followers to express their appreciation and admiration for the leader. Recognition of this kind only reinforces desirable leadership behavior. Although some may argue that praising a leader is a form of ingratiation easily used to influence the leader, when sincere, it can help to build a positive leader–follower exchange relationship.

Keep the Leader Informed

Accurate and timely information enables a leader to make good decisions and to have a complete picture of where things stand in the organization. Leaders who appear not to know what is going on in their organizations do feel and look incompetent in front of their peers and superiors. It is embarrassing for a leader to hear about events or changes taking place within his or her unit from others. This responsibility of relaying information to the leader includes both positive and negative information. Some followers tend to withhold bad news from their leaders. This is just as detrimental as providing no information at all.

Resist Inappropriate Influence from the Leader

A leader may be tempted to use his or her power to influence the follower in ways that are inappropriate (legally or ethically). Despite the power gap between the leader and follower, the follower is not required to comply with inappropriate influence attempts, or to be exploited by an abusive leader.[82] Effective followers challenge the leader in a firm, tactful, and diplomatic way. Reminding the leader of his or her ethical responsibilities, insisting on your rights, and pointing out the negative consequences of complying are various ways in which a follower can resist inappropriate influence attempts by a leader. It is important to challenge such behavior early, before it becomes habitual, and to do it without personal hostility. Taking a moral stand may sometimes require the follower to psychologically and/or physically separate from the leader.

CONCEPT APPLICATION 7-2

Guidelines to Becoming an Effective Follower

Identify each guideline using the letters a–i from Exhibit 7.2 on page 244:

_____ 10. I understand the leader's needs, goals, and constraints, and I work hard to help meet them.

_____ 11. I make a point to internally question the wisdom of the leader's decision rather than just doing what I am told.

_____ 12. When the leader asks me to do something that runs contrary to my professional or personal preferences, I do you say "no" rather than "yes."

_____ 13. I do you assert my views on important issues, especially when I know it will help the organization achieve its goals, even though it might mean conflict with my group.

_____ 14. I am actively developing my abilities in some critical areas so that I can become more valuable to the leader and the organization.

_____ 15. We have a new boss, and I've been filling her in on how we do things in our department.

_____ 16. We only have performance reviews once a year. But I wanted to know what my boss thinks of my work sooner, so we had a meeting to discuss my performance.

_____ 17. My boss hinted about having a sexual relationship, so I reminded her that I was happily married and clearly told her I was not interested and not to talk about it again.

_____ 18. We started a new project today but I did not understand what I was supposed to be doing or expected to do. So I went to talk to my boss about what to do.

Learning Outcome 6   *Briefly describe the three factors than can enhance a follower's influence.*

Factors That Can Enhance Follower Influence

In every organization or work setting, some followers seem to have more influence over their peers (and even their leaders) than others. These are the followers that command respect, trust, and loyalty from everyone, including the leader. They are opinion leaders amongst their peers. It is not uncommon for a follower of such stature to exert greater influence over other followers than even the leader of the group can. Leaders who understand this "follower–follower" dynamic can use it to their advantage.

It is not always the case that influential followers use their influence appropriately. Some may employ their influence in negative ways to make the leader's job difficult. This section examines some of the key factors that have been found to enhance follower influence. We will discuss the follower's relative power position, locus of control, and education/experience (see Exhibit 7.3).

EXHIBIT 7.3

Factors That Can Enhance Follower Influence

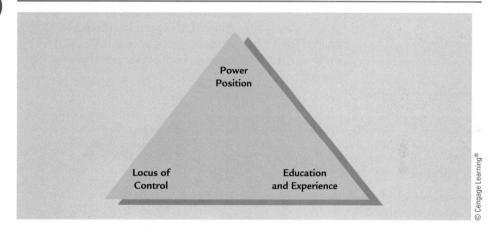

© Cengage Learning®

Power Position

Leaders need to realize that they are no longer the sole possessors of power and influence in their work units. The new reality is that no matter what position a person holds in the workplace, they can be a force for change. Some followers distinguish themselves as innovators, self-managers, or risk-takers. These are terms that have traditionally been reserved for describing leaders, not followers. Some followers may have personal, referent, expert, information, and connection power that can be used to boost upward influence. These power sources are discussed in Chapter 5. Any of these sources of power can give the follower the ability to influence others at different levels of the organization. As more and more employees come to rely on a particular follower for information, expertise, or simply because of his or her personality, the follower's relative power position increases.[83] These are the followers that can influence other followers to slow down performance, file grievances, stage demonstrations, or even sabotage operations—all actions that can hurt a leader's reputation.

Locus of Control

As discussed in Chapter 2, **locus of control** *is on a continuum between an external and internal belief over who has control of a person's destiny.* People who believe they are "masters of their own destiny" are said to have an *internal locus of control;* they believe that they can influence people and events in their workplace. People who believe they are "pawns of fate" (*external locus of control*) tend to believe they have no influence or control at work. The literature mostly supports the view that leadership qualities are predominantly present in those with an internal locus of control. [84] Followers with an internal locus of control prefer a work environment that encourages honest and open communication with leaders, participation in decision making, and opportunities to be creative.

They are likely to be more influential with other followers than are those with external locus of control.

Education and Experience

Not all followers have the same level of education and/or experience. These differences can have a major impact on the influencing ability of followers. Followers with valuable skills and experience may be able to use their expert power to influence other followers and even the leader. Leaders have to create opportunities to learn from others, including followers. Today's workforce is far more educated, mobile, diverse, and younger than the workforce of 30 years ago. The experienced and educated follower can be much more influential with other followers than can the leader.

As workers' education and experience increase, they tend to reject top-down directive leadership. Leaders who ignore this fact will face higher employee dissatisfaction and turnover and miss out on the benefits of utilizing the talents of effective followers.

CONCEPT APPLICATION 7-4

Determinants of Follower Influence

Identify the specific follower-influencing characteristic in each of these statements.

a. power position   b. locus of control   c. education and experience

_____ 19. Given my technical background and long tenure in my department, I do help out other coworkers, making them look good, even when I don't get any credit.

_____ 20. I try to solve the tough problems (technical or organizational), rather than look to the leader or others to do it for me.

_____ 21. I believe that no matter what I do to try to get ahead, there are always people out there trying to sabotage my plans.

_____ 22. Many of my peers depend on me for technical assistance because I am the only one in the department who has been trained to work with this new machine successfully.

_____ 23. When it comes to selling my points to peers, I easily get them to see things my way rather than the boss's way due to my seniority and popularity in this division.

OPENING CASE Application

5. The text discusses factors that can determine follower influence, when applied to Facebook employees; which factor(s) in your opinion stands out?

It is clear from the case that Facebook employees are highly skilled and experienced software engineers. They are highly sought-after in the tech world. As mentioned in the case, everyone at Facebook was a star somewhere else and you don't find a lot of shy, retiring types there. They are described as "power nerds." Even those who have left Facebook have gone on to create their own ventures. Facebook employees have expert, connection, and referent power. By all indications, they have internal locus of control. Finally, Facebook employees are highly educated and experienced given the competitive and high-tech environment in which they operate.

Dual Role of Being a Leader and a Follower

As the guidelines for becoming an effective follower reveal, effective leadership is found in highly effective followers. It is important to recognize that even when someone is identified as a leader, the same person is also a follower to someone higher up the organizational hierarchy.[85] It is not at all uncommon to switch between being a leader and being a follower several times during the course of a day's work. For example, within an organization, mid-level managers answer to vice presidents, who answer to the CEO, who answers to the board of directors; within the school system, teachers answer to the principal, who answers to the school superintendent, who answers to school board members. Regardless of one's position in an organization, we are all in a follower role to someone else. To execute both roles effectively is a challenge, but one that can be done effectively.

Delegation

We now focus on developing followers by delegating tasks to them. **Delegation** *is the process of assigning responsibility and authority for accomplishing objectives.* Telling employees to perform the tasks that are part of their job design is issuing orders, not delegating. *Delegating* refers to giving employees new tasks. The new task may become a part of a redesigned job, or it may simply be a onetime task. The true art of delegation lies in a manager's ability to know what cannot be delegated and what should be delegated. Some management experts believe that if there were a top ten list of managerial mistakes, failure to delegate would be one of them.[86] In this section, we discuss delegating, delegation decisions, and delegating with a model.

Delegating

Effective delegation requires that a leader carefully consider several factors relating to the task, time requirement, and follower characteristics before delegating.[87] A leader should delegate work when there is not enough time to attend to priority tasks, when followers desire more challenges and opportunities, and when the tasks match follower skill levels and experiences. Also a leader must find the proper person for the job and provide careful instructions. Effective delegation allows people to prosper in their own uniqueness.

Let's begin by discussing the benefits of delegation, the obstacles to delegation, and signs of delegating too little.

Benefits of Delegation

When managers delegate, they have more time to perform high-priority tasks. Delegation gets tasks accomplished and increases productivity. Delegation can empower followers and give them more confidence.[88] Delegating both responsibility and authority pushes decision making down the ladder, encourages input from operational employees who are closest to problems, and promotes a participative work environment. It enables leaders to mobilize resources and secure better results than they could have gotten alone. Delegation trains employees and improves their self-esteem, as well as eases the stress and burden on managers. By delegating responsibilities, leaders can focus on doing a few tasks well instead of many tasks less effectively. Consequently, they improve their management and leadership potential while training others to succeed them. It is a means of developing followers by enriching their jobs. From the organization's perspective, delegating can result in increased performance and work outcomes.[89] It can also lead to more communication between leaders and followers, thus encouraging followers to voice their opinions on how to improve the work environment.[90]

Obstacles to Delegation

Managers become used to doing things themselves. They forget part of leadership is "getting work done through others."[91] Managers fear that employees will fail to accomplish tasks. You can delegate responsibility and authority but not your accountability. Managers believe they can perform tasks more efficiently than others. Some managers don't realize that delegation is an important part of their job, others don't know what to delegate, and some don't know how to delegate. Effective delegation greatly improves a leader's time management, without which efficiency and effectiveness suffer. If you let anything keep you from delegating, you could end up like Dr. Rudenstine, former president of Harvard University, who became ill due to job stress by trying to do too much by himself.

Signs of Delegating Too Little

Certain behaviors are associated with leaders who are reluctant to delegate to their subordinates. These behaviors are signs that a leader is delegating too little. Some of these behaviors include taking work home, performing employee tasks, being behind in work, a continual feeling of pressure and stress, rushing to meet deadlines, and requiring that employees seek approval before acting. Leaders who can't disengage from the office and delegate authority and responsibility undermine employees' confidence to make decisions and take responsibility for their actions.[92] Unfortunately, in many of today's cost-cutting environments, you don't always have someone you can delegate some of your tasks to.

WORK
Application **7-7**

Describe an obstacle to delegation, or sign of delegating too little, that you have observed on the job.

Learning Outcome 7   *List five things a leader should delegate.*

Delegation Decisions

As mentioned earlier, an important part of delegation is knowing which tasks to delegate. Successful delegation is often based on selecting what task to delegate and whom to delegate it to.

What to Delegate

As a general guide, use your prioritized to-do list and delegate anything that you don't have to be personally involved with because of your unique knowledge or skill. Some possibilities include the following:

- *Paperwork.* Have others prepare reports, memos, letters, and so on.
- *Routine tasks.* Delegate checking inventory, scheduling, ordering, and so on.
- *Technical matters.* Have top employees deal with technical questions and problems.
- *Tasks with developmental potential.* Give employees the opportunity to learn new things. Prepare them for advancement by enriching their jobs.
- *Employees' problems.* Train employees to solve their own problems; don't solve problems for them, unless their capability is low.

What Not to Delegate

As a general guide, do not delegate anything that you need to be personally involved with because of your unique knowledge or skill.[93] Here are some typical examples:

- *Personnel matters.* Performance appraisals, counseling, disciplining, firing, resolving conflicts, and so on.

- *Confidential activities.* Unless you have permission to do so.
- *Crises.* There is no time to delegate.
- *Activities delegated to you personally.* For example, if you are assigned to a committee, do not assign someone else without permission.

Determining to Whom to Delegate

Once you have decided what to delegate, you must select an employee to do the task. When selecting an employee to delegate to, be sure that he or she has the capability to get the job done right by the deadline. Consider your employees' talents and interests when making a selection. You may consult with several employees to determine their interests before making the final choice.[94]

Before you learn how to delegate with the use of a model, complete Self-Assessment 7-5 to learn how your personality may affect your followership and delegation.

SELF-ASSESSMENT 7-5   **Followership and Personality**

Personality Differences

Generally, if you have an agreeableness Big Five personality type, which is a high need for affiliation, you will have a good relationship with your manager, because having a good relationship with everyone helps you to meet your needs. If you have a lower need for power, you prefer to be a follower, rather than a leader. Generally, you will be willing to delegate authority.

If you have a surgency/high need for power, you may have some problems getting along with your manager. You prefer to be in control, or to be a leader rather than a follower. However, if you don't get along well with your manager, you will have difficulty climbing the corporate ladder. You may have some reluctance to delegate authority because you like to be in control—and when you delegate, you lose some control.

If you have a conscientiousness/high need for achievement, you may not be concerned about your relationship with your manager, other than getting what you need to get the job done. However, if you don't get along well with your manager, you will have difficulty getting what you want. You may also be reluctant to delegate tasks that you like to do, because you get satisfaction from doing the job itself, rather than having someone else to do it.

Being well adjusted also helps you have a good relationship with your manager. Being open to experience, which includes an internal locus of control (Chapter 2), helps you to get along with others since you are willing to try new things.

Gender Differences

Although there are exceptions, generally women tend to seek relationships that are on a more personal level than those favored by men. For example, two women who work together are more apt to talk about their family lives than two men. Men do socialize, but it is more frequently about other interests such as sports. It is not unusual for women who have worked together for months to know more about each other's personal and family lives than men who have worked together for years. Men who do enjoy talking about their personal lives tend to talk more about their families in dyads with women than in those with men. One of the reasons men enjoy working with women is because they often bring a personal-level relationship to the job.

How does your personality affect your dyadic relationships, followership, and delegation?

_____

_____

_____

_____

YOU
Make the
ETHICAL
Call

7.2

On May 3, 2011, Senator John Ensign of Nevada resigned. Ensign admitted to having an affair in 2009 with Cynthia Hampton—a past campaign aide and the wife of Doug Hampton. During a two-year inquiry into possible violations by Ensign, the Senate Ethics Committee found that he violated campaign finance laws and obscured justice to cover up his affair.

Senator Tom Coburn of Oklahoma, a friend of Ensign's who confronted him about the adultery, became involved as an intermediary in negotiations between Ensign and Doug Hampton. The former aide is said to have sought some kind of financial settlement from Ensign soon after he became aware of the affair. Senator Coburn was the go-between in trying to negotiate settlement terms. According to reports, Ensign's father eventually gave the Hamptons $96,000 as a gift, which the Ethics Committee determined to be in violation of campaign finance laws.[95]

1. Is it ethically responsible for Senator Coburn to be trying to help his friend Senator Ensign pay off the Hamptons in a deal that is seen as a violation of campaign finance laws?

2. What would you do if your boss asked you to cover up evidence of wrongdoing by your organization? (Some options include the following: just do it, don't say anything but don't do it, question the motives, look closely at what you are asked to destroy, go to your boss's boss to make sure it's okay to do it, tell the boss you will not do it, ask the boss to do it him- or herself, blow the whistle to an outside source like the government or media.)

3. If you went to court for trying to cover up a violation like Senator Coburn was doing, do you believe you would have a good ethical defense by saying "I was not directly involved"?

Delegating with the Use of a Model

After determining what to delegate and to whom, you must plan for and delegate the tasks. *The* **delegation model** *steps are (1) explain the need for delegating and the reasons for selecting the employee; (2) set objectives that define responsibility, level of authority, and deadline; (3) develop a plan; and (4) establish control checkpoints and hold employees accountable.*[96] Following these four steps can increase your chances of successfully delegating. As you read on, you will see how the delegation model is used with the job characteristics model, core job dimensions, and critical psychological states to influence performance and work outcomes.

Step 1. Explain the need for delegating and the reasons for selecting the employee. It is helpful for the employee to understand why the assignment must be completed. In other words, how will the department or organization benefit? Informing employees helps them realize the importance of the task (experienced meaningfulness of work). Telling the employee why he or she was selected should make him or her feel valued. Don't use the "it's a lousy job, but someone has to do it" approach. Be positive; make employees aware of how they will benefit from the assignment. If step 1 is completed successfully, the employee should be motivated, or at least willing, to do the assignment.

Step 2. Set objectives that define responsibility, level of authority, and deadline. The objectives should clearly state the end result the employee is responsible for achieving by a specific deadline. You should also define the level of authority the employee has, as the following choices illustrate:

- Make a list of all supplies on hand, and present it to me each Friday at 2:00 (inform authority).
- Fill out a supply purchase order, and present it to me each Friday at 2:00 (recommend authority).

- Fill out and sign a purchase order for supplies; send it to the purchasing department with a copy put in my in-basket each Friday by 2:00 (report authority).
- Fill out and sign a purchase order for supplies, and send it to the purchasing department each Friday by 2:00, keeping a copy (full authority).

Step 3. Develop a plan. Once the objective is set, a plan is needed to achieve it. It is helpful to write out the objective, specifying the level of authority and the plan. When developing a plan, be sure to identify the resources needed to achieve the objectives, and give the employee the authority necessary to obtain the resources. Inform all parties of the employee's authority and with whom the employee must work. For example, if an employee is doing a marketing report, you should contact the marketing department and tell them the employee must have access to the necessary information.

Step 4. Establish control checkpoints and hold employees accountable. For simple, short tasks, a deadline without control checkpoints is appropriate. However, it is often advisable to check progress at predetermined times (control checkpoints) for tasks that have multiple steps or will take some time to complete. This builds information flow into the delegation system right from the start. You and the employee should agree on the form (phone call, visit, memo, or detailed report) and time frame (daily, weekly, or after specific steps are completed but before going on to the next step) for information regarding the assignment. When establishing control, consider the employee's capability level. The lower the capability, the more frequent the checks; the higher the capability, the less frequent the checks.

WORK
Application **7-8**

Select a manager you work or have worked for, and analyze how well he or she implements the four steps of delegation. Which steps does the manager typically follow and not follow?

It is helpful to list the control checkpoints in writing on an operational planning sheet, making copies of the finished plan so that the parties involved and you as the delegating manager have a record to refer to. In addition, all parties involved should record the control checkpoints on their calendars. If the employee to whom the task was delegated does not report as scheduled, follow up to find out why the person did not report, and get the information. You should evaluate performance at each control checkpoint, and upon completion provide feedback that develops knowledge of the results of work.

Providing praise for progress and completion of the task motivates employees to do a good job. You will recall that Chapter 6 discussed how to give praise.

The four steps of the delegation process are summarized in Model 7.1. In Developing Your Leadership Skills Exercise 1, you will have the opportunity to use the model to delegate a task and to develop your delegation skills.

Steps in the Delegation Process

MODEL 7.1

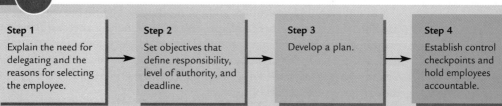

Step 1	Step 2	Step 3	Step 4
Explain the need for delegating and the reasons for selecting the employee.	Set objectives that define responsibility, level of authority, and deadline.	Develop a plan.	Establish control checkpoints and hold employees accountable.

© Cengage Learning®

Learning Outcome **8** *An effective evaluation should accomplish at least three things. Name them.*

Evaluating Followers: Guidelines for Success

Past research on employee evaluation and feedback has shown that when employees feel they are treated fairly, positive outcomes result and negative outcomes can be avoided. Evaluation and feedback is usually given to the employee by his superior, and represents an assessment of the employee's job performance and efforts in the assigned task. Therefore, it should be seen as a tool for professional learning and growth for the employee or subordinate.

It is an important leadership responsibility that ought to be part of regular leadership training and development programs.[97] Leader and subordinate personality traits, self-efficacy, self-esteem, locus of control, and emotional stability have been shown to affect the feedback process.[98] People in general tend to be defensive when being evaluated, especially when the evaluation is not very positive. To some followers, a negative evaluation questions their abilities and threatens their self-esteem. Some leaders are uncomfortable confronting followers who underperform because of this sentiment and the fear of hurting their relationship with the follower. However, addressing a follower's performance deficiencies is required to help the follower address weaknesses, but the way it is done can preserve or strain the leader–follower relationship.[99]

Researchers and practitioners generally agree that followers admire and respect leaders who show honesty, caring, understanding, and empathy during the evaluation process.[100] Followers also want to be convinced that the evaluation is fair and effective.[101] That's why the 360-degree multi-rater evaluation method is highly recommended. This evaluation tool uses multiple sources (self, peer, superior, customers, suppliers, etc.) to evaluate an individual.[102] It goes by different names such as the 360-degree feedback, multi-source feedback, or crowdsourced performance reviews.[103]

A leader must learn to stay calm and professional when followers overreact to a negative evaluation. The leader must be specific in stating the deficiency, calmly explaining the impact of poor performance on team or organizational objectives, involving the follower in identifying the reasons for negative evaluation, and work with the follower to suggest remedies for change. At the conclusion of an evaluation session, the follower must come away believing that the leader showed a genuine desire to be of help and that both parties mutually agreed on specific action steps for improvement. The follower's self-confidence should remain intact or be enhanced through evaluation and feedback, rather than being shattered. This is an indication that not only was the evaluation done well, but the feedback between the leader and follower was equally effective.[104]

An effective evaluation should accomplish three things:[105]

- Describe behavior, performance, and results the leader has observed.
- Explain, illustrate, and support the leader's conclusions.
- Tell employees clearly what they are doing well and describe what they need to improve.

Careful planning, execution, and monitoring of the process are required. Therefore, Exhibit 7.4 presents a three-step process for conducting successful evaluation; where planning is the pre-evaluation and feedback step, execution is the actual evaluation and feedback phase, and post-evaluation is the monitoring phase. We should note here that Chapter 6 has an expanded discussion on feedback. Other approaches for providing feedback are presented as part of coaching.

WORK
Application **7-9**

Recall the last time you were evaluated on the job by your manager. Describe how you felt at the end of the session. What factors accounted for your feelings? See if some of the factors discussed in this section apply in your particular situation.

EXHIBIT 7.4

Effective Evaluation and Feedback

Pre-Evaluation and Feedback—Leader should:

- Have an agenda that specifies time and place
- Gather accurate facts on follower performance

During Evaluation and Feedback Session—Leader should:

- Be specific in stating performance deficiency
- Explain negative impact of poor performance
- Help follower identify reasons for poor performance
- Ask follower to suggest remedies
- Arrive at mutual agreement on specific action steps

Post-Evaluation and Feedback—Leader should:

- Follow up to ensure implementation of action steps
- Show desire to be of help to follower
- Build follower's self-confidence

© Cengage Learning®

"Take It To The Net". Access student resources at www.cengagebrain.com. Search for Lussier, Leadership 6e to find student study tools.

Chapter Summary

The chapter summary is organized to answer the 8 learning outcomes for this chapter.

① **Describe the two subgroups that can form under VDL Theory.**

Leaders develop positive social exchanges with a select subset of followers known as the in-group. With another subgroup known as the out-group, leaders develop economic-based authority relationships. Leaders primarily use expert, referent, and reward power to influence members of the in-group. Out-group members are more likely to be managed according to the requirements of the employment contract. As long as such compliance is forthcoming, the out-group follower receives the standard benefits for the job (such as a salary) and no more.

② **Define the two kinds of relationships that can occur between a leader and followers under Leader–Member Exchange Theory.**

Leaders form *high-quality social exchanges* (based on trust and liking) with some members and *low-quality economic exchanges* with others.

③ **Describe the role of the leader and follower in influencing LMX relationships**

The Leader's Role. The leader's ability or willingness to develop a working relationship with a follower that goes

beyond an economic-based exchange (which is strictly contractual in nature) to a socially based exchange relationship (characterized by friendship, mutual trust, loyalty, and respect between the leader and the follower) is critical in influencing the LMX relationship. Other factors such as a leader's resource strength, span of control, and ability to create a supportive work climate or environment will also greatly influence LMX relationships.

The Follower's Role. Proactive followers who want to influence LMX relationships with their leaders can employ tactics such as impressions management, ingratiation and self-promotion.

④ **Discuss the main criticisms of LMX Theory.**

The main criticisms of LMX theory are measurement issues and attribution bias and its predictive power. The main instrument for measuring LMX quality is the LMX-7. A criticism of LMX-7 is that it determines the quality of the exchange relationship solely from the follower's perspective. The leader's input is not taken into account. A second criticism of LMX is its attribution bias in favor of in-group members. Given the variability in a leader's treatment of in-group and out-group members, it is quite possible that a leader's favorable impressions toward in-group members may well translate into favorable performance evaluations and feedback for such members. Finally, there have been criticisms of the predictive power of LMX theory. For example, the research evidence on staff turnover is mix at best and reservations about the performance measures used.

❺ Describe the two behaviors identified in the Kelley model and the resulting five follower types.

Using a combination of two types of behavior—independent critical thinking and level of involvement in organizational affairs—Kelley groups followers into five categories. The independent critical-thinking variable is on a continuum from low to high and the level of involvement on a continuum from low to high as well. The five basic follower types are: alienated, passive, conformist, pragmatic, and effective follower.

❻ Briefly describe the three factors than can enhance a follower's influence.

The three follower-influencing characteristics are: (1) Relative power position—leaders need to realize that followers also have the power to influence them. (2) Locus of control—followers can have an internal or external locus of control, based on their belief about who is the master of their destiny. Thus, leader–member exchanges should be different based on locus of control. (3) Education and experience—leaders need to realize that followers may have different levels of education and experience and that they need to supervise them differently.

❼ List five things a leader should delegate.

A leader should delegate paperwork, routine tasks, technical matters, tasks with developmental potential, and employees' own problems.

❽ An effective evaluation should accomplish at least three things. Name them.

An effective evaluation should:

- Describe behavior, performance, and results the leader has observed
- Explain, illustrate, and support the leader's conclusions
- Tell employees clearly what they are doing well and describe what they need to improve.

Key Terms

alienated follower, 242

conformist follower, 241

delegation, 249

delegation model, 252

dyad, 232

dyadic theory, 232

effective follower, 242

follower, 240

followership, 240

impressions management, 237

ingratiation, 237

in-group, 232

leader–member exchange (LMX), 234

locus of control, 247

organizational citizenship behavior, 236

out-group, 233

passive follower, 241

pragmatic follower, 242

self-efficacy, 243

self-promotion, 237

social capital, 238

social identity 236

Review Questions

❶ What are the differences between in-groups and out-groups?

❷ How do high-quality leader–member exchange relationships influence follower behavior?

❸ Describe the inherent bias of LMX theory and how it can lead to unintended consequences.

❹ How do education and experience, described as follower-influencing characteristics, affect effective followership?

❺ What are some of the benefits of delegating?

❻ What are some things that a leader should not delegate?

Critical-Thinking Questions

The following critical-thinking questions can be used for class discussion and/or as written assignments to develop communication skills. Be sure to give complete explanations for all questions.

1 In your opinion, can a leader maintain a personal friendship with some members of his or her work group or team without creating the perception of in-groups (those in his or her social circle) and out-groups (those outside his or her social circle)?

2 What should a leader do to dispel any notion or misperception that there are in-groups and out-groups in his or her work unit?

3 High-quality LMX relationships create a circle of reciprocity where followers feel like they should go the extra mile for a leader who supports them and the leader feels like he or she should offer the followers more support and benefits to keep their loyalty. Do you believe this is the case in the real world or is it something different?

4 Movies dealing with the prison or college environment often depict one or two prisoners or students who seem to have more influence over other prisoners or students than even the guards or administrators. Can you think of one such case and explain why the individual was influential over other prisoners or students?

5 What do you say to those who argue that tactics used by followers to get noticed by their leader (such as impressions management, ingratiation, and self-promotion) are shameful and self-serving and should be avoided?

6 Can someone have a successful career by aspiring to be an effective follower? Explain.

7 As a leader, how will you motivate the alienated follower?

CASE

W. L. Gore & Associates

Terri Kelly is the president and CEO of W. L. Gore & Associates. For the past 16 years, Gore has consistently been named among the "100 Best Companies to Work For" in the United States by *Fortune* magazine. Gore is now one of only a few companies to appear on all of the U.S. "100 Best Companies to Work For" lists since its initiation in 1984. In a recent interview, Ms. Kelly was asked what would be the most distinctive elements of the Gore management model to an outsider. She listed four factors: "We don't operate in a hierarchy; we try to resist titles; our associates, who are all owners in the company, self-commit to what they want to do; and our leaders have positions of authority because they have followers." According to CEO Kelly, these four attributes enable Gore to maximize individual potential while cultivating an environment that fosters creativity and also to operate with high integrity. She is quick to remind everyone that all of Gore's practices and ways of doing business reflect the innovative and entrepreneurial spirit of its founders.

Those founders are Bill and Vieve Gore, who in 1958 set out to create a business where innovation was a way of life and not a by-product. They founded W. L. Gore & Associates. There is no doubt that the Gores' vision has been realized. Gore is a uniquely managed, privately owned, family business. Today Gore is best known for its Gore-Tex range of high-performance fabrics and Elixir Strings for guitars. Gore is the leading manufacturer of thousands of advanced technology products for the medical, electronics, industrial, and fabrics markets. With annual revenues of $3.2 billion, the company employs more than 10,000 employees, called associates at more than 50 facilities around the world. Gore is truly a modern day success story.

CEO Kelly attributes Gore's success to its unique culture. How work is conducted at Gore and how employees relate to one another sets Gore apart. There are no titles, no bosses, and no formal hierarchy. Compensation and promotion decisions are determined by peer rankings of each other's performance. To avoid dampening employee creativity, the company has an organizational structure and culture that goes against conventional wisdom. W. L. Gore & Associates has been described as not only unmanaged but also unstructured. Bill Gore (the founder) referred to the company's structure as a "lattice organization."

Gore's lattice structure includes the following features:[106]

- Direct lines of communication—person to person—with no intermediary
- No fixed or assigned authority

- Sponsors, not bosses
- Natural leadership as evidenced by the willingness of others to follow
- Objectives set by those who must "make them happen"
- Tasks and functions organized through commitments
- Complete avoidance of the hierarchical command and control structure

The lattice structure as described by the people at Gore encourages hands-on innovation and discourages bureaucratic red tape by involving those closest to a project in decision making. Instead of a pyramid of bosses and managers, Gore has a flat organizational structure. There are no chains of command, no predetermined channels of communication. It sounds very much like a self-managed team at a much broader scale.

Why has Gore achieved such remarkable success? W. L. Gore & Associates prefers to think of the various people who play key roles in the organization as being leaders, not managers. While Bill Gore did not believe in smothering the company in thick layers of formal management, he also knew that as the company grew, he had to find ways to assist new people and to follow their progress. Thus, W. L. Gore & Associates came up with its "sponsor" program. The sponsor program is a dyadic relationship between an incumbent, experienced employee and a newly hired, inexperienced employee. Before a candidate is hired, an associate has to agree to be his or her sponsor or what others refer to as a mentor. The sponsor's role is to take a personal interest in the new associate's contributions, problems, and goals, acting as both a coach and an advocate. The sponsor tracks the new associate's progress, offers help and encouragement, points out weaknesses and suggests ways to correct them, and concentrates on how the associate might better exploit his or her strengths.

Sponsoring is not a short-term commitment. All associates have sponsors, and many have more than one. When individuals are hired, at first they are likely to have a sponsor in their immediate work area. As associates' commitments change or grow, it's normal for them to acquire additional sponsors. For instance, if they move to a new job in another area of the company, they typically gain a sponsor there. Sponsors help associates chart a course in the organization that will offer personal fulfillment while maximizing their contribution to the enterprise. Leaders emerge naturally by demonstrating special knowledge, skill, or experience that advances a business objective.

An internal memo describes the three kinds of sponsorship and how they might work:

- **Starting sponsor**—a sponsor who helps a new associate get started on his or her first job at Gore, or helps a present associate get started on a new job.
- **Advocate sponsor**—a sponsor who sees to it that the associate being sponsored gets credit and recognition for contributions and accomplishments.
- **Compensation sponsor**—a sponsor who sees to it that the associate being sponsored is fairly paid for contributions to the success of the enterprise.

An associate can perform any one or all three kinds of sponsorship. Quite frequently, a sponsoring associate is a good friend, and it's not uncommon for two associates to sponsor each other as advocates.

Being an associate is a natural commitment to four basic principles articulated by Bill Gore and still a key belief of the company: fairness to each other and everyone we come in contact with; freedom to encourage, help, and allow other associates to grow in knowledge, skill, and scope of responsibility; the ability to make one's own commitments and keep them; and consultation with other associates before undertaking actions that could affect the reputation of the company.

Over the years, W. L. Gore & Associates has faced a number of unionization drives. The company neither tries to dissuade associates from attending organizational meetings nor retaliates against associates who pass out union flyers. However, Bill Gore believes there is no need for third-party representation under the lattice structure. He asks, "Why would associates join a union when they own the company? It seems rather absurd."

Commitment is seen as a two-way street at W. L. Gore & Associates—while associates are expected to commit to making a contribution to the company's success, the company is committed to providing a challenging, opportunity-rich work environment, and reasonable job security. The company tries to avoid laying off associates. If a workforce reduction becomes necessary, the company uses a system of temporary transfers within a plant or cluster of plants, and requests voluntary layoffs. According to CEO Kelly, Gore's structure, systems, and culture have continued to yield impressive results for the company. In the more than 50 years that Gore has been in business, it has never made a loss.[107]

GO TO THE INTERNET: To learn more about W. L. Gore & Associates, visit its Web site **(http://www.gore.com)**.

Support your answers to the following questions with specific information from the case and text or with other information you get from the Web or other sources.

1. What theories from this chapter are revealed through the case?

2. How did Gore's "sponsors" program facilitate the creation of high-quality relationships among leaders, sponsors, and associates?

3. Evaluate followership at W. L. Gore & Associates. What company actions and/or policies account for the quality of followership?

CUMULATIVE CASE QUESTIONS

4. Would you characterize the leadership style at W. L. Gore & Associates as job-centered or employee-centered (Chapter 3)? Support your answer.

5. Based on the types of power discussed in the text, what type(s) of power do sponsors have in their relationships with associates (Chapter 5)?

6. What role, if any, does coaching play in W. L. Gore's lattice structure (Chapter 6)?

CASE EXERCISE AND ROLE-PLAY

Preparation: You are part of an organization that evaluates its employees at the end of each year. The month of the year when evaluations need to be completed by all leaders and managers is approaching. Your task is to play the role of a leader evaluating your followers, and then play the role of follower being evaluated by your own manager. Based on your understanding of the discussion of guidelines for effective leader feedback and guidelines for effective followership, (1) present a scenario of an effective and an ineffective feedback session, applying at least three of the guidelines discussed in the text and (2) present a scenario of effective and ineffective followership, applying at least three of the guidelines discussed in the text.

Role-Play: The instructor forms students into leader–follower pairs and has each pair dramatize scenarios 1 and 2 in front of the rest of the class. After each scenario, the class is to contrast the two approaches (effective versus ineffective feedback) by identifying the guidelines that the presenters or actors employed in making their points. Different student teams should try the exercise by employing different guidelines to both scenarios.

VIDEO ▶ CASE

Delegation at Boyne USA Resorts

Detroit native Everett Kircher moved to northern Michigan in 1947 and purchased land (for the price of $1) necessary to start his first ski resort known today as Boyne Mountain. Kircher practiced a traditional chain of command in a vertical organizational structure. Every decision came from his desk. As his company expanded, additional people were needed to manage the different locations. For Kircher, it was the beginning of a partial decentralization and delegation of his leadership and decision making. In 2002, Everett Kircher died at the age of 85, but his legacy lives on. The company's reorganization in 2004 paved the way for the "Boyne Brand" to grow while maintaining organizational integrity. General managers were hired at each resort location to oversee operations. In addition, vice presidents known as "subject matter experts" were hired. The VPs share critical information with the general managers to help each resort operation. The general managers fold these experts into the decision-making process and help provide policy.

1. Describe leader–follower relations at Boyne USA Resorts.

2. Why was decentralization and delegation necessary to Boyne's future despite the success with Everett Kircher at the helm of a vertical structure?

Developing Your Leadership Skills 7-1

Improving Dyadic Relationships—Followership

Preparing for This Exercise

Based on your reading of effective leader–member exchange relationships, how can you improve your current or future relationship with your manager?

Be sure to list specific things you plan to do.

_____

_____

Based on Self-Assessment 7-4 on page 243, "Effective Followers," how can you improve your followership skills with your present or future manager? Be sure to list specific things you plan to do.

_____

_____

Doing This Exercise in Class

Objective

To develop a plan to improve your dyadic relationship with your manager and to improve your followership skills

AACSB General Skills Area

The primary AACSB learning standard skills developed through this exercise are reflective thinking and analytic skills.

Preparation

You should have completed a plan in the preparation part of this exercise.

Experience

You will share your plan in a small group to provide further development.

Procedure 1 *(8–12 minutes)* Option A: Break into groups of three or four and share your plans. Offer each other ideas for improving plans.

Option B: Same as Option A, but add a spokesperson to record some of the best ideas from each group member.

Procedure 2 *(10–20 minutes)* Option B, each spokesperson reports to the entire class.

Conclusion

The instructor leads a class discussion and/or makes concluding remarks.

Apply It *(2–4 minutes)* What did I learn from this exercise? When will I implement my plan?

_____

_____

Sharing

In the group, or to the entire class, volunteers may give their answers to the "Apply It" questions.

Behavior Model Skills Training

In this behavior model skills training session, you will perform three activities:

1 Read the section, "Delegation," in this chapter (to learn how to use Model 7.1, page 253).

2 Watch Behavior Model Video 7.1, "Delegating."

3 Complete Developing Your Leadership Skills Exercise 2 (to develop your delegating skills).

For further practice, use the delegation model in your personal and professional life.

The Delegation Model

Step 1 Explain the need for delegating and the reasons for selecting the employee.

Step 2 Set objectives that define responsibility, level of authority, and deadline.

Step 3 Develop a plan.

Step 4 Establish control checkpoints and hold employees accountable.

Behavior Model Video 7.1

Delegating

Objective

To observe a manager delegating a task to an employee

Video *(4½ minutes)* Overview

You will watch a production manager, Steve, delegate the completion of a production output form to Dale.

Developing Your Leadership Skills 7-2

Delegating

Preparing for This Exercise

You should have read and understood the material on delegation.

Doing This Exercise in Class

Objective

To experience and develop skills in delegating a task

AACSB General Skills Area

The primary AACSB skill developed through this exercise is analytic skills and application of knowledge.

Experience

You will delegate, be delegated to, and observe the delegation of a task, and then evaluate the effectiveness of the delegated task. You may also see a video example of how to delegate using the delegation model.

Procedure 1 *(4–8 minutes)* Break into as many groups of three as possible, with the remainder in groups of two. Each person in the group picks a number 1, 2, or 3. Number 1 will be the first to delegate a task, then 2, and then 3. The level of difficulty of the delegation will increase with the number.

Each person then reads his or her delegation situation below (1, 2, or 3) and plans how he or she will delegate the task. If you prefer, you can use an actual delegation from a past or present job. Just be sure to fully explain the situation to the delegatee. Be sure to follow the four delegation steps in this chapter. An observer sheet is included at the end of this exercise for giving feedback on each delegation.

Delegation Situation 1

Delegator 1, you are a college student with a paper due in three days for your 10:00 a.m. class. It must be typed. You don't type well, so you have decided to hire someone to do it for you. The going rate is $1.50 per page. Think of an actual paper you have written in the past or will write in the future. Plan to delegate. Be sure to include the course name, paper title, special typing instructions, and so on. Assume that you are meeting the typ-

ist for the first time. He or she doesn't know you and doesn't expect you.

Delegator 2, assume that you do typing and are willing to do the job if the delegation is acceptable to you.

Delegation Situation 2

Delegator 2, you are the manager of a fast-food restaurant. In the past, you have scheduled the workers. Your policy is to keep changing the workers' schedules. You have decided to delegate the scheduling to your assistant manager. This person has never done any scheduling but appears to be very willing and confident about taking on new responsibility. Plan your delegation.

Delegator 3, assume that you are interested in doing the scheduling if the manager delegates the task effectively.

Delegation Situation 3

Delegator 3, you own and manage your own business. You have eight employees, one of whom is the organization's secretary. The secretary currently uses an old computer, which needs to be replaced. You have not kept up with the latest technology and don't know what to buy. You can spend $1,200. You try to keep costs down and get the most for your money. Because the secretary will use the new machine, you believe that this employee should be involved or maybe even make the decision. The secretary has never purchased equipment, and you believe he or she will be somewhat insecure about the assignment. Plan your delegation.

Delegator 1, assume that you are able to do the job but are somewhat insecure. Accept the task if the delegator "participates" effectively.

Procedure 2 *(7–10 minutes)*

a. *Delegation 1.* Delegator 1 delegates the task (role-play) to number 2. Number 3 is the observer. As the delegation takes place, the observer uses the form at the end of this exercise to provide feedback on the effectiveness of the delegator. Answer the questions on the form.

b. *Integration.* The observer (or number 3) leads a discussion of the effectiveness of the delegation, although all team members should participate. Do not continue until you are told to do so.

Procedure 3 *(7–10 minutes)*

a. *Delegation 2.* Follow procedure 2A, except number 2 is now the delegator, number 3 is the delegatee, and number 1 is the observer.

b. *Integration.* Follow procedure 2B with number 1 as the observer. Do not continue until you are told to do so.

Procedure 4 *(7–10 minutes)*

a. *Delegation 3.* Follow procedure 2A, except number 3 is now the delegator, number 1 is the delegatee, and number 2 is the observer. If you are in a group of two, be an additional observer for another group.

b. *Integration.* Follow procedure 2B with number 2 as the observer.

Conclusion

The instructor may lead a class discussion and make concluding remarks.

Apply It *(2–4 minutes)* What did I learn from this experience? When will I delegate using the model?

_____

_____

Sharing

In the group, or to the entire class, volunteers may give their answers to the "Apply It" questions.

Note: Remember that the process does not end with delegating the task; you must control (check progress at control points and help when needed) to ensure that the task is completed as scheduled.

OBSERVER FORM

During the delegation process, the observer checks off the items performed by the delegators. Items not checked were not performed. After the delegation, the delegator and delegatee also check off the items.

This sheet is used for all three situations. Use the appropriate column for each situation.

Delegation items for all situations	Situation 1	2	3

Did the delegator follow these steps?

Step 1. Explain the need for delegating and the reasons for selecting the person.

Step 2. Set an objective that defines responsibility, level of authority, and deadline.

Step 3. Develop a plan.

Step 4. Establish control checkpoints and hold the person accountable.

Process

Did the delegate clearly understand what was expected of him or her and know how to follow the plan?

_____

_____

Improvements

How could the delegation be improved if done again?

_____

_____

_____

Endnotes

1 C. Guglielmo, "Facebook's Mark Zuckerberg Tops Apple's Tim Cook as Best CEO of 2013," Forbes.com (March 15, 2013): 6; Mac R. "Mark Zuckerberg's Net Worth Up $3.7 Billion as Facebook Shares Soar Following Earnings," Forbes.com (July 25, 2013): 14; R. Stengel, "Person of the Year," *Time* (December 15, 2010); J. A. Vargas, "The Face of Facebook," *The New Yorker* (September, 20, 2010); "M. Zuckerberg," *New York Times* (January 3, 2011).

2 B. J. Avolio, "Promoting More Integrative Strategies for Leadership Theory Building," *American Psychologist 62* (2007): 25–33; G. B. Graen & M. Uhl-Bien, "Relationship-Based Approach to Leadership: Development of Leader–Member Exchange (LMX) Theory of Leadership over 25 Years: Applying a Multi-Level Multi-Domain Perspective," *Leadership Quarterly 6* (1995): 219–247; G. B. Graen & T. A. Scandura, "Toward a Psychology of Dyadic Organizing: Research in Organizational Behavior," In L. L. Cummings & B. Staw (Eds.), *Research in Organizational Behavior 9* (1987): 175–208.

3 T. Smith & B. Kirkman, "Understanding Leadership: The Followers' Influence on Leader Effectiveness," *Academy of Management Annual Meeting Proceedings,* (January 2012): 1.

4 T. Rockstuhl, A. Soon, J. Dulebohn, & L. Shore, "Leader–Member Exchange (LMX) and Culture: A Meta-Analysis of Correlates of LMX across 23 Countries," *Journal of Applied Psychology 97*(6) (November 2012): 1097–1130.

5 J. Shweta, & J. Srirang, "Leader-Member Exchange: A Critique of Theory & Practice," *Journal of Management & Public Policy 4*(2) (June 2013): 42–53.

6 D. Sluss & B. Thompson, "Socializing the Newcomer: The Mediating Role of Leader–Member Exchange," *Organizational Behavior & Human Decision Processes 119*(1) (September 2012): 114–125.

7 R. Zhang, L. Tsingan, & L. Zhang, "Role Stressors and Job Attitudes: A Mediated Model of Leader–Member Exchange," *Journal of Social Psychology 153*(5) (September 2013): 560–576.

8 J. DeConinck, "The Effects of Leader-Member Exchange and Organizational Identification on Performance and Turnover among Salespeople," *Journal of Personal Selling & Sales Management 31*(1) (Winter 2011): 21–34.

9 J. Volmer, D. Spurk, & C. Niessen, "Leader–Member Exchange (LMX), Job Autonomy, and Creative Work Involvement," *Leadership Quarterly 23*(3) (June 2012): 456–465.

10 M. Biron & C. Boon. "Performance and Turnover Intentions: A Social Exchange Perspective," *Journal of Managerial Psychology 28*(5) (September 2013): 511–531.

11 L. Raymond, M. Yina, & N. Hang-yue, "Linking Leader-Member Exchange and Employee Work Outcomes: The Mediating Role of Organizational Social and Economic Exchange," *Management & Organization Review 5*(3) (2009): 401–422.

12 G. B. Graen & M. Uhl-Bien, "Relationship-Based Approach to Leadership: Development of Leader-Member Exchange (LMX) Theory of Leadership over 25 Years: Applying a Multi-Level Multi-Domain Perspective," *Leadership Quarterly 6* (1995): 219–247.

13 A. Perumalu, I. Kandan, & I. Ali, "A Correlation Study of Leader-Member Exchange and Organizational Citizenship Behavior in a Public Sector Organization," *Journal of Global Business & Economics 1*(1) (2010): 62–78.

14 D. S. Kang & J. Stewart, "Leader-Member Exchange (LMX) Theory of Leadership and HRD: Development of Units of Theory and Laws of Interaction," *Leadership & Organizational Journal 28*(6) (2007): 531–551.

15 J. Manzoni & J. Barsoux, *The Set-Up-to-Fail Syndrome: How Good Managers Cause Great People to Fail* (Boston: Harvard Business School Press, 2002).

16 F. Dansereau, G. B. Graen, & W. J. Haga, "A Vertical Dyad Linkage Approach to Leadership within Formal Organizations," *Organizational Behavior and Human Performance 13* (1975): 46–78.

17 G. B. Graen, M. A. Novak, & P. Sommerkamp, "The Effects of Leader-Member Exchange and Job Design on Productivity and Satisfaction: Testing the Dual Attachment Model," *Organizational Behavior and Human Performance 30* (1982): 109–131.

18 R. C. Liden & G. B. Graen, "Generalizability of the Vertical Dyad Linkage Model of Leadership." *Academy of Management Journal 23*(3), 451–465.

19 C. A. Schriessheim, S. L. Castro, X. Zhou, & F. J. Yamarino, "The Folly of Theorizing "A" but Testing "B": A Selective Level-of-Analysis View of the Field and Detailed Leader-Member Exchange Illustrations," *Leadership Quarterly* (Winter 2001): 515–551.

20 D. Krasikova & J. LeBreton, "Just the Two of Us: Misalignment of Theory and Methods in Examining Dyadic Phenomena." *Journal of Applied Psychology 97*(4) (July 2012): 739–757.

21 W. van Breukelen, R. van der Leeden, W. Wesselius, & M. Hoes, "Differential Treatment within Sports Teams, Leader-Member (Coach-Player) Exchange Quality, Team Atmosphere, and Team Performance," *Journal of Organizational Behavior 33*(1) (January 2012): 43–63.

22 V. Fernandez, P. Simo, M. Enache, & J. Sallan. "The Frequency of the Dyadic Influence Tactics according to Communication Media," *Behaviour & Information Technology* 31(6) (June 2012): 577–586.

23 J. Volmer, C. Niessen, D. Spurk, A. Linz, & A. Abele, "Reciprocal Relationships between Leader-Member Exchange (LMX) and Job Satisfaction: A Cross-Lagged Analysis," *Applied Psychology: An International Review* 60(4) (October 2011): 522–545.

24 A. Joshi, H. Liao, & S. Jackson, "Cross-Level Effects of Workplace Diversity on Sales Performance and Pay," *Academy of Management Journal* 49(3) (2006): 459–481.

25 B. Erdogan, R. Liden, & L. Kraimer, "Justice and Leader–Member Exchange: The Moderating Role of Organizational Culture," *Academy of Management Journal* 149 (2006): 395–406.

26 B. Kuvaas, R. Buch, A. Dysvik, & T. Haerem, "Economic and Social Leader–Member Exchange Relationships and Follower Performance," *Leadership Quarterly* 23(5) (October 2012): 756–765.

27 J. B. Wu, A. S. Tsui, & A. J. Kinicki, "Consequences of Differentiated Leadership in Groups," *Academy of Management Journal* 53(1) (2010): 90–106.

28 R. L Loi, Y. M. Mao, & H. Ngo, "Linking Leader-Member Exchange and Employee Work Outcomes: The Mediating Role of Organizational Social and Economic Exchange," *Management & Organization Review* 5(3) (2009): 401–422.

29 R. Zhang, L. Tsingan, & L. Zhang, "Role Stressors and Job Attitudes: A Mediated Model of Leader-Member Exchange," *Journal of Social Psychology* 153(5) (September 2013):560–576; D. Ariani, "Leader-Member Exchanges as a Mediator of the Effect of Job Satisfaction on Affective Organizational Commitment: An Empirical Test," *International Journal of Management* 29(1) (March 2012): 46–56; T. Rockstuhl, A. Soon, J. Dulebohn, & L. Shore, "Leader-Member Exchange (LMX) and Culture: A Meta-Analysis of Correlates of LMX across 23 Countries," *Journal of Applied Psychology* 97(6) (November 2012): 1097–1130; J. Volmer, C. Niessen, D. Spurk, A. Linz, & A. Abele, "Reciprocal Relationships between Leader-Member Exchange (LMX) and Job Satisfaction: A Cross-Lagged Analysis," *Applied Psychology: An International Review* 60(4) (October 2011): 522–545; M. Biron & C. Boon, "Performance and Turnover Intentions: A Social Exchange Perspective," *Journal of Managerial Psychology* 28(5) (September 2013): 511–531; J. Shweta & J. Srirang, "Leader-Member Exchange: A Critique of Theory & Practice," *Journal of Management & Public Policy* 4(2) (June 2013): 42–45; J. Volmer, D. Spurk, & C. Niessen, "Leader–Member Exchange (LMX), Job Autonomy, and Creative Work Involvement," *Leadership Quarterly* 23(3) (June 2012): 456–465.

30 J. Volmer, C. Niessen, D. Spurk, A. Linz, & A. Abele, "Reciprocal Relationships between Leader-Member Exchange (LMX) and Job Satisfaction: A Cross-Lagged Analysis," *Applied Psychology: An International Review* 60(4) (October 2011): 522–545.

31 K. M. Sherony & S. G. Green, "Co-Worker Exchange Relationships between Co-Workers, Leader-Member Exchange, and Work Attitudes," *Journal of Applied Psychology* 87(3) (2002): 542–548.

32 T. Rockstuhl, A. Soon, J. Dulebohn, & L. Shore, "Leader-Member Exchange (LMX) and Culture: A Meta-Analysis of Correlates of LMX across 23 Countries," *Journal of Applied Psychology* 97(6) (November 2012): 1097–1130.

33 F. Walumbwa, R. Cropanzano, & B. Goldman, "How Leader-Member Exchange Influences Effective Work Behaviors: Social Exchange and Internal-External Efficacy Perspectives," *Personnel Psychology* 64(3) (September 2011): 739–770.

34 M. Biron & C. Boon, "Performance and Turnover Intentions: A Social Exchange Perspective," *Journal of Managerial Psychology* 28(5) (September 2013): 511–531.

35 T. Rockstuhl, A. Soon, J. Dulebohn, & L. Shore, "Leader-Member Exchange (LMX) and Culture: A Meta-Analysis of Correlates of LMX across 23 Countries," *Journal of Applied Psychology* 97(6) (November 2012): 1097–1130.

36 E. Jackson & R. Johnson, "When Opposites Do (and Do Not) Attract: Interplay of Leader and Follower Self-Identities and Its Consequences for Leader–Member Exchange," *Leadership Quarterly* 23(3) (June 2012): 488–501.

37 J. DeConinck, "The Effects of Leader-Member Exchange and Organizational Identification on Performance and Turnover among Salespeople," *Journal of Personal Selling & Sales Management* 31(1) (Winter 2011): 21–34.

38 M. Farrell & E. Oczkowski, "Organisational Identification and Leader Member Exchange Influences on Customer Orientation and Organisational Citizenship Behaviours," *Journal of Strategic Marketing* 20(4) (July 2012): 365–377.

39 S. M. S. Malar, "Right Attitude: Grab It!" *IUP Journal of Soft Skills 3* (September 2009): 19–25.

40 J. Westphal, S. Park, M. McDonald, & M. Hayward, "Helping Other CEOs Avoid Bad Press: Social Exchange and Impression Management Support among CEOs in Communications with Journalists," *Administrative Science Quarterly,* 57(2) (June 2012): 217–268.

41 W. Lam, X. Huang, & E. Snape, "Feedback Seeking Behavior and Leader–Member Exchange: Do Supervisor Attributed Motives Matter?" *Academy of Management Journal 50* (2007): 348–363.

42 D. Paulhus, B. Westlake, S. Calvez, & P. Harms, "Self-Presentation Style in Job Interviews: The Role of Personality and Culture," *Journal of Applied Social Psychology 43*(10) (October 2013): 2042–2059.

43 J. Volmer, C. Niessen, D. Spurk, A. Linz, & A. Abele, "Reciprocal Relationships between Leader-Member Exchange (LMX) and Job Satisfaction: A Cross-Lagged Analysis," *Applied Psychology: An International Review 60*(4) (October 2011): 522–545.

44 L. Wu, H. Kwan, L. Wei, & J. Liu, "Ingratiation in the Workplace: The Role of Subordinate and Supervisor Political Skill," *Journal of Management Studies 50*(6) (September 2013): 991–1017.

45 C. Sue-Chan, A. Au, & R. Hackett, "Trust as a Mediator of the Relationship between Leader/Member Behavior and Leader-Member-Exchange Quality," *Journal of World Business 47*(3) (July 2012): 459–468.

46 F. Walumbwa, R. Cropanzano, & B. Goldman, "How Leader-Member Exchange Influences Effective Work Behaviors: Social Exchange and Internal-External Efficacy Perspectives," *Personnel Psychology 64*(3) (September 2011): 739–770.

47 J. Shweta & J. Srirang, "Leader-Member Exchange: A Critique of Theory & Practice," *Journal of Management & Public Policy 4*(2) (June 2013): 42–53.

48 E. L. Mouriño-Ruiz, "Leader-Member Exchange (LMX): The Impact of Leader-Employee Relationships in the 21st Century Workplace (Implications for Research on Latinos in the Workforce)," *The Business Journal of Hispanic Research 4*(1) (2010): 35–42.

49 J. Volmer, C. Niessen, D. Spurk, A. Linz, & A. Abele, "Reciprocal Relationships between Leader-Member Exchange (LMX) and Job Satisfaction: A Cross-Lagged Analysis," *Applied Psychology: An International Review 60*(4) (October 2011): 522–545.

50 M. Brewer, "The Importance of Being We: Human Nature and Intergroup Relations," *The American Psychologist 62* (2007): 728–738.

51 H. Oh, M.-H. Chung, & G. Labianca, "Group Social Capital and Group Effectiveness: The Role of Informal Socializing Ties," *Academy of Management Review 4*(7) (2004): 860–875.

52 E. McKenna, *Business Psychology and Organizational Behavior* (5/e) (Hove & New York: Psychology Press, 2012).

53 J. Dulebohn, W. Bommer, R. Liden, R. Brouer, & G. Ferris, "A Meta-Analysis of Antecedents and Consequences of Leader-Member Exchange: Integrating the Past with an Eye toward the Future," *Journal Of Management 38*(6) (November 2012): 1715–1759.

54 T. Smith & B. Kirkman, "Understanding Leadership: The Followers' Influence on Leader Effectiveness," *Academy of Management Annual Meeting Proceedings* (January 2012): 1.

55 I. Chaleff, *The Courageous Follower: Standing up to and for Our Leaders* (2nd ed.) (San Francisco, CA: Berrett-Koehler Publishers, Inc, 2003); B. Kellerman, "Followership: How Followers Are Creating Change and Changing Leaders" (Boston, MA: Harvard Business Press, 2004).

56 R. Jerry, II., "Leadership and Followership," *University of Toledo Law Review 44*(2) (Winter 2013): 345–354.

57 W. Bennis, "Art of Followership," *Leadership Excellence 27*(1) (January 2010): 3–4.

58 C. Crippen, "Enhancing Authentic Leadership–Followership: Strengthening School Relationships," *Management in Education* (Sage Publications, Ltd.) *26*(4) (October 2012): 192–198.

59 J. Whitlock, "The Value of Active Followership," *Nursing Management–UK 20*(2) (May 2013): 20–23.

60 D. Kirchhubel, "Effective 'Followership' How to Manage Upwards," *Manager: British Journal of Administrative Management* (72) (Fall 2010): 18.

61 H. Greyvenstein & F. Cilliers, "Followership's Experiences of Organisational Leadership: A Systems Psychodynamic Perspective," *South African Journal of Industrial Psychology 38*(2) (June 2012): 1–10.

62 R. E. Kelley, *Power of Followership: How to Create Leaders People Want to Follow and Followers Who Want to Lead Themselves,* (New York: Doubleday, 1991).

63 I. Cox, G. Plagens, & K. Sylla, "The Leadership-Followership Dynamic: Making the Choice to Follow," *International Journal of Interdisciplinary Social Sciences 5*(8) (December 2010): 37–51.

64 R. E. Kelley, *The Power of Followership* (New York: Doubleday, 1992).

65 I. Chaleff, "Courageous Followers," *Leadership Excellence 28*(4) (April 2011): 19.

66 I. Chaleff, "The Courageous Follower: Standing Up to and for Our Leaders, Third Edition," *T+D 64*(2) (February 2010): 75.

67 J. Kohles, M. Bligh, & M. Carsten, A Follower-Centric Approach to the Vision Integration Process," *Leadership Quarterly* 23(3) (June 2012): 476–487.

68 R. Kelley, "In Praise of Followers," *Harvard Business Review* (November–December 1988): 142–148.

69 M. Carsten, M. Uhl-Bien, B. West, J. Patera, & R. McGregor, "Exploring Social Constructions of Followership: A Qualitative Study," *Leadership Quarterly* 21(3) (June 2010): 543–562.

70 B. Kellerman, "What Every Leader Needs to Know about Followers," *Harvard Business Review* 85 (December 2007): 84–91.

71 R. E. Kelley, "In Praise of Followers," *Harvard Business Review* (November/December 1988): 142–148.

72 M. Carsten, M. Uhl-Bien, B. West, J. Patera, & R. McGregor, "Exploring Social Constructions of Followership: A Qualitative Study," *Leadership Quarterly* 21(3) (June 2010): 543–562.

73 B. Kaufman, "Speak Truth to Power," *Leadership Excellence* 28(6) (June 2011): 6.

74 D.B. Zoogak, D.H. Agboh, & L. Leyland, "Determinants of Strategic Followership: An African Perspective," *Journal of International Business & Economics* 10(4) (July 2010): 137–148.

75 J. M. Howell & B. Shamir, "The Role of Followers in the Charismatic Leadership Process: Relationships and Their Consequences," *Academy of Management Review* 30(1) (2005): 96–112.

76 A. Bandura, "Self-Efficacy," in V.S. Ramachaudran (Ed.), *Encyclopedia of Human Behavior* (Vol. 4, pp. 71–81) (New York: Academic Press); repr. in H. Friedman [Ed.], *Encyclopedia of Mental Health* (San Diego: Academic Press, 1998).

77 S. Norman, B. Avolio, & F. Luthans, "The Impact of Positivity and Transparency on Trust in Leaders and Their Perceived Effectiveness," *Leadership Quarterly* 21(3) (June 2010): 350–364.

78 C. Crippen, "Enhancing Authentic Leadership–Followership: Strengthening School Relationships," *Management in Education (Sage Publications, Ltd.)* 26(4) (October 2012): 192–198.

79 D. Kirchhubel, "Effective 'Followership': How to Manage Upwards," *Manager: British Journal of Administrative Management* (72) (Fall 2010): 18.

80 G. Abudi, "The Fine Art of Followership," *PM Network* 24(10) (October 2010): 64–65.

81 A. J. DeLellis, "Clarifying the Concept of Respect: Implications for Leadership," *Journal of Leadership Studies* 7 (Spring 2000): 2–37.

82 C. Thoroughgood, A. Padilla, S. Hunter, & B. Tate, "The Susceptible Circle: A Taxonomy of Followers Associated with Destructive Leadership," *Leadership Quarterly* 23(5) (October 2012): 897–917.

83 A. Martinez, R. Kane, G. Ferris, & C. Brooks, "Power in Leader–Follower Work Relationships," *Journal of Leadership & Organizational Studies (Sage Publications Inc.)* 19(2) (May 2012): 142–151.

84 K. April, B. Dharani, & K. Peters, "Impact of Locus of Control Expectancy on Level of Well-Being," *Review of European Studies* 4(2) (June 2012): 124–137.

85 D. Cavell, "Leadership or Followership: One or Both? All Successful Leaders Need Good Followers," *Healthcare Financial Management* 61 (November 2007): 142–143.

86 P. M. Buhler, "Managing in the New Millennium: The Top Ten Managerial Mistakes," *Supervision* 65 (August 2004): 15–18.

87 S. Chevrier & M. Viegas-Pires, "Delegating Effectively across Cultures," *Journal of World Business* [serial online] 48(3) (July 2013): 431–439.

88 N. Lorinkova, M. Pearsall, & H. Sims Jr., "Examining the Differential Longitudinal Performance of Directive versus Empowering Leadership in Teams," *Academy of Management Journal* 56(2) (April 2013): 573–596.

89 F. Csaszar & J. Eggers, "Organizational Decision Making: An Information Aggregation View," *Management Science* 50(10) (October 2013): 2257–2277.

90 G. Charness, R. Cobo-Reyes, N. Jiménez, J. Lacomba, & F. Lagos, "The Hidden Advantage of Delegation: Pareto Improvements in a Gift Exchange Game," *American Economic Review* 102(5) (August 2012): 2358–2379.

91 P. Danby, "Setting the Right Direction," *Business Strategy Review* 20(4) (Winter 2009): 58–63.

92 C. Hymowitz, "A Vacationing Boss Should Take a Break; Let Staffers Step Up," *The Wall Street Journal* (August 20, 2007): B1.

93 V. Thiele, "Subjective Performance Evaluations, Collusion, and Organizational Design," *Journal of Law, Economics & Organization* 29(1) (February 2013): 35–59.

94 V. Thiele, "Subjective Performance Evaluations, Collusion, and Organizational Design," *Journal of Law, Economics & Organization* 29(1) (February 2013): 35–59.

95　www.huffingtonpost.com/.../tom-coburn-john-ensign_n_861287.html, accessed May 25, 2011.

96　S. Chevrier & M. Viegas-Pires, "Delegating Effectively across Cultures," *Journal of World Business* [serial online] 48(3) (July 2013): 431–439.

97　Q. Li, R. Zhou, H. Xiao, et al. "Pre-Training Evaluation and Feedback Improved Skills Retention of Basic Life Support in Medical Students," *Resuscitation* 84(9) (September 2013): 1274–1278.

98　B. Krenn, S. Wuerth, & A. Hergovich, "Individual Differences Concerning the Impact of Feedback: Specifying the Role of Core Self-Evaluations," *Studia Psychologica* 55(2) (April 2013): 95–110.

99　C. Westerman & D. Westerman, "What's Fair? Public and Private Delivery of Project Feedback," *Journal of Business Communication* 50(2) (April 2013): 190–207.

100　J. Kollée, S. Giessner, & D. van Knippenberg, "Leader Evaluations after Performance Feedback: The Role of Follower Mood," *Leadership Quarterly* 24(1) (February 2013): 203–214.

101　C. Westerman, & D. Westerman, "What's Fair? Public and Private Delivery of Project Feedback," *Journal of Business Communication* 50(2) (April 2013): 190–207.

102　L. Darling-Hammond, "When Teachers Support & Evaluate Their Peers," *Educational Leadership* 71 (2) (October 2013): 24–29.

103　A. Fisher, "Should Performance Reviews Be Crowdsourced?" Fortune.com [serial online] (October 9, 2013): 1.

104　R. Wolf, "Personal Feedback as a Tool for Good Management," *Mustang Journal of Business & Ethics* (3) (August 2012): 113–121.

105　P. Harms, & D. Roebuck, "Teaching the Art and Craft of Giving and Receiving Feedback," *Business Communication Quarterly* 73(4) (December 2010): 413–431.

106　Information taken from the W. L. Gore & Associates Web site: www.gore.com accessed July 8, 2008. Update to May 2011.

107　G. Hamel, "W. L. Gore: Lessons from a Management Revolutionary," *The Wall Street Journal* (March 18, 2010); G. Hamel, "W. L. Gore: Lessons from a Management Revolutionary, Part 2," *The Wall Street Journal* (April 2, 2010).

CHAPTER OUTLINE

Team Leadership and Self-Managed Teams

Learning Outcomes

After studying this chapter, you should be able to:

1. Discuss the benefits and limitations of working in teams. p. 272

2. Identify and explain the ten characteristics of highly effective teams. p. 276

3. What role can a team leader play in creating an effective team? p. 279

4. Describe how organizational culture can influence team creativity. p. 281

5. Outline the three parts of conducting effective meetings. p. 291

6. Explain the differences between conventional and self-managed teams. p. 294

7. Describe the benefits of using self-managed teams in organizations. p. 295

8. Describe top management's role in improving the success rate of self-managed teams. p. 296

9. Describe the challenges of implementing effective self-managed teams. p. 299

OPENING CASE Application

For more than four decades, Dallas-based Southwest Airlines continues to differentiate itself from other airlines with top-of-the-line customer service delivered by more than 45,000 employees to more than 100 million customers annually. Key to this success is Southwest's teamwork and a people-centered culture. In his 2012 Southwest Airlines One Report, CEO Gary Kelly reiterated the company's team philosophy: "Our Employees are passionate about our Purpose to connect people . . . We couldn't be who we are without our dedicated Employees." As he puts it, at Southwest, "We believe in Living the Southwest Way, which is to have a Warrior Spirit, a Servant's Heart, and a Fun-LUVing Attitude."

Southwest has an extensive training and development program for its employees that focuses on building their leadership and teamwork skills. The University for People and the Manager-in-Training (MIT) are two flagship programs that make this possible. According to the company's Web site, the University for People is a state-of-the-art training facility that offers employees training and development for every stage of their careers. Offerings include orientation sessions for hires, leadership for frontline and management-level employees, oral and written communication, performance appraisals, and even a Myers-Briggs personality assessment to help teams better appreciate individual differences and work more cohesively.

The MIT program focuses on employees with high potential for leadership and interest in a long-term career at Southwest Airlines. MIT I is designed for employees at the supervisor, team leader, and manager levels. MIT II is designed for managers and directors who aspire to higher leadership positions. Participants learn how to become strategic leaders.

At Southwest, each department has a dedicated team working together to create action plans to realize its mission and vision. On May 3, 2013, CEO Kelly captured the essence of Southwest's team approach with this closing statement in his annual report to employees and shareholders: "As we look to our future in building LUV ("LUV" is the ticker symbol for Southwest on the New York Stock Exchange), our priority is to maintain the excellence we have built . . . with our brand, Culture, Customer Service, operational excellence, and consecutive annual profits. I am enthusiastic about our 2013 plan and believe our transformation efforts will make us better, stronger, and more competitive. And, the outstanding efforts, commitment, and dedication of our People give me confidence in our ability to successfully execute our plan." Southwest has ranked on *Fortune*'s World's Most Admired Companies list every year since 1994. They upheld this record with the recent recognition in 2013 as the seventh most admired company in the world.[1]

OPENING CASE QUESTIONS:

1. What does it say about Gary Kelly's leadership philosophy when he categorically proclaims, "Our people are our single greatest strength and most enduring long-term competitive advantage"?

2. How can you match our definition of team effectiveness as a multivariable concept involving three components (task performance, group process, and individual satisfaction) to this statement by Mr. Kelly: "We believe in Living the Southwest Way, which is to have a Warrior Spirit, a Servant's Heart, and a Fun-LUVing Attitude"?

3. What is the evidence that there is strong organizational support for teamwork at Southwest?

4. In what way has Southwest shown that it understands the connection between team leadership and team success?

5. Southwest encourages its teams to be creative problem solvers. What are some examples of creative problem solving by Southwest teams?

6. Of the four types of teams discussed, which type(s) do you think Southwest is using?

7. Do you think Gary Kelly is the type of leader who would embrace the self-managed team concept? Explain your answer.

Can you answer any of these questions? You'll find answers to these questions and learn more about Southwest Airlines and team leadership throughout the chapter.

To learn more about Gary Kelly and Southwest Airlines, visit Southwest's Web site at **http://www.southwest.com**.

Many organizations have adopted the team approach in response to the growing trend toward eliminating functional boundaries common when work was mostly organized along functional or departmental lines.[2,3] There is general agreement that functional boundaries tend to inhibit the flow of information and limit opportunities for cross-functional cooperation and coordination.[4] This limitation of the functional structure was also impacting another trend, which is the fact that many more value chain activities are conducted in project teams requiring input from employees with different expertise, background, education, and experience.[5] The reason for this is the increasing realization that teams typically outperform individuals in tasks requiring multiple skills, abilities, and experiences. As a result, employers are requiring new hires to show evidence that they can function well in a team environment. Team leadership competency is now becoming a key requirement in hiring new leaders and managers.[6]

The first half of the chapter focuses on the team concept. We will discuss the growing use of teams in organizations, review some of the more popular types of teams, explore decision making in teams and explain how to plan and conduct effective team meetings. The second half of the chapter focuses on self-managed teams (SMTs). We discuss the nature of SMTs, the difference between SMTs and conventional teams, the benefits of using SMTs and how to improve SMT effectiveness.

The Use of Teams in Organizations

As mentioned in the introduction, teamwork is a way of life in the postmodern organization.[7] There was a time when the use of teams in production processes made news because few companies were doing it. Today, it's just the opposite. It's the organization that does not use teams that has become newsworthy. Through the years, organizations have adopted team-based structures as the tool to promote cooperation and coordination of actions and, thus, enhance performance.[8] The basic message behind teamwork is that teams offer the best opportunity for better organizational performance in the form of increased productivity and profits. In other words, the synergistic benefits of teamwork are such that members of a team working cooperatively with one another can achieve more in output than those working independently. As such, teams have become the basic unit of empowerment[9]—large enough for the collective strength and synergy of diverse talents and small enough for effective participation and bonding.[10,11] This is discussed in greater depth as part of the presentation on the benefits and limitations of working in teams.

Since the early 1990s, various studies have reported greater numbers of U.S. corporations using teams to accomplish organizational tasks.[12] According to some estimates, over 50 percent of all organizations and 80 percent of organizations with more than 100 employees use some form of teams.[13] Many organizations have reengineered their work processes and procedures to be performed by teams.[14] The reasons for this trend are obvious. Many companies, large and small, face serious challenges from a dynamic and complex global economy—challenges that have put in question the effectiveness of individual or non-team efforts to getting work done.[15] As a consequence, many more organizations are seeking leaders who possess team leadership skills. Employers expect colleges and universities to be at the forefront of preparing graduates to effectively work in teams. They are actively looking for applicants who possess teamwork skills and abilities.[16]

However, not all team efforts have resulted in success. In some cases, the use of teams has resulted in such negative outcomes as increased costs, stress, and lower group cohesion.[17,18] To avoid these negative outcomes, it is recommended that an organization ask critical questions of itself before embracing the team approach. Examples of such questions include the following:

- Will the use of teams diffuse important organizational capabilities?
- How much infrastructure realignment will be required?
- Will leaders embrace the team concept and change their styles to suit?[19]
- Can teams carry out tasks previously performed by individuals or functional units?
- How difficult it will be to develop team problem-solving capabilities?

These questions are addressed later in the chapter as part of the discussion on the role of top management, organizational culture, and the team leader in creating effective teams. But first, a brief review of the distinction between a group and a team. We take the view that they are not synonymous.

Is It a Group or a Team?

All teams are groups, but not all groups are teams. A manager can put together a group of people and never build a team. A **group** *is a collection of individuals who interact primarily to share information and to make decisions that enable each member to perform within his or her area of responsibility.* As such, group performance is merely the summation of each group member's individual contribution. There is no synergy. A team creates synergy. That is, the collective efforts of the members result in a level of performance that is greater than the sum of the individual inputs. In other words, the whole is greater than the sum of its parts (1+1=3). A team brings together individuals from varied backgrounds to contribute toward a collective output. Team members have both individual and collective accountability for team outcomes. Therefore, we define a **team** as *a unit of interdependent individuals with complementary skills who are committed to a common purpose and set of performance outcomes and to common expectations, for which they hold themselves accountable.*[20] In their comprehensive study of work groups and teams, Kozlowski and Bell describe teams as "collectives who exist to perform organizationally-relevant tasks, share one or more common goals, interact socially, exhibit task interdependencies, maintain and manage boundaries and are embedded in an organizational context that sets boundaries, constrains the team and influences exchanges with other units in the broader entity."[21] This supports and reinforces our definition of a team.

Whereas groups focus on individual performance and goals, and reliance on individual abilities, teams have a collective mentality that focuses on the following: (1) shared mission; (2) common objectives; (3) sharing information, insights, and perspectives; (4) making decisions that support each individual to do his or her own job better; and (5) reinforcing each other's efforts.[22]

The leadership style in a group tends to be boss-centered, whereas in a team it is more participative or empowerment-oriented. In a team, incentives are team-based; in contrast, a group is more likely to be characterized by self-interest, with a mentality of "what's in it for me." In the best teams, there are no stars, and everyone suppresses individual ego for the good of the whole.

WORK
Application **8-1**

Think of a past or present job. Based on your knowledge of the distinction between a group and a team, would you say you were part of a team or a group? Explain.

OPENING CASE Application

I. What does it say about Gary Kelly's leadership philosophy when he categorically proclaims, "Our people are our single greatest strength and most enduring long-term competitive advantage"?

It demonstrates his people-centered leadership style. With his strong belief in the value of his employees to the company's success, it is not surprising that his orders are for each department to have a dedicated team working together to create action plans to make Southwest a happy place to work. Teamwork is a way of life at Southwest and this is a direct result of the commitment of the CEO to this approach to structuring tasks.

CONCEPT APPLICATION 8-1

Group or Team

Based on each statement, identify it as characteristic of a group or a team. Write the appropriate letter in the blank before each item.

a. group   b. team

_____ 1. We have a collective mentality that focuses on a shared mission.

_____ 2. We all have a common objective that focuses our energies and resources.

_____ 3. Here every individual does his or her tasks separately and we add up our outputs at the end.

_____ 4. In our department, each person is rewarded for what they accomplish as an individual rather than what they contribute to the team effort.

_____ 5. My compensation is based primarily on my department's performance and there is shared responsibility.

_____ 6. We are just a collection of about 30 people working individually on an assigned project.

_____ 7. Our tasks are interconnected, and we make decisions that support each individual to do his or her own job better.

> **Learning Outcome 1**   *Discuss the benefits and limitations of working in teams.*

Benefits and Limitations of Teamwork

Teamwork *is an understanding and commitment to a common goal on the part of all team members.* The increased acceptance and use of teams suggests that their usage offers many benefits. However, there are inherent limitations associated with the use of teams. Let's start with the benefits of working in teams.

Benefits of Using Teams

There are several benefits of teamwork:

1. Teams offer synergistic benefits that non-team arrangements fail to offer.[23] *Synergy* is when a team's total output exceeds the sum of the various members' contributions. It involves the creative cooperation of people working together to achieve something beyond the capacities of individuals working alone.[24]

WORK
Application **8-2**

Identify a team you were or are a part of and describe the benefits that you derived from being a member of the team.

2. Team members can help each other avoid major errors. This tendency of mutual support and peer review of ideas helps teams make better decisions and can provide immunity for an organization against disruptive surprises.

3. Teams offer more opportunities for new ideas that advance innovation.[25]

4. Teams offer a work environment in which people feel empowered and satisfied with their jobs.[26] Job satisfaction is important because it is associated with other positive organizational outcomes. For example, employees who are satisfied with their jobs are said to be less likely to quit their jobs, are absent less, and are more likely to display organizational citizenship behavior.[27,28] Being a member of a team makes it possible to satisfy one's social need for affiliation. Team members develop trust for each other and come to see the team as a social network that fulfills other needs.[29]

Limitations of Using Teams

Employing the team approach has some potential limitations for both organizations and individuals:

1. There is the possibility that members face pressure to conform to team standards of performance and conduct, even if it goes against the individual's or organization's interest.[30] For example, a team member may be ostracized for being much more productive than his or her coworkers if the team's goal is to slow down production. This can lead to intra-team conflict.

2. Shirking of individual responsibility, also known as social loafing, is another limitation of teams. **Social loafing** *is the conscious or unconscious tendency by some team members to shirk responsibility by withholding effort toward team goals when they are not individually accountable for their work.*[31] Many students who have worked on team projects (like group term papers) have encountered a social loafer. Social loafing is likely to result when individual effort is not recognized and assessed.[32,33] Individual performance evaluations can help discourage social loafing by holding each team member accountable for assigned tasks; however, this goes against the argument that team-based performance measures are necessary for a strong team identity. It's a conundrum in that while instituting individual accountability may help reduce social loafing, it risks jeopardizing team accountability for shared goals—a critical characteristic of effective teams.

3. Another well-known disadvantage associated with highly cohesive teams is a mindset known as groupthink. **Groupthink** *is when members of a cohesive group tend to agree on a decision not on the basis of its merit but because they are less willing to risk rejection for questioning a majority viewpoint or presenting a dissenting opinion.* The team values getting along more than getting things done. The team often becomes more concerned with striving for unanimity than with objectively appraising different courses of action. Dissenting views are suppressed in favor of consensus.[34]

4. Though cohesiveness is a desirable quality of teams, teams that are extremely cohesive can also become, at their worst, a source of intra-team and inter-team conflict.[35] A team may become so cohesive that it resembles a clique. A clan culture develops with each team (clan) fighting for dominance. There is pressure for members to stand by their teammates and to achieve the team's goals at any cost. Even within teams, sub-groups could form and create fault lines that impede team success. When a team possesses strong fault lines in which one subset of members shares the same attributes while another subset of members shares a different set of attributes, its effectiveness is compromised.[36,37]

WORK
Application **8-3**

Based on Self-Assessment 8-1, list some things that a team could do to improve its level of teamwork. Use experiences associated with a present or past job.

_____

_____

_____

_____

Effective team leaders find ways to maximize the benefits of teams and to minimize the limitations of teams. Suggested methods for accomplishing this include an understanding of the significance of culture, norms, and beliefs; recognition of fault line triggers; use of suitable leadership styles; development of team incentives and recognition; and effective use of intra-team communications.[38] More on these when we discuss the characteristics of effective teams and the role of top management and team leaders in creating effective teams.

Complete Self-Assessment 8-1 to evaluate teamwork from your own work experience.

SELF-ASSESSMENT 8-1   Assessing Teamwork in Your Group

Based on experiences you have or have had with teams, indicate whether your team has (or had) the following characteristics by placing a checkmark in the appropriate column:

In my team:

	Mostly True	Mostly False
1. There is a common understanding and commitment to group goals on the part of all team members.	____	____
2. Members support and provide constructive feedback to one another's ideas.	____	____
3. Members do not feel the pressure to conform to group standards of performance and conduct.	____	____
4. Dissenting views are accepted and discussed rather than suppressed in favor of consensus.	____	____
5. The level of interpersonal interaction among members is high.	____	____
6. Much of the responsibility and authority for making important decisions is turned over to the team.	____	____
7. There is an open communication channel for all members to voice their opinions.	____	____

	Mostly True	Mostly False
8. Members are provided with the opportunity for continuous learning and training in appropriate skills.	____	____
9. Every team member is treated equally.	____	____
10. Members are more likely to provide backup and support for one another without the team leader's instruction.	____	____
11. Rewards and recognition are linked to individual as well as team results.	____	____
12. Roles and responsibilities for performing various tasks are clearly established.	____	____

Scoring

Add up the number of mostly true answers and place the total on the continuum below.

12 — 11 — 10 — 9 — 8— 7 — 6 — 5 — 4— 3 — 2 — 1
Effective teamwork   _Ineffective teamwork_

Interpreting the Score

The higher the score, the more effective is the teamwork. Self-assessment exercises like this can be used by groups during team building to improve teamwork. You will learn more about the team leader's role in building effective teams in the next section and about SMTs later in the chapter.

YOU
Make the
ETHICAL
Call

8.1 *He Is Not a Team Player*

The story is told of a company that took a drastic decision to not interview a candidate for a job because of the feedback from the employee who picked up the candidate from the airport. The company prides itself on a culture that highly values its employees and teamwork approach to doing work. It's a culture that takes the happiness of its employees seriously and everyone feels a sense of being part of a fun-loving team. On her way back to the company headquarters with a prospective candidate for a leadership position, she tried unsuccessfully to get the candidate to acknowledge her or even respond to her attempts at "small talk." The candidate seemed unwilling to acknowledge or engage in conversation with someone much lower in status than himself. Upon arrival back at headquarters, the employee reported her feeling to her boss. She said that she didn't think the candidate will make a good team player or fit in with the open, friendly, and fun-loving culture of the company. That was all it took for the candidate to be returned to the airport.

1. Is being a team player really necessary to be a successful employee?

2. Is it ethical and socially responsible of the company in this case to reject job candidates because they are considered not to be good team players?

3. Would you act the same way if you were the driver picking up the candidate?

What Is an Effective Team?

In a teamwork environment, team members are required to be able to form positive exchange relationships not only with the team leader but also with each other. The former is what we have referred to as leader–member exchange (LMX) in Chapter 7, and the latter describes what has come to be known as **team-member exchange (TMX)**. TMX is defined as *a team member's social exchanges with peers in terms of the mutual exchange of ideas, support, camaraderie, and feedback.* High-quality LMX and TMX relations enhance group identification and collective efficacy, which positively contributes to team effectiveness.[39,40]

The obvious question then becomes, what makes one team effective and another ineffective? One model of team effectiveness focused on internal team processes such as group learning, team efficacy, self-leadership, interdependency, and team cohesion.[41,42] According to this model, teams that excel in all these areas are said to be effective. Another model examined three contextual factors—team design, organizational resources and rewards, and process assistance—as determinants of team effectiveness.[43] From these two models, we present **team effectiveness** as *a construct consisting of three components: (1) task performance—the degree to which the team's output (product or service) meets the needs and expectations of those who use it; (2) group process—the degree to which members interact or relate in ways that allow the team to work increasingly well together over time; and (3) individual satisfaction—the degree to which the group experience, on balance, is more satisfying than frustrating to team members.*[44]

This definition embodies a number of performance outcomes that others have used as a basis for evaluating team effectiveness. These include innovation, efficiency, quality, and employee satisfaction. *Innovative teams* are those with the capability to rapidly respond to new problems and changes with creative solutions. They are teams that have mastered what some refer to as "team learning."[45] **Team learning** *is the collective acquisition, combination, creation, and sharing of knowledge.*[46] *Efficient teams* enable the organization to achieve its goals with fewer resources. *Quality* is the team's ability to produce outputs that meet or exceed customer expectations. *Satisfaction* measures the team's ability to achieve not only the team's goals (team satisfaction) but also satisfy the personal needs of its members (individual satisfaction).

OPENING CASE Application

2. **How can you match our definition of team effectiveness as a multivariable concept involving three components (task performance, group process, and individual satisfaction) to this statement by Mr. Kelly: "We believe in Living the Southwest Way, which is to have a Warrior Spirit, a Servant's Heart, and a Fun-LUVing Attitude"?**

The "Southwest way" is the team spirit that every employee of the company shares. Having a "warrior spirit" is the overwhelming desire to succeed at whatever your task requires. Having a "servant's heart" is the way employees treat each other and the customer. It's about everyone working together toward a common end. A good servant is a giver, a selfless and gracious individual. Finally, a "Fun-LUVing Attitude" is about the individual. People should love what they are doing and be satisfied doing it.

Learning Outcome 2 *Identify and explain the ten characteristics of highly effective teams.*

Characteristics of Highly Effective Teams

The team approach, though beneficial in many ways, also presents organizations with many challenges, including the need for effective communication; resolving personality conflicts and egos; establishing unifying goals, direction, and focus; specifying an appropriate reward and incentive systems; providing effective team leadership; and having the right team mix, autonomy, and accountability[47,48,49]. Failure to effectively address these challenges often results in dysfunctional or ineffective teams. Such dysfunctions create an environment where there is a lack of trust, fear of conflict, lack of commitment, lack of accountability, and inattention to result.[50] Exhibit 8.1 highlights ten characteristics of effective teams that address these challenges and dysfunctions. It should be noted that this is not a finite list of characteristics.

EXHIBIT 8.1

Characteristics of Highly Effective Teams

1. Team charter and norms
2. Widely shared team goals
3. Team cohesion and task interdependence
4. Team demographics and size
5. Clearly define team member roles and responsibilities
6. Positive interpersonal relationships
7. Clearly stated operating procedures
8. Effective conflict resolution strategies
9. High-level interpersonal communications
10. Strong top management support

Team Charter and Norms

A team charter is a governing document that should be jointly developed by team members and should specify the rules by which they agree to be governed. Norms evolve out of a team charter and become the framework for the decision-making process within the team, thus providing the underpinnings for team cohesion. **Team norms** are *acceptable standards of behavior that are shared by team members*. For example, a team norm might specify cooperative over competitive behavior. This may be reflected by the level of importance members place on shared pursuits, objectives, and mutual interests rather than personal interests. The reward structure must match this cooperative norm.

YOU
Make the
ETHICAL
Call

8.2   Norms

One or a few employees can break the norms and cause disastrous consequences for not only one organization but also entire industries. On the other hand, one or a few people can blow the whistle to disclose illegal and unethical business practices, which can lead to decreasing unethical behavior, such as at Enron. At the team level, employees influence each other's behavior through developing and enforcing norms; we can also call it peer pressure.

1. Should employees be able to do their own thing without the group enforcing norms?
2. Is it ethical and socially responsible for teams to develop and enforce norms? If so, what type of ethical standards should a team have?

Widely Shared Team Goals

When team members all share the same goals and each member clearly understands his or her role in helping achieve the goals, performance is enhanced. It is often the case that when team goals conflict, tensions can appear within the team, and "the whole is no longer greater than the sum of its parts."[51] Therefore, setting team goals should be an inclusive process.[52] The process should allow for open and honest exchange of ideas. Effective teams strive for consensus, consistency, and agreement on team goals. There is a sense of ownership in the goals of the team and thus greater accountability for team actions.

Team Cohesion and Task Interdependence

Members of effective teams are able to collaborate and work well with each other.[53] This happens when there is a high level of team cohesion and interdependence.[54] Teams that have a history of working together in this way are more likely to succeed, confirming the importance of esprit de corps within the team.[55,56] **Team cohesion** *is the extent to which team members band together and remain committed to achieving team goals*. Team cohesion is increased when team members share similar attitudes and values and strong interpersonal relations and self-identification with the team.[57] Teams that show a high degree of agreeableness between team members also show higher levels of cohesion and team performance.[58]

The degree to which team members depend on each other for information, resources, and other inputs to complete their own tasks determines the level of task interdependence.[59] The higher level of interdependency, the greater the responsibility members feel toward each other.[60] With interdependence comes the need for coordination to ensure that the team functions as a unified whole.

Team Demographics and Size

An effective team is more than just a bunch of people brought together to accomplish a goal. Team demographics focus on the diversity in culture, knowledge, skills, gender, personality, background, and experiences of team members.[61,62] The findings of one study revealed that top management team diversity is positively related to performance; and this effect is stronger in longer tenured teams, highly internationalized firms, and munificent environments.[63] Two other studies found that teams with an equal gender mix perform better than male-dominated teams in terms of sales and profits.[64,65] Teams that have experience working together tend to demonstrate greater task proficiency and teamwork effectiveness.

Size may affect team members' ability to form close interpersonal relationships with other members. Small teams, typically fewer than 12 people, are generally more effective than larger teams. In small teams, conflicts and differences are more manageable. In larger teams, it is much more difficult for members to interact and share ideas with each other. As a general rule, teams that participants perceive as too small or too large relative to the task at hand are deemed to have failed the size test and are generally less effective.

Clearly Defined Team Member Roles and Responsibilities

There is a greater chance of realizing team goals and objectives when team members clearly understand their roles and responsibilities.[66] In other words, team members know their specific task(s) and each individual's task contributes to meeting team goals. As someone once said, "You know team roles and responsibilities are clearly defined when each team member is able to state, in one sentence: My job on this team is to help us get to our goal of X by doing Y or, I know I am doing my job when Z happens."[67] The benefits of having clearly defined roles and responsibilities are that team members are more likely to accept personal responsibility and not assign blame when things go wrong. They are more accountable for their actions. These are the kinds of teams where team members tend to be their own toughest critics.

Positive Interpersonal Relationships

Positive interpersonal relationships exist when there is mutual respect and trust, support, inclusion, collaboration, and open and honest communication between team members. Isolation from your team—such as not getting information, being excluded from team meetings, your work going unnoticed, your suggestions going unanswered, or the team leader playing favorites—is symptomatic of poor or negative interpersonal relationships. This can lead to feelings of insecurity, low self-esteem and even depression. Positive interpersonal relationships give members a sense of belonging in the team.[68]

Clearly Stated Operating Procedures

An effective team starts out by laying down the operating rules and procedures that will govern how the team carries out its work together. Setting and abiding by the team's rules and operating procedures will assure consistency in behavior among team members and reduce the chance of mistakes or conflict that can jeopardize team success.[69]

Effective Conflict Resolution Strategies

Conflict is an inevitable consequence of working with other people; however, it does not have to be dysfunctional.[70] In any given team, differences on goals, needs/aspirations, opinions, values, and personality provide more than enough grounds for disagreement and conflict. Conflict can be task, relationship, or process based.[71] Disagreements can have both positive and negative consequences on team effectiveness. On the positive side, constructive disagreement is actually part of the reason why teams can be so effective; the more perspectives that go into a decision, the better the end result. On the negative side, allowing disagreements to get out of hand can cause unnecessary disruption and lead to breakdowns in working relationships.[72] Such breakdowns can result in intra-team conflicts, lack of communication, and ultimately lack of team spirit. Effective teams are proactive in developing conflict resolution strategies that apply to all team members.

High-Level Interpersonal Communications

Communication is "like the circulatory system in the human body."[73] Effective teams have open and honest communication with each other. Team members of effective teams tend to show a high competency in oral and written communication skills. Effective communication involves not just what is said but how it is said. Hurtful and insensitive ways of communicating can damage relations in a team. Other roadblocks to effective communication—such as information overload, lack of filtering, defensiveness, and cultural differences—can be overcome by effective listening, applying feedback, being sensitive to others, and simplifying communication.

Strong Top Management Support

Effective teams are those that have strong support from the upper-level management.[74] After all, team resources and rewards come from top management. When teams are not achieving expected results, top management must determine if all or most of the characteristics of effective teams described above are present. Also, top management must create an organizational culture that supports teamwork and has reward programs that motivate and reinforce team behavior.[75] This is discussed in greater depth in the next two sections.

WORK
Application **8-4**

Recall a team you have worked with that you would characterize as effective. Which of the characteristics discussed and listed in Exhibit 8.1 did your team possess?

OPENING CASE Application

3. What is the evidence that there is strong organizational support for teamwork at Southwest?

At Southwest, there is the "University for People." The University for People is a state-of-the-art training facility led by Southwest Airlines facilitators and senior leaders as guest professors. Here the company offers training and development for its employees at every stage of their careers. For example, the curriculum includes a Myers-Briggs personality assessment seminar to help teams better appreciate individual differences and work more cohesively.

Learning Outcome **3**   *What role can a team leader play in creating an effective team?*

Team Leadership

Increasing organizational reliance on teams to perform complex tasks has led to a corresponding increase in interest toward understanding the important role of leaders in improving team performance.[76,77] Studies have shown that when leaders are trained to develop and nurture high-quality relationships with all of their followers, the results on follower performance are dramatic.[78,79] To fully understand the factors that add to the quality of the working relationship between a leader and his or her team members, it is important not only to pay attention to the general leadership style of the leader toward the team as a whole but also to his or her specific behaviors toward various team members, described in Chapter 7 as the leader–member exchange relationship. A team leader's empowering or directive style of leadership will impact team performance.[80] Team leaders must manage not just the work but also team member relations across diverse functional and cultural boundaries.[81,82] Without effective team leaders, teams can get off course, go too far or not far enough, lose sight of their mission, and become meshed by interpersonal conflict.[83]

The team leader's role in creating effective teams is critical. Here are some examples:

- The team leader as *chief motivator*. Through the leader's support, encouragement, and training, followers feel a sense of self-worth, appreciation, and value for their work, and they respond with high performance.[84,85] As these relationships mature, the entire work group becomes more cohesive, and the payoffs only increase.
- The team leader as *coach and mentor*. Team-based organizations need leaders who are good at coaching and mentoring followers, especially new team members. Like any good coach, they are experienced and knowledgeable in the team process and are capable of developing trust and teamwork norms in team members.[86]
- The team leader as a *role model*. A team leader must model the behavior that he/she wants to see in team members. For instance, a leader's self-sacrificing behavior and display of self-confidence do influence team members. Self-sacrificing leaders are those who go above and beyond what's expected of them. They don't just issue orders; they get involved in making things happen.[87] Being a role model helps develop trust, commitment, and confidence in the leader.
- The team leader as team *culture enforcer*. The team leader plays a leading role in fostering a team culture that supports the team's goals and operational strategies. A team culture specifies standards and values that govern team member behavior. The leader for example may insist on team incentives over individual incentives to promote team performance.[88]
- The team leader as *cheerleader*. Leaders with strong social skills tend to have greater influencing abilities and relate well with team members.[89] As the team's leading cheerleader, the leader inspires and motivates team members to achieve higher levels of performance. When a team leader can leverage his/her social skills to obtain resources for the team, he or she is said to possess social capital. The leader can use social capital to resolve team conflict, encourage greater communication, and build a stronger commitment to the team effort.
- The team leader as *resource person*. The team leader's role is to be the resource person that recognizes team needs and attends to them in a timely fashion. The team leader's knowledge of the team's capabilities enables him or her to address areas of weaknesses so the team can function more effectively and efficiently.

Although some individuals are skilled in all these areas and appear to have been born to be team leaders, the majority of aspiring leaders can benefit from team leadership development programs designed to assess and improve their effectiveness in team leadership.[90]

WORK
Application **8-5**

Interview someone you have worked with or know who is a team leader. Ask him or her to provide specific examples for some of the roles discussed in the text.

OPENING CASE Application

4. In what way has Southwest shown that it understands the connection between team leadership and team success?

Southwest has a program called Manager-in-Training (MIT) aimed at identifying employees with a high potential for leadership and interest in a long-term career with the company. Among the courses offered, there is one specifically designed for team leaders. The first course is called MIT I, designed for employees at the supervisor, team leader, and manager levels. This is a clear indication that top management takes team leadership seriously.

Learning Outcome **4** | *Describe how organizational culture can influence team creativity.*

Organizational Culture and Team Creativity

Creativity is one of the most complex mental functions. It requires the whole spectrum of affective experiences (positive and negative), and the cognitive processes they elicit between team members. Creativity feeds innovation, which is fast becoming a critical requirement for success in any type of business (profit or not-for-profit)—particularly for those organizations operating in highly volatile, competitive and dynamic market environments. Today's economy has been rightly described as a "knowledge-based economy" because more companies are gaining competitive advantages based on knowledge rather than on physical or financial resources alone. It will take both physical and financial resources and a highly creative workforce to be competitive.

Creativity is generally viewed as the actions of individual employees exchanging ideas and information with each other.[91] In the context of a team-based environment, team creativity entails being able to access and use each member's unique talents to perform effectively. Harnessing the creativity of each team member is what team creativity is all about.[92,93] Teams promote creativity through their effective cross-fertilization of ideas.[94] Teams that are able to dynamically integrate member ideas into creative innovations are said to possess knowledge-integration capabilities.[95] Knowledge-integration capabilities unleash employees' innate creative talents. Such creative ideas do become the building blocks for organizational innovation and change.[96,97]

Therefore, we define **team creativity** as *the creation of something that is valuable, useful, and novel by individuals working together in a complex social system.* Top management plays a significant role in fostering a culture of learning and creativity.[98] Creating an organizational culture that supports and encourages creativity provides the protection that team members need to take creative risks.[99] Another organizational factor that influences team creativity is a commitment to team diversity. Diverse teams feature differences in thinking styles, knowledge, skills, values, and beliefs among individual team members, which enhances creativity.[100]

Encouraging inter-team rivalries does stimulate creativity because the competition challenges teams to bring out their best. Inter-team rivalries can turn a team into a vortex of creativity. The goal is to create a team culture where there is simultaneous cooperative and competitive behavior within and between teams. Evidence shows that this dual competitive model does drive high-quality knowledge creation and sharing among cross-functional team members.[101]

Organizations that have a culture that supports and promotes team creativity have a team-goal orientation, team-centered recognition and rewards programs, team-centered resource allocation policies, flexible operating procedures, team diversity, and a team-centered leadership development program.[102,103,104]

WORK Application **8-6**

Think of a work situation in which you were required to do a lot of creative thinking, or in which your job required doing a lot of very creative things. In what ways did the organization and your immediate supervisor or leader facilitate or hinder your effectiveness?

Self-Assessment 8-2 should help you assess the culture for creativity in your organization or institution.

SELF-ASSESSMENT 8-2   Assessing the Culture for Creativity

Place a checkmark in the appropriate column for each question.

In my team:	Mostly Agree	Mostly Disagree
1. Organizational practices generally encourage creativity.	____	____
2. The reward system has been carefully designed to encourage creativity.	____	____
3. People are not restricted by rules and regulations or many layers of approval when they want to try new ideas.	____	____
4. "Doing things the way they have always been done" is not a slogan that applies in this organization.	____	____
5. People are able to experiment and dream outside their regular functional area on company time.	____	____
6. The organization's culture values and appreciates input from members.	____	____
7. People feel they have been properly matched with tasks that fit their skills, interests, and experiences.	____	____

	Mostly Agree	Mostly Disagree
8. Employees have greater autonomy to think and act freely than they would in another organization.	____	____
9. In looking around, it is certain that the work environment has been carefully designed to encourage creativity.	____	____
10. Managerial practices in this organization would lead to the conclusion that creativity and innovation are highly valued at all levels.	____	____

Scoring

Begin by placing a checkmark in the appropriate column for each question. Add up the number of "mostly agree" checkmarks and place the sum on the continuum below.

10 — 9 — 8 — 7 — 6 — 5 — 4 — 3 — 2 — 1
Supportive climate   *Unsupportive climate*

Interpreting the Score

The higher the score, the more supportive the organizational culture is of creativity and innovation. Self-assessment exercises like this can be used to encourage students to relate their work environments to the concepts in ways that others can benefit from their experience.

OPENING CASE Application

5. Southwest encourages its teams to be creative problem solvers. What are some examples of creative problem solving by Southwest teams?

Southwest employees have teamed up to find better ways of performing their task. Working together, Southwest employees found better and faster ways to turn around their planes in just 25 minutes, one of the fastest in the industry. There are also countless customer accounts of Southwest employees going out of their way to help them. In many of the cases, the employees took it upon themselves to find a solution to the customer's problem without waiting for managerial approval. The company definitely encourages its employees to find creative, yet efficient, ways to accomplish their tasks and this is showing in the company's bottom line.

CONCEPT APPLICATION **8-2**

Managing Creative Teams

Identify which statement is likely to favor greater team creativity or lessen team creativity:

a. may favor greater team creativity   b. may lessen team creativity

_____ 8. A team policy dictates strict adherence to standard operating procedures.

_____ 9. A certain amount of our work day is left up to us to do whatever we chose—like experimenting and sharing new ideas.

_____ 10. Our work schedule is so hectic and regimented in a way that there is very little room for thinking "out of the box" in this team.

_____ 11. Our organization has different levels of team recognition and rewards programs for taking meaningful risks.

_____ 12. Our organization discourages inter-team rivalries because of the potential for internal conflict.

_____ 13. In our team, we have a suggestion box and team members can receive up to $500 in a gift certificate for good ideas.

Types of Teams

Structural metamorphosis seems to be the one constant in organizational life today. Traditional organizational structures, known for their stable designs, are changing in favor of more fluid designs that can respond to external opportunities and threats. A manufacturing enterprise might, for example, make use of a variety of teams, such as a quality improvement team, customer service team, self-managed team, cross-functional team, technology integration team, virtual team, new product development team, or safety teams; instead of relying on the old functional department form to get work done. In this section, we focus on four team types that are common across organizations today: the functional team, the cross-functional team, the virtual team, and the self-managed team.

Functional Team

One hundred years ago, Frederick Taylor, called the "father of scientific management," espoused a leadership approach whereby managers made themselves functional experts, divided work processes into simple repetitive tasks, and treated workers as interchangeable parts. The functional team is mostly made up of a functional manager and a small group of frontline employees within that functional area or department. *Therefore, we define a* **functional team** *as a group of employees belonging to the same functional department, such as marketing, R&D, production, human resources, or information systems, who have a common objective.*

Over time, the drawbacks of this approach became evident, as workers suffered from boredom due to the repetitive nature of their jobs. The structure of the functional team is generally more hierarchical, with the functional leader making all the decisions and expecting followers to implement them. Another drawback of the functional team, although unintended, is the tendency for team members to focus on their local area of specialization and ignore or downplay the overall organizational mission. This can lead to a lack of cooperation between functional teams, resulting in poor overall organization performance. In fact, rivalry, rather than cooperation, is what often happens between functional teams that don't interact with each other.

Over the years, the use of functional teams has been in decline. Cross-functional teams became popular in the late 1980s, when companies started to readjust their organizational structures to make them more flexible and competitive.

Cross-Functional Team

In today's dynamic business environment, organizations are realizing that to effectively respond to market and competitive challenges, there has to be cooperation across functional boundaries. Team leaders are under pressure to dismantle walls separating functional units and form cross-functional teams for the purpose of accomplishing organizational objectives.[105,106] We define a **cross-functional team** as one *composed of members from different functional departments of an organization who are brought together to perform unique tasks to create new and non-routine products or services*.[107] Team members may also include representatives from outside the organization, such as suppliers, clients, and joint-venture partners.

The appeal of the cross-functional team concept is that interaction, cooperation, coordination, information sharing, and cross-fertilization of ideas among people from different functional areas produces better outcomes such as better-quality products/services with shorter developmental cycles.[108]

As cross-functional teams have become popular, interest in their effectiveness has also kept pace. In one study, researchers interviewed 75 current and previous leaders of cross-functional teams in Hewlett-Packard's marketing, R&D, manufacturing, and information systems units. The interviews focused on identifying factors that were critical to the optimal performance of the teams.[109] In another study, a survey of frontline managers on the barriers and gateways to management cooperation and teamwork identified five keys or gateways for getting frontline managers to work effectively in cross-functional teams.[110] The factors or gateways for improving the effectiveness of cross-functional teams identified in these studies are no different from those discussed earlier as characteristics of effective teams.[111]

Cross-functional teams offer many potential benefits to an organization. For example:

WORK
Application **8-7**

Recall any experience you have had or currently have working with individuals from different disciplines or technical specialties outside of yours. How did you get along with these individuals? Describe the positives and negatives of your experience.

- Bringing together the right mix of people gives the team a rich and diverse base of knowledge and creative potential that far exceeds anything a single functional team could come up with.
- Coordination is improved and many problems are avoided when people from different functional specialties come together to work on a project at the same time, rather than working in separate units.[112]
- The cross-functional makeup of a team offers the benefit of multiple sources of information and perspectives and contacts outside of one's functional specialty; these are critical for success in globally competitive, high-technology markets.[113]
- Members learn new skills that are carried back to their functional units and to subsequent teams.
- Finally, the positive synergy that occurs in effective cross-functional teams can help them achieve a level of performance that far exceeds the sum of the individual performances of members.[114]

Cross-functional teams are often an organization's first step toward greater employee participation and empowerment. These teams may gradually evolve into virtual or self-managed teams, depending on the type of environmental challenges or opportunities the organization faces.

Virtual Team

Virtual teams are probably the most recent structural innovation of the 21st century.[115] An increasing number of organizations are using virtual teams to provide human resource flexibility, customer service responsiveness, innovation, and speed in project completion.[116] Increasingly, companies are investing in virtual teams to enhance their performance and competitiveness.[117]

Globalization and technological advances are driving organizations to adopt virtual teams.[118] Virtual cross-functional teams are growing at a much faster rate in companies with global operations for obvious reasons. Global virtual team leaders are counseled to employ success strategies, such as building trust-based relationships, encouraging members to show respect for other cultures and languages, and promoting diversity as a team strength and not a weakness.[119]

Virtual teams enable organizations to pool the talents and expertise of employees and nonemployees by eliminating time and space barriers. In particular, new and advanced technologies are providing the means for work that is dispersed (carried out in different locations) and asynchronous (carried out at different times) to still be performed in team settings.[120] The virtual team can be organized along functional or cross-functional lines. We define a **virtual team** as one *whose members are geographically dispersed, requiring them to work together through electronic means with minimal face-to-face interaction.*

In the United States, it is estimated that among companies with 5,000 or more employees, more than half of them use virtual teams.[121] Another survey by the Gartner Group revealed that more than 60 percent of professional employees now work in virtual teams.[122] A recent report revealed that 102,900 federal employees worked in a telecommuting environment in 2008.[123]

Virtual teams present significant collaboration, communication, and leadership challenges that if not handled properly can potentially hinder team cohesion, information sharing, and knowledge integration—all critical to success.[124,125] Recommendations for dealing with these challenges include focusing attention on both technological and interpersonal issues, with team leaders staying alert to relational and communication problems.[126] Leaders of successful virtual teams establish and maintain trust and commitment in their teams by making sure that the necessary technology, support, and reward systems are in place.[127] The fourth type of team is called the self-managed team SMT.

Self-Managed Team (SMT)

With self-managed (autonomous) work teams, a group of people work together without a leader to plan, coordinate, and evaluate each other's work. We define **self-managed teams (SMTs)** as *relatively autonomous teams whose members share or rotate leadership responsibilities and hold one another mutually responsible for a set of performance targets assigned by top management.* The SMT concept is discussed in greater depth later in the chapter.

WORK
Application **8-8**

Recall a present or past job. Describe what type of team you are in or have been in— functional, cross-functional, or self-managed.

OPENING CASE Application

6. Of the four types of teams discussed, which type(s) do you think Southwest is using?

At Southwest, you get the sense that there are no walls separating the different departments—what some have called "silos." There is evidence of cross-functional teamwork at different levels. The effort to achieve a 25-minute turnaround time for each arriving flight takes a highly integrated and coordinated cross-functional team to accomplish.

CONCEPT APPLICATION 8-3

Type of Team

Identify each statement as characteristic of the following team types:

a. functional
b. cross-functional
c. virtual
d. self-managed

_____ 14. We are in the marketing department and our primary task is to deal with customer related problems.

_____ 15. We don't really have a conventional boss in our team; instead we share leadership responsibilities.

_____ 16. We are developing a multi-specialty work team to speed up processing our orders, and we are including two other departments in the mix.

_____ 17. Members of my team are dispersed all over the country and even overseas, yet we conduct meetings and get our work done using the Internet and videoconferencing technologies.

_____ 18. Our team has been charged with developing a new product within three months, and we get to decide many job-related issues on our own.

Decision Making in Teams

More and more, organizations are finding out that the leader-centered decision-making model does not work well in organizations professing to be team-oriented. Instead, there is greater acceptance and appreciation for the team-centered decision-making model. For work teams to be effective, leaders must relinquish some of the decision-making responsibilities to team members. Exactly how this can be done effectively is the focus of this section.

Recall that in Chapter 4, we discussed the normative leadership model. Also, recall that the normative models (Exhibits 4.9 and 4.10 on pages 125 and 126) and Chapter 4's Developing Your Leadership Skills Exercise 4-2 (p.140) apply to group decision making, because the models are used to determine the level of follower participation in a given decision. Developing Your Leadership Skills Exercise 8-1 (on p. 304) presents a contingency leadership decision-making model that is adapted from the normative leadership model. It is a simpler model and uses the same leadership styles as situational communications (Developing Your Leadership Skills Exercise 6-2 in Chapter 6 on p.222) to help you determine the appropriate level of participation to use in a given situation.

Normative Leadership Model

The normative leadership model has a time-driven and development-driven decision tree that enables the user to select one of five leadership styles (decide, consult individually, consult group, facilitate, and delegate) appropriate for the situation to maximize decision outcomes. Each of the five leadership styles affects the level of participation in the decision by followers. Leaders who employ the "facilitate" and "delegate" leadership styles allow greater team participation in decision making. This is what some have described as empowering leadership. Unlike directive leadership that is characterized by behaviors aimed at strict adherence to structure through clear directions and instructions, empowering leadership gives team members a sense of psychological ownership of their task with greater latitude in decision making.[128]

Team-Centered Decision-Making Model

The team-centered decision-making model is preferred when (a) relevant information and expertise are scattered among different people, (b) participation is needed to obtain necessary commitment, (c) concentrating power in a single individual hurts the team, and (d) unpopular decisions need to be made.[129] The team-centered approach empowers team members to make decisions and follow through.[130] Advocates of the team-centered approach argue that empowerment results in a more dedicated, energetic, and creative workforce. Further, they maintain that employees can be trusted to make decisions about their work, that they can be trained to acquire the skills and abilities needed to do so, and that organizational effectiveness is enhanced through this approach.[131] The role of the leader in a team-centered decision-making model is to serve as a consultant, advisor, coach, or facilitator for the team.[132]

Advantages and Disadvantages of Team-Centered Decision Making

Some **advantages** of team-centered decision making include the following:

- It can improve decision quality.
- Exposure to team decision making has strong positive spillovers on the quality of individual decisions.[133]
- It shifts much of the decision-making action away from the leader, thereby freeing him or her to focus on more strategic issues.
- It allows responsibility to be diffused among several people, thereby facilitating support for some types of unpopular decisions.
- It results in higher commitment by team members to implement decisions as compared to decisions made alone by a leader.

Some **disadvantages** of team-centered decision making include the following:

- It can take longer than decisions made alone by a manager.
- It can be self-serving and contrary to the best interests of the organization, if team members have objectives and/or priorities that are different from those of the team or organization.
- It can end up being a poor compromise rather than an optimal solution when team members cannot agree among themselves.
- Leaders who are accustomed to making most or all team decisions may not want to give up this power or fear that if they do, they will appear weak or incompetent. This can lead to confusion and conflict in the team.
- Also, resistance may come from team members who prefer to avoid assuming more responsibility for leadership functions in the team.

WORK
Application **8-9**

Recall a team decision that you were a part of, and describe the team leader's role during the process leading up to the final decision. Would you characterize the leader's role as leader-centered or team-centered?

Despite these potential problems, empowering team members to make team decisions is a far better approach than concentrating such power in a single individual.

There is general agreement that personality traits of team members affect their effectiveness in decision making. Team members with similar traits and experiences will more likely share a common frame of reference when making decisions.[134] We should note that the characteristics of effective teams discussed earlier will also contribute toward effective decision making. Complete Self-Assessment 8-3 to better understand how your personality will affect your teamwork. An important part of a leader's job is conducting team meetings. The next section focuses on conducting team meetings.

SELF-ASSESSMENT 8-3   **Personality Traits and Teams**

Answer the following two questions, and then read how your personality profile can affect your teamwork.

I enjoy being part of a team and working with others more than working alone.

7 — 6 — 5 — 4 — 3 — 2 — 1
Strongly agree   *Strongly disagree*

I enjoy achieving team goals more than individual accomplishments.

7 — 6 — 5 — 4 — 3 — 2 — 1
Strongly agree   *Strongly disagree*

The stronger you agree with the two statements, the higher the probability that you will be a good team player. However, lower scores do not mean that you are not a good team player. The following is some information on how Big Five personality dimensions and their related motive needs can affect your teamwork.

Surgency—high need for power. If you have a high need for power, whether you are the team leader or not, you have to be careful not to dominate the group. Seek others' input, and know when to lead and when to follow. Even when you have great ideas, be sensitive to others so they don't feel that you are bullying them, and stay calm (adjustment) as you influence them. Be aware of your motives to make sure you use socialized, rather than personalized, power. You have the potential to make a positive contribution to the team with your influencing leadership skills. If you have a low need for power, try to be assertive so that others don't take advantage of you, and speak up when you have good ideas.

Agreeableness—high need for affiliation. If you have a high need for affiliation, you tend to be a good team player. However, don't let the fear of hurting relationships get in the way of your influencing the team when you have good ideas. Don't be too quick to give in to others; it doesn't help the performance of the team when you have a better idea that is not implemented. You have the potential to be a valuable asset to the team as you contribute your skills of working well with others and making them feel important. If you have a low need for affiliation, be careful to be sensitive to others.

Conscientiousness—high need for achievement. If you have a high need for achievement, you have to watch your natural tendency to be more individualistic than team oriented. It's good to have your own goals; but if the team and organization fail, so do you. Remember that there is usually more than one good way to do anything; your way is not always the best. In a related issue, don't be a perfectionist, as you can cause problems with team members. Being conscientious, you have the potential to help the team do a good job and reach its full potential. If you have a low need for achievement, push yourself to be a valuable contributor to the group, or pull your own weight.

Conducting Effective Team Meetings

In a team-oriented organization, leaders spend a great deal of time conducting meetings. Therefore, the need for conducting effective team meetings is stronger than ever.[135] The success of meetings depends on the leader's skill at managing the process. The most common complaints about meetings are that *there are too many of them*, *they are too long*, and *they are unproductive*. Meeting leadership skills can lead to more productive meetings. A few years back, Ford Motor Company spent $500,000 to send 280 employees to a three-day training session on developing meeting leadership skills, with three one-day sessions to follow. After the training, fewer employees complained of meetings being too long or unproductive. Managers had gained the necessary meeting leadership skills and were putting this knowledge into practice. Ford's investment had obviously paid off. In this section, we learn how to plan and conduct a meeting and how to handle problem team members.

Planning Meetings

Leader and member preparations for a meeting have a direct effect on the meeting. Unprepared leaders tend to conduct unproductive meetings. Planning is needed in at least five areas: objectives, selecting participants and making assignments, the agenda, the time and place for the meeting, and leadership. A written copy of the plan should be sent to members prior to the meeting (see Exhibit 8.2).

Meeting Plans

- **Time.** List date, place (if it changes), and time (both beginning and ending).
- **Objective.** State the objectives and/or purpose of the meeting. The objectives can be listed with agenda items, as shown below, rather than as a separate section. However, be sure objectives are specific.
- **Participation and Assignments.** If all members have the same assignment, list it. If different members have different assignments, list their names and assignments. Assignments may be listed as agenda items, as shown below for Ted and Karen.
- **Agenda.** List each item to be covered, in order of priority, with its approximate time limit. Accepting the minutes of the preceding meeting may be an agenda item. Here is an example agenda:

GOLD TEAM MEETING
November 22, 2013, Gold room, 9:00 a.m. to 10:00 a.m.

Participation and Assignments
All members will attend and should have read the six computer brochures enclosed before the meeting. Be ready to discuss your preferences.

Agenda
1. Discussion and selection of two PCs to be presented to the team at a later date by PC representatives—45 minutes. (Note that this is the major objective; the actual selection takes place later.)
2. Ted will give the Venus project report—5 minutes.
3. Karen will present an idea for changing the product process slightly, without discussion—5 minutes. Discussion will take place at the next meeting, after members have given the idea some thought.

© Cengage Learning®

Objectives

Probably the single greatest mistake made by those who call meetings is that they often have no clear idea and purpose for the meeting. Before calling a meeting, clearly define its purpose and set objectives to be accomplished during the meeting. The only exceptions may be at regularly scheduled information-dissemination or brainstorming meetings.

Participants and Assignments

Before calling the meeting, decide who should attend. The more members who attend a meeting, the less the chance that any work will get done. Does the full group/team need to attend? Should some non-group specialist be invited to provide input? On controversial issues, the leader may find it wiser to meet with the key members before the meeting to discuss the issue. Participants should know in advance what is expected of them at the meeting. If any preparation is expected (read material, do some research, make a report, and so forth), they should have adequate advance notice.

Agenda

Before calling the meeting, identify the activities that will take place during the meeting to achieve the objective. The agenda tells the members what is expected and how the meeting will progress. Having a set time limit for each agenda item helps keep the group on target; needless discussion and getting off the subject are common at all meetings. However, you need to be flexible and allow more time when really needed. Agenda items may also be submitted from members. If you get agenda items that require action, they should have objectives.

Place agenda items in order of priority. That way, if the group does not have time to cover every item, the least important items carry forward. In meetings in which the agenda items are not prioritized, the tendency is for the leader to put all the so-called quick items first. When this happens, the group gets bogged down and either rushes through the important items or puts them off until later.

Date, Time, and Place

To determine which day(s) and time(s) of the week are best for meetings, get members' input. Members tend to be more alert early in the day. When members are working in the same office or nearby, it is better to have more frequent shorter meetings focusing on one or just a few items. However, when members have to travel, fewer but longer meetings are needed. Be sure to select an appropriate place for the meeting, and plan for the physical comfort of the group. Be sure seating provides eye contact for small discussion groups, and plan enough time so that the members do not have to rush. If reservations are needed for the meeting place, make them far enough in advance to get a proper meeting room.

With advances in technology, telephone conferences are becoming quite common. Videoconferences are also gaining popularity. These techniques have saved travel costs and time and have resulted in better and quicker decisions. The majority of companies (big and small) today use videoconferencing and teleconferencing technologies to conduct meetings. The personal computer has been said to be the most useful tool for running meetings since *Robert's Rules of Order*. The personal computer can be turned into a large-screen "intelligent chalkboard" that can dramatically change meeting results. Minutes (notes on what took place during the last meeting) can be taken on the personal computer and distributed at the end of the meeting.

Leadership

The leader should determine the appropriate leadership style for the meeting. It is recommended that leaders play the role of facilitators, which involves guiding the process of the meeting while not influencing the content. Each agenda item may need to be handled differently. For example, some items may simply call for disseminating information; others require a discussion, vote, or consensus; other items require a simple, quick report from a member, and so forth. An effective way to develop group members' ability is to rotate the role of the group moderator/leader for each meeting.

Conducting Meetings

The First Meeting

At the first meeting, the group is in the orientation stage. The leader should use the high-task role. However, the members should be given the opportunity to spend some time getting to know one another. Introductions set the stage for subsequent interactions. A simple technique is to start with introductions and then move on to the group's purpose and objectives and members' job roles. Sometime during or following this procedure, have a break that enables members to interact informally. If members find that their social needs will not be met, dissatisfaction may occur quickly.

Learning Outcome **5** *Outline the three parts of conducting effective meetings.*

The Three Parts of a Meeting

Each meeting should cover the following:

1. *Identifying objectives.* Begin the meeting on time; waiting for late members penalizes the members who are on time and develops a norm for arriving late. Begin by reviewing progress to date, the group's objectives, and the purpose/objective for the specific meeting. If minutes are recorded, they are usually approved at the beginning of the next meeting. For most meetings it is recommended that a secretary be appointed to take minutes.

2. *Covering agenda items.* Be sure to cover agenda items in priority order. Try to keep to the approximate times but be flexible. If the discussion is constructive and members need more time, give it to them; however, if the discussion becomes more of a destructive argument, move ahead.

3. *Summarizing and reviewing assignments.* End the meeting on time. The leader should summarize what took place during the meeting. Were the meeting's objectives achieved? Review all of the assignments given during the meeting. Get a commitment to the task that each member should perform for the next or a specific future meeting. The secretary and/or leader should record all assignments. If there is no accountability and follow-up on assignments, members may not complete them.

The team leader needs to focus on group structure, process, and development. As stated, the leadership style needs to change with the group's level of development. The leader must be sure to provide the appropriate task and/or maintenance behavior when it is needed.

Handling Problem Members

As members work together, personality types tend to emerge. Certain personality types can cause the group to be less efficient. Some of the problem members you may have in your group are the following: silent, talker, wanderer, bored, and arguer.

Silent

To have a fully effective meeting, all group members should participate. If members are silent, the group does not get the benefit of their input. It is the leader's responsibility to encourage the silent member to participate without being obvious or overdoing it. One technique the leader can use is the rotation method, in which all members take turns giving their input. This method is generally less threatening than directly calling on people. However, the rotation method is not always appropriate. To build up the silent members' confidence, call on them with questions they can easily answer. When you believe they have convictions, ask them to express them. Watch their nonverbal communication as indicators of when to call on them. If you are a silent type, try to participate more often. Know when to stand up for your views and be assertive. Silent types generally do not make good leaders.

Talker

Talkers have something to say about everything. They like to dominate the discussion. However, if they do dominate, the other members do not get to participate. The talker can cause intragroup problems, such as low cohesiveness and conflicts. It is the leader's responsibility to slow talkers down, not to shut them up. Do not let them dominate the group. The rotation technique is also effective with talkers. They have to wait their turn. When not using a rotation method, gently interrupt the talker and present your own ideas or call on other members to present their ideas. Prefacing questions with statements like "let's give those who have not answered yet a chance" can also slow the talker down. If you tend to be a talker, try to slow down. Give others a chance to talk and do things for themselves. Good leaders develop others' abilities in these areas.

Wanderer

Wanderers distract the group from the agenda items; they tend to change the subject and often like to complain. The leader is responsible for keeping the group on track. If the wanderer wants to socialize, cut it off. Be kind; thank the member for the contribution, and then throw a question out to the group to get it back on track. If the wanderer has a complaint that is legitimate and solvable, allow the group to discuss it. Group structure issues should be addressed and resolved. However, if an issue is not resolvable, get the group back on track. Griping without resolving anything tends to reduce morale and commitment to task accomplishment. If the wanderer complains about irresolvable issues, make statements like "We may be underpaid, but we have no control over our pay. Complaining will not get us a raise; let's get back to the issue at hand." If you tend to be a wanderer, try to be aware of your behavior and stay on the subject at hand.

Bored

Your group may have one or more members who are not interested in the job. The bored person may be preoccupied with other issues and not pay attention or participate in the group meeting. The bored member may also feel superior and wonder why the group is spending so much time on the obvious.

The leader is responsible for keeping members motivated. Assign the bored member a task like recording ideas on the board and recording the minutes. Call on bored members; bring them into the group. If you allow them to sit back, things may get worse and others may decide not to participate either. If you tend to be bored, try to find ways to help motivate yourself. Work at becoming more patient and in control of behavior that can have negative effects on other members.

Arguer

Like the talker, the arguer likes to be the center of attention. This behavior can occur when you use the devil's advocate approach, which is helpful in developing and selecting alternative courses of action. However, arguers enjoy arguing for the sake of arguing, rather than helping the group. They turn things into a win–lose situation, and they can not stand losing.

The leader should resolve conflict but not in an argumentative way. Do not get into an argument with arguers; that is exactly what they want to happen. If an argument starts, bring others into the discussion. If it is personal, cut it off. Personal attacks only hurt the group. Keep the discussion moving on target. If you tend to be an arguer, strive to convey your views in an assertive debate format, not as an aggressive argument. Listen to others' views and be willing to change if they have better ideas.

CONCEPT APPLICATION 8-4

Group Problem People

Identify the problem type as:

a. silent   b. talker   c. wanderer   d. bored   e. arguer

_____ 19. Marcy is usually reluctant to share her ideas. When asked to expand on her ideas, Marcy often shrugs and declines further comment.

_____ 20. A usually very active team member, Frank seems very absent-minded today and not very engaged in the discussion. The other members are doing all the discussing and volunteering for assignments.

_____ 21. David seems to enjoy challenging members' viewpoints on every issue so much so that other team members are getting really frustrated with him.

_____ 22. As the team is trying to resolve a crisis, Johnny's focus was on trying to inform everyone about the company owner and the female mailroom clerk.

_____ 23. Charlie is always first or second to volunteer his ideas. He is long-winded in his presentations, which draws whispers from others about his "clueless" attitude.

Working with Group Members

Whenever you work in a group, do not embarrass, intimidate, or argue with any members, no matter how they provoke you. If you do, the result will make a martyr of them and a bully of you to the group. If you have serious problem members who do not respond to the above techniques, confront them individually outside of the group. Get them to agree to work in a cooperative way.

The remainder of this chapter will focus on the concept of SMTs, an innovative extension of the team concept.

WORK
Application **8-10**

Recall a meeting you attended. Did you receive an agenda prior to the meeting? How well did the leader conduct the meeting? Give ideas on how the meeting could have been improved. Did the group have any problem members? How well did the leader handle them?

Self-Managed Teams

As work increases in complexity and domestic economies become part of the global economy, the desire to find new and more effective ways of organizing employees grows accordingly. During the latter part of the 20th century to the present, the use of teams has been the competitive weapon of choice for many organizations (for-profit and not-for-profit). Lately, many of these organizations are experimenting with an innovative extension of the team concept called the *self-managed team (SMT).*[136] Proponents of the SMT concept argue that autonomy in the form of shared control over critical task-related decisions does enable SMTs to perform better than conventional teams.[137] It is the belief that team members who have such autonomy are more likely to feel invested in the process and be dedicated to accomplishing the stated goals. SMTs go by many different names: self-directed, autonomous, self-leading, self-maintaining, or self-regulating.[138]

This section examines the nature of SMTs by highlighting the differences between SMTs and conventional teams, the benefits of using SMTs, guidelines for improving their effectiveness, the role of leadership in the SMT concept, and the challenges of incorporating SMTs into an organization's structure.

The Nature of Self-Managed Teams

In the quest to remain competitive in new product/service development, companies are finding out that effectively managing human interactions and the rapid transfer of technology/ideas among individuals and functional units is key to staying competitive. Selecting, training, and rewarding employees as well as giving them autonomy in the form of collective control over critical task-related decisions can enable SMTs to perform more effectively.[139] To better understand the nature of SMTs, we call attention to a few key differences between SMTs and traditional teams.

Learning Outcome	6	*Explain the differences between conventional and self-managed teams.*

How Are SMTs Different from Conventional Teams?

Self-managed teams differ from conventional teams in a number of ways. In conventional teams, decision making resides in the hands of a leader who provides the team with direction and maintains control over work-related decisions. In contrast, SMTs have a significant amount of decision-making authority. Members are charged with duties such as managing themselves, self-appraisals, planning and scheduling work, making production- or service-related decisions, peer evaluation, and conflict resolution. Members take responsibility for outlining how they will achieve the team's objectives.[140]

The leadership function in a SMT is different from that in a conventional team. SMT members share or rotate leadership responsibilities and hold themselves mutually responsible for meeting team goals. Roles interchange frequently as members learn to be followers as well as leaders. Rather than being specialized, SMT members develop multi-skilled capabilities that make them very flexible in performing various tasks within the team. SMTs give all team members a voice in making decisions about the design of work, as well as greater autonomy and discretion in task accomplishment. Members operate without direct managerial supervision—an idea almost unthinkable a generation ago.[141]

The nature of SMTs is one of team rather than individual empowerment and accountability.[142] Team accountability is a significant responsibility, because SMT members are responsible not only for their own performance but for that of other team members as well. In successful SMTs, members have come to see that what they collectively gain is greater than what they could achieve individually. It is the case that those who do well in SMT settings are good problem solvers, effective communicators, able to deal with conflict, very adaptive, and possess an internal locus of control.

Depending on the types of decisions, the amount of authority vested in an SMT varies from one organization to another. For instance, in some organizations, SMTs are given the primary responsibility for personnel decisions such as hiring and firing team members, conducting performance appraisals, and determining compensation (within specified limits); in other organizations, such decisions are left to top management.[143] Teams in this later setting are usually allowed to make small expenditures for supplies and equipment without prior approval, but like in most organizations, any action involving large purchases must be approved by top management. Exhibit 8.5 summarizes the key differences between conventional and SMT.

WORK
Application **8-11**

Based on your own experience, or asking someone who has been part of an SMT, describe some of the self-managing activities of the team that made it a truly self-managing team as opposed to a traditional team.

EXHIBIT   **8.3**

Differences between Conventional and Self-Managed Teams

Characteristics	Self-Managed Teams	Conventional Teams
Leadership	Shared/Distributed	Singular/Sole
Team member role	Interchangeable	Fixed
Accountability	Team	Individual
Work design	Inter-dependent	Task Oriented
Job Descriptions	Flexible	Fixed
Skills	Multi-skilled	Specialized

© Cengage Learning®

CONCEPT APPLICATION 8-5

Types of Teams

Identify each statement below with one of these key terms.

a. group
b. functional team
c. cross-functional team
d. self-managed team

_____ 24. I have been assigned to a team where leadership roles are rotated and shared, with the team responsible for its own planning and execution of plans.

_____ 25. At Solomon's Technology Solutions, an integrated team with members from R&D, design, finance, customer service, and quality control oversaw an ambitious information system for a big client.

_____ 26. At the Furniture Factory, the quality control department headed by a manager is in charge of checking a sample of all finished furniture to make sure there are no defective items going to the retail customers.

_____ 27. In my organization, a number of us usually get together with no specific objective or purpose to discuss work-related and sometimes non-work-related matters.

Learning Outcome **7**   *Describe the benefits of using self-managed teams in organizations.*

The Benefits of Self-Managed Teams

A primary reason for growth in popularity of the SMT concept is the reported benefits by organizations (large and small) that have adopted it. Self-managed work teams are praised for bringing about results such as *increased productivity, accelerated new product development and process improvements, greater product/service quality, improved worker participation, and better decisions overall.*[144] These outcomes do lead to *increases in job satisfaction*, which in turn have been associated with other positive organizational and employee outcomes, such as *lower absenteeism rates, less turnover, higher motivation levels and self-esteem, increased organizational citizenship behavior, and, ultimately, increased levels of profitability.*[145,146]

WORK
Application **8-12**

If you have been part of an SMT, describe the benefits that you derived from being part of the team. Be specific, matching your description to the list in Exhibit 8.4.

SMTs do create a context for a shared and emotionally grounded identity that allows for a common set of guiding principles for decision making and action. *Because any agreed-upon course of action is taken collectively, there is a strong commitment among all team members to make it successful.*[147] Pride in the team's accomplishment and a strong sense of belonging inspire SMT members to connect with their organization's vision and mission.

SMTs *reduce costs because of the reductions in managerial ranks throughout the organization.* In a study examining the economic benefits of organizing field technicians into SMTs, it was found that SMTs absorb the monitoring and coordination tasks of supervisors, substantially reducing indirect labor costs but without adversely affecting quality and productivity.[148]

It should be noted that SMTs do exhibit the same general advantages of teamwork discussed earlier in the chapter. It's a question of how much further these benefits go when conventional teams are replaced with SMTs. Exhibit 8.6 summarizes the benefits of SMTs. The next section discusses options for improving SMT effectiveness and addresses organizational-level factors that can impact SMT success.

◄ EXHIBIT 8.4

Benefits of Self-Managed Teams

- Greater improvements in quality, speed, process, and innovation.
- A strong sense of belonging and ownership in one's work.
- Greater employee motivation.
- Accelerated new product development.
- Greater employee participation.
- Reduced operational costs because of reductions in managerial ranks and greater efficiencies.
- Greater employee job satisfaction, commitment, and productivity, and lower turnover and absenteeism rates.

© Cengage Learning®

OPENING CASE Application

7. Do you think Gary Kelly is the type of leader who would embrace the SMT concept? Explain your answer.

In 2008 and 2010, Mr. Kelly asked the Mercer Group, a management-consulting firm, to conduct an employee survey to determine how employees felt about the company and areas of improvement. This shows that the CEO is willing to listen to his followers and take their suggestions seriously. Reflecting on the careers of some of his young managers, whom he hired as entry-level employees, Gary Kelly said, "It is not such a stretch to feel that you've helped raised these people. They helped raise me, for that matter." Coupled with Mr. Kelly's objective to make Southwest a happy place for its employees and make work fun, it is a good bet that he would readily embrace SMTs if employees wanted to give it a try. He seems to be a leader who will be adaptable and willing to learn from his followers.

| Learning Outcome | 8 | *Describe top management's role in improving the success rate of self-managed teams.* |

Top Management and Self-Managed Team Success

Despite the documented benefits of SMTs, there is still much that needs to be done to improve their success rate. Many things can go wrong with SMTs, and adjusting to new behavioral expectations can be difficult. Many SMT initiatives are eventually abandoned.[149] For SMTs to succeed there has to be strong and sustained top management support. The introduction of SMTs does threaten the positions of managers who are asked to function as team members instead of team leaders. Some rank-and-file employees may not be ready to handle the responsibility, authority, and accountability that SMTs put on them. The SMT concept may go against the organization's old way of doing things and thus encounter resistance and even sabotage from other employees. Therefore, in planning the introduction of SMTs into the organization's structure, top management should abide by the following recommendations to ensure a higher rate of success:[150]

- Ensure that there is an organization-wide support and acceptance of the SMT concept. This can be done by confronting critical structural and cultural questions such as: Does the SMT have sufficient autonomy to perform its task and have access to information? Have conditions been created in which authority can shift between members to appropriately match the demands of their task? Are SMT participants adequately motivated and supported? Are there any psychological or functional walls preventing unity of purpose and action? This structural-cultural alignment with the SMT concept increases the chances of success.
- Have a champion to support and defend the SMT from opponents who are threatened by the new concept and what it represents. *A **self-managed team champion** is an advocate of the SMT concept whose responsibility is to help the team obtain necessary resources, gain political support from top management and other stakeholders of the organization, and defend it from enemy attacks.* This advocacy role is especially critical when there is hostility and distrust by other managers who are afraid the SMTs will cause major shifts of power and authority in the organization. The SMT champion is therefore constantly engaged in getting others to "buy in" and gaining commitment at all levels, while communicating the benefits of the SMT.[151]
- Allow adequate time for training so team members can bond with one another and form team skills. Effective team-building interventions will break down barriers and create opportunities for greater cooperation.
- Selecting members for SMTs should be a careful and judicious process. Team member skills and experiences should match task requirements. Team diversity should be emphasized.[152]
- Provide specific goals and incentives.
- Ensure that the organization has the necessary resources in time, money and people to commit to this kind of change.
- Avoid overreacting at the first sign of crisis. Team-building experts caution against overreacting when an SMT starts experiencing problems. Top management should resist the urge to pull the plug on the new program or the tendency to micromanage it. Instead, a careful review and analysis of problem areas should be done before any action is taken.

The next sections examine the changing role of leadership in SMTs and the challenges of implementing SMTs.

CONCEPT APPLICATION 8-6

Improving the Success Rate of SMTs

Identify which guideline for improving the success rate of SMTs is implied by each statement below.

a. top management support and commitment
b. specific goals and incentives
c. SMT Champion
d. adequate and necessary resources
e. team composition
f. matching culture and structure
g. adequate team training time

_____ 28. Management expects us to get the job done but has not created the kind of environment that supports and values our unique set up and way of doing things.

_____ 29. The thing that frustrates me is the fact that we don't have all that we need to meet our team objectives.

_____ 30. I got frustrated with my team because no two team members could agree on what we were supposed to be doing or how we will be evaluated for compensation.

_____ 31. The team members are not taking our new self-directed status seriously, because they believe SMTs are just the latest fad and those in charge will drop it for the next hot topic.

_____ 32. There are still a lot of people in this organization who don't know why we operate differently from other traditional teams and thus are not very supportive of our efforts. We need someone to defend and promote us.

The Changing Role of Leadership in Self-Managed Teams

If, as we defined it, SMTs are relatively autonomous teams whose members share or rotate leadership responsibilities and hold themselves mutually responsible for meeting team goals, then the obvious question becomes, what type of leadership does the SMT embody if at all? The answer lies in a leadership form that is not authority-determined or hierarchical.[153] Members have been highly trained to handle leadership responsibilities such as hiring, discipline, firing, motivation, performance appraisals, and training. Different persons lead as the needs of the team demand. We call this distributed or shared leadership.[154,155] *In* **distributed leadership**, *multiple leaders take complementary leadership roles in rotation within the same SMT, according to their area of expertise or interest.*[156,157] In other words, different members of the SMT assume different leadership roles as circumstances and task requirements warrant. It is what some have described as peer leadership.[158]

Some organizations do assign a facilitator to SMTs. Where this is the case, the SMT reports to the facilitator. The purpose of the facilitator is to define the "broad parameters" for the SMT, clear the path in the organization for the team, and offer advice and counsel as needed. It is just as critical that the SMT facilitator possess the requisite skills and ability to effectively lead as was the case with conventional teams. The **SMT facilitator** is *the external leader of an SMT, whose job is to create optimal working conditions so that team members take on responsibilities to work productively and solve complex problems on their own.*

A summary of the SMT facilitator's team-building activities is presented in Exhibit 8.5. Employing these team-building activities will generate greater identification with the team, especially as pride in the team's accomplishments grows.

WORK
Application **8-13**

Describe which of the SMT Facilitator's team-building activities (see Exhibit 8.5) have been employed in a team that you are or had been a member.

_____

_____

_____

_____

EXHIBIT 8.5

SMT Facilitator: Team-Building Activities

- Providing avenues for resolving interpersonal conflicts.
- Creating opportunities for social interaction.
- Increasing cohesiveness and cooperation among team members.
- Facilitating high level communication among team members.
- Highlighting mutual interest, not differences, of team members.
- Using ceremonies, rituals, and symbols to build team identify and bonding.
- Employing team-oriented incentives to foster team spirit.

© Cengage Learning®

Learning Outcome 9

Describe the challenges of implementing effective self-managed teams.

The Challenges of Implementing Self-Managed Teams

To observe a highly effective SMT at work is truly a sight to behold. However, it is a difficult concept to implement. There are many reasons for this, not the least of which is the fact that management usually will not get out of the way. Some managers see the SMT as a threat to their future. Some have gone as far as to suggest that the use of self-managed work teams may signal the end of the middle manager.[159]

Even among members of the non-managerial ranks, the transition to SMTs has as much potential for frustrations and problems as it does for managers. This is usually due to unfamiliarity with the new structure and new routines, and adjusting to team responsibilities. Team members must learn new behaviors. The need to adapt to a new working arrangement in which the definition of teamwork requires a fundamental adjustment, may be too much for some members, and thus lead to personality and behavior conflicts. The greatest challenge may lie in setting and enforcing new behavioral expectations made necessary by the absence of a conventional leader and the presence of new employee rights and responsibilities.

Some of the disadvantages of working in teams in general discussed earlier in the chapter—such as social loafing and groupthink—are also likely to occur in poorly designed SMTs.

The decision to use SMTs as a tool for re-engineering work in an organization is not always a guaranteed success. It requires a great deal of commitment, effort, and support from all members of the organization, especially senior management. In organizations where there has been careful planning, former managers become SMT facilitators and are retrained to function differently than they did in their previous role.

Many of the difficulties associated with SMTs stem from the inability of some managers to transition from a conventional command-and-control leadership role to a shared role in self-managed teams.[160] Ultimately, when former managers now working as part of an SMT worry more about their egos and avoid communicating with other members, they set a poor example for the rest of the team. This can lead to increased workplace conflict and political activity, ill will, and decrease in morale. Changing old attitudes and mindsets is therefore a major challenge to implementing SMTs.

It is the case that managers who have become accustomed to traditional, autocratic management and jaded at management fads that come and go may resist or undermine an SMT launch. In the long run, the benefits of SMTs such as improved employee morale, productivity, quality, and economic savings are well worth the growing pains.

WORK
Application **8-14**

Have you worked in a team in which former managers have been reassigned to function simply as members of the team? What was your experience with the behavior and attitude of these former managers in their new role as team members?

"Take It To The Net". Access student resources at www.cengagebrain.com. Search for Lussier, Leadership 6e to find student study tools.

Chapter Summary

The chapter summary is organized to answer the nine learning outcomes for this chapter.

1 Discuss the benefits and limitations of working in teams.

Benefits: In a team situation it is possible to achieve synergy, whereby the team's total output exceeds the sum of individual member contributions. Team members often evaluate and add to one another's thinking, so there are fewer chances of errors and the quality of the decisions is improved. A team atmosphere contributes well toward effective problem solving, continuous improvement, and innovation. Also, being a team member makes it possible for someone to satisfy more needs than working alone; among these are the need for affiliation, security, self-esteem, and self-fulfillment.

Limitations: Some teams have the unhealthy practice of pressuring members to conform to lower group standards of performance and conduct. For example, a team member may be ostracized for being more productive than his or her coworkers. Shirking of individual responsibility, or social loafing, is another problem frequently noted in teams. Another well-known problem common in teams is the practice of groupthink, which happens when the team values getting along so much that dissenting views are quickly suppressed in favor of group consensus.

2 Identify and explain the ten characteristics of highly effective teams.

See Exhibit 8.1 and the ensuing discussion of each characteristic in the text.

3 What role can a team leader play in creating an effective team?

The team leader's role in creating an effective team include being the (1) chief motivator, (2) team coach and mentor, (3) role model, (4) team culture enforcer, (5) cheerleader, and (6) resource person.

4 Describe how organizational culture can influence team creativity.

Creating the right organizational culture is the responsibility of top management. Creativity does not work in hierarchical command-and-control environments. Top management has the responsibility to create the appropriate setting and support systems that foster and nourish creativity. Creating an organizational culture that supports and encourages creativity provides the protection that team members need to take creative risks. Another organizational factor that influences team creativity is a commitment to team diversity. Diverse teams feature differences in thinking styles, knowledge, skills, values, and beliefs among individual team members, which enhances creativity.

5 Outline the three parts of conducting effective meetings.

Each meeting should cover the following:

1. *Identify objectives.* Begin the meeting on time. Begin by reviewing progress to date, the group's objectives, and the purpose/objective for the specific meeting. If minutes are recorded, they are usually approved at the beginning of the next meeting.

2. *Cover agenda items.* Be sure to cover agenda items in priority order. Try to keep to the approximate times, but be flexible. If the discussion is constructive and members need more time, give it to them; however, if the discussion is more of a destructive argument, move ahead.

3. *Summarize and review assignments.* End the meeting on time. The leader should summarize what took place during the meeting. Were the meeting's objectives achieved? Review all of the assignments given during the meeting. Get a commitment to the task that each member should perform for the next or a specific future meeting. The secretary and/or leader should record all assignments.

6 Explain the differences between conventional and self-managed teams.

SMTs differ from traditional teams in a number of ways. In SMTs, roles interchange frequently as members learn to be followers as well as leaders. Rather than functioning in their specialized units, SMT members develop multi-skilled capabilities that make them very flexible in performing various tasks within the team. The nature of SMTs is one of team empowerment and accountability rather than individual empowerment and accountability. Team accountability is a significant responsibility, especially because SMT members determine how they will organize themselves to get the work done and are responsible not only for their own performance but for that of other team members as well. See Exhibit 8.3.

7 Describe the benefits of using self-managed teams in organizations.

SMTs (1) create a stronger sense of commitment to the work effort among team members; (2) improve quality, speed, and innovation; (3) have more satisfied employees and lower turnover and absenteeism; (4) facilitate faster new-product development; (5) allow cross-trained team members greater flexibility in dealing with personnel shortages due to illness or turnover; and (6) keep operational costs down because of reductions in managerial ranks and increased efficiencies.

8 **Describe top management's role in improving the success rate of self-managed teams.**

Senior management has the principal responsibility to create the right environment in which SMTs can grow and thrive. This involves undertaking activities to ensure that there is organization-wide support and acceptance of the SMT concept, appoint a champion to support and defend the SMT from opponents who are threatened by the new concept and what it represents, allow adequate time for training so team members can bond with one another and form team skills, carefully and judiciously select team members so their skills and experiences match task requirements, provide specific goals and incentives,

insure the availability of adequate resources, and avoid overreacting at the first sign of a crisis.

9 **Describe the challenges of implementing effective self-managed teams.**

Many of the challenges of implementing SMTs stem from the difficulties of transitioning from a traditional command-and-control work environment to SMTs. Managers who have become accustomed to traditional, autocratic management and jaded by management fads that come and go may resist or undermine a team approach. Even among members of the non-managerial ranks, the transition to SMTs has as much potential for frustrations and problems as it does for managers. This is usually due to unfamiliarity with the new structure and new routines and adjusting to team responsibilities. The greatest challenge may lie in setting and enforcing new behavioral expectations, made necessary by the absence of a traditional leader and the presence of new employee rights and responsibilities.

Key Terms

cross-functional team, 284

distributed leadership, 298

functional team, 283

group, 271

groupthink, 273

self-managed team champion, 297

SMT facilitator, 298

self-managed teams (SMTs), 285

social loafing, 273

team, 271

team cohesion, 277

team creativity, 281

team effectiveness, 275

team learning, 275

team-member exchange (TMX), 275

team norms, 277

teamwork, 272

virtual team, 285

Review Questions

1 What is groupthink, and under what conditions is it most likely to occur?

2 Describe the factors that generally contribute to high levels of team cohesion.

3 Creativity is usually thought of as a characteristic of individuals, but are some teams more creative than individuals?

4 What is team-centered leadership, and how does it differ from the leader-centered approach?

5 Describe how a leader can avoid conducting nonproductive meetings.

6 Describe the level of decision-making latitude commonly found in self-managed teams?

7 Briefly discuss some of the potential benefits and drawbacks of using self-managed teams.

Critical Thinking Questions

The following critical-thinking questions can be used for class discussion and/or as written assignments to develop critical thinking skills. Be sure to give complete explanations for all questions.

1 Teams are often credited with making better decisions than individuals, yet they are also criticized for groupthink. What are some strategies for creating effective teams that don't fall victim to the groupthink phenomenon?

2 Identify and describe any team you have been a member of, or know about otherwise, that has a strong norm of teamwork that all members support. What role did the team leader play in making this possible?

3 What are some of the key indicators of team dysfunction?

4 What is the key to creating cross-functional teams in which team members put the good of the team ahead of functional self-interest?

5 How can virtual teams work well together from far apart?

6 What would you describe as some of the dos and don'ts of team leadership?

7 Describe an organization whose culture, structure, and leadership philosophy clearly support creativity and innovation.

CASE

Frederick W. Smith—FedEx

FedEx has built what is the most seamless global air and ground network in its industry, connecting more than 90 percent of the world's economic activity. It is evident that FedEx's open, flexible, and team-based organizational structure and culture has been instrumental in keeping the company's lead position in overnight package service. According to its founding CEO Fred Smith, teamwork and team leadership deserves much of the credit.

FedEx has expanded far beyond what Mr. Smith started with back in 1971. With annual revenues of $43 billion, FedEx has continued to strengthen its industry leadership in global transportation services. Federal Express was the first service company to win the Malcolm Baldrige National Quality Award in 1990. In addition, FedEx has consistently been ranked on *Fortune* magazine's industry lists, including "World's Most Admired Companies," "America's Most Admired Companies," "100 Best Companies to Work For," and "Blue Ribbon Companies."

With growth have come difficulties of coordination, maintaining efficiency, meeting customer expectations, and managing employees. Smith realized that a rigid hierarchy of command-and-control leadership would only magnify these difficulties. To give his employees the flexibility and freedom they need to move quickly and help FedEx remain the dominant overnight delivery service in the world, Smith decided to restructure FedEx by emphasizing the *team approach* to getting work done. The phrase "*FedEx Team*" is common throughout the corporate literature and represents the way they view themselves. CEO Smith directed his executive team to create and empower more teams by giving them the authority and the responsibility to make the changes needed to improve productivity and customer satisfaction throughout the FedEx system. As described on the corporation's Web site, FedEx's operating strategy works seamlessly—and simultaneously—on three levels:

- **Compete collectively** by standing as one brand worldwide and speaking with one voice.

- **Operate independently** by focusing on our independent networks to meet distinct customer needs.

- **Manage collaboratively** by working together to sustain loyal relationships with our workforce, customers, and investors.

An example of the successful implementation of Mr. Smith's vision can be found in Springfield, Virginia. With strong support from their managers, employees formed the Quality Action Team to overhaul their package-sorting techniques. The improvements they introduced put couriers on the road 12 minutes earlier than before and halved the number of packages they delivered late. The success of teams at departmental or local levels encouraged the CEO and his leadership team to also assign employee teams to companywide projects. Facing growing competition from United Parcel Service, the U.S. Postal Service, and Airborne Express, FedEx organized its clerical employees into "super-teams" of up to 10 people. These teams operated as SMTs with little direct supervision from managers. One team cut service glitches, such as incorrect bills and lost packages by 13 percent. Another team spotted—and worked until they eventually solved—a billing problem that had been costing the company $2.1 million a year.

FedEx teams have worked so well because Fred Smith sets stretch goals and then incentivizes his followers to achieve them. He spearheaded the concept of the "golden package," the idea that every package FedEx handles is criti-cal and must be delivered on time. Whenever there's a crisis, whether due to operational failures or to Mother Nature threatening to ground the company's planes, the team with the golden package takes charge to figure out how to make the delivery on time. Smith reinforces group performance by presenting a monthly Circle of Excellence award to the best FedEx station. He encourages innovative thinking by creat-ing a "job-secure environment." He takes the position that "if you hang people who try to do something that doesn't quite work, you'll get people who don't do anything."

Managers are by no means obsolete at FedEx. Mr. Smith has redefined their roles. There has been a shift in mindset from the traditional leader-centric model to the team-cen-tered leadership approach. Managers are expected to for-mulate clear, attainable goals for their teams, solicit employee ideas, and act on the best employee suggestions. FedEx man-agers perceive their role as facilitators—and sometimes they are players. During emergencies at the Memphis hub, senior managers have been known to hurry down from the execu-tive suite to help load packages onto the conveyor belts that feed the company's planes. They practice team leadership by doing, not by telling.

Mr. Smith is responsible for providing strategic vision for all FedEx Corporation operating companies, including FedEx Ser-vices, FedEx Express, FedEx Ground, and FedEx Freight. FedEx serves more than 220 countries and territories with opera-tions that include 634 aircraft and over 90,000 vehicles. FedEx inspires its more than 300,000 team members to remain "ab-solutely, positively" focused on safety, the highest ethical and professional standards and the needs of their customers and communities.[161]

GO TO THE INTERNET: To learn more about Fred Smith and FedEx, visit the Web site **(http://www .fedex.com)**.

Support your answers to the following questions with specific information from the case and text or with other information you get from the Web or other sources.

1. How do the standards set by Fred Smith for FedEx teams improve organizational performance?

2. What motivates the members of FedEx to remain highly engaged in their teams?

3. Describe the role FedEx managers play in facilitating team effectiveness.

4. What type of teams does FedEx use? Provide evidence from the case to support your answer.

5. Leaders play a critical role in building effective teams. Cite evidence from the case that FedEx managers per-formed some of these roles in developing effective teams.

CUMULATIVE CASE QUESTIONS

6. The Big Five model of personality categorizes traits into dimensions of surgency, agreeableness, adjust-ment, conscientiousness, and openness to experience (Chapter 2). Which of these dimensions do you think Fred Smith possesses?

7. The normative leadership model identifies five leader-ship styles appropriate for different situations that us-ers can select to maximize decisions (Chapter 4). Which of the five leadership styles is practiced by FedEx team leaders?

8. The case reveals that at the Memphis hub senior man-agers have been known to hurry down from the execu-tive suite to help load packages during emergencies to get the plane off on time. FedEx leaders want to be seen as coaches, not managers. Specific guidelines can help a leader become an effective coach (Chapter 6). Which of the guideline(s) does the example above represent?

9. Research on followership describes five types of followers (see Exhibit 7.1). Which of these types will work best in FedEx's team environment as described in the case, and why?

CASE EXERCISE AND ROLE-PLAY

Preparation: You are senior vice president for operations at FedEx. FedEx's monthly Circle of Excellence Award is presented to the best FedEx station. This time the best station was one that truly represented the spirit of teamwork in problem solving. The station manager spotted a loading problem that was costing the company millions of dollars a year and decided to leave it up to the station as a group to find ways of solving the problem. After a series of group meetings and key decisions, a solution was found that successfully took care of the loading problem and was adopted by the rest of the company. It has come to Fred Smith's attention that a key reason for the station's success is the leadership role played by the team leader during this process. Smith has asked that you use the award ceremony as an opportunity to highlight the virtues of the team-centered approach of leadership,

particularly with respect to decision making in teams. Develop the key parts of the speech you will give on this occasion.

Your instructor may elect to break the class into groups to share ideas and put together the speech or simply ask each student to prepare an independent speech. If you do a group speech, select one leader to present the speech to the entire class.

Role-Play: One person (representing oneself or a group) may give the speech to the entire class, or break into groups of five or six and deliver speeches one at a time.

VIDEO ▶ CASE

The NEADS Team: People and Dogs

The National Education for Assistance Dog Services (NEADS) functions with teams of people. But another type of teamwork is also central to the mission of NEADS: the team of human and dog. NEADS acquires, raises, trains, and matches service dogs to meet the needs of people with limited physical mobility or deafness. It takes about two years to train a service dog—and that requires a lot of teamwork. Volunteer families become part of the team when, at four months of age, the puppies are placed in foster care. These families agree to feed, love, and raise the puppies so they become accustomed to the distractions and energy of the real world. Professional dog trainers from NEADS visit regularly to work with the families and dogs to ensure that the dogs receive the proper training in preparation for their

later work. The puppies live in their foster homes until they are about a year and a half old; then they return to the NEADS farm to continue their education. Here, they receive advanced training from professional dog trainers. When a dog's training is complete, its new owner arrives on campus for a two-week stay, during which the person and the dog become a team. The person and dog have been matched through an extensive interview process that involves a team of people interviewers and dog trainers.

1. Describe the characteristics of a typical NEADS team, using the information discussed in the chapter.

2. What factors determine the cohesiveness of NEADS teams?

Behavior Model Skills Training 8-1

This behavior model skills training on leadership decision making has four parts. You should first read how to use the model. Then, you may view the behavior model video that illustrates all four decision-making styles for the same decision. Parts III and IV are together in Developing Your Leadership Skills Exercise

8-1, which gives you the opportunity to develop your ability to select the leadership decision-making style most appropriate for a given situation. Lastly, you further develop this skill by using the model in your personal and professional life.

Leadership Decision-Making Model

(Part I)

Deciding Which Leadership Decision-Making Style to Use

Read the instructions for using the leadership decision-making model, and see Model 8.1. You may want to refer to the model as you read.

Managers today realize the trend toward participation in decision making, and managers are open to using participation. It is sometimes difficult for managers to decide when to use participation and when not to, and what level of participation to use. You are about to learn how to use a model that will develop your skill at selecting the appropriate leadership style to meet the needs of the situation. First, let's examine ways in which groups can be used to generate solutions.

Selecting the Appropriate Leadership Decision Style

We have the same four variables as in the Situational Communication Model 6.6—time, information, acceptance, and capability level.

Step 1   Diagnose the situation. The first step you follow as a leader involves diagnosing the situational variables—including time, information, acceptance, and follower capability.

Time. You must determine whether there is enough time to include followers in decision making. Time is viewed as yes (you have time to use participation) or no (there is no time to use participation). If there is no time, you should use the autocratic style (S1A in Model 6.6), regardless of preference. When there is no time to include employees in problem solving and decision making, you ignore the other three variables; they are irrelevant if there is no time. If you say yes there is time, then the consultative, participative, or empowerment styles may be appropriate. You use the other three variables to select the style.

Time is a relative term. In one situation, a few minutes may be considered a short time period, but in another a month may be a short period of time. Time is not wasted when the potential advantages of using participation are realized.

Information. You must decide if you have enough information to make a quality decision alone. The more information you have, the less need for participation; the less information you have, the greater the need for participation. If you have all the necessary information, there is no need for follower participation, and the autocratic style (S1A) is appropriate. When you have some information, but need more, which can be obtained by asking questions, the consultative style (S2C) may be appropriate. If you have little information, the appropriate style may be participative (S3P—group discussion) or empowerment (S4E—group makes the decision).

Acceptance. You must decide whether employee acceptance of the decision is critical to implementation of the decision. The more the followers will like a decision, the less need there is for participation; the more the followers will dislike a decision, the greater the need for participation. If you make the decision alone, will the follower or group willingly implement it? If the follower or group will be accepting, the appropriate style is probably autocratic (S1A). If the follower or group will be reluctant, the appropriate style may be consultative (S2C) or participative (S3P). If they will probably reject the decision, the participative (S3P) or empowerment style (S4E) may be appropriate. When teams make decisions, they are more understanding, accepting, and committed to implementing the decision.

Capability. You must decide whether the follower or group has the ability and motivation to be involved in problem solving and decision making. Does the follower or group have the experience and information needed to be involved? Will followers put the organization's or department's goals ahead of personal goals? Do the followers want to be involved in problem solving and decision making? Followers are more willing to participate when the decisions personally affect them. If the follower or group capability level is low (C1), an autocratic style (S1A) may be appropriate. When capability is moderate (C2), a consultative style (S2C) may be appropriate. If capability level is high (C3), a participative style (S3P) might be adopted. If capability is outstanding (C4), choose the empowerment style (S4E). Remember that an employee's or group's capability level can change from situation to situation.

Step 2   Select the appropriate leadership style. After considering the four variables, you select the appropriate style. In some situations, all variables will indicate that the same style is appropriate, whereas in other cases, the appropriate style is not so clear. For example, you could be in a situation in which you have time to use any style, may have all the information necessary (autocratic), followers may be reluctant (consultative or participative), and their capability may be moderate (consultative). In situations where different styles are indicated for different variables, you must determine which variables should be given more weight. In the above example, assume that acceptance was critical for successful implementation of the decision. Acceptance takes precedence over information. Because the followers involved have moderate capability, the consultative style would be appropriate. Again, Model 8.1 summarizes use of the four situational communication styles in decision making.

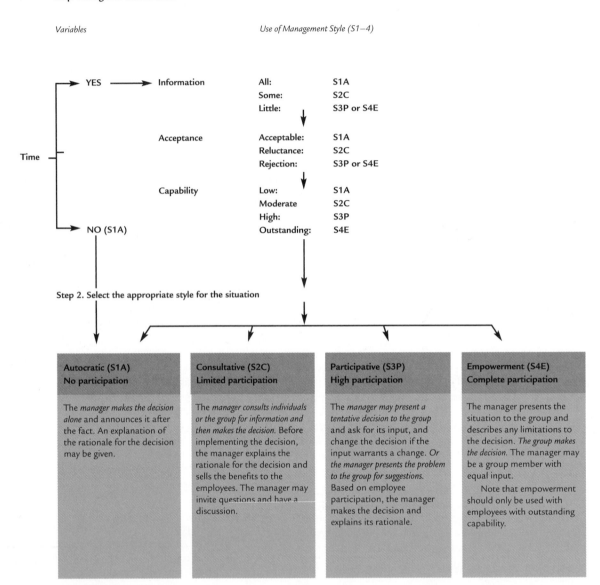

MODEL 8-1

Leadership Decision Making

Step 1. Diagnose the situation

Variables   *Use of Management Style (S1—4)*

YES → Information	All:	S1A
	Some:	S2C
	Little:	S3P or S4E
Acceptance	Acceptable:	S1A
	Reluctance:	S2C
	Rejection:	S3P or S4E
Time Capability	Low:	S1A
	Moderate	S2C
	High:	S3P
NO (S1A)	Outstanding:	S4E

Step 2. Select the appropriate style for the situation

Autocratic (S1A) **No participation**	**Consultative (S2C)** **Limited participation**	**Participative (S3P)** **High participation**	**Empowerment (S4E)** **Complete participation**
The *manager makes the decision alone* and announces it after the fact. An explanation of the rationale for the decision may be given.	The *manager consults individuals or the group for information and then makes the decision.* Before implementing the decision, the manager explains the rationale for the decision and sells the benefits to the employees. The manager may invite questions and have a discussion.	The *manager may present a tentative decision to the group* and ask for its input, and change the decision if the input warrants a change. *Or the manager presents the problem to the group for suggestions.* Based on employee participation, the manager makes the decision and explains its rationale.	The manager presents the situation to the group and describes any limitations to the decision. *The group makes the decision.* The manager may be a group member with equal input. Note that empowerment should only be used with employees with outstanding capability.

———————————————— Level of Participation ————————————————→

Note that with autocratic, consultative, and participative styles the manager retains the power to make the decision; with empowerment the group makes the decision.

Using the Leadership Decision-Making Model

We will apply the model to the following situation; additional similar situations are presented later with the skill-development exercise.

Manager Ben can give one of his followers a merit pay raise. He has a week to make the decision. Ben knows how well each employee performed over the past year. The followers really have no option but to accept getting or not getting the pay raise, but they can complain to upper management about the selection. The followers' capability levels vary, but as a group they have a high capability level under normal circumstances.

time _____ information _____ acceptance _____ capability
Leadership style _____

Step 1 **Diagnose the situation.** Ben has plenty of time to use any level of participation (place a Y for yes on the "time" line below the situation). He has all the information needed to make the decision (place S1A on the "information" line). Followers have no choice but to accept the decision (place S1A on the "acceptance" line). And the group's capability level is normally high (place S3P on the "capability" line).

Step 2 **Select the Appropriate Style for the Situation.** There are conflicting styles to choose from (autocratic and participative): yes time; S1A information; S1A acceptance; S3P capability.

The variable that should be given precedence is information. The followers are normally capable, but in a situation like this they may not put the department's goals ahead of their own. In other words, even if followers know who deserves the raise, they may fight for it anyway. Such a conflict could cause future problems. Some ways to make the decision could include the following:

Autocratic (S1A) The manager would select the person to be given the raise without discussing it with any followers. Ben would simply announce the decision after submitting it to the payroll department.

Consultative (S2C). The manager would get information from the followers concerning who should get the raise. Ben would then decide who would get the raise. He would announce the decision and explain the rationale for it. He may invite questions and discussion.

Participative (S3P). The manager could tentatively select the employee who gets the raise, but be open to change if a group member convinces him that someone else should. Or Ben could explain the situation to the group and lead a discussion concerning who should get the raise. After considering their input, Ben would make the decision and explain the rationale for it. Notice that the consultative style does not allow for discussion as the participative style does.

Empowerment (S4E). The manager would explain the situation and allow the group to decide who gets the raise. Ben may be a group member. Notice that this is the only style that allows the group to make the decision.

The autocratic style is appropriate for this situation. The consultative style is also a good approach. However, the participative and empowerment styles use too much participation for the situation. Your skill at selecting the appropriate decision-making leadership style should improve through using the model for the ten situations in the skill-development exercise. However, the next step is to view the behavior video model.

Behavior Model Video 8-1 and Video Exercise

(Part II)

Deciding Which Leadership Decision-Making Style to Use

Objectives

To better understand the four leadership decision-making styles, and to select the most appropriate style for a given situation.

Video (13 minutes) Overview

The video begins by telling you how to use the model. Then it shows the human resources director, Richard, meeting with a supervisor, Denise, to discuss training changes. Each of the four styles is shown to illustrate how all four styles can be used in the same situation. Thus, you gain a better understanding of the four styles. During the video you will be asked to identify each of the four styles being used by Richard. The answers will be given by your instructor during or at the end of the video. In viewing the video, you should also realize that some styles are more appropriate than others for this situation. As a class, you may discuss which style would be the most effective, and at the end of the video, the recommended style is stated.

Preparation

You should have read the "Leadership Decision-Making Model" section of this leadership behavior-modeling skills training.

Procedure 1 (10–20 minutes) The instructor shows (or you view on your own) the video, "Decision Making." As you view each of the four scenes, identify the four leadership decision-making styles being used by Richard. Write the letters and number of the style on the line after each scene.

Scene 1. _____ Autocratic (S1A)

Scene 2. _____ Consultative (S2C)

Scene 3. _____ Participative (S3P)

Scene 4. _____ Empowerment (S4E)

Option A: View all four scenes and identify the style used by Richard. Select the one style that you would use in this situation. Are other styles also appropriate? Which style would you not use (is not appropriate) for this situation? Next to each style listed above, write the letter "a" for appropriate or "n" for not appropriate. After everyone is finished the instructor leads a class discussion and/or gives the correct answers.

Option B: After each scene the class discusses the style used by Richard. The instructor states the correct answer after each of the four scenes. Then discuss which style is the most effective for the situation.

Option C: Simply view the entire video without any discussion.

Conclusion

The instructor may lead a class discussion and/or make concluding remarks.

Developing Your Leadership Skills (8-1

(Parts III & IV)

Deciding Which Leadership Decision-Making Style to Use

Preparation for This Exercise

Below are ten situations calling for a decision. Select the appropriate decision-making style for each. Be sure to use Model 8.1 when determining the style to use. First determine the answers to the variables (S1A, S2C, S3P, S4E) and write them on the lines below the situation. Then place the selected style on the "Leadership style" line.

S1A autocratic   S2C consultative

S3P participative   S4E empowerment

1 You have developed a new work procedure that will increase productivity. Your boss likes the idea and wants you to try it in a few weeks. You view your followers as fairly capable and believe that they will be receptive to the change.

__ time __ information __ acceptance __ capability
Leadership style _____

2 There is new competition in your industry. Your organization's revenues have been dropping. You have been told to lay off 3 of your 15 followers in two weeks. You have been supervisor for over three years. Normally, your followers are very capable.

time __ information __ acceptance __ capability
Leadership style _____

3 Your department has been facing a problem for several months. Many solutions have been tried and have failed. You've finally thought of a solution, but you're not sure of the possible consequences of the change required, or of acceptance by your highly capable followers.

time __ information __ acceptance __ capability
Leadership style _____

4 Flextime has become popular in your organization. Some departments let each employee start and end work when he or she chooses. However, because of the cooperation required of your followers, they must all work the same eight hours. You're not sure of the level of interest in changing the hours. Your followers are a very capable group and like to make decisions.

time __ information __ acceptance __ capability
Leadership style _____

5 The technology in your industry is changing too fast for the members of your organization to keep up. Top management hired a consultant who has made recommendations. You have two weeks to decide what to do about the recommendations. Your followers are usually capable; they enjoy participating in the decision-making process.

time __ information __ acceptance __ capability
Leadership style _____

6 Top management has handed down a change. How you implement it is your decision. The change takes effect in one month. It will affect everyone in your department. Their acceptance is critical to the success of the change. Your followers are usually not interested in making routine decisions.

time __ information __ acceptance __ capability
Leadership style _____

7 Your boss called to tell you that someone requested an order for your department's product; the delivery date is very short. She asked you to call her back in 15 minutes with a decision about taking the order. Looking over the work schedule, you realize that it will be very difficult to deliver the order on time. Your followers will have to push hard to make it. They are cooperative, capable, and enjoy being involved in decision making.

time ___ information ___ acceptance ___ capability
Leadership style _____

8 Top management has decided to make a change that will affect all of your followers. You know that they will be upset because it will cause them hardship. One or two may even quit. The change goes into effect in 30 days. Your followers are very capable.

time ___ information ___ acceptance ___ capability
Leadership style _____

9 You believe that productivity in your department could be increased. You have thought of some ways to increase it, but you're not sure of them. Your followers are very experienced; almost all of them have been in the department longer than you have.

time ___ information ___ acceptance ___ capability
Leadership style _____

10 A customer offered you a contract for your product with a quick delivery date. The offer is open for two days. To meet the contract deadline, followers would have to work nights and weekends for six weeks. You cannot require them to work overtime. Filling this profitable contract could help get you the raise you want and feel you deserve. However, if you take the contract and don't deliver on time, it will hurt your chances of getting a big raise. Your followers are very capable.

time ___ information ___ acceptance ___ capability
Leadership style _____

Doing This Exercise in Class

Objective

To develop your skill at knowing which level of participation to use in a given decision-making situation. You will learn to use the leadership decision-making model.

AACSB General Skills Area

The primary AACSB skills developed through this exercise are interpersonal relations and teamwork skills, analytic and reflective thinking skills and application of knowledge.

Experience

You will try to select the appropriate decision-making style for each of ten situations in preparation for this exercise.

Preparation

You should have completed the preparation for this exercise, unless told not to do so by your instructor. There is an option to do the preparation in class as part of the exercise.

Procedure 1 *(8–12 minutes)* The instructor may review the leadership decision-making model (Model 8.1) and will explain how to use it to select the appropriate leadership style for the first situation.

Procedure 2 *(4–8 minutes)* Students, working alone, complete situation 2 using the model, followed by the instructor going over the recommend answers. If the instructor will be testing you on leadership decision making, you may be told the details.

Procedure 3 *(10–20 minutes)* Break into teams of two or three. Apply the model to situations 3 through 5 as a team. You may decide to change your original answers. The instructor goes over the recommended answers and scoring for situations 3 through 5. Your instructor may tell you not to continue on to situation 6 until he or she goes over the answers to situations 3 through 5.

Procedure 4 *(10–20 minutes)* In the same teams, select decision-making styles for situations 6 through 10. The instructor will go over the recommended answers and scoring.

Conclusion

The instructor may lead a class discussion and/or make concluding remarks.

Apply It *(2–4 minutes)* What did I learn from this experience? How will I use this knowledge in the future? Identify when you will practice this skill.

_____
_____
_____

Sharing

In the group, or to the entire class, volunteers may give their answers to the "Apply It" questions.

Developing Your Leadership Skills (8-2)

Individual versus Group Decision Making

Preparation for This Exercise

To complete this exercise you must answer the questions in Concept Applications 1 through 4 in the chapter.

Doing This Exercise in Class

Objective

To compare individual and group decision making, to better understand when to use a group to make decisions

AACSB General Skills Area

The primary AACSB skills developed through this exercise are interpersonal relations and teamwork skills, analytic and reflective thinking skills and application of knowledge.

Preparation

As preparation, you should have answered the questions in Concept Applications 1 through 4.

Experience

You will work in a group, each member of which will answer the same 20 questions, and then analyze the results to determine if the group or one (or more) of its members had the higher score.

Procedure 1 *(1–2 minutes)* Place your answers to the 20 questions in the "Individual Answer" column in the table on page 320.

Procedure 2 *(15–20 minutes)* Break into teams of five, with smaller or larger groups as necessary. As a group, come to an agreement on the answers to the 20 questions. Place the group answers in the "Group Answer" column. Try to use consensus rather than voting or majority in arriving at the answers.

Procedure 3 *(4–6 minutes)* **Scoring.** The instructor will give the recommended answers. Determine how many you got right as an individual and as a group. Total your individual and the group's score.

Compute the *average* individual score by adding all the individual scores and dividing by the number of group members. Write it here:___.

Now calculate the difference between the average individual score and the group score. If the group's score is higher than the average individual score, you have a gain (+) of points; if the group score is lower, you have a loss (−) of points. Write it here, and circle one (+ or −).

Determine the highest individual score. Write it here: ___.

Determine the number of individuals who scored higher than the group's score: ___.

Procedure 4 *(5–10 minutes)* **Integration.** As a group, discuss the advantages or disadvantages of being in a group while making the decisions in this exercise. Go back to the text and review the advantages and disadvantages of team-centered decision making listed on pages 295–296 and discuss. Then try to agree on which of the advantages and disadvantages your group had. Overall, were the advantages of using a group greater than the disadvantages? If your group were to continue to work together, how could it improve its decision-making ability? Write your answer below.

_____

_____

_____

Conclusion

The instructor may lead a class discussion and/or make concluding remarks.

Apply It *(2–4 minutes)* What did I learn from this experience? How will I use this knowledge in the future? Specifically, what will I do the next time I'm in a group to help it make better decisions? When will I have the opportunity?

_____

_____

_____

Sharing

In the group, or to the entire class, volunteers may give their answers to the "Apply It" questions.

Question Number		Individual Answer	Group Answer	Recommended Answer	Individual Score	Group Score
CA 1	1					
	2					
	3					
	4					
	5					
CA 2	6					
	7					
	8					
	9					
	10					
CA 3	11					
	12					
	13					
	14					
	15					
CA 4	16					
	17					
	18					
	19					
	20					
Total scores						

Endnotes

1. www.southwest.com; Building LUV - 2013 Southwest Airlines One report; L. Betty, G. Kelly, CEO, Southwest Airlines, Is Interviewed. *Bloomberg Transcripts* [serial online] (n.d.); Available from: Newspaper Source Plus, Ipswich, MA. Accessed January 1, 2014; PR N. Webcast Alert: Southwest Airlines Co. Annual Meeting of Shareholders. *PR Newswire US* [serial online]. (2013, May 8); Available from: Newspaper Source Plus, Ipswich, MA. Accessed January 1, 2014 and Event Brief of Q2 2013 Southwest Airlines Earnings Conference Call - Final. *Fair Disclosure Wire (Quarterly Earnings Reports)* [serial online]. n.d.; Available from: Newspaper Source Plus, Ipswich, MA. Accessed January 1, 2014.

2. K. Lanaj, J. Hollenbeck, D. Ilgen, C. Barnes, and S. Harmon, "The Double-Edged Sword of Decentralized Planning in Multiteam Systems," *Academy of Management Journal* [serial online] 56(3) (2013, June): 735–757.

3. J. Kleinert, J. Ohlert, M. Sulprizio, et al., "Group Dynamics in Sports: An Overview and Recommendations on Diagnostic and Intervention," *Sport Psychologist* 26(3) (2012, September): 412–434.

4. A.A. Thompson, M.A. Peteraf, J.E. Gamble, and A.J. Strickland, *Crafting & Executing Strategy – The Quest for Competitive Advantage* (19/e) (New York: McGraw-Hill Irwin Publishing, 2014).

5. K. Lanaj, J. Hollenbeck, D. Ilgen, C. Barnes, S. Harmon, "The Double-Edged Sword of Decentralized Planning in Multiteam Systems. *Academy of Management Journal* 56(3) (2013, June): 735–757.

6. H. Gardner, B. Staats, and F. Gino, "Dynamically Integrating Knowledge in Teams: Transforming Resources into Performance. *Academy of Management Journal* [serial online] 55(4) (2012, August): 998–1022.

7. N. Lorinkova, M. Pearsall, H. Sims Jr., "Examining the Differential Longitudinal Performance of Directive Versus Empowering Leadership in Teams. *Academy of Management Journal* 56(2) (2013, April): 573–596.

8. A. Seers, "Interpersonal Workplace Theory at a Crossroads," In G. B. Graen (Ed.), *New Frontiers of Leadership, LMX Leadership:* The series, 2: 1–31 (Greenwich, CT: Information Age, 2004); T. L. Baker and T. G. Hunt, "An Exploratory Investigation into the Effects of Team Composition on Moral Orientation," *Journal of Managerial Issues* 15 (2003, Spring): 106–120; E. E. Lawler, III, S. A. Mohrman, and G. E. Ledford, Jr., *Creating High Performance Organizations: Practices and Results of Employee Involvement and Total Quality Management in Fortune 1000 Companies* (San Francisco, CA: Jossey-Bass Publishers, 1995); and J. Gordon, "Work Teams: How Far Have They Come?" *Training* 29 (1992): 59–65.

9. N. Lorinkova, M. Pearsall, H. Sims Jr., "Examining the Differential Longitudinal Performance of Directive versus Empowering Leadership in Teams. *Academy of Management Journal* 56(2) (2013, April): 573–596.

10. D. C. Jones and K. Takao, "The Impact of Teams on Output, Quality, and Downtime: An Empirical Analysis Using Individual Panel Data," *Industrial & Labor Relations Review* 64(2) (2011, January): 215–240.

11. C. Huey-Wen, L. Yu-Hsun, and C. Shyan-Bin, "Team Cognition, Collective Efficacy, and Performance in Strategic Decision-Making Teams," *Social Behavior & Personality: An International* 40(3) (2012, April): 381–394.

12. R. Th. A. J. Leenders, J.M.L. van Engelen, and J. Kratzer, "Systematic Design Methods and the Creative Performance of New Product Teams: Do They Contradict or Complement Each Other?" *Journal of Product Innovation Management* 24 (2007): 166–179; E. E. Lawler, S. A. Mohrman, and G. E. Ledford, *Creating High Performance Organizations: Practices and Results of Employee Involvement and Total Quality Management in Fortune 1000 companies* (San Francisco: Jossey-Bass, 1995).

13. G.B. Graen, C. Hui, and E.A. Taylor, "Experience-Based Learning about LMX Leadership and Fairness in Project Teams: A Dyadic Directional Approach," *Academy of Management Learning & Education* 5(4) (2006): 448–460.

14. H. E. Harding, et al., "The Impact of Preparing Faculty in the Effective Use of Student Teams," *College Student Journal* 44(3) (2010): 752–761.

15. J. Lai, L. Lam, S. Lam, "Organizational Citizenship Behavior in Work Groups: A Team Cultural Perspective," *Journal of Organizational Behavior* 34(7) (2013, October): 1039–1056.

16. M.E. Burbach, G.S. Matkin, K.M. Gambrell, K.M., and H.E. Harding, "The Impact of Preparing Faculty in the Effective Use of Student Teams," *College Student Journal* 44(3) (2010): 752–761.

17. D. Naranjo-Gil, G. Cuevas-Rodriguez, Á. López-Cabrales, and J. Sánchez, "The Effects of Incentive System and Cognitive Orientation on Teams' Performance," *Behavioral Research in Accounting* 24(2) (2012, June): 177–191.

18. M. Butler, "Our HR Columnist," *People Management* 13 (2007, November): 43.

19. N. Lorinkova, M. Pearsall, H. Sims Jr., "Examining the Differential Longitudinal Performance of Directive versus Empowering Leadership in Teams," *Academy of Management Journal* 56(2) (2013, April): 573–596.

20. A. Ellis, "System Breakdown: The Role of Mental Models and Transactive Memory in the Relationship between Acute

Stress and Team Performance," *Academy of Management Review* 49(3) (2006): 576–589.

21 S.W.J. Kozlowski, and B.S.Bell, (2003), "Work Groups and Teams in Organizations," in W. C. Borman, D. R. Ilgen and R. J. Klimoski (eds), *Handbook of Psychology: Industrial and Organizational Psychology*, Vol. 12 (Hoboken, NJ: John Wiley & Sons), pp. 333–375.

22 J. Allen, "Building a Group into a Team," *Internet Journal of Healthcare Administration* 6(1) (2009): 3.

23 N. Meslec, and P. Curşeu, "Too Close or Too Far Hurts: Cognitive Distance and Group Cognitive Synergy," *Small Group Research* 44(5) (2013, October): 471–497.

24 K. Lanaj, J. Hollenbeck, D. Ilgen, C. Barnes, and S. Harmon, "The Double-Edged Sword of Decentralized Planning in Multiteam Systems," *Academy of Management Journal* 56(3) (2013, June): 735–757.

25 L. Hsieh and S. Chen, "A Study of Cross-Functional Collaboration in New Produce Development: A Social Capital Perspective," *International Journal of Productivity and Quality Management* 2 (2006, November): 23.

26 Y. Badir, B. Büchel, and C. Tucci, "A Conceptual Framework of the Impact of NPD Project Team and Leader Empowerment on Communication and Performance: An Alliance Case Context," *International Journal of Project Management* 30(8) (2012, November): 914–926.

27 J. Lai, L. Lam, and S. Lam, "Organizational Citizenship Behavior in Work Groups: A Team Cultural Perspective," *Journal of Organizational Behavior* 34(7) (2013, October): 1039–1056.

28 L. Cheng-Chen, and P. Tai-Kuang, "From Organizational Citizenship Behaviour to Team Performance: The Mediation of Group Cohesion and Collective Efficacy," *Management & Organization Review* 6(1) (2010): 55–75.

29 C. Hopp, and L. Zenk, "Collaborative Team Networks and Implications for Strategic HRM," *International Journal of Human Resource Management* 23(14) (2012, July 15): 2975–2994.

30 D. Naranjo-Gil, G. Cuevas-Rodríguez, Á. López-Cabrales, and J. Sánchez, "The Effects of Incentive System and Cognitive Orientation on Teams' Performance," *Behavioral Research In Accounting* 24(2) (2012, June): 177–191.

31 R. Kidwell and S. Valentine, "Positive Group Context, Work Attitudes, and Organizational Misbehavior: The Case of Withholding Job Effort," *Journal of Business Ethics* 86(1) (2009): 15–28.

32 K. Price, D. Harrison, and J. Gavin, "Withholding Inputs in Team Contexts: Member Composition, Interaction Processes, Evaluation Structure, and Social Loafing," *Journal of Applied Psychology* 91 (2006, November): 1375–1384.

33 E. Stark, J. Shaw, and M. Duffy, "Preference for Group Work, Winning Orientation, and Social Loafing Behavior Groups," *Group & Organization Management* 32 (2007, December): 699–723.

34 K. McFarland, "Where Group-Think Is Good; Groups Often Provide the Best Answers to Business Problems— Provided You Know How to Structure the Team," *Business Week Online* (April 2007).

35 K. Lanaj, J. Hollenbeck, D. Ilgen, C. Barnes, & S. Harmon, "The Double-Edged Sword of Decentralized Planning in Multiteam Systems," *Academy of Management Journal* 56(3) (2013, June): 735–757.

36 A. Carton and J. Cummings, "A Theory of Subgroups in Work Teams," *Academy of Management Review* [serial online] 37(3) (2012, July): 441–470.

37 K. Lanaj, J. Hollenbeck, D. Ilgen, C. Barnes, and S. Harmon, "The Double-Edged Sword of Decentralized Planning in Multiteam Systems," *Academy of Management Journal* 56(3) (2013, June): 735–757.

38 Hall J. "Managing Teams with Diverse Compositions: Implications for Managers from Research on the Faultline Model," *SAM Advanced Management Journal* (07497075) 78(1) (2013, winter): 4–10.

39 J. B Wu, A. S Tsui, and A. J. Kinicki, "Consequences of Differentiated Leadership in Groups," *Academy of Management Journal* 53(1) (2010, February): 90–106.

40 J. Summers, S. Humphrey, and G. Ferris, "Team Member Change, Flux in Coordination, and Performance: Effects of Strategic Core Roles, Information Transfer, and Cognitive Ability," *Academy of Management Journal* 55(2) (2012, April): 314–338.

41 K. Lanaj, J. Hollenbeck, D. Ilgen, C. Barnes, S. Harmon, "The Double-Edged Sword of Decentralized Planning in Multiteam Systems," *Academy of Management Journal* 56(3) (2013, June): 735–757.

42 J. Kleinert, J. Ohlert, M. Sulprizio, et al., "Group Dynamics in Sports: An Overview and Recommendations on Diagnostic and Intervention," *Sport Psychologist* 26(3) (2012, September): 412–434

43 M. Pryor, L. Singleton, S. Taneja, and L. Toombs, "Teaming as a Strategic and Tactical Tool: An Analysis with Recommendations," *International Journal of Management* 26(2): 320–333.

44 L. Lynam, M. McCord, and L. Michaelsen, "Designing Effective Team Assignments: Kolb's Learning Cycle Modified by the 4 S Method," *Business Education Innovation Journal* 2(1) (2010): 67–75.

45 G. Yaping, K. Tae-Yeol, L. Deog-Ro, and Z. Jing, "A Multilevel Model of Team Goal Orientation, Information Exchange,

and Creativity," *Academy of Management Journal* 56(3) (2013, June): 827–851.

46 D. Vashdi, P. Bamberger, and M. Erez, "Can Surgical Teams Ever Learn? The Role of Coordination, Complexity, and Transitivity in Action Team Learning," *Academy of Management Journal* 56(4) (2013, August): 945–971.

47 C. Huey-Wen, L. Yu-Hsun, and C. Shyan-Bin, "Team Cognition, Collective Efficacy, and Performance in Strategic Decision-Making Teams," *Social Behavior & Personality: An International* 40(3) (2012, April): 381–394.

48 N. Sivasubramaniam, S. Liebowitz, and C. Lackman, "Determinants of New Product Development Team Performance: A Meta-Analytic Review," *Journal of Product Innovation Management* 29(5) (2012, September): 803–820.

49 Hall J. "Managing Teams with Diverse Compositions: Implications for Managers from Research on the Faultline Model," *SAM Advanced Management Journal (07497075)* 78(1) (2013, winter): 4–10.

50 P. Lencioni, "The Five Dysfunctions of a Team: A Leadership Fable," Reviewed by J. R. Hackman and E. Pierce, *Academy of Management Perspectives* 20 (2006): 122–125.

51 D. Naranjo-Gil, G. Cuevas-Rodrıguez, Á. López-Cabrales, and J. Sánchez, "The Effects of Incentive System and Cognitive Orientation on Teams' Performance," *Behavioral Research In Accounting* 24(2) (2012, June): 177–191.

52 D. Jones, P. Kalmi, and A. Kauhanen, "How Does Employee Involvement Stack Up? The Effects of Human Resource Management Policies on Performance in a Retail Firm," *Industrial Relations* 49(1) (2010): 1–21.

53 C. Hopp and L. Zenk, "Collaborative Team Networks and Implications for Strategic HRM," *International Journal of Human Resource Management* 23(14) (2012, July 15): 2975–2994.

54 T. Brahm and F. Kunze, "The Role of Trust Climate in Virtual Teams," *Journal of Managerial Psychology* 27(6) (2012, October): 595–614.

55 D. Vashdi, P. Bamberger, and M. Erez, "Can Surgical Teams Ever Learn? The Role of Coordination, Complexity, and Transitivity in Action Team Learning," *Academy of Management Journal* 56(4) (2013, August): 945–971.

56 N. Sivasubramaniam, S. Liebowitz, and C. Lackman, "Determinants of New Product Development Team Performance: A Meta-Analytic Review," *Journal of Product Innovation Management* 29(5) (2012, September): 803–820.

57 A. Pescosolido and R. Saavedra, "Cohesion and Sports Teams: A Review," *Small Group Research* 43(6) (2012, December): 744–758.

58 B. Bradley, J. Baur, C. Banford, and B. Postlethwaite, "Team Players and Collective Performance: How Agreeableness Affects Team Performance over Time," *Small Group* 44(6) (2013, December): 680–711.

59 T. Kline and J. O'Grady, "Team Member Personality, Team Processes and Outcomes: Relationships within a Graduate Student Project Team Sample," *North American Journal of Psychology* 11(2) (2009): 369–382.

60 L. Wei and L. Wu, "What a Diverse Top Management Team Means: Testing an Integrated Model," *Journal of Management Studies* 50(3) (2013, May): 389–412.

61 C. Hopp and L. Zenk, "Collaborative Team Networks and Implications for Strategic HRM," *International Journal of Human Resource Management* 23(14) (2012, July 15): 2975–2994.

62 A. Nederveen Pieterse, D. van Knippenberg, and D. van Dierendonck, "Cultural Diversity and Team Performance: The Role of Team Member Goal Orientation," *Academy of Management Journal* 56(3) (2013, June): 782–804.

63 B. Nielsen and S. Nielsen, "Top Management Team Nationality Diversity and Firm Performance: A Multilevel Study," *Strategic Management Journal* 34(3) (2013, March): 373–382.

64 S. Hoogendoorn, H. Oosterbeek, and M. van Praag, "The Impact of Gender Diversity on the Performance of Business Teams: Evidence from a Field Experiment," *Management Science* 59(7) (2013, July): 1514–1528.

65 S. Jee Young and H. Doo-Seung, "Gender Diversity: How Can We Facilitate Its Positive Effects on Teams?" *Social Behavior & Personality: An International Journal* 41(3) (2013, March): 497–507.

66 R. Hollister and C. Mejia, "Navigating Team Whirlpools," *Journal of the Quality Assurance Institute* 23(2) (2009): 16–19.

67 G. Clark, "The Seeds of Excellence," *Profit* 28(5) (2009): 19.

68 M. Triana, C. Porter, S. DeGrassi, and M. Bergman, "We're All in This Together...Except for You: The Effects of Workload, Performance Feedback, and Racial Distance on Helping Behavior in Teams," *Journal of Organizational Behavior* 34(8) (2013, November): 1124–1144.

69 K. Eisenhardt, "Top Management Teams and the Performance of Entrepreneurial Firms," *Small Business Economics* [serial online] 40(4) (2013, May): 805–816.

70 M. Lang, "Conflict Management: A Gap in Business Education Curricula," *Journal of Education for Business* 84(4) (2009): 240–245.

71. T. O'Neill, N. Allen, and S. Hastings, "Examining the 'Pros' and 'Cons' of Team Conflict: A Team-Level Meta-Analysis of Task, Relationship, and Process Conflict," *Human Performance* 26(3) (2013, July): 236–260.

72. C. Shu-Cheng Steve, H. Chiung-Yi, and C. Artemis, "Safety Climate and Relational Conflict in the Eyes of Team Members: Examining the Role of Need for Closure," *Social Behavior & Personality: An International Journal* 38(1) (2010): 103–114.

73. D. Sethi and M. Seth, "Interpersonal Communication: Lifeblood of an Organization," *IUP Journal of Soft Skills* 3 (2009, September): 32–40.

74. C. Kauffman, "Employee Involvement: A New Blueprint for Success," *Journal of Accountancy* 209 (2010, May): 46–49.

75. J. Kleinert, J. Ohlert, M. Sulprizio, et al., "Group Dynamics in Sports: An Overview and Recommendations on Diagnostic and Intervention," *Sport Psychologist* 26(3) (2012, September): 412–434

76. N. Lorinkova, M. Pearsall, H. Sims Jr., "Examining the Differential Longitudinal Performance of Directive versus Empowering Leadership in Teams," *Academy of Management Journal* [serial online] 56(2) (2013, April): 573–596.

77. J. Kleinert, J. Ohlert, M. Sulprizio, et al., "Group Dynamics in Sports: An Overview and Recommendations on Diagnostic and Intervention," *Sport* 26(3) (2012, September): 412–434.

78. D. Bhatnagar and D. Tjosvold, "Leader Values for Constructive Controversy and Team Effectiveness in India," *International Journal of Human Resource Management* 23(1) (2012, January): 109–125.

79. M. Brodke, "Management Training to Ensure Excellent Team Performance," *Industrial & Commercial Training* 45(7) (2013, December): 428–432.

80. N. Lorinkova, M. Pearsall, and H. Sims Jr., "Examining the Differential Longitudinal Performance of Directive versus Empowering Leadership in Teams," *Academy of Management Journal* 56(2) (2013, April): 573–596.

81. V. S. Anantatmula, "Project Manager Leadership Role in Improving Project Performance," *Engineering Management Journal* 22(1) (2010): 13–22.

82. S. Sarin and G. O'Connor, "First Among Equals: The Effect of Team Leader Characteristics on the Internal Dynamics of Cross-Functional Product Development Teams," *Journal of Product Innovation Management* 26(2) (2009): 188–205.

83. N. Lorinkova, M. Pearsall, and H. Sims Jr., "Examining the Differential Longitudinal Performance of Directive versus Empowering Leadership in Teams," *Academy of Management Journal* 56(2) (2013, April): 573–596.

84. D. Bhatnagar and D. Tjosvold, "Leader Values for Constructive Controversy and Team Effectiveness in India," *International Journal of Human Resource Management* 23(1) (2012, January): 109–125.

85. H. Liao, D. Liu, and R. Loi "Looking at Both Sides of the Social Exchange Coin: A Social Cognitive Perspective on the Joint Effects of Relationship Quality and Differentiation on Creativity," *Academy of Management Journal* 53(5) (2010): 1090–1109.

86. P. Wellington and N. Foster, "21st Century Teamwork," *Engineering & Technology (17509637)* 4(118) (2009): 72–75.

87. S. Ruggieri and C. Abbate, "Leadership Style, Self-Sacrifice, and Team Identification," *Social Behavior & Personality: An International Journal* 41(7) (2013, August): 1171–1178.

88. N. R. Rothenberg, "Teams, Leaders, and Performance Measures," *Contemporary Accounting Research* 28(4) (2011): 1123–1140.

89. D. Derue, J. Hollenbeck, D. Ilgen, D. Feltz, "Efficacy Dispersion in Teams: Moving Beyond Agreement and Aggregation," *Personnel Psychology* 63(1) (2010): 1–40.

90. M. Brodke, "Management Training to Ensure Excellent Team Performance," *Industrial & Commercial Training* 45(7) (2013, December): 428–432.

91. G. Yaping, K. Tae-Yeol, L. Deog-Ro, and Z. Jing, "A Multilevel Model of Team Goal Orientation, Information Exchange, and Creativity," *Academy of Management Journal* 56(3) (2013, June): 827–851.

92. D. Vashdi, P. Bamberger, and M. Erez, "Can Surgical Teams Ever Learn? The Role of Coordination, Complexity, and Transitivity in Action Team Learning," *Academy of Management Journal* 56(4) (2013, August): 945–971.

93. H. Gardner, B. Staats, and F. Gino, "Dynamically Integrating Knowledge in Teams: Transforming Resources into Performance," *Academy of Management Journal* 55(4) (2012, August): 998–1022.

94. W. Tsai, N. Chi, A. Grandey, and S. Fung, "Positive Group Affective Tone and Team Creativity: Negative Group Affective Tone and Team Trust as Boundary Conditions," *Journal of Organizational Behavior* 33(5) (2012, July): 638–656.

95. H. Gardner, B. Staats, and F. Gino, "Dynamically Integrating Knowledge in Teams: Transforming Resources into Performance," *Academy of Management Journal* 55(4) (2012, August): 998–1022.

96. G. Yaping, K. Tae-Yeol, L. Deog-Ro, and Z. Jing, "A Multilevel Model of Team Goal Orientation, Information Exchange, and Creativity," *Academy of Management Journal* 56(3) (2013, June): 827–851.

97. B. Joo, J. Song, D. Lim, and S. Yoon, "Team Creativity: The Effects of Perceived Learning Culture, Developmental Feedback and Team Cohesion," *International Journal of Training & Development* 16(2) (2012, June): 77–91.

98. M. Yueru, C. Weibo, B. Ribbens, and Z. Juanmei, "Linking Ethical Leadership to Employee Creativity: Knowledge Sharing and Self-Efficacy as Mediators," *Social Behavior & Personality: An International Journal* 41(9) (2013, October): 1409–1420.

99. B. Joo, J. Song, D. Lim, and S. Yoon, "Team Creativity: The Effects of Perceived Learning Culture, Developmental Feedback and Team Cohesion," *International Journal of Training & Development* 16(2) (2012, June): 77–91.

100. S. Shin, T. Kim, J. Lee, and L. Bian, "Cognitive Team Diversity and Individual Team Member Creativity: A Cross-Level Interaction," *Academy of Management Journal* 55(1) (2012, February): 197–212.

101. S. Ghobadi and J. D'Ambra, "Modeling High-Quality Knowledge Sharing in Cross-Functional Software Development Teams," *Information Processing & Management* 49(1):138-157

102. G. Yaping, K. Tae-Yeol, L. Deog-Ro, and Z. Jing, "A Multilevel Model of Team Goal Orientation, Information Exchange, and Creativity," *Academy of Management Journal* 56(3) (2013, June): 827–851.

103. S. Shin, T. Kim, J. Lee, and L. Bian, "Cognitive Team Diversity and Individual Team Member Creativity: A Cross-Level Interaction," *Academy of Management Journal* 55(1) (2012, February): 197–212.

104. B. Joo, J. Song, D. Lim, and S. Yoon, "Team Creativity: The Effects of Perceived Learning Culture, Developmental Feedback and Team Cohesion," *International Journal of Training & Development* 16(2) (2012, June): 77–91.

105. V. Vad Baunsgaard and S. Clegg, "'Walls or Boxes': The Effects of Professional Identity, Power and Rationality on Strategies for Cross-Functional Integration," *Organization Studies* 34(9) (2013, September): 1299–1325.

106. N. Piercy, W. Phillips, and M. Lewis, "Change Management in the Public Sector: The Use of Cross-Functional Teams," *Production Planning & Control* 24(10/11) (2013, November): 976–987.

107. A. Carr, H. Kaynak, and S. Muthusamy, "The Cross-Functional Coordination Between Operations, Marketing, Purchasing, and Engineering and the Impact on Performance," *International Journal of Manufacturing Technology and Management* 13 (2007, December): 55.

108. H. Bruns, "Working Alone Together: Coordination in Collaboration across Domains of Expertise," *Academy of Management Journal* 56(1) (2013, February): 62–83.

109. T. L. Legare, "How Hewlett-Packard Used Cross-Functional Teams to Deliver Healthcare Industry Solutions," *Journal of Organizational Excellence* 20(4) (2001, Autumn): 29–38.

110. C. O. Longenecker, and M. Neubert, "Barriers and Gateways to Management Cooperation and Teamwork," *Business Horizons* 43(5) (2000, September/October): 37–44.

111. N. Piercy, W. Phillips, and M. Lewis, "Change Management in the Public Sector: The Use of Cross-Functional Teams," *Production Planning & Control* 24(10/11) (2013, November): 976–987.

112. E. Jones and J. Kelly, "The Psychological Costs of Knowledge Specialization in Groups: Unique Expertise Leaves You Out of the Loop," *Organizational Behavior & Human Decision Processes* 121(2) (2013, July): 174–182.

113. A. Joshi, N. Pandey, and G. Han, "Bracketing Team Boundary Spanning: An Examination of Task-Based, Team-Level, and Contextual Antecedents," *Journal of Organizational Behavior* 30(6) (2009): 731–759.

114. H. Bruns, "Working Alone Together: Coordination in Collaboration across Domains of Expertise," *Academy of Management Journal* 56(1) (2013, February): 62–83.

115. D. D. Greenand and G. E. Roberts, "Personnel Implications of Public Sector Virtual Organizations," *Public Personnel Management* 39(1) (2010): 47–57.

116. M. Scott, "'Communicate through the Roof': A Case Study Analysis of the Communicative Rules and Resources of an Effective Global Virtual Team," *Communication Quarterly* 61(3) (2013, July): 301–318.

117. P. Ferreira, E. Lima, and S. da Costa, "Perception of Virtual Team's Performance: A Multinational Exercise," *International Journal of Production Economics* 140(1) (2012, November): 416–430.

118. A. Klitmøller and J. Lauring, "When Global Virtual Teams Share Knowledge: Media Richness, Cultural Difference and Language Commonality," *Journal of World Business* 48(3) (2013, July): 398–406.

119. T. Brahm and F. Kunze, "The Role of Trust Climate in Virtual Teams," *Journal of Managerial Psychology* 27(6) (2012, October): 595–614.

120. M. Scott, "'Communicate through the Roof': A Case Study Analysis of the Communicative Rules and Resources of an Effective Global Virtual Team," *Communication* 61(3) (2013, July): 301–318.

121. S. A. Furst, M. Reeves, B. Rosen, and R. S. Blackburn, "Managing the Life Cycle of Virtual Teams," *Academy of Management Executive* (May 2004): 6–20; L. L. Martins, L. L. Gilson, and M T. Maynard, "Virtual Teams: What Do We Know and Where Do We Go from Here," *Journal of Management* 30(6) (2004): 805–835.

122 C.B. Gibson and J.L. Gibbs, "Unpacking the Concept of Virtuality: The Effects of Geographic Dispersion, Electronic Dependence, Dynamic Structure, and National Diversity on Team Innovation," *Administrative Science Quarterly* (2006, September): 451–495.

123 United States Office of Personnel Management. (2009). *Status of Telework in the Federal Government*, http://www.telework.gov/Reports

124 P. Ferreira, E. Lima, and S. da Costa, "Perception of Virtual Team's Performance: A Multinational Exercise," *International Journal of Production Economics* 140(1) (2012, November): 416–430.

125 L. Gilson, M. Maynard, and E. Bergiel, "Virtual Team Effectiveness: An Experiential Activity," *Small Group Research* 44(4) (2013, August): 412–427.

126 Y. Tong, X. Yang, and H. Teo, "Spontaneous Virtual Teams: Improving Organizational Performance through Information and Communication Technology," *Business Horizons* 56(3) (2013, May): 361–375.

127 T. Brahm and F. Kunze, "The Role of Trust Climate in Virtual Teams," *Journal of Managerial Psychology* 27(6) (2012, October): 595–614.

128 N. Lorinkova, M. Pearsall, and H. Sims Jr., "Examining the Differential Longitudinal Performance of Directive versus Empowering Leadership in Teams," *Academy of Management Journal* 56(2) (2013, April): 573–596.

129 A. Ismail, N. Zainuddin, and Z. Ibrahim, "Linking Participative and Consultative Leadership Styles to Organizational Commitment as an Antecedent of Job Satisfaction," *UNITAR e-Journal* 6(1) (2010): 11–26.

130 P. Carbonell and A. Rodriguez-Escudero, "Management Control, Role Expectations and Job Satisfaction of New Product Development Teams: The Moderating Effect of Participative Decision-Making," *Industrial Marketing Management* 42(2) (2013, February): 248–259.

131 Y. Badir, B. Büchel, and C. Tucci, "A Conceptual Framework of the Impact of NPD Project Team and Leader Empowerment on Communication and Performance: An Alliance Case Context," *International Journal of Project Management* 30(8) (2012, November): 914–926.

132 N. Lorinkova, M. Pearsall, and H. Sims Jr., "Examining the Differential Longitudinal Performance of Directive versus Empowering Leadership in Teams," *Academy of Management Journal* 56(2) (2013, April): 573–596.

133 B. Maciejovsky, M. Sutter, D. Budescu, and P. Bernau, "Teams Make You Smarter: How Exposure to Teams Improves Individual Decisions in Probability and Reasoning Tasks," *Management Science* 59(6) (2013, June): 1255–1270.

134 M. Seo and L. Barrett, "Being Emotional During Decision Making—Good or Bad? An Empirical Investigation," *Academy of Management Journal* 50 (2007): 923–940.

135 I. Bens, "Facilitating with Ease! Core Skills for Facilitators, Team Leaders and Members, Managers, Consultants, and Trainers," Reviewed by J. K. Williams, *Academy of Management Learning & Education* 6(2) (June 2007): 294.

136 Q. Roberson and I. Williamson, "Justice in Self-Managing Teams: The Role of Social Networks in the Emergence of Procedural Justice Climates," *Academy of Management Journal* 55(3) (2012, June): 685–701.

137 H. McIntyre and R. Foti, "The Impact of Shared Leadership on Teamwork Mental Models and Performance in Self-Directed Teams," *Group Processes & Intergroup Relations* 16(1) (2013, January): 46–57.

138 B. Hawkins, "Gendering the Eye of the Norm: Exploring Gendered Concertive Control Processes in Two Self-Managing Teams," *Gender, Work & Organization* 20(1) (2013, January): 113–126.

139 Q. Roberson and I. Williamson, "Justice in Self-Managing Teams: The Role of Social Networks in the Emergence of Procedural Justice Climates," *Academy of Management Journal* 55(3) (2012, June): 685–701.

140 N. Watersand and M. Beruvides, "An Empirical Study Analyzing Traditional Work Schemes versus Work Teams," *Engineering Management Journal* 21(4) (2009): 36–43.

141 Q. Roberson and I. Williamson, "Justice in Self-Managing Teams: The Role of Social Networks in the Emergence of Procedural Justice Climates," *Academy of Management Journal* 55(3) (2012, June): 685–701.

142 Y. Badir, B. Büchel, and C. Tucci, "A Conceptual Framework of the Impact of NPD Project Team and Leader Empowerment on Communication and Performance: An Alliance Case Context," *International Journal of Project Management* 30(8) (2012, November): 914–926.

143 Q. Roberson and I. Williamson, "Justice in Self-Managing Teams: The Role of Social Networks in the Emergence of Procedural Justice Climates," *Academy of Management Journal* 55(3) (2012, June): 685–701.

144 I. P. Vlachos, "The Effects of Human Resource Practices on Firm Growth," *International Journal of Business Science & Applied Management* 4(2) (2009): 17–34.

145 A. Fazzariand J. Mosca, "'Partners in Perfection': Human Resources Facilitating Creation and Ongoing Implementation of Self-Managed Manufacturing Teams in a Small Medium Enterprise," *Human Resource Development Quarterly* 20(3) (2009): 353–376.

146. Z. Omar, A. Zainal, F. Omar, and R. Khairudin, "The Influence of Leadership Behaviour on Organisational Citizenship Behaviour in Self-Managed Work Teams in Malaysia," *South African Journal of Human Resource Management* 7(1) (2009): 196–206.

147. H. McIntyre and R. Foti, "The Impact of Shared Leadership on Teamwork Mental Models and Performance in Self-Directed Teams," *Group Processes & Intergroup Relations* 16(1) (2013, January): 46–57.

148. Q. Roberson and I. Williamson, "Justice in Self-Managing Teams: The Role of Social Networks in the Emergence of Procedural Justice Climates," *Academy of Management Journal* 55(3) (2012, June): 685–701.

149. C. Langfred, "The Downside of Self-Management: A Longitudinal Study of the Effects of Conflict on Trust, Autonomy, and Task Interdependence in Self-Managing Teams," *Academy of Management Journal* 50 (2007): 885–900.

150. M. Moravec, O. J. Johannessen, and T. A. Hjelmas, "The Well-Managed SMT," *Management Review* 87 (June 1998): 56–58.

151. J. Ingvaldsen and M. Rolfsen, "Autonomous Work Groups and the Challenge of Inter-Group Coordination," *Human Relations* 65(7) (2012, July): 861–881.

152. A. Nederveen Pieterse, D. van Knippenberg, and D. van Dierendonck, "Cultural Diversity and Team Performance: The Role of Team Member Goal Orientation," *Academy of Management Journal* 56(3) (2013, June): 782–804.

153. Q. Roberson and I. Williamson, "Justice in Self-Managing Teams: The Role of Social Networks in the Emergence of Procedural Justice Climates," *Academy of Management Journal* 55(3) (2012, June): 685–701.

154. H. McIntyre and R. Foti, "The Impact of Shared Leadership on Teamwork Mental Models and Performance in Self-directed Teams," *Group Processes & Intergroup Relations* 16(1) (2013, January): 46–57.

155. J. Ingvaldsen and M. Rolfsen, "Autonomous Work Groups and the Challenge of Inter-Group Coordination," *Human Relations* 65(7) (2012, July): 861–881.

156. H. McIntyre and R. Foti, "The Impact of Shared Leadership on Teamwork Mental Models and Performance in Self-Directed Teams," *Group Processes & Intergroup Relations* 16(1) (2013, January): 46–57.

157. R. Bolden, "Distributed Leadership in Organizations: A Review of Theory and Research," *International Journal of Management Reviews* 13(3) (2011, September): 251–269.

158. J. Ingvaldsen and M. Rolfsen, "Autonomous Work Groups and the Challenge of Inter-Group Coordination," *Human Relations* 65(7) (2012, July): 861–881.

159. L. Gratton, "The End of the Middle Manager," *Harvard Business Review* 89(11/2) (2011): 36.

160. Q. Roberson and I. Williamson, "Justice in Self-Managing Teams: The Role of Social Networks in the Emergence of Procedural Justice Climates," *Academy of Management Journal* 55(3) (2012, June): 685–701.

161. http://news.van.fedex.com/Holiday2013; "The Purple Promise," *Smart Business Orange County* [serial online] 8(2) (2013, June): 22; "The Purple Promise," *Smart Business Houston* [serial online] 7(12) (2013, June): 10; W. Risher, "FedEx Marks 40th Anniversary," *The Commercial Appeal*, April 18, 2013.

9

Charismatic and Transformational Leadership

Learning Outcomes

After studying this chapter, you should be able to:

1 Briefly explain Max Weber's conceptualization of charisma. p. 321

2 Explain what is meant by the "locus of charismatic leadership." p. 322

3 Discuss the effects of charismatic leadership on followers. p. 323

4 Discuss how one can acquire charismatic qualities. p. 324

5 Distinguish between socialized and personalized charismatic leader types. p. 326

6 Explain the four stages of the transformation process. p. 331

7 List the qualities of effective charismatic and transformational leaders. p. 333

8 Describe the four behavior dimensions associated with transformational and charismatic leaders. p. 337

9 Distinguish between charismatic and transformational leadership. p. 338

10 Explain the basis of stewardship and servant leadership. p. 342

CHAPTER OUTLINE

Charismatic Leadership

Weber's Conceptualization of Charisma

Locus of Charismatic Leadership

The Effects of Charismatic Leaders on Followers

How One Acquires Charismatic Qualities

Charisma: A Double-Edged Sword

Transformational Leadership

The Effects of Transformational Leadership

Transformational and Transactional Leadership

The Transformation Process

Charismatic-Transformational Leadership

Qualities of Effective Charismatic and Transformational Leadership

Transformational and Charismatic Leader Behaviors

Charismatic and Transformational Leadership: What's the Difference?

Stewardship and Servant Leadership

Stewardship and Attributes of the Effective Steward Leader

Servant Leadership and Attributes of the Effective Servant Leader

OPENING CASE Application

Oprah Winfrey and OWN

From childhood poverty and sexual abuse and her battle with weight loss, Oprah's drive and charisma have made her the "near-perfect spokesperson for eternal optimism" in the psyche of her followers. Her influence is unparalleled. *The Oprah Winfrey Show* has been described as one of the most successful daytime programs in TV history. She launched *O* magazine that boasts a circulation rate of about 2.5 million, launched the TV careers of now-famous TV personalities like Dr. Oz, Dr. Phil, and Rachael Ray, and the designer Nate Berkus. Anything she endorses or mentions in a favorable light becomes an instant best seller in its category. As one writer puts it, "Her brand could sell everything from croissants to refrigerators." It is estimated that Oprah's net worth is about $3 billion.

In January 2008, Oprah and Discovery Channel announced the launching of OWN (Oprah Winfrey Network). It is a 50–50 partnership in which Discovery would invest $100 million in the new network that would focus on Oprah's mantra—"Live Your Best Life." Experts point out that "startups in today's fragmented media market tend to be moguls' pipe dreams." They cite the struggles of Rupert Murdock and Martha Stewart as examples. So, why would this charismatic figure after 25 years of ruling daytime TV give it all up to take the biggest risk and gamble of her professional life? The answer according to Oprah is that she is ready to get "out of the chairs and into the hearts of peoples' lives." She adds, "I want to expand Americans' views of people in the world." Her vision is to use OWN as the platform to impact as many people as possible. Asked how she would define success in her next chapter, Oprah said, "The truth is … I'm not one of those people who says 'Oh, if I change just one person's life…. Nope, not satisfied with just a few. I want millions of people!"

Since its launch, the network's average viewership has fallen from 204,000 to 153,000 people as of May 15, 2011.

According to David Zaslav, CEO of Discovery, which owns half of OWN, "the ratings have been below expectations." After such a rough start and many changes by Oprah, OWN began to show signs of growth and profitability in 2013. She has surprised industry experts, who did not think she could do it. Oprah is showing that she has the leadership skills to transform a failing network, thus earning her claim as not just a charismatic but a transformational leader as well.[1]

OPENING CASE QUESTIONS:

1. Why was Oprah (and possibly still is) such a popular and admired figure on TV?

2. Is Oprah's charisma more of a function of her personal qualities or the environment?

3. What effects has Oprah's charisma had on her followers?

4. Does Oprah embody the example of a socialized charismatic leader or a personalized charismatic leader?

5. What qualities of charismatic leadership does Oprah possess?

6. Is Oprah a transformational leader, a charismatic leader, or both?

7. Oprah seems to have a clear sense of her personal meaning or purpose in life. What factors do you think have contributed to her understanding?

Can you answer any of these questions? You'll find answers to these questions and learn more about Oprah Winfrey's businesses and leadership style throughout the chapter. To learn more about Oprah Winfrey, visit her Web site at **http://www.oprah.com**.

Charismatic and transformational theories return our focus to organizational leadership. These theories shine the light on exemplary leaders whose influence impacts entire social, cultural, economic, and political systems. Charismatic and transformational leaders are able to influence followers to rally toward a shared goal(s). They generate emotion, energy, and excitement that cause followers to make significant personal sacrifices in the interest of the organization.

In this chapter, we will start by discussing charismatic leadership; second, we will discuss transformational leadership; third, we will take a combined approach in examining issues common to both charismatic and transformational leadership; and finally, we will briefly explore the related topics of stewardship and servant leadership.

OPENING CASE Application

1. Why was Oprah (and possibly still is) such a popular and admired figure on TV?

Because of the values she espouses and the causes she champions. She has used her celebrity status to push for social change in our society. She has championed the cause for child abuse, poverty, domestic violence, illiteracy, and much more. Through her television show and magazine, she has entertained, enlightened, and empowered millions of viewers not just in the United States but also around the world.

Learning Outcome ❶   *Briefly explain Max Weber's conceptualization of charisma.*

Charismatic Leadership

Charismatic leadership has generally been analyzed in terms of the effects the leader has on followers, or in terms of the relationship between leaders and followers. In this section, we will review Max Weber's conceptualization of charisma, explain the locus of charismatic leadership, discuss the effects of charismatic leaders on followers, explore how anyone can develop charismatic qualities, and examine the notion of charisma as a double-edged sword.

Weber's Conceptualization of Charisma

The Greek word *charisma* means "divinely inspired gift." Like the term *leadership* itself, charisma has roots in many disciplines, including politics, economics, social movements, and religion. Of the early theories of charisma, the sociologist Max Weber made what is probably the single most important contribution.[2] Weber used the term "charisma" to explain a form of influence based not on traditional or legal–rational authority systems but rather on follower perceptions that a leader is endowed with the gift of divine inspiration or supernatural qualities.[3] As such, charismatic leadership might be less a "gift from God" and more a "gift from followers."[4] Weber saw in a charismatic leader someone who single-handedly visualizes a transcendent vision or course of action that is not only appealing to potential followers but also compels them to act on it because they believe the leader is extraordinarily gifted.[5] **Vision** *is the ability to imagine different and better conditions and the ways to achieve them.* Other attributes of charisma identified in the political and sociological literature include acts of heroism, an ability to inspire and build confidence, espousing of revolutionary ideals, oratorical ability, and a "powerful aura."[6]

Charisma has been called "a fire that ignites followers' energy and commitment, producing results above and beyond the ordinary."[7] It is relational in nature. Charisma is not something found solely in the leader as a psychological phenomenon, nor is it totally

WORK
Application **9-1**

Think of a leader from your work experience or education whom you believe has charisma. Explain why.

situation determined. Instead, charisma manifests itself in the interplay between a leader (his or her traits and behaviors) and followers (their values, needs, perceptions, and beliefs). **Charisma** is therefore defined as *a social construct between the leader and follower, in which the leader offers a transformative vision or ideal that exceeds the status quo and then convinces followers to accept this course of action not because of its rational likelihood of success, but because of their implicit belief in the extraordinary qualities of the leader*[8]

Learning Outcome **2**   *Explain what is meant by the "locus of charismatic leadership."*

Locus of Charismatic Leadership

The locus of charismatic leadership focuses on one question: what is the basis of charisma? This question centers on the debate over whether charisma is primarily the result of (a) the situation or social climate facing the leader, (b) the leader's extraordinary qualities, or (c) a combination of the situation and the leader's qualities.

There are those who believe that charismatic leadership could not take place unless the society was in a state of crisis—that charisma is situationally determined. For those sharing this viewpoint, the charismatic leader is simply an opportunist who capitalizes on a crisis situation. Proponents of this view argue that before an individual with extraordinary qualities could be perceived as a charismatic leader, the social situation presents the opportunity for followers to recognize the need for the leader's qualities. And thus, absent a crisis or situation, such an individual may never be known to possess charismatic qualities. The sociological literature, led by Weber, supports this viewpoint, emphasizing that charismatic leadership is born out of stressful situations. Under stressful situations, charismatic leaders are able to express sentiments that are different from the established order, and also inspire others to buy into their vision of a better future. Advocates of this position would then argue that Martin Luther King Jr., Nelson Mandela, Adolph Hitler, or Gandhi would not have emerged as charismatic leaders without the prevailing socio-economic and political crises in their respective countries.

On the other side of the debate are those who argue that charisma need not be born out of distress but rather that charisma is primarily the result of leaders' innate attributes as seen by their followers. These attributes include a strong sense of vision, exceptional communication skills, strong conviction, trustworthiness, high self-confidence, intelligence, energy and a proactive orientation. Advocates of this position would argue that none of the leaders mentioned earlier would have earned the label of charisma if they did not possess these qualities, regardless of the situation.[9]

OPENING CASE Application

2. Is Oprah's charisma more of a function of her personal qualities or the environment?

The locus of Oprah's charisma can be attributed to her extraordinary qualities rather than to her environment. "Knowledge is power! With knowledge you can soar and reach as high as your dreams can take you," said Oprah. This belief has guided Oprah Winfrey on her brilliant journey from a troubled youth to international fame. Oprah Winfrey is a success story that the everyday person can relate to. She is an effective communicator and a passionate individual. She has the ability to inspire trust and loyalty. Her personal story is inspirational and pulls people in to form strong emotional bonds with her.

Finally, there are those who believe that charismatic leadership does not depend on the leader's innate qualities or the presence of a crisis alone, but rather that it is the interaction of the two. Advocates view charisma as the result of follower attributions, influenced not only by actual leader characteristics and behavior but also by the context of the situation.

| Learning Outcome 3 | *Discuss the effects of charismatic leadership on followers.* |

The Effects of Charismatic Leaders on Followers

An area of interest for many scholars of charisma concerns the effects that charismatic leadership has on follower motivations, job performance, and satisfaction, as well as on an organization's overall performance.[10]

Followers of charismatic leaders often develop a *strong sense of trust and bonding* with the leader that is hard to find in other leader–follower relationships.[11] The relationship between the charismatic leader and the followers is comparable to that of disciples to a master. Such a strong emotional bond is possible because the charismatic leader is believed to have the power to effect radical change by virtue of his or her *transcendent vision*—one that is different from the status quo.[12] Followers stay with the charismatic leader, not out of fear or monetary inducement, but out of love, passionate devotion, trust, and commitment.[13] There is the effect of *unconditional acceptance* of the charismatic leader by his/her followers that is not often seen with other types of leaders. Charismatic leaders are seen as generally more positive in their personality than noncharismatic leaders. This type of positiveness and the leader's capacity to spread it has an effect on followers. Followers develop a *strong sense of self-confidence and self-efficacy* as they work to realize the leader's vision. By observing the leader display self-confidence, followers develop self-confidence as well. When this happens, a positive atmosphere permeates the organization and fuels excitement and energy for the leader's cause. Some scholars have found that this cycle of influence ultimately *increases followers' organizational citizenship behavior and empowerment*.[14]

Followers of charismatic leaders tend to *assume greater risk* than they would with other types of leaders. Followers are willing to suffer whatever fate awaits the charismatic leader as he or she fights to change the status quo. They have absolute trust in the leader and his or her cause. There is an *unquestioning loyalty and obedience to the leader*.[15] This was the case with Gandhi and Martin Luther King Jr.'s followers, as they fought to bring about equality and freedom for all. They completely bought into these two leaders' philosophy of nonviolent resistance even when faced with violence from their opponents.

Another effect of charismatic leadership on followers is to motivate them *to set or aim for higher goals and ideals* and have greater confidence in their ability to achieve such goals.[16] The charismatic leader is seen as an object of identification by followers who try to emulate his or her behavior. When the character of the leader is grounded on such core values as integrity, hard work, responsibility, respect, and accountability, it has an effect on followers who already *desire to align their beliefs, self-concept, cognitions, and values with those of their leader*. We are all aware of business leaders—such as Oprah Winfrey (OWN), Richard Branson (the Virgin Group), and Mark Zuckerberg (Facebook)—who command an extraordinary level of respect and affection from their followers. The effect of the leader's charisma on followers is seen by some as more critical than any other leadership qualities the leader may possess.

WORK
Application **9-2**

Refer back to Work Application 9-1 on the leader you thought has charisma. Briefly discuss examples of the effect his or her charisma had on your work ethic, job performance, or job satisfaction.

At the organizational level, there is an ongoing debate in academic circles on charismatic CEOs and their effect on performance. The question is whether charismatic CEOs achieve better organizational performance than their less charismatic counterparts. The results are mixed; some studies revealed that charismatic leadership showed a positive relationship to financial performance[17] and others seemed to show no effect. According to the findings of one study, supervisors' charismatic leadership style influenced subordinates' work performance and turnover intention.[18] There are also those who say a charismatic leader may indeed make the organization more attractive to outside stakeholders such as investors, customers, suppliers, and activists groups.[19] Exhibit 9.1 summarizes these effects.

The Effects of Charismatic Leaders on Followers

EXHIBIT 9.1

a. Followers are inspired by the "rightness" of the leader's vision and a strong bond develops
b. Unconditional acceptance of the leader
c. Increased follower self-confidence and self-efficacy
d. Follower acceptance of higher or challenging goals
e. Increase in followers' organizational citizenship behavior
f. Tendency of followers to assume greater risks
g. Strong loyalty and obedience to the leader
h. Increased follower motivation to set or aim for higher goals
i. Follower desire to align their beliefs, self-concept, cognitions, and values with those of the leader

Source: Based on R. J. House, and M. L. Baetx (1979). "Leadership: Some Empirical Generalizations and New Research Directions." In B.M. Staw (Ed.), *Research in Organizational behavior*, vol. I (Greenwich, CT: JAI Press, 1979), 399–401.

© Cengage Learning®

OPENING CASE Application

3. What effects has Oprah's charisma had on her followers?

The effects of charismatic leadership summarized in Exhibit 9.1 are very much applicable to Oprah and her followers. Oprah's followers and supporters seem to have an unquestioning loyalty to her and all that she stands for. There is a strong affection and unconditional acceptance of her and a willingness to trust in the "rightness" of whatever cause she champions.

Learning Outcome 4 *Discuss how one can acquire charismatic qualities.*

How One Acquires Charismatic Qualities

There are those who believe that charisma, the ability to inspire and captivate an audience, is an innate quality that cannot be trained into someone. However, there are also those who believe that charismatic qualities can be acquired—that everyone has the potential to develop charismatic qualities.[20] It is possible through training to improve

CONCEPT APPLICATION 9-1

The Effects of Charismatic Leaders on Followers

Referring to Exhibit 9.1 on page 324, align each statement with the effect(s) it illustrates using the letters a–i.

_____ 1. According to one writer, over the years, Oprah has stoked a number of controversies, "yet these embarrassments barely affected Winfrey's standing. Her moral character hasn't been questioned." What effect(s) does this example reveal?

_____ 2. At Facebook, the cult of Zuckerberg is described as "downright Jobsian in its intensity. Engineers are romanced by the size and scope of his vision and for many, winning his approval is its own reward." What effect(s) does this example reveal?

_____ 3. In our church, the relationship between some members and the pastor is comparable to that of disciples to a master. These followers obey every instruction he utters.

_____ 4. The members of the church referred to in No. 3 believe that the pastor has the power to effect radical change by virtue of his transcendent vision, which is different from the status quo.

_____ 5. Our leader, who is very charismatic, has somehow convinced every one of us that we can do anything if only we believe in ourselves.

_____ 6. Your friend tells you that she is very uncomfortable with some of the comments her CEO makes about gays and minorities but does not want to say anything because of her strong commitment to his overall mission.

_____ 7. Every few months, Facebook holds an all-night workfest called the "hackathon." It's a test of their mettle. As one engineer describes it, "Your body's like, 'I'm hungry; I'm tired; I want to go home.' Your brain's like, 'No, no, no this can become something real.'" What effect(s) does this example reveal?

one's communication skills, build self-confidence, and learn techniques to inspire others. There have been great charismatic leaders who did not reveal their charismatic qualities until much later in life. Hitler certainly was not born with charismatic qualities. He was living life on the fringes of society and failed in most of his early endeavors. However, he gradually developed his oratorical and interpersonal skills when he had the opportunity to influence others of like-minded thinking. Richard Branson (CEO and founder of the Virgin Group) and Jack Welch (former CEO of GE) are two very effective leaders who have been described as charismatic and transformational; yet they both overcame stuttering, a speech impediment that causes many others to avoid public speaking. In 2011, the best picture in the Oscar awards ceremony went to *The King's Speech,* a movie about the King of England who had a terrible speech impediment and only through the help of a speech coach did he overcome this weakness. He became an effective speaker and gave some inspiring speeches during World War II.

Nelson Mandela, John F. Kennedy, and Martin Luther King Jr., on the other hand, seemed to have had charismatic qualities early on as young adults that carried on into their mature years as leaders. Suggested strategies for acquiring or enhancing one's charismatic qualities include:

- Through training and practice, you can improve your communication and interpersonal skills. A coach or speech therapist can help you overcome a speech impediment such as stuttering that may be hindering you from communicating effectively. An expert on interpersonal relationships can help you learn how to relate to others in a positive and inspiring way.

- Through education, you can develop your visionary skills by practicing the act of creating a vision in a college course like this one. The role-play exercise at the end of this chapter is directed at this issue.
- You can practice being candid. Although not insensitive, the charismatic person is typically forthright in giving his or her assessment of a situation, whether the assessment is positive or negative. Charismatic leaders are direct in their approach, so that there is no ambiguity about their position on issues.
- Through a leadership development workshop or seminar, you can develop an attractive, enthusiastic, optimistic, and energetic personality profile. A major behavior pattern of charismatic leaders is their combination of vision, enthusiasm, optimism, and a high energy level that they bring to the situation. As mentioned earlier, charisma is a relational concept and ultimately comes from the attributions of followers.

> **Learning Outcome 5** *Distinguish between socialized and personalized charismatic leader types.*

Charisma: A Double-Edged Sword

Most people agree that charisma can be a double-edged sword capable of producing both positive and negative outcomes. It is possible in reading about the personal magnetism, vision, self-confidence, masterful rhetorical skills, and empowering style of charismatic leaders to conclude that they are all good moral leaders whom others should emulate. We live in a society where hero worship is a common occurrence. It is foolish and even dangerous to follow a leader just because he/she is charismatic. Leaders such as Nelson Mandela, Gandhi, Martin Luther King Jr., John F. Kennedy, and Winston Churchill exhibited tremendous charisma.[21] So did leaders such as Osama bin Laden, Charles Manson, David Koresh, Adolph Hitler, and the Reverend Jim Jones of the People's Temple. This latter group of charismatic leaders represents the dark side of charisma.[22] These leaders and many others like them are prone to extreme narcissism that leads them to promote highly self-serving and grandiose goals. Therefore, charisma can cut both ways; it is not always used in the service of a greater good, thus our description of charisma as a "double-edged sword."

A meaningful approach for differentiating between positive and negative charisma is in terms of the values and motives of the leader. Values research proposes that two opposing but complementary motives drive an individual's behavior: *self-glorification* and *self-transcendence*. The *self-glorification motive* is about the self-maintenance and self-enhancement of the leader. It seeks to protect, maintain, and enhance the leader's self-esteem and is consistent with negative or destructive charisma.[23] On the other hand, the *self-transcendence motive* is about the collective interest or good of the broader society. It seeks to build mutually supportive relationships with followers and is consistent with altruistic and empowering orientations of positive or constructive charisma.

Based on this construct of positive and negative charisma, two types of charismatic leaders are identified: the socialized or positive charismatic leader and the personalized or negative charismatic leader. The **socialized charismatic leader (SCL)** *is one who possesses an egalitarian, self-transcendent, and empowering personality and uses charisma for the benefit of others.*[24] The **personalized charismatic leader (PCL)** *is one who possesses a dominant, self-centered, self-aggrandizing, and narcissistic personality and uses charisma for self-glorification.*

SCLs pursue organization-driven goals and promote empowerment, personal growth, and equal participation for followers, whereas PCLs pursue leader-driven goals

WORK
Application **9-4**

Describe a leader in your work experience who manifested positive or negative charismatic qualities. How did this affect your relationship with the leader?

and promote obedience, dependency, and submission.[25] The PCL has a tendency to be authoritarian and exploitative.

With socialized charismatic leaders, rewards are used to reinforce behavior that is consistent with the vision and mission of the organization; personalized charismatic leaders use rewards and punishment to manipulate and control followers, and information is restricted or used to preserve the image of the leader or to exaggerate external threats to the organization. Socialized charismatic leaders tend to have followers who are part of a cohesive team. They convey a values-based message that aligns with the mission and objectives of the organization.[26]

Personalized or negative charismatic leaders emphasize devotion to themselves more than to ideals. Decisions of these leaders are often self-serving. Group accomplishments are used for self-glorification. Ideological appeals are only a ploy to gain power, after which the ideology is ignored or arbitrarily changed to serve the leader's self-interest. In contrast, socialized or positive charismatic leaders seek to instill devotion to ideology more than devotion to self.[27]

OPENING CASE Application

4. Does Oprah embody the example of a socialized charismatic leader or a personalized charismatic leader?

Oprah's philanthropic activities and the way she conducts herself would suggest that she is definitely a socialized charismatic leader. The Oprah Winfrey Foundation was established to support the inspiration, empowerment, education, and well-being of women, children, and families around the world. Through this private charity, Oprah has directly served the needs of low-opportunity people and has awarded hundreds of grants to organizations that carry out this mission. She has contributed millions of dollars toward providing a better education for underprivileged students who have merit but no means. She created the "Oprah Winfrey Scholars Program," which gives scholarships to students determined to use their education to give back to their communities in the United States and abroad.

YOU Make the ETHICAL Call

9.1 Obesity and Charismatic Ads

The federal government has reported that obesity might overtake tobacco as the leading cause of death in the United States.[28] Some social activists are blaming part of the obesity problem on marketing junk food to kids,[29] and food makers and ad agencies are defending advertising to children.[30] Some companies use charismatic star performers and athletes to promote their junk food products to get people to eat more. At the same time, American health officials are trying to persuade people to lose weight. The government has taken out public service ads to convince people to get in shape and eat right. Part of the ads' success depends on whether people take personal responsibility for their own health and weight.

1. What is the reason for the increase in obesity in the United States? Are junk food ads using charismatic stars to promote their products contributing to the obesity problem?

2. Is it ethical for junk food sellers to use charismatic stars to promote their products?

3. Is it ethical and socially responsible for the government to try to get people to lose weight, through ads and other methods?

CONCEPT APPLICATION 9-2

Socialized versus Personalized Charismatic Leaders

Identify each statement as being more characteristic of one or the other type of charismatic leadership:

a. socialized charismatic leader   b. personalized charismatic leader

____ 8. A leader like the late Nelson Mandela who advocated peace and forgiveness toward the white-dominated apartheid government that had imprisoned him for 27 years.

____ 9. An organization where information is restricted and only used to preserve the image of the leader or to exaggerate external threats to the organization.

____ 10. A leader whose primary motive is self-glorification and self-aggrandizement.

____ 11. A leader whose primary motive is to achieve collective interest through close supportive relationships with all follower.

____ 12. A leader who is more interested in protecting, maintaining, and enhancing his or her self-image.

____ 13. A leader who wants obedience, dependency, and submission from his followers.

Transformational Leadership

J. M. Burns first articulated the idea of transformational leadership in 1978 before Bernard Bass expanded on it almost a decade later. Burns proposed two leadership approaches for getting work done: transactional and transformational.[31] Transformational leaders are less a function of follower attributions; rather, they earn their reputation as transformational leaders from their known accomplishments. Transformational leaders are known for moving and changing organizations "in a big way," by communicating to followers an inspiring vision of the future and, like charismatic leaders, tapping into followers' higher ideals and desire for change. The transformational leader seeks to transform a mediocre organization by influencing followers to buy into a new vision and new possibilities.[32]

Effective transformational leaders know that to move forward, they must first earn the trust, commitment, and respect of followers. When this happens, the transformational leader is more likely to achieve a collective "buy-in" to his vision. Followers willingly expend exceptional effort in achieving organizational goals. Therefore, **transformational leadership** *seeks to change the status quo by articulating to followers the problems in the current system and a compelling vision of what a new organization could be,* whereas **transactional leadership** *seeks to maintain stability within an organization through regular economic and social exchanges that achieve specific goals for both leaders and their followers.*

In this section, we will focus attention on the effects of transformational leaders on followers, similar to the discussion on charismatic leaders. We will also differentiate between transactional and transformational leadership and review key stages in the transformation process.

The Effects of Transformational Leadership

As organizations continue to face global challenges, there is greater need for leaders who can successfully craft and implement bold strategies that will enable an organization to achieve above average returns and competitiveness.[33] Transformational leadership describes a process of bold vision creation and articulation that changes and transforms organizations and individuals.[34,35] A number of studies have highlighted the effects of transformational leadership on various organizational and follower outcomes.

At the organizational level, studies have found that transformational leadership has *positive effects on organizational performance,* [36,37] *culture, and learning.* [38] Transformational leaders are more likely to be strong advocates of teamwork, cooperation, and innovation—all ingredients of a learning culture.[39,40,41]

At the individual level, transformational leadership has been found to *positively affect follower organizational commitment* and organizational commitment reflects the extent to which members are loyal and willing to work hard toward achieving organizational objectives. [42,43] Organizational commitment has direct implications on employee *turnover rates, performance,* and *citizenship behavior.*[44] An effective transformational leader has the effect of influencing followers to *shift from a focus on self-interest to a focus on collective interests.*[45,46] Effective transformational leaders use their charisma and power to inspire and motivate followers to *trust and work hard to achieve the organization's objectives.*[47,48] They generate *excitement and energy* by presenting a compelling and inspiring vision of the future. [49] Followers associated with transformational leaders report *higher levels of job satisfaction and empowerment and lower levels of turnover and stress.*[50,51,52] In certain work situations, transformational leadership is associated with *increased employee cognitive abilities, which in turn improve creativity and decision quality.*[53,54]

Transformational versus Transactional Leadership

Begin this section by completing Self-Assessment 9-1 to determine if you are more of a transactional or a transformational leader.

SELF-ASSESSMENT 9-1   Are You More of a Transformational Leader?

Complete the following questions based on how you will act (or have acted) in a typical work or school situation. Use the following scale:

1 — 2 — 3 — 4 — 5

Disagree   Agree

_____ 1. I enjoy change and see myself as a change agent.

_____ 2. I am better at inspiring employees toward a new future than motivating them to perform their current jobs.

_____ 3. I have/had a vision of how an organization can change for the better.

_____ 4. I see myself as someone who is comfortable encouraging people to express ideas and opinions that differ from my own.

_____ 5. I enjoy taking risks, but I'm not reckless.

_____ 6. I enjoy spending time developing new solutions to old problems rather than implementing existing solutions.

_____ 7. I deliberate carefully before acting; I'm not impulsive.

_____ 8. I like to support change initiatives, even when the idea may not work.

_____ 9. I learn from my experience; I don't repeat the same mistakes.

_____ 10. I believe the effort to change something for the better should be rewarded, even if the final outcome is disappointing.

Add up the numbers on lines 1–10 and place your total score here and on the continuum below.

10 — 20 — 30 — 40 — 50
Transactional leader   *Transformational leader*

The higher the score, generally, the more you exhibit transformational leader qualities. However, transformational leaders also perform transactional behaviors. It is also generally easier to be transformational at higher levels of management than at lower levels.

In today's globally competitive environment, experts and scholars agree that employee creativity and innovative behavior is imperative for organizations' survival. Transformational leadership has been determined to be particularly effective in engendering **follower** innovative behavior and innovation happens to be a driving force in transforming organizations.[55] Therefore, transformational leadership is about *changing the status quo.* The transformational leader wants to change the status quo by articulating to followers the problems in the current system and a compelling vision of what a new organization could be.

The transactional leadership process involves an exchange of valued benefits, based on defined expectations and motivations of both leaders and followers. The transactional leader enters into specific contractual arrangements with followers. In exchange for meeting specific objectives or performing certain duties, the leader provides benefits that satisfy followers' needs and expectations.[56] It is akin to the leader–member exchange (LMX) process in which the leader rewards the follower for specific behaviors and performance that meets with expectations and punishes behavior or performance that does not.[57] Such exchanges represent defined contingent reward and punishment behaviors that cater to the self-interest of the followers in exchange for performance that benefits the immediate needs of the organization.

Therefore, transformational leaders are described as *vision-oriented,* whereas transactional leaders are described as *task and reward-oriented.* Transformational leaders *value change,* especially change that improves on the status quo. Transactional leaders *value stability,* especially stability in the efficiency and effectiveness of the enterprise as it works to achieve its short- and long-term objectives. Transactional leaders *manage* the daily ongoing transactions that help further the leader's vision. Transactional leadership tends to be *transitory* in that once a transaction is completed the relationship between the parties may end or be redefined. Transformational leadership puts the emphasis on the

CONCEPT APPLICATION 9-3

Transformational or Transactional Leadership

Identify each statement as being more characteristic of one or the other style:

a. transformational leadership   b. transactional leadership

_____ 14. Oprah's determination to inspire her followers to live their best lives is an example of what type of leadership?

_____ 15. As the head of my unit, I believe my primary responsibility is to maintain the steady progress we have been making with this current strategy.

_____ 16. Facebook has a guiding philosophy called the "hacker way." The hacker way is about continuous improvement and iteration. According to Mark Zuckerberg (Facebook CEO), if the hacker way has one enemy, it's the status quo. This example illustrates what type of leadership?

_____ 17. I like to think that as a leader, I inspire my followers to focus on higher ideals and organizational accomplishments rather than self-interest.

_____ 18. My vision is one that changes the status quo of this organization to something bigger and better.

_____ 19. My job is to fulfill specific contractual arrangements with my employees, one individual and one project at a time.

_____ 20. My job is to insure that my team efficiently and effectively meets daily task requirements by using the right mix of rewards and incentives to motivate team members.

_____ 21. As a leader, I believe my job is to exploit current opportunities rather than chasing new opportunities that may not materialize.

WORK
Application **9-5**

Identify a leader you have worked for or working with now. In your opinion, is this leader more of a transformational or transactional leader? Explain why and include examples

long-term future of the organization, thus it is more *enduring*.[58] In studies comparing the influential abilities of transformational and transactional leaders on employees' creativity and innovative behavior, transformational leadership led to greater employee creativity and innovative behavior.[59,60]

Because of the attention paid to both charismatic and transformational leaders, the tendency for some has been to diminish the importance that transactional leaders have on organizational success. Recent studies, however, are revealing that transactional leadership does have substantial effects on employee attitudes, commitment, organizational citizenship behavior, and job performance.[61,62] Bernard Bass argued that contrary to Burns's assertion that transformational and transactional leadership are at opposite ends of a single continuum of leadership, the two approaches are actually interdependent and complementary. A meta-analytic test of the relative validity of transformational and transactional leadership styles confirmed Bass's assertion. The study revealed that both are valid approaches for achieving organizational objectives, with transformational leadership showing the highest overall results and transactional or contingent reward leadership a close second.[63,64]

Learning Outcome 6 *Explain the four stages of the transformation process.*

The Transformation Process

Transformational leaders are usually brought into an organization that is experiencing a decline or in need of a major change in direction. The transformation leader is brought in to institute turnaround strategies that can transform the organization and put it on a path to prosperity. This often involves fundamental changes in vision, mission, strategies, and policies. The transformational leader usually employs his/her charisma and/or power to influence follower behaviors and work ethic. A successful transformation process involves broad participation among organizational stakeholders with the ultimate goal of embracing a shared vision, negotiating and communicating priorities, minimizing risk, and creating action plans and commitments for change.[65] It is not an ad hoc, serendipitous process. We present a four-part process that starts with the transformational leader's ability to (1) challenge the status quo and make a convincing case for change, (2) present an inspiring vision of the future, (3) provide effective leadership during the transformation, and (4) institutionalize the change. Exhibit 9.2 presents the four stages of the transformation process with suggested activities in each stage.

The Transformation Process

◀ EXHIBIT 9.2

Stages	Suggested Activities
1. Make a compelling case for change	• Increase sensitivity and awareness to environmental opportunities and threats. • Challenge the status quo. • Identify attractive new trends.
2. Present a shared vision	• Encourage everyone to think of a new and brighter future. • Involve others in seeing and moving toward the vision. • Express new vision in ideological, not just economic terms. • Inspire followers.

(continued)

The Transformation Process (continued)

EXHIBIT 9.2

Stages	Suggested Activities
3. Lead the transformation	Instill a sense of urgency for the change.
	Empower, support, foster collaboration, and strengthen followers.
	Help followers understand need for change.
	Increase followers' self-confidence and optimism.
	Establish priorities.
	Minimize risk.
	Avoid the temptation of a "quick fix."
	Recognize and deal openly with conflict and resistance.
4. Institutionalize the change	Enable and strengthen followers with a "greatness attitude"; for example, recognize and celebrate accomplishments.
	Help followers find self-fulfillment with new vision.
	Help followers look beyond self-interests to collective interests.
	Change appraisal procedures and reward systems.
	Implement team-building interventions and personnel changes.
	Appoint a special task force to monitor progress.
	Encourage top leaders and managers to model the way.

Source: Based on Carolyn Hines and William Hines Jr., "Seminar on the Essence of Transformational Leadership (Leadership Training Institute)," *Nation's Cities Weekly* 25(9) (March 4, 2002): 8.

© Cengage Learning®

YOU
Make the
ETHICAL
Call

9.2 *Breach of Privacy*

Recent news that smart phone devices like the iPhone and iPad had been recording and retaining locational information generated a lot of anger from customers, privacy advocates, and government officials. There is great concern that keeping a detailed history of users' geographical locations without consent violates their privacy. Apple, the maker of these devices, argued that the purpose of maintaining a comprehensive location database is to ensure quicker and more precise location services to its iPhone and iPad customers.[66]

The dilemma for Apple is that while for some customers, privacy supersedes all other considerations, for others, location data provides the services they want and expect. For these users, finding the location of an appointment, a restaurant in a new part of town, or networking with a friend, the geolocation feature is a must-have. For others who worry about privacy, this feature could be a problem when, for example, an abusive spouse is involved or when an overzealous government agency can collect information on an individual without legal authorization like a search warrant. Both sides want the government and/or Apple to take steps to address their worries.[67]

1. Is it ethical for Apple to record and store location data for its customers without their consent?

2. What about the rights of those who want this location feature? What if taking out the location feature causes these customers to switch phone brands? Will this be fair to Apple?

3. In your opinion, what is the ethical thing for Apple to do?

Charismatic-Transformational Leadership

In the literature, both charismatic and transformational leadership forms have been presented as one construct called charismatic-transformational leadership.[68] Both leadership types share similarities in terms of the qualities that describe each, the effects that they have on followers and in the nature of the relationships (influencing behavior) that exist between them and their followers. Some would argue that the election of President Obama illustrates how he was able to use his transformational and charismatic qualities to influence the electorate to make such a cultural shift in the 2008 presidential elections.[69] Therefore, this section examines the qualities of effectiveness common to both charismatic and transformational leadership types, the leader behaviors they share in common, and what sets them apart.

Learning Outcome 7 | *List the qualities of effective charismatic and transformational leaders.*

Qualities of Effective Charismatic and Transformational Leadership

Effective charismatic and transformational leaders share certain qualities. Exhibit 9.3 lists these qualities. Some of these qualities may have greater application to one leadership type and not the other; however, both share the majority of them. We will briefly discuss each quality and point out similarities and variations associated with either leadership type.

EXHIBIT 9.3

Qualities of Effective Charismatic and Transformational Leaders

a. Vision
b. Superb communication skills
c. Self-confidence and moral conviction
d. Ability to inspire trust
e. High risk orientation
f. High energy and action orientation
g. Relational power base
h. Achievement orientation
i. Ability to empower followers
j. Self-promoting personality

© Cengage Learning®

Vision

Researchers have consistently emphasized the role of vision in charismatic and transformational leadership. Both leadership types articulate a transcendent vision that becomes the rallying cry of a movement or a cause. Charismatic and transformational leaders have the ability to articulate an idealized vision of a future that is significantly better than the present. They are able to recognize and articulate fundamental discrepancies between the status quo and the way things can (or should) be.[70] An effective vision should uplift and rally followers to a shared purpose, something charismatic and transformational leaders do very well.

Superb Communication Skills

In addition to having a vision, charismatic and transformational leaders are known for their ability to communicate effectively.[71] In fact, this is one quality that sets charismatic leaders apart. Not only are they effective communicators, they are also excellent orators when it comes to delivery of their message. The charismatic leader's eloquent, imaginative, and passionate presentations awaken followers' desire for change and inspire them to embrace the leader's vision.[72] Charismatic leaders use their superior oratorical skills to stir dissatisfaction with the status quo while they build support for their vision of a new future. They employ rhetorical techniques such as metaphors, analogies, similes; stories and anecdotes; contrasts; rhetorical questions; and expressions of moral conviction to drive home their points so that their message will have a profound impact on followers;[73] all along, conveying confidence that their vision and goals can be achieved. Fitting examples here include Martin Luther King Jr.'s "I Have a Dream" speech, Hitler's "Thousand-year Reich" speech, or John F. Kennedy's inaugural speech in 1961.[74]

Transformational leaders are able to make their case for change but not always with the same oratorical eloquence and style known for charismatic leaders. Both leadership types are good at knowing what (facts) followers need to know, when (timing) they need to know, who (appropriate audience) needs to know, and where (media choice) the information needs to be for access. The distinction between the two leadership types often lies in how (oratorical ability) the information is delivered. Transformational leaders who are not very charismatic may use other means (written communication or a spokesperson) to communicate their ideas.

Self-Confidence and Moral Conviction

Charismatic and transformational leaders display an unshakable self-confidence and optimism as part of their persona. Charismatic leaders are, however, known to espouse messages of change that have religious and/or political overtones, thus emphasizing their strong faith and moral conviction in the message.[75] These qualities are critical in everyday interactions with followers, and all the more so for a leader who must convince others to join his or her cause.

Followers feel connected to leaders who are themselves optimistic and confident in the ultimate success of their mission. The leader's moral conviction in the rightness of his or her cause inspires followers' faith in the leader. Martin Luther King Jr.'s "I Have a Dream" speech is an example of how a leader's self-confidence, faith, optimism, and strong moral conviction can inspire hope and faith in a better future and move an entire nation.

Ability to Inspire Trust

Trust is critical in any relationship but even more so for transformational and charismatic leaders because of the magnitude of change they often present to their followers. Constituents have to believe very strongly in the integrity of charismatic and transformational leaders to risk their careers, and even lives in some cases, for them. Charismatic and transformational leaders build support and trust by being honest with followers. Also, these leaders "talk the talk and walk the walk"; in other words, they model what they desire of their followers. This builds credibility with their followers and garners the support and cooperation of everyone. Effective charismatic and transformational leaders want to be role models to a new value system that is congruent with their articulations.

Gandhi represents an outstanding example of such systematic and intentional role modeling. He preached self-sacrifice, brotherly love, and nonviolent resistance to British rule. Repeatedly he engaged in self-sacrificing behaviors, such as giving up his lucrative law practice to live the life of a peasant, engaging in civil disobedience, fasting, and refusing to accept the ordinary conveniences offered to him by others.

High-Risk Orientation

Charismatic and transformational leaders are willing to take greater risk than the average leader. From a business standpoint, transformational leaders understand the risk–return relationship. They know that to earn high returns, one must take higher but calculated risks. Charismatic leaders on their part are willing to incur great personal risk to realize their vision. The fearlessness of the charismatic leader romanticizes death as an honorable outcome. People admire the courage of those who take high risk. Putting themselves on the line is one way charismatic leaders affirm self-advocacy for their vision and thus gain the admiration and respect of their followers. It has been reported that Martin Luther King Jr. received death threats against himself and his family almost every day during the civil rights movement. Yet he persisted with his mission until his assassination.

In addition to assuming great risk, transformational and charismatic leaders use unconventional means to achieve success. Martin Luther King Jr. and his nonviolent campaign against angry violent opponents was a novel idea in the United States when he started. Contemporary examples of transformational leaders who have used unconventional methods to inspire followers include Herb Kelleher, former CEO of Southwest Airlines. Kelleher encouraged employees to break the rules, maintain their individuality, and have fun—a style he called "management by fooling around." It is a follower-centric style that has made Southwest Airlines employees the most productive in the industry. This is very similar to the laissez-faire leadership approach employed by Richard Branson of Virgin Airlines.

High Energy and Action Orientation

Charismatic and transformational leaders believe time is not on their side and thus are always on the move. There is urgency in the way they express courage and conviction about their vision. Few people can match the daily routines of these leaders.

WORK
Application **9-6**

As part of your general education requirements, you have taken courses in the natural sciences, history, and literature. Identify a leader from any of these disciplines who you believe was either a transformational or charismatic leader. How many of the qualities of charismatic and transformational leaders found in Exhibit 9.3, can you assign to your chosen leader?

Relational Power Base

Effective leaders in general have close working relationships with followers. However, as mentioned earlier, a key part of charismatic leadership is the close emotional bond the leader has with followers.[76] Unlike other types of leadership, it is intensely relational and based almost entirely on soft power bases, even when the leader occupies a formal organizational position.[77] Followers are often in awe of the charismatic leader. There is a powerful identification with and emulation of such a magnetic personality and an unquestioning acceptance of and affection for him or her. The transformational leader's power source is typically positional. They have reward and punishment power. However, effective transformational leaders do not rely solely on their positional power to influence followers; they try to develop close relations with their followers similar to the charismatic leader.[78]

Achievement Orientation

Typically, charismatic and transformational leaders have a strong belief in the "rightness" of their cause, which explains why they persist and stay the course, even through setbacks. Because of this conviction, they experience less internal conflict and discomfort even when faced with resistance and threats to themselves and their families. This is much more so with charismatic leaders who have given up their lives or freedom for what they believe.

Ability to Empower Followers

Transformational and charismatic leaders understand that they cannot achieve their vision alone. They need help and support from their followers. Effective charismatic and transformational leaders empower their followers to do what has to be done to achieve organizational goals. They are good at transforming followers into highly effective team players with the message that together, great things can be accomplished. They do this not with extrinsic rewards but with intrinsic rewards such as pride from accomplishing great things.

Self-Promoting Personality

Even if no one will take up their cause, transformational and charismatic leaders are frequently out in media circles, promoting their vision. Richard Branson and Donald Trump have relied on self-promotion to help build their business empires. These leaders are "not afraid to toot their own horn."

OPENING CASE Application

5. What qualities of charismatic leadership does Oprah possess?

As one writer puts it, Oprah is the "near-perfect peddler of a relentless optimism." Her message is one of self-improvement, doing good, and controlling your own destiny. Her mantra is "live your best life." Oprah is a vision-driven leader. She is a superb communicator. She has self-confidence and a strong sense of moral conviction in everything she does. She has inspired and empowered millions of people through her show and magazine. She is of high energy. Oprah is described by those close to her as inspirational, brilliant, and personable. Oprah exemplifies all or most of the qualities of charismatic and transformational leaders listed in Exhibit 9.3 on page 333.

CONCEPT APPLICATION 9-4

Qualities of Effective Charismatic and Transformational Leaders

Referring to the qualities listed in Exhibit 9.3 on page 333 identify each statement by the quality or qualities it highlights using the letters a–j.

_____ 22. Of all the gutsy moves Oprah has made throughout her career, none is as bold and risky as the decision to launch her own very cable network—OWN. Which quality(s) does this move reveal of Oprah?

_____ 23. As CEO of this company, I see a future that is much better than the status quo. Let us grab the opportunity before it's too late.

_____ 24. Jordan's honesty, sincerity, and integrity have had a significant impact on her followers; they seem to have more faith when it comes to following her directives. What does this say about Jordan as a leader?

_____ 25. As the leader of his fraternity, Justin has a way of using eloquent, imaginative, and passionate presentations to inspire his fraternity brothers.

_____ 26. Brooke has convinced each member of her cycling team that they have what it takes to win the Tour de France without resorting to using banned substances—that is, doping. What effect does this have on Brooke's followers?

_____ 27. Unlike her peer managers, Mrs. Smith has given her followers greater latitude and freedom in decisions affecting their jobs.

Learning Outcome **8**   *Describe the four behavior dimensions associated with transformational and charismatic leaders.*

Transformational and Charismatic Leader Behaviors

To achieve their mission and objectives, transformational and charismatic leaders engage in a variety of behaviors.[79,80] This section focuses on some of these shared behavior dimensions.

Bass and Avilio proposed that transformational leadership is composed of four behavior dimensions; they referred to them as the "four Is"—*idealized influence, inspirational motivation, individual consideration,* and *intellectual stimulation.*[81] Both leadership types are well known for using these behavior dimensions to influence followers and advance their visions. The four behavior dimensions are discussed below.

- *Idealized influence* is a powerful tool used by transformational and charismatic leaders. They possess the ability to develop great symbolic power that is then used to influence followers. Followers idealize such leaders and often develop a strong emotional attachment to their vision. The charismatic and transformational leader engages in behavior that infuses followers with a strong sense of idealism.
- The second behavior dimension is *inspirational motivation*. Transformational and charismatic leaders have the ability to passionately communicate a future idealistic vision that is a much better alternative to the status quo.[82] Both leadership types employ compelling visionary explanations to depict what the work group can accomplish and what it will mean to them. Excited followers are then motivated and inspired to achieve challenging organizational goals.
- The third behavior dimension, *individual consideration,* is about the mentoring role often assumed by charismatic and transformational leaders.[83] They serve as mentors to their followers. Effective charismatic and transformational leaders use an individualized developmental model that responds to follower needs and concerns. Studies have found that in dyadic relationships characterized by strong individualized leader–follower exchanges, followers felt a greater sense of self-worth. Transformational leaders were found to support the development of these exchange relationships in greater measure.[84]
- Finally, *intellectual stimulation* describes the charismatic and transformational leader's creative and out-of-the-box way of thinking. They encourage followers to approach old and familiar problems in new ways. By stimulating novel thinking, charismatic and transformational leaders inspire followers to question their own assumptions and learn to solve problems creatively. In a fast-changing environment such as we have today, innovation has come to be seen as a strategic imperative for organizational survival. Because of the strategic significance of innovation, leader behaviors must focus on intellectual stimulation of followers. Leaders have to take a leading role in building and enhancing innovative capabilities of the organization. This includes an emphasis on creativity, risk taking, and experimentation. The organizational culture should embrace change and constantly challenge the status quo.[85] Charismatic and transformational leaders lead the pack in this area.

A leader who exemplifies these four behavior dimensions is the late Nelson Mandela. Nelson Mandela led the change that is depolarizing a nation racially polarized for decades. Mandela's transformational leadership humanized apartheid South Africa and

WORK
Application **9-7**

Think of a leader in our society today who is generally perceived to be a charismatic or transformational leader. In your opinion, which of the behavioral dimensions of charismatic and transformational leadership described in the text can be attributed to him or her?

----

led to the emergence of a nation deserving of global recognition. His charismatic effects softened the hardest stances of the "haves" and "have-nots" and aligned them in pursuit of a constructive common purpose.

Martin Luther King Jr. was both a charismatic and a transformational leader like Nelson Mandela. A study focused on examining his legacy concluded that he personified the four behavior dimensions listed earlier. The study emphasized Martin Luther King Jr.'s efforts at building follower confidence (individualized consideration), challenging taken-for-granted assumptions (intellectual stimulation), developing follower needs (inspirational motivation), and upholding high moral values (idealized influence).[86]

EXHIBIT 9.4

Transformational and Charismatic Leader Behaviors

Behavioral Dimension	Description
Idealized Influence	Behavior that conveys an ideal future that is much better than the present. The leader's behavior is aimed at inspiring followers to share in his or her vision.
Inspirational Motivation	Passionate communications of better days ahead that motivates followers to buy into the leader's vision.
Individual Consideration	Behavior that employs an individualized developmental model that responds to follower needs and concerns
Intellectual Stimulation	Behavior that challenges followers to think "outside of the box" and re-examine old ways and methods

Source: Based on B.M. Bass and B.J. Avilio, *Improving Organizational Effectiveness through Transformational Leadership* (Thousand Oaks, CA: Sage, 1994); and P.M. Podsakoff, S.B. Mackenzie, R.H. Moorman, and R. Fetter, "Transformational Leader Behaviors and Their Effects on Followers' Trust in Leader, Satisfaction, and Organizational Citizenship Behavior," *Leadership Quarterly* 1(2) (1990): 107–142.

© Cengage Learning®

OPENING CASE Application

6. Is Oprah a transformational leader, a charismatic leader, or both?

Oprah's current venture into cable network TV with the launch of OWN and her success so far in is transforming the network is an example of her transformational leadership qualities. Oprah is a transformational leader with charismatic qualities. She embodies both leadership styles.

Learning Outcome **9** *Distinguish between charismatic and transformational leadership.*

Charismatic and Transformational Leadership: What's the Difference?

Some authors make no distinction between the charismatic and the transformational leader, preferring to combine them into one model of leadership. They refer to the combined model as charismatic leadership because charisma is a central theme in both, either explicitly or implicitly. The thinking behind this viewpoint is that charismatic leaders are by nature transformational. Their vision is almost always about transforming from the status quo to something else. Also, supporters of the combined theory approach make the case that transformational leaders share a lot of the qualities associated with charismatic leaders such as vision, honesty, optimism, inspiration, communication skills, confidence, and, yes, charisma itself.

From this perspective, it would appear that charismatic and transformational leadership theories are one and the same. However, a closer examination does reveal some key differences between the two theories. The first notable area of difference is that though charismatic and transformational leadership theories are about change, *not all transformational leaders are charismatic.* There are many examples of very successful transformational leaders who achieved great transforming results but not through the charismatic effects of their personalities. These leaders are lacking in charisma but very effective as transformational leaders. Many will agree that leaders like Bill Gates, Warren Buffet, Abraham Lincoln, or Jack Welch are transformational, but few will label them as charismatic.[87] A more recent example is Mark Zuckerberg, the founder and CEO of Facebook. Not only is he leading the transformation of Facebook in the social network media industry, but he is also transforming our society in the ways we relate and communicate with each other. Yet he is described as shy, a recluse, a loner, and not very comfortable with the public.[88] No one will label him today as a charismatic leader; maybe he will develop charismatic qualities later in life. On the other hand, there are leaders such as Martin Luther King Jr., John F. Kennedy, Adolf Hitler, Mahatma Gandhi, Nelson Mandela, Ronald Reagan, Bill Clinton, Richard Branson, and many others whose successful transforming results are to a great extent attributed to their charismatic qualities. These leaders for the most part live by the tenets of consultation, teamwork, persuasion, and cooperation, and they shun coercion and domination.

A second area of difference is *how one achieves the label of charisma or transformer.* Attribution theory states that *followers make attributions* of heroic or extraordinary leadership qualities when they observe certain behaviors in their leader. These attributions form the basis upon which a leader is seen as possessing or not possessing charisma.[89] Such attributions of charisma then become the reason for follower unconditional loyalty, devotion, self-sacrifice, obedience, and commitment to the leader and his or her cause.[90] Transformational leaders, on the other hand, do not achieve their label from follower attributions. They are labeled as transformational leaders because they actually transformed the organizations they led. It is a reputation or label based on an individual's *track record of past accomplishments and training;* not follower attributions.[91]

A third area of difference is on *the mind-set of charismatic and transformational leaders.* Charismatic leaders tend to have a more *activist mind-set.* They see political and social causes as opportunities to influence change and provide a better life for their followers. Pursuing these causes provide charismatic leaders with meaning or sense of purpose for their existence. Charismatic leaders have a greater sensitivity to political, cultural, and economic conditions that are ripe for change. They magnify a climate of dissatisfaction by encouraging activism that heightens followers' willingness to change the status quo. *When followers are going through periods of turmoil and collective stress, they may respond to a leader who is able to give meaning to their experiences in terms of a new social or political order.* For example, Oprah's commitment to children led her to initiate the National Child Protection Act in 1991, when she testified before the U.S. Senate Judiciary Committee to establish a national database of convicted child abusers. On December 20, 1993, President Clinton signed the national "Oprah Bill" into law. *Transformational leaders are more strategic in their approach. They find and exploit opportunities that maximize their gains and avoid threats.* In fact, they try to steer away from political controversy. *They are mostly driven by economic factors.*

A fourth area of difference is on *the career path that each leadership type is likely to follow.* Transformational leaders do follow an organic career path of promotions and growth that ultimately puts them in a position of top leadership where they can showcase their transformational qualities. In contrast, charismatic leaders are more likely to emerge in the throes of a crisis, when an organization or society is in turmoil because of conflicting values or belief systems. It is also the case that a leader could emerge from obscurity to prominence with or without a crisis simply because of his or her charismatic qualities. Such a leader could go on to pursue a career in public speaking without any track record of specific achievements. It's a more inorganic career path.

A fifth area of difference between charismatic and transformational leaders is how each perceives their *personal meaning or purpose in life.* Charismatic leaders tend to express their personal meaning or purpose in life at a much earlier age and use it as a driving force behind their vision. We define **personal meaning** as *the degree to which people's lives make emotional sense and to which the demands confronted by them are perceived as being worthy of their energy and commitment.* Personal meaning influences behavior especially for individuals facing challenges. It is more often cited as the motivational force behind charismatic leader behaviors than transformational leader behaviors. You don't hear a transformational leader say their purpose in life has always been to become the CEO of Ford and turn it around. But you will hear a charismatic leader like Nelson Mandela say that peace and freedom for South Africa has always been his purpose in life—a cause that has dominated his entire life.

Finally, the sixth area of difference between the charismatic and transformational leader is the *degree of risk each faces from opponents of their vision.* Often, the emotional levels of resistance and conflict toward charismatic leaders are more extreme than those toward transformational leaders. There is more polarization between supporters and opponents for a charismatic leader's vision. They either love or hate the charismatic leader for what he/she stands for; there is very little in between. Resistance to the transformational leader's vision is less emotional. This may explain why more charismatic leaders have met with violent deaths (such as Martin Luther King Jr., John F. Kennedy, Mussolini, Hitler, and Mahatma Gandhi) than transformational leaders. Mostly, transformational leaders lose their job or resign in the face of unrelenting resistance or conflict.

WORK
Application **9-8**

Identify a leader you have worked with or are working with now. In your opinion, is this leader more of a transformational or charismatic leader? Explain why and include examples.

OPENING CASE Application

7. Oprah seems to have a clear sense of her personal meaning or purpose in life. What factors do you think have contributed to her understanding?

Oprah believes her purpose or personal meaning is to help others achieve their full potential in life. Oprah's life experiences, her values, and faith have been instrumental in shaping her sense of personal meaning. Oprah speaks openly of her strong faith and spirituality.

SELF-ASSESSMENT 9-2   Are You More Charismatic, Transformational, or Both?

There are no right or wrong answers, so be honest and you will really increase your self-awareness. We suggest doing this exercise in pencil or making a copy before you write on it. We will explain why later.

Using the scale below, rate each of the 20 statements according to how accurately it describes you. Place a number from 1 to 7 on the line before each statement.

Like me			Somewhat like me			Not like me
7	6	5	4	3	2	1

_____ 1. I do enjoy getting up in front of audiences and giving passionate presentations on topics I care about.

_____ 2. I tend to associate my faith and religious values to issues I care very much about.

_____ 3. I enjoy change and see myself as a change agent.

_____ 4. I have always seen myself as someone who has the ability to inspire trust with my fellow students.

_____ 5. On occasions when I have made a difficult moral decision (or if I had to make a moral decision), I was (or will be) guided by the desire to not seem like a hypocrite if my actions became public.

_____ 6. I see myself as someone who, if given a leadership opportunity, will influence my followers and colleagues based on who I am (my vision and values), not what I am (my position).

_____ 7. When I walk into a room of people (other students), I generally feel like my presence evokes a "powerful aura" or immediate attention.

_____ 8. I make friends easily and feel like I am extraordinarily gifted in more ways than others.

_____ 9. I am pretty good at making people feel empowered and self-confident.

_____ 10. If I believe in something, I will not give up trying to achieve it even if my life is threatened because of it.

_____ 11. I want to be remembered for something special I did beyond just being a loving member of my family.

_____ 12. I am better at inspiring employees toward a new future than motivating them to perform their current jobs.

_____ 13. I have/had a vision of how an organization can change for the better.

_____ 14. I see myself as someone who is comfortable encouraging people to express ideas and opinions that differ from my own.

_____ 15. I enjoy taking risks but I'm not reckless.

_____ 16. I enjoy spending time developing new solutions to old problems rather than implementing existing solutions.

_____ 17. I deliberate carefully before acting; I'm not impulsive.

_____ 18. Being in a position to turn a struggling organization around will be more attractive to me than leading a stable (no big changes required) type organization.

To determine whether you are more charismatic, transformational, or both: (1) In the blanks, place a number from 1 to 7 that represents your score for each statement. (2) Add up each column. Your total should be a number from 5 to 35. (3) On the number scale, circle the number that is closest to your total score. Each column in the chart represents an attribute of charismatic or transformational leadership.

1 Charismatic		2 Transformational		3 Both	
35	35	35			
30				30	30
_____ 1.	25	_____ 12.	25	_____ 3.	25
_____ 2.	20	_____ 14.	20	_____ 4.	20
_____ 7.	15	_____ 15.	15	_____ 5.	15

(Self-Assessment 2 continued)

____ 8.	10	____ 16.	10	____ 6.	10
____ 10.	5	____ 17.	5	____ 9.	5
____ 11.	____	____ 18.	____	____ 13.	____
____ Total	Scale	____ Total	Scale	____ Total	Scale

The higher the total number, the stronger you are in that particular leadership type. As discussed in the text, you can always improve your weak areas if you want to be a better charismatic or transformational leader or both.

Learning Outcome **10**   *Explain the basis of stewardship and servant leadership.*

Stewardship and Servant Leadership

Stewardship and servant leadership represent a shift in the leadership paradigm from a focus on leading to a focus on serving. Traditional leadership theories elevate the leader and his or her role in effecting organizational success. The leader is the authority from whom followers take their orders. Advocates of stewardship and servant leadership view the leader as a steward and servant of the people. They believe that leadership has less to do with directing other people and more to do with serving people by placing others' needs ahead of the leader's.[92] Servant leadership and stewardship have their roots in ethics, virtues and morality.[93] Stewardship and servant leadership describe leaders who lead from positions of moral influence, not power, and who are very follower-centric. Both leadership types call for empathy, kindness, honesty, humility, equality, moral integrity, empowerment, and respect for others, especially the less powerful or influential.[94] These attributes are important in identifying leaders who can be effective in the role of servant leader or stewardship. Some have used the term *values-based leadership* to describe these two leadership types. Values-based leadership is the moral foundation underlying the decisions and actions of servant and steward leaders.[95,96]

Though some may view these two leadership types as one and the same, they are not exactly identical. The cognitive and behavioral disposition of leaders with a **servant** profile and the organizational contexts that influence it are not exactly the same for steward leadership.[97] While both shine the spotlight on followers, servant leadership goes a step further. Servant leadership calls for the highest level of selflessness—a level that some doubt exists in the real world or at best can only be found in a few individuals.

Therefore, we define **stewardship** as *an employee-focused form of leadership that empowers followers to make decisions and have control over their jobs.* We define **servant leadership** as *leadership that transcends self-interest to serve the needs of others, by helping them grow professionally and personally.* Both stewardship and servant leadership advocate moral imperatives related to public policy, such as the need to address poverty and economic exploitation.[98,99] They remind followers to be good stewards of resources (especially natural resources) so future generations are not short-changed and also to serve those in need.[100]

In this section, we examine the cognitive and behavioral disposition of leaders with servant and steward identities and the organizational contexts that influence each type. We conclude with a discussion of the attributes of effectiveness for the steward and servant leader.

Stewardship and Attributes of the Effective Steward Leader

Leaders who embody the stewardship philosophy have a particular structural and psychological frame of mind that influences their thinking and behavior.[101] They are sincerely concerned about their followers and want to assist them to grow, develop, and achieve both personal and organizational goals.[102] A central theme of stewardship is commitment to people's growth and building community.[103] An effective steward leader creates the environment for individual and team empowerment where decision making is highly decentralized. Therefore, stewardship is more about facilitating than actively leading. Another critical element in steward leadership is trust. Ethical stewardship is when followers perceive the leader's behavior as trustworthy.[104] Exhibit 9.5 highlights four attributes of effective stewardship.

Attributes of Effective Stewardship

EXHIBIT 9.5

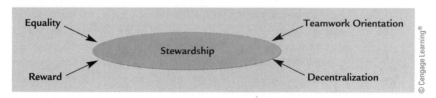

© Cengage Learning®

Strong Team Orientation

Steward leadership works best in environments where leaders and followers come together as a team to formulate goals, strategies, and policies for achieving a collective vision.[105] Here, the steward leader's role is less dominant and more supportive of the process. Where a strong team spirit is present, the steward leader is just one of the team members. His or her job is more of a coach or facilitator than leader of the team.[106]

Decentralized Decision Making and Power

The steward leader is most effective when authority and decision making is decentralized and brought to the level where work gets done and followers are encouraged to take an active role in self-leadership.[107] In this environment, the steward leader is highly effective, given the empowered status of followers and the positive exchange relationship between the steward leader and followers.[108]

Equality

Stewardship works best when there is equality between the steward leader and followers. It is a partnership of equals rather than a hierarchical leader–follower command and control relationship. The role of the steward leader is to find opportunities to empower followers to serve rather than dictate orders.[109] Honesty, respect, and mutual trust prevail when there is equality; these are values that enhance the success of stewardship. The absence of equality makes stewardship almost inoperable.

Reward

Stewardship puts greater responsibility in the hands of employees. Increased responsibilities should be matched with appropriate rewards. Employees with more responsibility and authority who are compensated accordingly flourish under stewardship because they are motivated and committed to the organization's mission. Without rewards that are aligned with performance, it is hard to sustain stewardship.

Stewardship leaders are known not only for their great deeds but for empowering others to achieve great deeds as well. These leaders don't lead; they coach (Chapter 6) followers to do the leading. This encourages followers to be more involved and committed to their jobs. In a study measuring the impact of stewardship on employer–employee relationships, the authors found that **stewardship** significantly impacted feelings of trust, commitment, satisfaction, and balanced power between the employer and the employee. Additionally, they also revealed that increased use of **stewardship** resulted in increased involvement by employees.[110]

Servant Leadership and Attributes of the Effective Servant Leader

Servant leadership is linked to ethics, virtues, and morality. At the core of servant leadership is self-sacrifice for others without regard to what one might receive in return. The leader makes a conscious decision to hold followers in high regard. The leader is driven to serve, not to be served. According to Robert K. Greenleaf, servant leadership begins with the natural feeling that one wants to serve. Robert Greenleaf first introduced the concept of the leader as a servant more than three decades ago. Today, there is a Greenleaf Center for Servant Leadership with a global reach that includes 11 branch offices located around the world.[111]

Servant leaders approach leadership from a strong moral perspective. The servant leader operates from the viewpoint that we all have a moral duty to one another and that as leaders, we have to both serve and lead. Leadership is seen as an opportunity to serve at the ground level, not to direct orders from the top. It is a leadership approach that is centered on a strong service orientation and moral–spiritual grounding. Servant leaders exhibit personality traits high on agreeableness, active listening, empathy, and integrity.[112,113]

Right from the first few moments of his appearance as head of the Roman Catholic Church, Pope Francis I showed humility through his demeanor as well as his words. It is reported that after that first public appearance as the new pope, for instance, he waited and took the last bus back to the bishops' lodgings instead of hopping into a waiting limo. He is clearly representing himself as a servant of the people. His decision to wash the feet of women on Holy Thursday was a clear signal that he intended to be a servant of his followers. Many observers admire his humbleness for not choosing to live in the apostolic palace, his refusal to wear symbols of monarchy, and his desire to eat in the common dining room and celebrate mass with common people.[114]

Another example of servant leadership is the late Mother Teresa who founded the Missionaries of Charity, a Catholic order of nuns dedicated to helping the less fortunate. Begun in Kolkata (formerly Calcutta), India, the Missionaries of Charity grew to help the poor, the dying, orphans, lepers, and AIDS sufferers in over a hundred countries. Mother Teresa's selfless effort to help those in need is a true model of servant leadership. From a performance standpoint, a recent study revealed that servant leadership enhances profits through reduced customer turnover and increased organizational trust, and also that employee satisfaction increases in organizations where leaders see themselves as **servants** first.[115] Other studies have corroborated this finding of higher performance and servant leadership.[116,117,118] Exhibit 9.6 highlights four attributes of the effective servant leader.

Helping Others Discover Their Inner Spirit

The servant leader's role is to help followers discover the strength of their inner spirit and their potential to make a difference. This requires servant leaders to be empathetic to the circumstances of others.[119] Servant leaders are not afraid to show their vulnerabilities. Mother Teresa was able to inspire hundreds of followers to join her order and serve others.

Attributes of the Effective Servant Leader

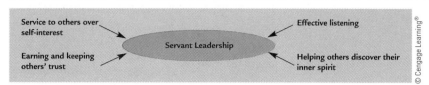

Earning and Keeping Others' Trust

Servant leaders earn followers' trust by being honest and true to their word. They work hard to preserve their integrity. They don't have any hidden agendas, and they are not afraid to give up power, recognition, or control to followers if it helps move the organization forward. It is how servant leaders build strong working relationships with followers. Servant leadership is about influence that is based on trust, not power.[120]

Service over Self-Interest

The hallmark of servant leadership is the desire to help others, rather than the desire to attain power and control over others. Doing what's right for others takes precedence over protecting one's position. Servant leaders make decisions to further the interests of the group rather than their own interests.[121]

Effective Listening

Servant leaders do not impose their will on the team; rather, they listen carefully to the problems others are facing and then engage the team to find solutions. They show love, acceptance, and encouragement for their followers and are very empathetic.[122]

   The discussion in this chapter has emphasized two leadership approaches (charismatic and transformational leadership) that operate under the thesis that maintaining the status quo in a changing environment is a recipe for organizational decline and ultimate irrelevance. We also examined two relevant, yet not very popular, approaches to leadership—Stewardship and Servant Leadership—that are very follower-centric. Self-Assessment 9-3 provides the opportunity to link these leadership approaches to one personality type.

WORK
Application **9-9**

In your college or work experience, identify one leader you have come across whom you can say fits the bill of either a steward or servant leader. Explain why.

_____

_____

_____

_____

SELF-ASSESSMENT 9-3   **Personality and Charismatic and Transformational Leadership**

Charismatic leaders have charisma based on personality and other personal traits that cut across all of the Big Five personality types. Review the ten qualities of charismatic leaders in Exhibit 9.3 on page 333. Which traits do you have?

_____

_____

   If you have a high surgency Big Five personality style and a high need for power, you need to focus on

using socialized, rather than personalized, charismatic leadership.

   Transformational leaders tend to be charismatic as well. In Self-Assessment 9-1 on page 329 you determined if you were more transformational or transactional. How does your personality affect your transformational and transactional leadership styles?

_____

_____

"Take It To The Net". Access student resources at www.cengagebrain.com. Search for Lussier, Leadership 6e to find student study tools.

Chapter Summary

The chapter summary is organized to answer the 10 learning outcomes for this chapter.

1 Briefly explain Max Weber's conceptualization of charisma.

Weber used the term *charisma* to explain a form of influence based on follower perceptions that the leader is endowed with the gift of divine inspiration, not a traditional or legal mandate of authority. This gift of divine inspiration is the force behind a charismatic leader's ability to focus society's attention on both the crisis it faces and the leader's vision for a new and better future. According to Weber, charismatic individuals emerge as leaders during times of great social crisis and inspire people to do more than they would under normal circumstances.

2 Explain what is meant by the "locus of charismatic leadership."

The question scholars have entertained since Weber's conceptualization of charisma is whether charisma is a function of the prevailing social climate, the leader's extraordinary qualities, or the confluence of the two. Supporters of the view that charismatic leadership could not take place unless the society were in a tumultuous, unstable situation argue that without a crisis and followers' need for change, a leader's charismatic qualities would be hard to notice or appreciate. Therefore, for proponents of this viewpoint, the locus of charismatic leadership is external from the leader. Others argue that charismatic leadership is primarily the result of leader attributes (internal), not the situation. They maintain that leader characteristics such as vision, exceptional communication skills, trustworthiness, self-confidence, and focus on empowering others are what qualify someone as a charismatic leader regardless of the external situation. Finally, there is an emerging view that charismatic leadership is a convergence of follower perceptions and reactions influenced by leader characteristics and the prevailing social situation.

3 Discuss the effects of charismatic leadership on followers.

Charismatic leaders tend to have a strong emotional bond with their followers. The effects of such a bond are that followers are inspired to give unconditional loyalty, devotion, obedience, and commitment to the leader and to the cause the leader represents. A sense of fulfillment and satisfaction is derived from the pursuit of worthwhile activities and goals and having positive beliefs and values about life as presented by the charismatic leader. Implicitly, the charismatic leader is seen as an object of identification by which a follower emulates his or her behavior; thus, followers model their behavior, values, and cognitions after the leader. For example, followers are more likely to set or accept higher goals and have greater confidence in their ability to contribute to the achievement of such goals. By observing the leader display self-confidence, followers develop self-confidence as well.

4 Discuss how one can acquire charismatic qualities.

There are suggested strategies for acquiring or enhancing charismatic qualities. Through training and education, people can enhance their communication skills and learn techniques of crafting visionary statements, as well as how to empower followers. Through practice and self-discipline, an individual can build his or her self-confidence and develop a personality profile that is warm, positive, enthusiastic, and optimistic.

5 Distinguish between socialized and personalized charismatic leader types.

The charismatic leader seeks to achieve the unconditional commitment and devotion of followers to his or her vision. However, negative charismatic leaders emphasize devotion to themselves more than to ideals, and positive charismatic leaders seek the opposite. Negative charismatics are said to have a personalized power orientation and positive charismatics have a socialized power orientation. In the former, ideological appeals are only a ploy to gain power and manipulate and control followers. In the latter, ideological appeals are organization-driven and seek to empower followers to achieve the vision and mission of the organization. Personalized (negative) charismatic leaders seek self-glorification, and socialized (positive) charismatic leaders seek organizational transformation through empowerment of followers.

6 Explain the four stages of the transformation process.

A transformational leader who is brought into an organization facing a serious crisis or approaching total collapse has to institute a turnaround strategy. Turnaround strategies are often radical transformations that put the organization on a different path for future growth and prosperity. The magnitude of the task and the high risk of failure require that it be approached in a systematic fashion. Thus, the transformation process is a four stage approach that *starts with the recognition of the need for change*. This provides the opportunity for the leader to formulate and introduce a *new vision* for the organization that promises a better and brighter future than the present. Once there is *acceptance of the leader's vision,* the third stage involves *implementing the new vision and effectively managing the transition.* Here, instilling in managers a sense of urgency for change, raising followers' self-confidence and optimism, and recognizing and dealing with resistance will greatly increase the chances of a successful transformation. The last stage is *institutionalizing the change* so that it is not a short-lived transformation. Effective strategies for institutionalizing change are outlined in the text.

7 **List the qualities of effective charismatic and transformational leaders.**

The qualities that effective charismatic and transformational leader share are vision, superb communication skills, self-confidence and moral conviction, ability to inspire trust, high risk orientation, high energy and action orientation, relational power base, minimum internal conflict, ability to empower others, self-promoting personality, selflessness, and having an activist mind-set.

8 **Describe the four behavior dimensions associated with transformational and charismatic leaders.**

The four behavior dimensions, also known as the "four Is" are idealized influence, inspirational motivation, individual consideration, and intellectual stimulation.

Idealized Influence—behavior that conveys an ideal future that is much better than the present. The leader's behavior is aimed at inspiring followers to share in his or her vision.

Inspirational Motivation—passionate communications of better days ahead that motivates followers to buy into the leader's vision.

Individual Consideration—behavior that employs an individualized developmental model that responds to follower needs and concerns.

Intellectual Stimulation—behavior that challenges followers to think "outside of the box" and reexamine old ways and methods. It implores followers to be creative and innovate.

9 **Distinguish between charismatic and transformational leadership.**

The two leadership types are similar in that charisma and vision are central concepts in both of them. Also, both leadership types share the ability to influence followers to believe in their vision. They are different in many ways:

- Charismatic leaders are by nature transformational (regardless of the kind of transformation they seek), but not all transformational leaders are charismatic. How one achieves the label of charisma or transformation is different for the two. Charisma is attributed to an individual by followers who believe he or she possesses charismatic qualities. Transformational is an earned title based on past accomplishments.

- Charismatic leaders tend to have a more activist mind-set than transformational leaders. They use political and social causes as opportunities to influence change and provide a better life for their followers. Transformational leaders are more strategic in their approach.

- Charismatic leaders tend to have a sense of their purpose or personal meaning much earlier in life than transformational leaders. Transformational leaders follow a career path that brings them to the point of leadership where they then display their transformational abilities.

- The level of resistance and conflict toward charismatic leaders are more extreme than those toward transformational leaders. This may explain why more charismatic leaders have met with violent deaths than have transformational leaders.

10 **Explain the basis of stewardship and servant leadership.**

Both leadership types are based on placing others ahead of oneself. Servant leadership and stewardship have their roots in ethics, virtues, and morality. Stewardship and servant leadership describe leaders who lead from positions of moral influence, not power, and who are very follower-centric. Both leadership styles call for empathy, kindness, honesty, humility, equality, moral integrity, empowerment, and respect for others, especially the less powerful or influential.

Key Terms

charisma, 322

personalized charismatic leader (PCL), 326

personal meaning, 340

servant leadership, 342

socialized charismatic leader (SCL), 326

stewardship, 342

transformational leadership, 328

transactional leadership, 328

vision, 321

Review Questions

1. Citing specific examples, explain how a charismatic leader can use vision and superb communication skills to make his/her case.

2. Describe the leading characteristics of charismatic leaders.

3. Martin Luther King Jr., Gandhi, John F. Kennedy, Adolph Hitler, Nelson Mandela, David Koresh (of the Branch Davidians), Herb Kelleher (of Southwest Airlines), and Richard Branson (of the Virgin Group) are/were charismatic leaders. Can you associate with each name a characteristic (see Exhibit 9.3 on page 333) of charisma you think best describes the individual? Note: If you are not familiar with these individuals, do library or Internet research on them before attempting an answer.

4. Why is the theory of charisma described as a double-edged sword?

5. Describe the limitations of charismatic leadership theory.

6. Describe four key behaviors characteristic of transformational and charismatic leaders.

7. Describe some key attributes/qualities of charismatic and transformational leaders.

8. What is servant leadership?

Critical-Thinking Questions

The following critical-thinking questions can be used for class discussion and/or as written assignments to develop communication skills. Be sure to give complete explanations for all questions.

1. A strong emotional attachment and loyalty to a charismatic leader can have both beneficial and detrimental effects on followers. Explain both types of effects on followers.

2. Charismatic leaders are said to possess special traits that influence their behaviors. Three such traits described in the chapter are envisioning, empathy, and empowerment. Explain how each of these traits influences how followers perceive the charismatic leader.

3. In Chapter 5, different types of power—legitimate, reward, coercive, referent, expert, connection, and information power—and influencing tactics were discussed. What type of power is the charismatic leader most likely to be associated with and why?

4. Explain the importance of effective communication skills for charismatic and transformational leaders.

5. Servant leadership emphasizes being able to serve and lead. In your opinion, is this contradictory or doable?

6. Do you believe everyone has the same capability to become a servant leader, or are some people by their nature more inclined to be servant leaders?

CASE

Ursula Burns: Xerox's Chairwoman and CEO

Ms. Burns joined Xerox in 1980 as a mechanical engineer and worked her way to the top, becoming the chairwoman and CEO in 2009. Alongside then CEO and her former boss, Anne Mulcahy, Ms. Burns worked to restructure Xerox through its transformation and turnaround. She is just one of 21 women who hold the title of an S&P 500 CEO. That's just 4 percent. Xerox Corporation is a $23 billion global enterprise for business process and document management.

Ursula Burns's elevation marked two milestones: the first time an African American woman was named CEO of a major American corporation and the first time a woman succeeded another woman in the top job at a company of this size.[123] Ms. Burns's story is the quintessential tale of the American Dream. She has defied the odds. She was raised in a housing project on Manhattan's Lower East Side by a hard-working single mother, who cleaned, ironed, did child care—anything to see that Ursula and her siblings got a good education. She attended all-girls Catholic High School in New York. She then went on to obtain a BS in mechanical engineering from the Polytechnic Institute of NYU in 1980 and a master's in mechanical engineering from Columbia University a year later. Burns describes her mother as a values-driven single mother who believed in the mantra "where you are is not who you are" and who viewed a good education as a way "up and out."

Asked to describe her leadership approach, Burns said there are two tenets guiding how she leads the company—the customer and innovation. She went on to describe the culture at Xerox as extremely collaborative. "We try to make people win. We try to have winners in the organization, versus winners and losers. We try to have parity in the organization so that we can get the best out of the group." She encourages participation in decision making and frowns on compartmentalization, where people mostly think along functional or departmental lines. She advises her managers to check at the door their functional affiliation as the primary thought process by which they give her input. She is team-oriented and wants everyone to focus on the customer, competitors, employees, and shareholders. Burns preaches a "can do" attitude. She describes Xerox's culture in one word—"possibility." "We actually believe that there's not a challenge that we cannot undertake. When there's a big challenge or a huge opportunity, we have a culture that says, yes, let's go after it."

It is obvious that Ms. Burns is not comfortable being in the spotlight or getting all the recognition and praise that the media and others have heaped on her since being named to the top job at Xerox. "The accolades that I get for doing absolutely nothing are amazing—I've been named to every list, literally, since I became the CEO," Ms. Burns says. "In the first 30 days, I was named to a list of the most impressive XYZ. The accolades are good for five minutes, but then it takes kind of a shine off the real story. The real story is not Ursula Burns. I just happen to be the person standing up at this point representing Xerox."

Ms. Burns is emphatic on the values that she wants Xerox employees to espouse. Describing how Xerox goes about in the conduct of its business with stakeholders, Burns said they put a huge premium on "means." As she puts it, "Are we contributing or taking away? If you have the wrong means, you can probably knock the ball out of the park for a while, but you wouldn't be able to do it in a sustainable way."

In talking about the problems that have plagued Xerox in the recent past, Ms. Burns said that there was a disconnect between formulated strategies and implementation. "We had no way to screen through what capability our organization had to do some of the things we wanted to do. You can't just wish it and expect it to come out without enabling." There was a sense that Xerox had become bureaucratic and less responsive to changing circumstances. She had to redefine core concepts like collaboration and teamwork that had assumed a negative context among her followers. "Teamwork doesn't mean everybody agrees 100 percent," she said. She advocated teamwork and fearlessness as tools to implement decisions with agility and to take corrective action when necessary.

Ms. Burns does not believe leading and managing are synonymous. As she puts it, "lead" does not mean "manage." She describes the early years with Anne Mulcahy (her predecessor) as the "bunker" years. "During the bunker days, for both Anne and me, and probably the top ten people of the company, 80 percent of what we did was managing." Now, under her tenure, it's totally switched, with 20 percent managing and 80 percent leading, because the company has been stabilized. This is a clear illustration of the distinction we drew in the text between leadership and management and also between transformational and transactional leadership. Managers maintain the status quo and leaders bring about change through their vision. Transformational leaders lead, and transactional leaders manage.

There is no doubt that Ursula Burns sees her role as that of vision setter for Xerox. Asked if there has been any change in Xerox's purpose, vision, and values in recent years, Burns said she has had to change the purpose and vision in the intermediate term but not the values. She believes that vision formulation should be an ongoing exercise because of the changing business environment. When one purpose and vision is fulfilled, there is an urgent need for the leader to usher in a new vision; else, as she puts it, "People look up and say, now what? If you don't define it clearly, then people actually make up their own. Then you can forget it. Then you just stagnate."

About accomplishments that have taken place since Burns became CEO, such as major product announcements, launches of new businesses, acquisitions, and major operational efficiencies, she said they are all the "collective accomplishments of Team Xerox." According to the *Wall Street Journal*, the cornerstone of Ms. Burns's strategy, which she dubbed Xerox 2010, was the acquisition of Dallas-based service company Affiliated Computer Services (ACS) for $6.4 billion. The service sector of Xerox is now bringing in nearly half of the company's total revenue. Recently, Lynn Blodgett, former CEO of ACS who's now president of Xerox Services, remarked on the terrific job Ms. Burns had done in getting the right level of integration and at the same time preserving the entrepreneurial spirit that made ACS such a great company. This is important because many analysts and investors had criticized her for taking this action. They said it was the wrong move because it was too costly in the midst of a recession and too large—ACS had 74,000 employees compared to Xerox's 54,000 at the time.

Asked to defined great leadership in a sentence or two, she said it is about persons who can *define a purpose, select a great team, empower that team appropriately, enable them to understand what greatness is about*, and then *let them go*.[124]

GO TO THE INTERNET: To learn more about Ursula Burns and Xerox, visit the latter's Web site (**http://www.xerox.com**). Support your answers to the following questions with specific information from the case and text or with other information you get from the Web or other sources.

1. In your opinion is Ursula Burns more of a charismatic, transformational, or transactional leader? Or is she all of these leadership types?

2. Exhibit 9.4 identifies transformational and charismatic leader behaviors. In your opinion, which of the behavioral components does Ms. Burns exemplify?

3. A key attribute of servant leadership is that it transcends self-interest to serve the needs of others. Does Ursula Burns fit this bill?

4. Exhibit 9.3 identifies the qualities of charismatic and transformational leaders. Based on your knowledge of Ms. Burns, which of the ten qualities can you directly attribute to her?

5. What is the evidence that Ms. Burns employed the transformation process described and outline (see Exhibit 9.2) in the text?

CUMULATIVE CASE QUESTIONS

6. According to the leadership continuum model of Tannenbaum and Schmidt, where would you put Ursula Burns based on the facts of the case (see Chapter 4)?

7. Communication is a major competency for leaders (Chapter 6). Would you agree that this is a quality that Burns likely possesses, to have been as effective as she has been so far?

8. One of the characteristics of effective teams is the presence of a capable and competent team leader (Chapter 8). Chapter 8 describes different activities of the team leader in creating an effective team (see Exhibit 8.1 on page 276), including turning obstacles into opportunities. Would you describe Ursula Burns as an effective team leader?

CASE EXERCISE AND ROLE-PLAY

Preparation: Assume you are part of the leadership of an organization or organizational unit that is in need of redirection in a changing market environment. Your task is to formulate a new vision and mission statement that would transform your organization.

In-Class Groups: Break into groups of four to six members and develop an inspiring vision of no more than 15 words and a mission statement of no more than 100 words.

Role-Play: One student (representing the group) will present the team's vision and mission statement before other members of the class. At the end of the presentations, the professor should call for a vote on who has the most inspiring and compelling vision and mission.

Here are some guidelines:

1. Identify key environmental trends or changes that have influenced your group's vision.

2. Make up a list of core values that your organization holds, or you would want it to have, and incorporate these in your mission statement.

VIDEO ▶ CASE

Timbuk2: Former CEO Sets a Course

Making decisions is a big part of any manager's job. Making decisions that determine the direction a company will take is the job of a CEO. Mark Dwight, former CEO of Timbuk2, a manufacturer of bicycle messenger bags, was comfortable with this role, even though it meant sometimes making unpopular decisions—or even making mistakes. Most of the decisions Dwight made at Timbuk2 were non-programmed decisions—such as the design of a new product or the type of fabric to use. These decisions can affect sales, the brand image, and even overall performance of the company. "Mark is the guy with the vision," said marketing manager Macy Allatt. "He will drive decision making, but he's very open to taking input from other people. When decisions need to be made,

everyone sits down and we hash it out, and when we come out of the room, we feel like we're going to make some progress." Just about every decision Mark Dwight faced at Timbuk2 had some degree of uncertainty. He knew that he wanted Timbuk2 to achieve $25 million in sales in five years; he knew that he wanted the firm to reach new markets; he knew that the firm needed to find new distribution channels. But there was no guarantee that a single decision would be the right one.

1. Would you describe Timbuk2's former CEO Mark Dwight as a charismatic leader? Why or why not?

2. Does Mark Dwight possess any characteristics of a transformational leader? If so, what are they?

Developing Your Leadership Skills 9-1

Is the President of the United States a Charismatic Leader?

Preparing for This Exercise

Rate the current president of the United States on each of the ten characteristics of charismatic leaders. For each characteristic, rate the president as high (H), medium (M), or low (L). Be sure to provide a specific example (what the president did or said) for why you rate the president as H, M, or L for each characteristic.

1. Vision
2. Superb communication skills
3. Self-confidence and moral conviction
4. Ability to inspire trust
5. High-risk orientation
6. High energy and action orientation
7. Relational power base
8. Achievement orientation
9. Ability to empower others
10. Self-promoting personality

Based on the text, what specific things do you recommend the president do or say to improve his skills as a charismatic leader?

Preparing for This Exercise in Class

Objective

To develop your ability to assess a leader's charismatic qualities or lack thereof.

AACSB General Skills Area

The primary AACSB learning skills developed through this exercise are analytic skills and reflective thinking.

Procedure *(10–30 minutes)* Option A: As a class, go over the preparation and rate the president as high, medium, or low on each charismatic leadership characteristic, and give an overall rating.

Option B: Break into groups of four to six, go over the preparation, and rate the president as high, medium, or low on each charismatic leadership characteristic, giving an overall rating. Be sure to provide a specific example (what the president did or said) for why your group rated the president as H, M, or L for each characteristic.

Option C: Same as B, but also select a spokesperson to present the group's answers to the entire class.

Conclusion

The instructor may lead a class discussion and/or make concluding remarks.

Apply It *(2–4 minutes)* What did I learn from this experience? How will I use this knowledge in the future?

_____

_____

_____

Sharing

In the group, or to the entire class, volunteers may give their answers to the "Apply It" questions.

Endnotes

1. S. Berfield, "Marketing Lessons from Brand Oprah," *Bloomberg Businessweek* (4230) (2011, May 23): 20–22.; M. Townsend, "Riding the Oprah Wave, Ready or Not," *Bloomberg Businessweek* (4230) (2011, May 23): 24; R. Grover and A. Fixmer, "Is Cable One Market Oprah Can't Conquer?" *Bloomberg Businessweek* (4230) (2011, May 23): 25–26; and P. Sellers, "Oprah's Next Act," (cover story). *Fortune* 162(6) (2010, October 18): 116–126.

2. M. Weber, (1947) *Max Weber: The Theory of Social and Economic Organization*. Translated by A. M. Henderson & Talcott Parsons. New York: The Free Press.

3. J. Taylor, "Max Weber Revisited: Charisma and Institution at the Origins of Christianity," *Australian E-Journal of Theology* 19(3) (2012, December): 195–208.

4. S. Kempster and K. Parry, "Charismatic Leadership through the Eyes of Followers," *Strategic HR Review* 13(1) (2014, January): 20–23

5. C. Adair-Toteff, "Max Weber's Charisma," *Journal of Classical Sociology* 5(2) (2005): 189–204, Academic Search Complete, EBSCOhost, retrieved June 6, 2011.

6. M. G. Scott, "Max Weber: On Charisma and Institution Building (Book)," *British Journal of Sociology* 21(4) (1970): 458–460, Academic Search Complete, EBSCOhost, retrieved June 6, 2011.

7. A. B. Seligman, "Charisma and the Transformation of Grace in the Early Modern Era," *Social Research* 58(3) (1991): 591–620.

8. T. E. Dow, Jr., "The Theory of Charisma," *Sociological Quarterly* 10 (1969): 306–318.

9. M. Bligh and J. Robinson, "Was Gandhi 'Charismatic?' Exploring the Rhetorical Leadership of Mahatma Gandhi," *Leadership Quarterly* 21(5) (2010): 844–855.

10. C. Wilderom, P. van den Berg, and U. Wiersma, "A Longitudinal Study of the Effects of Charismatic Leadership and Organizational Culture on Objective and Perceived Corporate Performance," *Leadership Quarterly* 23(5) (2012, October): 835–848.

11. B. Michaelis, R. Stegmaier, and K. Sonntag, "Affective Commitment to Change and Innovation Implementation Behavior: The Role of Charismatic Leadership and Employees' Trust in Top Management," *Journal of Change Management* 9(4) (2009): 399–417.

12. C. Nohe, B. Michaelis, J. Menges, Z. Zhang, and K. Sonntag, "Charisma and Organizational Change: A Multilevel Study of Perceived Charisma, Commitment to Change, and Team

Performance," *Leadership Quarterly* 24(2) (2013, April): 378–389.

13. S. Kempster and K. Parry, "Charismatic Leadership through the Eyes of Followers," *Strategic HR Review* 13(1) (2014, January): 20–23.

14. W. Kwak, "Charismatic Leadership Influence on Empowered and Less Empowered Followers' Voice: A Mediated Moderation Model," *Journal of Leadership, Accountability & Ethics* 9(1) (2012, January): 56–70.

15. A. Samnani and P. Singh, "When Leaders Victimize: The Role of Charismatic Leaders in Facilitating Group Pressures," *Leadership Quarterly* 24(1) (2013, February): 189–202.

16. W. Kwak, "Charismatic Leadership Influence on Empowered and Less Empowered Followers' Voice: A Mediated Moderation Model," *Journal of Leadership, Accountability & Ethics* 9(1) (2012, January): 56–70.

17. C. Wilderom, P. van den Berg, and U. Wiersma, "A Longitudinal Study of the Effects of Charismatic Leadership and Organizational Culture on Objective and Perceived Corporate Performance," *Leadership Quarterly* 23(5) (2012, October): 835–848.

18. M. Wu and J. Wang, "Developing a Charismatic Leadership Model for Chinese Organizations: The Mediating Role of Loyalty to Supervisors," *International Journal of Human Resource Management* 23(19) (2012, November): 4069–4084.

19. P. Vlachos, N. Panagopoulos, and A. Rapp, "Feeling Good by Doing Good: Employee CSR-Induced Attributions, Job Satisfaction, and the Role of Charismatic Leadership," *Journal of Business Ethics* 118(3) (2013, December 15): 577–588.

20. J. Antonakis, M. Fenley, and S. Liechti, "Learning Charisma," *Harvard Business Review* 90(6) (2012, June): 127–130.

21. M. Bligh and J. Robinson "Was Gandhi 'Charismatic'? Exploring the Rhetorical Leadership of Mahatma Gandhi," *Leadership Quarterly* 21(5) (2010): 844–855.

22. A. Samnani and P. Singh, "When Leaders Victimize: The Role of Charismatic Leaders in Facilitating Group Pressures," *Leadership Quarterly* 24(1) (2013, February): 189–202.

23. J. Humphreys, D. Zhao, K. Ingram, J. Gladstone, and L. Basham, "Situational Narcissism and Charismatic Leadership: A Conceptual Framework," *Journal of Behavioral & Applied Management* 11(2) (2010): 118–136.

24. R. Nielsen, J. Marrone, and H. Slay, "A New Look at Humility: Exploring the Humility Concept and Its Role in

Socialized Charismatic Leadership," *Journal of Leadership & Organizational Studies* 17(1) (2010): 33–43.

25 P. Varella, M. Javidan, and Dr. Waldman, "Leadership, Group Behavior, and Density of Instrumental Ties in Organizational Groups," *Academy of Management Annual Meeting Proceedings* (2010): 1–5.

26 M. Brown and L. Trevifio, "Leader-Follower Values Congruence: Are Socialized Charismatic Leaders Better Able to Achieve It?" *Journal of Applied Psychology* 94(2) (2009): 478–490.

27 A. Samnani, and P. Singh, "When Leaders Victimize: The Role of Charismatic Leaders in Facilitating Group Pressures," *Leadership Quarterly* 24(1) (2013, February): 189–202.

28 www.cdc.gov, retrieved June 3, 2011.

29 http://www.thehealthcarecenter.com/child_obesity_from_fast_food.html, retrieved June 3, 2011.

30 www.fastfoodmarketing.org, retrieved June 3, 2011.

31 J. M. Burns, *Leadership* (New York: Harper & Row, 1978).

32 H. Tse, and W. Chiu, "Transformational Leadership and Job Performance: A Social Identity Perspective," *Journal of Business Research* 67(1) (2014, January): 2827–2835.

33 H. Tse, and W. Chiu, "Transformational Leadership and Job Performance: A Social Identity Perspective," *Journal of Business Research* 67(1) (2014, January): 2827–2835.

34 A. Grant, "Leading with Meaning: Beneficiary Contact, Prosocial Impact, and the Performance Effects of Transformational Leadership," *Academy of Management Journal* 55(2) (2012, April): 458–476.

35 D. Bealer, and R. Bhanugopan, "Transactional and Transformational Leadership Behaviour of Expatriate and National Managers in the UAE: A Cross-Cultural Comparative Analysis," *International Journal of Human Resource Management* 25(1/2) (2014, January 19): 293–316.

36 S. Braun, C. Peus, S. Weisweiler, and D. Frey, "Transformational Leadership, Job Satisfaction, and Team Performance: A Multilevel Mediation Model of Trust," *Leadership Quarterly* [serial online] 24(1) (2013, February): 270–283.

37 A. Choudhary, S. Akhtar, and A. Zaheer, "Impact of Transformational and Servant Leadership on Organizational Performance: A Comparative Analysis," *Journal of Business Ethics* 116(2) (2013, August 5): 433–440.

38 V. García-Morales, M. Jiménez-Barrionuevo, and L. Gutiérrez-Gutiérrez, "Transformational Leadership Influence on Organizational Performance through Organizational Learning and Innovation," *Journal of Business Research* 65(7) (2012, July): 1040–1050.

39 S. Eisenbeiß and S. Boerner, "A Double-Edged Sword: Transformational Leadership and Individual Creativity," *British Journal of Management* 24(1) (2013, March): 54–68.

40 H. Tse and W. Chiu, "Transformational Leadership and Job Performance: A Social Identity Perspective," *Journal of Business Research* 67(1) (2014, January): 2827–2835.

41 N. Paulsen, V. Callan, O. Ayoko, and D. Saunders, "Transformational Leadership and Innovation in an R&D Organization Experiencing Major Change," *Journal of Organizational Change Management* 26(3) (2013, May): 595–610.

42 S. Kovjanic, S. Schuh, and K. Jonas, "Transformational Leadership and Performance: An Experimental Investigation of the Mediating Effects of Basic Needs Satisfaction and Work Engagement," *Journal of Occupational & Organizational Psychology* 86(4) (2013, December): 543–555.

43 T. Dvir, D. Eden, B. Avolio, and B. Shamir, "Impact of Transformational Leadership on Follower Development and Performance: A Field Experiment," *Academy of Management Journal* 45(4) (2002, August): 735–744.

44 A. Pierro, B. Raven, C. Amato, and J. Bélanger, "Bases of Social Power, Leadership Styles, and Organizational Commitment," *International Journal of Psychology* 48(6) (2013, December): 1122–1134.

45 A. Colbert, A. Kristof-Brown, B. Bradley, and M. Barrick, "CEO Transformational Leadership: The Role of Goal Importance Congruence in Top Management Teams," *Academy of Management Journal* 51(1) (2008, February): 81–96.

46 J. Caillier, "Do Employees Feel Comfortable Blowing the Whistle When Their Supervisors Practice Transformational Leadership?" *International Journal of Public Administration* 36(14) (2013, December): 1020–1028.

47 C. Schwepker Jr. and D. Good, "Improving Salespeople's Trust in the Organization, Moral Judgment and Performance through Transformational Leadership," *Journal of Business & Industrial Marketing* 28(7) (2013, November): 535–546.

48 H. Shih, Y. Chiang, and T. Chen, "Transformational Leadership, Trusting Climate, and Knowledge-Exchange Behaviors in Taiwan," *International Journal of Human Resource Management* 23(6) (2012, March 15): 1057–1073.

49 A. Grant, "Leading with Meaning: Beneficiary Contact, Prosocial Impact, and the Performance Effects of Transformational Leadership," *Academy of Management Journal* 55(2) (2012, April): 458–476.

50 A. Pierro, B. Raven, C. Amato, and J. Bélanger, "Bases of Social Power, Leadership Styles, and Organizational Commitment," *International Journal of Psychology* 48(6) (2013, December): 1122–1134.

51 J. Caillier, "Do Employees Feel Comfortable Blowing the Whistle When Their Supervisors Practice Transformational Leadership?" *International Journal of Public Administration* 36(14) (2013, December): 1020–1028.

52 S. Jha, "Managerial Practices, Transformational Leadership, Customer Satisfaction and Self Efficacy as Antecedents of Psychological Empowerment," *Journal of Management Research (09725814)* 13(2) (2013, April): 105–117.

53 S. Kahai, R. Jestire, and H. Rui, "Effects of Transformational and Transactional Leadership on Cognitive Effort and Outcomes during Collaborative Learning within a Virtual World," *British Journal of Educational Technology* 44(6) (2013, November): 969–985.

54 S. Si and F. Wei, "Transformational and Transactional Leaderships, Empowerment Climate, and Innovation Performance: A Multilevel Analysis in the Chinese Context," *European Journal of Work & Organizational Psychology* 21(2) (2012, April): 299–320.

55 A. Pieterse, D. van Knippenberg, M. Schippers, and D. Stam, "Transformational and Transactional Leadership and Innovative Behavior: The Moderating Role of Psychological Empowerment," *Journal of Organizational Behavior* [serial online] 31(4) (2010, May): 609–623. Available from: Business Source Complete, Ipswich, MA. Accessed November 17, 2013.

56 A. Ismail, M. Mohamad, H. Mohamed, N. Rafiuddin, and K. Zhen, "Transformational and Transactional Leadership Styles as a Predictor of Individual Outcomes," *Theoretical & Applied Economics* 17(6) (2010): 89–104.

57 R. L. Loi, Y. M. Mao, and H. Ngo, "Linking Leader-Member Exchange and Employee Work Outcomes: The Mediating Role of Organizational Social and Economic Exchange," *Management & Organization Review* 5(3) (2009): 401–422.

58 S. Ruggieri and C. Abbate, "Leadership Style, Self-Sacrifice, and Team Identification," *Social Behavior & Personality: An International Journal* [serial online] 41(7) (2013, August): 1171–1178.

59 S. Si and F. Wei, "Transformational and Transactional Leaderships, Empowerment Climate, and Innovation Performance: A Multilevel Analysis in the Chinese Context," *European Journal of Work & Organizational Psychology* 21(2) (2012, April): 299–320.

60 S. Kahai, R. Jestire, and H. Rui, "Effects of Transformational and Transactional Leadership on Cognitive Effort and Outcomes during Collaborative Learning within a Virtual World," *British Journal of Educational Technology* 44(6) (2013, November): 969–985.

61 S. Ruggieri and C. Abbate, "Leadership Style, Self-Sacrifice, and Team Identification," *Social Behavior & Personality: An International Journal* [serial online] 41(7) (2013, August): 1171–1178.

62 N. Podsakoff, P. Podsakoff, and V. Kuskova, "Dispelling Misconceptions and Providing Guidelines for Leader Reward and Punishment Behavior," *Business Horizons* 53(3) (2010): 291–303.

63 B. M. Bass, B. J. Avolio, D. I. Jung, and Y. Berson, "Predicting Unit Performance by Assessing Transformational and Transactional Leadership," *Journal of Applied Psychology* 88(2) (April 2003): 207–219.

64 T. Judge and R. Piccolo, "Transformational and Transactional Leadership: A Meta-Analytic Test of Their Relative Validity," *Journal of Applied Psychology* 89(5) (2004, October): 755–768.

65 E. Davis, J. Kee, and K. Newcomer, "Strategic Transformation Process: Toward Purpose, People, Process and Power," *Organization Management Journal* 7(1) (2010): 66–80.

66 A. Thierer, "Apple, The iPhone and a Locational Privacy Techno-Panic," *Forbes* (2011, May).

67 S. Thurm and Y. I. Kane, "Your Apps Are Watching You: A WSJ Investigation Finds That iPhone and Android Apps Are Breaching the Privacy of Smartphone Users," *Wall Street Journal* (2010, December 17).

68 D. van Knippenberg and S. Sitkin, "A Critical Assessment of Charismatic—Transformational Leadership Research: Back to the Drawing Board?" *Academy of Management Annals* 7(1) (2013, June): 1–60.

69 D. Green and G. Roberts, "Transformational Leadership in a Postmodern World: The Presidential Election of Barack Obama," *Academy of Strategic Management Journal* 11(1) (2012, January): 9–25.

70 C. Nohe, B. Michaelis, J. Menges, Z. Zhang, and K. Sonntag, "Charisma and Organizational Change: A Multilevel Study of Perceived Charisma, Commitment to Change, and Team Performance," *Leadership Quarterly* 24(2) (2013, April): 378–389.

71 Levine, R. Muenchen, and A. Brooks, "Measuring Transformational and Charismatic Leadership: Why Isn't Charisma Measured?" *Communication Monographs* 77(4) (2010): 576–591.

72 K. Davis and W. Gardner, "Charisma under Crisis Revisited: Presidential Leadership, Perceived Leader Effectiveness,

and Contextual Influences," *Leadership Quarterly* 23(5) (2012, October): 918–933.

73 J. Antonakis, M. Fenley, and S. Liechti, "Learning Charisma," *Harvard Business Review* 90(6) (2012, June): 127–130.

74 J. Robinson and D. Topping, "The Rhetoric of Power: A Comparison of Hitler and Martin Luther King Jr," *Journal of Management Inquiry* 22(2) (2013, April): 194–210.

75 J. Sosik, J. Juzbasich, and J. Chun, "Effects of Moral Reasoning and Management Level on Ratings of Charismatic Leadership, In-Role and Extra-Role Performance of Managers: A Multi-Source Examination," *Leadership Quarterly* 22(2) (2011): 434–450.

76 B. Galvin, P. Balkundi, and D. Waldman, "Spreading the Word: The Role of Surrogates in Charismatic Leadership Process," *Academy of Management Review* 35(3) (2010): 477–494.

77 A. Pierro, B. Raven, C. Amato, and J. Bélanger, "Bases of Social Power, Leadership Styles, and Organizational Commitment," *International Journal of Psychology* 48(6) (2013, December): 1122–1134.

78 R. Rubin, D. Munz, and W. Bommer, "Leading from Within: The Effects of Emotion Recognition and Personality on Transformational Leadership Behavior," *Academy of Management Journal* 48(5) (2005, October): 845–858.

79 C. Davidson, "Leadership: Do You Have It?" *Employee Benefit Adviser* [serial online] 10(2) (2012, February): 58–59. Available from: Business Source Complete, Ipswich, MA. Accessed November 17, 2013.

80 F. Walter and H. Bruch, "An Affective Events Model of Charismatic Leadership Behavior: A Review, Theoretical Integration, and Research Agenda," *Journal of Management* 35(6) (2009): 1428–1452.

81 B. M. Bass and B. J. Avilio, *Improving Organizational Effectiveness through Transformational Leadership* (Thousand Oaks, CA: Sage, 1994).

82 R. De Vries, A. Bakker-Pieper, and W. Oostenveld, "Leadership = Communication? The Relations of Leaders' Communication Styles with Leadership Styles, Knowledge Sharing and Leadership Outcomes," *Journal of Business & Psychology* 25(3) (2010): 367–380.

83 S. Eisenbeiß, and S. Boerner, "A Double-Edged Sword: Transformational Leadership and Individual Creativity," *British Journal of Management* [serial online] 24(1) (2013, March): 54–68. Available from: Business Source Complete, Ipswich, MA. Accessed November 16, 2013.

84 N. Wallis, F. Yammarino, and A. Feyerherm, "Individualized Leadership: A Qualitative Study of Senior Executive Leaders," *Leadership Quarterly* 22(1) (2011): 182–206.

85 A. Oke, N. Munsh, and F. Walumbwa, "The Influence of Leadership on Innovation Processes and Activities," *Organizational Dynamics* 38(1) (2009): 64–72.

86 D. McGuire and K. Hutchings, "Portrait of a Transformational Leader: The Legacy of Dr. Martin Luther King Jr.," *Leadership & Organization Development Journal* 28 (2007): 154–166.

87 M. Cusumano, "Technology Strategy and Management: The Legacy of Bill Gates," *Communications of the ACM* 52(1) (2009): 25–26.

88 R. Stengel, "Person of the Year," *Time* (Wednesday, 2010, December 15); J.A. Vargas, "The Face of Facebook," *The New Yorker* (2010, September 20); "M. Zuckerberg," *New York Times* (2011, January 3).

89 D. Jung and J. Sosik, "Who Are the Spellbinders? Identifying Personal Attributes of Charismatic Leaders," *Journal of Leadership & Organizational Studies* 12 (2006): 12–26.

90 J. M. Howell and B. Shamir, "The Role of Followers in the Charismatic Leadership Process: Relationships and Their Consequences," *Academy of Management Review* 30(1) (2005, January): 96–112.

91 R. Hassan, B. Fuwad, and A. Rauf, "Pre-Training Motivation and the Effectiveness of Transformational Leadership Training: An Experiment," *Academy of Strategic Management Journal* 9(2) (2010, June): 1–8.

92 M. McCuddy and M. Cavin, "The Demographic Context of Servant Leadership," *Journal of the Academy of Business & Economics* 9(2) (2009): 129–139.

93 D. Parris and J. Peachey, "A Systematic Literature Review of Servant Leadership Theory in Organizational Contexts," *Journal of Business Ethics* 113(3) (2013, March 11): 377–393.

94 R. Mittal and P. Dorfman, "Servant Leadership across Cultures," *Journal of World Business* 47(4) (2012, October): 555–570.

95 D. Parris and J. Peachey, "A Systematic Literature Review of Servant Leadership Theory in Organizational Contexts," *Journal of Business Ethics* 113(3) (2013, March 11): 377–393.

96 M. Ahn, L. Ettner, and A. Loupin, "From Classical to Contemporary Leadership Challenges," *Journal of Leadership Studies* 5(1) (2011): 6–22.

97 P. Sun, "The Servant Identity: Influences on the Cognition and Behavior of Servant Leaders," *Leadership Quarterly* 24(4) (2013, August): 544–557.

98 A. Choudhary, S. Akhtar, and A. Zaheer, "Impact of Transformational and Servant Leadership on Organizational

Performance: A Comparative Analysis," *Journal of Business Ethics* [serial online] 116(2) (2013, August 5): 433–440.

99 S. Dutta, R. Lawson, and D. Marcinko, "Paradigms for Sustainable Development: Implications of Management Theory," *Corporate Social Responsibility & Environmental Management* 19(1) (2012, January): 1–10.

100 H. Walsh and T. Dowding, "Sustainability and the Coca-Cola Company: The Global Water Crisis and Coca-Cola's Business Case for Water Stewardship," *International Journal of Business Insights & Transformation* 4 (Special Issue) (2012, January): 106–118.

101 M. Hernandez, "Toward an Understanding of the Psychology of Stewardship," *Academy of Management Review* 37(2) (2012, April): 172–193.

102 R. Waters, D. Bortree, and N. Tindall, "Can Public Relations Improve the Workplace? Measuring the Impact of Stewardship on the Employer-Employee Relationship," *Employee Relations* 35(6) (2013, December): 613–629.

103 B. Vanourek and G. Vanourek, "Financial Executives as Leadership Stewards," *Financial Executive* 29(1) (2013, January): 36–39.

104 B. Vanourek and G. Vanourek, "Financial Executives as Leadership Stewards," *Financial Executive* 29(1) (2013, January): 36–39.

105 R. Waters, D. Bortree, and N. Tindall, "Can Public Relations Improve the Workplace? Measuring the Impact of Stewardship on the Employer-Employee Relationship," *Employee Relations* 35(6) (2013, December): 613–629.

106 M. Hernandez, "Toward an Understanding of the Psychology of Stewardship," *Academy of Management Review* 37(2) (2012, April): 172–193.

107 R. Waters, D. Bortree, and N. Tindall, "Can Public Relations Improve the Workplace? Measuring the Impact of Stewardship on the Employer-Employee Relationship," *Employee Relations* 35(6) (2013, December): 613–629.

108 M. Hernandez, "Toward an Understanding of the Psychology of Stewardship," *Academy of Management Review* 37(2) (2012, April): 172–193.

109 M. Hernandez, "Toward an Understanding of the Psychology of Stewardship," *Academy of Management Review* 37(2) (2012, April): 172–193.

110 R. Waters, D. Bortree, and N. Tindall, "Can Public Relations Improve the Workplace? Measuring the Impact of Stewardship on the Employer-Employee Relationship," *Employee Relations* 35(6) (2013, December): 613–629.

111 R. K. Greenleaf, *Servant Leadership: A Journey into the Nature of Legitimate Power and Greatness* (Mahwah, NJ: Paulist Press, 1977), p. 7.

112 D. Parris and J. Peachey, "A Systematic Literature Review of Servant Leadership Theory in Organizational Contexts," *Journal of Business Ethics* 113(3) (2013, March 11): 377–393.

113 R. Rai and A. Prakash, "A Relational Perspective to Knowledge Creation: Role of Servant Leadership," *Journal of Leadership Studies* 6(2) (2012, summer): 61–85.

114 R. Berger, "The Pope We've Been Waiting For?" *Sojourners Magazine* [serial online] 42(6) (2013, June): 31.

115 D. Jones, "Does Servant Leadership Lead to Greater Customer Focus and Employee Satisfaction?" *Business Studies Journal* 4(2) (2012, July): 21–35.

116 S. Peterson, B. Galvin, and D. Lange, "CEO Servant Leadership: Exploring Executive Characteristics and Firm Performance," *Personnel Psychology* 65(3) (2012, September): 565–596.

117 R. Rai and A. Prakash, "A Relational Perspective to Knowledge Creation: Role of Servant Leadership," *Journal of Leadership Studies* 6(2) (2012, summer): 61–85.

118 D. Jones, "Servant Leadership's Impact on Profit, Employee Satisfaction, and Empowerment within the Framework of a Participative Culture in Business," *Business Studies Journal* 4(1) (2012, January): 35–49.

119 R. Mittal and P. Dorfman, "Servant Leadership across Cultures," *Journal of World Business* 47(4) (2012, October): 555–570.

120 R. Mittal and P. Dorfman, "Servant Leadership across Cultures," *Journal of World Business* 47(4) (2012, October): 555–570.

121 R. Mittal and P. Dorfman, "Servant Leadership across Cultures," *Journal of World Business* 47(4) (2012, October): 555–570.

122 R. Rai and A. Prakash, "A Relational Perspective to Knowledge Creation: Role of Servant Leadership," *Journal of Leadership Studies* 6(2) (2012, summer): 61–85.

123 A. Bryant, "Xerox's New Chief Tries to Redefine Its Culture," *New York Times* (2010, February 20).

124 http://triplecrownleadership.com/a-vision-of-great-leadership/—Interview with Ursula Burns, Chairman and CEO, Xerox Leaders Speak Series. December 03, 2012; Bob and Gregg Vanourek, *Triple Crown Leadership: Building Excellent, Ethical, and Enduring Organizations* (New York: McGraw-Hill, 2012); http://www.dallasnews.com/business/columnists/cheryl-hall/20130504-ceo-leads-xerox-in-a-new-direction-with-acs-deal.ece?nclick_check=1; http://wbusinesstoday.intoday.in/story/interview-with-xerox-ursula-burns/1/198431.html.

10

Leadership of Culture, Ethics, and Diversity

Learning Outcomes

After studying this chapter, you should be able to:

1 Explain the power of culture to an organization's effectiveness, both internally and externally. p. 360

2 Describe the characteristics of strong versus weak cultures. p. 361

3 Distinguish between symbolic and substantive leadership actions for shaping organizational culture. p. 364

4 Identify and briefly describe the four types of culture commonly found in organizations. p. 366

5 Describe Hofstede's theory on National Culture Identities. p. 369

6 Identify organizational practices that do foster an ethical work environment. p. 372

7 Explain how authentic leadership has its roots in moral and ethical theory of leadership. p. 374

8 Explain the benefits of embracing diversity. p. 376

9 What leadership actions can support and sustain a pro-diversity culture? p. 378

What Is Organizational Culture?

Culture Creation and Sustainability

The Power of Culture

Strong versus Weak Cultures

The Leader's Role in Influencing Culture

Types of Cultures

National Culture Identities—
Hofstede's Value Dimensions

Organizational Ethics

Fostering an Ethical Work Environment

Authentic Leadership

Diversity Leadership

The Changing Work Place

Benefits of Embracing Diversity

Creating a Pro-Diversity
Organizational Culture

The Effects of Globalization
on Diversity Leadership

OPENING CASE Application

Sheri McCoy is the CEO of Avon Corporation. Prior to joining Avon, she worked at Johnson and Johnson, where she was responsible for the pharmaceutical and consumer business divisions of the company. In 2013, she was named by *Fortune* magazine as the 20th woman on their list of "50 Most Powerful Women in Business." Looking ahead, she said her vision is to restore Avon's image as an iconic beauty brand and its leadership position in global direct selling. She is a big believer in Avon's mission of empowering women.

Avon is the world's largest direct seller, with six million representatives in more than 100 countries, and the world's fifth-largest beauty company. Lately, there has not been much to celebrate at Avon. Over the last five years, the stock has fallen more than 50 percent and net income has plunged as well. Compounding its weakening financial situation is a pending regulatory investigation. The Securities and Exchange Commission is examining whether Avon officials made illicit payments to officials of foreign governments, actions that could amount to bribery in violation of the Foreign Corrupt Practices Act.

A few months after she took over, CEO McCoy announced her turnaround plan: cut 1,500 jobs, pull out of struggling markets such as Vietnam and South Korea, invest $200 million to update its information systems, embrace digital and social media as contemporary selling tools, increase sales in hard-hit markets like the United States and the United Kingdom, and push premium brands like its anti-aging line Anew. She emphasized that the focus of her strategy is the Avon sales representative and the customers.

CEO McCoy sees technology as the biggest difference in terms of changing the buying and selling experience of customers and Avon reps. She believes that Avon's future survival will depend on its ability to evolve and adapt to changing market and economic conditions. Asked to describe her leadership style, Ms. McCoy said she is thoughtful, disciplined, and deliberate. She is a people-centered leader. As she puts it, "I like to think I set aspirational but reasonable goals and encourage my team to achieve them. I clearly recognize that people drive results, and it's about getting the right people around you and giving them the support." Throughout her career, she has consistently promoted employee engagement, leadership development, and diversity of thought. She is committed to Avon's culture and its five core values of trust, respect, belief, humility, and integrity.[1]

OPENING CASE QUESTIONS:

1. **Is Avon's culture a contributing factor to its recent struggles? Explain.**

2. **The text points out that an organization's culture serves two important functions: (1) it creates internal unity and (2) it helps the organization adapt to changes in the external environment. Has this been the case at Avon?**

3. **The chapter discusses the characteristics of high-performance (or strong) and low-performing (or weak) cultures. How will you describe Avon's culture?**

4. **Is Avon's culture more of a competitive, adaptive, bureaucratic, or cooperative type?**

5. **What role can CEO McCoy play in fostering a climate of strict ethical standards at Avon?**

6. **What is Avon's stance on diversity?**

Can you answer any of these questions? You'll find answers to these questions and learn more about Avon and its leadership throughout the chapter.

To learn more about Avon and Sheri McCoy, visit Avon's Web site at **http://www.avoncompany.com**.

I n this chapter, we examine issues of organizational culture, ethics, and diversity—and the leader's role in shaping them. Regardless of the type of business or the size, organizations that consistently achieve outstanding results also have what we call a strong or high-performing culture.[2] Organizations with strong cultures have an unmistakable profile that sets them apart from average performers—a profile that includes distinctive characteristics of a shared value system, a reputation for ethical leadership, and a talented, motivated, and diversified workforce.[3]

What Is Organizational Culture?

The concept of culture traces its roots to anthropology and sociology. An organization's culture is manifested in the structures, rules, routines, values, norms, and expectations that leaders preach and practice; in its employees' attitudes and behavior; in ethical guidelines; in operating policies; and in the stories people repeat about key events in the organization.[4] Culture gives meaning to each individual's membership in the workplace and, in so doing, describes the organization's essential nature. Organizational culture gives identity to an organization.[5] Culture can guide and constrain behavior in that it clarifies and reinforces standards of behavior.

An organization's culture is the operating system that gives meaning to the underlying core values of the organization.[6] Organizational culture has been described as a "shared mental model" or the "social glue" that holds an organization together. Therefore, we define **culture** as *the aggregate of beliefs, norms, attitudes, values, assumptions, and ways of doing things that is shared by members of an organization and taught to new members.*[7] Beliefs, morals, customs, and practices make up the cultural DNA that gives organizations and individuals their identities.[8] For a deeper appreciation and understanding of the concept, we will focus our discussion in the following areas: culture creation and sustainability, the power of culture, strong versus weak cultures, the role of leadership in influencing culture, and culture types.

Culture Creation and Sustainability

Culture creation and sustainability highlights top management's role in this area.[9] The effectiveness of top management in influencing follower behavior is partly determined by the type of organizational culture in place. Culture is created either by intentional design or by default.

By design, culture can be imposed on an organization by a new leader's intentions to change or adapt an existing culture so it aligns with his or her vision, values, objectives, and strategies. An essential challenge of a new culture implantation is to smoothly and quickly incorporate new behaviors into one's cultural orientation, described by one source as "cultural retooling." Accordingly, this process of cultural retooling can unfold over three distinct phases—conflict, ambivalence, and authenticity. And the outcome for individuals going through the process can take one of three paths—regress, stagnate, or transform.[10] This underscores the difficulty and complexity of effecting a successful culture change and why so many attempts end in failure.

It can be a difficult undertaking if the new leader's proposed cultural changes are incongruent with those of the organization's members. Unwelcomed changes to an entrenched culture can provoke negative emotional reactions, often of an intense nature. This can create conflict and ambivalence amongst organization members. However, when followers' values are congruent with those of the leader, they tend to react to change more positively, thus believing in the authenticity of the leader and embracing the new culture. So, rather than regressing or stagnating, they transform into the new culture.[11]

Culture creation can also happen by default as a slowly evolving process. An organization's core values and beliefs can come about from the experiences gained or lessons learned during trying times of the organization's life. The lessons learned during these hard times ultimately serve as the basis for role expectations that guide future behavior and become embedded in the memory bank of organizational members. Shared by leaders and followers, these expectations persist as new employees are encouraged to embrace them. This shared memory of core values may include hard work, commitment, loyalty, honesty, perseverance, trustworthiness, and respect. Eventually, these values become so deeply rooted in the culture that organizational members are no longer consciously aware of them. We should note that cultural values and norms can also be learned during positive times of growth and prosperity. This organic process is consistent with the long-held view that culture emerges from the history and experiences of individuals and groups in a particular organization's context.

A culture is sustained as each successive generation of leaders and followers embraces and passes it to the next through mechanisms such as stories, artifacts, rituals, slogans, symbols, and special ceremonies.[12] These mechanisms reproduce as well as reinforce the accepted culture. Top management must play a central role in sustaining an organization's culture. An example of this would be Sam Walton's conception of Walmart's culture from its early years. The essence of Walmart's culture is a commitment to customer satisfaction, zealous pursuit of low costs, and a strong work ethic. To show his commitment to upholding these cultural values, Sam Walton instituted his ritualistic Saturday morning executive meetings at headquarters to exchange ideas and review problems. Also, he required company executives to visit stores, talk to customers, and solicit suggestions from employees. This tradition has carried on long after Mr. Walton's death. Creating and sustaining a high-performing culture at Walmart has been critical to its success.

OPENING CASE Application

1. Is Avon's culture a contributing factor to its struggles? Explain.

The culture of Avon is encapsulated in what it calls "The Five Values of Avon," which are trust, respect, integrity, belief, and humility. According to the company's management, these five values have served as a continuing source of strength throughout Avon's proud history and will remain at the heart of who they are as a company. Avon enjoys a proud legacy and commitment to women. It is not certain at this time that Avon's culture is contributing to its financial weakness and the pending regulatory investigation. If anything, Avon's culture should be a strength on which the new CEO can build.

Learning Outcome *Explain the power of culture to an organization's effectiveness, both internally and externally.*

The Power of Culture

An organization's culture determines the way that it responds to changes in its environment. Experts and scholars on organizational culture have long maintained that culture serves two important functions in organizations: (1) it creates internal unity and (2) it helps the organization adapt to changes in its environment.[13]

Internal Unity

Organizational culture defines a normative order that serves as a source of consistent behavior inside an organization. To the extent that culture provides organizational members with a way of making sense of their daily lives and establishes guidelines and rules for how to behave, it is a social control mechanism. A supportive culture provides a system of rules and peer pressures, which can be very powerful in influencing behavior, thus affecting organizational performance. A strong culture is a tool that regulates behavior and promotes strong employee identification with the organization's vision, mission, goals, and strategy. Culturally approved behavior thrives and is rewarded, whereas culturally disapproved behavior is discouraged and even punished. Culture offers a shared understanding about the identity of an organization. The right culture can make employees feel that they are valued participants and become self-motivated to take on the challenges of realizing the organization's mission, resulting in a unified workforce.[14] The right culture can transform an organization's workforce into a source of creativity and innovative solutions.[15]

External Adaptation

Culture determines how the organization responds to changes in its environment. Depending on the volatility in the business environment, some changes are significant enough to threaten an organization's competitiveness and even its long-term survival. Culture plays a key role in informing sense-making or meaning when external changes are severe enough to force members to reevaluate aspects of their organizational identity and purpose.[16] Having the right culture can ensure that an organization responds quickly to rapidly changing environmental conditions in the market place.[17] There has to be a strategy-culture fit for performance to be optimized. For example, if the competitive environment requires a strategy of superior customer service, the organizational culture should encourage and support such values as listening to customers, empowering employees to address customer problems, and rewarding employees for outstanding customer service deeds. In such a case, the organization is said to exhibit a high degree of fit or alignment between strategy and culture. A low degree (or absence) of fit between strategy and an organization's culture is a recipe for failure.[18] Despite the empirical evidence of a strong correlation between organizational culture and performance, many organizations still don't have a credible claim to owning a strong or high-performing culture. The next section examines the characteristics of strong versus weak cultures.

OPENING CASE Application

2. The text points out that an organization's culture serves two important functions: (1) it creates internal unity and (2) it helps the organization adapt to the external environment. Has this been the case at Avon?

Avon strives to create a work environment that values and encourages the uniqueness of each individual, and it is committed to creating a culture that supports associates as they balance their many, and sometimes competing work and personal responsibilities. The culture of Avon is certainly a factor in explaining the strong bond or internal unity that exists among company employees and also between sales representatives and their customers. As CEO McCoy reiterated recently, Avon must evolve and adapt to changing market and economic situations.

Learning Outcome 2 *Describe the characteristics of strong versus weak cultures.*

Strong versus Weak Cultures

A growing body of literature documents the economic benefits of investing in a strong culture. A strong culture is a performance-oriented culture.[19] Organizational culture has been found to influence such performance outcomes as quality, customer satisfaction, innovation, turnover and absenteeism rates, workforce productivity, employee job satisfaction, creativity, commitment, and learning.[20,21,22,23] A unique corporate culture is hard to duplicate or imitate and thus can be the source of a firm's competitive advantage. The strength of any culture depends on the degree to which behavioral norms and practices are widely shared and strongly held throughout the organization.[24] Therefore, a **weak culture** symbolizes a lack of agreement or shared mind-set on key values and norms, whereas a **strong culture** symbolizes a complete agreement or shared mind-set on key values and norms, with leaders playing a key role. The strong culture is described as distinctive and very tight—so much so that members whose values don't match the organization's values are more likely to have a short tenure because they are either forced to quit or voluntarily quit.[25] Let us examine in greater depth the characteristics of weak and strong performing cultures.

Characteristics of Weak (Low) Performing Cultures

Weak cultures are generally associated with low performance. An organization's culture is weak when there is little or no agreement on the values, beliefs, and norms governing member behavior. There is a low degree of fit between practice and an organization's culture.[26] Negative behaviors like gossiping, manipulation, favoritism, lack of communication, and internal conflict prevail in a weak culture.

In a weak culture, the internal environment is highly politicized. Many issues or problems get resolved along the lines of power. Vocal support or opposition by powerful individuals, as well as personal lobbying by key individuals or groups with vested interests in a particular outcome, may stifle important change. Also, because of such a politicized internal environment, unhealthy promotion and other career-related practices abound. For example, no effort is made to match the skills and capabilities of candidates to the tasks requirements of a new position; instead, promotions are based on personal considerations (friendship, family ties, favoritism, etc.). What's best for the organization is secondary to the self-interests of individual players or groups.

Weak cultures suffer from insular or inward thinking. There is a tendency to want to stick with the existing way of doing things even if external conditions call for a change. They resist any efforts to change the old culture.

In a weak culture, members of the organization typically show no deeply felt sense of identity with the organization's vision, mission, objectives, and strategy. There is a general absence of passion and goal orientation. Without knowledge of what the organization stands for or ownership and pride in its mission, followers work against managerial aspirations.

Lack of trust, closed-mindedness, low expectations, and absence of accountability and integrity are defining features of relationships between leaders and their followers in weak or low-performing cultures.[27] See a summary list of characteristics of weak cultures in Exhibit 10.1.

EXHIBIT 10.1

Characteristics of Weak (Low) Performing Cultures

- Insular thinking
- Resistance to change
- Politicized internal environment
- Unhealthy promotion practices
- Lack of shared values
- Low expectations and lack of passion for achievement

© Cengage Learning®

Characteristics of Strong (High) Performing Cultures

Strong cultures are generally associated with high performance.[28] An organization's culture is considered strong and cohesive when it conducts its business according to a clear and explicit set of principles and values that are widely shared. In this culture, management commits considerable time to communicating these principles and values and explaining how they relate to the mission and strategies of the organization. There is a higher degree of fit between practice and the organization's culture.[29]

In a strong culture, leaders use ceremonies, rewards, rituals, symbols, stories, and other social events to reinforce dramatic examples of what the company values. Ceremonies recognize and celebrate high-performing employees. Leaders tell stories to new employees to illustrate the company's primary values, which then creates a shared understanding among workers. They also use symbols, rituals, and specialized language (such as slogans) to convey meaning and values.

Ultimately, strong cultures have what can only be described as a culture of discipline—where everyone is responsible and accountable to the mission of the company. There is a "can-do" spirit amongst all employees of the organization. It is a very results-oriented culture.[30] Everyone takes ownership of their goals and as such demonstrate a higher commitment and motivation to achieve them. Goals form the basis of leader–follower performance evaluations and feedback. Leaders seek out reasons and opportunities to give out pins, buttons, badges, certificates, and medals to those who stand out in their performance. Leaders reinforce high performance with matching rewards.

In a strong culture, there is an emphasis on excellence. Management pursues policies that benchmark best practices in the industry.[31] There is a passion for achieving and employees are encouraged to take measured risks. Mistakes are seen as opportunities to learn and not reasons for punishment.[32]

Finally, strong or high-performing cultures are very people-centered. They see their employees as their number one asset. They treat employees with dignity and respect, grant them greater autonomy, involve them in decision making, celebrate their achievements, and use the full range of rewards and punishment to enforce high performance standards. A reciprocal relationship develops because such employees are more likely to behave in ways that help the organization succeed. This cycle of success is like a "virtuous spiral" that reinforces the reciprocal pattern again and again. Trust, openness, responsibility, accountability, and integrity are defining features of relationships between leaders and their followers in strong or high-performing cultures.[33, 34] These culture attributes offer firm-specific benefits that provide unique value and, because they are hard for competitors to imitate, present the best means for building and sustaining a competitive advantage. See the characteristics shared by strong cultures in Exhibit 10.2

Characteristics of Strong (High) Performing Cultures

EXHIBIT 10.2

- Strong performance with a passion for achieving
- Intensely people oriented with a "can-do" spirit
- Results oriented and goal driven
- Emphasis on excellence
- Learn from mistakes
- Reinforce performance with matching rewards

© Cengage Learning®

OPENING CASE Application

3. The chapter discusses the characteristics of high-performing (strong) and low-performing (weak) cultures. How will you describe Avon's culture?

Everyone at Avon seems to share the same dream and aspiration. There is an emotional bond with the mission of the company, and every employee works hard to realize the long-term goals set by the CEO and her senior leadership team. At Avon, leaders and managers at various levels are encouraged to communicate with the rank and file openly and frequently. Though Avon has struggled to perform in the past five years and is facing allegations of regulatory violations, its culture as represented in policies, principles, and values suggest strength and may provide the foundation for its recovery.

CONCEPT APPLICATION 10-1

Characteristics of Strong versus Weak Cultures

a. Strong performance with a passion for achieving
b. Intensely people oriented
c. Results oriented and goal driven
d. Emphasis on excellence
e. Shared values and beliefs

f. Insular thinking
g. Resistance to change
h. Politicized internal environment
i. Unhealthy promotion practices
j. Reinforce performance with matching rewards

Identify each statement with a characteristic associated with a strong versus weak culture. Write the appropriate letter in the blank before each item.

____ 1. In our organization, management "talks the talk" and "walks the walk" in how it treats employees.

____ 2. I wonder how many of the top executives here got to where they are today on merit?

____ 3. We have always done things here in a certain way and it's worked so far. I see no need to change that which is not broken.

____ 4. Here, you have a big role in setting your own goals, but once they are set, you are held to them.

____ 5. In our organization, management pursues policies that benchmark best practices in the industry.

____ 6. In our organization, there is little or no agreement on the values, beliefs, and norms governing member behavior and negative behaviors like gossiping, manipulation, favoritism, lack of communication, and internal conflict prevail.

____ 7. In our company, we have a "can-do" spirit with a healthy level of internal competition between departments.

____ 8. I think every department in the company has a copy of the mission and values statement on the wall somewhere.

____ 9. In our organization, leaders seek out reasons and opportunities to reward those who stand out in their performance.

____ 10. Every division here is striving to be No. 1 or 2 in its industry; it is very challenging, yet motivating.

Learning Outcome 3 — *Distinguish between symbolic and substantive leadership actions for shaping organizational culture*

The Leader's Role in Influencing Culture

Leaders have many different tools at their disposal for changing, modifying or sustaining culture. Some of these may include new policies, programs or practices. Some of these actions are substantive, whereas others are simply symbolic; yet taken together, they can shape the culture of an organization according to the expectations of the leader.

Substantive actions are explicit and highly visible and are indicative of management's commitment to a new way of doing things. These are actions that everyone will understand and are intended to establish a new culture more in tune with the organization's mission and strategy. *Symbolic actions* are valuable for the signals they send about the kinds of behavior and expectations leaders wish to encourage and promote. In his book *Organizational Culture and Leadership,* author Edgar Schein uses the terms *primary* and *secondary mechanisms* to distinguish between symbolic and substantive actions.[35]

Substantive Actions

Substantive actions that a leader can employ to influence culture include aligning cultural values and principles to HR policies and practices, strategy, and structure; matching rewards/incentives to the culture indicators; and designing physical work environments that match espoused cultural norms. Let us briefly examine each of these matching relationships.

The strongest sign that management is truly committed to creating a new culture is replacing current members who are unwilling to change with a new breed of employees. This can be accomplished through new HR criteria for recruiting, selecting, promoting, and firing employees. These new criteria should match the values and expectations of the new culture. A lack of "fit" will hinder or constrain strategy execution. Existing policies and practices that impede the execution of new strategies must be scrapped. Through these actions, leaders let followers know what is important.

Creating a strategy-culture fit is another substantive action leaders can take. In rapidly changing business environments, the capacity to introduce new strategies is a necessity if a company is to perform well over long periods of time. Strategic agility and fast organizational response to new opportunities and threats require a culture that quickly adapts to environmental change rather than a culture that resists change. Another name for this type of culture is the *organizational learning culture.* Chapter 12 examines in greater depth the organizational learning culture. Thus, if the strategy calls for rapid new product innovation and the culture is one that resist change and risk-taking, there is a lack of fit between strategy and culture.

Tying rewards and incentive programs directly to new performance metrics is another substantive culture-shaping action because it gives the leader leverage to reward only those performances that are supportive of the strategy and culture. It is often the case that in many organizations, when strategies change, changes in the reward structure tend to lag behind. Imagine an organization in which the CEO has articulated an integration-based strategy that will require leaders at all levels to think and act across departmental or divisional boundaries and act on behalf of the entire enterprise. However, the organizational reward system only offers incentives for achieving unit success. Such reward/incentive misalignments weaken an organization's culture.

Finally, leaders can design the physical work environment to reflect the values they want to promote within the organization. For example, having common eating facilities for all employees, no special parking areas, and similar offices is consistent with a value of equality. An open office layout with fewer walls separating employees is consistent with a value for open communication. In designing its headquarters, Google wanted to provide open work spaces and an environment that promoted coworker contact and interaction. Google succeeded in communicating an employee-friendly culture through its facility design, with the architecture and comfort of the setting reinforced by the cultural and aesthetic elements in the building.

Symbolic Actions

Symbolic actions that a leader can employ to influence culture include modeling expected behavior, recognizing and celebrating accomplishments, and being visible.

Senior executives are role models, and the stories they tell, decisions they make, and actions they take reveal an implicit cultural expectation for followers. Employees learn what is valued most in an organization by watching what attitudes and behaviors leaders pay attention to and reward and whether the leaders' own behaviors match the espoused values.[36] Employees want to see that their leaders "walk the walk." For example, when top executives lead a cost-reduction effort by curtailing executive perks, or when they emphasize the importance of responding to customers' needs by requiring members of the top management team (TMT) to spend a portion of each week talking with customers and understanding their needs, these actions set a good example. The message employees get when a leader institutes a policy but fails to act in accordance with it is that the policy is really not important or necessary.[37]

Leaders can schedule ceremonies to celebrate and honor people whose actions and performance exemplify what is called for in the new culture. Ceremonies reinforce specific values and create emotional bonds by allowing employees to share in important moments. A culture that celebrates accomplishments helps retain valued employees.

Another symbolic action a leader can use to influence culture is simply being visible. A leader who appears at ceremonial functions to praise followers who exemplify the values and practices of the new culture is making a symbolic, yet instructive, gesture. Effective leaders will also make special appearances at non-ceremonial events (such as employee training workshops) to stress key priorities, values, norms, and ethical principles. To followers, the mere appearance of the executive—and the things he or she chooses to emphasize—clearly communicates management's commitment to the new culture.[38] Exhibit 10.3 summarizes the substantive and symbolic actions that leaders can use to influence or shape organizational culture.

WORK
Application **10-2**

Identify and briefly explain which of the leadership actions for shaping culture have been used by a leader where you work or have worked.

EXHIBIT 10.3

Leadership Actions for Shaping Culture

Substantive Actions

a. Instituting new policies and practices

b. Aligning strategy and structure to culture

c. Matching rewards/incentives to the culture

d. Matching work environment design to culture

Symbolic Actions

a. Modeling expected behavior

b. Recognizing and celebrating accomplishments

c. Being visible

© Cengage Learning®

Learning Outcome **4**   *Identify and briefly describe the four types of culture commonly found in organizations.*

Types of Culture

There is no one best organizational culture. The ideal culture is that which supports the organization's mission and strategy. In the academic community, we hear names such as *learning, innovative, team, clan,* and *market or adhocracy cultures.*[39] Each of these names is intended to communicate something about the core values, principles, and expectations of an organization. We will focus on four often mentioned culture types that encompass these other labels: the *cooperative, adaptive, competitive*, and *bureaucratic* cultures. These culture types are not mutually exclusive; an organization's culture may reveal characteristics that will fit one or more of these types. However, high-performing organizations with strong cohesive cultures tend to emphasize or lean more toward one particular culture type—a shared mind-set.

Cooperative Culture

The **cooperative culture** *represents a leadership belief in strong, mutually reinforcing exchanges and linkages between employees and departments.* In this type of culture, operating policies, beliefs, norms, and practices are all designed with one goal in mind—to encourage cooperation, teamwork, power sharing, and camaraderie among employees. Management thinking is predicated on the belief that organizational success is influenced more by effective cooperative relationships inside the organization than by external relationships. It is an internally focused culture. Proponents of the cooperative culture argue that in today's dynamic work setting—characterized by constant changes and fluid projects—creating a work setting in which workers collaborate with each other and work in highly effective teams, leads to synergy and increases productivity. It is a culture where employees are empowered to act and think like owners rather than hired hands. A company like Southwest Airlines puts a high premium on cooperation and teamwork amongst its employees and defines its culture along these lines.

Adaptive Culture

The **adaptive culture** *represents a leadership belief in active monitoring of the external environment for emerging opportunities and threats and adapting to them.* In this type of culture, existing policies, beliefs, norms, and practices are designed with the purpose to support employees' ability to respond quickly to changing environmental conditions. In adaptive cultures, members are encouraged to take risks, experiment, innovate, and learn from these experiences.

Management thinking is predicated on the belief that organizational success is influenced more by events outside the organization than by internal factors. Therefore, employees are empowered to make decisions and act quickly to take advantage of emerging opportunities and avoid threats. There is greater individual autonomy and tolerance for failure. There is a spirit of doing what is necessary to ensure both short- and long-term organizational success, provided core values and business principles are upheld in the process. The adaptive culture is generally known for its flexibility and innovativeness. The core principles of the adaptive culture are similar to those of organizational learning culture (OLC) discussed in Chapter 12. Companies like Google, Facebook, 3M, Apple, Nike, Tesla Motors, and many others are known for their adaptive or innovative cultures. These companies pursue a strategy of differentiation.

Competitive Culture

The **competitive culture** *represents a leadership mind-set that encourages and values a highly competitive work environment.* Organizational policies, beliefs, norms, and work practices are all designed to foster both internal competition (employee versus employee, department versus department, or division versus division) and external competition (company versus competitors). An organization with a competitive culture operates in a mature market environment in which competition for customers is intense. It is the type of culture that some have described as the market-oriented culture.[40] The drive to win either against one another internally or against an external competitor is what holds the organization together.

PepsiCo and Coca-Cola are two companies that exemplify the competitive culture. We all remember the "cola wars." Each company socializes its members to view the other's

WORK
Application **10-3**

Describe which of the four types of organizational cultures exist where you work or have worked. Does it lean toward one type or is it a compilation of the four types?

employees as enemies and to do whatever is necessary to defeat them in the marketplace. High performance standards and tough reviews are used to weed out the weak and reward the strong. At PepsiCo, for example, former CEO Wayne Calloway was known to set backbreaking standards and then systematically raise them each year. Executives who met his standards were generously rewarded—stock options, bonuses, rapid promotions—and those who did not felt the pressure to produce or risk negative consequences such as demotions, transfers, or job termination.

Bureaucratic Culture

The **bureaucratic culture** *represents a leadership mind-set that values order, stability, status, and efficiency.* Bureaucratic cultures emphasizes strict adherence to set rules, policies, and procedures, which ensure an orderly way of doing business. Organizations with bureaucratic cultures are highly structured and efficiency driven. The bureaucratic culture may work for an organization pursuing a low-cost leadership strategy (like Walmart and other discount retailers) but not for one pursuing a differentiation strategy (like Nordstrom's and other high-end department store retailers). The bureaucratic culture is becoming increasingly less attractive even for low–cost driven companies. Faced with the increasing threat of competition from domestic and global competitors, many leaders are forced to make the shift away from bureaucratic cultures because of the need for greater flexibility and adaptation.

OPENING CASE Application

4. Is Avon's culture more of a competitive, adaptive, bureaucratic, or cooperative type?

Avon's culture fits with three of the four culture types. Avon wants its sales reps to share ideas with each other and to work together as a team. To facilitate this, Avon provides opportunities for employees to network among themselves. This qualifies Avon as having a cooperative culture. However, Avon is also cognizant of the need to adapt to market and technological changes. Avon can also be described as having a competitive culture in the sense that the company is aware of its competitors and is constantly positioning and repositioning its marketing strategies vis-à-vis its competitors. In essence, Avon's culture is a little bit of the cooperative, competitive, and adaptive types.

CONCEPT APPLICATION 10-2

Type of Organizational Culture

Identify each statement as characteristic of one of the types of organizational culture. Write the appropriate letter in the blank before each item.

a. competitive   c. bureaucratic   e. team
b. adaptive   d. cooperative   f. clan

_____ 11. Google has been described as a company where employees have a lot of flexibility and are empowered to pursue creative solutions to customer problems.

_____ 12. In our company, there is a set way of doing things and our managers hold firm to these practices because they have been found to improve efficiency and keep cost down.

_____ 13. In our industry, every action draws a counteraction from competitors; thus we keep a close eye on our competitors to make sure they are not stealing our customers.

_____ 14. Being a small family business, we want our employees to work collaboratively with each other and share ideas/information.

Learning Outcome **5**   *Describe Hofstede's theory on National Culture Identities.*

National Culture Identities— Hofstede's Value Dimensions

Whether culture is analyzed from an organizational or national context, it is still a product of values, beliefs, and norms that people use to guide and control behavior. Relationships between leaders and members of an organization are based on shared values and beliefs. On a national level, there are unique cultural identities associated with different countries. An organization's cultural archetype may have its roots or some of its roots in the national culture.[42] The people of a particular country are socialized into the national culture as they grow up and, thus, are influenced by it. A well-known study on this subject is that of Geert Hofstede. Hofstede developed five value dimensions that distinguish a nation's culture from other nations.[43] Exhibit 10.4 summarizes these value dimensions, which are briefly discussed along with leadership implications. Each of these five dimensions contains two opposing values that are at opposite ends.

EXHIBIT 10.4

Hofstede's Value Dimensions for Understanding National Cultural Differences

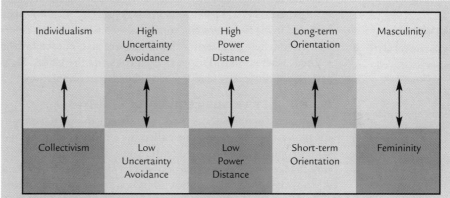

Source: Based on G. Hofstede, "Cultural Constraints in Management Theories," *Academy of Management Executive 7* (1993), pp. 81–94.

© Cengage Learning®

Individualistic versus Collectivistic Cultures

This dimension involves a person's source of identity in society. Some societies value individualism more than collectivism, and vice versa. **Individualism** *is a psychological state in which people see themselves first as individuals and believe their own interest and values are primary.* Other names for the individualistic culture are the autonomy culture or the self-expression culture. **Collectivism** *is the state of mind wherein the values and goals of the group—whether extended family, ethnic group, company, or community—are primary.* The United States, Great Britain, and Canada have been described as individualistic cultures, whereas Greece, Japan, and Mexico are said to have collectivistic cultures.

High- versus Low-Uncertainty-Avoidance Cultures

A society with a **high-uncertainty-avoidance culture** has *a majority of people who do not tolerate risk, avoid the unknown, and are comfortable when the future is relatively predictable and certain.* In a high-uncertainty-avoidance country like Japan, managers prefer well-structured and predictable situations. The other end of the continuum is a society where the majority of the people have low uncertainty avoidance. A **low-uncertainty-avoidance culture** *has a majority of* people *who are comfortable with and accepting of the unknown, and tolerate risk and unpredictability.* The United States, Australia, and Canada are associated with low-uncertainty-avoidance cultures, whereas Argentina, Italy, Japan, and Israel are associated with high-uncertainty-avoidance cultures.

High- versus Low-Power-Distance Cultures

This dimension deals with a society's view on power and status. The way in which people of different social standing (status), power, or authority should relate to each other as equals or unequals is referred to as power distance. In a **high-power-distance culture**, *leaders and followers rarely interact as equals,* whereas in a **low-power-distance culture**, *leaders and their followers interact on several levels as equals.* It is also called the egalitarian culture. High-power-distance cultures include Mexico, Japan, Spain, and France. Low-power-distance cultures include Germany, the United States, and Ireland.

Long- versus Short-Term Orientation

This dimension refers to a society's long- or short-term orientation toward life and work. People from a culture with a **long-term orientation** *have a future-oriented view of life and thus are thrifty (saving for the future) and persistent in achieving goals.* A **short-term orientation** *derives from values that express a concern for maintaining personal happiness and living in the present.* Immediate gratification is a priority. Most Asian countries, known for their long-term orientation, are also known for their high rate of per capita savings, whereas most European countries and the United States tend to spend more and save less because they tend to have a short-term orientation.

Masculinity versus Femininity Cultures

This value dimension was used by Hofstede to make the distinction between the quest for material assets (which he called masculinity) and the quest for social connections with people (which he called femininity). In this context, **masculinity** *describes a culture that emphasizes assertiveness and a competitive drive for money and material objects.* At the other end of the continuum is **femininity**, which *describes a culture that emphasizes developing and nurturing personal relationships and a high quality of life.* Countries with masculine cultures include Japan and Italy; feminine cultures include Sweden and Denmark.

Implications for Leadership

The growing diversity of the workforce and the increasing globalization of the marketplace create the need for leaders with multicultural backgrounds and experiences. This trend explains why the Association to Advance Collegiate Schools of Business (AACSB) lists among required knowledge and skill areas the dynamics of the global economy and multicultural diversity understanding.[44] In the academic community, there is greater recognition that future leaders need diversity competencies to effectively leverage a diverse workforce. Leaders have to recognize, for example, that although employers in the United States may reward and encourage individual achievements, a different norm may apply in Japan, where team recognition and rewards are paramount. In the United States, competition between work-group members for career advancement is desirable. In collectivistic cultures, however, members may resist competing with peers for rewards or promotions to avoid disrupting the harmony of the group or appearing self-centered.

Cross-cultural and international joint venture (IJV) studies often identify cultural differences as the cause of many interpersonal difficulties, including conflict and poor performance in post–merger and acquisition deals.[45] More and more organizations are relying on leaders with international experience to lead a multicultural workforce and compete in the global marketplace.

YOU
Make the
ETHICAL
Call

10.1   *Buy American*

Organizational culture is also based on national culture. People tend to believe their country or company is the best. You most likely have heard the slogan "Buy American." Unions tend to ask Americans to buy products made in the United States to help save their jobs. On the other hand, some Americans ask why they should buy American products, especially if they cost more or they are inferior in quality or style to foreign-made products. Many (or most) Americans don't know the country of ownership of many products they buy, and some domestic products are made with more than half of the components coming from other countries—so is the product really made in America?

1. Is it ethical and socially responsible to ask people to buy American or from their home country?

2. Is it ethical and socially responsible to buy foreign products?

Organizational Ethics

Leadership and culture does relate to ethical cognitions and behaviors of followers in an organization.[46] Organizational core values influence ethics. Ethics influence behavior and the combination of core values and ethics describe an organization's culture.[47] An ethical organizational culture encourages a different set of behaviors from one that has the opposite culture.[48] The importance of organizational ethics can be seen in the crises of the recent past. These crises revealed huge, and in some cases criminal failures of both ethics and leadership in the banking and finance industry, the real estate sub-prime market, and government. The AACSB lists ethical understanding and reasoning as important leadership competencies. This may explain why quite a few colleges and universities are adding ethics courses in their curriculum. **Ethics** *are the standards of right and wrong that influence behavior.* Ethics provide guidelines for judging conduct and decision making.[49] The discussion of ethics in Chapter 3 was from the individual's perspective. The emphasis was on how an individual's personality traits and attitudes, level of moral development, and the situational context affect their ethical behavior.[50]

In this chapter, we examine ethics from an organizational perspective by focusing on the role of leadership in creating an ethical work environment. The absence of an ethical work environment can lead to severe consequences for the organizations involved. Enron, Tyco, and WorldCom did not happen in a vacuum. The ethical and legal violations that took place at these companies cannot be explained as simply one or two individuals who were morally corrupt. The ethical breakdowns that occurred in these companies happened over a period of time, involved numerous individuals both inside and outside of the organization, and brought about the implosion of these companies.[51] Organizational ethics applies not only to larger corporations but also small- and medium-sized enterprises.

Therefore, we will focus our discussion on organizational practices that can foster an ethical work environment. We also discuss the related concept of authentic leadership. Before we begin, complete Self-Assessment 10-1 to determine your personal values in eight areas.

SELF-ASSESSMENT 10-1   **Personal Values**

Below are 16 items. Rate how important each one is to you on a scale of 0 (not important) to 100 (very important). Write the numbers 0–100 on the line to the left of each item.

0 — 10 — 20 — 30 — 40 — 50 — 60 — 70 — 80—90 — 100
Not important   Some what important   Very important

_____ 1. An enjoyable, satisfying job

_____ 2. A high-paying job

_____ 3. A good marriage

_____ 4. Meeting new people, social events

_____ 5. Involvement in community activities

_____ 6. My relationship with God/my religion

_____ 7. Exercising, playing sports

_____ 8. Intellectual development

_____ 9. A career with challenging opportunities

_____ 10. Nice cars, clothes, home, and so on

_____ 11. Spending time with family

_____ 12. Having several close friends

_____ 13. Volunteer work for not-for-profit organizations like the Cancer Society

_____ 14. Meditation, quiet time to think, pray, and so on

_____ 15. A healthy, balanced diet

_____ 16. Educational reading, self-improvement programs, TV, and so on

Next, transfer your rating numbers for each of the 16 items to the appropriate columns. Then add the two numbers in each column.

	Professional	Financial	Family	Social
	1. ____	2. ____	3. ____	4. ____
	9. ____	10. ____	11. ____	12. ____
Totals	____	____	____	____

	Community	Spiritual	Physical	Intellectual
	5. ____	6. ____	7. ____	8. ____
	13. ____	14. ____	15. ____	16. ____
Totals	____	____	____	____

The higher the total in any area, the higher the value you place on that particular area. The closer the numbers are in all eight areas, the better rounded you are.

Think about the time and effort you put forth in your top three values. Is it sufficient to allow you to achieve the level of success you want in each of those areas? If not, what can you do to change? Is there any area in which you feel you should have a higher value total? If yes, which, and what can you do to change?

Learning Outcome 6   *Identify organizational practices that do foster an ethical work environment.*

Fostering an Ethical Work Environment

For an organization to display consistently high ethical and socially responsible behavior, its leaders must create and maintain a culture of ethics that permeates the entire organization.[52,53] The influences of ethical leadership occur not only directly, between leaders and followers within work units, but also indirectly, across hierarchical levels, through senior leaders' influences on subordinate–leader behavior.[54] An ethical work environment is mission and values-driven, stakeholder balanced, and effectively managed.[55,56] Some of the tools available for creating and fostering this type of ethical work environment are discussed below.

Code of Ethics

Many organizations have a written code of ethics or code of conduct that displays the values and principles governing employee behavior. Written statements have the advantage of explicitly stating the company's position on ethical and moral issues, and they serve as benchmarks for judging both company decisions and actions and individual conduct.[57] A growing number of organizations have added a code of ethics to their list of formal statements and public pronouncements. They are seen as tools for highlighting an organization's ethical and socially responsible culture.

Leaders must constantly communicate to members the value of not only observing ethical codes but also reporting ethical violations. "Gray areas" must be identified and openly discussed with members, and leaders should offer guidelines on what to do when disagreements arise. It is generally believed that the more an organization's employees are informed of ethical expectations, the more likely they are to do the right thing. A code of ethics is of no consequence if a supportive corporate culture and leadership are lacking.[58]

Ethics Committees

Having a code of ethics is no guarantee that everyone will behave ethically. Enforcing the ethical code is critical. To ensure compliance with the code of ethics, effective leaders also require the creation of ethics committees charged with resolving ethical violations and updating ethical standards. In other organizations the responsibility is given to an ombudsperson. An **ethics ombudsperson** *is a single person entrusted with the responsibility of acting as the organization's conscience.* He or she hears and investigates complaints and points out potential ethics gaps to top management. In many large corporations, ethics departments with full-time staff are now part of the organizational setup and charged with helping employees deal with day-to-day ethical problems or questions.

Training and Education Programs

Training and education provide the opportunity for everyone in the organization to be informed and educated on the company's code of ethics and social responsibility obligations. Training teaches employees how to incorporate ethics into daily behavior. In short, training helps align member behaviors with the organization's values. Educators at every level need to play a greater role in instilling ethical values in their students, who are, after all, future business leaders. Organizations must train their employees to focus not only on the economic imperative of profit generation but also the fiduciary imperative of ethically anchored and socially responsible behavior.[59]

Disclosure Mechanisms

As part of enforcing ethical conduct, proactive organizations have also instituted disclosure mechanisms to encourage employees to report any knowledge of ethical violations. **Whistle-blowing** *is employee disclosure of illegal or unethical practices within an organization.* Whistle-blowing can be risky for those who choose to do it—they have been known to suffer consequences, including being ostracized by coworkers, demoted or transferred to less-desirable jobs, and even losing their jobs. Policies that protect employees from going through these setbacks will signal management's genuine commitment to enforce ethical standards.[60] Some organizations have done this by setting up hotlines to give employees a confidential way to report unethical or illegal actions.

WORK Application 10-5

In your school, look around or investigate if any of the tools discussed here for enforcing an ethical and socially responsible work environment is present. Describe briefly what it is, where it is located, and what behavior it regulates.

OPENING CASE Application

5. What role can Sheri McCoy play in fostering a climate of strict ethical standards at Avon?

First of all, let us start by identifying Avon's ethical standards. On its Web site, the following declaration is posted: "At Avon, we strive always to maintain the highest standards of integrity and ethical conduct, consistent with our Company values and in compliance with both the letter and spirit of all applicable laws and regulations. Each Avon Associate is individually responsible for strict compliance with the policies applicable to their work. Information published on this site reflects our commitment to upholding the highest of standards in the area of ethics, corporate governance and compliance." CEO McCoy will have to be out front reiterating Avon's ethical standards and being a role model for them.

YOU
Make the
ETHICAL
Call

10.2 Avon Bribe Investigation

In a *Wall Street Journal* article on May 5, 2011, it was reported that Avon was widening its internal investigation into possible bribery of foreign officials. A person familiar with the case said that internal investigators at the door-to-door beauty seller have turned up millions of dollars of questionable payments to officials in Brazil, Mexico, Argentina, India, and Japan in amounts that are "not insignificant."[61]

This is a violation that falls under the Foreign Corrupt Practices Act, which basically says that it is illegal and a criminal act for U.S. company officials to bribe foreign government officials to curry business favors. Over the years, many have questioned this law given that other countries don't punish or forbid the same practice. If anything, it is encouraged. The view of opponents of the law is that it puts American businesses at a disadvantage since bribery is a way of doing business in many cultures; especially developing countries.

1. Do you think this law is fair to American businesses?

2. An Avon official has already been suspended. Is Avon doing the right thing?

3. Is it ethical that other countries are allowing or even encouraging this practice?

Learning
Outcome **7**

Explain how authentic leadership has its roots in moral and ethical theory of leadership.

Authentic Leadership

In the wake of corporate scandals involving companies like JPMorgan, Tyco, Enron, Bank of America, and many others, trust in leadership is at an all-time low.[62] With frequent headlines on corruption, deceit, and ethical lapses, a common occurrence, there are calls for leaders to be more transparent and truthful, and lead with authenticity and integrity.[63] We need authentic leaders, people of the highest integrity, committed to building enduring organizations—leaders who have a deep sense of purpose and are true to their values. We need leaders who have the courage to tell their followers the hard truths even if it's not what they want to hear. Authentic leadership is a values-based concept. Earning the trust and loyalty of followers lays the groundwork for a high-performing, motivated, and engaged workforce.[64] To fully understand this leadership approach, we focus our discussion on the personality profile of an authentic leader and his/her impact on follower behavior, attitudes, and performance.

Personality Profile of the Authentic Leader

Authenticity is about genuineness. It is a leadership approach that focuses on knowing and acting in accordance with one's core values, beliefs, emotions, and preferences. The authentic leader holds him- or herself to a higher standard of integrity and accountability. It is rooted in the notion of a "true self."[65] Authentic leadership has an introspective quality that allows leaders to reflect on whether their actions are consistent with who they are, ensuring that their values and ethics take precedence over external pressures and not vice versa. Authentic leaders try to convey a message of hopefulness, optimism, and resiliency to their followers.

Authentic leadership theory is grounded in moral and ethical foundations of leadership.[66] The authentic leader is driven by a value system that calls for being truthful to others, focusing on what is ethical or the right thing to do, staying the course even at personal risk, making empowerment of others a priority, and maintaining open communication with all followers. It is closely associated with other positive leadership models such as charismatic, transformational, and servant leadership.

Authentic leadership is also about courage and character. Character provides the moral compass for decision making, especially for the tough decisions. When faced with difficult decisions, authentic leaders know what they stand for, and they have the courage to act on their principles even if the decision is unpopular. Courageous leaders are able to speak out to right wrongs, admit to personal weaknesses, and own up to mistakes.[67] They don't shy away from making tough decisions, because they are motivated not by the desire to be liked but by their values and purpose. They don't allow social influences or pressures within the organization to affect their ethics when tough decisions have to be made.[68]

How Authentic Leaders Influence Follower Behaviors and Attitudes

How a leader's authenticity influences follower behavior and attitudes is an important consideration and a worthwhile discussion.[69] Followers take their cue from the leader, which is why the role of the leader in creating an ethical work environment is so critical. Trust is seen as the primary intervening variable linking authentic leadership to follower attitudes and behaviors.[70] Authentic leaders understand that trust must be earned. Therefore, authentic leadership emphasizes a transparent and high-quality exchange relationship between leaders and followers. This allows for the formation of positive leader–member exchange relationships. This increases follower organizational citizenship behavior, job satisfaction, and retention. These are the outcomes that do lead to high levels of team spirit and productivity among employees and the bases of a sustainable competitive advantage. Because authentic leaders are consistent in their behavior, followers know what to expect from their leader and what is expected of them. Leader authenticity leads to higher levels of follower identification with the leader.[71]

Diversity Leadership

Diversity leadership focuses on the role that leaders, especially those at the top, play in fostering diversity in their organizations. Without a strong leadership influence, diversity initiatives are shallow and ineffective.[72,73,74] **Diversity** *is the inclusion of all groups at all levels in an organization.* During the past three decades, the U.S. workplace has become more multiculturally diverse.[75] A number of factors have contributed to this trend; among these are the Civil Rights Acts, which outlawed most types of employment discrimination; increased immigration, which has resulted in a more racially and ethnically mixed population; changing demographics; and the passage of the Americans with Disabilities Act (ADA) that has further broadened the scope of diversity in the workplace.

In this section, we explore changing demographics and its impact on workforce diversity, the benefits of embracing diversity, creating a pro-diversity organizational culture, and the effects of globalization on diversity leadership.

The Changing Work Place

Major demographic changes, as well as greater minority representation in the workforce, have accounted for the most significant increase in workforce diversity.[76] The last census revealed an increasing number of Hispanics, African Americans, and Asians in the U.S. workforce. The population of these minority groups is growing at a faster rate than the overall population, thus accelerating the cultural diversity of the U.S. population. The 2010 U.S. Census revealed that the number of Hispanics now stands at 16.3 percent (a 43 percent increase from 2000 to 2010). It is now the largest minority group and growing the fastest. The percentage of African-Americans is 12.6 percent, a 12.3 percent increase from 2000 to 2010. Longer term, Caucasians are projected to become a minority by 2050. Four states (California, Hawaii, New Mexico, and Texas) currently have the distinction of having a combined minority population greater than white populations, which only grew by 5.7 percent in the last census.

In the new work environment, workers must often share work duties and space with co-workers who are disabled. The passage of the ADA has further broadened the scope of diversity in the workplace.

Another demographic trend is the age and gender mix. There are more women entering the workforce today than at any other time in recent memory.[77] This trend is only going to continue as more young women earn college degrees than their male counterparts.[78] The aging trend has now created what some have called generational or age diversity in the workplace.[79] For the first time, four distinct generations comprise today's workforce—the Traditionalists (1900–1945), the Baby Boomers (1946–1964), the Generation Xers (1965–1980), and the Millennials (1981–2000). Different generations have different attitudes and values, making the job of managing a team of mixed generations challenging to say the least.[80]

A greater likelihood exists that individuals will find themselves leading or under the leadership of someone demographically different from them.[81] As the U.S. workforce diversity continues to grow rapidly, effective leaders must create a workplace culture that allows workers from diverse backgrounds to succeed.[82] There is a growing interest in adding diversity management competency as part of leadership development programs.[83] [84] Diversity competency training will enable leaders to understand how various leadership styles interact with followers' cultural value orientations to influence their affective, cognitive, and behavioral outcomes.[85] Also, more corporate boards are recommending that TMTs be diversified. [86]

WORK
Application 10-6

Describe diversity where you work or have worked. For example, approximately what percentages are male versus female, Caucasian versus non-Caucasian, older versus younger, and so on?

Learning Outcome **8**

Explain the benefits of embracing diversity.

Benefits of Embracing Diversity

Decades of research have confirmed what many in the business world already know—that diversity makes for good business.[87,88] From a purely humanistic perspective, many of us believe that there is an ethical and moral imperative to pursue a policy of inclusion rather than exclusion.[89] Advocates of this viewpoint believe that it is a matter of fairness and that an inclusionary policy signals a company's commitment to uphold the dignity of every person regardless of their circumstance.

From a legal perspective, embracing diversity is in compliance with laws that have precedent and historical foundations. From a practical perspective, shifting demographics and increasing globalization have significantly changed the composition of the workforce, forcing corporations to respond or suffer economic loss. Organizations are forced to change their views and their approach to diversity to reflect this new reality.

Regardless of the moral, legal, or practical imperative of diversity, it must also have a positive link to the "bottom line." Many studies have examined the relationship between workforce diversity and organizational performance. There is a general acknowledgment that effective management of diversity initiatives/programs does produce positive outcomes.[90,91] Diversity initiatives that succeed in the short and long term are those that have a tangible impact on shareholder, customer, and employee value. Some of the economic benefits or value that make the case for embracing diversity include the following:

1. Embracing diversity offers a company a marketing advantage. More organizations are competing for talent and customers in a tight labor market, and they recognize that demographic shifts are going to dramatically change their marketplace over the next 20 years. A diversified workforce may offer a greater understanding on how to meet the needs of diverse customers. A diversified workforce is suitable to serve a diversified market place because employees who share similar cultural traits with the customers may be able to develop better, longer-lasting customer relationships. Diversity, therefore, can enable a company to gain access in markets that others may not find easy to penetrate.

2. Companies that embrace diversity are able to recruit from a larger pool, train and retain superior performers, and maximize the benefits of a diverse workforce. When an organization has a reputation for valuing diversity, it tends to attract the best job candidates among women and other culturally diverse groups. For example, many HR recruiters have discovered that focusing on diversity in recruitment advertising helps attract more applicants from diverse backgrounds. Minority job seekers may feel more comfortable applying for employment with companies that have a proven diversity record.

3. Embracing diversity has cost implications. Organizations that wholeheartedly embrace diversity and make everyone feel valued for their contributions can increase the job satisfaction of diverse groups, thus decreasing turnover and absenteeism and their associated costs. An organization's commitment to not only manage but also truly value diversity can lead to positive effects on employees' commitment and performance.[92]

4. Embracing diversity provides an organization with a broader and deeper base of creative problem solvers and decision makers. Creative solutions to problems are more likely to be reached in diverse work groups than homogeneous groups. In diverse groups, people bring different perspectives, knowledge, information, expertise, and skills to problems—resulting in better solutions and greater innovation.[93] In innovative companies, leaders are challenged to create organizational environments that nurture and support creative thinking and the sharing of diverse viewpoints.

5. Diverse teams have been found to outperform non-diverse teams. According to the findings of one study, cultural diversity is more positive for team performance because of the aforementioned benefits of greater diverse inputs, cross-learning, and creativity.[94,95]

We should caution that simply responding to legislative mandates does not automatically result in meaningful, substantive changes in behaviors and attitudes. Rather, diversity initiatives must have top management support and commitment, have broad participation through empowerment, and require constant reinforcement.

Left unmanaged, workforce diversity is more likely to damage morale and creativity, increase turnover, and cause communication difficulties and ultimately conflict.[96] This may occur because people generally feel more comfortable dealing with others who are like themselves. Rather than a unified team, distrust toward one another may characterize a diverse work environment and ultimately lead to a decline in performance.[97] The next section focuses on organizational practices that are characteristic of a pro-diversity culture. The kind of practices that can lower the risk of diversity initiatives turning into a dysfunction.

Learning Outcome 9

What leadership actions can support and sustain a pro-diversity culture?

Creating a Pro-Diversity Organizational Culture

There are still reported accounts of racial and minority groups experiencing feelings of discomfort, alienation, and frustration as they try to assimilate into the workplace.[98] At the executive level, there is still the persistent underrepresentation of women and other minorities among those who are seen as members of the "corporate elite."[99] For organizations to embrace and value diversity, the concept itself must be embedded in the culture of the organization and led from the top.[100]

An organization that has a strong pro-diversity culture has a commitment to attract, retain, and promote employees of minority backgrounds and offers a system that rewards diversity initiatives throughout the organization. The best companies look beyond diversity compliance (with its focus on simply managing the numbers) to diversity institutionalization (with its focus on results). Saying you have a pro-diversity culture and being a diversified organization are two different things. It is the gap that exists between public diversity pronouncements and actual practices that distinguishes the two. Some organizations publicize compliance programs that are nothing but window dressing, symbolic gestures designed to give the appearance of satisfying regulatory, and social responsibility expectations without changing their practices substantively. That is why diversity proponents emphasize the importance of executive leadership and organization-wide

EXHIBIT 10.5

Factors That Support and Sustain a Pro-Diversity Culture

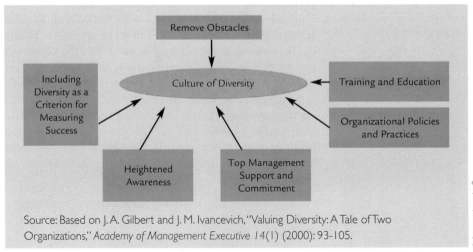

Source: Based on J. A. Gilbert and J. M. Ivancevich, "Valuing Diversity: A Tale of Two Organizations," *Academy of Management Executive* 14(1) (2000): 93-105.

© Cengage Learning®

participation.[101] Exhibit 10.5 identifies key factors that can enhance and promote a strong culture of diversity.

Top Management Support and Commitment

Publishing a statement that says an organization supports diversity does not guarantee success, unless it is woven into the fabric of organizational life in such a way that all employees, regardless of race, creed, age, or gender, feel welcomed to be a part of the organization. This is where top management support and commitment make a big difference. The commitment of the CEO and his or her executive team to diversity will filter down the organizational hierarchy, thus making diversity an institutionalized concept. Leaders who talk diversity must "walk the walk." CEO commitment is considered to be the cornerstone of any successful diversity initiative. Diversity must start from the boardroom downward. The Board of directors and TMT diversity send a clear message where the organization stands on the subject. Studies have found a strong correlation between TMT **diversity** and firm performance.[102]

To achieve full diversity, leaders are challenged to institute policies that provide women, African Americans, Hispanics, and other minorities equal opportunities to move up the corporate ladder into leadership positions.[103] Though slowly changing, it is still the case that top leadership positions in most of corporate America are occupied by white males, despite the growing population of women and other minorities in the workplace.[104]

Remove Obstacles

Organizations with a pro-diversity culture make every effort to remove diversity blockers or obstacles.[105] Diversity blockers are company policies and practices that result in unintended consequences such as stereotypes and prejudices, ethnocentric beliefs, the "glass ceiling" effect, and, ultimately, an unfriendly work environment.

A stereotype is an assumption, without evidence, that people who are not part of the mainstream culture (Hispanics, African Americans, and other minorities) are inherently inferior, less competent at their jobs, and less suitable for leadership positions. Unchecked, stereotypes can lead to prejudice and discrimination. **Ethnocentrism** *is the belief that one's own group or subculture is naturally superior to other groups and cultures.* It is easy to see how this kind of mind-set can be an obstacle to diversity and, at its worst, lead to discrimination.

The "glass ceiling" effect is the concentration of women and minorities at the lower rungs of the corporate ladder, where their skills and talents are not fully utilized.[106] The **glass ceiling** *is defined as an invisible barrier that separate women and minorities from top leadership positions.* The truth is that women and minorities are still vastly underrepresented in the board rooms and upper management positions.[107] Despite college and graduate school enrollments among women that exceed those of men and despite a workforce participation rate since the mid-1960s that has resulted in three-fourths of all working-age women now in the labor force, the upper echelon of most U.S. corporations is still a decidedly male bastion.[108]

Organizational Policies and Practices

Policies express an organization's intentions and provide a blueprint for action. One could argue that policies on diversity document the organization's "diversity talk," whereas practices represent the organization's "diversity walk." Unfortunately, it is not always the case that the two go hand in hand. We've all heard of the phrase "talk is cheap." To ensure that organizations "talk the talk" and "walk the walk," top leaders must put in place pro-diversity policies and practices. As such, policies on recruitment, hiring, training, promotion, compensation, and layoffs must be examined to make sure that minorities are not unfairly treated by actions taken in these areas.

WORK
Application **10-7**

Identify and briefly explain which of the obstacles to diversity exist and/or have been removed where you work or have worked.

The work environment for many minorities can be a lonely, unfriendly, and stressful place, particularly at the executive level where Caucasian men outnumber women and minorities.[109] Sexual harassment, intimidation, bullying, and social rejection are all examples of behavior that make the work place unfriendly. Minorities and women may be excluded from social activities in or out of the office, which often leads to feelings of alienation and despair. This in turn often leads to job dissatisfaction and high turnover among minority groups. Organizational practices such as periodic audits of recruitment, retention, compensation, performance appraisal, employee development, and promotion would ensure that diversity gains are not reversed.

Heightened Awareness

Organizational communication in the form of newsletters, posters, calendars, or coffee mugs celebrating diversity achievements, and regular surveys of employee attitudes and opinions, are ways to heighten awareness of diversity. Repeated exposure to diversity themes would help promote the message that diversity is a normal and accepted part of everyday life in the organization.

Include Diversity as a Criterion for Measuring Success

Creating a culture that supports diversity also means including diversity as a performance metric. Rewards and incentives must be tied to diversity goal metrics and progress. Organizational objectives such as recruiting and promoting more minorities into managerial positions, developing and implementing regular diversity refresher workshops, or addressing diversity concerns in a timely manner can be tied to managerial compensation by requiring that a certain percentage of the manager's compensation be dependent on meeting these diversity targets. Not rewarding accomplishment of diversity goals could send a message that diversity is not a top management priority.

Training and Education

Finally, sustaining a culture of diversity takes continuous training and education.[110] New employees are oriented on the organization's diversity culture while existing employees undergo refresher courses to keep them from backsliding into old habits.[111] Diversity training can include but is not limited to activities such as:

- Role-playing, in which participants act out appropriate and inappropriate ways to deal with diverse employees
- Self-assessment activities, in which participants discover how their own hidden or overt biases influences their thinking about specific individuals and groups
- Sensitivity projects in which participants learn about others who differ from them in race, gender, culture, and so on.

Diversity training is most likely to be successful when it is not a onetime event, but an ongoing activity, and when there are follow-up activities to evaluate behavior post training.

As recommended by the AACSB, colleges and universities should incorporate multicultural and diversity understanding in their curriculum. Through education, students develop their knowledge of different cultures and ethnicities. They learn that diversity is a strength, not a weakness. Through education, diversity blockers like stereotypes, prejudice, ethnocentrism, and other negative attitudes that can lead to discrimination are removed.

WORK Application 10-8

Identify and briefly explain which of the six factors related to creating a pro-diversity culture exist or do not exist where you work or have worked.

WORK Application 10-9

Does the organization you work or have worked for offer diversity-awareness training and education? If you are not sure, contact the human resources department to find out. If it does, briefly describe the program.

YOU
Make the
ETHICAL
Call

10.3   Gender Discrimination

On June 20, 2011, the Supreme Court ruled that a class action lawsuit filed against Walmart could not go forward. The majority opinion said that each case was different from the other, casting doubt on the claim that it was an intentional company-wide policy to discriminate against women.[112] Therefore, the case did not meet the standard for a class action lawsuit. The plaintiffs can still pursue the case but on an individual basis. Walmart had been accused of denying women workers equal pay and opportunities for promotion. The suit claimed that even if Walmart policies were not clearly discriminatory, its organizational culture perpetuated gender stereotypes that lead to differences in pay and promotion between men and women. It is estimated that up to 1.6 million women had join the class action suit. Walmart strongly disagreed with the lower court's decision to proceed with a class action lawsuit and appealed to the Supreme Court. Since the lawsuit was filed, Walmart's CEO Lee Scott has initiated workplace-diversity moves to achieve full diversity. Walmart hired a director of diversity and set diversity targets, and executive bonuses are cut if the company doesn't meet the objectives. Walmart now posts management openings on its company-wide computer network.

1. Do you believe that organizational culture can lead to discrimination? Why or why not?

2. Do you agree with the Supreme Court ruling?

3. What's your opinion of Walmart's actions on diversity after the lawsuit was filed? Do you believe Walmart would have initiated the changes without the lawsuit?

CONCEPT APPLICATION 10-3

Factors That Support and Sustain a Pro-Diversity Culture

Match each statement to one of the factors below. These are factors that show the extent to which an organization's policies and practices support a pro-diversity culture. Write the appropriate letter in the blank before each item.

a. Top Management Support and Commitment
b. Remove Obstacles
c. Organizational Policies and Practices
d. Heightened Awareness
e. Diversity as a Criterion for Measuring Success
f. Training and Education

_____ 15. Using newsletters, posters calendars, and conducting regular surveys of employee attitudes and opinions on diversity issues is part of which factor?

_____ 16. Making sure that hiring, training, promotion, compensation, and retirement or layoffs decisions don't unfairly affect minorities is an example of which factor?

_____ 17. Taking action to prevent behaviors or practices that can result in an unfriendly work environment are part of which factor?

_____ 18. A company-wide mind-set that views diversity as a strategic imperative to the organization's success refers to which factor?

_____ 19. Though many factors are involved, this particular factor is considered to be the cornerstone of any successful diversity initiative.

_____ 20. Using diversity metrics as part of leadership performance evaluations is associated with which factor?

The Effects of Globalization on Diversity Leadership

Corporations are becoming more global and hence more ethnically diverse. Globalization has led firms to originate, produce, and market their products and services worldwide. A global labor market is emerging, dominated by Brazil, Russia, India, and China ("BRIC" countries). U.S.-based companies such as Pepsi-Cola, Coca-Cola, Procter & Gamble, and many others have established a significant presence in China and India, partly motivated by cheap labor and a sizable consumer market. They face competition from European companies such as Daimler-Benz, Nestlé of Switzerland, Canada's Northern Telecom, and many others with a significant presence in the United States. These corporations have to deal with a diverse cross-cultural workforce, customers, competitors, suppliers, and financial institutions. The formation of regional trading blocks like NAFTA or the EU are one way to overcome the growing threat of nationalism—the tendency to want to purchase products from one's own country rather than a foreign country.[113]

In this global environment, understanding cultural differences and learning to deal effectively with partners from different cultures will be critical. This may partially explain why the number of foreign-born managers being appointed to lead U.S. companies is increasing. More and more, multinational companies are recruiting and hiring leaders who have multicultural experiences.[114]

OPENING CASE Application

6. What is Avon's stance on diversity?

Avon embraces diversity in the workforce and continues to be a leader in taking affirmative action to ensure that doors are open to talented individuals, and that all associates and employees have opportunities for development and advancement. Avon has more women in management positions than any other Fortune 500 company, and half of its board of directors is women. In the United States and elsewhere, Avon has internal networks of associates, including a Parents' Network, a Hispanic Network, a Black Professional Association, an Asian network, and a Gay and Lesbian network. The networks act as liaisons between associates and management, to bring voice to critical issues that impact the workplace and the marketplace.

Now that you have learned about culture and diversity as described in this chapter, you may find it interesting to see how your own personality traits match up. Complete Self-Assessment 10-2.

SELF-ASSESSMENT 10-2 Personality, Culture, Values, and Diversity

Culture and Values

If you scored high on the Big Five personality dimension of conscientiousness (high need for achievement), you tend to be a conformist and will most likely feel comfortable in an organization with a strong culture. If you have a high agreeableness (high need for affiliation) personality, you tend to get along well with people, can fit into a strong culture, and would do well in a cooperative culture that values collectivism, low power distance, and femininity. If you have surgency (high need for power), you like to dominate and may not like to fit into a strong culture that does not reflect the values you have. You would tend to do well in a competitive culture that values individualism, high-power distance (if you have it), and masculinity.

On the Big Five, if you are open to new experiences you will do well in an adaptive culture that values low-uncertainty-avoidance, whereas if you are closed to new experiences, you will tend to do well in a bureaucratic culture that values high-uncertainty-avoidance. Would you like to work in an organization with a weak or strong culture? What type of culture and values interest you?

Diversity

If you have a Big Five agreeableness personality type (high need for affiliation), are open to experience, and are well adjusted, you will tend to embrace diversity and get along well with people who are different from you. However, if you have a surgency personality type (high need for power), are closed to experience, and are not well adjusted, you will tend to want to have things done your way and may have problems with a diverse group of people who don't want to give you the power. If you have a conscientiousness personality type (high need for achievement), are well adjusted, and have openness to experience, you will tend to work with those who share your achievement values regardless of other differences. Do you enjoy working with a diversity of people?

_____

_____

"Take It To The Net". Access student resources at www.cengagebrain.com. Search for Lussier, Leadership 6e to find student study tools.

Chapter Summary

The chapter summary is organized to answer the nine learning outcomes for Chapter 10.

1 Explain the power of culture to an organization's effectiveness, both internally and externally.

An organization's culture determines the way that it responds to changes in its external and internal environments. The two important functions served by culture are directly tied to this concept: (1) that *culture creates internal unity* and (2) that *culture helps the organization adapt* to the external environment. Culture provides a value system in which to operate, and when all employees buy into such a value system, there is internal unity. Culture determines how the organization responds to changes in its external environment.

2 Describe the characteristics of strong versus weak cultures.

When there is little or no consensus on a set of values and norms governing member behavior, we describe it as a low-performing or weak cultures. Strong cultures are ones in which core values are widely shared across the organization, from top management to rank-and-file

employees. The characteristics of low-performance cultures include insular thinking, resistance to change, a highly politicized internal environment, and poorly conceived promotion or advancement practices for employees. The characteristics of high-performance cultures include a reputation for valuing their employees, being very results-oriented, and constantly pushing for outstanding performance and excellence.

3 Distinguish between symbolic and substantive leadership actions for shaping organizational culture.

Leaders can initiate many different types of policies, programs, and practices to change, modify, or sustain an organization's culture. Some of these actions are *substantive*, whereas others are simply *symbolic*; yet taken together, they can shape the culture of an organization according to the expectations of the leader. Substantive actions are explicit and highly visible and are indicative of management's commitment to a particular way of doing things. Symbolic actions are valuable for the signals they send about the kinds of behavior and expectations leaders wish to encourage and promote.

4 **Identify and briefly describe the four types of culture commonly found in organizations.**

The *cooperative* culture emphasizes teamwork amongst its employees. Collaboration is seen as critical to achieving organizational goals. The belief is that empowering, respecting, rewarding, and trusting employees is the key to capitalizing on external opportunities. The *adaptive* and cooperative cultures are often referred to as cultures of innovation, for their flexibility and creativity in responding to environmental changes. *Competitive* cultures are common in mature markets in which the emphasis is on the achievement of specific targets (such as market share, revenue growth, and profitability). The *bureaucratic* culture emphasizes strict adherence to set rules, procedures, and authority lines. Organizations with bureaucratic cultures are highly structured and efficiency driven. Change is slow in bureaucratic cultures.

5 **Describe Hofstede's theory on national culture identities.**

The conceptual framework for understanding global cultural differences proposes that national cultures differ by the values they espouse. Researchers have associated different value dimensions with the cultures of different nationalities and/or regions of the world. Leading this effort is the work of Geert Hofstede, whose research identified five value dimensions for understanding global cultural differences. Each value dimension represents a continuum of two opposite ends. The five value dimensions making up the framework are the following:
a. Individualism–collectivism
b. High–low uncertainty avoidance
c. High–low power distance
d. Long-term–short-term orientation
e. Masculinity–femininity

6 **Identify organizational practices that do foster an ethical work environment.**

Organizational practices that can promote an ethical work environment include the following: a jointly developed code of ethics that everyone is well informed of its contents, creating ethics committees to oversee and process ethical violations, making ethical training part of employee development programs, and ensuring that there are available and safe disclosure mechanisms such as a whistle-blowing program for reporting ethical violations.

7 **Explain how authentic leadership has its roots in moral and ethical theory of leadership.**

Authenticity is a psychological construct that focuses on knowing, accepting, and acting in accordance with one's core values, beliefs, emotions, and preferences. The authentic leader holds him-or herself to a higher moral standard. Authentic leadership theory has an introspective quality that allows leaders to reflect on whether their actions are consistent with who they are, ensuring that their values and ethics take precedence over external pressures and not vice versa. The authentic leader is driven by a value system that calls for being moral and focusing on what is ethical or the right thing to do.

8 **Explain the benefits of embracing diversity.**

The value of diversity is evident in studies that have found, among other things, that a diversified workforce offers an advantage in understanding and meeting the needs of diverse customers; some of the best job candidates are found among women and other culturally diverse groups; embracing and valuing diversity can lower an organization's cost attributed to high turnover and/or absenteeism among minority groups; and diverse work groups are more creative and innovative than homogeneous work groups.

9 **What leadership actions can support and sustain a pro-diversity culture?**

An organization that has a strong culture of diversity has a commitment to attract, retain, and promote employees of minority backgrounds and a system that rewards diversity initiatives throughout the organization. The best companies look beyond diversity compliance (with its focus on simply managing the numbers) to diversity institutionalization (with its focus on results). Some of the factors that promote a culture of diversity include top management support and commitment, removing obstacles, including diversity as a criterion for assessing and rewarding managerial performance, organizational awareness, organizational practices and policies, and regular training and education on diversity.

Key Terms

Review Questions

1. What are the similarities and differences between the co-operative culture and the adaptive culture?

2. How does a code of ethics help enforce ethical behavior in an organization?

3. What potential problems could develop in a case in which a leader is from a high-power-distance culture, but his followers are from a low-power-distance culture?

4. Describe the personality profile of an authentic leader.

5. What are the major obstacles often encountered in trying to achieve diversity?

Critical-Thinking Questions

The following critical-thinking questions can be used for class discussion and/or as written assignments to develop communication skills. Be sure to give complete explanations for all questions.

1. Based on your knowledge of the Enron case (Google it), what part did culture play in its actions and ultimate demise?

2. Describe some of the practices, policies, and norms that you would expect to find in an organization that prides itself on building a culture of respect and trust.

3. Describe the different generations that make up what some people are now referring to as "generational diversity" and identify their unique characteristics. What are the implications of generational diversity on effective leadership?

4. Despite the benefits of diversity, some have described it as a "double-edged sword." Explain why.

5. What is the difference between diversity compliance and diversity institutionalization?

6. In your opinion, what would be some strategies for developing a diversity sensitive orientation (DSO)?

CASE

Mary Barra—New CEO of General Motors

On January 15, 2014, Mary Barra became the chief executive officer (CEO) of General Motors, the first female CEO of a major global automaker. She is also a member of the GM board of directors. Commenting on her appointment, Hillary Clinton, former secretary of state, said, "I guess you could say she broke through the steel ceiling, not the glass ceiling."

Ms. Barra is not new to GM. She is an engineer who rose through the ranks, serving in a wide variety of jobs, including plant manager and vice president roles in manufacturing, engineering, human resources, and new product development. She has been with GM since 1980, when she first came as an intern. She is seen as someone with great smart skills, and toughness. Barra represents the new face of GM and an end to old thinking about the car maker.

Asked to describe her management style, CEO Barra answered with one word, "collaborative." She is a strong believer in the power of teamwork. "We come together as a team," she said. "Putting a car, truck or crossover on the road is a team sport, and I just view myself as part of the team." Given the tough decisions that have to be made on GM's direction and strategies, Barra says she welcomes the constructive tension that comes with vigorous debates. "I try to create an environment where people feel they could voice their concerns and that we can get the best ideas on the table and then make the right decision. But at the end of the day, when the decision has to be made, if we don't have complete unanimity, I have no qualms about making it. But I want that tension in a constructive way to make sure we evaluate things from every angle."

Barra inherits a company that is much stronger in many ways but still with significant weaknesses. GM's losses in Europe continue to mount (though they may have leveled off) as it fights to hold on to its gains in China against a resurgent Volkswagen. GM has to reestablish itself as a technology leader after losing more than a billion dollars on the failed Chevrolet Volt. Just about all the experts or analysts believe that she is highly qualified to deal with these issues. She proved herself in the restructuring of Europe's Opel. Her engineering background and ability to get involved will allow her to efficiently supervise the rebuilding of GM's product portfolio. And her earlier appointment as head of human resources gives her rare and valuable insights into GM's still-evolving employee culture.

Some say her biggest challenge will be to win over surviving GM traditionalists, those who either wanted her job or wanted someone from the old-boy network to get the job. Ms. Barra says she will know she has become successful when people stop referring to her as a "car girl" and just call her "boss." Under her leadership, GM is striving to become the global industry leader in automobile design and technology, product quality, customer service, and profitability. Her goal is to make sure that GM is profitable and "wins" in every segment of the market where it competes.

Barra credits her parents for instilling core values about integrity and the importance of hard work; values that she has taken with her to every job she has ever held. On being a role model for aspiring young women, she said if by being a woman CEO, she can encourage young women who like math and science to not shy away from it, and to pursue technical careers, she has no hesitation doing that.[115]

GO TO THE INTERNET: To learn more about CEO Mary Barra, visit the official Web site of General Motors at **http://www.gm.com**.

Support your answers to the following questions with specific information from the case and text or with information you get from the Web or another source.

1. In your opinion, what culture type is CEO Barra bringing to GM? Support your answer with evidence from the case.

2. In what ways has GM's governing board shown that it embraces and supports diversity?

3. What is the evidence in the case to support the assertion that CEO Barra exemplifies the principles of authentic leadership?

4. What are some the factors in Mary Barra's life that have influenced her values?

CUMULATIVE CASE QUESTIONS

5. Based on what you know so far of Mary Barra, describe the quality of the exchange relationship (Chapter 7) she would most likely have with her followers. Explain your answer.

6. In Chapter 8, we discussed how organizational climate can influence team creativity and the role of top leaders in creating such a climate. Is Mary Barra the kind of CEO that can make this happen at GM? Support your answer.

7. Transformational versus transactional leadership describes two leadership styles commonly associated with senior leaders of corporations (Chapter 9). Which of these leadership types is more representative of Mary Barra? Support your answer.

CASE EXERCISE AND ROLE-PLAY

Preparation: Put yourself in CEO Barra's position. Since the announcement that she was GM's new CEO, she has been featured in media outlets across the globe and bombarded by reporters, photographers, and TV crews on her reaction to being the first female to lead a major automaker. She wants to craft a short and insightful statement that she can give every time the question is asked so she can move on to other things. Prepare the exact wording of such a statement.

In-Class Groups: Break into groups of four to six members to share ideas and develop the response.

Role-Play: One student (representing themselves or their group) may give the response to the entire class, with the class acting like members of the media.

VIDEO CASE

Diversity at PepsiCo

Imagine trying to manage and accommodate the needs of more than 185,000 people at once. Imagine a variety of voices, languages, cultures, ethnic backgrounds, families, lifestyles, ages, and geographies all vying for attention, all bearing the name PepsiCo. From the top down, PepsiCo embraces diversity and inclusion in its worldwide workforce. Top executives believe that nurturing diversity in the organization is not only a matter of responsible ethics but also good business. The Frito-Lay North American Diversity/Inclusion Model is a good example of how PepsiCo builds a measurable framework for

diversity. The model addresses five key areas, ranging from "evolving the culture" to "leveraging our people systems." By following a structure, the human resources department and other managers can develop and implement specific programs to meet the needs of their employees.

1. Why is it important for upper-level managers at PepsiCo to receive diversity and inclusion training?

2. Do you think that PepsiCo's encouragement of employee networks actually works against diversity and the formation of multicultural teams? Why or why not?

Developing Your Leadership Skills 10-1

Identifying and Improving Organizational Culture

Preparing for This Exercise

1 Select one organization you work for or have worked for. Identify its culture by providing your responses to the following Work Applications (WA) in the text: WA 1 (is it a high- or low-performance culture?), WA 2 (which of the leadership actions for shaping culture are used?), WA 3 (which of the four types of organizational cultures does it have?), and WA 4 (Which of the five value dimensions of national culture does it reveal?). For Work Application 4, your answer can be between the two poles (on each of the five dimensions); however, try to identify which end of the spectrum the culture is closest to.

2 What are the mission and values of the organization? Does the culture support the mission and values of the organization? Explain why or why not. If the organization does not have a clearly written mission and values statement, that would be a good starting point.

3 Based on the organization's mission and values, how can the culture be improved? Be specific.

Doing This Exercise in Class

Objective

To improve your ability to identify and improve an organization's culture to support its mission and values

AACSB General Skills Area

The primary AACSB learning standard skill developed through this exercise is global and multicultural trends, diversity, and ethics.

Preparation

You should have completed the preparation for this exercise.

Procedure (10–45 minutes)

A The instructor calls on students to give their answers to the preparation, with or without a class discussion.

B Break into groups of four to six and share your answers to the preparation.

C Same as B, but select one group member to present their answer to the entire class.

Conclusion

The instructor may lead a class discussion and/or make concluding remarks.

Apply It (2–4 minutes) What did I learn from this exercise? When will I implement my plan?

_____

_____

_____

Sharing

In the group, or to the entire class, volunteers may give their answers to the "Apply It" questions.

Developing Your Leadership Skills (10-2)

Diversity Training

Preparing for This Exercise

In preparation for the in-class exercise, write out the answers to the following questions.

Race and Ethnicity

1. I am of _____ race and ethnicity(ies).

2. My name is _____. It is significant because it means _____ and/or I was named after _____.

3. One positive thing about being this race/ethnicity is _____.

4. One difficult or challenging thing is _____.

Religion

1. I am of _____ religion/nonreligious/atheist.

2. One positive thing about it is _____.

3. One difficult or challenging thing about it is _____.

Gender

1. I am of _____ gender.

2. One positive thing about being this gender is _____ .

3. One difficult or challenging thing is _____.

4. Men and women are primarily different in _____ because _____.

Age

1. I am _____ years old.

2. One positive thing about this age is _____.

3. One difficult or embarrassing thing about being this age is _____ and on the job. I do/don't have a disability.

Ability

1. I am of _____ (high, medium, low) ability in college and on the job. I do/don't have a disability.

2. One positive thing about being of this ability is _____.

3. One difficult or challenging thing about being of this ability is _____.

Other

1. The major other way(s) in which I'm different than other people is _____.

2. One positive thing about being different in this way is _____.

3. One difficult or challenging thing about being different in this way is _____.

Prejudice, Stereotypes, Discrimination

Identify how you have been prejudged, stereotyped, and discriminated against.

_____

_____

_____

Doing This Exercise in Class

Objective

To increase your understanding of the value of diversity and being different. The more you value diversity, the more effort you will place on developing good human relations with a diversity of people.

The primary AACSB learning standard skill developed through this exercise is global and multicultural trends, diversity, and ethics.

Preparation

You should have answered the preparation questions for this exercise.

Procedure 1 *(2–3 minutes)* Break into groups of four to six with as much diversity as possible. The instructor will check the diversity levels and reassign people to groups to improve diversity, if necessary. Select a spokesperson to give the group's best one or two answers to the "Prejudice, Stereotype, Discrimination" question; it is not necessary to report on any other areas.

Procedure 2 *(10–30 minutes)* The instructor sets a time limit

Procedure 3 *(5–20 minutes)* The spokesperson from each group gives the one or two best examples of prejudice, stereotypes, and discrimination.

Conclusion

The instructor may lead a class discussion and/or make concluding remarks.

Apply It *(2–4 minutes)* What did I learn from this experience? How will I use this knowledge in the future? More specifically, what will I do differently to personally embrace diversity? How will I encourage others to embrace diversity?

_____

_____

_____

Sharing

In the group, or to the entire class, volunteers may give their answers to the "Apply It" questions.

Developing Your Leadership Skills 10-3

Developing an Effective Multicultural Team

Preparing for This Exercise

Assume you are part of a team and your task is to develop a brand new product called the Mind Reader 2010. It will make it possible for you to tell what someone is thinking by simply focusing the device in their direction. There is currently no product or substitute like it on the market—but time is of the essence and this product has to be on the market within a very short time; otherwise, other competing groups will beat you to it. You are a multicultural team with members from the following countries: the United States, Japan, Argentina, Mexico, and Sweden. As discussed in the text section (pp. 369), "National Culture Identities—Hofstede's Value Dimensions," researchers have found key dimensions that explain broad cultural differences among selected nationalities. The following table (see below) summarizes the value dimensions of five countries from which team members are to be selected.

Doing This Exercise in Class

Objective

To learn how to deal with the different values, norms, and attitudes that characterize different cultures. Leaders have to recognize that cultural differences can lead to conflicts in multicultural team settings, and finding common ground where value differences exist is key to effective teamwork.

The primary AACSB learning standard skills developed through this exercise are teamwork and global and multicultural trends, diversity, and ethics.

Preparation

Read and understand the meaning of each value dimension in Exhibit 10.4 on page 369. Review the table in this exercise for the particular value dimensions of each country.

Procedure 1 *(3–5 minutes)* Break up into groups of four to six with as much diversity as possible. The instructor will check to ensure that each group is well diversified and reassign students to groups needing more diversity, if possible. Select a leader who will present the findings of the group's deliberations.

Procedure 2 *(10–20 minutes)* The instructor sets a time limit on the deliberations. If quality, teamwork, and speed are critical to successfully completing this project, what adaptations in behavior would your group have to make, given the different countries your group members are from? Be mindful of the values associated with each country and team member. For example, somebody from an individualistic culture or a high-uncertainty avoidance culture may have difficulty working as part of a team or working with people who are comfortable with and accepting of the unknown, and who tolerate risk and unpredictability. What ideas does the group have to help this individual adapt to the needs of the team to finish the project on time? Other potential areas of conflict exist. Identify them based on the composition of your team, and deliberate on possible solutions, keeping the objective in mind.

Procedure 3 *(15–20 minutes)* The leader from each group presents the potential conflicts introduced by the differences

Country	Femininity	Time Orientation		Individualism	Collectivism	Uncertainty Avoidance		Power Distance	
		Long Term	Short Term			High	Low	High	Low
United States		X		X					
Japan	X		X		X	X			
Argentina							X		
Mexico					X			X	
Sweden	X						X		X

in the value dimensions of team members and the team's solutions for dealing with such conflicts to achieve the desired objectives.

Conclusion

The instructor may lead a class discussion and/or make concluding remarks.

Apply It *(2–4 minutes)*

What did I learn from this experience? How will I use this knowledge in the future?

_____

_____

_____

Apply It *(2–4 minutes)*

What did I learn from this experience? How will I use this knowledge in the future?

Sharing

In the group, or to the entire class, volunteers may give their answers to the "Apply It" questions.

Endnotes

1. G. Jenna, "New Avon CEO Vows to Restore the 126-Year-Old Beauty Company to Former Glory," *Forbes* (February 27, 2013); www.avon.com; http://dealbook.nytimes.com/2012/04/09/avon-appoints-new-chief-executive/?_php=true&_type=blogs&_r=0

2. A. Mushtaq, F. Ahmad, and A. Tanveer, "Organizational Culture in Hotel Industry: Perceptions and Preferences among Staff," *Advances in Management* 6(5): 55–60.

3. C. Panico, "Naked Leadership: Lead to Win Hearts and Minds," *Business & Professional Ethics Journal* 32(3/4) (2013, September): 259– 270.

4. J. Gehman, L. Treviño, and R. Garud, "Values Work: A Process Study of the Emergence and Performance of Organizational Values Practices," *Academy Of Management Journal* 56(1) (2013, February): 84–112.

5. C. Chih-Chung and Y. Baiyin, "Structure and Mechanism of Organizational Cultural Identification in a Chinese Business Context," *Social Behavior & Personality: An International Journal* 41(8) (2013, September): 1347–1358.

6. H. Bourne and M. Jenkins, "Organizational Values: A Dynamic Perspective," *Organization Studies* (01708406) 34(4) (2013, April): 495–514.

7. E. H. Schein, (2004). *Organizational Culture and Leadership*, 3rd ed. (San Francisco, CA: Jossey-Bass, 2004).

8. C. Chih-Chung and Y. Baiyin, "Structure and Mechanism of Organizational Cultural Identification in a Chinese Business Context," *Social Behavior & Personality: An International Journal* 41(8) (2013, September): 1347–1358.

9. Q. Hu, T. Dinev, P. Hart, D. Cooke, *Decision Sciences* 43 (4) (2012, August): 615–660.

10. A. Molinsky, "The Psychological Processes of Cultural Retooling," *Academy of Management Journal* [serial online] 56(3) (2013, June): 683–710.

11. A. Molinsky, "The Psychological Processes of Cultural Retooling," *Academy of Management Journal* [serial online] 56(3) (2013, June): 683–710.

12. S. Dolan and Y. Bao, "Sharing the Culture: Embedding Storytelling and Ethics in the Culture Change Management Process," *Journal of Management & Change* 29(1) (2012, June): 10–23.

13. E. Schien, *Organizational Culture and Leadership*, 2nd ed. (San Francisco, CA: Jossey-Bass, 1992).

14. G. Sharoni, A. Tziner, E. C. Fein, T. Shultz, K. Shaul, and L. Zilberman, *Journal of Applied Social Psychology* 42 (Supplement) (2012, December): pE267–E294.

15. V. Cristian-Liviu, "Organizational Culture and Strategy. How Does It Work? An Empirical Research," *Annals of the University of Oradea, Economic Science Series* 22(1) (2013, July): 1690–1696.

16. P. Duncan, M. Green, and R. Herrera, "Culture Predicting Leadership," *Business Studies Journal* 4 (2012, January 2): 71–84.

17 A. Canato, D. Ravasi, and N. Phillips, "Coerced Practice Implementation in Cases of Low Cultural Fit: Cultural Change and Practice Adaptation during the Implementation of Six Sigma at 3M," *Academy of Management Journal* 56(6) (2013, December): 1724–1753.

18 A. Canato, D. Ravasi, and N. Phillips, "Coerced Practice Implementation in Cases of Low Cultural Fit: Cultural Change and Practice Adaptation during the Implementation of Six Sigma at 3M," *Academy of Management Journal* 56(6) (2013, December): 1724–1753.

19 S. Ramakrishnan, "Vital Missing Link in Organizational Transformation," *Industrial Management* 55(1) (2013, January): 8–9.

20 J. Gimenez-Espin, D. Jiménez-Jiménez, and M. Martínez-Costa, "Organizational Culture for Total Quality Management," *Total Quality Management & Business Excellence* 24(5/6) (2013, June): 678–692.

21 Sudarmo, "Influence Business Principles, Organizational Culture, Fundamental Safe Work Practices, Operational Excellence Expectations, and Corporate Commitment to the Tenets of Corporate Operations and Corporate Performance Oil and Gas Chevron Indonesia," *Journal of Accounting, Business & Management* 20(1) (2013, April): 71–90.

22 I. Cho, J. K. Kim, C. Park, N.-H. Cho, *Total Quality Management & Business Excellence* 24(7/8) (2013, August): 753–768.

23 E. Berman, M. Sabharwal, R. Gomes, et al., "The Impact of Societal Culture on the Use of Performance Strategies in East Asia: Evidence from a Comparative Survey," *Public Management Review* 15(8) (2013, November): 1065–1089.

24 "Build a Confident Employee Culture," *Marketing Health Services* 32(1) (2012, winter): 28–29.

25 P. Ruiz-Palomino and R. Martínez-Cañas, "Ethical Culture, Ethical Intent, and Organizational Citizenship Behavior: The Moderating and Mediating Role of Person-Organization Fit," *Journal of Business Ethics* 120(1) (2014, March): 95–108.

26 A. Canato, D. Ravasi, and N. Phillips, "Coerced Practice Implementation in Cases of Low Cultural Fit: Cultural Change and Practice Adaptation during the Implementation of Six Sigma at 3M," *Academy of Management Journal* 56(6) (2013, December): 1724–1753.

27 K. Jin, R. Drozdenko, and S. DeLoughy, "The Role of Corporate Value Clusters in Ethics, Social Responsibility, and Performance: A Study of Financial Professionals and Implications for the Financial Meltdown," *Journal of Business Ethics* 112(1) (2013, January): 15–24.

28 A. Mushtaq, F. Ahmad, and A. Tanveer, "Organizational Culture in Hotel Industry: Perceptions and Preferences among Staff." *Advances in Management* 6(5): 55–60.

29 A. Canato, D. Ravasi, and N. Phillips, "Coerced Practice Implementation in Cases of Low Cultural Fit: Cultural Change and Practice Adaptation during the Implementation of Six Sigma at 3M," *Academy of Management Journal* 56(6) (2013, December): 1724–1753.

30 M. V. Davis, E. Mahanna, B. Joly, M. Zelek, W. Riley, P. Verma, and J. Solomon Fisher, *American Journal of Public Health* 104(1) (2014, January): e98–e104.

31 M. V. Davis, E. Mahanna, B. Joly, M. Zelek, W. Riley, P. Verma, and J. Solomon Fisher, *American Journal of Public Health* 104(1) (2014, January): e98–e104.

32 H. Darvish and E. A. Nazari, *Economic Insights—Trends & Challenges* 65(1) (2013): 1–16.

33 K. Jin, R. Drozdenko, and S. DeLoughy, "The Role of Corporate Value Clusters in Ethics, Social Responsibility, and Performance: A Study of Financial Professionals and Implications for the Financial Meltdown," *Journal of Business Ethics* 112(1) (2013, January): 15–24.

34 R. Scotney, "Good Leadership: Where Do We Begin?" *Human Resources Magazine* 17(4) (2012, October): 14–15.

35 E. H. Schein, (2004). *Organizational Culture and Leadership*, 3rd ed. (San Francisco, CA: Jossey-Bass, 2004).

36 J. Gehman, L. Treviño, and R. Garud, "Values Work: A Process Study of the Emergence and Performance of Organizational Values Practices," *Academy Of Management Journal* 56(1) (2013, February): 84–112.

37 J. Kottke and K. Pelletier, "Measuring and Differentiating Perceptions of Supervisor and Top Leader Ethics," *Journal of Business Ethics* 113(3) (2013, March 11): 415–428.

38 J. Kottke and K. Pelletier, "Measuring and Differentiating Perceptions of Supervisor and Top Leader Ethics," *Journal of Business Ethics* 113(3) (2013, March 11): 415–428.

39 J. Gimenez-Espin, D. Jiménez-Jiménez, and M. Martínez-Costa, "Organizational Culture for Total Quality Management," *Total Quality Management & Business Excellence* 24(5/6) (2013, June): 678–692.

40 J. Gimenez-Espin, D. Jiménez-Jiménez, and M. Martínez-Costa, "Organizational Culture for Total Quality Management," *Total Quality Management & Business Excellence* 24(5/6) (2013, June): 678–692.

41 P. Yu-Shu, D. Altan-Uya, and C. Hsiang Lin, "National Culture and Firm's CSR Engagement: A Cross-Nation Study," *Journal of Marketing & Management* 5(1) (2014, May): 38–49.

42 D. Rottig and A. Rubens, "A Conceptual Model of Strategic Leadership and Employee Perception of Inequity," *Academy of Management Annual Meeting Proceedings* (2012, January): 1.

43 G. Hofstede, "Cultural Constraints in Management Theories," *Academy of Management Executive* 7(1) (February, 1993): 81–94.

44 http://www.aacsb.edu/accreditation/2013standards/

45 L. Pinto, C. Cabral-Cardoso, and W. Werther, "Why Solidarity Matters (and Sociability Doesn't): The Effects of Perceived Organizational Culture on Expatriation Adjustment," *Thunderbird International Business Review* 53(3) (2011): 377–389.

46 J. Schaubroeck, S. Hannah, and A. Peng, et al., "Embedding Ethical Leadership within and across Organization Levels," *Academy of Management Journal* 55(5) (2012, October): 1053–1078.

47 M. Pitesa and S. Thau, "Compliant Sinners, Obstinate Saints: How Power and Self-Focus Determine the Effectiveness of Social Influences in Ethical Decision Making," *Academy of Management Journal* [serial online] 56(3) (2013, June): 635–658.

48 M. Huhtala, T. Feldt, K. Hyvönen, and S. Mauno, "Ethical Organisational Culture as a Context for Managers' Personal Work Goals," *Journal of Business Ethics* 114(2) (2013, May): 265–282.

49 N. McClaren, "The Personal Selling and Sales Management Ethics Research: Managerial Implications and Research Directions from a Comprehensive Review of the Empirical Literature," *Journal of Business Ethics* 112(1) (2013, January): 101–125.

50 C. Matherne, III and S. Litchfield, "Investigating the Relationship between Affective Commitment and Unethical Pro-Organizational Behaviors: The Role of Moral Identity," *Journal of Leadership, Accountability & Ethics* 9(5) (2012, November): 35–46.

51 R. Jackson, C. Wood, and J. Zboja, "The Dissolution of Ethical Decision-Making in Organizations: A Comprehensive Review and Model," *Journal of Business Ethics* 116(2) (2013, August 5): 233–250.

52 J. Schaubroeck, S. Hannah, and A. Peng, et al., "Embedding Ethical Leadership within and across Organization Levels," *Academy of Management Journal* 55(5) (2012, October): 1053–1078.

53 H. Baird, "A Word from the President," *Financial Management (14719185)* (2012, May): 3.

54 J. Schaubroeck, S. Hannah, and A. Peng, et al., "Embedding Ethical Leadership within and across Organization Levels,"

Academy of Management Journal 55(5) (2012, October): 1053–1078.

55 M. Huhtala, T. Feldt, K. Hyvönen, and S. Mauno, "Ethical Organisational Culture as a Context for Managers' Personal Work Goals," *Journal of Business Ethics* 114(2) (2013, May): 265–282.

56 M. Painter-Morland, "The Relationship between Identity Crises and Crises of Control," *Journal of Business Ethics* 114(1) (2013, April 8): 1–14.

57 H. Baird, "A Word from the President," *Financial Management (14719185)* (2012, May): 3.

58 C. Jurkiewicz, "Developing a Multicultural Organizational Code of Ethics Rooted in the Moral Obligations of Citizenry," *Public Organization Review* 12(3) (2012, September): 243–249.

59 B. Bayley, "Organizational Ethics Training," *Journal for Quality & Participation* 35(2) (2012, July): 15–19.

60 K. Loyens, "Towards a Custom-Made Whistle Blowing Policy. Using Grid-Group Cultural Theory to Match Policy Measures to Different Styles of Peer Reporting," *Journal of Business Ethics* 114(2) (2013, May): 239–249.

61 E. Byron, "Avon Bribe Investigation Widens," *Wall Street Journal* (Thursday, May 5, 2011).

62 C. Panico, "Naked Leadership: Lead to Win Hearts and Minds," *Business & Professional Ethics Journal* 32(3/4) (2013, September): 259–270.

63 C. Peus, J. Wesche, B. Streicher, S. Braun, and D. Frey, "Authentic Leadership: An Empirical Test of Its Antecedents, Consequences, and Mediating Mechanisms," *Journal of Business Ethics* 107(3) (2012, May 15): 331–348.

64 J. Schaubroeck, A. Chunyan Peng, and S. Hannah, "Developing Trust with Peers and Leaders: Impacts on Organizational Identification and Performance during Entry," *Academy of Management Journal* 56(4) (2013, August): 1148–1168.

65 C. Peus, J. Wesche, B. Streicher, S. Braun, and D. Frey, "Authentic Leadership: An Empirical Test of Its Antecedents, Consequences, and Mediating Mechanisms," *Journal of Business Ethics* 107(3) (2012, May 15): 331–348.

66 C. Caldwell, R. Dixon, L. Floyd, J. Chaudoin, J. Post, and G. Cheokas, "Transformative Leadership: Achieving Unparalleled Excellence," *Journal of Business Ethics* 109(2) (2012, August 20): 175–187.

67 C. Caldwell, R. Dixon, L. Floyd, J. Chaudoin, J. Post, and G. Cheokas, "Transformative Leadership: Achieving Unparalleled Excellence," *Journal of Business Ethics* 109(2) (2012, August 20): 175–187.

68 M. Pitesa, and S. Thau, "Compliant Sinners, Obstinate Saints: How Power and Self-Focus Determine the Effectiveness of Social Influences in Ethical Decision Making," *Academy of Management Journal* [serial online] 56(3) (2013, June): 635–658.

69 S. Peterson, F. Walumbwa, B. Avolio, and S. Hannah, "The Relationship between Authentic Leadership and Follower Job Performance: The Mediating Role of Follower Positivity in Extreme Contexts," *Leadership Quarterly* 23(3) (2012, June): 502–516.

70 J. Schaubroeck, A. Chunyan Peng, and S. Hannah, "Developing Trust with Peers and Leaders: Impacts on Organizational Identification and Performance during Entry," *Academy of Management Journal* 56(4) (2013, August): 1148–1168.

71 J. Schaubroeck, A. Chunyan Peng, and S. Hannah, "Developing Trust with Peers and Leaders: Impacts on Organizational Identification and Performance during Entry," *Academy of Management Journal* 56(4) (2013, August): 1148–1168.

72 "Working toward More Diverse Leadership," *Financial Executive* 28(5) (2012, June): 6.

73 M. Coleman, "Leadership and Diversity," *Educational Management Administration & Leadership* 40(5) (2012, September): 592–609.

74 E. A. Ewoh, "Managing and Valuing Diversity: Challenges to Public Managers in the 21st Century," *Public Personnel Management* 42(2) (2013, June): 107–122.

75 P. A. Nederveen, D. Van Knippenberg, D. Van Dierendonck, "Cultural Diversity and Team Performance: The Role of Team Member Goal Orientation," *Academy of Management Journal* 56(3) (2013, June): 782–804.

76 P. A. Nederveen, D. Van Knippenberg, D. Van Dierendonck, "Cultural Diversity and Team Performance: The Role of Team Member Goal Orientation," *Academy of Management Journal* 56(3) (2013, June): 782–804.

77 L. Nishii, "The Benefits of Climate for Inclusion for Gender-Diverse Groups," *Academy of Management Journal* 56(6) (2013, December): 1754–1774.

78 H. Rosin, "The End of Men and the Rise of Women," *Boston University Law Review* 93(3) (2013, May): 667–680.

79 J. Hendricks and V. Cope, "Generational Diversity: What Nurse Managers Need to Know," *Journal of Advanced Nursing* 69(3) (2013, March): 717–725.

80 E. A. Ewoh, "Managing and Valuing Diversity: Challenges to Public Managers in the 21st Century," *Public Personnel Management* 42(2) (2013, June): 107–122.

81 M. Virick and C. Greer, "Gender Diversity in Leadership Succession: Preparing for the Future," *Human Resource Management* 51(4) (2012, July): 575–600.

82 M. Mcdonald and J. Westphal, "Access Denied: Low Mentoring of Women and Minority First-Time Directors and Its Negative Effects on Appointments to Additional Boards," *Academy of Management Journal* 56(4) (2013, August): 1169–1198.

83 "Working toward More Diverse Leadership," *Financial Executive* 28(5) (2012, June): 6.

84 E. A. Ewoh, "Managing and Valuing Diversity: Challenges to Public Managers in the 21st Century," *Public Personnel Management* 42(2) (2013, June): 107–122.

85 C. Butts, B. Trejo, K. Parks, and D. McDonald, "The Integration of Diversity and Cross-Cultural Work: Competencies and Commonalities," *Industrial & Organizational Psychology* 5(3) (2012, September): 361–364.

86 M. Mcdonald and J. Westphal, "Access Denied: Low Mentoring of Women and Minority First-Time Directors and Its Negative Effects on Appointments to Additional Boards," *Academy of Management Journal* 56(4) (2013, August): 1169–1198.

87 D. Chrobot-Mason and N. Aramovich, "The Psychological Benefits of Creating an Affirming Climate for Workplace Diversity," *Group & Organization Management* 38(6) (2013, December): 659–689.

88 P. A. Nederveen, D. Van Knippenberg, D. Van Dierendonck, "Cultural Diversity and Team Performance: The Role of Team Member Goal Orientation," *Academy of Management Journal* 56(3) (2013, June): 782–804.

89 L. Nishii, "The Benefits of Climate for Inclusion for Gender-Diverse Groups," *Academy of Management Journal* 56(6) (2013, December): 1754–1774.

90 P. A. Nederveen, D. Van Knippenberg, D. Van Dierendonck, "Cultural Diversity and Team Performance: The Role of Team Member Goal Orientation," *Academy of Management Journal* 56(3) (2013, June): 782–804.

91 V. Senichev, "Human Resource Diversity and Performance within the Frame of Organizations, Teams and Individuals," *Business: Theory & Practice* 14(4) (2013, December): 337–345.

92 E. A. Ewoh, "Managing and Valuing Diversity: Challenges to Public Managers in the 21st Century," *Public Personnel Management* 42(2) (2013, June): 107–122.

93 L. Nishii, "The Benefits of Climate for Inclusion for Gender-Diverse Groups," *Academy of Management Journal* 56(6) (2013, December): 1754–1774.

94 P. A. Nederveen, D. Van Knippenberg, and D. Van Dierendonck, "Cultural Diversity and Team Performance: The Role of Team Member Goal Orientation," *Academy of Management Journal* 56(3) (2013, June): 782–804.

95 S. Shin, T. Kim, J. Lee, and L. Bian, "Cognitive Team Diversity and Individual Team Member Creativity: A Cross-Level Interaction," *Academy Of Management Journal* 55(1) (2012, February): 197–212.

96 E. A. Ewoh, "Managing and Valuing Diversity: Challenges to Public Managers in the 21st Century," *Public Personnel Management* 42(2) (2013, June): 107–122.

97 R. Chua, "The Costs of Ambient Cultural Disharmony: Indirect Intercultural Conflicts in Social Environment Undermine Creativity," *Academy of Management Journal* 56(6) (2013, December): 1545–1577.

98 M. Mcdonald and J. Westphal, "Access Denied: Low Mentoring of Women and Minority First-Time Directors and Its Negative Effects on Appointments to Additional Boards," *Academy of Management Journal* 56(4) (2013, August): 1169–1198.

99 M. Mcdonald and J. Westphal, "Access Denied: Low Mentoring of Women and Minority First-Time Directors and Its Negative Effects on Appointments to Additional Boards," *Academy of Management Journal* 56(4) (2013, August): 1169–1198.

100 E. Ng and G. Sears, "CEO Leadership Styles and the Implementation of Organizational Diversity Practices: Moderating Effects of Social Values and Age," *Journal of Business Ethics* 105(1) (2012, January): 41–52.

101 E. A. Ewoh, "Managing and Valuing Diversity: Challenges to Public Managers in the 21st Century," *Public Personnel Management* 42(2) (2013, June): 107–122.

102 B. Nielsen and S. Nielsen, "Top Management Team Nationality Diversity and Firm Performance: A Multilevel Study," *Strategic Management Journal* 34(3) (2013, March): 373–382.

103 C. Dezsö and D. Ross, "Does Female Representation in Top Management Improve Firm Performance? A Panel Data Investigation," *Strategic Management Journal* 33(9) (2012, September): 1072–1089.

104 B. Luscombe, "The Rise of the Sheconomy," *Time* 176(21) (2010, November 22): 58–61.

105 T. Dolan, "Increasing Diversity in Governance and Management," *Journal of Healthcare Management* 58(2) (2013, March): 84–86.

106 L. Clevenger and N. Singh, "Exploring Barriers That Lead to the Glass Ceiling Effect for Women in the U.S. Hospitality Industry," *Journal Of Human Resources in Hospitality & Tourism* 12(4) (2013, October): 376–399.

107 A. Cook and C. Glass, "Women and Top Leadership Positions: Towards an Institutional Analysis," *Gender, Work & Organization* 21(1) (2014, January): 91–103.

108 C. Dezsö and D. Ross, "Does Female Representation in Top Management Improve Firm Performance? A Panel Data Investigation," *Strategic Management Journal* 33(9) (2012, September): 1072–1089.

109 M. Mcdonald and J. Westphal, "Access Denied: Low Mentoring of Women and Minority First-Time Directors and Its Negative Effects on Appointments to Additional Boards," *Academy of Management Journal* 56(4) (2013, August): 1169–1198.

110 A. Lee, R. Williams, and R. Kilaberia, "Engaging Diversity in First-Year College Classrooms," *Innovative Higher Education*. June 2012; 37(3):199–213.

111 K. Bezrukova, K. Jehn, and C. Spell, "Reviewing Diversity Training: Where We Have Been and Where We Should Go," *Academy Of Management Learning & Education* 11(2) (2012, June): 207–227.

112 J. Bravin and A. Zimmerman, "Wal-Mart Ruling to Have Wide Reach," *Wall Street Journal* (Tuesday, June 21, 2011).

113 M. Wright and T. Reeskens, "Of What Cloth Are the Ties That Bind? National Identity and Support for the Welfare State across 29 European Countries," *Journal of European Public Policy* 20(10) (2013, December 10): 1443–1463.

114 B. Nielsen and S. Nielsen, "Top Management Team Nationality Diversity and Firm Performance: A Multilevel Study," *Strategic Management Journal* 34(3) (2013, March): 373–382.

115 http://www.gm.com/company/corporate-officers/mary-barra; http://www.latimes.com/business/autos/la-fi-hy-mary-barra-gm-ceo-20131211,0,6764014.story#axzz2u6lnLXWf; http://www.business2community.com/leadership/mary-barra-new-general-motors-ceo-worthy-role-model-women-business-0783707#!wUYWh; http://www.businessweek.com/news/2014-01-27/clinton-says-gm-s-barra-broke-steel-ceiling-as-sector-recovers; http://www.forbes.com/sites/joannmuller/2014/02/06/mary-barras-to-do-list-at-general-motors/.

Strategic Leadership and Change Management

Learning Outcomes

After studying this chapter, you should be able to:

1 Discuss the role of strategic leadership in the strategic management process. p. 399

2 Identify the five major decision categories in the strategic management process. p. 402

3 Explain the relationship between objectives and strategies. p. 404

4 Describe the relevance of analyzing an organization's internal and external environment as part of strategy formulation. p. 405

5 Explain the importance of strategy evaluation in the strategic management process. p. 411

6 Describe the change management process using Kurt Lewin's force-field model of change. p. 413

7 Identify the major reasons for resisting change. p. 414

8 Discuss some of the recommendations for minimizing resistance to change. p. 416

OPENING CASE Application

As chief executive officer, Larry Page is responsible for Google's product development and technology strategy. Sergey Brin co-founded Google Inc. with Larry Page in 1998. Today, he directs special projects. Eric Schmidt, former CEO, is the executive chairman of the board. Together, these three men provide strategic leadership at Google.

Google's mission is to organize the world's information and make it universally accessible and useful. By providing the best user experience, Google and its leadership team believe that they can build a company that will create more value, not just for its users but ultimately for its shareholders. Its business model is based on providing a free information search engine to millions of subscribers in exchange for the sale of ads that appear alongside its search engine results. Google's advertising programs range from simple text ads to rich media ads that help businesses find customers and help publishers make money off of their content. The company also provides cloud computing tools for businesses that save money and help organizations be more productive.

Google has on its Web site a page titled "*Ten things we know to be true.*" The 10th item states, "*Great just isn't good enough.*" This 10th item discusses Google's goal-setting strategy: "We set ourselves goals we know we can't reach yet, because we know that by stretching to meet them we can get further than we expected." Google sets stretch goals, a mark of strategic leaders whose vision stretches way beyond what others think is possible. Through innovation and iteration, Google aims to take things that work well and improve upon them in unexpected ways. "We try to anticipate needs not yet articulated by our global audience, and meet them with products and services that set new standards." This is the essence of strategic leadership—anticipating customer needs and then designing innovative products/services that will satisfy those needs. The strategic management process is about having the right vision, setting challenging objectives, and formulating the right strategies to achieve these objectives and keep moving toward the vision. Google is certainly pursuing a differentiation strategy. Google is always looking for new opportunities where it can make a difference. "Ultimately, our constant dissatisfaction with the way things are becomes the driving force behind everything we do."

In other words, Google is a change-driven, not a status-quo, organization.

Google certainly strives for a strategy-culture fit. As Google's leadership sees it, great, creative things are more likely to happen with the right company culture. At Google, there is an emphasis on team achievements and pride in individual accomplishments that contribute to its success. The company puts great stock in its employees who are described as energetic and passionate. Google strongly believes in diversity. Its employees come from diverse backgrounds with creative approaches to work and play. The company's culture is adaptive, yet casual and very informal. This culture type is key to Google's success as an innovator. Idea generation is the first step to new product development. At Google, it is not uncommon for a new idea to emerge in a café line, at a team meeting, or at the gym. What sets Google apart from its competitors is the dizzying speed with which new ideas are traded, tested, and put into practice.

Google is one of the world's most dominant companies. Google can be accessed in 120 languages and available in 50 countries worldwide. *By any standard or metric, Google is a standout company, and perhaps the main reason for its superiority is its remarkable style of leadership.* Google's results speak for its performance. The company reached $1 billion in revenue in six years, ten years faster than Microsoft. The Google brand is valued at $100 billion, making it the world's first "one-hundred billion" brand.

OPENING CASE QUESTIONS:

1. **How effective has the executive leadership team of Schmidt, Page, and Brin been in providing the kind of strategic leadership that Google has seen so far?**

2. **Critique Google's mission statement.**

3. **How well do Google's long-term objectives balance with the interests of its stakeholders?**

4. **Describe Google's business environment. How well is Google adapting to it?**

5. **What type of strategy is Google pursuing, and why do you think the leadership team has chosen such a course rather than the alternatives?**

6. What are some of the factors contributing to Google's effective strategy implementation?

7. Why have Schmidt, Page, and Brin encountered less resistance in bringing about changes at Google than most companies experience?

Can you answer any of these questions? You'll find answers to these questions and learn more about Google and its leadership throughout the chapter.

To learn more about Google and its leadership team, visit the company's Web site at **http://www.google.com**.

Strategic Leadership

In the past two decades, the spread of globalization and the Internet have generated unprecedented changes in ways organizations are managed. These changes have produced new requirements for competition and forced a new emphasis on strategic thinking and leadership.[1]

Although there are varying definitions of the concept of strategic leadership, they all seem to revolve around the same themes: vision, change, people, and performance. Strategic leadership is the responsibility of the CEO and top management. Top management will include the vice presidents of divisions or strategic business units. They take the lead in crafting the organization's vision, mission, core values, objectives, and strategies. Strategic leaders are responsible for the organization's near-term performance, as well as for creating conditions that will ensure the organization's long-term competitiveness.[2] There is ample evidence supporting the hypothesis that strategic leaders have positive effects on firm performance because of their leading role in planning and executing firm strategies.[3,4]

In their study involving more than 20,000 executives, Shoemaker, Krupp, and Howland identified six skills that, when mastered and used in concert, allow leaders to think strategically and navigate the unknown effectively. They are the abilities to *anticipate, challenge, interpret, decide, align, and learn.*[5] Along with these abilities, the effective strategic leader must be capable of the following:[6]

- Anticipating and forecasting events in the external environment that have the potential to impact business performance—they observe from the outside in.
- Finding and sustaining competitive advantage by building core competencies and selecting the right entrepreneurial opportunities to pursue.[7]
- Evaluating strategy implementation and results systematically, and making strategic adjustments.
- Building a highly effective, efficient, and motivated team of employees.[8]
- Selecting, developing, and mentoring a talented team of top leaders who can sense, capture, and shape market opportunities for firm growth.[9]
- Deciding on appropriate goals and priorities.
- Communicating effectively.

Therefore, we define **strategic leadership** as *a leader's ability to anticipate, envision, maintain flexibility, think strategically, and work with others to initiate changes that will create a viable future for an organization.*[10,11] It is a process of providing the leadership and inspiration necessary to create and implement a firm's vision, mission, and strategies to achieve organizational objectives.[12]

The focus of this chapter is on strategic leadership and the strategic management process, and change management. However, before delving into these topics, we will briefly explore two related topics: globalization and environmental sustainability.

SELF-ASSESSMENT 11-1   ## Strategic Leadership

Identify each of the 16 statements according to how accurately it describes you. Place a number from 1 to 5 on the line before each statement.

$$5 \;—\; 4 \;—\; 3 \;—\; 2 \;—\; 1$$
More like me   Less like me   Not me at all

_____ 1. I have a tendency to plan ahead instead of waiting until the last minute before acting on issues/problems.

_____ 2. I am a very flexible person when it comes to dealing with people or issues.

_____ 3. As a student, I often find myself playing the role of a leader rather than a follower.

_____ 4. When the stakes are high, I am comfortable being the one to make the final decision.

_____ 5. I am very good at setting personal goals and prioritizing events in my life.

_____ 6. I tend to consider the long-term consequences of my decisions and actions today rather than just the immediate consequences.

_____ 7. When I contact businesspeople who can help me, I praise their accomplishments.

_____ 8. I am the type that likes to sit back and try to envision my future to see where or what I will be in ten years.

_____ 9. When it comes to working with others, I am more of a team player than a loner.

_____ 10. I am the type that would want the ball with the play clock counting down to zero and the chance to make the winning basket.

_____ 11. I am the type that would be very comfortable mentoring, training, and motivating others to meet team goals.

_____ 12. When it comes to interacting with people, I can communicate effectively with all kinds of people.

_____ 13. When it comes to solving problems or completing group projects, I will describe myself as more analytical than most of my peers.

_____ 14. I like to keep things the way they are (especially if they are working just fine) rather than trying to change them.

_____ 15. I have a strong desire to one day become the CEO of an organization.

_____ 16. I am a very ethical person when it comes to dealing with others or acting according to accepted norms.

Add up your score and place it here _____ and on the continuum below.

$$80 \;—\; 70 \;—\; 60 \;—\; 50 \;—\; 40 \;—\; 30 \;—\; 16$$
Strong Strategic Leadership   Weak Strategic Leadership
Potential   Potential

This self-assessment exercise is similar to the first one in Chapter 1 except this focuses on your potential to lead from the top. Generally, the higher your score on the continuum above, the greater your potential for strategic leadership. However, the key to realizing your aspirations is education, hard work, and persistence, not simply potential. You can develop your strategic leadership ability through this course by applying the principles and theories to your personal and professional life.

OPENING CASE Application

1. How effective has the executive leadership team of Schmidt, Page, and Brin been in providing the kind of strategic leadership that Google has utilized so far?

Together, this trio has created a profitable business model built around keyword advertising. Since going public in 2004, Google has exceeded analysts' estimates for its financial performance in all but one quarter. Google's stock is currently trading at over $1,200 per share. The trio of strategic leaders is performing exceptionally well in all the areas identified above. Evidence of this can be seen in the market standing of the company today.

Globalization and Environmental Sustainability

One area in which change is unmistakable is the increasingly global competitive marketplace.[13] Virtually every company, large or small, faces competition for critical resources and market opportunities, not just from competitors in the home market but also more and more from distant and often little-understood regions of the world.[14,15] In his book *The World Is Flat,* Thomas Friedman eloquently makes the case that labor, jobs, information, knowledge, and capital readily move across borders with far less restrictions and at greater speed than was possible only a few years ago, a view that has been supported by many others.[16,17,18] How successful a company is at exploiting emerging opportunities and dealing with associated threats depends crucially on leadership's ability to cultivate a global mind-set among managers and their followers.[19] International experience is now considered key for anyone aspiring to top leadership in many organizations. There is a renewed interest in the development of global leadership and intercultural competency.[20,21]

Beginning in the later part of the 20th century, there has been increasing attention paid to the idea of environmental sustainability.[22] There seems to be emerging a collective understanding that the natural environment (which includes physical resources, wildlife, and climate) cannot sustain itself if human behavior toward the air, water, land, natural resources, flora, and fauna does not change.[23] Leaders today have a responsibility to ensure that they reduce side effects such as pollution, deforestation, and greenhouse gas emissions. Sustainability is about conservation of natural resources and minimization of waste in operations through actions such as recycling. The common phrase used nowadays to refer to this trend is "going green."[24] Companies are increasingly seeking to develop and market environmentally friendly products.[25] Stakeholder groups (customers, shareholders, activists, and policymakers) are increasingly demanding improved environmental performance from firms globally.[26] As such, organizations are paying greater attention to the environmental impact of their business activities. This has led to calls for strategic leaders to formulate strategies that will help sustain the environment. Top management's active involvement and support are needed for environmental sustainability initiatives to succeed.[27] The extent to which firms are willing to compromise on short-term profit maximization for the larger good of society is directly tied to the vision and commitment of top management.[28] Environmental sustainability is a part of the broader concept of corporate social responsibility (CSR). CSR is about the ethical and discretionary responsibilities an organization owes its stakeholders.[29]

Being pro-environment is also financially good for business. It's called "green marketing" and more companies are doing well selling products that are environmentally friendly like cars (Tesla Motors and Toyota), packaging for consumer goods (Procter & Gamble and General Mills), and shoes (Nike). The importance of environmental sustainability can be seen in the growing number of higher education programs focused on sustainability.[30,31] In fact, there is now an Association for the Advancement of Sustainability in Higher Education. Although it is still the goal of strategic leaders to develop and grow their businesses, there is now talk of sustainable development—development that caters to the needs of today's generation without shortchanging the ability of future generations to meet their own needs.[32]

| Learning Outcome 1 | *Discuss the role of strategic leadership in the strategic management process.* |

Strategic Leadership and the Strategic Management Process

The link between leadership and strategy was firmly established in the early 1960s with the application of strategy to business planning. However, by the mid-1960s, there were attempts to separate the two as some dismissed the role of leadership in strategic planning in favor of objective analyses of the external environment that eliminated any need for leadership skills, judgment, values, or intuition.[33] Today, the reverse is taking place. More and more, there is the realization that leadership and the strategic management process are interconnected.[34] You need an experienced strategist to lead the process and when this has happened, the outcome has been positive for the organization.[35] The leader makes a difference by maintaining a strong sense of purpose, refocusing the organization when it starts to stray off track, and repositioning it when its original vision has run its course and a new vision is warranted.[36] We should note that the leader's role in leading the strategic management process applies to for-profit as well as not-for-profit organizations.[37] Some of the key questions requiring top management input and leadership during the strategic management process include the following:[38]

- What's our vision?
- What's our mission?
- What are our objectives—short and long term? Is there company-wide clarity about our objectives?
- Who is our customer(s) and what are their needs?
- Do we have a viable and competitive business model?
- What are the changes/trends taking place in our industry and broader environment and why?
- Do we understand where these changes will take the market (and us)?
- Who are our competitors (direct and indirect) and how do they rank against us?
- Do we understand our competitors' strategies? Can we find ways to outcompete them?
- What is our core strategy? Are we innovative and bold with our strategy? Are we taking appropriate risks? Do we understand what needs to be done and who will be accountable for specific parts of the plan?
- As we get to the execution phase of our strategy, do we have the right people to execute the strategy? Do we have the right kinds and level of resources to execute our strategy? What is our compensation structure? What are the performance targets for tracking success?[39]
- In terms of our positioning, how are we different? What's our culture and is it strong or weak?
- How does our overall strategic road map look? Do all the parts fit together? Will it satisfy our stakeholders? Are we on the right track to realizing our vision?
- What contingency plans do we have if the bets we make prove unsuccessful?[40]

Taking the leading role in addressing these and other questions is what strategic leadership is about.[41] Some describe it as strategic thinking.[42,43] These questions provide content for the strategic management framework, which consists of five key decision categories (see Exhibit 11.1): *Crafting a strategic vision and mission statement, setting objectives, strategy formulation, strategy execution, and strategy evaluation and control.*

An effective strategic leader seeks the participation of a broad coalition of employees throughout the strategic management process because followers who participate in the process take ownership in it and are more committed to its success.[44] We now turn our attention to the strategic management process.

Learning Outcome **2**   *Identify the five major decision categories in the strategic management process.*

The Strategic Management Process

The **strategic management process** consists of *the set of decisions and actions used to formulate and implement specific strategies that are aligned with the organization's capabilities and its environment, to achieve organizational goals.*[45] Formulating and executing strategy is the central theme of strategic leadership in any organization. How to perform this task proficiently is what distinguishes effective from ineffective strategic leaders.[46] As mentioned earlier, the strategic management process consists of five key decision areas: craft a strategic vision and mission statement, set objectives, formulate, execute, and evaluate and control strategy (see Exhibit 11.1). We examine each of these decision categories, focusing on the role of the strategic leader in bringing together everyone to participate in filling in the details and thus putting in place a strategic road map for the entire organization.

The Strategic Management Process

EXHIBIT 11.1

Step 1: Crafting a Strategic Vision and Mission Statement
- What is our long-term direction? (Where are we going and why?)
- What's our present business and purpose? (Who are we and what do we do?)
- Who is our customer(s) and what are their needs?
- Do we have a viable and competitive business model?
- What values and principles should govern our behavior?

Step 2: Setting Objectives
- What are our strategic and financial objectives/outcomes—short and long term? Is there company-wide clarity about our objectives?
- Does every department and manager understand what objectives/outcomes they are responsible for and their accountability?

Step 3: Strategy Formulation
- What are the changes/trends taking place in our industry and broader environment and why?
- Do we understand where these changes will take the market (and us)?
- Who are our competitors (direct and indirect) and how do they rank against us?
- Do we understand their strategies? Can we find ways to outcompete them?
- What is our core strategy? Are we innovative and bold with our strategy?
- Is it the right strategy for capturing emerging opportunities, meeting our customers' needs, and defending against our competitors? Are we taking appropriate risks?

Step 4: Strategy Execution
- As we get to the execution phase of our strategy, do we have the right people to execute the strategy? Do we have the right kinds and level of resources to execute our strategy? What is our compensation structure? Is there a strategy-resource fit? What are the performance targets for tracking success?

© Cengage Learning®

The Strategic Management Process (*continued*)

- In terms of our positioning, how are we different? What's our culture and is it strong or weak? Is there a strategy-culture fit? Do we have the appropriate structure for executing our strategy? Is there a strategy-structure fit?

Step 5: Strategy Evaluation & Control
- How does our overall strategic road map look? Do all the parts fit together? Will it satisfy our stakeholders? Are we on the right track to realizing our vision?
- How well did our strategy perform this quarter? Did we meet our quarterly milestones?
- What corrective actions do we need to take to address weaknesses in our strategy?

YOU Make the ETHICAL Call

11.1 *Strategic Leadership and Management*

An important part of strategic leadership and management is creating the business model of how the business competes. The University of Miami Online High School (UMOHS) is in partnership with the University of Miami. UMOHS is for young athletes and performers (grades 8–12) who are too busy to attend traditional classes; it gives them more time to train and to travel to compete/perform. It wants to become the establishment school in the sports and performing world. UMOHS also accepts international students who want an American diploma. Some argue that online high school deprives a child of a traditional education and prevents a kid from being a kid and enjoying childhood.

1. How do you feel about high school students enrolling in an online school and missing the experience of attending traditional classes? Do you agree with the mission of UMOHS?

2. Is it ethical and socially responsible to offer an online high school for athletes and performers?

Crafting a Vision and Mission Statement

Strategic leadership starts with communicating what direction the organization wants to go. It is generally believed that a leader's inspiring vision motivates followers to focus on reaching a desirable future state that is better than the present state.

A mission statement on the other hand specifies an organization's present purpose—its market niche (customers), product/service offerings, operating principles, and business model. So, a vision statement represents a future aspiration, whereas the mission statement represents the enduring purpose of the organization in the present. The job of strategic leadership is to ensure that the best vision and mission statements are put forth and that they are widely shared and embraced by members of the organization. Mission and vision statements provide identity and a road map of the future for an organization.[47]

Getting the behaviors of diverse workers to coalesce around a common purpose and future path is a major challenge for top management. The values espoused as part of the mission and vision can act as a powerful force in bringing people together to perform effectively.[48,49] So, let's focus on crafting a strategic vision, mission, and values statements.

Crafting a Strategic Vision

A **strategic vision** is defined as *an ambitious view of the future that everyone in the organization can believe in and that is not readily attainable, yet offers a future that is better in* *important ways than what now exists.*[50] It is important for the CEO to convey a vision of the organization's future and to do it in such a way that followers accept it as their vision as well.[51] The leader must have a clear idea of where he or she wants to take the organization and the strength to persist even in the face of setbacks and even failures.

John F. Kennedy demonstrated vision when he promised that an American would land on the moon during the 1960s, because at the time of his announcement, NASA was in its infancy and the state-of-the-art technology for space exploration was *Sputnik*.

To be motivating, a vision must be expressed in ideological terms, not just in economic terms, to help people develop a personal connection with the organization.

To be widely accepted, vision creation should be a shared experience. The role of the leader in bringing together all the key players to the visioning process is critical. To make a difference, a vision must be based on the input of employees representing different functional units or divisions and levels of the organizational hierarchy. Other stakeholder groups such as the shareholders, customers, suppliers, and the board of directors should also be represented. A well-crafted vision is one that is the result of a broad consensus. It should be simple enough to be understood, appealing enough to energize and garner commitment, and credible enough to be accepted as realistic and attainable. During a period of crisis or transformation, a vision statement helps to provide direction.[52]

Some examples of companies with simple, yet inspiring, vision statements include the following:

- Google: To organize the world's information and make it universally accessible and useful.
- Komatsu: "Encircle Caterpillar"
- Pepsi: "To put into action through programs and a focus on environmental stewardship, activities to benefit society, and a commitment to build shareholder value by making PepsiCo a truly sustainable company."
- American Express: "To be the world's most respected service brand"

Crafting a Mission Statement

A **mission statement** *is an enduring statement of purpose that distinguishes one organization from other similar enterprises.* It is the organization's core purpose and reason for existence.[53] It answers the question "What business are we in?"[54] It is in a company's mission statement that its business model (or at least part of it) is revealed. A business model specifies an organization's customer value proposition and its profit formula. In other words, what is the company proposing to offer its customers and can it earn a reasonable return or profit in the process? The customer value proposition doesn't just describe goods and services; it describes the broad needs (immediate and anticipated) of the people served by the organization's products or services. This is very much the purpose of the organization. The job of the strategic leader is to ensure that the company has a sound and sustainable business mission.

Examples abound of organizations that have been adversely affected by poorly crafted mission statements. The railroad industry almost brought about its own demise by defining its mission as being in the railroad business rather than the transportation business. The March of Dimes' original mission was "to cure polio," until a cure was discovered and the organization found itself without a purpose. Today, its mission is to advance human health.

The mission should be broad but not so broad that it does not distinguish the organization from its competitors. It should be specific but not so specific that it creates rigidity and resistance to new ideas.[55] It is generally believed that mission-driven organizations stand a better chance of succeeding and thus creating long-term shareholder value than those that are not mission driven. Studies that have examined the relationship between mission statements and performance found that organizations with well-crafted mission statements showed higher returns on certain financial measures than companies that did not have well-crafted mission statements.[56]

A well-crafted mission statement can provide other benefits to an organization, including providing direction and focus, forming the basis for objectives and strategies, inspiring positive emotions about the organization, ensuring unanimity of purpose, and helping resolve divergent views among managers.[57]

OPENING CASE Application

2. Critique Google's mission statement.

Google's mission *is to organize the world's information and make it universally accessible and useful.* It succinctly identifies Google's purpose. It focuses on the need (information) that Google's product/service (search engine technology) provides. It is neither too broad nor too narrow. Of the two components often featured in mission statements—core values and core purpose—Google's mission statement only identifies its core purpose; however, Google has a separate document called "Google's Code of Conduct" that identifies its core values. Overall, Google's mission statement is well designed.

Crafting a Values Statement

A **values statement** *is the set of beliefs, traits, and behavioral norms that management has determined should guide the pursuit of its vision and mission.*[58] Also known as *core values,* they outline the guiding principles and ethical standards by which company personnel will conduct business. Avon Corporation's five core values are trust, respect, belief, humility, and integrity. Strategic leaders who truly believe that core values should be practiced rather than just serve as window-dressing incorporate core values into the culture of the organization. They model the principles embodied in the core values and insist that everyone else does the same. The values are institutionalized and become the way of life in the organization.

Learning Outcome 3   *Explain the relationship between objectives and strategies.*

Setting Organizational Objectives

Objectives are the desired immediate and long-term outcomes that an organization seeks to achieve for its various stakeholders—employees, customers, shareholders, and others.[59] They represent a clear and unambiguous articulation of what the organization seeks to achieve.[60]

Companies develop both financial and strategic objectives. Financial objectives may include measures such as return on investment, sales, profits, earnings per share, or return on equity. Strategic goals may include acquiring new customers, opening new market, or creating new products. Meeting one's strategic objectives does contribute to the overall performance of a successful company.[61]

Commitment to organizational outcomes is achieved when there is broad participation in goal setting, and rewards are linked to goal achievement.[62] According to goal-setting theory, people with **s**pecific, **m**easurable, **a**chievable, **r**elevant, and **t**ime-specific goals perform better than those with vague goals (such as "do your best") or easily attained goals. Effective strategic leadership is about setting "SMART" goals. Refer to Chapter 3 for details on how to write good objectives (see Model 3.1 in Chapter 3).

Goals are essential because they help focus everyone in the same direction; they offer feedback on how well an organization's strategy is working; they create synergy; they are the means by which organizations reveal their priorities; and they are the basis for making corrective adjustments.[63]

OPENING CASE Application

3. How well do Google's long-term objectives balance the interests of its stakeholders?

Google's executive leadership team under CEO Larry Page believes that in the long term, Google's obligation is to maximize shareholder and customer value by providing the best user experience. Google is a company that has remained relentlessly focused on the end user by continuously improving on the quality of its search results. To accomplish this, Google has brought together a highly talented and motivated workforce. The media has regularly featured stories touting Google's generous incentives and compensation package for its employees. The focus on quality has brought in more users and consequently more advertising revenues and profits. Google's philanthropic causes include disease prediction and prevention and improvement of public services by informing and empowering people. These examples illustrate how stakeholder-centric Google is in its business strategy.

Learning Outcome 4 — *Describe the relevance of analyzing an organization's internal and external environment as part of strategy formulation.*

Strategy Formulation

Strategy formulation is about selecting appropriate strategies for achieving an organization's objectives. Therefore, strategies are the means to the ends (objectives). Simply put, a **strategy** *is an organization's chosen plan of action for outperforming its competitors and achieving superior outcomes.* Before formulating a core strategy, an organization must first complete an analysis of its environment, also called a situation analysis. Thus, let's start with a discussion of what it entails.

Environmental or Situation Analysis

A situation analysis focuses on an organization's internal environment (for its strengths and weaknesses) and its external environment (for opportunities and threats). The external environment focuses on the industry and general environments. They determine the attractiveness or unattractiveness of the industry or competitive environment. Awareness of the trends taking place in the economic, political, technological, sociocultural, industry and competitive sectors provides critical input for selecting an appropriate strategy or strategies. As one author puts it, every leader needs to cultivate a triad of awareness, in abundance and in the proper balance, because *a failure to focus inward leaves one rudderless, a failure to focus on others renders one clueless, and a failure to focus outward may cause one to be blindsided.*[64] A good strategist knows where the organization is headed (vision), knows what the competitors are doing or plan to do (competitor intelligence), and is aware and prepared for newly emerging opportunities and threats before competitors.

The combined analysis of the external and internal environment is commonly referred to as SWOT (strengths, weaknesses, opportunities, and threats) analysis. The effectiveness of an organization's strategies is influenced by the degree of fit or alignment between the organization's internal capabilities/resources (strengths) and its opportunities.[65] The outcome of an environmental analysis can also lead to a fine-turning of the strategic vision and long-term objectives.

OPENING CASE Application

4. Describe Google's business environment. How well is Google adapting to it?

Google operates in a high-tech environment, a sector that is undergoing significant transformations every day. The competition between Google, Facebook, Yahoo!, and Microsoft for supremacy is intense. The technologies for serving user needs in the industry are constantly changing. Major demographic changes are taking place among the user market. The world's economy is now one boundary-less global market with as much universality as diversity in customer needs. Google has adapted well to this turbulent business environment. Their focus on technological innovation and operating efficiency has created a search engine that is currently number one in its industry.

Selecting from Alternative Strategies

An organization's core strategy is the source of its competitive advantage and is how the organization differentiates itself from its competitors. There are three generic core strategies that strategic leaders can select from:[66]

- Broad or Niche Differentiation Strategy: Develop innovative products or exceptional services ahead of your competitors that are difficult to imitate or copy (think Apple, Google, Facebook, 3M, Nike, BMW, etc.).
- Broad or Niche Low-Cost Strategy (Operational efficiency): Gain a cost advantage through relentless attention to productivity improvement and cost management (think Wal-Mart, SW Airlines, Costco, Dollar General, etc.).
- Best-Cost or Value-Based Strategy: This strategy aims to satisfy the value-conscious customer who desires upscale products and services, though not as high as those of the differentiator and is willing a pay a little more than the low-cost providers are charging. It is called a hybrid strategy because it is positioned between the differentiation and low-cost provider strategies. The problem with trying to be great at two things at once is that your competitors who have pick one or the other will be better than you at each.

A strategic leader's decisions about what to invest in, what kind of people to hire, and what markets to pursue should determine what core strategy to select. Having more than one core strategy is common among large companies but for a small enterprise with limited resources, focusing on more than one core strategy may lead to resources getting diluted and competitive advantage diminished.

Accurate and timely interpretation of environmental trends plays a large part in the future actions and the continuing effectiveness of an organization's strategy. The importance of speed in recognizing and responding to environmental trends has been dramatically accentuated by the highly competitive landscape facing most organizations. As a result, some strategic leaders believe that it is much better to be a *first-mover* or *pioneer* and make mistakes occasionally than to be a *follower*.[67] In this type of turbulent business environment, the leader's ability to think quickly and navigate the unknown is critical.

WORK
Application **11-3**

Think of your college or university. Prepare a SWOT analysis that identifies one opportunity and one threat facing your institution in the next five years. Also identify a strength and a weakness that you think your institution has.

For the highly effective strategic leaders with good instincts, the more the uncertainty there is in the environment, the greater the opportunities to be exploited.[68]

Other related decisions involving core strategy include deciding whether to adopt a *defender, prospector, analyzer, or reactor* posture. Defenders seldom search for new opportunities. They are content with establishing a stable position in a limited operating domain and improving their cost competitiveness. In contrast, prospectors continuously search for market opportunities. They are constantly searching for new product markets and profit opportunities. Analyzers carefully deliberate and decide upon the optimum timing of investment to seize upon market opportunities using their existing technology. They are like prospectors but more deliberate in their approach. Reactors are those pursuing a late-follower strategy. They tend to delay actions until much later when they are convinced the strategy is working for others.[69]

Delivering value to the customer is the central premise of any strategy. **Customer value** *is the perceived benefits received to the perceived price paid by the customer.* At the end of the day, every strategy is designed to satisfy the needs or expectations of a firm's customers. Firms that meet or exceed the customer's expectations are the ones leading their competitors in the market place.

OPENING CASE Application

5. What type of strategy is Google pursuing, and why do you think the leadership team has chosen such a course rather than the alternatives?

Google is pursuing a differentiation strategy. It's all about innovation and new products/services for its users. It is evident from its actions in the market place that Google is a prospector not a defender or reactor. Google is actively pursuing merger and acquisition opportunities with other related businesses. This strategy is preferred because it allows Google to quickly adopt new technologies and processes rather than trying to develop them internally.

CONCEPT APPLICATION 11-1

Strategic Management Process

Match each statement to one of the strategic management concepts (a through h) below.

a. threat/opportunity   d. objective   g. core competency
b. vision   e. strategy   h. strength/weakness
c. mission   f. customer value

_____ 1. GM: To increase revenue by 10 percent from 2013 to 2014.

_____ 2. YMCA: We are the only child care provider to offer gym and swim classes as part of our programs.

_____ 3. Discover: Our small-business credit card is the only one that will give you 5 percent back on your office supplies and gas purchases.

_____ 4. Google: We are number 1 because we offer the best search engine for free to our users.

_____ 5. Motorola: The Apple iPhone is taking away our sales.

_____ 6. Microsoft: A personal computer on every desk in every home.

_____ 7. UVA's College at Wise: We educate students in spirit, mind, and body for leadership in service to humanity.

(continued)

CONCEPT APPLICATION 11-1

____ 8. Jiffy Lube: We have the lowest cost in the industry and this gives us the lowest price our services in the oil change market space.

____ 9. InBev: We are focused on developing unique, high-quality products that meet our customers' needs

____ 10. Avon Cosmetics: To give unlimited opportunity to women.

Strategy Execution

Strategy execution is the primary domain of operational leaders—those who are in charge of functional departments such as marketing, production, finance, human resources, and R&D. They provide the leadership necessary to convert plans into actions.

An excellent strategy that is poorly executed will yield the same poor results as a bad strategy.[70] Therefore, careful consideration must be paid not just to strategy formulation but to its implementation as well.[71] Strategy implementation takes place through the basic organizational architecture (structure, culture, policies, procedures, systems, incentives, and governance) that makes things happen. Strategy execution has been described as the most important and most difficult step of the strategic management process.

As mentioned, there are a number of factors that need to be present for strategy execution to progress successfully. They include having the right front-line leadership and skilled employees to execute the strategy, creating a strategy-supportive organizational structure, provide adequate resources and capabilities, institute the right policies and procedures, create appropriate reward and incentive package, adopt best practices, and instill a culture that supports good strategy execution. A few of these are highlighted below:

Strong Leadership and Competent Managers

Strong leadership is a critical requirement for successful strategy implementation. A strong leadership team and an abundance of skilled and well trained operational leaders/managers make a difference. An internal study at Google identified eight qualities of leaders/managers (listed in the order of importance) that contribute to successful strategy execution. They are:[72]

1. Be a good coach.
2. Empower your team and don't micromanage.
3. Express interest in your team members' success and well-being.
4. Be productive and results-oriented.
5. Be a good communicator and listen to your team.
6. Help your employees with career development.
7. Have a clear vision and strategy for the team.
8. Have technical skills so you can advise the team.

These qualities are not unique to Google. They are applicable to any organization that aims for effective strategy execution. Successful strategy execution requires galvanizing the organization's employees and managers at all levels to turn formulated strategies into action.

Appropriate Policies and Procedure

Policies provide guidance for employees in the workplace. The policies and procedures of an organization regulate behavior and help set the tone of the work climate. They contribute to an understanding of "how we do things around here" mentality. Policies and procedures insure consistency in how employees do their jobs because they standardize the way specific strategy-execution tasks are performed. This insures the quality and reliability of the strategy execution process.[73] With a new strategy, there is often a need to review existing policies and procedures to make sure they are supportive of the strategy.

Adequate Organizational Capabilities

Resources are the foundation of a company's capabilities and core competencies. Building a company's capabilities into core competencies and further into distinctive core competencies is a key responsibility of strategic leadership. Strategies that are based on a company's unique or distinctive core competencies are hard to copy and not easily substitutable, and as such have a better chance of sustaining the company's competitive advantage.[74] Therefore, a **distinctive core competence** *is a capability that allows an organization to perform extremely well in comparison to competitors and is the basis for a competitive advantage.*

WORK
Application **11-4**

Identify a core competence of an organization you work or worked for. Explain how it differentiates the organization from its competitors.

Arguably, the most distinctive and hard-to-imitate resource available to firms is knowledge, especially people-based knowledge. Unlike physical resources, which are depleted when used, core competencies increase (in terms of their efficient application) as they are used. Such employee-based competencies are what some have referred to as *human capital.* Human capital is among key organizational resources that are hard to imitate; therefore, maintaining and developing it is crucial for organizations to stay ahead of the competition.[75]

Another resource that can affect strategy execution is time. Time is of the essence in strategy execution. Being careful and rational during strategy formulation is important but not sufficient if managers are slow to initiate actions. Managers must avoid becoming trapped in the vicious cycle of rigidity and inaction that prevents them from acting in a timely fashion. We call it "paralysis by analysis."

Having the Right Corporate Culture

An organization's **culture** is *the aggregate of beliefs, norms, attitudes, values, assumptions, and ways of doing things that is shared by members of an organization and taught to new members.*[76] The shared actions and interactions of employees across functional boundaries help create an organizational identity that differentiates the organization from rivals. A supportive organizational culture enhances the success of strategy execution.[77] **Organizational identity** is *the members' consensual understanding of "who we are as an organization" that emerges from that which is central, distinctive, and enduring to the organization as a whole.* Organizations like Southwest Airlines, Nike, Walmart, Google, Facebook, and many others are well known for fostering an identity and culture that separates them from their competitors.

Appropriate Rewards and Incentives

An appropriate reward structure must go hand in hand with a new strategy. Rewards and incentives are powerful motivating tools that can greatly enhance strategy execution. Rewards and other forms of compensation must be aligned with the objectives that employees are seeking to accomplish. The right package of financial and nonfinancial incentives will drive up employee commitment, hard work, speed, quality, and satisfaction, leading to greater output and profitability.

Underlining the discussion of successful strategy execution is the concept of "strategic alignment" or "fit" with various components of a firm's strategic framework.[78] Let's illustrate with an example. A company pursuing a strategy of differentiation through innovation in a bureaucratic and hierarchical structure will be an example of a misalignment or lack of fit between strategy and structure. A strategy of differentiation works best with an adaptive or flexible structure. However, a company pursuing a strategy of operational efficiency and stability, aimed at offering customers lower prices than competitors (low-cost leadership), is more likely to succeed with this type of centralized hierarchical structure because of its strict controls on cost containment. Other strategic "fits" that can enhance firm performance are a strategy-culture fit, a strategy-capability fit, and a strategy-leadership fit.[79,80] Assessing the extent to which stated goals or expectations have been achieved or not achieved after implementation is strategy evaluation.

OPENING CASE Application

6. What are some of the factors contributing to Google's effective strategy execution?

Granting employees the freedom to implement strategy is one part of Google's people-management system. The other is to provide the employees with a hassle-free environment so that they can concentrate fully on work. In other words, the goal is to strip away everything that gets in the employees' way. The company provides a standard package of benefits to employees that it tops up with a seemingly endless and highly enviable array of perks—just about anything a hardworking employee might want to be taken care of while he/she is at work. In fact, employees don't even have to worry much about getting dressed up, as Google's corporate vision includes such axioms as "You can be serious without a suit." Leadership's policy of empowering and facilitating employees' work has led to a large number of innovations and, consequently, to the explosive growth of the company.

CONCEPT APPLICATION 11-2

Strategic Leadership

Identify in each statement if the view expressed is reflective of a strategic leader or operational leader/manager.

a. strategic leader   b. operational leader/manager

____ 11. My goal is to motivate and lead my team to meet our production quota every week and not worry about other departments.

____ 12. In our business, the environment changes very quickly. Therefore, we have to constantly monitor it for emerging opportunities and threats.

____ 13. It is my responsibility to ensure that we have the right strategy to achieve our long-term objectives and mission.

____ 14. I am concerned that our technology is not keeping up with the latest technological trends and our culture is not aligned with strategy.

____ 15. I am not worried about the future because our current portfolio of products is meeting our customers' present needs just fine.

____ 16. I get paid to deliver results today, not to worry about the future.

____ 17. My job is to motivate and challenge my team to meet our monthly targets.

____ 18. I worry if our strategy is bold and innovative relative to our competitors.

____ 19. We are not concerned about developing future capabilities and other resources that we don't not need today.

____ 20. I am responsible for setting the future direction for my company.

Learning Outcome **5** | *Explain the importance of strategy evaluation in the strategic management process.*

Strategy Evaluation and Control

Strategy evaluation and control is the last and final phase of the strategic management process. This phase compares actual results (outcomes) with expected results (stated objectives), which then provides feedback for necessary adjustments throughout the process. It is the primary means of determining the overall effectiveness or success of a strategy. Effective strategy evaluation is a three-step process: (1) reviewing internal and external factors that are the bases for the current strategy, (2) measuring actual performance against stated objectives, and (3) taking corrective action.[81] When step two reveals that actual performance did not meet expected or set targets, it is the responsibility of strategic and operational leaders to take corrective actions. Another tool used to measure the effectiveness of executed strategies is the balance scorecard. The balance scorecard evaluates the company's financial and strategic objectives.[82] Feedback from strategy evaluation should be shared throughout the organization and necessary changes acted upon. We now turn our attention to leading and managing change.

Leading Organizational Change

Rapid environmental changes are causing fundamental dislocations that are having a dramatic impact on organizations and presenting new opportunities and threats for leadership. Organizational or institutional change is an alteration of not only structures, systems, and processes but also a cognitive leadership reorientation. There is little doubt that implementing strategic change is an important responsibility of any strategic leader.[83] Leaders must be ready and able to make necessary changes when conditions warrant such actions. Successful implementation of strategic change can re-energize a business, whereas failure can lead to loss of confidence among employees.

Organizational change can be transformational or incremental, and sometimes an incremental change can amplify into a much larger and radical change than was first anticipated. A transformational change can be as radical as changing an organization's entire business model or as simple as changing a company policy. Our focus here is on organizational or institutional change—change that affects the entire organization.

Ultimately, organizational change is about changes in human behavior. It is about people doing things differently—for example, re-engineering business practices, learning new processes or systems, adopting new technologies, or acquiring new skills and capabilities. In this section, we discuss the need for organizational change, the role of strategic leaders in implementing change, the change management process, why people resist change, and strategies for minimizing resistance to change.

YOU Make the **ETHICAL** Call

11.2   Change through Upgrading

SAP is a leading software company in the world, headquartered in Germany. Fluor Corporation is one of the world's largest publicly owned engineering, procurement, construction, and maintenance services organizations.

Fluor and other businesses have accused SAP and other software companies of forcing them to upgrade their software. Fluor claims that SAP upgrades are often minor and not needed, yet Fluor is required to purchase the upgrades. In fact, Fluor dropped part of the products it had licensed from SAP and tried to take over its own software, hiring its own chief information officer (CIO) at a cost of about $13 million. However, SAP told Fluor that it would have to install a new version or pay even higher annual fees to get updates, fixes for bugs, and access to SAP's technicians.

1. Do you believe that companies come out with upgrades just to make more money (sometimes called planned obsolescence), or do you believe companies are being honestly innovative and customers are just resistant to change?

2. As a sales rep, would you push selling an upgrade to a customer who doesn't really need one so that you can make a commission?

3. What would you do if your boss pressured you to sell unneeded upgrades?

4. Is it ethical and socially responsible to "require" updates to continue using a product or service?

The Need for Organizational Change

A key first step in managing change is for the leader to identify and explain to followers the need for change.[84,85] The need for change may be triggered by weaknesses in an organization's internal environment or because of threats in its external environment.

Externally, threats in the form of direct competition from key rivals, new technologies and innovations that render a company's existing technologies or processes obsolete, weakness in the economy and consequent effects on an organization's performance, new regulations with strategic implications for an organization, or major changes in consumer attitudes and buying behavior that negatively affect demand for a company's products/ services. The need for change may also be triggered by emerging opportunities in the external environment that a company is not prepared or capable of exploiting.

Internally, the need for change may be triggered by a leadership change, such as when a long-time CEO retires and a new CEO is brought in or a current CEO is fired for poor performance. This in itself could then lead to many other internal change initiatives (such as in personnel, culture, or strategy) by the new CEO.[86,87] A company's internal assessment may also reveal weaknesses in its capabilities or competencies that need to be addressed.

It is the leader's responsibility to communicate the need for change, especially when the organization is in a crisis state. People need to know that change is needed—now—and why. The leader has to create a sense of urgency or what Edgar Schein—a leading scholar on change management—referred to as "survival anxiety." **Survival anxiety** *is the feeling that unless an organization makes a change, it is going to be out of business or fail to achieve some important goals.* However, Professor Schein cautions that even if survival anxiety increases acceptance of the need for change, another type of anxiety may be a counterforce creating resistance to change. Change often requires new skills, capabilities, and knowledge. According to Professor Schein, the prospect of learning something new creates "learning anxiety." Therefore, communicating the urgency for change is critical, but leaders have to also acknowledge the anxiety that learning new skills and technologies can create. Left unmanaged, learning anxiety can create strong resistance even when the need to survive is high. The next section examines the role of leadership in managing change.

The Role of Top Leaders in Managing Change

Studies on institutional change have stressed the role of change agents (leaders) in effectively managing the process, focusing on how they need to infuse new values, expectations, and beliefs into the organization's social structure. The top leader's role is to garner collective action in support of a change initiative.[88,89] It is one thing to talk about making a major change; it is quite another to actually execute it successfully. To insure successful change execution, effective leaders stay engaged and do things such as:

- Continuing to articulate a compelling reason for the change.
- Eliminate policies, procedures, and behaviors that undermine change efforts.
- Maintaining adequate human, financial and material resources.
- Forming a coalition of supporters and experts to counter any opposition.
- Celebrating milestones along the way.
- Staying the course in spite of perceived difficulties.
- Incentivizing workers with recognition and rewards.
- Keeping the process transparent.

Effective leaders are role models for change. A leader must embody the change that he or she wants to see in followers.[90] Gandhi put it best when he said "We must become the change we want to see." Effective change agents must be good listeners. Listening helps a leader have a better understanding of the root causes of resistance.

An organized and systematic change management process enhances the chances of successful change implementation and the likelihood that more people will support and commit to the change rather than resist it. The next section focuses on the change management process.

The Change Management Process

Not every change initiative succeeds. Some fail miserably. Employing the change management process is one way to mitigate the chances of failure. It requires moving through key steps and executing specific tasks at each step to achieve a desired end result.

One of the earliest and most widely used change management process theories is Kurt Lewin's classic theory of *planned change,* also known as the *force-field model of change.* The three steps in the force-field model of change are (1) "unfreezing" an existing state, (2) moving to a new and desirable state, and then (3) "refreezing" new state.[91,92]

> **Learning Outcome 6**
>
> *Describe the change management process using Kurt Lewin's force-field model of change.*

Step 1: Unfreeze

The earlier discussion on establishing the need for change is a major part of unfreezing the current state. The key here is to identify the threats facing the organization that call for an urgent need to change. It is important to invest the time at this early stage to explain not just the threat but also its root cause(s). When followers are not convinced of the need for change or don't understand it, there is a greater likelihood of resistance. Step two is the actual implementation of the change initiative.

Step 2: Change

This step is about execution of the change. The key is developing new attitudes, values, and behaviors that are aligned with the proposed change. People look to the leader for a plan of action. Some specific actions include forming a powerful coalition of supporters, consistently communicating the rationale for the change, empowering followers to act on it, insuring the availability of needed resources, celebrating short-term wins, and consolidating gains for greater change.

Step 3: Refreeze

For any change to become permanent and accepted into the everyday practices of an organization, the leader must follow through to the final stage of refreezing the new change. A variety of things can be done to achieve this including new norms, practices, traditions, regulations, and reward schemes to institutionalize the new changes and increase desired behaviors. This will prevent a reversion to the old ways post implementation. Complete transformation can only occur when the desired changes in behavior become habitual. As the saying goes, "old habits die hard." Resistance that may have been resolved during the changing phase can re-surface in the form of resentment toward those who supported and committed to the change.

Though the three steps in the change process generally overlap, each step is critical for success. An attempt to start the changing phase without first unfreezing old attitudes and behaviors is likely to meet with strong resistance. Not refreezing new attitudes and behaviors may result in the change being reversed soon after implementation. Understanding these steps is important for change-minded leaders, who must exercise good judgment throughout the process.

It should be noted that following these steps does not guarantee success; it only enhances the chances of success. It increases the likelihood that the majority of organizational members will commit to, rather than resist, the change. Even with the best change implementation efforts, a few people will always resist any change. However, it is generally the case that these holdouts tend to come around when confronted by fellow group members whose majority membership is committed to the change and also when the holdouts begin to see the positive effects of the change.

Learning Outcome 7 *Identify the major reasons for resisting change.*

Why People Resist Change

Although indispensable for long-term economic growth, organizational changes are frequently met with resistance. Change can disrupt the status quo and lead to stress, discomfort, and, for some, even dislocation. These negative outcomes often motivate people to resist change. Cultural inertia can also be a big factor. Cultural inertia is a rigid, outdated culture that works against anything new or different from the status quo. Whether it's because of personal factors or cultural inertia, resistance is a natural response by those who want to protect their self-interest in the organization. For these employees, change is perceived as a win–lose proposition. Change has to be perceived as a win–win proposition for both leaders and followers. Exhibit 11.2 summarizes some of the reasons why people resist change.

EXHIBIT 11.2

Reasons for Resisting Change

a. Threat to one's self-interest
b. Uncertainty
c. Lack of confidence that change will succeed
d. Lack of conviction that change is necessary
e. Distrust of leadership
f. Threat to Existing Cultural values
g. Fear of being manipulated

© Cengage Learning®

Threat to One's Self-Interest

An employee's self-interest in protecting his or her power, position, prestige, pay, and other company benefits is a major reason for opposing change. When an organization embarks on a major change, such as pursuing a new strategy, it often results in a shift in the relative power structure and the status of individuals and units within the organization. For example, changes in job design or technology may require knowledge and skills not currently possessed by employees. For these employees, the fear of losing their jobs or status is a major impetus for resisting change, regardless of the benefits to the organization. Fear of having to learn new skills and capabilities may create learning anxiety.

Uncertainty

Uncertainty represents a fear of the unknown. Lack of information about a change initiative creates a sense of uncertainty. When employees don't have full knowledge of how a proposed change will affect them, they are less likely to support the change and more likely to resist.

Lack of Confidence That Change Will Succeed

A proposed change may require such a radical transformation from the old ways of doing things that some will question its likelihood of succeeding. In this case, even though there may be a general acknowledgment of problems and the need for change, the lack of confidence that the change will succeed creates resistance. Also, if there have been instances of past failures, this may create cynicism and doubt for future change initiatives. This cynicism does affect employee attitudes and behavior toward any proposed change.[93]

Lack of Conviction That Change Is Necessary

People may resist change if the leader has failed to articulate a real need and urgency for change-described earlier as the unfreezing step in the change management process. This is especially true in cases where employees believe that the current strategy is working just fine and there is no need to change. It's that old adage of "if it's not broken, don't fix it."

Distrust of Leadership

Trust between parties is the basic requirement for sustaining any relationship. Change is resisted if people suspect that there are hidden consequences or motives that management is not revealing. Trust is a valuable currency for leaders to have, because it is the foundation upon which the benefits of a proposed change can be sold to employees who may suffer personal losses from such action. Employees may be skeptical of corporate change initiatives but are willing to put their trust in change proposals that are supported by influential peers or trusted leaders.

WORK Application **11-6**

Give an example of when you were resistant to change. Be sure to identify your resistance with one of the seven reasons in Exhibit 11.2.

Threat to Existing Cultural Values

When a proposed change threatens an organization's existing values, it ignites powerful feelings that fuel resistance to the change. Any proposed change must take into account its impact on the values of those who are affected by the change, especially values that are closely aligned with an entrenched organizational culture. If threatened, values that are aligned with an entrenched organizational culture will ignite resistance that is organization-wide rather than isolated.

Fear of Being Manipulated

When people perceive change as an attempt by management to manipulate them, they will resist. However, when people understand and accept the need for change and believe that they have a voice in determining how to implement the change, resistance is lessened.

In the end, leaders who regard resistance as a distraction rather than a real and legitimate concern will find it hard to move beyond the first step of the change management model. Effective leaders will not only follow the steps in the model but also employ the best strategies to minimize employee resistance.

OPENING CASE Application

7. Why have Page, Schmidt, and Brin encountered less resistance in bringing about changes at Google than most companies experience?

Google's leadership style and its culture have largely contributed to the lack of resistance. Though Eric Schmidt came from a corporate background, his leadership style had many things in common with the culture already created and put in place by the founders of Google. Since Page took over, not much has changed in the culture. At Google, there is a sense of "we are in this together." There is little in the way of corporate hierarchy, and everyone wears several hats. Everyone realizes that they are an important part of Google's success. Though growing rapidly, Google still maintains a small-company feel. At its headquarters, almost everyone eats in the Google café (known as "Charlie's Cafe"), sitting at whatever table has an opening and enjoying conversations with Googlers from different departments. Google's culture of transparency and open communication minimizes resistance to change initiatives.

CONCEPT APPLICATION 11-3

Resistance to Change

Using the letters "a" through "g" that accompany the reasons listed in Exhibit 11.2, identify which reason for resisting change explains each employee statement.

_____ 21. I'm not too sure about this new program. Is it really going to make a difference or just another fad?

_____ 22. Why should we adopt the culture of the company we are merging with? Their values and principles rub me the wrong way.

_____ 23. If we get these new machines, we will need fewer operators and there goes my job.

_____ 24. Why do we have to put in a new system when the current one is only a year old and is working fine?

_____ 25. How can management ask us to take a pay cut when they are the ones who are making all the money? We shouldn't let them take advantage of us.

Learning Outcome 8

Discuss some of the recommendations for minimizing resistance to change.

Minimizing Resistance to Change

Effective leaders do not downplay resistance or perceive it as a discipline problem to be dealt with through punishment or coercion. Turning resistance into positive momentum can focus the energy where it will do the most good. One way to do this is for leaders to become good listeners and be open to feedback from followers. People want to be heard when they express their feelings and they want validation. From this humanistic point of view, resistance to change is said to have a cognitive, emotional, and behavioral dimension.

From a cognitive perspective, there is a rational calculation from both sides (supporters and non-supporters) that change cannot occur unless the forces driving the need for change are stronger than the forces resisting it. When there is a concerted effort to increase the forces of resistance against the forces of support, resistance wins. This is why leaders should form a powerful coalition of supporters and experts during the early stages of the change process to counter the forces of resistance. From an emotional perspective, the fear of loss (status, position, job, pay, etc.) and fear of the unknown cause a lot of frustration and anger. Capitalizing on such anger can really heighten resistance. Resistance to change as a behavior focuses on the actions of members opposed to the change. Examples of such actions include sabotage and intentional work slowdowns. Effective leaders have to be aware of these behaviors and find ways to neutralize them before they become bigger problems

Effective communication before, during, and after a change has been implemented will prevent misunderstandings, false rumors, and conflict. It is important that those to be affected by change not learn about it from secondhand sources. Employees should be informed of *what* is changing, *why* it is changing, *who* is affected, *how* the change will affect individuals, and *when* the change will start and end. Another way to put this is for change agents to pay attention to the "5 Ps"—*purpose, priorities, people, process, and proof.* A stated purpose describes what is changing with specific targets identified and prioritized, people potentially affected by the change, a process that employs appropriate levels of participation and consultation, and proof that the change will accomplish its stated goals. Taking this approach can mitigate any attempts of sabotage or work slowdowns by those opposing change.

Ultimately it all comes down to creating an organizational climate that supports change and addresses the fears of those opposing it.[94] This involves leaders making process, policy, and structural changes in the organization. For example, adopting flatter, more agile structures or empowering teams/individuals to make decisions within stated guidelines are better ways of minimizing resistance to change. Although it is time-consuming, getting employees involved in designing change activities pays off in that it gives them a sense of control. Exhibit 11.3 presents recommendations that leaders can employ to minimize resistance to change.

Recommendations for Minimizing Resistance

◄ **EXHIBIT** (**11.3**

To minimize resistance to change, effective leaders:

- Show relentless support and unquestionable commitment to the change process.
- Communicate the need and the urgency for change to everyone.
- Maintain ongoing communication about the progress of change.
- Avoid micromanaging and empower people to implement the change.
- Ensure that change efforts are adequately staffed and funded.
- Anticipate and prepare people for the necessary adjustments that change will trigger. Provide career counseling and/or retraining.
- Create an organizational climate that supports change.

© Cengage Learning®

Now that you have learned about strategic leadership and change leadership, complete Self-Assessment 11-1 to determine how your personality affects your strategic planning and ability to change.

SELF-ASSESSMENT 11-2   Personality, Leadership, and Change

Strategic leadership is less based on personality than is charismatic or transformational leadership. Management level also has a lot to do with strategic planning and leadership, as it is primarily a function of top-level managers. Are you a strategic thinker with a focus on long term planning? Do you have any business or personal plans for three to five years from now, or do you take things as they come without planning for the future?

_____

_____

_____

Change leadership is based on the Big Five personality dimension of openness to experience. Charismatic, transformational, and strategic leadership all require being receptive to change and influencing others to change. Are you open to trying new things and to change, or do you tend to like the status quo and resist change? Do you attempt to influence others to try new things?

_____

_____

_____

"Take It To The Net". Access student resources at www.cengagebrain.com. Search for Lussier, Leadership 6e to find student study tools.

Chapter Summary

The chapter summary is organized to answer the eight learning outcomes for this chapter.

1 Discuss the role of strategic leadership in the strategic management process.

Strategic leaders establish organizational direction through vision and strategy. They lead the strategic management process by crafting a vision everyone can believe in and work toward. Strategic leaders encourage a team effort through the entire strategic management process, knowing when to be actively involved and when to simply facilitate. They understand that broad participation is key to success but that ultimate responsibility rest on them.

2 Identify the five major decision categories in the strategic management process.

The five key decision categories are: (1) craft a strategic vision and mission statement, (2) set strategic objectives, (3) formulate strategy or strategies, (4) execute strategy, and (5) evaluate and control strategy.

3 Explain the relationship between objectives and strategies.

Corporate objectives are the desired outcomes that an organization seeks to achieve for its various

stakeholders. Strategies are the means by which objectives will be realized. It is for this reason that the vision, mission, and objectives of an organization are established before the strategy formulation step in the strategic management process.

4 Describe the relevance of analyzing an organization's internal and external environment as part of strategy formulation.

The basic premise of an environmental (situation) analysis is that organizations need to formulate strategies to take advantage of external opportunities and to avoid or reduce the negative impact of external threats. Monitoring the industry and competitive environment presents emerging opportunities or threats that can influence the choice of strategies to pursue. Analyzing the internal environment focuses on assessing an organization's financial position, employee capabilities and core competencies, culture, and the organization's structure. This analysis reveals the organization's strengths and weaknesses. The combined analysis of the external and internal environment is commonly referred to as SWOT or situation analysis. The best strategies are those that rely on the organization's strengths to exploit opportunities and avert threats. A strategy that relies on the weaknesses of the organization for its execution is doomed to fail.

5 **Explain the importance of strategy evaluation in the strategic management process.**

Strategy evaluation involves three fundamental activities: (1) reviewing internal and external factors that are the bases for the current strategies, (2) measuring performance against stated objectives, and (3) taking corrective action. Corrective action utilizes the feedback that results from the strategy evaluation process.

6 **Describe the change management process using Kurt Lewin's force-field model of change.**

The force-field model proposes that the change process can be divided into three phases: unfreezing, changing, and refreezing. During the unfreezing phase, the leader establishes the need for change by communicating the problems associated with the current situation and presenting a vision of a better future. Awareness of the need for change and acceptance of a new direction sets the stage for the changing phase. It is during the second step that the proposed change is implemented. It is action oriented. The leader must empower followers to act on the change by giving them resources, information, and discretion to make decisions. The leader removes obstacles to change, which may include policies, procedures, and structures that are counterproductive to the change effort. The third phase, refreezing, involves institutionalizing the change so that it is not reversed soon

after implementation. Because of refreezing, old habits, values, customs, and attitudes are permanently replaced.

7 **Identify the major reasons for resisting change.**

Change is not a risk-free proposition. Change often brings with it pain and stress. Some people get demoted, reassigned, relocated, or even fired from their jobs. With all of these negative possibilities, the first reaction of most people is to resist any attempts at making a change. Some of the major reasons why people resist change are the threat to one's self-interest, lack of conviction that change is necessary, fear of being manipulated, threat to existing cultural values, lack of confidence that change will succeed, distrust of leadership, and uncertainty.

8 **Discuss some of the recommendations for minimizing resistance to change.**

To overcome resistance to change, effective leaders must do the following: Anticipate change and prepare people for the necessary adjustments that change will trigger, avoid micromanaging and empower people to implement the change, ensure that change efforts are adequately staffed and funded, communicate a strong message about the urgency for change, celebrate and maintain ongoing communication about the progress of change, and show a strong commitment to the change process.

Key Terms

change leadership, 418

distinctive core competence, 409

culture, 409

customer value, 407

mission statement, 403

organizational identity, 409

strategy, 405

strategic leadership, 418

strategic management process, 401

strategic vision, 402

survival anxiety, 412

values statement, 404

Review Questions

1 Discuss how an organization's objectives may affect its search for opportunities.

2 What are the key elements of the strategic management process?

3 What is the difference between a strategic vision and a mission statement?

4 The essence of the strategic management process is adapting to change. Discuss.

5 Describe the role of leadership in successful change implementation.

6 Why is organizational change often perceived as a win–lose proposition between leaders and followers?

Critical Thinking Questions

The following critical-thinking questions can be used for class discussion and/or as written assignments to develop communication skills. Be sure to give complete explanations for all questions.

1 What in your opinion, were the risks and benefits of the previous leadership arrangement at Google, where the two founders (Larry Page and Sergey Brin) elected to bring in Eric Schmidt to be the CEO while they functioned as presidents under him?

2 Comment on this statement: "Google is so successful it does not need to change anything in its strategic framework."

3 As leaders make strategic decisions, they must balance the interests of various stakeholders—employees, customers, shareholders, suppliers, unions/activists, and the community. Describe the best approach for doing this.

4 Many decisions made by strategic leaders benefit some people at the expense of others, thus raising ethical issues. Give specific examples for each of the following categories of unethical behavior:

- Breaking laws or evading regulations
- Legal but unethical behavior
- Acts of omission rather than commission

5 For CEOs and many other senior executives, strategic leadership is an important role they must perform well. Briefly describe some of the specific actions or responsibilities of the CEO that strategic leadership entails.

6 Resistance to change is more likely to succeed if the forces resisting the change are stronger than the forces driving the need for change. Describe some of the specific tactics that resisters could employ to thwart change efforts.

CASE

Nike in the Era of CEO Mark Parker

Behind a great company are strong leaders. This is certainly true for Nike and Mark Parker. Since assuming the role of CEO of Nike in 2006, Parker and his team have overhauled the way Nike runs, shifting the brand away from the previous sub-brand and product-based structure to a customer-driven structure. He has structured Nike into six "customer-focused" categories, such as running, basketball, and women's fitness. Parker has personally shaped Nike's innovation processes. Nike's mission is to bring inspiration and innovation to every athlete in the world.

Mark Parker took the helm of Nike at a time when the stakes in the U.S. athletic footwear market were particularly high, especially as Adidas was becoming more powerful with the acquisition of Reebok. Parker said at the time that he believed he was the right person to lead Nike through the challenges of the future. He said it was his job to help carry the torch into the future. He has always maintained that all Nike employees work for one boss—the consumer. Mark's greatest strength lies in his ability to synthesize the input of disparate influences, from lab engineers to downtown artists.[95] Nike's commitment to diversity is unmatched. Its Web site proudly proclaims, "Most companies embrace diversity. Not Nike. We soak it up. We squeeze it out. We want it to drip over everything Nike does." Nike's mission is to harness diversity and inclusion to inspire ideas and ignite innovation.

Commenting on his 30-year career at Nike, Mark Parker acknowledged that it has been a long time but quickly added that some things haven't changed. As he put it, "I think our success has been based on our commitment to innovation and great design, which really in our case starts with our commitment to the athlete—and really understanding the athlete and the insights we get from that relationship."[96]

Nike has what it calls "Nike Sustainable Business + Innovation" program. Nike believes it can use the power of its brand, the energy and passion of its people, and the scale of its business to create meaningful change. Nike believes the opportunity is greater than ever for sustainable principles and practices to deliver business returns and create a positive social and environmental impact in the world.[97]

Parker isn't an attention-seeking sort of CEO, so until now it has been hard to get a sense of him. But the imprint he is making as CEO is turning out to be as meaningful as his design

(continued)

work. Parker has reorganized the company into units based on particular sports, "a conscious decision to sharpen each piece of the business so we're not some big fat dumb company," he says; he reshuffled its regions to put new emphasis on China and Japan; streamlined the reporting process and removed regional middle management, and handled a rare round of layoffs.

Since his appointment in 2006, Nike has reached annual revenues of $24 billion, up 60 percent. "At Nike we run a complete offense, and it's based on a core commitment to innovation. That's how we stay opportunistic, serve the athlete, reward our shareholders, and continue to lead our industry," said Mark Parker. These statements in particular and the case in general are the essence of strategic leadership and the strategic management process as presented in this chapter.

GO TO THE INTERNET: (http://www.nike.com) Support your answers to the following questions with specific information from the case and text or with other information you get from the Web or other sources.

1. What external and internal pressures did Mark Parker face when he assumed the leadership of Nike, and how did he respond to these challenges?

2. Strategic management is about formulating strategies that align an organization's internal capabilities with external opportunities while avoiding or minimizing threats. How effective has Mark Parker been as a strategist so far?

3. What is the evidence that Mark Parker and Nike understand the impact of environmental sustainability on Nike's business practices?

4. An effective strategist develops strategies that (1) enhance value to its customers, (2) create synergistic opportunities, and (3) build on the company's core competencies. What evidence shows that Mark Parker is pursuing this course or shares this viewpoint?

CUMULATIVE CASE QUESTIONS

5. According to the Big Five Model of Personality, what traits would Mark Parker consider critical for his managers to possess (Chapter 2)?

6. Communication, coaching, and conflict management are said to be skills that have a direct and significant impact on a leader's career success (Chapter 6). Given the weak market and financial position that Nike was in prior to Mark Parker's appointment, how critical are these skills in his efforts to reposition the company and address its weaknesses?

CASE EXERCISE AND ROLE-PLAY

Preparation: Assume you are part of the leadership of an organization or organizational unit whose objective is to train the management team of its foreign subsidiary to embrace and practice diversity at the highest levels. Assume your parent company's diversity strategy is no different from Nike's. Under Mark Parker, Nike is leading the way in diversity. Nike's vision is for every team to be high performing, diverse, and inclusive. To achieve this vision, Nike's strategy is to:

- Cultivate diversity and inclusion to develop world-class, high-performing teams
- Ignite change and inspire critical conversations around diversity, inclusion, and innovation
- Create venues and environments for open dialogue, diverse opinions, and a multitude of perspectives

A multinational corporation like Nike wants to ensure that all its subsidiaries around the world have high diversity standards (visit Nike's Web site at **www.nike.com** for more information).

Your task is to help your foreign subsidiary develop diversity standards for its respective units that are in congruence with the overall diversity standards of the parent corporation.

In-Class Groups: Break into groups of four to six members. Select a spokesperson to record the diversity statement.

Role-Play: One person from each group at a time presents the group's crafted statement to the rest of the class. The statement is to be no more than 100 words. During and/or after the presentation, Nike representatives (played by other students) and/or committee members ask questions and make comments on each statement. Are the ideas in line with Nike's diversity vision? After the presentations and Q&A, the class then votes on who has the best diversity statement.

VIDEO ▶ CASE

Original Penguin Spreads Its Wings

Chris Kolbe is a master of change. Now president of Original Penguin, Kolbe essentially runs the division for its parent company, Perry Ellis International. Original Penguin was a 1950s icon—the penguin logo appeared on Munsingwear Penguin knit sport shirts for men. Eventually, its popularity faded, and Perry Ellis International later acquired the brand. Chris Kolbe was working in merchandising at retailer Urban Outfitters when he conceived the idea of rejuvenating the penguin—but with a new twist and for a new market. Starting with a few new shirts, which sold out almost immediately, the "new" Original Penguin began to grow, and Perry Ellis tapped Kolbe to complete the transformation as head of a new venture team. Kolbe recognizes that the fashion industry is a hotbed of change—and any clothing company that wants to survive must embrace innovation. He also understands that change takes time and patience.

1. Why has it been important for Perry Ellis International to give freedom to a new venture team to launch Original Penguin?

2. In what respects does Original Penguin represent a cultural change for Perry Ellis?

Developing Your Leadership Skills 11-1

Strategic Planning

Preparing for This Exercise

Think of a business that you would like to start someday. Develop a simple strategic plan for your proposed business by following steps 1 through 4 below. If you cannot think of a business you would like to start, select an existing business. Do not select a company if you are familiar with their strategic plan. What is the name and location of the business?

_____

1 What would be some of your strengths and weaknesses, opportunities and threats, compared to your competitors? It may be helpful to think about your answer to step 4 below before doing your SWOT analysis.

_____

_____

2 Develop a vision statement for your business.

_____

3 Develop a mission statement for your business.

_____

_____

4 As part of the strategy formulation, identify your core competencies. Be sure they answer the questions "What will your business do better or different than your competitors? and Why should someone do business with you rather than your competitors?" This stage is related to the SWOT analysis in step 1 above.

_____

_____

Doing This Exercise in Class

Objective

To develop a simple strategic plan for a business you would like to start someday

AACSB General Skills Area

The primary AACSB skills developed through this exercise are communication, using analytical thinking to select appropriate strategies—application of knowledge.

Procedure *(10–30 minutes)*

Option A: Break into groups of three to six and share your strategic plans. Offer each other suggestions for improvements.

Option B: Same as A, but select the best strategy from the group to be presented to the entire class. Each group's selected strategy is presented to the class.

Conclusion

The instructor may make concluding remarks.

Apply It *(2–4 minutes)* What did I learn from this exercise? How will I use this knowledge in the future?

_____

_____

_____

Sharing

In the group, or to the entire class, volunteers may give their answers to the "Apply It" questions.

Developing Your Leadership Skills 11-2

Planning a Change Using the Force-Field Model

Preparing This Exercise

Select a change at work or in your personal life that you would like to make, and develop a plan as follows.

1 Unfreezing. Briefly describe the change and why it is needed.

_____

_____

2 Changing. State the beginning-of-change date and end-of-change date. Develop a plan for making the change.

_____

_____

_____

_____

_____

3 Refreezing. Identify plans for maintaining the new change.

_____

_____

_____

Doing This Exercise in Class

Objective

To develop a personal plan for change

AACSB General Skills Area

The primary AACSB skills developed through this exercise are communication, analytical thinking and problem solving (i.e., implementing change).

Procedure (10–30 minutes)

Option A: Break into groups of three to six and share your change plans. Offer each other suggestions for improvements.

Option B: Same as A, but select the best plan from the group to be presented to the entire class. Each group's selected plan is presented to the class.

Conclusion

The instructor may make concluding remarks.

Apply It (2–4 minutes) What did I learn from this experience? How will I use this knowledge in the future? Relist your beginning and ending target dates for the change.

_____

_____

_____

Sharing

In the group, or to the entire class, volunteers may give their answers to the "Apply It" questions.

Developing Your Leadership Skills 11-3

Managing Change at Your College

Doing This Exercise in Class

Objective

To develop a large-scale plan for change

AACSB General Skills Area

The primary AACSB skills developed through this exercise are communication, analytical thinking, and problem solving (i.e., implementing change)

Procedures (10–30 minutes)

As an individual, group, or class, select a change you would like to see implemented at your college. Answer the following questions and conduct the force-field analysis.

1 State the change you want.

_____

2 Identify possible resistance to the change.

_____

_____

3 Select strategies for overcoming the resistance.

_____

_____

_____

4 Conduct a force-field analysis for the change. Below, write the present situation in the center and the forces that hinder the change and the forces that can help get the change implemented.

Hindering Forces   Present Situation   Driving Forces

Conclusion

The instructor may make concluding remarks.

Apply It *(2–4 minutes)* What did I learn from this experience? How will I use this knowledge in the future?

_____

_____

_____

Sharing

In the group, or to the entire class, volunteers may give their answers to the "Apply It" questions.

Endnotes

1. T. Mészáros, "Traditional and New Elements in Strategic Thinking," *International Journal of Management Cases* [serial online] 14(1) (2012, January): 134–152.

2. P. Schoemaker, S. Krupp, and S. Howland, "Strategic Leadership: The Essential Skills," *Harvard Business Review* [serial online] 91(1) (2013, January): 131–134.

3. H. Wang, D. Waldman, and H. Zhang, "Strategic Leadership across Cultures: Current Findings and Future Research Directions," *Journal of World Business* [serial online] 47(4) (2012, October): 571–580.

4. S. Dunn, and B. Avolio, "Monetizing Leadership Quality," *People & Strategy* [serial online] 36(1) (2013, January): 12.

5. P. Schoemaker, S. Krupp, and S. Howland, "Strategic Leadership: The Essential Skills," *Harvard Business Review* [serial online] 91(1) (2013, January): 131–134.

6. H. Wang, D. Waldman, and H. Zhang, "Strategic Leadership across Cultures: Current Findings and Future Research Directions," *Journal of World Business* [serial online] 47(4) (2012, October): 571–580.

7. S. Abdelgawad, S. Zahra, S. Svejenova, and H. Sapienza, "Strategic Leadership and Entrepreneurial Capability for Game Change," *Journal of Leadership & Organizational Studies* (Sage Publications Inc.) [serial online] 20(4) (2013, November): 394–407.

8. C. Brumm, and S. Drury, "Leadership That Empowers: How Strategic Planning Relates to Followership," *Engineering Management Journal* [serial online] 25(4) (2013, December): 17–32.

9. S. Abdelgawad, S. Zahra, S. Svejenova, and H. Sapienza, "Strategic Leadership and Entrepreneurial Capability for Game Change," *Journal of Leadership & Organizational Studies* (Sage Publications Inc.) [serial online] 20(4) (2013, November): 394–407.

10. P. Schoemaker, S. Krupp, and S. Howland, "Strategic Leadership: The Essential Skills," *Harvard Business Review* [serial online] 91(1) (2013, January): 131–134.

11. M. Salleh and D. Grunewald, "Organizational Leadership—The Strategic Role of the Chief Exec," *Journal of Leadership, Accountability & Ethics* [serial online] 10(5) (2013, December): 9–20.

12. M. Salleh and D. Grunewald, "Organizational Leadership—The Strategic Role of the Chief Exec," *Journal of Leadership, Accountability & Ethics* [serial online] 10(5) (2013, December): 9–20.

13. N. J. Emami, "The Short and Long-Run Impact of Globalization if Firms Differ in Factor Input Ratios," *Journal of Economic Dynamics & Control* [serial online] 38 (2014, January): 37–64.

14. L. Heng, J. Xu, Z. Jianqi, and Z. Xinglu, "Strategic Flexibility and International Venturing by Emerging Market Firms: The Moderating Effects of Institutional and Relational Factors," *Journal of International Marketing* [serial online] 21(2) (2013, June): 79–98.

15. E. Van Genderen, "The Trendy World in Which We Live: 'Flat', 'Spiky', or 'Wavy'?" *Middle East Journal of Business* [serial online] 8(1) (2013, January): 4–6.

16. T. L. Friedman, *The World Is Flat* (New York: Farrar, Strauss & Giroux, 2005).

17. L. Ramrattan and M. Szenberg, "A Generalized Model for Foreign Direct Investment Flows to All Countries," *Journal of Developing Areas* [serial online] 48(1) (2014, winter): 165–175.

18. M. Timmer, B. Los, R. Stehrer, and G. Vries, "Fragmentation, Incomes and Jobs: An Analysis of European Competitiveness," *Economic Policy* [serial online] 28(76) (2013, October): 613–661.

19. S. Khavul, M. Peterson, D. Mullens, and A. Rasheed, "Going Global with Innovations from Emerging Economies: Investment in Customer Support Capabilities Pays Off," *Journal of International Marketing* 18(4) (2010): 22–42.

20. A. Andenoro, "Introduction," *Journal of Leadership Studies* [serial online] 6(1) (2012, spring): 50–51.

21 A. Brown and D. Snower, "Skills Development: Rethinking the Future," *OECD Observer* [serial online] (290/291) (2012, May): 47–48.

22 E. Van der Heijden and E. Moxnes, "Leading by Example to Protect the Environment: Do the Costs of Leading Matter?" *Journal of Conflict Resolution* [serial online] 57(2) (2013, April): 307–326.

23 J. Robertson and J. Barling, "Greening Organizations through Leaders' Influence on Employees' Pro-Environmental Behaviors," *Journal of Organizational Behavior* [serial online] 34(2) (2013, February): 176–194.

24 J. Robertson and J. Barling, "Greening Organizations through Leaders' Influence on Employees' Pro-Environmental Behaviors," *Journal of Organizational Behavior* [serial online] 34(2) (2013, February): 176–194.

25 M. Pagell, F. Wiengarten, and B. Fynes, "Institutional Effects and the Decision to Make Environmental Investments," *International Journal of Production Research* [serial online] 51(2) (2013, January 15): 427–446.

26 Thompson, Peteraf, Gamble & Strickland, Crafting & Executing, *Strategy: The Quest for Competitive Advantage*, 19th ed. (New York: McGraw-Hill, 2014).

27 J. Robertson and J. Barling, "Greening Organizations through Leaders' Influence on Employees' Pro-Environmental Behaviors," *Journal of Organizational Behavior* [serial online] 34(2) (2013, February): 176–194.

28 Y. Nini, C. Colvin, and W. Yim-Yu, "Navigating Corporate Social Responsibility Components and Strategic Options: The IHR Perspective," *Academy of Strategic Management Journal* [serial online] 12(1) (2013, January): 39–58.

29 Thompson, Peteraf, Gamble & Strickland, and Crafting & Executing, *Strategy: The Quest for Competitive Advantage*, 19th ed. (New York: McGraw-Hill, 2014).

30 P. Shrivastava, "Pedagogy of Passion for Sustainability," *Academy of Management Learning & Education* 9(3) (2010): 443–455.

31 S. Benn and A. Martin, "Learning and Change for Sustainability Reconsidered: A Role for Boundary Objects," *Academy of Management Learning & Education* 9(3) (2010): 397–412.

32 M. Pagell, F. Wiengarten, and B. Fynes, "Institutional Effects and the Decision to Make Environmental Investments," *International Journal of Production Research* [serial online] 51(2) (2013, January 15): 427–446.

33 T. Marx, "Teaching Leadership and Strategy," *Business Education Innovation Journal* [serial online] 5(2) (2013, December): 12–19.

34 S. Kumar, V. Adhish, and N. Deoki, "Introduction to Strategic Management and Leadership for Health Professionals," *Indian Journal of Community Medicine* [serial online] 39(1) (2014, January): 13–16.

35 "Institute Hosts 2013 Leadership Academy Class," *Journal of Accountancy* [serial online] 216(6) (2013, December): 1–2.

36 B. Leavy, "Updating a Classic Formula for Strategic Success: Focus, Alignment, Repeatability and Leadership," *Strategy & Leadership* [serial online] 41(1) (2013, January): 18–28.

37 P. Markiewicz, "Methodical Aspects of Applying Strategy Map in an Organization," *Business, Management & Education / Verslas, Vadyba Ir Studijos* [serial online] 11(1) (2013, June): 153–167.

38 R. Olie, A. van Iterson, and Z. Simsek, "When Do CEOs versus Top Management Teams Matter in Explaining Strategic Decision-Making Processes?" *International Studies of Management & Organization* [serial online] 42(4) (2012, winter): 86–105.

39 A. Adams, "Mapping a Strategic Approach to HR Leadership," *Strategic HR Review* [serial online] 11(1) (2012, January): 31–36.

40 "Put Your Strategy to the Test," *Sunday Times* [serial online] (2013, September 29): 3.

41 M. Salleh and D. Grunewald, "Organizational Leadership— The Strategic Role of the Chief Exec," *Journal of Leadership, Accountability & Ethics* [serial online] 10(5) (2013, December): 9–20.

42 C. Markides, "Think Again: Fine-Tuning Your Strategic Thinking," *Business Strategy Review* [serial online] 23(4) (2012, winter): 80–85.

43 S. Krupp and S. Howland, "Strategic Leadership," *Leadership Excellence* [serial online] 30(5) (2013, May): 17.

44 C. Brumm, and S. Drury, "Leadership That Empowers: How Strategic Planning Relates to Followership," *Engineering Management Journal* [serial online] 25(4) (2013, December): 17–32.

45 P. Daewoo, R. Chinta, M. Lee, J. Turner, and L. Kilbourne, "Macro-Fit versus Micro-Fit of the Organization with Its Environment: Implications for Strategic Leadership," *International Journal of Management* 28(2) (2011): 488–492.

46 M. Salleh and D. Grunewald, "Organizational Leadership— The Strategic Role of the Chief Exec," *Journal of Leadership, Accountability & Ethics* [serial online] 10(5) (2013, December): 9–20.

47 A. Choudhary, "Mission 'Trust,'" *Academy of Strategic Management Journal* [serial online] 11(1) (2012, January): 101–113.

48 A. Choudhary, "Mission 'Trust,'" *Academy of Strategic Management Journal* [serial online] 11(1) (2012, January): 101–113.

49 "Mission, Vision, and Values Statements," *NAMTA Journal* [serial online] (2012, August 2): 85–106.

50 S. Kantabutra and G. Avery, "The Power of Vision: Statements That Resonate," *Journal of Business Strategy* 31(1) (2010): 37–45.

51 F. Slack, J. Orife, and F. Anderson, "Effects of Commitment to Corporate Vision on Employee Satisfaction with Their Organization: An Empirical Study in the United States," *International Journal of Management* 27(3) (2010): 421–436.

52 M. L. Kukkurainen, S. Tarja, R. Sirkku, H. Eeva, and K. Liisa, "Organizational Vision: Experience at the Unit Level," *Journal of Nursing Management* 20(7) (2012): 868–876.

53 D. King and C. M. K. Case, "2012 Mission Statements: A Ten Country Global Analysis," *Academy of Strategic Management Journal* [serial online] 12(1) (2013, January): 77–93.

54 I. Anitsal, M. Anitsal, and T. Girard, "Retail Mission Statements: Top 100 Global Retailers," *Academy of Strategic Management Journal* [serial online] 12(1) (2013, January): 1–20.

55 J. Rajasekar, "A Comparative Analysis of Mission Statement Content and Readability," *Journal of Management Policy & Practice* [serial online] 14(6) (2013, December): 131–147.

56 I. Anitsal, M. Anitsal, and T. Girard, "Retail Mission Statements: Top 100 Global Retailers," *Academy of Strategic Management Journal* [serial online] 12(1) (2013, January): 1–20.

57 D. King and C. M. K. Case, "2012 Mission Statements: A Ten Country Global Analysis," *Academy of Strategic Management Journal* [serial online] 12(1) (2013, January): 77–93.

58 Thompson, Peteraf, Gamble & Strickland, *Crafting & Executing, Strategy: The Quest for Competitive Advantage*, 19th ed. (New York: McGraw-Hill, 2014).

59 H. Sundin, M. Granlund, and D. Brown, "Balancing Multiple Competing Objectives with a Balanced Scorecard," *European Accounting Review* 19(2) (2010): 203–246.

60 D. Stacks and S. Bowen, "The Strategic Approach: Writing Measurable Objectives," *Public Relations Tactics* 18(5) (2011): 14.

61 F. Mitchell, L. Nielsen, H. Nørreklit, and L. Nørreklit, "Scoring Strategic Performance: A Pragmatic Constructivist Approach to Strategic Performance Measurement," *Journal of Management & Governance* [serial online] 17(1) (2013, February): 5–34.

62 N. Foss and S. Lindenberg, "Microfoundations for Strategy: A Goal-Framing Perspective on the Drivers of Value Creation," *Academy of Management Perspectives* [serial online] 27(2) (2013, May): 85–102.

63 N. Foss and S. Lindenberg, "Microfoundations for Strategy: A Goal-Framing Perspective on the Drivers of Value Creation," *Academy of Management Perspectives* [serial online] 27(2) (2013, May): 85–102.

64 D. Goleman, "The Focused Leader," (cover story). *Harvard Business Review* [serial online] 91(12) (2013, December): 50–60.

65 L. Pleshko and R. Heiens, "The Market Share Impact of the Fit between Market Leadership Efforts and Overall Strategic Aggressiveness," *Business & Economics Research Journal* [serial online] 3(3) (2012, July): 1–15.

66 Thompson, Peteraf, Gamble & Strickland, and Crafting & Executing, *Strategy: The Quest for Competitive Advantage*, 19th ed. (New York: McGraw-Hill, 2014).

67 Thompson, Peteraf, Gamble & Strickland, and Crafting & Executing, *Strategy: The Quest for Competitive Advantage*, 19th ed. (New York: McGraw-Hill, 2014).

68 P. Schoemaker, S. Krupp, and S. Howland, "Strategic Leadership: The Essential Skills," *Harvard Business Review* [serial online] 91(1) (2013, January): 131–134.

69 N. Shimizu and A. Tamura, "Connecting Capital Budgeting Practice with the Miles-Snow Strategic Type: A Novel Managerial Accounting Approach," *Global Conference on Business & Finance Proceedings* [serial online] 7(1) (2012, January): 45–56.

70 T. Poister, L. Edwards, O. Pasha, and J. Edwards, "Strategy Formulation and Performance," *Public Performance & Management Review* [serial online] 36(4) (2013, June): 585–615.

71 B. Ramaseshan, A. Ishak, and R. Kingshott, "Interactive Effects of Marketing Strategy Formulation and Implementation upon Firm Performance," *Journal of Marketing Management* [serial online] 29(11/12) (2013, August): 1224–1250.

72 http://iveybusinessjournal.com/topics/leadership/distributed-leadership-at-google-lessons-from-the-billion-dollar-brand#.UxfFLzYo5Vc

73 Thompson, Peteraf, Gamble & Strickland, and Crafting & Executing, *Strategy: The Quest for Competitive Advantage*, 19th ed. (New York: McGraw-Hill, 2014).

74 Thompson, Peteraf, Gamble & Strickland, and Crafting & Executing, *Strategy: The Quest for Competitive Advantage*, 19th ed. (New York: McGraw-Hill, 2014).

75 E. Ndinguri, L. Prieto, and K. Machtmes, "Human Capital Development Dynamics: The Knowledge Based Approach,"

Academy of Strategic Management Journal [serial online] 11(2) (2012, June): 121–136.

76 E. H. Schein, *Organizational Culture and Leadership*, 3rd ed. (San Francisco, CA: Jossey-Bass, 2004).

77 A. Toaldo, S. Didonet, and F. Luce, "The Influence of Innovative Organizational Culture on Marketing Strategy Formulation and Results," *Latin American Business Review* [serial online] 14(3/4) (2013, July): 251–269.

78 L. Pleshko and R. Heiens, "The Market Share Impact of the Fit between Market Leadership Efforts and Overall Strategic Aggressiveness," *Business & Economics Research Journal* [serial online] 3(3) (2012, July): 1–15.

79 L. Pleshko and R. Heiens, "The Market Share Impact of the Fit between Market Leadership Efforts and Overall Strategic Aggressiveness," *Business & Economics Research Journal* [serial online] 3(3) (2012, July): 1–15.

80 D. Blettner, F. Chaddad, and R. Bettis, "The CEO Performance Effect: Statistical Issues and a Complex Fit Perspective," *Strategic Management Journal* [serial online] 33(8) (2012, August): 986–999.

81 Thompson, Peteraf, Gamble & Strickland, Crafting & Executing, *Strategy: The Quest for Competitive Advantage*, 19th ed. (New York: McGraw-Hill, 2014).

82 P. Markiewicz, "Methodical Aspects of Applying Strategy Map in an Organization," *Business, Management & Education / Verslas, Vadyba Ir Studijos* [serial online] 11(1) (2013, June): 153–167.

83 A. Karaevli and E. Zajac, "When Do Outsider CEOs Generate Strategic Change? The Enabling Role of Corporate Stability," *Journal of Management Studies* [serial online] 50(7) (2013, November): 1267–1294.

84 P. Yeoh, "Internationalization and Performance Outcomes of Entrepreneurial Family SMEs: The Role of Outside CEOs, Technology Sourcing, and Innovation," *Thunderbird International Business Review* [serial online] 56(1) (2014, January): 77–96.

85 J. Younger, R. Sorensen, C. Cleemann, A. Younger, A. Freed, and S. Moller, "Accelerating Strategic Change through Action Learning," *Strategic HR Review* [serial online] 12(4) (2013, July): 177–184.

86 A. Karaevli and E. Zajac, "When Do Outsider CEOs Generate Strategic Change? The Enabling Role of Corporate Stability," *Journal of Management Studies* [serial online] 50(7) (2013, November): 1267–1294.

87 P. Yeoh, "Internationalization and Performance Outcomes of Entrepreneurial Family SMEs: The Role of Outside CEOs, Technology Sourcing, and Innovation," *Thunderbird International Business Review* [serial online] 56(1) (2014, January): 77–96.

88 A. Karaevli and E. Zajac, "When Do Outsider CEOs Generate Strategic Change? The Enabling Role of Corporate Stability," *Journal of Management Studies* [serial online] 50(7) (2013, November): 1267–1294.

89 P. Yeoh, "Internationalization and Performance Outcomes of Entrepreneurial Family SMEs: The Role of Outside CEOs, Technology Sourcing, and Innovation," *Thunderbird International Business Review* [serial online] 56(1) (2014, January): 77–96.

90 M. Shirey, "Strategic Leadership for Organizational Change. Executive Presence for Strategic Influence," *Journal of Nursing Administration* [serial online] 43(7/8) (2013, July): 373–376.

91 M. Shirey, "Strategic Leadership for Organizational Change. Lewin's Theory of Planned Change as a Strategic Resource," *Journal of Nursing Administration* [serial online] 43(2) (2013, February): 69–72.

92 E. H. Schein, "Kurt Lewin's Change Theory in the Field and in the Classroom: Notes Toward a Model of Managed Learning," www.a2zpsychology.com/articles/Kurt_Lewin's_Change_Theory.htm

93 K. DeCelles, P. Tesluk, and F. Taxman, "A Field Investigation of Multilevel Cynicism toward Change," *Organization Science* [serial online] 24(1) (2013, January): 154–171.

94 A. S. Lutz, J. Smith, and N. Da Silva, "Leadership Style in Relation to Organizational Change and Organizational Creativity: Perceptions from Nonprofit Organizational Members," *Nonprofit Management & Leadership* [serial online] 24(1) (2013, Fall): 23–42.

95 http://online.wsj.com/news/articles/SB10001424052702303376904579135802125126572.

96 http://www.fastcompany.com/3022912/bottom-line/nike-ceo-mark-parker-on-how-insight-and-innovation-intersect

97 www.nikemedia.com

Crisis Leadership and the Learning Organization

Learning Outcomes

After studying this chapter, you should be able to:

1 Explain why crisis leadership competency is an important consideration when hiring new leaders. p. 430

2 What are the benefits of having a crisis management plan in advance of a crisis? p. 432

3 Briefly describe the three stages of a crisis management plan. p. 433

4 Describe the role of top management during a crisis. p. 435

5 Describe the five-step process for crisis risk assessment. p. 437

6 Describe the importance of effective communication during a crisis. p. 440

7 Describe the key characteristics of a learning organization. p. 444

8 Distinguish between the traditional and the learning organization. p. 446

9 Describe the role of leadership in creating a learning organization culture. p. 449

OPENING CASE Application

Antonio Perez—Eastman Kodak

Antonio Perez, one of only seven Latino CEO's in Fortune 500 companies, took over as chairman and CEO of Eastman Kodak in 2005. Perez is an American, born in Spain. His father was a fisherman. From this humble beginning, Perez went on to graduate from college and start a career at Hewlett-Packard (HP), where he worked for 25 years before leaving to join Eastman Kodak in 2003. He was instrumental in transforming HP's inkjet printer business division from a money-losing to a money-making operation. HP increased its market share to over 60 percent around the world. Despite his accomplishments, Perez was passed over as a choice to the company's CEO position in 2003, so he resigned.

Kodak, the once-innovative digital giant with 17,000 patents worth between $2 and $3 billion, was on a fast slide downward. Its stock price, once worth around $25, had plunged to just cents to the dollar.[1] The company that gave birth to the first digital camera in 1975 was now being left behind in the digital revolution. Kodak had turned to a slow-moving bureaucratic company. It was losing ground to competitors like Sony, Nikon, Canon, and Olympus in the digital imaging business. These companies were much faster at innovating and responding to market demands.

On January 19, 2012, Perez announced that Eastman Kodak was filing for Chapter 11 bankruptcy protection. Along with this filing, Perez embarked on an aggressive restructuring strategy to cut cost while diversifying into new business sectors to increase revenues. Despite these actions, many investors believe Perez was not acting fast enough in his transformation plans. He was criticized for acting too slow in winding down operations and making the layoffs that the company needed to survive before it was in an unavoidable bankruptcy.[2] However, the board of directors thought differently. Perez, it said, will remain CEO for one year post-bankruptcy emergence, or until the post-emergence board of directors elects his successor, whichever is sooner.[3] Kodak emerged from bankruptcy and its restructuring on September 3, 2013.

Kodak is coming out of what has been one of the most trying periods in the company's history. It has transformed into a business-to-business company focused on imaging. It

describes itself as a company centered on disruptive technologies and breakthrough solutions for the product goods packaging, graphic communications, and functional printing industries.[4] As a result of Perez's reorganization strategy, Kodak today is leaner, financially stronger, and ready to grow. The stock price that once traded for just cents to the dollar is now back over $27 a share. It seems Perez is proving his critics wrong. For those who thought Perez was risking his own survival by taking a stake at Kodak's survival, time may prove them wrong. He would soon be leaving Kodak with his reputation intact.

OPENING CASE QUESTIONS:

1. Describe the nature of the crisis that Kodak has been going through since Perez took over as CEO in 2005?

2. In your opinion, could this crisis have been avoided?

3. How effective has CEO Perez been in managing the crisis so far?

4. In your opinion, has Mr. Perez been an effective communicator in the way he has handled the crisis?

5. What are some of the changes Mr. Perez has instituted to avoid a repeat of a similar crisis in the future?

6. Describe the threats facing Kodak in its external environment. Do these threats justify or go against adopting a learning organizational culture?

7. In your opinion, does Kodak represent the traditional organization or the learning organization?

8. What additional steps will you recommend that Antonio Perez take to make Kodak more of a learning organization?

Can you answer any of these questions? You'll find answers to these questions and learn more about Kodak and its leadership throughout the chapter.

To learn more about Eastman Kodak and Antonio Perez, visit Kodak's Web site at **http://www.kodak.com**.

A **crisis** is a low-probability but high-impact event that threatens the viability of an organization and is characterized by ambiguity of cause, effect, and means of resolution, as well as by a belief that decisions must be made swiftly.[5] Crises are omnipresent in today's environment.[6] A crisis by its very nature is an event that could not be predicted or anticipated prior to its occurrence. Therefore, avoidance is rarely possible. Crisis leadership is now an integral part of effective organizational leadership.[7]

Crises are indeed damaging to an organization if not properly managed.[8] A crisis that is mismanaged can damage an organization's reputation, personal careers, and diminish consumer confidence in the organization, and in some cases have led to its demise altogether.[9] Increasingly, organizations are investing significant resources in developing crises response plans.[10,11]

Crises come in many forms—natural disasters (the 2011 earthquake in Japan and subsequent nuclear accident), mass shootings (December 2012, Sandy Hook Elementary School in Newtown), product failures (GM's recall crisis of 2014), human error disasters (Bangladesh factory collapse in 2014 that killed 1,100 workers), and system failures (the disastrous debut of Healthcare.gov in 2013).[12] Also, many crises don't always make the front pages of newspapers or aren't featured in the TV news, such as sexual harassment, executive misconduct, sabotage, and succession crisis.

Regardless of the nature of the crises or the type of organization, what they all have in common is the stress and pressure they place on organizational resources and systems. Any weaknesses that may have been present in the system prior to a crisis are exposed. It is therefore imperative that organizations prepare their leaders on managing a crisis.

The most recent example of a corporate crisis involves General Motors. A House panel will investigate the response of General Motors and U.S. regulators to consumer complaints about ignition-switch failures that led to the recall of 1.6 million vehicles and are linked to at least 13 deaths. The issue is emerging as the first major test in crisis management for GM's chief executive officer Mary Barra, who was promoted to the position two weeks before an internal company decision on January 31, 2014, to do a recall. She is personally leading senior executives who are monitoring progress on the recall, which includes Chevrolet Cobalt and Pontiac G5 small cars.[13]

The first half of this chapter discusses crisis leadership. The second half of the chapter focuses on organizational learning and knowledge management. The learning organization is one that emphasizes creativity, innovation, and knowledge creation as a way of maintaining its competitive edge.

Learning Outcome 1

Explain why crisis leadership competency is an important consideration when hiring new leaders.

Crisis Leadership

Crisis leadership is about being prepared with a plan to follow when a crisis occurs. It is about the role of corporate leaders in **crisis** prevention and preparedness. Unfortunately, many leaders never think this is a critical part of their job until a crisis happens. These are the leaders who are surprised by events and become very reactive in their approach. They apply knee-jerk, shoot-from-the-hip solutions. According to experts in the field, effective crisis leadership is about having the foresight and proper pre-crisis planning for managing a crisis.[14] It is a proactive approach to crisis management.

Today, more than ever, there is a great need for leaders from all walks of life to show that they possess the skills and competence to lead during times of crisis.[15] Mismanaging a crisis has ended the careers of many executives. Proactive organizations have found it prudent to designate a specific individual or unit with the task of scanning and monitoring the internal and external environments for potential threats or warning signs of a crisis.[16]

In the event of a crisis, the leader must be visible, in control, and overseeing all aspects of the plan's execution. The ultimate responsibility of the crisis leader is to plan for a crisis and lead during a crisis. In planning for a crisis, the leader has to focus on five integrated tasks:

1. *Formulate an overarching vision of crisis management for the organization.*
2. *Establish strategic goals and program objectives for crisis management.*
3. *Coordinate the creation of a crisis management plan.*
4. *Establish a communication plan for notification and mobilization when needed.*
5. *Develop a pre-crisis simulation and drill plan for the crisis team and the entire organization.*

Leaders who develop proficiency in performing these tasks have a greater success rate at resolving crisis than those without these competencies.[17] It is worth noting that these five tasks are closely related to the tasks needed for successful strategic leadership of an organization that we outlined and discussed in Chapter 11. Therefore, top management or strategic leaders should require that crisis planning be incorporated into the strategic framework of their organizations. This would insure that crisis planning is an ongoing exercise and not a once-in-a-while practice.

These five tasks point to the *essential competencies* of crisis leaders, which are the ability to:

- *Craft a vision.*
- *Set objectives.*
- *Formulate, Execute, and Evaluate crisis plan.*
- *Communicate.*
- *Manage people.*

To be effective, a crisis leader must have the power, resources, position, and stature to influence events when a crisis erupts. For example, an organization must empower the crisis leader to make a critical decision such as shutting down a production line if a defect is suspected, or halting operations on an assembly line if multiple injuries or malfunctions have occurred. The ability of crisis leaders to grasp the impact of events in the early stages of development has helped some organizations avert a crisis and has even helped others turn would-be crises into opportunities.[18,19]

According to Warren Bennis, a well-known scholar in leadership research, crises are always crucibles of leadership in that sooner or later some transformative event or experience comes along that is central to finding one's voice, learning how to engage others through shared meaning, and acquiring other skills of leadership.[20]

Crisis leadership training and development programs should be available for leaders to learn and hone the competencies outlined above. Leaders who develop these competencies are more self-confident in their abilities to resolve any future crisis. The Three-Stage Crisis Management Plan (Exhibit 12.2) and Effective Crisis Communication (Exhibit 12.3), discussed later in the chapter are effective tools for crises leadership training.

Crisis Communication in the Age of Social Media

Advances in communications technologies now allow millions to analyze and critique virtually every aspect of an organization's response to a crisis—such as a violent act on the job, a major accident, or a product recall. *Technologies such as e-mail, Web pages, cable news, and social-networking sites (such Facebook, Twitter, YouTube, or Snapchat) are* weapons for affected organizations and the outside world to use during a crisis.[21] Social networks must be part of an integrated communication strategy that ensures that all affected parties are receiving a coherent and consistent message.[22]

A crisis is instantly visible and viral with the potential to inflict terminal damage on the affected organization. These technologies have diminished an organization's ability to control crisis communications by opening alternate channels that others can use to disseminate their views and build support.[23]

A company today may have only minutes, not hours, to contain a crisis. In many cases, there is a minute-by-minute real-time analysis of the financial implications of a crisis by investors, customers, and analysts, as Internet and cable television are linked with investment portfolios. Stakeholders may have more information at their fingertips about an ongoing crisis than the company. To stay ahead, effective leaders are incorporating crisis management into their strategic and operating plans and updating their skills in crisis leadership.[24]

Anticipating the kinds of crises that an organization can encounter is not an easy task for any leader. Literally thousands of incidents can turn into crises and handicap an organization's attempts to achieve its financial and strategic goals. The challenge is detecting the signals that warn of a crisis before it hits. Many organizations are presented with early warning signals of an impending crisis but fail to recognize and heed them like in the case of Kodak in the opening case. Therefore, the same degree of care invested in putting together a strategic plan for growth must be devoted to pre-crisis planning.

A crisis can present the opportunity for an organization to learn and adapt when the next crisis hits. Some leaders start paying attention to pre-crisis planning only after they encounter a crisis. Up until a crisis hits, it is an often neglected part of leadership in most organizations.[25] This approach is dangerous because there may not always be a second chance to learn from your mistakes. The next section discusses crisis management planning using the three-stage crisis planning model.

OPENING CASE Application

I. Describe the nature of the crisis that Kodak was in prior to Mr. Perez's appointment.

Eastman Kodak's problems did not start with the digital revolution. As one writer put it, "The company has been one of the longest drawn out train wrecks that has taken about 15 years to play out as the digital age destroyed its core markets."[26] For many years prior to Perez joining the company in 2003, Kodak had become a slow-moving bureaucratic company with a workforce that reached nearly 150,000 employees in 1998. It had been living off its patents and lawsuits against competitors for decades, burning cash, and not finding new ways to generate genuine earnings. Kodak's traditional business model did not move fast enough to confront fierce competition from companies like Sony, Nikon, Canon, Olympus, and other smaller manufacturers in the digital imaging business.

Learning Outcome ②   *Identify the benefits of having a crisis management plan in advance of a crisis.*

Formulating a Crisis Plan

Many people seldom contemplate the possibility that a fire, coworker violence, robbery, or natural disaster could occur where they work. The tendency is to develop a mental detachment from the issue—it happens to other people, not to me or our organization. Some leaders rationalize that the present systems are adequate to deal with such crises should they arise, whereas others find solace in the "positive thinking" (nothing bad will happen) approach. Denial of the occurrence of these low-probability, high-impact events makes thinking the unthinkable a major leadership challenge. Leaders who are able to overcome these psychological roadblocks and perceive risks realistically can approach crisis management planning in a logical and systematic way.

The literature suggests that organizations with early crisis identification systems and crisis management plans already in place before the occurrence of a crisis are significantly better prepared to manage and survive a crisis event. In addition, these better prepared organizations have the opportunity to reposition themselves and turn a crisis event into a strategic opportunity.[27] Therefore, an organization's readiness to respond to a crisis is a function of the following:

- The skills, abilities, and experience of a designated crisis leader
- A trained and well-prepared crisis team
- Organizational preparedness through regular drills and training
- Adequate organizational resources
- Top management support and commitment

Crises by nature are not part of the regular work experience; therefore, effectively managing crisis situations requires leaders to be well prepared for the unknown. There are benefits to putting a crisis plan in place.

The Benefits of a Crisis Plan

Though suffering some loss is almost unavoidable, having a crisis plan in the event of an actual crisis has several benefits. Having a crisis plan in place can: (a) reduce the duration of a crisis, (b) enhance or retain a corporation's image and reputation, (c) allow for quick and effective responses, (d) improve communications, (e) enhance coordination and cooperation, (f) ensure ready and available resources, (g) ensure fewer costly mistakes, (h) ensure less panic, (i) ensure quicker resolution of the crisis, and (j) limit or protect financial loss.

During a crisis, the leader is responsible for the safety and security of both employees and the organization. In the event of a crisis, the leader must be visible, in control, and overseeing all aspects of the plan's execution.

In the next section, we propose a three-stage crisis response plan for managing a crisis.

Learning Outcome **3** | *Briefly describe the three stages of crisis planning and management.*

The Three-Stage Crisis Management Plan

The three-stage crisis management plan consists of *pre-crisis planning, leading during a crisis, and adapting after a crisis* (see Exhibit 12.1).

Pre-Crisis Planning

Every organization (large, small, for-profit, or nonprofit) should have a pre-crisis plan. Although no one can develop a pre-crisis plan that would accurately anticipate and address every possibility in the future, such a plan is still the best way to mitigate the

EXHIBIT **12.1**

Three-Stage Crisis Management Plan

Pre-Crisis Planning
- Form Crisis Response Team
- Develop Crisis Plan

Leading during a Crisis
- The Role of Senior Leaders
- Effective Crisis Communication
- Crisis Resolution

Adapting after a Crisis
- Evaluation of Crisis Response
- Lessons Learned
- Preventing a Future Crisis

© Cengage Learning®

WORK
Application **12-1**

Find out if your college or university has a pre-crisis plan. If you find one, read and critique it for its effectiveness and present your findings to your classmates. If there is none, present an argument for having one.

negative consequences of any crisis. The message in pre-crisis planning is to *hope for the best and plan for the worst*. A pre-crisis plan enables leaders and their followers to make good decisions under the most difficult and unpleasant circumstances.[28] Pre-crisis planning addresses three key questions: (1) *Do we have a crisis response team and who is on it?* (2) *What is our crisis plan of action?* and (3) *Do we have all the necessary resources in place?*

On the first question, having a standing *crisis response team* increases an organization's ability to respond to a crisis in a timely and effective manner. A crisis response team should involve a good mix of representatives from all parts of the organization. Diversity in the makeup of the crisis response team increases diverse input that contributes to better decisions.[29]

In the event of a crisis, a leader wants a team that has trained and worked together.[30] Unfortunately, it is often the case that during a crisis, people who must work together have no history of doing so because they have never practiced or rehearsed the plan; thus, they have no understanding of each other's roles and responsibilities. During pre-crisis planning, questions on information flow and chains of command are addressed.

On the second question, *developing a crisis plan of action* involves imagining the worst possible scenarios that could happen to the organization and the impact on employees, customers, and other stakeholders. To be well prepared, the crisis plan must incorporate as many potential emergency situations as possible. The crisis leader and the team should then assess the risk of these potential events, and evaluate their possible ramifications. For each crisis scenario, the crisis team tries to imagine the responses of different stakeholder groups—this includes stockholders, customers, employees, activist groups, the media, and the community. Anticipating what each of these groups might need from the organization during a crisis enhances preparation and reduces the level of confusion, anxiety, and frustration that often ensues. We will discuss crisis scenario and risk assessment analysis in greater detail when we examine the five-step risk assessment model later in the chapter.

On the third question of *resources,* having the right quantity and quality of resources is critical for success. Both financial and non-financial resources are needed. It is often the case that during a crisis, resources (people, technology, and equipment) that are brought to bear may never have been deployed to see how well they function together. This underscores the importance of training and drills that simulate actual crisis situations or scenarios.

Another aspect of pre-crisis planning is deciding on the appropriate communications strategy when a crisis hits. Decisions on who will take charge of news conferences with the media and who will handle ongoing daily communications with outside groups are finalized. For example, while the CEO or some other designated senior executive handles major news conferences, public relations staff may field questions from other stakeholder groups and the legal staff responds to legal inquiries. A well-coordinated crisis communication plan helps avoid both the mistake of putting out mixed messages from multiple sources and potential power struggles over jurisdiction.[31] These problems affect crisis response effectiveness.[32]

In the event of a crisis, the pre-crisis plan is put into action. The crisis leader and his team have to step forward and manage the crisis effectively.

Learning Outcome 4   *Describe the role of top management during a crisis.*

WORK
Application **12-2**

Identify someone who has been or is part of a crisis prevention and management team, preferably someone on your campus's crisis prevention and management team. Ask him or her to describe the makeup and function of the team.

_____

_____

_____

Leading during a Crisis

When a crisis erupts, a rapid response is vital. The crisis leader must step forward and lead. The effective leader focuses on three key areas: *goals, people, and resources.* The *goals* define the "What"—that is, the specific outcomes and objectives of the crisis intervention. *People* define the "Who"—getting the right people in the right positions with the right teams.[33] *Resources* define the "how"—determining how resources will be allocated to the right people and how they will employ such resources. These are issues that should already be spelled out in the pre-crisis plan. The crisis leader should avoid the temptation of micromanaging or denying that there is a crisis. Some leaders go into denial about the urgency and severity of a crisis. This hampers an immediate and effective response to a crisis.

During a crisis, effective leaders employ a team effort. They take advantage of the crisis team. A team with a balance of complementary skills and talents can move quickly and effectively. Not only should a leader seek wise counsel from the team; he or she should also instill a sense of "togetherness" among all employees by allowing them to share their emotions and feelings with each other in group settings.[34] This is where pre-crisis planning and risk assessment pay big dividends. Effective leaders understand that their job during a crisis includes showing compassion for employees, customers, and other affected parties.

Within minutes of becoming aware that a crisis situation may exist, company officials must be prepared to issue an initial statement to the media and other key stakeholder groups—providing facts as they are known and an indication of when additional details will be made available. At the local, state, and federal level, government agencies are mandated to utilize Incident Command Systems (ICS) to structure on-scene response efforts.[35] The purpose of an immediate response on the part of the affected organization is to fill an information vacuum with facts and perspectives. Such quick action can help preserve the credibility and reputation of the organization and its leaders during the crisis. Experience has shown that the longer companies wait, the more likely the vacuum will be filled with inaccurate statements and outright misinformation that becomes accepted as truth.[36]

Effective leadership from the top is critical during a crisis.[37] During a crisis, employees will look to the CEO or other top management executives on how to cope with the situation.[38] Unfortunately, some senior leaders have been known to retreat behind closed doors when a crisis hits. They rely totally on the crisis leader or manager to handle the crisis. The crisis leader becomes the face of the organization as far as the media is concerned. This is a questionable approach at best. CEO or other top executives who dig deeper into their foxhole or adopt a bunker mentality during a crisis reminds us of the familiar tale of Nero playing the fiddle while Rome burned. A strategic leader's physical presence is a matter of moral importance even when it lacks immediate practical value. Being there conveys moral solidarity, commitment, and concern, apart from the leader's actual empathy or sensitivity.[39,40]

When all is said and done, there are three key principles of crisis leadership: (1) *stay engaged and lead from the front*, (2) *focus on the big picture and communicate the vision*, and (3) *work with the crisis management team*. The message of crisis leadership is to prepare for crises, respond quickly, act with integrity, and disclose fully. Another way of saying this is for the crisis leader to be mindful of the *"three As"—acknowledge, action*, and *avoid. Acknowledge* or admit the crisis, specify what *action* you are taking to contain or repair the damage, and tell the public what you are going to do to *avoid* a repeat in the future.

Adapting after a Crisis

An effective post-crisis evaluation can turn a negative event into a growth and learning experience.[41] Most forward-looking organizations do a postmortem. That is, in the aftermath of a crisis, top management authorizes a review (preferably conducted by an objective third party) of the organization's effectiveness in resolving the crisis. The whole purpose of the review is to determine which parts of the crisis response plan worked and which parts failed.[42]

The review should include performance indicators such as the following:

- Effectiveness in communicating with key stakeholder groups
- Effectiveness in addressing the root cause(s) of the crisis
- Crisis team effectiveness
- Leadership effectiveness
- Effectiveness in dealing with victims and family members

It is about looking beyond the present crisis and into the future. The information generated from the post-crisis evaluation can help prevent future crises or improve the effectiveness with which future crisis are handled. Actively communicating post-crisis evaluation information with key stakeholder groups can be very effective in protecting positive corporate reputation than a no-message or a justification strategy.[43]

Developing a crisis plan such as the one introduced above is a cross-functional activity that affects different departments and maybe even outside groups. It is a multifaceted

OPENING CASE Application

5. What are some of the changes Mr. Perez has instituted to avoid a repeat of a similar crisis in the future?

It was under Perez's leadership that Kodak began a massive, four-year restructuring that saw it shed thousands of jobs, demolish numerous buildings at Eastman Business Park, and sell off such business lines as health imaging. While in bankruptcy, Kodak has eliminated health care benefits for retirees and ended its digital camera and desktop inkjet printer lines. The decision to eliminate health care benefits for retirees resolved large, longstanding legacy liabilities that the company could no longer maintain. Through these actions, Kodak today is a leaner and financially stronger company, ready to grow.

activity that requires systemic thinking. A risk assessment model provides the best tool for developing a comprehensive crisis plan. So, the next section focuses on the five-step risk assessment model for developing crisis plans.

> **Learning Outcome 5** Describe the five-step process for crisis risk assessment.

The Five-Step Crisis Risk Assessment Model

The five-step crisis risk assessment model is a scenario analysis and planning tool that highlights different contingencies. It is the tool used to put together a crisis management action plan discussed earlier. For example, members may entertain questions such as "what could happen?" "where are we vulnerable?" "what is the worst-case scenario?" and "what are the short- and long- term outlooks?" The five-steps in the crisis risk assessment model are: (1) risk identification, (2) risk assessment and ranking, (3) risk reduction, (4) crisis prevention, and (5) crisis management. (See Exhibit 12.2.)

Five-Step Risk Crisis Assessment Model

EXHIBIT 12.2

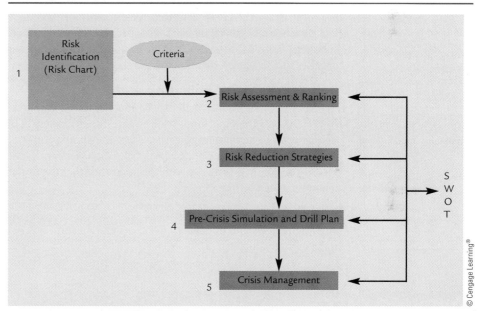

© Cengage Learning®

Step 1. Risk identification

Crisis team members begin pre-crisis planning by first identifying the worst-case incidents that could have severe consequences on people, the organization's financial position, or its image. It is a "what-if" scenario analysis that focuses on identifying realistic incidents under various crisis situations. This first step is akin to the analytical process of monitoring an organization's internal operations and core businesses to identify potential weaknesses/strengths and industry trends (to identify threats and opportunities) that could impact its business model. For the strategist, such an analysis is a form of crisis aversion.[44] This first step does result in the creation of a risk chart that features all the potential crisis incidents that could materialize and negatively impact the organization.

Step 2. Risk assessment and ranking

Next, these incidents are analyzed and ranked using criteria such as loss of life, injuries, emotional trauma, or minimal inconvenience for each incident's human impact. On the financial and image side, ranking criteria such as extraordinary impact (i.e., it will bankrupt the organization), serious but insured (i.e., we are covered), or small impact (i.e., nothing to worry about) may be employed. This information is then used as the basis for launching the third step, which is risk reduction.

Step 3. Risk reduction

During the risk reduction step, the crisis leader shares the risk chart with larger audiences, and they begin debating and formulating strategies for countering top-ranked potential crisis or threat. SWOT analysis comes into play as a tool in determining what resources and capabilities are available or needed to better manage each crisis. For instance, assume the organization is a chemical plant. An item on the risk chart may indicate the risk of a "poisonous gas leak" as a likely event. A SWOT analysis of this particular risk may progress as follows: The crisis team identifies strengths the organization has if such an incident should occur (such as scientists who have experience working with poison gas), weaknesses (such as the present lack of a poisonous gas leak response plan), opportunities (such as community support for the plant because of its economic impact on the area), and threats (such as environmentalists who are likely to protest and demand that the plant be closed). Based on this analysis, the crisis team may recommend a risk-reduction plan that calls on the organization to begin safety awareness programs and conduct joint meetings with local emergency response teams such as the hospital or fire department. The process is repeated for other risk scenarios identified on the chart.

Step 4. Pre-Crisis Simulation and Drill Plan

Pre-crisis simulations and drills are conducted to test employees' responsiveness. Again, SWOT analysis information is used to fine-tune this step. This step helps sensitize the organization to any potential crisis. After the simulations and drills and the resulting discussions, evaluations, and feedback from managers at all levels of the organization, the crisis team can then rest easy with the assurance that the organization is better prepared to handle such a crisis.

Step 5. Crisis management

Ongoing reviews and updates to the crisis plan become a regular part of doing business in the organization.

WORK
Application **12-4**

Using your college or university as a reference, identify five risk areas that could result in crisis if nothing is done now. Recommend a risk reduction plan or strategy that can help your school avert or deal with a crisis for one of these risk areas.

OPENING CASE Application

2. In your opinion, could the crisis at Kodak have been avoided?

The short answer is yes. Kodak's was a slow evolving crisis that previous leaders and the board failed to see until it was almost too late. Failure to restructure and diversify into new and attractive business sectors in a timely manner meant an over-reliance on an old business model that was no longer relevant for the technological revolution the industry was undergoing. It was a crisis brought on by a lack of leadership.

It is a fact of life that in spite of all the crisis-prevention planning that organizations undergo, sooner or later a crisis will emerge and an organization will have to deal with it.

Ultimately, the best gauge to determine an organization's readiness to respond to a crisis is how it rates according to the following five factors:[45]

1. Quality of crisis plan
2. Awareness and access to crisis management information
3. Readiness for an effective and timely response
4. Effective communication plan in place
5. Effective crisis leadership

As mentioned in step 4 and 5 of the crisis risk reduction model, unless the crisis response plan is rehearsed and practiced regularly, it becomes just another document collecting dust on the bookshelf.

How a company deals with a crisis from a communications standpoint can make or break it. The next section focuses on the importance of effective communication during a crisis.

YOU Make the **ETHICAL** Call

12.1 *Toyota Recall Crisis*

The Toyota recall crisis of 2010 prompted much criticism in media circles, national business forums, and automotive trade publications. The original complaint from some customers was that the brakes were failing and causing accidents. One such case was a driver on the freeway who had called 911 to report an ongoing crisis he was experiencing as his Toyota was not responding to repeated attempts to stop. Toyota did its own tests and kept saying that they had found nothing wrong with the brakes. At some point, as the media attention mounted, Toyota said they had concluded that the floor mats were causing the problem. Many lawsuits were filed against Toyota. Later, it was reported that the driver on the freeway had staged the supposed problem he was reporting about. There are those who think Toyota waited too long to take the complaints seriously and others who think it was unfair the way the American media targeted Toyota without waiting for the facts. It so happens that all this was happening at the same time that the American auto industry was going through its worst crisis. Some have speculated that the Toyota crisis did help the American auto manufacturers as many people switched from Toyota to American models.

A recent survey on this subject revealed the following: from a total of 109 participants that included 72 business college students and 37 adults from the local community, a majority (57 percent) of the sample felt that Toyota leadership's handling of the recall was somewhat disappointing or very poor. Moreover, few respondents (18 percent) had any confidence in the veracity of public statements from Toyota. With regard to ethics, 50 percent of the sample felt that Toyota's decision making is unethical to some degree. In addition, a majority (56 percent) expressed little faith in Toyota's transparency during this crisis. Noteworthy is that only 13 percent felt that Toyota would probably not regain its prominence in the auto sector.[46]

1. In your opinion, was the media coverage of the crisis fair and ethical?
2. What would you criticize of the survey results and the methodology for collecting the data?
3. If 50 percent of the sample felt that Toyota's decision making is unethical to some degree, why then is it that only 13 percent felt that Toyota would probably not regain its prominence in the auto sector?

OPENING CASE Application

3. How effective has CEO Perez been in managing the crisis he inherited?

The evidence so far indicates that Mr. Perez is successfully transforming Kodak. As a result of Perez's reorganization strategy, Kodak today is leaner, financially stronger, and ready to grow. The stock price that once traded for just cents to the dollar is now back over $27 a share.

Learning Outcome **6** | *Describe the importance of effective communication during a crisis.*

Effective Crisis Communication

Leaders must be able to communicate quickly and effectively during crises. It has become increasingly clear that opening communication lines with primary stakeholders—employees, customers, board members, the news media, and regulatory bodies—is critical for survival when a crisis hits. Four questions that often emerge after a crisis are: (1) *what happened?* (2) *how did it happen?* (3) *what's being done to address the crisis?* and (4) *what has been done to ensure it never happens again?* Providing honest, accurate, and timely answers to these questions is the essence of effective crisis communication.[49] The crisis response team must guard against releasing information too late or not countering rumors and myths in real time.[50]

Another potential problem with crisis communication is the seniority level of the person representing the organization. As mentioned before, it is important for the CEO or the most senior leader in the organization to show up rather than retreat to the background. The level of seniority demonstrates to the public the seriousness with which the incident is viewed. The organization does not want to send the message that it does not care or take the crisis seriously.[51] Leaders who retreat into their foxholes during a crisis are more likely to engage in a blame game—trying to assign responsibility and accountability to someone else.

Others, especially employees, can also play a critical role during crisis. To emotionally cope with a crisis, members of the community may need more than institutionally framed messages. They may seek information from employees or other sources. Therefore, well-informed employees can assist the organization in presenting accurate facts to the outside world on the current crisis.[52] They can only do this if they have been kept in the loop.

Internally, everyone should know what role(s) they would play in the event of a crisis and how communication will be handled within and between departments. There should be no power struggles over jurisdiction. It is important for everyone to be on the same page in communicating a unified message. Therefore, investing time and other resources in developing a comprehensive crisis communication system is necessary.[53]

Also, employees, even those at the lower levels of the organization, may have excellent insight on the incident and valuable suggestions on solution alternatives. Their immediate input may provide the pathway to a quick recovery. In the long term, this team approach will have won over the confidence, loyalty, and commitment of the employees who appreciate being included and listened to during the crisis. Employees' sense of belonging and self-worth is enhanced, and a culture of teamwork and cohesion is created. The post-crisis feeling of "we did it together" can carry over into other areas as the organization moves forward.

The literature is rich with several "dos" and "don'ts" when it comes to effective crisis communication. Some of these "dos" and "don'ts" are presented as part of the discussion on the guidelines to effective crisis communication. This is our next discussion.

OPENING CASE Application

4. In your opinion, has Mr. Perez been an effective communicator in the way he has handled the crisis?

Effective communication is the key. The CEO should be out there communicating the what, how, and when. People need to know the facts and what leadership is doing to address the crisis. On January 8, 2014, Perez—joined by customers and other Kodak leaders—rang the opening bell to kick off Kodak's new era and spotlight its return to NYSE. He is out communicating to key stakeholders (customers, employees, shareholders, and others) his vision and strategy for bringing Kodak out of its doldrums. His style of leadership and actions have endeared him to many including members of the Board of Directors who kept him on despite vocal calls for his removal.

Guidelines to Effective Crisis Communication

It is generally believed that the first 24 hours of a crisis are crucial because of the media's need to know what happened so they can tell their audiences. There is an information vacuum that, if left unfilled, will be filled by others. The longer organizations wait, the more likely falsehoods will become accepted as truths.[54] The key is to be open, straightforward, and transparent. Tell the truth and tell it quickly. Telling the truth up front is the simplest and most effective way of defusing public hostility, no matter how bad the incident.[55]

Rather than being preoccupied with protecting itself from liability, a company must demonstrate a strong sense of integrity, responsibility, and commitment. Getting out in front of the crisis with honest accounts of the facts and accepting responsibility will build confidence and credibility with all stakeholders.[56]

An organization can use a number of media and disclosure mechanisms to inform the public or tell its side of the story to weather the storm brought on by a crisis. These include press releases, press kits, news conferences, and one-on-one interviews with various media.[57] *A* **press release** *is a printed statement that describes how an organization is responding to a crisis and who is in charge.* A **press kit** *is a package of information about a company, including names and pictures of its executives, a fact sheet, and key milestones in the company's history.* In the event of a crisis, the last item included in the press kit is a specific press release related to the current incident. This package is ready for distribution to the media when a crisis breaks.

The public needs fast and accurate information so they are in the best possible position to cope with the shock of a crisis.[58] Telling what your organization is doing to address a crisis is especially important to family or close relatives of victims, especially a crisis that is the result of wrongdoing by an organization. These family members must be handled with utmost sensitivity. Leaders must avoid paternalistic attitudes that treat victims or the public as unintelligent or uninformed. The absence of genuine concern and empathy can lead to a perception of arrogance.[59] Exhibit 12.3 presents ten simple communication rules to remember during a crisis.

Effective Crisis Communication—Rules to Follow

EXHIBIT 12.3

a. Be present.

b. Don't "spin." Tell it like it is.

c. Communicate the plan of action for resolving the crisis.

d. Be sensitive with affected parties.

e. Avoid conflicting messages.

f. Show a plan for how you will avoid a repeat in the future.

g. Don't make excuses for yourself or the leader.

h. Go the extra mile. Go beyond the requirements of the situation.

i. When things are going good, take credit for it without being self-absorbed.

j. The media is your friend and link to the public. Be honest and straightforward with them.[60]

© Cengage Learning®

YOU Make the ETHICAL Call

12.2　*GM's Recall Crisis*

Refer to the discussion we presented at the beginning of this chapter on the GM recall. You can Google the topic for more information.

During a congressional hearing on the matter, Republicans and Democrats questioned GM's CEO Mary Barra on what she knew of the ignition problems, when she knew it, what she was doing so far to address the needs of those who have been hurt, and how she can prevent such a problem in the future. Many family members of the victims did not think she was being truthful. Some analysts thought her apologies went too far and may in the end jeopardize GM's legal defense case and expose it to higher levels of liability.

1. In your opinion, does the GM case have ethical implications and what are the ethical issues?

2. What is your opinion on the contrasting positions of family members of the victims and industry analysts regarding CEO Barra's public statements so far?

3. Based on what you have read on the media coverage of the crisis, how would you evaluate CEO Barra's communications strategy on the crisis so far?

4. In your opinion, will this issue be a major factor in investors' decision to buy or not buy GM's stock? Explain.

CONCEPT APPLICATION 12-1

Rules of Effective Crisis Communications

Using the letters a through j that accompany the guidelines in Exhibit 12.3, identify which guideline is explained by each statement below.

_____ 1. The public relations person addresses the media and says something that is later contradicted by the CEO in his own press conference.

_____ 2. After the Concorde crashed, the French authorities along with British Airways immediately grounded all Concorde flights until the designers came up with a fuel tank protection solution.

_____ 3. The accident happened because we relied on faulty instruments from our subcontractor who designed the part. Without their error, this would never have happened.

_____ 4. Family or close ones of victims, or those affected, are brought to a central location and provided with services such as counseling, support, and other facilities that might be needed to help them cope.

_____ 5. Information is held back or filtered to say only what the leaders or those in charge want you to know about a crisis.

_____ 6. The CEO of a company is on vacation when a crisis breaks out but refuses to cancel his vacation and return home to deal with the crisis.

_____ 7. The principal of a high school where a fatal shooting has just taken place appears before parents to explain what he and the security team are doing in response to the crisis. Many of the parents criticize him afterward for not having much to say about the incident.

_____ 8. Expect and treat victims and/or family members' emotional outbursts with empathy.

_____ 9. I don't like the press because they tend to overemphasize the negative as if we have never done anything good in this community. From now on, I will only tell them what they need to know.

_____ 10. After our post-crisis analysis, I realized that we did everything just right to address the crisis despite the criticisms that we received early on from some groups. It is a good thing we did not listen to them; after all what do they know about crisis management?

The Learning Organization and Knowledge Management

Today's organizations—large and small—are challenged by intense competitive pressure. Learning and knowledge management are widely seen as competencies able to support the management of complex situations in times of turbulence.[61] Organizational learning is the pathway to knowledge creation, and knowledge is seen as a strategic resource.[62]

Because of environmental complexities, organizations are increasingly dependent on innovation to create value for their customers. In a knowledge-based economy, learning and creativity are key to maintaining one's competitiveness.[63] For this to happen, leaders must develop knowledge-integration capabilities to dynamically coordinate and translate members' knowledge into higher performance.[64] The question for many leaders is how to continuously harness this human capacity for the growth and survival of the organization.[65]

In his book *The Fifth Discipline,* Peter Senge makes a compelling case that an organization's survival is linked to its ability to learn and adapt. He describes a learning organization as one that can develop not only new capabilities but also undergo a fundamental mind-set transformation.[66] To stay competitive, organizations must continuously innovate.

The responsibility of any organization desirous of change and innovation in a rapidly changing environment must be for its leaders to make it a priority to build and maintain a learning culture that engages employees in learning activities and that enables them to master new knowledge, skills, and abilities.[67]

In this section, we examine the concept of the learning organization, how a learning organization differs from a traditional organization, and the role of leadership in creating a learning organizational culture.

> Learning Outcome **7** *Describe the key characteristics of a learning organization.*

Learning Organization Characterisitcs

The learning organization describes a work environment with the following characteristics: (a) work patterns, structures, and routines are open to continuous adaptation and improvement, (b) everyone engages in continuous learning, (c) the culture is supportive of experimentation, creativity and innovation,[68] (d) knowledge creation and application is an imperative, and (e) decision making is informed by objective facts and analysis.

In rapidly changing environments, characterized by increasing globalization, intense competition, and continuous demographic and technological shifts, employee skills and abilities can quickly become obsolete and irrelevant. In this type of environment, there is increasing pressure on everyone to continuously upgrade their skills, abilities, and knowledge.[69] Learning organizations are constantly reinventing themselves so much so that the process itself is seen as a distinctive capability for those who do it exceptionally well.[70] For these organizations, change is a way of life. Employees who upgrade their skills package through continuous learning have better employment prospects than those who stick with their current knowledge base.

Organizations must learn to create and assimilate new knowledge at an increasing pace, share the knowledge, and learn to compete in new ways. This is more likely to happen in organizations that have adopted a learning organizational culture. A learning organization culture is one in which members have accepted and embraced continuous learning and knowledge creation as a way of life.[71,72] The results of one study showed a strong and statistically significant relationship between organizational learning culture and innovativeness.[73]

We define a **learning organization** as one that *is skilled at creating, acquiring, and transferring knowledge, and at modifying behavior to reflect new knowledge and insights.*[74] It is through learning that knowledge is created. In the past, organizations generally viewed learning as formal training programs that took place during specified periods of the year. However, many now recognize that learning should be an ongoing activity for every employee. Each assignment, job responsibility, temporary or permanent project, and other daily tasks are opportunities for expansive learning.[75]

Leaders, especially those in top positions, must create the type of environment that supports and nurtures collective learning (also known as organizational learning).[76] Only through learning do members acquire new knowledge and develop capabilities that result in new products/services.[77]

Organizational learning can occur from interactions that take place internally or externally. Externally, an organization can learn from its customers, suppliers, competitors, industry and academic publications, business partners, and consultants. Internally, organizations can learn from their employees. Every employee, especially those who work directly with customers, is a great source of new ideas.[78]

What Is Knowledge Management?

Creating, storing, and leveraging knowledge are integral to knowledge management processes.[79] **Organizational knowledge** *is the tacit and explicit know-how that individuals possess about products, services, systems, and processes.* Explicit or formal knowledge is expressed in a system of rules and is easily communicated and shared. It is often codified in manuals, databases, and information systems.

Tacit or informal knowledge is highly personal, difficult to communicate, strongly rooted in action, and highly contextual in nature. Unlike explicit knowledge, such as the design of a product or the description of a business process, tacit knowledge is the instinct and intuition that an experienced practitioner possesses.[80]

Organizational knowledge has been referred to as *intellectual or human capital* and is seen as a competitive asset for sustaining one's advantage in today's marketplace. Human capital is among key organizational resources that are hard to imitate; therefore, maintaining and developing it is crucial for organizations to stay competitive.[81] Superior performance is achieved when newly acquired knowledge is disseminated and integrated with existing knowledge and applied to solve problems. Therefore, the tendency by some to hide new knowledge from coworkers is counterproductive and creates other problems. The findings of one study revealed that when employees hide knowledge, they trigger a reciprocal distrust loop in which coworkers are unwilling to share knowledge with them and everyone suffers.[82] Organizations must invest in human capital development approaches that lead to knowledge creation and application.[83]

OPENING CASE Application

6. **Describe the threats facing Kodak in its external environment. Do these threats support or go against adopting a learning organizational culture?**

Kodak, like many other multinational corporations, is facing major threats from the technological, economic, and competitive environments. Kodak's industry is undergoing a digital revolution. As a result, the company is losing ground to competitors like Sony, Nikon, Canon, Olympus, and other smaller manufacturers in the digital imaging business who were much faster at innovating and responding to market demands. Mr. Perez attributed part of Kodak's economic decline to the weak economy. Today, Kodak describes itself as a company centered on disruptive technologies and breakthrough solutions—a clear indication that the company is returning to its roots as a learning or knowledge-based enterprise.

Before we get into the details of the learning organization and how it differs from the traditional organization, complete Self-Assessment 12-1.

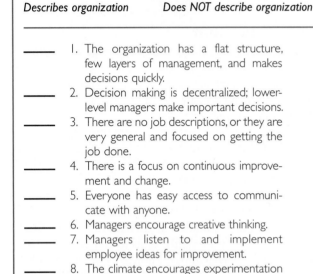

Learning Outcome 8   *Distinguish between the traditional and the learning organization.*

Traditional versus the Learning Organization

By all accounts, most organizations today operate in environments characterized by continuous change, and for some—like the bio- and high-tech companies—the level of change is discontinuous. **Discontinuous change** *occurs when anticipated or expected changes bear no resemblance to the present or the past.* In this type of environment, learning and innovation are critical.[84] In what used to be called stable environments, organizations focused on being efficient through highly structured command systems with strong vertical hierarchies and specialized jobs. However, given the realities of the current dynamic environment facing just about every industry, this traditional organization form is being replaced by the learning organization form. See Exhibit 12.4 for a comparison of the two organization types.

EXHIBIT 12.4

Key Differences between the Traditional and the Learning Organization

Traditional (efficiency driven)	Learning (innovation driven)
• Stable environment	• Changing environment
• Vertical bureaucratic structure	• Flat and flexible structure
• Strategy formulation is top-down	• Strategy formulation is collaborative
• Centralized decision making	• Decentralized decision making
• Rigidly defined and specialized tasks	• Loose, flexible, and adaptive roles
• Rigid organizational culture	• Adaptive organizational culture
• Top-down communication model	• Open, two-way communication model

© Cengage Learning®

Characteristics of the Traditional Organization

The traditional organization is based on the bureaucratic model that emphasizes a command-and-control structure, centralized decision making, highly formalized systems, and specialized tasks. These vertical bureaucratic structures are effective under stable environmental conditions where the pace of change is slow or incremental at best.

More often than not, the culture of the traditional organization is rigid and resistant to change. There is less openness and sharing of ideas. Rewards and other incentives are individualized. This fosters competition and less collaboration among individuals.

The mind-set of leaders in the traditional organization is that there is a "right way" to do things and a wrong way. There is an elaborate formal system of reporting that allows leaders to closely monitor work operations that are rigidly defined and specialized. This formal system is a powerful tool for controlling information and often acts as a filter in determining what information leaders pass down to lower-level employees. Because the traditional organization is efficiency driven, deviating from standard operating procedures is frowned upon and mistakes are punished. Therefore, employees don't take chances, and mistakes and problems are hidden.

Characteristics of the Learning Organization

The learning organization culture is open, adaptive, and innovation-driven. [85] In learning organizations, the vertical structure is abandoned for a flat and flexible structure. Flat and flexible structures are set up for greater participation and less bureaucratic red tape in decision making. Strategy formulation in these organizations is a collaborative process. This, in turn, leads to greater input and better decisions in the strategy-making process. [86]

Interdisciplinary teams and network systems are highly valued tools in learning organizations. [87] Network systems facilitate open communication and exchange throughout the organization and with other external entities. Networks that connect teams provide access to knowledge, resources, markets, and technologies. [88]

To encourage innovation and creativity in meeting current challenges, learning organizations are putting fewer restrictions on how things should be done. Responsibility and authority are decentralized to lower-level workers, empowering them to think, debate, create, learn, and solve problems at their level. [89]

A learning organization culture encourages individual, group, and organizational levels of analysis. [90] It involves multiple learning processes (experimentation, analysis, intuition, serendipity, or integration). There is a recognition that learning should flow

WORK
Application **12-5**

Explain whether where you work or have worked is more of a traditional organization or a learning organization. Identify some of the characteristics of the organization to justify your response.

forward (from those at the bottom to the top) and flow backward (from the top to those at the bottom). Learning is a *multilevel, organization-wide process*. The most successful learning organizations compound their learning advantage by encouraging employees at all levels to collect and share information across boundaries rather than hoarding it.[91] The infrastructure for these types of exchanges are communication and information hubs that facilitate the flow and exchange of information.

The learning organization takes the view that people will learn if encouraged to be creative, to experiment, and to reflect on their experiences.[92,93] Creating a sense of collective ownership of the learning process can be an important motivational force. In learning organizations, there is acknowledgement that people learn more from their mistakes than successes. This is supported by research findings that knowledge acquired through failure tends to depreciate slowly than knowledge acquired from successes.[94] Thus, failure does not draw the same negative reactions like in traditional organizations.

Examples of learning organizations today include Google, Facebook, Apple, Toyota, W. L. Gore & Associates, Xerox, 3M, Johnson & Johnson, Procter & Gamble, and many others. These companies are finding that success is more about nurturing the imagination, creativity, and passion of employees to solve customer problems than focusing on costs and profits.

OPENING CASE Application

7. In your opinion, does Kodak represent the traditional organization or the learning organization?

The company that gave birth to the first digital camera in 1975 was now being left behind in the digital revolution. Kodak had turned into a slow-moving bureaucratic company. Coming out of what has been one of the most trying periods in the company's history, Kodak has transformed into a business-to-business (B2B) company focused on its imaging business. Today, it describes itself as a company centered on disruptive technologies and breakthrough solutions. It is apparent that Kodak is returning to its roots as a learning organization.

CONCEPT APPLICATION 12-2

Differentiating between the traditional and learning organization

Identify each statement by the type of organization it illustrates. Write the appropriate letter in the blank before each item.

a. traditional
b. learning

_____ 11. In our organization, employees are encouraged to experiment and take risk without fear of punishment when they fail.

_____ 12. Top-level managers make all the important decisions around here.

_____ 13. Our organization's structure can be described as flat or horizontal with much decision-making responsibility delegated downward.

_____ 14. With a union, we have clearly defined jobs and are not allowed to do other work.

_____ 15. There aren't many levels of management in our company.

The Learning Organization Culture and Firm Performance

It is believed that a learning organization is more likely to develop and sustain its competitiveness because human capital assets are less substitutable and difficult to duplicate than other assets.[95] Increasingly, researchers are finding that the higher the level of learning and knowledge creation, the greater the level of firm financial and non-financial performance.[96] Here are a few examples:

- Studies investigating the relationship between knowledge creation and value creation found that a firm's ability to create and share knowledge is positively related to new product development success.
- Productivity and profits increase in organizations that embrace a learning culture.
- Organizational learning cultures have been found to have a positive and direct influence on a team's creativity and its collaborative knowledge creation practices.[97,98,99,100]
- Organizational learning and knowledge creation have a direct positive influence on the level of creativity and innovation.[101,102]
- The learning organization culture has been shown to have a direct positive impact on employee, customer, and supplier satisfaction levels.[103]
- The learning organization culture displays significantly higher levels of organizational citizenship behavior, knowledge-sharing intention, interpersonal trust, and organizational commitment amongst employees.[104]

Learning Outcome 9   *Describe the role of leadership in creating a learning organization culture.*

The Role of Leaders in Creating a Learning Organization Culture

Leaders are seen as the inspirational force behind employee engagement in learning activities that result in new knowledge.[105,106] On the flip side, leader behavior can also impede follower creativity and innovative behavior.[107] The learning organization is driven to innovate.

Leaders in learning organizations face a dual challenge to maintain efficient operations and create a flexible and adaptive organization at the same time.[108] For example, leaders have to balance the need to encouraging creativity and flexibility versus emphasizing efficiency and strict controls.[109] Exhibit 12.5 presents recommendations that leaders can employ to create conditions conducive to learning and knowledge creation.

Fostering a Learning Organizational Culture

EXHIBIT 12.5

- Encourage creative thinking.
- Create a climate where risk taking and failure are tolerated.
- Provide incentives for learning and innovation.
- Build confidence in followers' capacity to learn and adapt.
- Encourage systems thinking.
- Institute mechanisms for channeling and nurturing creative ideas for innovation.
- Create a shared vision for learning.
- Broaden employees' frame of reference.

© Cengage Learning®

Encourage Creative Thinking

Creative thinking can occur at the individual, group, and organizational level. At the individual level, leaders can enhance learning by encouraging members to "think outside the box"—in other words, consider possibilities that do not already exist. Rather than responding to known challenges, employees are encouraged to create the future.[110] People who advocate radical or different ideas must not be looked on as disruptive or troublesome. At the organizational and group level, creativity is affected by leadership style, culture, climate, structure, and systems that the organization has in place.[111] A facilitative leadership style, learning organization culture, supportive work climate, flexible structure, and adaptive systems can all contribute toward higher levels of creativity.

Create a Climate of Risk Taking and Tolerance for Failure

Some of the most important inventions or scientific breakthroughs resulted from investigating failed outcomes. Unfortunately, in many organizations, when experiments or full-scale ventures fail, the tendency is to immediately abandon the activity to save face or avoid negative consequences. This is often the wrong approach, because more learning takes place from things that go wrong than from things that go right. After all, when things turn out as expected, it just confirms existing theories or assumptions. New insights are more likely when there is an investigation into why expected outcomes were not realized. An organization that claims to support experimentation should not then turn around and punish employees for taking risks that are within accepted company guidelines.

Provide Incentives for Learning and Innovation

The use of incentives and rewards is a powerful tool that leaders can employ to encourage learning and innovation. Organizations are often criticized for proclaiming themselves as champions of learning and innovation but not able to provide matching incentives.

Build Confidence in Followers' Capacity to Learn and Adapt

Providing opportunities for employees to solve problems will increase their confidence and pride in the process especially when their successes are rewarded and celebrated. With each celebrated success comes greater confidence in dealing with new challenges. Over time, a habit of creativity and resulting innovation is institutionalized and becomes a way of life.[112]

Encourage Systems Thinking

To enhance broad-based learning, the leader should help members see the organization as a system in which everybody's work affects the work of everybody else. The emphasis on the whole system eliminates boundaries both within the organization and with other partners, which allows for collaboration and continuous learning.[113] Benchmarking of best practices is encouraged. **Benchmarking** *is a process that allows an organization to adopt the best practices of others.* An organization striving for excellence will even improve upon the best practices of competitors and launch innovations ahead of competitors.[114]

Institute Mechanisms for Channeling and Nurturing Creative Ideas for Innovation

The birth of a new idea or knowledge begins with the individual. Knowledge that is shared has a multiplying or cumulative effect. Ideas generated within or outside an organization may become the source of new products or innovations. Venture teams, task forces, information systems networks, seminars, and workshops are mechanisms that can be used to diffuse knowledge and to channel creative ideas to appropriate locations for evaluation and application.[115]

Create a Shared Vision for Learning

Creating a shared vision enhances learning as organization members develop a common purpose and commitment to make learning an ongoing part of the organization. If employees all believe that the organization is headed toward greatness, they will be motivated to be part of it by learning and contributing their best ideas and solutions.[116]

Broaden Employees' Frame of Reference

A person's frame of reference determines how he or she sees the world. The ways we gather, analyze, and interpret information—and how we make decisions based on such information—are affected by our personal frames of reference. A frame of reference influences people's assumptions, and those assumptions, consciously or unconsciously, affect how they interpret events. To enhance employees' ability to learn, it is important for leaders to broaden the lens through which employees see the organization and the world around them. Exposing employees to different experiences and practices outside of their normal environment is one way to broaden their frame of reference. A manufacturing business, for example, may take its employees to observe how a NASCAR pit crew functions during races. Or, a retail chain may take its staff to Las Vegas to observe how casino and hotel staff perform their jobs.

Learning is a never-ending exercise. Leaders must communicate the message that learning and continuous improvements are imperative in today's highly dynamic business environment. Leaders must take the lead in challenging the status quo and creating organizational conditions that are conducive to learning and continuous innovation.[117]

WORK
Application **12-6**

The workplace should be a place of learning but some critics argue that not all of them have a culture that encourages learning. Of the eight recommendations for fostering a learning organizational culture in Exhibit 12.5, how many would you say are true of your current or past workplace?

YOU
Make the
ETHICAL
Call

12.3 *Departmentalization*

Colleges and universities are known to have rigid departments, such as economics, management, marketing, accounting, and finance. At some schools, these departments are more concerned about themselves (related to budgets and number of faculty and courses) than serving students and cooperating with other departments. For example, some economics faculty have stated that they are concerned with theory and don't need to teach anything practical. There is also overlap in some courses offered by different departments, such as strategy being taught in management and marketing courses. In the business world, there is a trend to break down the barriers between departments and to be much more cooperative. However, academia doesn't seem to be following this trend.

1. Should the faculty's top priority be students, their department, or cooperating with other departments?
2. Should faculty move away from a focus on theory to more practical applications to business?
3. Should colleges follow the business trend of breaking away from departments and cooperate more? Or are they different from businesses, thus needing clear departments differentiated by discipline?

OPENING CASE Application

8. What additional steps will you recommend that Mr. Perez take to make Kodak more of a learning organization?

CEO Perez can employ many of the guidelines for enhancing organizational learning listed in Exhibit 12.5 and described in this section. Action on all or any number of these guidelines will increase Kodak's efforts to become a successful learning organization.

Now that you have learned about crisis leadership and the learning organization, you may find it interesting to see how your own personality traits match up. Complete Self-Assessment 12-2.

SELF-ASSESSMENT 12-2 — Personality and Crisis and the Learning Organization

Crisis

When facing a crisis, surgency personalities tend to take the leadership position to solve the crisis, and agreeableness personalities are glad to follow. Those with adjustment problems tend to get emotional under the pressure of a crisis and often get defensive and deny there is a problem, whereas conscientious personalities with an openness to experience tend to want to resolve the crisis. How do you handle crisis situations? How can you improve?

_____

_____

Learning Organization

The key personality trait that differs between the traditional organization and the learning organization is openness to new experience. If you are closed to new experience, you will tend to like a traditional organization in which change is slow and top management makes the decisions. If you are open to new experiences, you will tend to enjoy a learning organization in which you are encouraged and valued for implementing change and making many of your own decisions. Would you be more comfortable in a traditional or learning organization? Why?

_____

"Take It To The Net". Access student resources at www.cengagebrain.com. Search for Lussier, Leadership 6e to find student study tools.

Chapter Summary

The chapter summary is organized to answer the nine learning outcomes for this chapter.

① Explain why crisis leadership competency is an important consideration when hiring new leaders.

Crises are inevitable. It is not a question of "if" a crisis will happen, but "when." A crisis can inflict severe damage to an organization if not properly managed. In a crisis, stock prices plummet and costs escalate, causing both short- and long-term financial losses. A crisis that is mismanaged can also damage an organization's reputation and diminish consumer confidence in the organization's mission, or in some cases can lead to its demise altogether. For these reasons, leaders must show some competency in crisis leadership and management.

2 **What are the benefits of having a crisis management plan in advance of a crisis.**

Pre-crisis planning buys you time. You are ready when a crisis strikes. Having a crisis management plan in place can (a) reduce the duration of a crisis, (b) enhance or retain a corporation's image and reputation, (c) allow for quick and effective responses, (d) improve communications, (e) enhance coordination and cooperation, (f) ensure ready and available resources, (g) ensure fewer costly mistakes, (h) ensure less panic, (i) ensure quicker resolution of the crisis, and (j) limit or protect financial loss

3 **Briefly describe the three stages of a crisis management plan.**

The three-stage crisis management plan consists of pre-crisis planning, leading during a crisis, and adapting after a crisis. **Pre-crisis planning** addresses two key questions: (1) *Do we have a crisis response team and who is on it?* and (2) *What is our crisis plan of action?* Having a standing *crisis response team* increases an organization's ability to respond to a crisis in a timely and effective manner. On the second question, *developing a crisis plan of action* involves imagining the worst possible scenarios that could happen to the organization and the impact on employees, customers, or operational systems. Action plans for high ranking crisis scenarios are developed and practiced. **Leading during a crisis** requires a rapid response. The crisis leader must step forward and lead. The leader's job is to insure that everyone plays their role as spelled out in the pre-crisis plan. **Adapting after a crisis** is about lessons learned. Most forward-looking organizations do a postmortem. That is, in the aftermath of a crisis, top management authorizes a review of the organization's effectiveness in managing the crisis.

4 **Describe the role of the top management during a crisis.**

When there is a crisis, employees will look to the CEO or other top management personnel on how to cope with the situation. During a crisis, top management should (1) stay engaged and lead from the front, (2) focus on the big picture and communicate the vision, and (3) work with the crisis leader and the crisis management team. Effective leaders understand that their job during a crisis includes showing compassion for victims, and other affected parties.

5 **Describe the five-step process for crisis risk assessment.**

The five-step process for risk assessment consists of: (1) risk identification, (2) risk assessment and ranking, (3) risk reduction strategies, (4) crisis prevention and simulations, and (5) crisis management. In step 1 (*risk identification*), crisis team members begin by identifying the worst-case scenarios that could have severe consequences on people, the organization's financial position, or its image. This process results in the creation of a risk chart. Step 2 (*risk assessment and ranking*), potential crisis incidents are analyzed and ranked. Step 3 (*risk reduction strategies*), there is debate and discussion of the crisis scenarios in step 2 and strategies for countering each incident are formulated. Step 4 (*crisis prevention simulations*), pre-crisis drills such as simulations are conducted to test employees' responsiveness. Step 5 (*crisis management*), the plan is reviewed and updated on a regular basis and ready to be put into action in the event of a real crisis.

6 **Describe the importance of effective communication during a crisis.**

Four questions that often emerge after a crisis are: (1) What happened? (2) How did it happen? (3) What's being done to address the crisis? and (4) What has been done to ensure it never happens again? Providing honest, accurate, and timely answers to these questions is the essence of effective crisis communication. Another potential problem during crisis communication is the seniority level of the person representing the organization. It is important for the CEO or the most senior leader in the organization to show up rather than retreat to the background. The level of seniority demonstrates to the public the seriousness with which the incident is viewed.

7 **Describe the key characteristics of a learning organization.**

The learning organization describes a work environment where (a) work patterns, structures, and routines are open to continuous adaptation and improvement, (b) everyone engages in continuous learning, (c) the culture is supportive of experimentation, creativity, and innovation, (d) knowledge creation and sharing are imperative, and (e) decision making is informed by objective facts and analysis

8 **Distinguish between the traditional and the learning organization.**

The following table highlights some of the differences between the traditional and the learning organization:

Traditional (efficiency driven)	Learning (innovation driven)
• Stable environment	• Changing environment
• Vertical bureaucratic structure	• Flat adaptive structure
• Strategy formulation is top-down	• Strategy formulation is collaborative.
• Centralized decision making	• Decentralized decision making

- Rigidly defined and specialized tasks
- Loose, flexible, and adaptive roles
- Rigid organizational culture
- Adaptive organizational culture
- Top-down communication model
- Open, two-way communication model

9 **Describe the role of leadership in creating a learning organization culture.**

In today's rapidly changing business environment, organizations must transform into active learning organisms or risk becoming extinct. To succeed, organizations must be proactive and anticipatory, which requires continuous adaptation and innovation. Thus, the traditional organization model that emphasizes efficiency and stability is being replaced by a model that is learning and knowledge driven. Leaders play a critical role in effecting this transformation. Without effective leadership from the top, it is hard to imagine how the learning organization can succeed. A shared vision and culture of learning are critical to the success of a learning organization, and this is the domain of the strategic leader. Leaders can play a key role in organizational learning by encouraging creative thinking, creating a climate in which experimentation and risk taking are encouraged, providing incentives for learning and innovation, building confidence in followers' capacity to learn and adapt, and encouraging systems thinking.

Key Terms

crisis, 430

benchmarking, 450

discontinuous change, 446

learning organization, 444

organizational knowledge, 445

press kit, 441

press release, 441

Review Questions

1 In planning for a crisis, the leader has to focus on five integrated tasks. Identify these tasks.

2 How has social media affected the way crises are managed in our society today?

3 What are the main components of a pre-crisis plan?

4 Pre-crisis planning is about asking and answering two critical questions. What are they?

5 The best indicator of an organization's readiness to respond to a crisis is how it rates in five areas of assessment. What are these five areas?

6 Briefly explain what a crisis management plan of action entails?

7 One of the characteristics of a learning organization's cultures is that learning is a multilevel, organization-wide process. What exactly do we mean by this statement?

8 Explain or illustrate how a leader can foster a learning organizational culture by creating a climate where risk taking and failure are tolerated?

Critical Thinking Questions

The following critical-thinking questions can be used for class discussion and/or as written assignments to develop communication skills. Be sure to give complete explanations for all questions.

1 Describe why a senior leader's physical presence is critical during a crisis.

2 What are the benefits of creating a comprehensive crisis response plan before a crisis happens?

3 What advice would you give to a leader who wants to improve his or her organization's communications function so that it is more effective during a crisis?

4 How important to an organization is internal (employee) communication during a crisis?

5 What message does it send when the organizational culture encourages employees to view mistakes/problems as opportunities for improvement rather than reasons to blame or punish those involved?

CASE

Merck CEO–Ken Frazier: First African American Leading a Major Pharmaceutical Company

Mr. Kenneth Frazier has been the CEO of Merck since January 1, 2011. In an industry dominated by white men who are either scientists or salesmen, Ken Frazier is an unlikely CEO. He is a lawyer by training and an African American who grew up in Philadelphia's inner city. He comes from a very humble background. His father was a janitor with a limited education who Frazier admires and adores. He describes his father as "one of the most intelligent men" he has ever met.

At the time of his appointment, many analysts saw Merck as a company in need of rejuvenation. Merck's mission is to save and improve lives around the world, and to uphold the highest standards of ethics and integrity. All indications were that Merck was having a difficult time fulfilling this mission. For a company that has introduced more new medicines in the past 60 years than any other company, Merck ranks only fifth in new drug approvals over the past 10 years. Since 2003 the company's stock has been up and down with no clear direction. Except for the purchase of Schering-Plough in 2009, organic growth has been stagnant. Merck has not launched a drug that has reached annual sales of more than $1 billion since 2007. Drug research is a high-risk and time-consuming process. Only one out of every 5,000–10,000 compounds screened becomes an approved drug. It takes an average of 10 to 15 years at an average cost of more than $1 billion to develop a successful medicine.[118] Mr. Frazier was seen as the candidate best suited to set things right.

Mr. Frazier's understanding of Merck's business comes from his 35-year career with the company; first as an outside attorney and then as the company's general counsel and top marketer. Frazier believes that Merck's competitive advantage is the quality of its research, and he worships its researchers, who can spend 15 or more years developing a single new medicine. "All I can do is create an environment where really talented, smart, committed people want to show up and (discover new drugs)," he once proclaimed.[119] Echoing this sentiment, one writer said of Mr. Frazier, "He professes a near-religious belief in letting his scientists do their jobs."[120]

After a slow start, Mr. Frazier has begun to make some real changes. A lot of his initiatives are right in line with our recommendations for fostering a learning organizational culture (see Exhibit 12-5). For example:

- Since assuming the leadership of Merck, Frazier has reiterated his desire to return Merck to a culture of innovation. In his 2012 annual report he said, "We believe that innovative and productive research and development is the only sustainable way to create true and enduring value for all of our stakeholders." He backed his commitment by increasing Merck's R&D budget for research. The world is changing, Mr. Frazier said, but Merck's focus on pursuing the best science and building a sustainable business is steadfast. One of the recommendations for fostering a culture of learning is to create a shared vision for learning.

- As a learning organization, Merck aims to promote a culture of professional development that will support its employees' growth while aligning their career aspirations with the company's strategic priorities. With its new professional development tool called *Career Maps*, employees have increased exposure to key competencies and skills for roles across the company. The competencies within Career Maps are linked to learning resources, empowering employees to focus their professional development on building and enhancing skills and helping them develop a plan to achieve their personal career goals. This is part of creating a culture conducive for individual and team learning, providing incentives for learning and innovation, instituting mechanisms for channeling and nurturing creative ideas, and building confidence in followers' capacity to learn and adapt.

- Merck recognizes that its employees are an invaluable source of ideas that can help transform it into a stronger, more innovative company. So, to take advantage of this asset, Merck created an annual event for collaboration among thousands of its employees globally. Over a three-day period, employees engage in an online brainstorming forum to tackle some of Merck's greatest transformational challenges. The round-the-clock format is designed to break down traditional divisional and geographic barriers and engage and inspire participants from all levels of the organization. At its latest gathering in 2012, some 24,000 employees from around the

(continued)

globe contributed more than 16,000 comments and ideas. This program encourages creative thinking, facilitates systems thinking, broadens employees' frame of reference, creates an environment in which people can share ideas and learn from each other, and is a great mechanism for channeling and nurturing creative ideas.

These programs and initiatives are all hallmarks of a learning and knowledge-based organization. Another hallmark of a learning and knowledge-based organization is innovation. Merck is dedicated to the highest level of scientific excellence. Merck's commitment is reflected in this direct quote from its Web site, "We strive to identify the most critical needs of consumers and customers, and through *continuous innovation*, we challenge ourselves to meet those needs."

Merck is a $44 billion company in revenues. It employs about 76,000 people worldwide. The stock is near its 52-week high at $59.84 a share, which occurred on May 1, 2014. According to information from its Web site, Merck has a robust pipeline of potential new drugs, with a wide range of product candidates across each phase of development. For those who said at his appointment that "only time will tell," there is evidence that Mr. Frazier's leadership is beginning to pay dividends. There is broad confidence in the long-term outlook of the company because of the strategies and changes that Ken Frazier is putting in place.

GO TO THE INTERNET: To learn more about Ken Frazier and Merck, visit **www.merck.com.**

Support your answers to the following questions with specific information from the case and text or with other information you get from the Web or other sources.

1. In what way(s) has Ken Frazier demonstrated his effectiveness as the leader of a learning and knowledge-based organization?

2. Given our discussion on the distinction between a traditional and learning organization, what type of organization is Merck? Support your answer.

3. Mr. Frazier has maintained that the pillar of Merck's strategy will remain innovation. Suggest some ideas he can institute to enhance innovation.

4. Describe the strategy that Ken Frazier has articulated for moving Merck forward.

5. Drug research is a high-risk and time-consuming process. What evidence is there to support this assertion?

6. What specific personality and leadership traits does Ken Frazier possess that align with leading a learning- and knowledge-driven organization like Merck?

CUMULATIVE CASE QUESTIONS

7. What is CEO Frazier's source of power? Also, what type of power and influencing tactics has he been using, and is it the appropriate power type? If not, which power type should he be using (Chapter 5)?

8. Chapter 6 discusses communication, coaching, and mentoring as ways to develop the leadership skills of underlings by senior leaders. Research the relationship between Ken Frazier and his predecessor. Based on your findings, is Mr. Frazier a beneficiary of effective mentoring and coaching?

9. Strategic leadership is about having a vision that aligns with future environmental trends and working with and through others to realize it (Chapter 11). What evidences is there that Ken Frazier is an effective strategic leader?

CASE EXERCISE AND ROLE-PLAY

Preparation: Put yourself in the position of Ken Frazier. There has been a major incident involving one of Merck's drugs. Patients using the drug have been experiencing some serious side effects. The lawsuits are beginning to mount. You and the crisis management team are getting ready for a news conference with the media on the crisis. Prepare a list of questions you anticipate the media will be asking and what your response should be. What other preparations do you have to make prior to the news conference?

In-Class Groups: Break into groups of four to six members, and discuss the prepared questions.

Role-Play: Taking turns, one group will represent the crisis management team led by Mr. Frazier. Let other groups play the role of the media. They should select no more than three questions from their prepared list to ask. The rest of the class should listen and judge the performance of the Merck crisis management team in addressing the media. Each group should take turns role-playing the media, the Merck crisis management team, or the judges. Each team playing the role of the media should ask a different set of questions, so the same questions are not repeated during each round.

Observer Role: As the rest of the class members watch the role-play, they should judge (1) the opening remarks of the crisis management team—their demeanor, body language, tone, style, and substance; (2) the quality of questions that the media team asked; and (3) the quality of responses given by

Mr. Frazier and his team—how honest and truthful they are with their answers. Did Mr. Frazier take a leading role or did he stay in the background and let others do the talking? Use the guidelines for effective crisis communication (Exhibit 12.3) as the tool to judge Merck's crisis management team performance during the news conference. Look for things that the person playing Mr. Frazier did well or did not do well during the news conference.

Discussion: After the role-plays, the class votes for the crisis management team that did the best job with its opening remarks and responding to questions. The instructor should weigh in with his or her opinion on which team did the best job in the questioning and which team did the best job in responding to the questions. Which team member playing Mr. Frazier did the best job and why? Where did the others fall short?

VIDEO ▶ CASE

Managing in Turbulent Times at Second City Theater

Managers today are expected to deal with uncertainty, unexpected events, diversity, and change. They must demonstrate flexibility, foster trust, and engage the hearts and minds of employees. The managers at Second City Theater have a leg up in developing these skills and dealing with these situations because Second City has been doing it for years—on stage. In 1975, owner and executive producer Andrew Alexander started the Second City television series (SCTV) in response to the new trend of television sketch comedy. Later, the company opened the Second City Training Center, an educational center offering classes in improvisation, acting, writing, and other skills. Most recently, Second City

opened a corporate communications division, which provides training in the areas of internal communications, external marketing and branding, and learning development. With its focus on human skills, Second City demonstrates all of the qualities of a learning organization. The managers at Second City foster a climate where experimentation and learning are encouraged.

1. Many students of the Second City Training Center are businesspeople looking to gain skills for the corporate context. What skills from the world of improvisational comedy would be valuable to a business manager?

2. What do you think would be the challenges of a manager in a learning organization? Why?

Developing Your Leadership Skills 12-1

Handling a Crisis

Preparation for This Exercise

Research the business news and find an organization that has just had a crisis. Below, identify the firm and the crisis. Also, read Procedure 2 below and think of your "Three As" response to the crisis.

_____

_____

_____

Doing This Exercise in Class

Objective

To develop your ability to handle a crisis

AACSB General Skills Area

The primary AACSB skills developed through this exercise are communication, analytical thinking, and problem solving.

Preparation

You should have selected a business in crisis.

Procedure 1 *(3–5 minutes)* Break into crisis teams of four to six and select one business crisis that the group will work on resolving.

Procedure 2 *(10–15 minutes)* Develop a crisis communication plan, identifying your "Three As."

Acknowledge: _____

Action: _____

_____

_____

Avoid: _____

_____

_____

Procedure 3 *(10–20 minutes)* Each crisis team selects a spokesperson who tells the class the organization chosen and its crisis, followed by the team's "Three As" plan.

Conclusion

The instructor may lead a class discussion and/or make concluding remarks.

Apply It *(2–4 minutes)* What did I learn from this experience? How will I use this knowledge in the future?

_____

_____

_____

Sharing

In the group, or to the entire class, volunteers may give their answers to the "Apply It" questions.

Developing Your Leadership Skills 12-2

The Learning Organization

Preparation for This Exercise

Return to Self-Assessment 12.1, Learning Organizations, on page 446. Below, identify the firm you assessed and its score.

_____

Select any 3 of the 15 characteristics of learning organization questions that can be improved. Below, list the numbers and develop a plan on how the organization can improve on each of the three characteristics.

_____

_____

_____

_____

_____

Doing This Exercise in Class

Objective

To develop your skill to improve a firm's ability to learn

AACSB General Skills Area

The primary AACSB skills developed through this exercise are communication, analytical thinking, and problem solving.

Preparation

You should have developed plans to improve learning on three characteristics of learning organizations.

Procedure 1 *(10–15 minutes)* Break into teams of four to six and share your preparation plans. Help each other improve the plans.

Procedure 2 *(10–20 minutes)* Each team selects a spokesperson who tells the class the organization chosen and the plans to improve learning.

Conclusion

The instructor may lead a class discussion and/or make concluding remarks.

Apply It *(2–4 minutes)* What did I learn from this experience? How will I use this knowledge in the future?

_____

_____

_____

Sharing

In the group, or to the entire class, volunteers may give their answers to the "Apply It" questions.

Endnotes

1 S. G. Baumann, "Antonio Perez' Struggle for Survival at Eastman Kodak," VOXXI, September 12, 2012. (http://voxxi.com /2012/09/12/antonio-perez-struggle-for-survival-eastman-kodak/)

2 S. G. Baumann, "Antonio Perez' Struggle for Survival at Eastman Kodak," VOXXI, September 12, 2012. (http:// voxxi.com/2012/09/12/antonio-perez-struggle-for-survival-eastman-kodak/)

3 http://247wallst.com/consumer-products/2013/07/31 /bankruptcy-mystery-antonio-perez-remains-kodak-ceo-for-yet-another-year-or-even-longer/

4 www.kodak.com

5 A. Carmeli and J. Schaubroeck, "Organizational Crisis-Preparedness: The Importance of Learning from Failures," *Long Range Planning* 41(2) (2008, April): 177–196.

6 C. Bergeron and F. Cooren, "The Collective Framing of Crisis Management: A Ventriloqual Analysis of Emergency Operations Centres," *Journal of Contingencies & Crisis Management* [serial online] 20(3) (2012, September): 120–137.

7 C. Bergeron and F. Cooren, "The Collective Framing of Crisis Management: A Ventriloqual Analysis of Emergency Operations Centres," *Journal of Contingencies & Crisis Management* [serial online] 20(3) (2012, September): 120–137.

8 S. Grebe, "Things Can Get Worse How Mismanagement of a Crisis Response Strategy Can Cause a Secondary or Double Crisis: The Example of the AWB Corporate Scandal," *Corporate Communications: An International Journal* [serial online] 18(1) (2013, February): 70–86.

9 A. Choudhary, "Mission 'Trust.'" *Academy of Strategic Management Journal* [serial online] 11(1) (2012, January): 101–113.

10 V. Cuñat, "Why Some Firms Thrive While Others Fail: Governance and Management Lessons from the Crisis," *Economica* [serial online] 81(321) (2014, January): 187–188.

11 V. Cuñat, "Why Some Firms Thrive While Others Fail: Governance and Management Lessons from the Crisis," *Economica* [serial online] 81(321) (2014, January): 187–188.

12 http://money.cnn.com/gallery/news/companies/2013/12/27 /business-scandals.fortune/6.html

13 J. Plungis and J. Green, "House Panel to Probe GM Recall of Vehicles for Ignition Switches," *Bloomberg News* (March 11, 2014).

14 www.ropella.com

15 T. Jaques, "Crisis Leadership: A View from the Executive Suite," *Journal of Public Affairs (14723891)* [serial online] 12(4) (2012, November): 366–372.

16 "The Art of Strategic Renewal," *MIT Sloan Management Review* [serial online] 55(2) (2014, Winter): 21–23.

17 T. Jaques, "Crisis Leadership: A View from the Executive Suite," *Journal of Public Affairs (14723891)* [serial online] 12(4) (2012, November): 366–372.

18 T. Coppens, "How to Turn a Planning Conflict into a Planning Success? Conditions for Constructive Conflict Management in the Case of Ruggeveld-Boterlaar-Silsburg in Antwerp, Belgium," *Planning Practice & Research* [serial online] 29(1) (2014, February): 96–111.

19 "Turning Crisis into Opportunity: The Key Role of Leadership," *Strategic Direction* [serial online] 29(4) (2013, April): 29–32.

20 W. Bennis, "Crises Reveal the Quality of Leadership," *Leader to Leader* (154) (2009): 27–31.

21 Y. Jin, B. Liu, and L. Austin, "Examining the Role of Social Media in Effective Crisis Management: The Effects of Crisis Origin, Information Form, and Source on Publics' Crisis Responses," *Communication Research* [serial online] 41(1) (2014, February): 74–94.

22 A. Coleman, "Managing a Crisis in the Era of Social Communication: How Greater Manchester Police Is Developing Community Engagement and Communication," *Journal of Brand Strategy* [serial online] 2(2) (2013, Summer): 128–133.

23 A. Pang, N. Hassan, and A. Chong, "Negotiating Crisis in the Social Media Environment: Evolution of Crises Online, Gaining Credibility Offline," *Corporate Communications: An International Journal* [serial online] 19(1) (2014, February): 96–118.

24 A. Zavyalova, M. Pfarrer, R. Reger, and D. Shapiro, "Managing the Message: The Effects of Firm Actions and Industry Spillovers on Media Coverage Following Wrongdoing," *Academy of Management Journal* [serial online] 55(5) (2012, October): 1079–1101.

25 J. A. Gruman, N. Chhinzer, and G. W. Smith, "An Exploratory Study of the Level of Disaster Preparedness in the Canadian Hospitality Industry," *International Journal of Hospitality & Tourism Administration* 12(1) (2011): 43–59.

26 http://www.marketwatch.com/story/bankruptcy-mystery-antonio-perez-remains-kodak-ceo-for-yet-another-year-or-even-longer-2013-07-31

27 S. Appelbaum, S. Keller, H. Alvarez, and C. Bédard, "Organizational Crisis: Lessons from Lehman Brothers and Paulson & Company," *International Journal of Commerce & Management* [serial online] 22(4) (2012, October): 286–305.

28 D. Bauman, "Evaluating Ethical Approaches to Crisis Leadership: Insights from Unintentional Harm Research," *Journal of Business Ethics* 98(2) (2011): 281–295.

29 D. Canyon, "Crisis Management Teams in Health Organisations," *Journal of Business Continuity & Emergency Planning* [serial online] 5(4) (2012, Spring): 365–372.

30 D. Canyon, "Crisis Management Teams in Health Organisations," *Journal of Business Continuity & Emergency Planning* [serial online] 5(4) (2012, Spring): 365–372.

31 W. Kahn, M. Barton, and S. Fellows, "Organizational Crises and the Disturbance of Relational Systems," *Academy of Management Review* [serial online] 38(3) (2013, July): 377–396.

32 W. Johansen, H. Aggerholm, and F. Frandsen, "Entering New Territory: A Study of Internal Crisis Management and Crisis Communication in Organizations," *Public Relations Review* [serial online] 38(2) (2012, June): 270–279.

33 www.ropella.com

34 P. Riddell, "Rallying the Troops: Crisis Communication and Reputation Management in Financial Services," *Journal of Brand Strategy* [serial online] 2(3) (2013, Fall): 222–227.

35 J. Jensen and W. Waugh, "The United States' Experience with the Incident Command System: What We Think We Know and What We Need to Know More About," *Journal of Contingencies & Crisis Management* [serial online] 22(1) (2014, March): 5–17.

36 P. Palttala, C. Boano, R. Lund, and M. Vos, "Communication Gaps in Disaster Management: Perceptions by Experts from Governmental and Non-Governmental Organizations," *Journal of Contingencies & Crisis Management* [serial online] 20(1) (2012, March): 2–12.

37 A. Carone and L. Di Iorio, "Crisis Management: An Extended Reference Framework for Decision Makers," *Journal of Business Continuity & Emergency Planning* [serial online] 6(4) (2013, Summer): 347–359.

38 K. Brumfield, "Succeeding in Crisis Leadership," *Financial Executive* [serial online] (October 2012): 45–47.

39 K. Brumfield, "Succeeding in Crisis Leadership," *Financial Executive* [serial online] (October 2012): 45–47.

40 A. Carone and L. Di Iorio, "Crisis Management: An Extended Reference Framework for Decision Makers," *Journal of Business Continuity & Emergency Planning* [serial online] 6(4) (2013, Summer): 347–359.

41 "Turning Crisis into Opportunity: The Key Role of Leadership," *Strategic Direction* [serial online] 29(4) (2013, April): 29–32.

42 C. Rongier, M. Lauras, F. Galasso, and D. Gourc, "Towards a Crisis Performance-Measurement System," *International Journal of Computer Integrated Manufacturing* [serial online] 26(11) (2013, November): 1087–1102.

43 S. Kim, "The Role of Prior Expectancies and Relational Satisfaction in Crisis," *Journalism & Mass Communication Quarterly* [serial online] 91(1) (2014, March): 139–158.

44 "The Art of Strategic Renewal," *MIT Sloan Management Review* [serial online] 55(2) (2014, Winter): 21–23.

45 W. Johansen, H. Aggerholm, and F. Frandsen, "Entering New Territory: A Study of Internal Crisis Management and Crisis Communication in Organizations," *Public Relations Review* [serial online] 38(2) (2012, June): 270–279.

46 P. Chris and R. W. Guyette, Jr., "Toyota Recall Crisis: Public Attitudes on Leadership and Ethics," *Organization Development Journal* 28(2) (2010): 89–97.

47 W. Kahn, M. Barton, & S. Fellows, "Organizational Crises and the Disturbance of Relational Systems," *Academy of Management Review* [serial online] 38(3) (2013, July): 377–396.

48 W. Johansen, H. Aggerholm, and F. Frandsen, "Entering New Territory: A Study of Internal Crisis Management and Crisis Communication in Organizations," *Public Relations Review* [serial online] 38(2) (2012, June): 270–279.

49 S. Kim, "The Role of Prior Expectancies and Relational Satisfaction in Crisis," *Journalism & Mass Communication Quarterly* [serial online] 91(1) (2014, March): 139–158.

50 P. Palttala, C. Boano, R. Lund, and M. Vos, "Communication Gaps in Disaster Management: Perceptions by Experts from Governmental and Non-Governmental Organizations," *Journal of Contingencies & Crisis Management* [serial online] 20(1) (2012, March): 2–12.

51 K. Brumfield, "Succeeding in Crisis Leadership," *Financial Executive* [serial online] (October 2012): 45–47.

52 T. Vihalemm, M. Kiisel, and H. Harro-Loit, "Citizens' Response Patterns to Warning Messages," *Journal of Contingencies & Crisis Management* [serial online] 20(1) (2012, March): 13–25.

53 W. Johansen, H. Aggerholm, and F. Frandsen, "Entering New Territory: A Study of Internal Crisis Management and Crisis

Communication in Organizations," *Public Relations Review* [serial online] 38(2) (2012, June): 270–279.

54 A. Pang, N. Hassan, and A. Chong, "Negotiating Crisis in the Social Media Environment: Evolution of Crises Online, Gaining Credibility Offline," *Corporate Communications: An International Journal* [serial online] 19(1) (2014, February): 96–118.

55 S. Stern, "Truth, Not Secrets, for Better Leadership," *Strategic Communication Management* 15(3) (2011): 11.

56 A. Zavyalova, M. Pfarrer, R. Reger, and D. Shapiro, "Managing the Message: The Effects of Firm Actions and Industry Spillovers on Media Coverage Following Wrongdoing," *Academy of Management Journal* [serial online] 55(5) (2012, October): 1079–1101.

57 P. Palttala and M. Vos, "Quality Indicators for Crisis Communication to Support Emergency Management by Public Authorities," *Journal of Contingencies & Crisis Management* [serial online] 20(1) (2012, March): 39–51.

58 A. Scholtens, J. Jorritsma, and I. Helsloot, "On the Need for a Paradigm Shift in the Dutch Command and Information System for the Acute Phase of Disasters," *Journal of Contingencies & Crisis Management* [serial online] 22(1) (2014, March): 39–51.

59 A. Zavyalova, M. Pfarrer, R. Reger, and D. Shapiro, "Managing the Message: The Effects of Firm Actions and Industry Spillovers on Media Coverage Following Wrongdoing," *Academy of Management Journal* [serial online] 55(5) (2012, October): 1079–1101.

60 A. Zavyalova, M. Pfarrer, R. Reger, and D. Shapiro, "Managing the Message: The Effects of Firm Actions and Industry Spillovers on Media Coverage Following Wrongdoing," *Academy of Management Journal* [serial online] 55(5) (2012, October): 1079–1101.

61 S. Ponis, and E. Koronis, "A Knowledge Management Process-Based Approach to Support Corporate Crisis Management," *Knowledge & Process Management* [serial online] 19(3) (2012, July): 148–159.

62 R. Nag and D. Gioia, "From Common to Uncommon Knowledge: Foundations of Firm-Specific Use of Knowledge as a Resource," *Academy of Management Journal* [serial online] 55(2) (2012, April): 421–457.

63 M. Černe, C. Nerstad, A. Dysvik, and M. Škerlavaj, "What Goes around Comes Around: Knowledge Hiding, Perceived Motivational Climate, and Creativity," *Academy of Management Journal* [serial online] 57(1) (2014, February): 172–192.

64 H. Gardner, B. Staats, and F. Gino, "Dynamically Integrating Knowledge in Teams: Transforming Resources into

Performance," *Academy of Management Journal* [serial online] 55(4) (2012, August): 998–1022.

65 R. Nag and D. Gioia, "From Common to Uncommon Knowledge: Foundations of Firm-Specific Use of Knowledge as a Resource," *Academy of Management Journal* [serial online] 55(2) (2012, April): 421–457.

66 P. M. Senge, *The Fifth Discipline: The Art and Practice of the Learning Organization* (Rev. ed.). (New York: Doubleday, 2006).

67 H. Darvish and E. A. Nazari, *Economic Insights—Trends & Challenges* 65(1) (2013): 1–16.

68 R. Chua, "The Costs of Ambient Cultural Disharmony: Indirect Intercultural Conflicts In Social Environment Undermine Creativity," *Academy of Management Journal* [serial online] 56(6) (2013, December): 1545–1577.

69 R. Mackay and R. Chia, "Choice, Chance, and Unintended Consequences in Strategic Change: A Process Understanding of the Rise and Fall of Northco Automotive," *Academy of Management Journal* [serial online] 56(1) (2013, February): 208–230.

70 P. Klarner and S. Raisch, "Move to the Beat—Rhythms of Change and Firm Performance," *Academy of Management Journal* [serial online] 56(1) (2013, February): 160–184.

71 M. Kalyar and N. Rafi, "'Organizational Learning Culture': An Ingenious Device for Promoting Firm's Innovativeness," *Service Industries Journal* [serial online] 33(12) (2013, November 5): 1135–1147.

72 H. Darvish and E. A. Nazari, *Economic Insights—Trends & Challenges* 65(1) (2013): 1–16.

73 H. Darvish and E. A. Nazari, *Economic Insights—Trends & Challenges* 65(1) (2013): 1–16.

74 P. M. Senge, *The Fifth Discipline: The Art and Practice of the Learning Organization* (Rev. ed.) (New York: Doubleday, 2006).

75 H. Darvish and E. A. Nazari, *Economic Insights—Trends & Challenges* 65(1) (2013): 1–16.

76 L. Qiang, P. Maggitti, K. Smith, P. Tesluk, and R. Katila, "Top Management Attention to Innovation: The Role of Search Selection and Intensity in New Product Introductions," *Academy of Management Journal* [serial online] 56(3) (2013, June): 893–916.

77 M. Kalyar and N. Rafi, "'Organizational Learning Culture': An Ingenious Device for Promoting Firm's Innovativeness," *Service Industries Journal* [serial online] 33(12) (2013, November 5): 1135–1147.

78 R. Funk, "Making the Most of Where You Are: Geography, Networks, and Innovation in Organizations," *Academy of*

Management Journal [serial online] 57(1) (2014, February): 193–222.

79 By: S.-H. Liao, W.-J. Chang, D.-C. Hu, and Y.-L. Yueh, *International Journal of Human Resource Management* 23(1) (2012, January): 52–70.

80 H. Bresman, "Changing Routines: A Process Model of Vicarious Group Learning in Pharmaceutical R&D," *Academy of Management Journal* [serial online] 56(1) (2013, February): 35–61.

81 E. Ndinguri, L. Prieto, and K. Machtmes, "Human Capital Development Dynamics: The Knowledge Based Approach," *Academy of Strategic Management Journal* [serial online] 11(2) (2012, June): 121–136.

82 M. Černe, C. Nerstad, A. Dysvik, and M. Škerlavaj, "What Goes around Comes Around: Knowledge Hiding, Perceived Motivational Climate, and Creativity," *Academy of Management Journal* [serial online] 57(1) (2014, February): 172–192.

83 E. Ndinguri, L. Prieto, and K. Machtmes, "Human Capital Development Dynamics: The Knowledge Based Approach," *Academy of Strategic Management Journal* [serial online] 11(2) (2012, June): 121–136.

84 E. Antonacopoulou and Z. Sheaffer, "Learning in Crisis: Rethinking the Relationship Between Organizational Learning and Crisis Management," *Journal of Management Inquiry* [serial online] 23(1) (2014, January): 5–21.

85 N. Akhtar and R. Khan, "Exploring the Paradox of Organizational Learning and Learning Organization," *Interdisciplinary Journal of Contemporary Research in Business* 2(9) (2011): 257–270.

86 H. Bruns, "Working Alone Together: Coordination in Collaboration across Domains of Expertise," *Academy of Management Journal* [serial online] 56(1) (2013, February): 62–83.

87 G. Yaping, K. Tae-Yeol, L. Deog-RO, and Z. Jing, "A Multilevel Model of Team Goal Orientation, Information Exchange, and Creativity," *Academy of Management Journal* [serial online] 56(3) (2013, June): 827–851.

88 M. Sytch and A. Tatarynowicz, "Exploring the Locus of Invention: The Dynamics of Network Communities and Firms' Invention Productivity," *Academy of Management Journal* [serial online] 57(1) (2014, February): 249–279.

89 M. Kalyar and N. Rafi, "'Organizational Learning Culture': An Ingenious Device for Promoting Firm's Innovativeness," *Service Industries Journal* [serial online] 33(12) (2013, November 5): 1135–1147.

90 G. Yaping, K. Tae-Yeol, L. Deog-RO, and Z. Jing, "A Multilevel Model of Team Goal Orientation, Information Exchange,

and Creativity," *Academy of Management Journal* [serial online] 56(3) (2013, June): 827–851.

91 M. Černe, C. Nerstad, A. Dysvik, and M. Škerlavaj, "What Goes around Comes Around: Knowledge Hiding, Perceived Motivational Climate, and Creativity," *Academy of Management Journal* [serial online] 57(1) (2014, February): 172–192.

92 L. Dong, L. Hui, and R. Loi, "The Dark Side of Leadership: A Three-Level Investigation of the Cascading Effect of Abusive Supervision on Employee Creativity," *Academy of Management Journal* [serial online] 55(5) (2012, October): 1187–1212.

93 M. Baer, "Putting Creativity to Work: The Implementation of Creative Ideas in Organizations," *Academy of Management Journal* [serial online] 55(5) (2012, October): 1102–1119.

94 P. M. Madsen and V. Desai, "Failing to Learn the Effects of Failure and Success on Organizational Learning in the Global Orbital Launch Vehicle Industry," *Academy of Management Journal* 53(3) (2010): 451–476.

95 E. Ndinguri, L. Prieto, and K. Machtmes, "Human Capital Development Dynamics: The Knowledge Based Approach," *Academy of Strategic Management Journal* [serial online] 11(2) (2012, June): 121–136.

96 M. Santos-Vijande, J. López-Sánchez, and J. Trespalacios, "How Organizational Learning Affects a Firm's Flexibility, Competitive Strategy, and Performance," *Journal of Business Research* [serial online] 65(8) (2012, August): 1079–1089.

97 R. Chua, "The Costs of Ambient Cultural Disharmony: Indirect Intercultural Conflicts in Social Environment Undermine Creativity," *Academy of Management Journal* [serial online] 56(6) (2013, December): 1545–1577.

98 G. Yaping, K. Tae-Yeol, L. Deog-RO, and Z. Jing, "A Multilevel Model of Team Goal Orientation, Information Exchange, and Creativity," *Academy of Management Journal* [serial online] 56(3) (2013, June): 827–851.

99 S. Liao, W. Chang, D. Hu, and Y. Yueh, "Relationships Among Organizational Culture, Knowledge Acquisition, Organizational Learning, and Organizational Innovation in Taiwan's Banking and Insurance Industries," *International Journal of Human Resource Management* [serial online] 23(1) (2012, January): 52–70.

100 L. Dong, L. Hui, and R. Loi, "The Dark Side of Leadership: A Three-Level Investigation of the Cascading Effect of Abusive Supervision on Employee Creativity," *Academy of Management Journal* [serial online] 55(5) (2012, October): 1187–1212.

101 M. Kalyar and N. Rafi, "'Organizational Learning Culture': An Ingenious Device for Promoting Firm's Innovativeness,"

Service Industries Journal [serial online] 33(12) (2013, November 5): 1135–1147.

102 M. Baer, "Putting Creativity to Work: The Implementation of Creative Ideas in Organizations," *Academy of Management Journal* [serial online] 55(5) (2012, October): 1102–1119.

103 S. Chich-Jen, "Study on the Relations among the Customer Knowledge Management, Learning Organization, and Organizational Performance," *Service Industries Journal* 31(5) (2011): 791–807.

104 J. Sung Jun and B. Joo, "Knowledge Sharing: The Influences of Learning Organization Culture, Organizational Commitment, and Organizational Citizenship Behaviors," *Journal of Leadership & Organizational Studies* 18(3) (2011): 353–364.

105 J. Sung Jun and B. Joo, "Knowledge Sharing: The Influences of Learning Organization Culture, Organizational Commitment, and Organizational Citizenship Behaviors," *Journal of Leadership & Organizational Studies* 18(3) (2011): 353–364.

106 S. Liao, W. Chang, D. Hu, and Y. Yueh, "Relationships among Organizational Culture, Knowledge Acquisition, Organizational Learning, and Organizational Innovation in Taiwan's Banking and Insurance Industries," *International Journal of Human Resource Management* [serial online] 23(1) (2012, January): 52–70.

107 L. Dong, L. Hui, and R. Loi, "The Dark Side of Leadership: A Three-Level Investigation of the Cascading Effect of Abusive Supervision on Employee Creativity," *Academy of Management Journal* [serial online] 55(5) (2012, October): 1187–1212.

108 M. Santos-Vijande, J. López-Sánchez, and J. Trespalacios, "How Organizational Learning Affects a Firm's Flexibility, Competitive Strategy, and Performance," *Journal of Business Research* [serial online] 65(8) (2012, August): 1079–1089.

109 M. Baer, "Putting Creativity to Work: The Implementation of Creative Ideas in Organizations," *Academy of Management Journal* [serial online] 55(5) (2012, October): 1102–1119.

110 M. Baer, "Putting Creativity to Work: The Implementation of Creative Ideas in Organizations," *Academy of Management Journal* [serial online] 55(5) (2012, October): 1102–1119.

111 R. Chua, "The Costs of Ambient Cultural Disharmony: Indirect Intercultural Conflicts in Social Environment Undermine Creativity," *Academy of Management Journal* [serial online] 56(6) (2013, December): 1545–1577.

112 M. Baer, "Putting Creativity to Work: The Implementation of Creative Ideas in Organizations," *Academy of Management Journal* [serial online] 55(5) (2012, October): 1102–1119.

113 H. Bruns, "Working Alone Together: Coordination in Collaboration across Domains of Expertise," *Academy of Management Journal* [serial online] 56(1) (2013, February): 62–83.

114 A. Toaldo, S. Didonet, and F. Luce, "The Influence of Innovative Organizational Culture on Marketing Strategy Formulation and Results," *Latin American Business Review* [serial online] 14(3/4) (2013, July): 251–269.

115 M. Baer, "Putting Creativity to Work: The Implementation of Creative Ideas in Organizations," *Academy of Management Journal* [serial online] 55(5) (2012, October): 1102–1119.

116 L. Qiang, P. Maggitti, K. Smith, P. Tesluk, and R. Katila, "Top Management Attention to Innovation: The Role of Search Selection and Intensity in New Product Introductions," *Academy of Management Journal* [serial online] 56(3) (2013, June): 893–916.

117 L. Qiang, P. Maggitti, K. Smith, P. Tesluk, and R. Katila, "Top Management Attention to Innovation: The Role of Search Selection and Intensity in New Product Introductions," *Academy of Management Journal* [serial online] 56(3) (2013, June): 893–916.

118 http://www.innovation.org/index.cfm/ToolsandResources/FactSheets/Innovation_by_the_Numbers

119 www.merck.com

120 H. Mathew, "Merck Could Return to Greatness if CEO Can Leave His Own Past Behind," *Forbes* (May 6, 2013). (http://www.forbes.com/sites/matthewherper/2013/04/17/merck-could-return-to-greatness-if-ceo-can-leave-his-own-past-behind/)

Appendix

Leadership and Spirituality in the Workplace

Judith Neal, PhD*

The purpose of this appendix is twofold: (1) It provides an overview of the concept of faith and spirituality in the workplace and (2) it provides spiritual principles that have been useful to many leaders in their personal and professional development.

Spirituality in the Workplace

Tom Aageson, former Director of Aid to Artisans—a nonprofit organization that helps artists in third-world countries—takes an annual retreat in which he contemplates questions about the purpose of his life, and evaluates how well he is living in alignment with his values. Angel Martinez, former CEO of Rockport Shoes, invited all his top executives to a retreat that included exploring the integration of each person's spiritual journey with his or her work journey. At Integrated Project Systems (IPS) in San Francisco, former CEO Bill Kern created a document called "The Corporate Stand" that is very explicit about "The Integrity of the Human Spirit." These are key principles that employees live by at IPS. Rodale Press, publisher of such well-known magazines as *Prevention, Men's Health, Runner's World*, and *Organic Gardening*, has a "kiva room" at corporate headquarters where employees may go to meditate, pray, or just spend quiet time when things get too stressful. ANZ Bank in Australia and New Zealand sends all its employees through personal transformation programs, conducts an audit based on levels of corporate consciousness, and allows each bank branch to design its own meditation/quiet room. Tyson Foods has over 120 workplace chaplains on the payroll and is committed to being a "faith-friendly workplace."

Stories like these are becoming more and more common in all kinds of workplaces. Academic and professional conferences are offering an increasing number of sessions that have words such as *Faith, Spirituality, Consciousness,* or *Soul* in the title. There is a new openness in management education to recognition of our spiritual nature. This recognition can be on a personal level, such as when a person explores his or her own spiritual

---

*Appendix written by Judith A. Neal, PhD, chairman, Edgewalkers International, http://edgewalkers.org/.
© 2011 by Judith Neal; used by permission of the author.

journey and struggles with what this means regarding work. It is also on a conceptual level, as both academics and practitioners explore the role that spirituality might have in bringing meaning, purpose, and increased performance to organizational life. A major change is going on in the personal and professional lives of leaders, as many of them more deeply integrate their spirituality and their work. And most would agree that this integration is leading to positive changes in their relationships and their effectiveness.

Defining Spirituality in the Workplace

Spirituality is difficult to define. The Latin origin of the word "spirit" is *spirare,* meaning "to breathe." At its most basic, then, spirit is what inhabits us when we are alive and breathing; it is the life force. Spirituality has been defined as "that which is traditionally believed to be the vital principle or animating force within living beings—that which constitutes one's unseen intangible being, or the real sense or significance of something."[1] A fairly comprehensive definition, part of which is provided here, is as follows:

> One's spirituality is the essence of who he or she is. It defines the inner self, separate from the body, but including the physical and intellectual self. . . . Spirituality also is the quality of being spiritual, of recognizing the intangible, life-affirming force in self and all human beings. It is a state of intimate relationship with the inner self of higher values and morality. It is a recognition of the truth of the inner nature of people. . . . Spirituality does not apply to particular religions, although the values of some religions may be a part of a person's spiritual focus. Said another way, spirituality is the song we all sing. Each religion has its own singer.[2]

Perhaps the difficulty people have had in defining spirituality is that they are trying to objectify and categorize an experience and way of being that is at its core very subjective and beyond categorizing. For this reason, some have resorted to poetry as a way of trying to capture the essence of the experience of spirituality. Lee Bolman did this very effectively in his keynote presentation on spirituality in the workplace to the Eastern Academy of Management in May 1995. He quoted the Persian poet Rumi:[3]

> All day I think about it, then at night I say it
> Where did I come from and what am I supposed to be doing? I have no idea
> My soul is elsewhere, I'm sure of that
> And I intend to end up there.

James Autry, a successful Fortune 500 executive, wrote a poem called "Threads." Here is an excerpt from that poem:[4]

> Listen.
> In every office
> You hear the threads
> of love and joy and fear and guilt,
> the cries for celebration and reassurance,
> and somehow you know that connecting those threads
> is what you are supposed to do
> and business takes care of itself.

Spirituality in the workplace is about people seeing their work as a spiritual path, as an opportunity to grow personally and to contribute to society in a meaningful way. It is about learning to be more caring and compassionate with fellow employees, with bosses, with subordinates and customers. It is about integrity, being true to oneself, and telling the truth to others. Spirituality in the workplace can refer to an individual's attempts to live his or her values more fully in the workplace. Or it can refer to the ways in which organizations structure themselves to support the spiritual growth of employees.

In the final analysis, the understanding of spirit and of spirituality in the workplace is a very individual and personal matter. There are as many expressions of these concepts as there are people who talk or write about them.

Approaches to Implementing Spirituality in the Workplace

In practice, organizations are implementing spirituality in the workplace utilizing one or more of the following four approaches:[5]

1: Individual Development

At this level, programs focus on helping the individual employee understand more about his or her values, spiritual principles, and sense of purpose. The organization is committed to helping individuals live in alignment with their faith and spiritual path, may offer meditation rooms or courses on spiritual practices and/or teachings, and may bring in speakers who talk about spiritual development. There is an understanding that if people can discover and respond to their own "calling" or sense of purpose, they will be more creative, committed, and service-oriented.

2: Leadership and Team Development

Organizations are offering courses to leaders with titles like "Authentic Leadership," "Leading with Soul," and "Spiritual Leadership." Leaders are encouraged to apply spiritual values such as humility, trust, courage, integrity, and faith to their work with teams. They may offer courses such as "Team Spirit" and "Noble Purpose" developed by Barry Heerman.[6] Some organizations are offering lunchtime Spirit at Work discussion groups. Others are offering team-building courses that incorporate spiritual values or practices.

3: Total System Development

A growing number of CEOs and organizational leaders have become personally committed to creating organizations that nurture the human spirit of the company's employees, customers, and other stakeholders. Several systemic approaches have been developed to help organizations evolve to a higher level of congruence with spiritual values. These include "Corporate Tools" by Richard Barrett,[7] "Spiral Dynamics" by Don Beck and Chris Cowan,[8] "Appreciative Inquiry" by David Cooperrider and colleagues,[9] "Positive Organizational Scholarship" and "The Abundance Framework" by Kim Cameron,[10] and "Open Space Technology" by Harrison Owen.[11] The key aim in each of these organizational development processes is to help an organization move beyond just a focus on profits and the bottom line to a commitment to human development and a positive contribution to society.

4: Redefining the Role of Business

A new paradigm is emerging among business leaders that redefines the purpose of business as the solution to solving problems in society and around the globe, rather than being a contributor to them. The focus is on using the creative energy and talent of their employees, along with their vast capital resources and international reach, to truly make a positive difference in the world. Willis Harman, cofounder of the Institute of Noetic Sciences and of the World Business Academy, was probably the first person to speak about the important role of business in increasing consciousness in the world.[12] More recently, Case Western Reserve's Wetherhead School of Management has created a Center of Excellence called the *Center of Business as an Agent of World Benefit (BAWB),* which has sponsored an ongoing inquiry research project into the ways business is making a positive difference in the world.

Each organization is unique in terms of its values, vision, and readiness for spirituality in the workplace, so there is no one formula that leaders can use to implement spiritual values and practices in their organizations. The best thing to do is to learn as much as possible from organizations that have been successful in this integration. A great place to start is to study the organizations that have received the International Spirit at Work Award for their explicit spiritual practices and commitment to nurturing the human spirit of their employees; for more information, go to http://edgewalkers.org.

Before we discuss guidelines for leading from a spiritual perspective, complete the self-assessment below to better know thyself.

SELF-ASSESSMENT I   Spiritual Intelligence at Work

Instructions: Please read each statement below and decide to what degree you either agree or disagree with the statement.

1 = Strongly Disagree
2 = Somewhat Disagree
3 = Neither Agree nor Disagree
4 = Somewhat Agree
5 = Strongly Agree

---

1. _____ I am very aware of my values and beliefs at work.

2. _____ It is important to accept that others in my workplace may not have the same values and beliefs that I do.

3. _____ I have had one or more transcendent experiences that have affected the way I feel about my work.

4. _____ People I work with describe me as calm and nonjudgmental.

5. _____ When someone has done something that makes me angry, I find it very difficult to forgive them.

6. _____ I try to have daily contact with my Higher Power, the Divine, God, or Universal Consciousness.

7. _____ In difficult situations, I find that a calm part of me can remain detached and observe my thoughts, feelings, and behaviors.

8. _____ I have a great deal of compassion for the leaders of my organization.

9. _____ When I need special help or guidance in my work, I turn to prayer, meditation, or other spiritual guidance.

10. _____ I do not feel the need to grow or develop myself at work.

11. _____ It is important to keep business life and personal life separate in my relationships at work.

12. _____ I feel divinely guided to the work I am doing.

13. _____ I have a regular spiritual or religious practice that I find helpful to me in my work.

14. _____ I often feel a real sense of love and caring work for the people I interact with at work.

15. _____ I do not believe that there is anything greater than myself and know that the only way to make it in my life and career is to rely on my own abilities.

16. _____ If I found myself in a work situation where I was asked to compromise my values, I would have to stick to my values, even if it hurt me or my career.

17. _____ My primary motivation at work is to be of service to others.

18. _____ I am deeply concerned about the effects of some business practices on the planet.

19. _____ The reality of business is that sometimes you just have to compromise your values for the sake of the company or for your career.

20. _____ Dealing with people at work is a great cause of frustration for me.

(continued)

(Self-Assessment 1 continued)

21. _____ It is important to me that my organization operate in a way that is respectful of all life.
22. _____ I have a real sense of calling about the work I do.
23. _____ I really try to get to know the people I work with on a deeper level than just work-related issues.
24. _____ I believe that my work is part of a larger divinely guided plan.
25. _____ My mission in life is very clear to me.
26. _____ People in my workplace often come to me to talk about personal or spiritual issues.
27. _____ I feel a sense of the sacred in my workplace.
28. _____ I often feel stressed at work.
29. _____ I work hard at having authentic and caring relationships with people at work.
30. _____ Because of my belief in something greater than myself, I try to live in alignment with key virtues such as trustworthiness, humility, justice, and unity.

Spiritual Intelligence at Work—

Scoring Key Instructions:

1. Transpose the numbers from the questionnaire to the columns below. For starred items (*), reverse the scoring by subtracting your answer from 6. For instance, if you responded to question 5 with a "4," 6 − 4 = 2, so put a "2" in item 5 below.
2. Add up the totals for each column.

Column A	Column B	Column C
1._____	2._____	3._____
4._____	*5._____	6._____
7._____	8._____	9._____
*10._____	*11._____	12._____
13._____	14._____	*15._____
16._____	17._____	18._____
*19._____	*20._____	21._____
22._____	23._____	24._____
25._____	26._____	27._____
*28._____	29._____	30._____

Totals:
Column A: _____ Column B: _____ Column C: _____

Spiritual Intelligence at Work—

Interpretation of Scores

Spiritual Intelligence is the ability to feel a connection to self, a connection to others, and a connection to something greater than oneself. Column A provides you the score for "Connection to Self," Column B for "Connection to Others," and Column C for "Connection to the Transcendent." Make note of your highest score and your lowest score and write your thoughts about that here:

_____
_____
_____

Connection to Self

Spiritual Intelligence must begin with some sense of self-awareness. As the Delphi Oracle declared, "Know Thyself." Of the five dimensions of work (physical, intellectual, emotional, volitional, and spiritual), "Connection to Self" is most related to the "Intellectual" dimension because of its emphasis on self-development. People who have a strong connection to self are in touch with their values and beliefs, have a strong degree of emotional intelligence, and have done enough spiritual practice or self-development work so that they can calmly observe themselves and gain mastery over their thoughts, feelings, and behaviors. Other people experience people who are high in connection to self as calm, able to act competently in chaotic situations, and as having serene competence.

40–50 You have a strong connection to self and may want to help others develop this capacity through your coaching or mentoring.

30–39 You are fairly self-aware with room for development. You may want to think about taking on a spiritual practice such as meditation or prayer, or receiving coaching or mentoring from someone who has a highly developed sense of connection to self.

20–29 You may often feel out of touch, confused by others' responses to you, and unsure of your sense of purpose or mission in life. It may be useful to take personal or spiritual growth workshops or to take time for a personal retreat where you can have time to reflect on yourself, your goals, and the kind of person you want to be.

0–19 You may feel fairly disconnected from yourself, and may be focusing most of your time and energy on external activities or on pleasing other people to your own detriment. You should give serious thought to the value of increasing your self-awareness of your beliefs, values, behavior, and goals in life. Therapy, spiritual direction, and support groups can all be very helpful in increasing your connection to self.

Connection to Others

It is not enough to just be self-aware and concerned with your own growth. People with high Spiritual Intelligence use this self-knowledge as a basis for understanding others better and for developing meaningful

(Self-Assessment | continued)

relationships. Of the five dimensions of work (physical, intellectual, emotional, volitional, and spiritual), "Connection to Others" is most related to the "Emotional" dimension because of its emphasis on the interpersonal aspects of the work environment. People who have a strong connection to others are very respectful of differences in values, beliefs, and cultural background and often curious to learn more. They are caring, compassionate, and able to forgive. They see the Divine in others and treat each person as unique and as a sacred being.

40–50 You have a strong connection to others and are probably good at team building and at creating a sense of community. People tend to trust you and you take that very seriously.

30–39 You are fairly good at relationship building with room for development. People are generally pretty comfortable with you and find you open and supportive. However, occasionally there may be things you say or do that are out of character. When this happens, take the time to reflect on your behavior and the underlying values, beliefs, or attitudes that you may want to change.

20–29 You may often feel uncomfortable in your relationships at work. You may either find yourself feeling angry or resentful a lot, or intimidated or unappreciated. It can be easy to blame others for this, but it may be worth taking a look at your own behavior. Consider taking courses or workshops in interpersonal skills such as communication, assertiveness training, or conflict resolution. It is also helpful to ask someone you trust for feedback on your behavior.

0–19 You may feel fairly isolated from others, and find yourself preferring to work alone to avoid the uncomfortableness of difficult relationships. It is helpful to spend time reflecting on how you can take responsibility for improving the situation. Interpersonal skills workshops, such as those mentioned above, may be helpful. You might also consider hiring a professional coach to help you improve your relationships.

Connection to the Transcendent

Perhaps the major element that distinguishes Spiritual Intelligence from other forms of human intelligence is its emphasis on the connection to something greater than ourselves—what people may refer to as God, the Universe, the Divine, the Transcendent, or similar terms. Of the five dimensions of work (physical, intellectual, emotional, volitional, and spiritual), "Connection to the Transcendent" is most related to the "Spiritual" dimension because of its emphasis on the sacredness of human beings and all life. People who are high in "Connection to the Transcendent" have a belief in something greater than themselves, and find themselves guided and led by the Transcendent. They tend to have a clear sense of their greater purpose in life and are concerned with moral issues such as justice and respect.

40–50 You have a strong connection to the Transcendent and find yourself guided by a greater wisdom. You see your work as part of a much larger plan that contributes to the human race and the good of the planet. Because of your vision and your spiritual connection, others turn to you for leadership and inspiration.

30–39 You value your connection to the Transcendent, but it may not be a part of your daily awareness. You have a desire to deepen this relationship but may either think you don't have the time to do this, or it may be that you don't know how. It may be helpful to explore the spiritual traditions of your childhood, or to read some of the inspiring books on the relationship to the Transcendent, such as "How to Know God," by Deepak Chopra.

20–29 You may feel somewhat disconnected from the spiritual dimension of your life, although you turn to your Higher Self or Higher Power on occasion when there are difficult situations at work. You are probably not that interested in larger issues of justice, respect, or morality at work, but may find yourself getting upset if you feel that a personal injustice has been done to you, or someone has shown you a lack of respect. It may be helpful to focus on some basic principles such as the Golden Rule (see Chapter 2) or the concept of Unity.

0–19 A connection to the Transcendent is not a big part of your life, and you may feel a lack of inspiration or sense of purpose about your work. It's possible that you may be dealing with basic survival issues and cannot focus on the bigger picture at this time. If you wish to enhance this part of your Spiritual Intelligence, you must develop the "Volitional" dimension of work—that is, the will to change for the better. To improve your connection to the Transcendent, you will need to make a commitment to a spiritual practice such as prayer, meditation, journaling, or spending time in nature. As part of your practice, ask the Transcendent for guidance on how to improve your connection. Make note of your reactions to your scores and list one or two areas you would like to develop further.

_____

_____

_____

Guidelines for Leading from a Spiritual Perspective

Following are five spiritual principles that have been useful to many leaders in their personal and professional development.

Know Thyself

All spiritual growth processes incorporate the principle of self-awareness. That is why we included the self-assessment on spiritual intelligence at work, and here are some other ways to know thyself. Leading provides a great opportunity to become more self-aware. Examine why you respond to situations the way you do. Take a moment in the morning to reflect on the kind of leader you would like to be today. At the end of the day, take quiet time to assess how well you did, and to what extent you were able to live in alignment with your most deeply held core values. It is also helpful to take personal and leadership assessment tools, such as the one in this appendix and the Myers-Briggs Type Indicator. You might also consider taking the *Spiritual Intelligence Assessment* developed by Cindy Wigglesworth at Deep Change.

Act with Authenticity and Congruency

Followers learn a lot more from who we are and how we behave than from what we say. Authenticity means being oneself, being fully congruent, and not playing a role. Many managers really get into the role of "leader," and they see managing as a place to assert their superiority and control. They would never want employees to see the more human, softer parts of them. Yet we are finding that managers who are more authentic, humble, and congruent tend to be more effective.[13]

It is a real challenge to be authentic and congruent in the workplace. Most people feel that if they are truly themselves, and if they say what they are really thinking, it will be the end of their careers. But I believe that if we don't do this, we sell a little bit of our souls every time we are inauthentic, and that saps our creative energy and our emotional intelligence. It also reduces our sense of commitment to the work we do, and we cannot perform at our highest level. Experiment with greater authenticity and with showing more of your humanness. You will be surprised at how positively people will respond.

It is also important to create a climate in which employees are encouraged to behave authentically and congruently. This means that they should be comfortable expressing feelings as well as thoughts and ideas. Contrary to popular opinion, humility accompanied by a strong will does create an enduring organization and is a much more powerful tool for success than a strong ego.

Respect and Honor the Beliefs of Others

It can be very risky and maybe even inappropriate to talk about your own spirituality in the workplace. Yet if spirituality is a guiding force in your life and your leading, and if you follow the guideline of authenticity and congruency, you cannot hide that part of yourself. It is a fine line to walk.

What seems to work best is to build a climate of trust and openness first, and to model an acceptance of opinions and ideas that are different from yours. Then, if an appropriate opportunity comes up in which you can mention something about your spiritual beliefs, you should emphasize that they are yours alone. Explain that people have different beliefs and that you respect those differences. It is extremely important that employees do not feel that you are imposing your belief system (spiritual, religious, or otherwise) on them.

At the same time, it is worthwhile to do anything that you can do to nurture spiritual and ethical development in your employees in a way that allows them to explore their own deepest values and beliefs.

WORK
Applications

A-1. Give an example of spirituality in the place where you work or have worked.

A-2. Have you or anyone you know struggled with spiritual journey and what this means for work? Explain.

Be as Trusting as You Can Be

This guideline operates on many levels. On the personal level, this guideline of "being as trusting as you can be" applies to trusting oneself, one's inner voice, or one's source of spiritual guidance. This means trusting that there is a Higher Power in your life and that if you ask you will receive guidance on important issues. It also operates on the interpersonal, team, and organizational level. If you truly learn to see yourself as trustworthy, and believe that it is our essential nature as humans to be trustworthy, then you will naturally feel trusting of colleagues and subordinates. And you will also feel more trusting that the processes and events that are happening have a higher purpose to them if you look for it and amplify it.

Maintain a Spiritual Practice

In a research study on people who integrate their spirituality and their work, the most frequently mentioned spiritual practice is spending time in nature. Examples of other practices are meditation, prayer, reading inspirational literature, hatha yoga, shamanistic practices, writing in a journal, and walking a labyrinth. People reported that it is very important for them to consistently commit to whatever individual spiritual practice they have chosen. The regular involvement in a chosen practice appears to be the best way to deepen one's spirituality.[14]

When leaders faithfully commit to a particular spiritual practice they are calmer, more creative, more in tune with employees and customers, and more compassionate.[15]

Resources on the Web

- *Center of Business as an Agent of World Benefit (BAWB)* at Case Western Reserve's Wetherhead School of Management. http://worldbenefit.case.edu
- *Spiritual Intelligence Assessment* developed by Cindy Wigglesworth at Deep Change, http://www.deepchange.com Note: The instrument is free if it is used as a part of a research project.
- *Tyson Center for Faith and Spirituality in the Workplace*, Sam M. Walton College of Business, University of Arkansas. http://tfsw.uark.edu. This Web site has research papers, dissertations, podcasts, videos, and many other resources for those interested in the integration of faith and spirituality in the workplace.

Appendix Summary

There is a growing trend to talk more openly about spirituality and to want to integrate spiritual principles into all aspects of life—relationships, community, and work. This appendix has presented some resources for leaders who are interested in more fully integrating their spirituality and their leadership. A newly emerging field expands beyond just the focus on spirituality in the workplace. It goes by such names as Faith at Work, Spiritual Capitalism, Compassionate Capitalism, and Conscious Capitalism. Leading edge thinkers are now exploring ideas about spiritual and humanistic values applied to economic and political systems.

Living more congruently with deeply held spiritual principles is never easy, but it is extremely rewarding and meaningful. I hope that some of the resources provided here will help to make the journey a little easier.

Review Questions

1. Spirituality is about learning to be more caring and compassionate in the workplace. Should we be more caring and compassionate with others at work? Why or why not?

2. Spirituality is about integrity, being true to oneself, and telling the truth to others in the workplace. Should we be honest with others at work? Why or why not?

3. Is knowing oneself important to leading from a spiritual perspective? Why or why not?

4. Should leaders let followers see the more human, softer parts of them (truly be themselves)? What effect would this have on productivity?

Critical-Thinking Questions

The following critical-thinking questions can be used for class discussion and/or as written assignments to develop communication skills. Be sure to give complete explanations for all questions.

1. There is no single accepted definition of spirituality in the workplace. What is your definition?

2. Are managers who have a spiritual practice more effective leaders than those who do not?

3. Do you have a spiritual practice? If yes, what is it?

4. If our capitalistic system were based on spiritual principles, what would it look like? How would business and government be different?

Endnotes

1. K. T. Scott, "Leadership and spirituality: A quest for reconciliation," in J. Conger (ed.), *Discovering the Spirituality in Leadership* (San Francisco: Jossey-Bass, 1994), 63–99.

2. G. Fairholm, *Capturing the heart of -leadership: Spirituality and community in the new American workplace.* (Westport, CT: Praeger), 1997.

3. C. Barks, *The Essential Rumi* (San Francisco: Harper, 1996).

4. J. Autry, *Love and profit: The art of caring leadership* (New York: Avon Books, 1991).

5. For details on the four levels of -spirituality in the workplace implementation, with case studies, worksheets, and assessments, the *Creating Enlightened Organizations Manual* by J. Neal can be ordered from the Association for Spirit at Work, http://www.spiritatwork.org.

6. B. Heermann, *Building team spirit: Activities for inspiring and energizing teams* (New York: McGraw-Hill, 1997). *Noble purpose: Igniting extraordinary passion for life and work* (Fairfax, VA: QSU Publishing, 2004).

7. R. Barrett, *Liberating the corporate soul: Building the visionary organization* (Cambridge, MA: Butterworth-Heinemann, 1998); http://www.corptools.com.

8. D. Beck and C. Cowen, *Spiral dynamics: Mastering values, leadership, and change* (Malden, MA: Blackwell Publishing, 1996); http://www.spiraldynamics.com.

9. David Cooperrider and Suresh Srivastva first developed the concept of Appreciative Inquiry in 1987, in D. Cooperrider and S. Srivastva, "Appreciative inquiry in -organizational life," in R. W. Woodman & W. A. Pasmore (eds.), *Research in -organizational change and development.* (Greenwich, CT: JAI Press, 1987). The most recent book in this field is D. Whitney, A. Trosten-Bloom, and D. Cooperrider, *The power of appreciative inquiry: A practical guide to positive change* (San Francisco: Berrett-Koehler, 2003); http://-appreciativeinquiry. cwru.edu/.

10. Kim Cameron coedited, with Jane Dutton and Robert Quinn, *Positive Organization Scholarship* (San Francisco: Berrett-Koehler, 2003). This book was widely acclaimed by the academic community; however the -business community responded that it was too "ivory tower." Cameron has recently -written a book for the business community called *The abundance framework* (in press); http://www.bus.umich.edu/Positive/.

⓫ H. Owen, *Open space technology: A user's guide,* 2nd ed. (San Francisco: -Berrett-Koehler, 1997); http://www.openspaceworld.org/.

⓬ W. Harman and J. Hormann, *Creative work: The constructive role of business in transforming society* (Indianapolis: Knowledge Systems, 1990).

⓭ J. Collins, *Good to great: Why some companies make the leap . . . and others don't* (NY: HarperBusiness, 2001). See Chapter 2 on "Level 5 Leadership," which documents the success of leaders who demonstrate the virtue of humility.

⓮ J. Neal, B. Lichtenstein, and D. Banner, "Spiritual perspectives on individual, -organizational, and societal -transformation," *Journal of Organizational Change Management,* 12(3), 175–185.

⓯ C. Schaefer and J. Darling, "Does spirit matter? A look at contemplative practice in the workplace," Spirit at Work newsletter, July 1997.

Glossary

360-degree feedback   It is based on receiving performance evaluations from many people.

achievement motivation theory   It attempts to explain and predict behavior and performance based on a person's need for achievement, power, and affiliation.

acquired needs theory   It proposes that people are motivated by their need for achievement, power, and affiliation.

adaptive culture   It represents a leadership belief in active monitoring of the external environment for emerging opportunities and threats and adapting to them.

adjustment personality dimension   It includes traits of emotional stability and self-confidence.

agreeableness personality dimension   It includes traits of sociability and emotional intelligence.

alienated follower   It is someone who is low on involvement, yet is high on critical thinking.

arbitrator   He/She is a neutral third party who makes a binding decision to resolve a conflict.

attribution theory   It is used to explain the process managers go through in determining the reasons for effective or ineffective performance and deciding what to do about it.

BCF model   It describes a conflict in terms of behavior, consequences, and feelings.

behavioral leadership theories   They attempt to explain distinctive styles used by effective leaders, or to define the nature of their work.

benchmarking   It is a process that allows an organization to adopt the best practices of others.

Big Five Model of Personality   It categorizes traits into the dimensions of surgency, agreeableness, adjustment, conscientiousness, and openness to experience.

bureaucratic culture   It represents a leadership mindset that values order, stability, status, and efficiency.

charisma   A social construct between the leader and follower, in which the leader offers a transformative vision or ideal that exceeds the status quo and then convinces followers to accept this course of action not because of its rational likelihood of success, but because of their implicit belief in the extraordinary qualities of the leader.

coaching   It is the process of giving motivational feedback to maintain and improve performance.

coaching feedback   It is based on a good, supportive relationship; it is specific and descriptive; and it is not judgmental criticism.

coercive power   It involves punishment and withholding of rewards to influence compliance.

collectivism   It is the state of mind wherein the values and goals of the group—whether extended family, ethnic group, company, or community—are primary.

communication   It is the process of conveying information and meaning.

competitive culture   It represents a leadership mindset that encourages and values a highly competitive work environment.

conflict   It exists whenever people are in disagreement and opposition.

conformist follower   It is someone who is high on involvement but low on critical thinking.

connection power   It is based on the user's relationships with influential people.

conscientiousness personality dimension   It includes traits of dependability and integrity.

content motivation theories   They focus on explaining and predicting behavior based on people's needs.

contingency leadership model   It is used to determine if a person's leadership style is task- or relationship-oriented, and if the situation (leader–member relationship, task structure, and position power) matches the leader's style to maximize performance

contingency leadership theories   They attempt to explain the appropriate leadership style based on the leader, followers, and situation.

cooperative culture   It represents a leadership belief in strong, mutually reinforcing exchanges and linkages between employees and departments.

crisis   It is a low-probability but high-impact event that threatens the viability of an organization and is characterized by ambiguity of cause, effect, and means of resolution, as well as by a belief that decisions must be made swiftly.

cross-functional team   It is composed of members from different functional departments of an organization who are brought together to perform unique tasks to create new and non-routine products or services.

culture   The aggregate of beliefs, norms, attitudes, values, assumptions, and ways of doing things that is shared by members of an organization and taught to new members.

decisional leadership roles   It includes entrepreneur, disturbance-handler, resource allocator, and negotiator.

decision-making skills   They are based on the ability to conceptualize situations and select alternatives to solve problems and take advantage of opportunities.

delegation   It is the process of assigning responsibility and authority for accomplishing objectives.

delegation model   The steps involved in delegation model are (1) explain the need for delegating and the

reasons for selecting the employee; (2) set objectives that define responsibility, level of authority, and deadline; (3) develop a plan; and (4) establish control checkpoints and hold employees accountable

descriptive leadership models   They identify contingency variables and leadership styles without specifying which style to use in a given situation.

discontinuous change   It occurs when anticipated or expected changes bear no resemblance to the present or the past.

distributed leadership   Here, multiple leaders take complementary leadership roles in rotation within the same SMT, according to their area of expertise or interest.

diversity   It is the inclusion of all groups at all levels in an organization.

dyad   It is defined as the individualized relationship between a leader and each follower in a work unit.

dyadic theory   It approaches leadership as an exchange relationship that develops between a leader and a follower over time during role-making activities.

effective follower   It is someone who is high on critical thinking and involvement.

equity theory   It proposes that people are motivated when their perceived inputs equal outputs.

ethics   They are the standards of right and wrong that influence behavior.

ethics   They are the standards of right and wrong that influence behavior.

ethics ombudsperson   It is a single person entrusted with the responsibility of acting as the organization's conscience.

ethnocentrism   It is the belief that one's own group or subculture is naturally superior to other groups and cultures.

evidence-based management   It means that decisions and organizational practices are based on the best available scientific evidence.

expectancy theory   It proposes that people are motivated when they believe they can accomplish the task, they will get the reward, and the rewards for doing the task are worth the effort

expert power   It is based on the user's skill and knowledge.

feedback   It is the process of verifying messages and determining if objectives are being met.

femininity   It describes a culture that emphasizes developing and nurturing personal relationships and a high quality of life.

follower   It is defined as someone who is under the direct influence and authority of a leader.

followership   It refers to the behavior of followers that result from the leader–follower mutual influencing relationship.

functional team   It is a group of employees belonging to the same functional department, such as marketing, R&D, production, human resources, or information systems, who have a common objective.

giving praise model   They are (1) Tell the employee exactly what was done correctly. (2) Tell the employee why the behavior is important. (3) Stop for a moment of silence. (4) Encourage repeat performance.

glass ceiling   It is defined as an invisible barrier that separate women and minorities from top leadership positions.

goal-setting theory   It proposes that specific, difficult goals motivate people.

group   It is a collection of individuals who interact primarily to share information and to make decisions that enable each member to perform within his or her area of responsibility.

groupthink   It is when members of a cohesive group tend to agree on a decision not on the basis of its merit but because they are less willing to risk rejection for questioning a majority viewpoint or presenting a dissenting opinion.

hierarchy of needs theory   It proposes that people are motivated through five levels of needs—physiological, safety, belongingness, esteem, and self-actualization.

high-power-distance culture   Leaders and followers rarely interact as equals here.

high-uncertainty-avoidance culture   A majority of people who do not tolerate risk, avoid the unknown, and are comfortable when the future is relatively predictable and certain.

impressions management   It is a follower's effort to project a favorable image to gain an immediate benefit or improve a long-term relationship with the leader.

individualism   It is a psychological state in which people see themselves first as individuals and believe their own interest and values are primary.

influencing   The process of a leader communicating ideas, gaining acceptance of them, and motivating followers to support and implement the ideas through change.

information power   It is based on the user's data desired by others.

informational leadership roles   It includes monitor, disseminator, and spokesperson.

ingratiation   It is the effort to appear supportive, appreciative, and respectful.

in-group   It includes followers with strong social ties to their leader in a supportive relationship characterized by high mutual trust, respect, loyalty, and influence.

initiating conflict resolution model   The steps are (1) plan a BCF statement

that maintains ownership of the problem; (2) present your BCF statement and agree on the conflict; (3) ask for, and/or give, alternative conflict resolutions; and (4) make an agreement for change.

integrative leadership theories   They attempt to combine the trait, behavioral, and contingency theories to explain successful, influencing leader–follower relationships.

interpersonal leadership roles   It includes figurehead, leader, and liaison.

interpersonal skills   It involves the ability to understand, communicate, and work well with individuals and groups through developing effective relationships

job instructional training (JIT)   The steps include (1) trainee receiving preparation; (2) trainer presenting the task; (3) trainee performing the task; and (4) trainer following up.

leader Motive Profile (LMP)   It includes a high need for power, which is socialized, that is greater than the need for affiliation and with a moderate need for achievement.

leader motive profile theory   It attempts to explain and predict leadership success based on a person's need for achievement, power, and affiliation.

leader–member exchange (LMX)   The quality of the exchange relationship between a leader and a follower.

leadership   The influencing process between leaders and followers to achieve organizational objectives through change.

leadership continuum model   It is used to determine which one of seven styles to select, based on the use of boss-centered versus subordinate-centered leadership, to meet the situation (boss, subordinates, situation/time) to maximize performance

leadership Grid   It identifies five leadership styles: 1,1 impoverished; 9,1 authority compliance; 1,9 country club; 5,5 middle of the road; and 9,9 team leader.

leadership model   It is an example of emulation or use in a given situation

leadership paradigm   It is a shared mindset that represents a fundamental way of thinking about, perceiving, studying, researching, and understanding leadership.

leadership style   It is the combination of traits, skills, and behaviors leaders use as they interact with followers.

leadership theory   It is an explanation of some aspect of leadership; theories have practical value because they are used to better understand, predict, and control successful leadership.

leadership theory classifications   They include trait, behavioral, contingency, and integrative theories.

leadership trait theories   They attempt to explain distinctive characteristics accounting for leadership effectiveness.

learning organization   It is one that is skilled at creating, acquiring, and transferring knowledge, and at modifying behavior to reflect new knowledge and insights.

legitimate power   It is based on the user's position power, given by the organization. It is also called the legitimization influencing tactic

levels of analysis of leadership theory   They are individual, group, and organizational.

locus of control   It is on a continuum between an external and internal belief over who has control of a person's destiny.

long-term orientation   They have a future-oriented view of life and thus are thrifty (saving for the future) and persistent in achieving goals.

low-power-distance culture   Leaders and their followers interact on several levels as equals.

low-uncertainty avoidance culture   It has a majority of people who are comfortable with and accepting of the unknown, and tolerate risk and unpredictability.

management to the leadership theory paradigm   It is a shift from the older autocratic management style to the newer participative leadership style of management.

managerial role categories   They are interpersonal, informational, and decisional.

masculinity   It describes a culture that emphasizes assertiveness and a competitive drive for money and material objects.

mediator   He/she is a neutral third party who helps resolve a conflict.

mentoring   It is a form of coaching in which a more experienced manager helps a less experienced protégé.

message-receiving process   It includes listening, analyzing, and checking understanding.

moral justification   It is the thinking process of rationalizing why unethical behavior is used.

motivation   It is anything that affects behavior in pursuing a certain outcome.

motivation process   In motivation process people go from need to motive to behavior to consequence to satisfaction or dissatisfaction.

negotiating   It is a process in which two or more parties have something the other wants and attempt to come to an agreement.

networking   It is the process of developing relationships for the purpose of socializing and politicking.

normative leadership model   It has a time-driven and development-driven decision tree that enables the user to select one of five leadership styles (decide, consult individually, consult group, facilitate, and delegate) appropriate for the situation (seven questions/variables) to maximize decisions.

Ohio State University Leadership Model   It identifies four leadership styles: low structure and high consideration, high structure and high consideration, low structure and low consideration, and high structure and low consideration.

one-minute self-sell   It is an opening statement used in networking that quickly summarizes your history and career plan and asks a question

openness-to-experience personality dimension   It includes traits of flexibility, intelligence, and internal locus of control.

oral message-sending process   (1) It develops rapport; (2) It states your communication objective; (3) It transmits your message; (4) It checks the receiver's understanding; and (5) gets a commitment and follow up.

organizational citizenship behavior   It is defined as individual behavior that is discretionary, not directly or explicitly recognized by the formal reward system, and that in the aggregate promotes the effective functioning of the organization.

organizational knowledge   It is the tacit and explicit know-how that individuals possess about products, services, systems, and processes.

out-group   It includes followers with few or no social ties to their leader, in a strictly task-centered relationship characterized by low exchange and top-down influence.

paraphrasing   It is the process of having the receiver restate the message in his or her own words.

passive follower   It is someone who is low on critical thinking and low on involvement.

path–goal leadership model   It is used to select the leadership style (directive, supportive, participative, or achievement-oriented) appropriate to the situation (subordinate and environment) to maximize both performance and job satisfaction

performance formula   It explains performance as a function of ability, motivation, and resources.

personal meaning   The degree to which people's lives make emotional sense and to which the demands confronted by them are perceived as being worthy of their energy and commitment.

personality   It is a combination of traits that classifies an individual's behavior.

personality profiles   They identify individual stronger and weaker traits.

personalized charismatic leader (PCL)   It is one who possesses a dominant, self-centered, self-aggrandizing, and narcissistic personality and uses charisma for self-glorification.

politics   It is the process of gaining and using power.

power   It is the leader's potential influence over followers

pragmatic follower   It exhibits a little of all four styles—depending on which style fits the prevailing situation.

prescriptive leadership models   They tell the user exactly which style to use in a given situation

press kit   It is a package of information about a company, including names and pictures of its executives, a fact sheet, and key milestones in the company's history.

press release   It is a printed statement that describes how an organization is responding to a crisis and who is in charge.

process motivation theories   It focus on understanding how people choose behavior to fulfill their needs.

Pygmalion effect   It proposes that leaders' attitudes toward and expectations of followers, and their treatment of them, explain and predict followers' behavior and performance.

reciprocity   It involves creating obligations and developing alliances, and using them to accomplish objectives.

referent power   It is based on the user's personal relationships with others.

reinforcement theory   It proposes that through the consequences for behavior, people will be motivated to behave in predetermined ways.

reward power   It is based on the user's ability to influence others with something of value to them.

self-concept   It refers to the positive or negative attitudes people have about themselves.

self-efficacy   It is defined as a person's beliefs in his or her capabilities to produce at a certain level of performance.

self-managed team champion   He/she is an advocate of the SMT concept whose responsibility is to help the team obtain necessary resources, gain political support from top management and other stakeholders of the organization, and defend it from enemy attacks.

self-managed teams(SMTs)   It is relatively autonomous teams whose members share or rotate leadership responsibilities and hold one another mutually responsible for a set of performance targets assigned by top management.

self-promotion   It is the effort to appear competent and dependable.

servant leadership   Leadership that transcends self-interest to serve the needs of others, by helping them grow professionally and personally

short-term orientation   It derives from values that express a concern for maintaining personal happiness and living in the present.

SMT facilitator   He/she is the external leader of an SMT, whose job is to create optimal working conditions so that team members take on responsibilities to work productively and solve complex problems on their own.

social capital   It is defined as the set of resources that inheres in the structure of relations between members of the group, which helps them get ahead.

social identity   It s the degree to which members form close social ties with the group and how it subsequently influences interactions within and between group members.

social loafing   It is the conscious or unconscious tendency by some team members to shirk responsibility by withholding effort toward team goals when they are not individually accountable for their work.

socialized charismatic leader (SCL)   It is one who possesses an egalitarian, self-transcendent, and empowering personality and uses charisma for the benefit of others.

stakeholder approach to ethics   One creates a win–win situation for relevant parties affected by the decision.

stewardship   An employee-focused form of leadership that empowers followers to make decisions and have control over their jobs.

strong culture   It symbolizes a complete agreement or shared mind-set on key values and norms, with leaders playing a key role.

substitutes for leadership   They include characteristics of the subordinate, task, and organization that replace the need for a leader or neutralize the leader's behavior

surgency personality dimension   It includes dominance, extraversion, and high energy with determination.

team   It is a unit of interdependent individuals with complementary skills who are committed to a common purpose and set of performance outcomes and to common expectations, for which they hold themselves accountable.

team cohesion   It is the extent to which team members band together and remain committed to achieving team goals.

team creativity   It is the creation of something that is valuable, useful, and novel by individuals working together in a complex social system.

team effectiveness   It is a construct consisting of three components: (1) task performance—the degree to which the team's output (product or service) meets the needs and expectations of those who use it; (2) group process—the degree to which members interact or relate in ways that allow the team to work increasingly well together over time; and (3) individual satisfaction—the degree to which the group experience, on balance, is more satisfying than frustrating to team members.

team learning   It is the collective acquisition, combination, creation, and sharing of knowledge.

team norms   They are acceptable standards of behavior that are shared by team members.

team-member exchange (TMX)   It is a team member's social exchanges with peers in terms of the mutual exchange of ideas, support, camaraderie, and feedback.

technical skills   It involves the ability to use methods and techniques to perform a task.

Theory X and Theory Y   It attempt to explain and predict leadership behavior and performance based on the leader's attitude about followers.

traits   They are distinguishing personal characteristics.

transactional leadership   It seeks to maintain stability within an organization through regular economic and social exchanges that achieve specific goals for both leaders and their followers.

transformational leadership   It seeks to change the status quo by articulating to followers the problems in the current system and a compelling vision of what a new organization could be.

two-factor theory   It proposes that people are motivated by motivators rather than maintenance factors.

University of Michigan Leadership Model   It identifies two leadership styles: job-centered and employee-centered.

virtual team   It is one whose members are geographically dispersed, requiring them to work together through electronic means with minimal face-to-face interaction."

vision   It is the ability to imagine different and better conditions and the ways to achieve them.

whistle-blowing   It is employee disclosure of illegal or unethical practices within an organization.

writing objectives model   They are (1) To + (2) action verb + (3) singular, specific, and measurable result to be achieved + (4) target date.

Index